# Fundamentals of Special Education

## What Every Teacher Needs to Know

**Richard A. Culatta**
Appalachian State University

**James R. Tompkins**
Applachian State University

Merrill,
an imprint of Prentice Hall
*Upper Saddle River, New Jersey*      Columbus, Ohio

**Library of Congress Cataloging-in-Publication Data**

Culatta, Richard A.

Fundamentals of special education: what every teacher needs to
know/Richard A. Culatta, James R. Tompkins.

p. cm.

Includes bibliographical references and index.

ISBN 0-13-256991-4

1. Special education—United States.   2. Exceptional children-
-United States.   3. Exceptional children—Services for—United
States.   I. Tompkins, James R., (date)   .   II. Title.

LC3981.C85   1999                                          98-17010

371.9'0973—dc21                                          CIP

Cover art: © Diana Ong, SuperStock
Editor: Ann Castel Davis
Production Editor: Sheryl Glicker Langner
Production Coordination: Linda Zuk, WordCrafters Editorial Services, Inc.
Photo Coordinator: Sandy Lenahan
Design Coordinator: Diane C. Lorenzo
Cover Designer: Dan Eckel
Production Manager: Laura Messerly
Electronic Text Management: Karen L. Bretz
Director of Marketing: Kevin Flanagan
Marketing Manager: Suzanne Stanton
Marketing Coordinator:  Krista Groshong
This book was set in Novarese Book by Carlisle Communications and was printed and bound by
Courier/Westford. The cover was printed by Phoenix ColorCorp.

© 1999 by Prentice-Hall, Inc.
Simon & Schuster/A Viacom Company
Upper Saddle River, New Jersey 07458

Photo credits: Pages 1, 23, 57, 83, 119, 185, 238, 274: Anne Vega; p. 17: Dan Floss; pp. 10, 43, 72, 229, 265,
357: Barbara Schwartz; pp. 33, 89, 101, 149, 165, 352, 400: Anthony Magnacca; pp. 51, 111, 137, 175, 209,
255, 307, 314, 332, 335, 381, 393: Scott Cunningham; p. 69: Prentice Hall College; pp. 78, 364: Tom
Watson; p. 105: George Dodson; pp. 142, 199, 295, 385: Todd Yarrington; p. 188: Jason Laure' p. 248:
Michael Heron; p. 284: Courtesy of Gallaudet University; p. 321 Michael Newman/Photo Edit; p. 349:
Doug Pensinger/Allsport Photography; p. 373: Silver Burdett Ginn.

Printed in the United States of America

10  9  8  7  6  5  4  3  2  1

ISBN: 0-13-256991-4

Prentice-Hall International (UK) Limited, *London*
Prentice-Hall of Australia Pty. Limited, *Sydney*
Prentice-Hall of Canada, Inc., *Toronto*
Prentice-Hall Hispanoamericana, S. A., *Mexico*
Prentice-Hall of India Private Limited, *New Delhi*
Prentice-Hall of Japan, Inc., *Tokyo*
Simon & Schuster Asia Pte. Ltd., *Singapore*
Editora Prentice-Hall do Brasil, Ltda., *Rio de Janeiro*

This book is dedicated to the children who fill our days:

Richard Edward,
whom I respect and admire more each day

Elizabeth Mary,
the lightness in my heart who makes each day worth living

Katherine Emily,
the imp out of the bottle more valuable than all possessions
and accomplishments who makes each day memorable

Timothy John,
whom I expect to see in Congress very soon

Mark Patrick,
my special dentist, graduation date 1998

And to the many other exceptional children who have contributed to our understanding of
their challenging lives.

# Preface

From the moment of conceptualization through the final editing of this text, the authors' guiding principle has not wavered. We have dedicated ourselves to presenting the fundamental knowledge necessary to understand the foundations upon which special education was constructed and the principles and practices that have evolved from that foundation. The structure for the chapters that have evolved included a uniform outline that could describe each exceptionality within a similar framework. It is from these similarly described basics for each exceptionality that the reader will be able to build a scaffold to understanding the complexities of each condition.

The authors share a combined total of 68 years of experience with exceptional children and youth. It is through this filter that the thinking of our predecessors and colleagues has been presented. By defining the basic parameters of exceptionality we have been able to explain the current issues driving the field, in what we hope is a concise and cogent manner.

Throughout this text we have attempted to confront problematic issues head on. Even at the introductory level, we believe that a knowledge of concerns and currently unanswered questions can be as informative as the explanation of the knowledge captured by the research efforts of our colleagues.

## ABOUT THIS BOOK

The purpose of this text is to gather in one source the most critical information needed to understand exceptional children and adolescents. We have tried to present this information as concisely yet completely as possible. The eleven separate but related chapters that follow should serve as a guide for the beginning student, the concerned parent, and the allied professional who seek introductory information about exceptionalities.

Chapter 1 introduces the reader to many of the basic concepts needed to understand exceptional children of all types. In it we define the special student, share relevant demographics, present a brief history of the special education movement, and show how the legislation that the federal government has seen fit to pass to protect exceptional people has formed the backbone of the service-provision structure in the schools where most services are initiated and provided. We will also highlight the

v

professional preparation standards that special educators must meet in order to provide the best educational experience possible for exceptional students.

Chapter 2 focuses on some of the most critical issues that are facing special educators, public schools, parents, and the many partnerships between parents, communities, and those responsible for providing direct and indirect service to people with exceptionalities. Once armed with this basic understanding, the reader may proceed to any of the nine separate chapters that deal with each exceptionality. In order, the chapters are:

Chapter 3: Children with Mental Retardation

Chapter 4: Children with Learning Disabilities

Chapter 5: Children with Emotional and Behavioral Disorders

Chapter 6: Children with Communication Disorders

Chapter 7: Children with Physical and Health Impairments

Chapter 8: Children with Hearing Impairments

Chapter 9: Children with Visual Impairments

Chapter 10: Children with Severe or Multiple Disabilities

Chapter 11: Children Who Are Gifted and Talented

In order to make each of the exceptionality chapters (Chapters 3–11) consistent and easy for the reader to follow, we have presented information using the same structure for each chapter. Each chapter will begin with a *definition* of the exceptional area to be discussed. As the reader will learn, defining each area of exceptionality is not as simple as the task may seem. Federal definitions, individual state definitions, and conceptualizations of scholars in each area are sometimes in conflict. We have attempted to highlight conflicting definitions and present the reader with those most commonly accepted.

Each chapter will present *prevalence* figures that will help the reader understand the magnitude of the exceptionality. Unfortunately, differing definitions often lead to different counts. We will present the conflicting data and explain how the different figures might occur.

The next section of each chapter will deal with the most salient *characteristics* that would identify a child as a member of an exceptionality group. This listing of observable behaviors or physical anomalies can help identify those children who are "at risk" for needing special services. We will repeatedly emphasize that most exceptional children are more like their nonexceptional age mates than they are different. However, an understanding of their most characteristic differences should provide the beginning reader with critical information in understanding each exceptionality.

The *etiology* or cause of each exceptionality will then be discussed. There may be multiple causes of a given exceptionality, or the causes may be unknown; in some instances the best information available can only provide the best guess we currently have as to the etiology of an exceptionality.

The *identification process* that is appropriate for each at-risk child will be discussed in detail. In this section of each chapter, the reader will learn what steps are necessary to fulfill both legal and professional requirements to include a child in an exceptionality category and allow that child to become eligible for the educational services and social benefits available to members of that exceptionality group.

We have next highlighted *programs* that are the most effective or widely used treatments or interventions used in the school context. Most often, the typical service-delivery format or model program is described to most concisely depict the intervention strategy.

While Chapter 2 discusses issues critical to special education in general, each categorical chapter has an *"Issues of Importance"* section that hones in on the specific concerns of students, teachers, parents, and other professionals who are concerned with individual exceptionalities. It is the goal of this section to sensitize the reader to the most compelling issues facing those seeking and providing service for the members of each specific exceptionality group and their parents. Throughout this text we have made it a point to differentiate cultural diversity from exceptionalities. The goal of special education is not to make everyone the same, but rather to enable children to achieve their potential while preserving their individual identities and cultural and ethnic heritage. However, there are often special considerations that service providers need to be knowledgeable of when dealing with culturally and linguistically diverse children. Each chapter has a section labeled *"Minority Concerns"* that highlights some of these issues.

A variety of professionals deal with children with exceptionalities. Obviously the special-education teacher will be critical for almost all students with exceptionalities. However, many other professionals, both educational and rehabilitative, will deal with any group of children with exceptionalities. A section entitled *"Professionals"* has been included in each chapter to help examine and explain the role that care providers in addition to special-education teachers provide for children identified as eligible for special education and related services.

The final sections of each exceptionality chapter provide the reader with sources for more information. The sections titled *"Professional Associations and Parent or Self-Help Groups"* identify a comprehensive listing of groups dedicated to improving all aspects of the lives of those who fall within their area of concern. The sections called *"References for Further Information"* are listings of professional publications, journals, and newsletters that are concerned with each exceptionality. The *bibliography* that appears at the end of each chapter identifies the sources that were critical in presenting the information in each chapter. The inclusion of separate bibliographies at the end of each chapter will simplify the search for further appropriate readings in each area.

Our goal throughout this text was to translate material that is often complex and contradictory into a format that could easily be understood by the novice reader. We are well aware of the potential dangers of oversimplification. We tried as best we could never to lose the essence of an issue or concern in a misguided attempt to make the information palatable. The reader will note throughout the text that supplementary readings are suggested to flesh out the necessary simplifications of an introductory work. In addition, the data base for this book was derived from studying the most accepted and accessible sources available to scholars and practitioners in special education and related fields. Although the authors bring a combined total of 68 years of experience to this text, we have tried to keep our opinions and personal feelings independent of the material presented in this overview, which presents the most commonly accepted information available at the date of publication. To do this, we have immersed ourselves in the writings of our expert colleagues who have presented the results of their studies in the literature. From this roundtable of experts, we have teased out a consensus of the current beliefs concerning the areas covered in each section of our text. At times, we were able to isolate and present divergent views. Thus the reader, while learning the most current beliefs driving the exceptionalities, should be able to quickly see how divergent views might develop into the lasting truths of the future.

A final caveat before the text begins. Only in textbooks are exceptionalities assigned one to a customer. In the real world, having one problem does not automatically excuse a person from all others. Thus, it is possible to be both gifted and visually impaired or learning disabled and behaviorally disordered. Often, exceptionalities may be related; other times they are not. Where there is a high correlation between exceptionalities—for example, between hearing impairment and speech sound articulation—we have alerted the reader to this possible mix. In addition, Chapter 10 is devoted to children with commonly defined multiple disabilities. However, in order to keep from mixing the boundaries of each exceptionality, we have most often treated them as discrete phenomena. This was done for the convenience of the reader, who we anticipate will be searching for guidelines, definitions, and a basic understanding of each exceptionality. The complexities of life will demand that the practitioner be alert and ever mindful of the possibility for co-existing exceptionalities.

## ACKNOWLEDGMENTS

While writing this text we have not worked in a vacuum. We were taught by our mentors, colleagues, students, and the children we have served. Our mentors helped us with the initial understanding of special education. Our colleagues have argued with us, shaped our thinking, and judged our contributions. Our students have taken us to task and forced us to clarify our thinking. The children we have attempted to serve have validated our professional lives. They are a constant reminder that we must do better for the next generation than we have for the past one. Given this wealth of experience, we feel fortunate to have been given the opportunity to synthesize our thinking with these experiences in producing this text. We have, of course, been as meticulous as possible in our attribution of thoughts, concepts, and techniques to their originators. If we have slighted anyone, it was not only unintentional, but a direct function of the synthesis of their truths into our lives. Julius E. Heuscher, quoted in *Newsweek* (1991), explains that borrowing often occurs in texts because "[s]ome ideas become so true that they become our own." We like to believe that we are learners before we are teachers.

This manuscript, in the format the reader is holding, is the direct result of the efforts of our editor, Ann Davis, who allowed us to write a text that could present and protect the dignity of the knowledge base without resorting to "dumbing down" the information in a misguided attempt to sugar it for readers. We are grateful to Ann; to Pat Grogg, her editorial assistant and calming influence; to Linda Zuk, our highly competent and refreshingly human production coordinator and her staff at WordCrafters, who flawlessly guided us through production; and to Merrill, for the meticulous care in the production of this text that included fourteen separate reviews prior to publication. We are especially grateful to Kathleen Briseno, College of DuPage and DeKalb County; Moon K. Chang, Alabama State University; Melanie B. Jephson, Stephen F. Austin State University; Pamela Laughon, University of North Carolina–Asheville; and Terry M. McLeod, North Georgia College and State University. Their insight and suggestions have saved us from oversights, unrecognized errors, and unfortunate assumptions.

# Contents

# 1

# Introduction to
# Special Education

Special education is individualized educational instruction designed to meet the unique educational and related needs of students with disabilities. Special education provides learning opportunities that are not provided in standard or regular school curricula or by regular school services. Special education programs are designed to be appropriate for the individual student and must be provided and paid for by the community, not the individual student and his or her family. The individualized programming that is the core of special education must be provided in settings that best meet each special student's needs. Typical settings for special education programs are public schools, special classes in public schools, special schools, homes, rehabilitation hospitals, and residential schools and institutions. Special education includes related instructional services such as speech, physical, and occupational therapy and transportation services. In addition, the special education movement supports the proposition that children and youth with disabilities need to be integrated or included in normal or regular educational services or programs to the extent that it is reasonable.

Kirk (1972) defines the exceptional child (including gifted and talented children as well as children with disabilities) as

> [the] child who deviates from the average or normal child (1) in mental characteristics, (2) in sensory abilities, (3) in neuromuscular or physical characteristics, (4) in social or emotional behavior, (5) in communication abilities, or (6) in multiple handicaps to such an extent that he requires a modification of school practices, or special education services, in order to develop to his maximum capacity. (p. 4)

Special education evolved when our society recognized and respected human differences and assumed the responsibility for the provision of individualized educational services for students with disabilities.

## INDIVIDUAL DIFFERENCES AND THE EXCEPTIONAL CHILD

All children exhibit differences from one another. Often the differences are quite apparent; in other instances, the differences may be more subtle. In addition, all students present different skill levels in academic subjects and different interest levels in educational activities. It is the degree of these differences that determines whether a child is exceptional and therefore eligible for special educational services.

The definition of "normal" or "acceptable" in our culture is elusive. One meaning is that a person is prepared to participate, in an independent fashion, in the American cultural mainstream or milieu. People within a group may be characterized as normal when they conform to the group's rules or values. When individuals meet the social and educational expectations of the group, they are considered normal.

Children display a wide variety of physical, emotional, and learning differences. When a child differs from the norm (what is considered normal) to such an extent that specialized and individualized educational programming is required to meet that child's unique needs, he or she is considered an exceptional child. Exceptional children are children who are below average intellectually, display learning and/or behavioral problems, or have physical or sensory impairments. Any given child may show multiple impairments that are combinations of any of the previously listed conditions. An exceptional child may also be gifted intellectually or show a remarkable talent. Special education is provided for children who are:

- Mentally retarded

- Learning disabled

- Emotionally or behaviorally disturbed

- Physically impaired

- Otherwise health impaired

- Communicatively disordered

- Hearing impaired

- Visually impaired

- Severely and multiply handicapped

- Gifted and talented

## CHILDREN AT RISK

In addition to those children who are identified as being exceptional, there are children who are referred to as *children at risk*. They are not yet identified as having a disability. However, they are considered to have a high probability of developing a disability. The term *at risk* is often used with the very young who, because of negative conditions surrounding their birth, nurturing, or environment, may be expected to experience developmental problems. At-risk students include students who are experiencing learning, socialization, and maturational difficulties in the regular classroom; are failing academic subjects; or are at risk of overall school failure and thus become identified as candidates for special-education services (Heward, 1996).

The terms defined in Box 1.1 will help the reader better understand the concepts being developed in this chapter.

### Box 1.1
### *WHAT EVERY TEACHER NEEDS TO KNOW*

### *Terms*

**classification**   A structured system that identifies and organizes characteristics to establish order; for example, characteristics of mental retardation or serious emotional disturbance.

**continuum** or **cascade of services**   The range of placement and service options available to meet the needs of individual students with disabilities.

**criterion-referenced tests**   Tests that compare individual performance to a set of defined objectives, tasks, behaviors, or competencies.

**curriculum-based assessment**   Assessment of students relative to the degree to which they are learning specific curriculum content.

**disability**   Reduced function or loss of a particular body part or organ; for example, a missing arm.

**handicap**   A limitation that individuals with impairments or disabilities have in their environments; for example, a person using a wheelchair.

**impairment**   The condition of diseased or defective tissue; for example, anoxia (lack of oxygen) may cause central nervous system impairment.

**incidence**   The number of new cases that occur within a certain time period.

**inclusion**   The process by which children with special needs receive remedial services in the least restricted environment, especially in the regular classroom. Inclusion presupposes collaboration between special educators and regular classroom teachers.

**labels**   The names or classifications used to describe individuals with special needs. The names or labels used also lead to the use of categories of special education; for example, mental retardation.

**mainstreaming**   The least restrictive environment for educational placement; for example, integration of students into the regular classroom for all or part of the school day.

**noncategorical** or **cross-categorical approach**   Declassification of individuals and emphasis on profiling their strengths or weaknesses or the classification of levels of disability; for example, mild, moderate, or severe.

**normalization**   Making available to individuals who are disabled life conditions that are as close as possible as the normal or regular circumstances and ways of life of society.

**norm-referenced tests**   Tests that compare a student's performance to that of the *norm group,* or the group of people on whom the test was standardized.

**prevalence**   The number of cases active at a given time.

**Regular Education Initiative (REI)**   Educational reform practices that place greater emphasis on educating students with disabilities in the regular classroom.

## HISTORY OF SPECIAL EDUCATION

Public education for exceptional students in the United States can be traced back to the establishment of free public education in the early 1800s. However, by the early 1900s, although institutional programs for students with sensory impairment and mental retardation were widespread in the United States; only a few public schools served students with disabilities who did not fit the available curriculum (Wynne & Conner, 1979).

From early 1900 to the 1970s, attempts to serve exceptional children within public schools took the form of special day schools, which educated students with physical impairments, mental retardation, and serious emotional disturbance. The independent self-contained special education classroom within a regular public school also emerged at this time (Wynne & Conner, 1979).

Special education has historically been supported by the U.S. Office of Education, which was a part of the former Department of Health, Education, and Welfare (HEW). It then evolved into the Bureau of Education for the Handicapped (BEH) in the Department of Health, Education, and Welfare. Currently, the BEH is identified as the Office of Special Education and Rehabilitation Services in the U.S. Department of Education. Along with the evolving bureaucracy, special-education leadership within and outside of the government began to re-evaluate the role of the popular but often isolated self-contained classroom programs for the education of exceptional students, along with supporting new programs focusing on preschool intervention, guaranteeing the legal rights of exceptional children, mainstreaming, resource room use, and the current attempt at full inclusion of exceptional children into the regular classroom.

It is reasonable to suggest that beginning in 1975 and continuing to the present, the special education movement has been experiencing a critical turning point. This is primarily due to the enactment of the federal laws that are referred to as the Bill of Rights for the Handicapped. They are Public Law 94-142, the Education for All Handicapped Children Act and its amendments, and PL 101-476, the Individuals with Disabilities Education Act (IDEA). PL 101-476 and its amendments provide a free, appropriate public education to all children and youth with disabilities. The major points described in these laws have become the specialized language of special education:

1. *Zero reject*—No child shall be refused an appropriate education by public schools.

2. *Nondiscriminatory evaluation*—Evaluations must be conducted in the child's native language.

3. *Least restrictive environment*—Each child must be mainstreamed whenever possible.

4. *Due process*—Fourteenth Amendment rights of the Constitution, which guarantee privacy, confidentiality of information, and protection of personal rights, are extended to those identified as handicapped or disabled.

5. *Individualized education program* (IEP)—Educators must plan individually tailored educational programs for each exceptional child.

6. *Preschool programs*—Early intervention programs for children from birth through age 3 must be developed and operational.

7. *Individualized transition program* (ITP)—Educators must plan individually tailored transition programs from school to employment and adult life.

These terms and the concepts they represent have become the backbone of the special education movement. We will refer to them repeatedly throughout this text and further define them as we proceed.

## LABELING CHILDREN

*Labeling* implies more than simply identifying children who need special educational services. There is a history of concern by special educators about the negative effects of labeling and categorization of exceptional children. Labeling has been viewed as demeaning, stigmatizing, and discriminatory, especially with regard to the potential to exclude children based on poverty or membership in ethnic and culturally diverse groups. These concerns have been balanced by recognizing that the labeling process facilitates the passage of legislation; governmental program administration; and eligibility for resources in treatment, education, research, and personnel preparation.

Criticisms of labeling, and professional activism against the labeling process, can be traced back to 1969, when special educators in the Council for Children with Behavioral Disorders, a subdivision of the Council for Exceptional Children, announced at the April 1969 International Convention in Denver, Colorado, that:

> We believe the following to be true, that the values and practices of professionals concerned with children produce schools which:
>
> 1. Deprive all children of the experience of self-fulfillment causing them to fail in school: to be excluded from school, to become impotent in education and society;
>
> 2. Create and maintain racist, and otherwise dehumanizing values in society; and
>
> 3. Use labels which place responsibility for failure on the child, his parents or on other factors unrelated to his school experiences.
>
> We further believe that Special Educators have allowed themselves to be used to perpetuate these means of harming children through practices which shield American education from its failures. Moreover, we believe that the Council for Exceptional Children and its divisions have permitted themselves to be used as one of the special arrangements for relieving individual and institutional guilt and responsibility. Now, therefore, the Council for Children with Behavioral Disorders calls upon the Council for Exceptional Children to:
>
> 1. Seek a definition of exceptionality that is educational in its origin and conception, and in its diagnostic and remedial implications.
>
> 2. Strongly affirm the inadequacy of the traditional special education model of remediation, and actively affirm the need for the development of a new model that involves the total system and all children. (CCBD, 1969).

This issue is far from resolved, and the almost 30-year-old resolution cited here has never been adopted as part of the bylaws of the Council for Exceptional Children.

## CASCADE OF SERVICES

The various special educational environments are often referred to as the *cascade of services*. The continuum of environments ranges from the least restricted environment of the regular classroom placement (full inclusion) to the most restrictive placement (institutionalization). Figure 1.1 is a graphic representation of this model. The philosophy guiding this continuum of service holds that to the maximum extent possible, children with special education needs shall be educated in regular class settings. Each child with special needs is to participate with children who are not disabled, and shall engage in activities to the maximum extent appropriate to the needs of the student in both non-academic and extracurricular services (meals, recess period, counseling services, recreational activities, special interest groups/clubs sponsored by the local school). In this context, the least restrictive environment (LRE) means that to the maximum extent possible, students with special needs shall be educated with children who are not handicapped or disabled. Among all the alternatives for placement within an educational system, students with special needs shall be placed where they can obtain appropriate educational services that meet their individual educational needs and are as

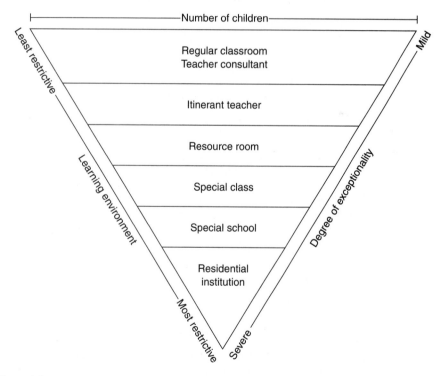

**Figure 1.1**

Cascade of Services: Special learning environments for exceptional children

Note: Hospital and homebound services provided for children with disabilities who may be confined for long periods of time fall within the realm of the residential-institution setting on the scale of special education learning environments.

Source: From "Special Education as Developmental Capital" by E. Deno, 1979, *Exceptional Children*, 37, pp. 229–237. Copyright 1970 by The Council for Exceptional Children. Reprinted with permission.

close to and as nearly like a regular classroom setting as possible. Those settings are defined as:

- *Regular class*, which includes students who receive the majority of their education program in a regular classroom and receive special education and related services outside the regular classroom for less than 21 percent of the school day. It includes children placed in a regular class and receiving special education within the regular class, as well as children placed in a regular class and receiving special education outside the regular class.

- *Resource rooms*, which include students who receive special education and related services outside the regular classroom for at least 21 percent but not more than 60 percent of the school day. This may include students placed in resource rooms who receive part-time instruction in a regular class.

- *Separate class placement*, which includes students who receive special education and related services outside the regular class for more than 60 percent of the school day. Students may be placed in self-contained special classrooms with part-time instruction in regular classes, or in self-contained classes full-time on a regular school campus.

- *Separate schools*, which include students who receive special education and related services for more than 50 percent of the school day in separate day schools for those with disabilities.

- *Residential facility placement*, which includes students who receive education in a public or private residential facility, at public expense, for more than 50 percent of the school day.

- *Homebound/hospital environments*, which include students receiving special education in hospital or homebound programs (U.S. Department of Education, 1997).

Table 1.1 presents the percentage of students age 6 through 21 with disabilities who are served in each of the educational environments just described.

## EDUCATIONAL PLACEMENTS

Each year since 1978, the Office of Special Education has reported on the number of students with disabilities age 6 through 21 served in each of six different educational environments: regular class, resource room, separate class (self-contained class), separate public or private school, public or private residential facility, and homebound/hospital placement (U.S. Department of Education, 1997). Table 1.2 lists the number and percentage change of students age 6 through 21 served under IDEA.

Table 1.1

Percentage of Students Age 6 though 21 with Disabilities Served in Different Educational Environments by Disability, School Year 1994–1995

| Disability | Regular Class | Resource Room | Separate Class | Separate School | Residential Facility | Homebound/ Hospital |
|---|---|---|---|---|---|---|
| Specific learning disabilities | 41.11 | 39.58 | 18.40 | 0.61 | 0.13 | 0.16 |
| Speech or language impairments | 87.36 | 7.69 | 4.53 | 0.32 | 0.03 | 0.06 |
| Mental retardation | 7.68 | 27.10 | 55.86 | 6.27 | 0.61 | 0.48 |
| Serious emotional disturbance | 22.05 | 24.01 | 35.21 | 13.61 | 3.31 | 1.82 |
| Other health impairments | 42.55 | 28.94 | 18.50 | 1.60 | 0.30 | 7.99 |
| Hearing impairments | 35.01 | 19.35 | 28.56 | 6.69 | 10.18 | 0.21 |
| Orthopedic impairments | 39.08 | 20.60 | 31.65 | 5.62 | 0.42 | 2.63 |
| Visual impairments | 45.94 | 21.08 | 17.23 | 4.80 | 10.42 | 0.53 |
| Autism | 10.68 | 9.32 | 54.99 | 21.58 | 3.87 | 0.55 |
| Deaf-blindness | 9.35 | 8.77 | 36.23 | 22.43 | 20.23 | 2.49 |
| Traumatic brain injury | 25.99 | 24.05 | 30.42 | 14.37 | 2.24 | 2.93 |
| Multiple disabilities | 8.98 | 11.80 | 51.32 | 21.89 | 3.51 | 2.49 |
| All disabilities | 50.68 | 9.31 | 31.69 | 5.54 | 0.18 | 2.60 |

*Source:* U.S. Department of Education, Office of Special Education, Data Analysis System (DANS).

Table 1.2

Number and Percentage Change of Students Ages 6 through 21 Served Under Part B and Chapter 1 (SOP): School Years 1994–95 through 1995–96

| Disability | Number of Students | | Change | |
|---|---|---|---|---|
| | *1994–95* | *1995–96* | *Number* | *Percent* |
| Specific learning disabilities | 2,503,967 | 2,595,004 | 91,037 | 3.64 |
| Speech or language impairments | 1,018,234 | 1,025,591 | 7,357 | .72 |
| Mental retardation | 569,196 | 584,406 | 15,210 | 2.67 |
| Serious emotional disturbance | 427,454 | 438,150 | 10,696 | 2.50 |
| Visual impairments | 24,663 | 25,443 | 780 | 3.16 |
| Hearing impairments | 65,070 | 67,994 | 2,924 | 4.49 |
| Orthopedic impairments | 60,415 | 63,158 | 2,743 | 4.54 |
| Other health impairments | 106,971 | 133,354 | 26,383 | 24.66 |
| Autism | 22,652 | 28,813 | 6,161 | 27.20 |
| Deaf-blindness | 1,315 | 1,352 | 37 | 2.81 |
| Traumatic brain injury | 7,248 | 9,439 | 2,191 | 30.23 |
| Multiple disabilities | 89,118 | 94,034 | 4,916 | 5.52 |
| All disabilities | 4,896,303 | 5,066,738 | 170,435 | 3.48 |

*Source:* U.S. Department of Education, 1997.

## INCLUSION

The concept of inclusion is simple to understand but complex in implementation. *Inclusion* refers to a special education reform that often requires school restructuring in general education. It involves altering curriculum and instruction, changing rules and beliefs of teachers, principals, and parents so that children with special needs can be integrated into regular classrooms. Although it may appear as simply another step along the special education continuum of services, it advances the proposition that general education is a source for supporting the kinds of profound changes required to accommodate special students with the collaborative remedial efforts of special and general educators.

## THE LAW AND SPECIAL EDUCATION

This section will identify some of the most critical legislation that has had an impact on special education. As we describe this important legislation, we will highlight some of the practical results each piece of legislation has had on routine service provision and ensuring the rights of exceptional students and their families. Many commonplace occurrences, such as writing an individualized education program (IEP) or including parents as part of the team that decides the best course for the exceptional child, did not occur until the enabling legislation was passed that mandated these

and other activities. Progress in providing appropriate educational experiences for exceptional children is directly related to the enabling legislation provided through legislative advocacy. Elected and appointed officials from federal, state, and local governments and school districts pass and implement laws and regulations that govern the operation of both public and private schools. They determine by financing (funding) and political policy what type of schools there should be, where they should be located, how they should be administered, what the curriculum content will be, who will teach, and who should or should not attend those schools. The state and local education agencies (SEAs and LEAs) maintain the major authority, unless federal legislation and funding stipulate specific directions for the use of monies given to the SEA or LEA. The states very often pass parallel legislative bills to match the federal legislative thrust; as a result, joint funding is often provided for needed educational programs (Meyen, 1996).

There is a rich history of legislative efforts by Congress for children and adults with disabilities. Table 1.3 highlights some of this legislation and identifies the years in which significant federal legislation was passed by Congress. This chronological summary of enabling legislation will help the reader understand where special education has its roots and the directions in which it is currently growing. However, the path has not always been a straight or narrow one. As a result, the summary in this section will by necessity include a potentially confusing criss-crossing of legislation and amendments. However, using Table 1.3 as a guide should help with the chronology.

Prior to World War II, there were few federal laws authorizing special benefits for people with disabilities. Children with disabilities were often excluded from schools in our nation's early history. Since the 1960s, however, there has been a great emergence of federal legislation in support of services and education for children and youth with disabilities. The many court decisions rendered and state and federal laws passed since the 1960s now protect the rights of children and youth with disabilities and guarantee that they receive a free, appropriate, publicly supported education (NICHCY, 1996).

## Early Federal Education Laws and Court Cases

Looking back, it is clear that federal guarantees of the educational rights of individuals with disabilities have been an evolving story. Throughout the 1800s, special education programs emerged for people with mental retardation, deafness, blindness, behavioral disorders, and physical disabilities. However, it was not until 1879, by way of Public Law 45-186, that Congress provided funds to develop braille materials for the American Printing House for the Blind. Years passed until Congress again acted on behalf of people with disabilities (PL 66-236) by providing vocational rehabilitation services for World War I veterans and extending these services to civilians (Smith & Luckasson, 1995). During the late 1950s there were limited and sporadic congressional attempts to assist individuals with mental retardation and deafness. There were also some early attempts at preparing personnel to assist people with exceptionalities. The 1960s initiated a productive era for the early emergence of legislation

**Table 1.3**
Federal Legislation for People with Disabilities

| Year | Legislation |
| --- | --- |
| 1879 | Funds to produce braille materials for the American Printing House for the Blind (PL 45-186) |
| 1920 | Vocational rehabilitation services authorized for World War I veterans are extended to civilians (PL 66-236) |
| 1961 | Provisions for production and distribution of captioned films for the deaf (PL 87-715) |
| 1963 | Funds to train teachers for all disabilities; research and demonstration projects are established to study education of exceptional children (PL 88-164) |
| 1965 | Provisions for extension of basic authorities allowing the development of research and demonstration centers (PL 89-105) |
| 1965 | Support to aid children with disabilities in state institutions (PL 89-313); National Technical Institute for the Deaf is established (PL 89-136) |
| 1966 | Authorization for establishing the Bureau of Education for the Handicapped and a National Advisory Committee on the Handicapped (PL 89-750) |
| 1968 | Experimental demonstration centers for preschoolers are established (PL 90-538); provisions are made for deaf-blind centers, resource centers, and expansion of media services for those with disabilities (PL 90-247) |
| 1970 | Facilities are required to be accessible to those with physical disabilities (PL 91-205) |
| 1970 | Consolidation into one act of all previously separate federal grant programs for children with disabilities. Known as Part B of the Education of the Handicapped Act (PL 91-230) |
| 1973 | Rights of individuals with disabilities in employment and educational institutions receiving federal funds are guaranteed through Section 504 of the Rehabilitation Act Amendments (PL 93-112) |
| 1974 | Authorization of the Family Educational Rights and Privacy Act giving parents the right to examine records kept in the student's files (PL 93-380) |
| 1975 | Free, appropriate public education and other procedural guarantees are mandated for all children with disabilities (PL 94-142) |
| 1978 | Gifted and Talented Children's Act (PL 95-561) authorizes minimum appropriations to state agencies for programs for gifted and talented children |
| 1983 | PL 94-142 amended to provide added emphasis on parent education and preschool, secondary, and postsecondary programs for children and youth with disabilities (PL 98-199); amended in 1986 to extend its provisions to infants and toddlers from birth through age 2 (PL 99-457) |
| 1984 | The Vocational Education Act (PL 98-524) supports vocational programs and the provision of such programs to students with disabilities |
| 1985 | The need for specialized temporary care is recognized by the Temporary Childcare for Handicapped Children and Crisis Nurseries Act (PL 99-401) |
| 1986 | Rehabilitation Act Amendments of 1986 provides programs in supported employment services for individuals with disabilities (PL 99-504) |
| 1987 | Developmental Disabilities and Bill of Rights Act establishes Developmental Disabilities Councils as a part of advocacy systems for people with developmental disabilities (PL 100-146) |
| 1988 | Authorization for the establishment of statewide assistive-technology services (PL 100-407) |
| 1990 | Discrimination against people with disabilities in employment is banned; public buildings, transportation, and communication systems must be made accessible (PL 101-335); PL 94-142 is amended to the Individuals with Disabilities Education Act (PL 101-476). |
| 1990 | Authorization of Early Intervention Programs for infants, toddlers, and preschoolers with disabilities (PL 102-119) |
| 1991 | The Carl D. Perkins Vocational and Applied Technology Education Act focuses on improving programs leading to providing the skills needed to work in a technological society PL 102-103. (1991) |
| 1994 | Reauthorization of PL 100-407 to develop a national classification system for easier access to assistive-technology devices and services (PL 103-218) |
| 1994 | Developmental Disabilities Assistance and Bill of Rights Act supports councils within states to help people with developmental disabilities achieve independence, productivity, and integration and inclusion into their communities (PL 103-230) |

*Sources:* From NICHCY, (1996, October). vol. 9, pp. 1–6; and *Exceptional Individuals in School, Community, and Work* (p. 27), by P. Wehman, 1997, Austin, TX: PRO-ED.

for individuals with disabilities. In 1961, PL 87-715 provided for funds to develop, produce, and distribute captioned films. In 1963, PL 88-164 expanded federal interest in training personnel to assist individuals in all the disability categories recognized at the time. Grants for research to learn more about each condition and demonstration projects to provide model service-delivery systems were also provided (Martin, 1968).

Direct federal support for the education of children with disabilities has its modern roots in the Elementary and Secondary Education Act of 1965 (ESEA), PL 89-105, which strengthened and improved educational quality and opportunity in the nation's elementary and secondary schools (DeStefano & Snauwaert, 1989). The key issue in the passage of PL 89-105 was that it encouraged the development of research and allowed for demonstration centers throughout the nation (Martin, 1968). Later, PL 89-105 was amended by PL 89-313, the Elementary and Secondary Education Act Amendments of 1965, which authorized the first federal grant programs specifically targeted for children and youth with disabilities. PL 89-313 authorized grants to state agencies to educate children with disabilities in state-operated or state-supported schools and institutions. During the next year, PL 89-750, the Elementary and Secondary Education Act Amendments of 1966, established the first federal grant program for the education of children with disabilities at the local school level. This law also established the Bureau of Education for the Handicapped (BEH) to administer all Office of Education programs for children and youth with disabilities. Its function was to help the states implement and monitor programs, support demonstration programs, conduct research, and evaluate federally funded programs. BEH was to (1) provide financial support for training special educators, other teachers, support personnel, and parents; and (2) support research, training, production, and distribution of educational media.

In 1968, PL 90-247, the Elementary and Secondary Education Act Amendments of 1968, established a set of programs that supplemented and supported the expansion and improvement of special education services, including funding for regional resource centers, centers and services for children with deaf-blindness, the expansion of instructional remedial programs, continued research in special education, and funds to establish a center to help improve the recruitment of education personnel and to disseminate information concerning education opportunities for children and youth with disabilities.

## Legislation from the 1970s to the Present

Following on the heels of this landmark legislation, Congress passed the Elementary and Secondary Education Act Amendments of 1970, PL 91-230. This law consolidated into one act a number of previously separate federal grant programs related to the education of children with disabilities. This new authorization, known as Part B, was titled the Education of the Handicapped Act (EHA) and was the precursor to the 1975 Education for All Handicapped Children Act, which would significantly expand the educational rights of children and youth with disabilities. The Rehabilitation Act of 1973, Section 504 (PL 93-112), provides qualified individuals with disabilities with basic civil rights protection in programs and activities that receive federal financial assistance. No qualified disabled individual in the United States shall, solely by reason of a disability, be excluded from the participation in, be denied the benefits of, or be subjected to discrimination under any program or activity receiving federal financial assistance. The U.S. Department of Education's implementation of Section 504 applies to preschool, elementary, secondary, postsecondary, vocational, and other programs and activities that receive or benefit from federal financial assistance. In essence, Section 504 prohibits discrimination against children and youth with disabilities in educational institutions receiving federal funds. PL 93-112 has been amended several times.

PL 93-380, the Family Educational Rights and Privacy Act (FERPA), passed in 1974, is often called the Buckley Amendment. It gives parents of students under the age of 18, and students age 18 and older, the right to examine records kept in the student's personal file. FERPA was designed to cover all students, including those in postsecondary education. The major provisions of the act are that:

- Parents and eligible students have the right to inspect and review the student's educational records.
- Schools must have written permission from the parent or eligible student before releasing any information from a student's records. While a school may disclose education records to others without consent—such as other school officials, schools to which a student is transferring, certain government officials, and state and local authorities—the school must keep track, within the student's files, of the requests for these records. The parent or eligible student may inspect this information.
- Parents and eligible students have the right to have the records explained and interpreted by school officials.
- School officials may not destroy any education records if there is an outstanding request to inspect and review them.
- Parents and eligible students who believe that information in the education records is inaccurate or misleading may request that the records be amended. The parent or eligible student must be advised if the school decides that the records should not be amended, and has the right to a hearing.

Finally, each school district must give parents or eligible students an annual notice to inform them of their rights under this law and of the right of parents or eligible students to file a complaint with the U.S. Department of Education. This legislation protects all families, in particular the families of exceptional children, from being subjected to arbitrary decisions that would affect the educational experience of their child.

Perhaps the single most far-reaching legislative act ever passed for children with exceptionalities is PL 94-142, the Education for All Handicapped Children Act. Congress passed this law in 1975 and has retitled it the Individuals with Disabilities Act (IDEA). It went into effect in October 1977, when the regulations were finalized. This act governs eligibility for special education services, parental rights, individualized education programs (IEPs), the requirement that children be served in the least restrictive environment, and the need to provide related (non-educational) services. Ballard, Ramirez, and Zantal-Weiner (1987) and DeStefano and Snauwaert (1989) write that the major purposes of PL 94-142 are:

- To guarantee that a "free appropriate education," including special education and related service programming, is available to all children and youth with disabilities who require it.
- To ensure that the rights of children and youth with disabilities and their parents or guardians are protected (for example, fairness, appropriateness, and due process in decision making about providing special education and related services to children and youth with disabilities).
- To assess and ensure the effectiveness of special education at all levels of government.
- To financially assist the efforts of state and local governments in providing full educational opportunities to all children and youth with disabilities through the use of federal funds.

The need for federal legislation for gifted and talented students was recognized in 1978 by PL 95-561, the Gifted and Talented Children's Act, which authorized a minimum appropriation of $50,000 for each state education agency (SEA) to assist their planning, development, operation, and improvement of programs for the education of gifted and talented children. This legislation was followed in August 1988 by Senate Bill 373, entitled the Jacob K. Javits Gifted and Talented Student Education Bill, which provided $8 million for the identification and service for gifted and talented students, training and professional development for teachers of the gifted, and the creation of the National Center for the Education of the Gifted.

In 1983, through the Education of the Handicapped Act Amendments of 1983 (PL 98-199), Congress changed the law to expand incentives for preschool special education programs, early intervention, and transition programs. All programs under the Education of the Handicapped Act (EHA) became the responsibility of the Office of Special Education Programs (OSEP), which by this time had replaced the Bureau of Education for the Handicapped (BEH).

The year 1984 saw the passage of PL 98-524, the Vocational Education Act, which is often referred to as the Carl D. Perkins Act or the Perkins Act. It authorized federal funds to support vocational education programs and to improve the access of those who either have been underserved in the past or who have greater-than-average education needs for these programs. This law is particularly important, because it requires that vocational education be provided for students with disabilities. The law states that individuals who are members of special populations (including individuals with disabilities) must be provided with equal access to recruitment, enrollment, and placement activities in vocational education. In addition, these individuals must be provided with equal access to the full range of vocational education programs available to others, including occupationally specific courses of study, cooperative education, apprenticeship programs, and, to the extent practical, comprehensive guidance and counseling services. Under the law, vocational education planning should be coordinated among public agencies, including vocational education, special education, and state vocational rehabilitation agencies.

The Temporary Childcare for Handicapped Children and Crisis Nurseries Act, PL 99-401, was first introduced in 1985 as part of an omnibus child-care bill and enacted by the 99th Congress in 1986. The act was later incorporated into the Children's Justice and Assistance Act of 1986 (PL 99-401). The act was most recently reauthorized and otherwise amended by the Child Abuse, Domestic Violence, Adoption and Family Services Act of 1992 (PL 102-295). This law provides funding through competitive grants to states and U.S. territories to develop nonmedical respite services (specialized temporary child care) for children with disabilities or chronic or terminal illnesses, and to develop crisis nursery services for children at risk of abuse and neglect. In addition to temporary child care, these programs also offer an array of family support services or referral to such services.

EHA was amended again through PL 99-457, the Education of the Handicapped Act Amendments of 1986, which lowered the age of eligibility for special education and related services for all children with disabilities to age 3. The law also established the Handicapped Infants and Toddlers Program (Part H). As specified by law, this program is directed to the needs of children, from birth to their third birthday, who need early intervention services. Under this program, the infant or toddler's family may receive services needed to help them assist in the development of their child. State definitions of eligibility under this program vary. PL 99-504, the Rehabilitation Act Amendment, was also passed in 1986. It provided programs for supported employment services for individuals with disabilities.

Along with health and educational services, the legal and civil rights of individuals with exceptionalities were a target for enabling legislation. The Mental Retardation Facilities and Community Mental Health Centers Construction Act of 1963 (PL 88-164) and the Developmental Disabilities and Bill of Rights Act Amendments of 1987 (PL 100-146) provided a Bill of Rights section for people with developmental disabilities, which was included in the 1987 amendments. People covered under these amendments included those with mental retardation, autism, cerebral palsy, and epilepsy. Grants were provided to states to establish Developmental Disabilities Councils to support the planning, coordination, and delivery of specialized services to people with developmental disabilities. The law also authorized formula awards to support the establishment and operation of state protection and advocacy systems. Discretionary grants were awarded to (1) university-affiliated programs that provide interdisciplinary training in the fields of developmental disabilities, and (2) projects of national significance aimed at increasing the independence, productivity, and community integration of people with developmental disabilities. The 1987 amendments also established a federal interagency committee to plan for and coordinate activities related to people with developmental disabilities. The act was amended in 1990 (PL 101-496) and in 1994 (PL 103-230) by the Developmental Disabilities Assistance and Bill of Rights Acts. The grants to support councils in the states are for promoting—through systematic change, capacity-building, and advocacy activities—the development of a comprehensive consumer- and family-centered system and a coordinated array of culturally competent services, supports, and other assistance designed to help those with developmental disabilities achieve independence, productivity, and integration and inclusion into the community. Another key provision of these amendments was the definition of *developmental disability*:

> a severe, chronic disability of an individual 5 years of age or older that: (a) is attributable to a mental or physical impairment or combination of mental and physical impairments; (b) is manifested before the person attains age 22; (c) is likely to continue indefinitely; (d) results in substantial functional limitation in three or more of the following areas of major life activity: (i) self-care; (ii) receptive and expressive language; (iii) learning; (iv) mobility; (v) self-direction; (vi) capacity for independent living; and (vii) economic sufficiency; and (e) reflects the individual's need for a combination and sequence of special interdisciplinary, or generic services, supports, or other assistance that is of lifelong or extended duration and is individually planned and coordinated. (NICHCY, 1996, 5-6).

The 1994 amendments make a specific exception to the age limitation for developmental disabilities, to include individuals from birth through age 5 who have substantial

developmental delays or specific congenital or acquired conditions with a high probability of resulting in developmental disabilities if services are not provided.

Programs, projects, and activities receiving assistance under the PL 103-230 must be carried out in a manner consistent with a number of principles, including: (1) that individuals with developmental disabilities, including those with the most severe developmental disabilities, are capable of achieving independence, productivity, and integration and inclusion into the community, given appropriate support; (2) that these individuals and their families are the primary decision makers regarding the services and supports to be received; and (3) that services, supports, and other assistance should be provided in a manner that demonstrates respect for individual dignity, personal preference, and cultural differences.

The Americans with Disabilities Act (ADA), PL 101-336, was signed into law by President Bush on July 26, 1990. The central purpose of the act is to extend to individuals with disabilities civil rights protections similar to those provided to individuals on the basis of race, sex, national origin, and religion. Based on the concepts of the Rehabilitation Act of 1973, the ADA guarantees equal opportunity for individuals with disabilities in employment, public accommodation, transportation, state and local government services, and telecommunications. The ADA is the most significant federal law ensuring the full civil rights of all individuals with disabilities.

Title II of the ADA prohibits discrimination on the basis of disability by state and local government entities. The Office of Civil Rights is responsible for enforcing Title II with respect to all programs, services, and regulatory activities related to the operation of public elementary and secondary education systems and institutions, public institutions of high education and vocational education (other than schools of medicine, dentistry and nursing; other health-related schools; and public libraries).

In 1990, Congress passed the Education of the Handicapped Act Amendments (PL 101-476) and changed EHA to the Individuals with Disabilities Education Act (IDEA). Some new discretionary programs, including special programs on transition, a new program to improve services for children and youth with serious emotional disturbance, and a research and information dissemination program on attention deficit disorder, were created. In addition, the law added transition services and assistive-technology services as new definitions of special education services that must be included in a student's IEP. Also, rehabilitation counseling and social-work services were included as related services under the law. Finally, the services and rights under this law were expanded to more fully include children with autism and traumatic brain injury.

The newest amendment, PL 102-119, primarily addressed the Part H program, now known as the Early Intervention Program for Infants and Toddlers with Disabilities. IDEA makes it possible for states and localities to receive federal funds to assist in the education of infants, toddlers, preschoolers, children, and youth with disabilities. Basically, in order to remain eligible for federal funds under the law, states must ensure that:

- All children and youth with disabilities, regardless of the severity of their disability, will receive a free, appropriate public education (FAPE) at public expense.

- Education of children and youth with disabilities will be based on a complete and individual evaluation and assessment of the specific, unique needs of each child.

- An Individualized Education Program (IEP) or an Individualized Family Services Plan (IFSP) will be drawn up for every child or youth found eligible for special education or early-intervention services, stating precisely what kinds of special education and related services, or the types of early-intervention services, each infant, toddler, preschooler, child, or youth will receive.
- To the maximum extent appropriate, all children and youth with disabilities will be educated in the regular education environment.

Children and youth receiving special education have the right to receive the related services necessary to benefit from special education instruction. Related services include:

> transportation and such developmental, corrective, and other supportive services as are required to assist a child with a disability to benefit from special education, and includes speech pathology and audiology, psychological services, physical and occupational therapy, recreation, early identification and assessment of disabilities in children, counseling services, including rehabilitation counseling, and medical services for diagnostic or evaluation purposes. The term also includes school health services, social work services in schools, and parent counseling and training. (NICCHY, 1996, 6)

Parents have the right to participate in every decision related to the identification, evaluation, and placement of their child or youth with a disability.

Parents must give consent for any initial evaluation, assessment, or placement; must be notified of any change in placement that may occur; must be included, along with teachers, in conferences and meetings held to draw up individualized programs; and must approve these plans before they go into effect for the first time. The right of parents to challenge and appeal any decision related to the identification, evaluation, and placement of their child, or any issue concerning the provision of FAPE, is fully protected by clearly spelled-out due-process procedures.

Parents have the right to confidentiality of information. No one may see a child's records unless the parents give their written permission. (The exception to this is school personnel with legitimate educational interests.)

In summary, the federal laws require that all students with disabilities be educated and that a student with disabilities receive a full individualized evaluation before being placed in special education. This evaluation must be nondiscriminatory and fair for every student, even nonverbal and nonreading students and those with different cultural backgrounds. Each student should be provided with an individualized education program devoted to the student's needs and, to the extent possible, should be educated with peers who are not disabled. Parents and legal guardians must be notified and give consent regarding the evaluation process and placement procedures. They have the right to a due-process hearing when an agreement cannot be reached between them and the school. Special education decisions are made by teams composed of parents and school personnel. Parental input is mandated and is a very essential part of the laws (NICHCY, 1996).

The federal government has also attempted to provide assistance for families who are dependent upon technology but may be confused about obtaining appropriate services or equipment by the bewildering array of devices and services available. The primary purpose of the Technology-Related Assistance for Individuals with Disabilities Act of 1988 (PL 100-407) was to assist states in developing comprehensive, consumer-oriented programs of technology-related assistance, and to increase the availability of assistive technology to individuals with disabilities and their families. In 1990 and 1991, Congress amended this law by passing PL 101-392 and PL 102-103, respectively. The name of the law was changed to the Carl D. Perkins Vocational and Applied Technology Education Act. This new legislation concentrates resources on improving educational programs leading to the academic and occupational skill competencies needed to work in a technologically advanced society. The new law expands the term *special population* to include individuals who are economically and educationally disadvantaged (including foster children), individuals with limited English proficiency, individuals who participate in programs to eliminate sex bias, and those in correctional institutions. The act was reauthorized in 1994 by PL 103-218. The reauthorization requires the development of a national classification system for assistive-technology devices and services.

*Assistive-technology device* is defined by the act as "any item, piece of equipment, or product system whether acquired off the shelf, modified or customized that is used to increase, maintain, or improve functional capabilities of individuals with disabilities." *Assistive technology services* are any services that directly assist an individual with a disability to select, acquire, or use an assistive-technology device. This includes evaluating the needs of the child, including a functional evaluation in the child's customary environment. PL 100-407 provides states with funds to develop a consumer-responsive state system of assistive-technology services. States receiving funds may develop or carry out any of the following: (1) model delivery systems; (2) statewide needs assessment; (3) support groups; (4) public-awareness programs; (5) training and technical assistance; (6) access to related information; (7) interagency agreements; and (8) other activities necessary for developing, implementing, or evaluating a statewide service-delivery system.

In 1997, both houses of Congress overwhelmingly reauthorized IDEA and President Clinton signed it into law. The most noteworthy features of the reauthorization deal with discipline, IEP modifications, mediation, funding, and professional development. Schools now have the authority to place students with exceptionalities in alternative placements if it is determined that the child's behavior was not a manifestation of the child's disability. This provision enables educators to more easily remove violent or dangerous children with disabilities from their current educational placement.

Individualized educational programs (IEPs) are to be more complex, requiring, among other mandates, statements of the student's current level of functioning, measurable short-term objectives, and annual goals. At age 14, transitional service needs must be specified and the IEP must detail how parents are to be regularly informed of their child's progress.

When mediation is needed to resolve differences about placement, individual states are required to establish a mediation system in which parents and schools may voluntarily participate. However, mediation may not be used to deprive parents of their rights to due process.

Funding formulas have been modified. Most significantly, the expense of special education for local school districts can now be shared among state education departments and public agencies. For example, a public agency other than the school district may be assigned the responsibility to pay for assistive technology devices or transitional services.

This latest IDEA also ensures that states will provide more mechanisms for general and special educators to avail themselves of professional development opportunities, enabling them to be current in the knowledge and skills necessary to meet the needs of exceptional children. Examples of professional development programs might include those that provide general and special educators content knowledge, collaborative skills, information about the latest research, or information about promising practices, materials, or technology (IDEA, 1997).

## Legal Reform

Since as early as 1954, litigation and legislation have worked in tandem to protect exceptional children. In the mid-1970s, legislative activism was joined with a burst of legal activism led by newly empowered parental and professional interest groups. Several cases that demanded the right to education for exceptional students were brought to courts in states all over the country. Two precedent-setting cases involving the education of children with disabilities took place in Pennsylvania and the District of Columbia. In Pennsylvania, the Pennsylvania Association for Retarded Citizens (PARC) and thirteen school-age children with mental retardation brought a class-action suit against the Commonwealth of Pennsylvania for its alleged failure to provide all of its school-age children with mental retardation with a publicly supported education (*Pennsylvania Association for Retarded Citizens v. Commonwealth of Pennsylvania*, 1972). The PARC suit was resolved by a consent agreement that specified that the state could not apply any law that would postpone, end, or deny children with mental retardation access to a publicly supported education. The agreement required the state to identify all school-age children with mental retardation who were excluded from the public schools and to place them in a "free public program of education and training appropriate to their capacity." The agreement claimed that it was highly desirable to educate these children in programs most like those available to children without disabilities.

In 1972, the parents and guardians of seven District of Columbia children brought a class-action suit against the District of Columbia Board of Education on behalf of all out-of-school children with disabilities (*Mills v. Board of Education*, 1972). Unlike the PARC case, *Mills* was resolved by a judgment against the district school board. The result was a court order that the District of Columbia must provide all children with a disability, regardless of the severity of their disability, with a publicly supported education.

The courts had become an ally in the quest for the best education possible for all students. Many similar cases followed. Table 1.4 is a brief summary of some major court cases that have influenced the development of special education and the betterment of the life circumstances of individuals with disabilities. The history of successful litigation sustains the proposition that disabled individuals are entitled to equal protection and rights for education and other services without discrimination.

**Table 1.4**
Selected History of Litigation of Special Education

| Year | Court Case |
|------|------------|
| 1954 | *Brown v. Board of Education of Topeka* (Kansas)<br>Established the right of all children to an equal opportunity for an education. |
| 1967 | *Hobson v. Hansen* (Washington, DC)<br>Declared the track system, which used standardized tests as a basis for special education placement, unconstitutional because it discriminated against African American and poor children. |
| 1970 | *Diana v. State Board of Education* (California)<br>Declared that children cannot be placed in special education on the basis of culturally biased tests or tests given in a language other than the child's native language. |
| 1972 | *Mills v. Board of Education of the District of Columbia*<br>Established the right of every child to an equal opportunity for education; declared that lack of funds was not an acceptable excuse for lack of educational opportunity. |
| 1972 | *Pennsylvania Association for Retarded Citizens v. the Commonwealth of Pennsylvania*<br>Class-action suit that established the right to free public education for all children with mental retardation. |
| 1972 | *Wyatt v. Stickney* (Alabama)<br>Declared that individuals in state institutions have the right to appropriate treatment within those institutions. |
| 1979 | *Larry P. v. Riles* (California)<br>First brought to court in 1972; ruled that IQ tests cannot be used as the sole basis for placing children in special classes. |
| 1982 | *Board of Education of the Hendrik Hudson Central School District v. Rowley* (New York)<br>Upheld for each child with a disability the right to a personalized program of instruction and necessary supportive services. |
| 1983 | *Abrahamson v. Hershman* (Massachusetts)<br>Ruled that residential placement in a private school was necessary for a child with multiple disabilities who needed around-the-clock training; required the school district to pay for the private placement. |
| 1984 | *Department of Education v. Katherine D.* (Hawaii)<br>Ruled that a homebound instructional program for a child with multiple health impairments did not meet the least-restrictive-environment standard; called for the child to be placed in a class with children without disabilities and provided with related medical services. |
| 1988 | *Honig v. Doe* (California)<br>Ruled that children with disabilities could not be excluded from school for any misbehavior that is "disability-related." |
| 1989 | *Timothy W. v. Rochester School District* (New Hampshire)<br>Required that all children with disabilities be provided with a free, appropriate public education. The three-judge appeals court overturned the decision of a district court judge, who had ruled that the local school district was not obligated to educate a 13-year-old boy with multiple and severe disabilities because he could not "benefit" from special education. |
| 1990 | *W.G. v. Target Range School District No. 23 Board of Trustees* (Montana)<br>Established that a parent is entitled to private-school cost reimbursement when a school district is in violation of EHA. |
| 1991 | *Community Consolidated School District No. 21 v. Illinois State Board of Education* (Illinois)<br>Established that the hostility of parents is of "obvious and direct relevance" in determining the benefits of an educational placement. |
| 1991 | *Theado v. Strongsville City School District* (Ohio)<br>Established that compensatory education may be awarded to an individual with a disability after age 21 if an appropriate education was denied during the tenure in public education. |
| 1991 | *Rachel Holland v. Board of Education, Sacramento City Unified School District* (California)<br>Established that any placement other than a regular-class placement can be made only after determining that the regular-class placement will be unsuccessful. |

| Year | Court Case |
|------|-----------|
| 1991 | *Corores v. Portsmouth School District* (New Hampshire)<br>Established the right to compensatory education when a district is found to have not provided a free and appropriate education to a student with a disability. |
| 1992 | *Oberti v. Board of Education of the Borough of Clementon School District* (New Jersey)<br>Established inclusion as a right, not a privilege, and found that in order to learn to function effectively, all children with disabilities need integration experiences. |
| 1992 | *Holland v. Sacramento City Unified School District* (California)<br>Established that the school district was required to accept an 11-year-old girl with an IQ of 44 in a regular class. In assessing the inclusion placement, the court considered benefits derived from full-time placement in regular classrooms, non-academic benefits, the impact of the exceptional student's presence on other students, and the costs of placement. |

*Sources:* From *Exceptional Children: An Introduction to Special Education* (pp. 18–25), by W. L. Heward, 1996, Upper Saddle River, NJ: Prentice-Hall/Merrill; and *Exceptional Children in Today's Schools* (3rd ed., pp. 80–84), by E. L. Meyen, 1996, Denver, CO: Love.

## Rights and Responsibilities Resulting from Legislation

The preceding section of the chapter outlined the step-by-step legal attainment of rights and responsibilities by children with disabilities and their parents. What follows is an explanation of how the legislation has been transformed into day-to-day procedures in providing services to exceptional children. Each of the following processes that form the structure of special education services can be traced back to the enabling legislation that made it a part of the education system for children with special needs.

## DUE PROCESS

Students with disabilities, their parents or guardians, and the schools are guaranteed procedural due process safeguards in the determination of needs for services, identification, and placement of students with disabilities. This means that at each of the various stages on the path to determining whether or not a child is eligible for special services, parents must be advised of their rights under the law and must give their consent to proceed with each step. Due process provides protection from arbitrary decision making and requires families to take appropriate responsibility in the determination of an educational plan for their children. Box 1.2 summarizes due process rights in an outline format that will help the reader understand the usual process for determining and providing for a child's educational needs.

## NONDISCRIMINATORY ASSESSMENT

Nondiscriminatory assessment is at the core of due process. Students with suspected disabilities must be assessed by public schools to determine whether the student is eligible for special education services. The majority of students are initially referred by the classroom teacher for evaluation. During evaluation and assessment procedures, educators must use, as best they can, tests and testing protocols that are culturally and racially fair or unbiased. The tests must be in the native language of the child. Use of multiple assessment tools and techniques safeguards against making judgments based on the results of one test only. Nondiscriminatory assessment procedures counteract the possibility of a child being included in a special education placement based on cultural or linguistic differences rather than identifiable disabilities.

## INDIVIDUALIZED EDUCATIONAL PROGRAM

All children who might be identified as eligible for special educational programming have the right to individual educational programming, which can result in an Individualized Educational Program (IEP) for each child. It must be developed by a team whose members meet, review the assessment information available about the child, and design an educational program to address the child's educational needs. This meeting, called an IEP *meeting*, must be held within 30 calendar days after the school district determines, through a multidisciplinary evaluation, that a child has a specified physical or mental impairment and needs special education and related services (North Carolina Department of Public Instruction, 1966). A child's IEP review must occur at least annually thereafter.

## Box 1.2
## *WHAT EVERY TEACHER NEEDS TO KNOW*

### Due Process Rights in a Nutshell

*Right to Know.* Parents must be informed before any action regarding:

1. Identification
2. Evaluation
3. Programming
4. Placement

*Guaranteed Active Participation in the IEP Process.* Parents must give permission for:

1. Release of health and educational records
2. Preplacement evaluation
3. Initial placement

*Appropriate Evaluation.* Testing and evaluation materials must be selected and administered so as not to be racially or culturally discriminatory, must be provided and administered in the child's native language, and must be valid for the purposes for which they are to be used:

1. Tests selected must accurately reflect the child's aptitude or achievement level and other factors they purport to measure
2. No single test may be used to determine educational programs
3. All areas that might have an impact on the disability must also be assessed

*Independent Evaluation.* If parents are concerned about team decisions, they may obtain an independent evaluation:

1. Usually at their own expense
2. At the school system's expense in some cases

*Placement Hearing Resolution.* If parents disagree with the school's plans for the child, and cannot resolve the disagreement informally, they are entitled to a hearing with an impartial hearing officer at no personal expense to help resolve differences.

*Input in the IEP.* The IEP lays out the goals for the child and the services to be provided, including the extent of participation in regular educational programs. Parents must have the opportunity to:

1. Attend each meeting of the IEP team
2. Be given advance notification of each meeting
3. Participate in planning
4. Schedule the meeting at a mutually agreeable time
5. Provide an interpreter if needed

*Communication of Team Decisions.* All decisions must be clearly and simply communicated in parents' native language and by a method of communication that can be understood by all members of the team. The school is responsible for providing all explanations required by team members.

*Right to Information.* Parents have the right to:

1. Review all educational records
2. Request copies of these records (there may be a charge)
3. Request removal of information they think is false or misleading

*Stay-Put Provision.* Once a placement has begun, it may be changed only by the IEP team. If consensus including parent agreement cannot be reached, the child must "stay put" until the hearing process is concluded. In extreme circumstances, the courts can change a placement.

*Right to Confidentiality.* All information on any child with a disability must be kept confidential.

*Right of Action in Federal Court.* Any party aggrieved by the decision of a hearing officer has the right to bring civil suit in federal court.

*Sources:* From NICHCY, (1996, October). Vol. 9, pp. 1–6; and 34 C.F.R., pt. 300, §.

According to the enabling legislation, the following people must be invited to attend the IEP meeting:

1. One or both of the child's parents.
2. The child's teacher(s). If the child has more than one teacher, state policy or law may specify which teacher(s) should participate.
3. A representative of the school other than the child's teacher (this person must be qualified to provide special education or supervise its provision).
4. Other individuals, at the discretion of the school or the parents.
5. The child, when appropriate.

Depending on the purpose of the meeting, other participants may be involved. For example, when a child is being evaluated for the first time, the school must ensure that a member of the evaluation team participates in the IEP meeting, so that someone knowledgeable about the evaluation procedures and results is present. If one of the purposes of the meeting is the consideration of transition services outside of the school setting for the student, then the school must also include the student and a representative of any other agency that will be responsible for providing or paying for the transition services. For all students age 16 or older, one of the purposes of the annual meeting will always be the planning of transition services, since transition services are a required component of the IEP for these students (North Carolina Department of Public Instruction, 1996).

An IEP must be developed for each student placed in a special education program. The plan developed by the team just described is formulated from the assessment procedures during evaluation. The procedures in the IEP process are outlined in Box 1.3.

Following the outline presented in Box 1.3 guarantees that the IEP team will follow all the procedures necessary to safeguard due process and to gather all the information needed to write an IEP. Once all the necessary information is gathered, it is time to construct the IEP. The following paradigm illustrates the ten steps in developing the IEP document:

1. Formulate a statement of the student's present level of educational performance.
2. Formulate a statement of annual goals.
3. Formulate short-term instructional objectives.
4. Formulate a statement of the specific special education services to be provided.
5. Determine the date when those services will begin and the length of time the services will be given.
6. Describe the extent to which the student will be able to participate in regular educational programs.
7. Provide a justification for the type of educational placement the student will receive.
8. Provide a list of the individuals responsible for implementation of the IEP.
9. Provide an outline of objective criteria, procedures, and timelines for evaluating whether the short-term objectives are being achieved.
10. Compile all information on the appropriate form(s).

*Box 1.3*
*WHAT EVERY TEACHER NEEDS TO KNOW*

*Steps in the IEP Process*

### I. EVALUATION

**Questions to Be Addressed**

1. Has parental consent been obtained?
2. What areas of concern are identified in the referral?
3. What data sources will be used?
4. Who should administer and gather the evaluation information?
5. Does the student qualify for special education services?

**Individuals Involved**

1. Classroom teacher
2. Special education teacher
3. LEA representative
4. Psychologist
5. Related service providers
6. Parents
7. Others when appropriate

### II. IEP DEVELOPMENT AND PLACEMENT

**Questions to Be Addressed**

1. How do the evaluation results translate into the student's present level of performance?
2. What are the final student program outcomes?
3. What goals can the student reasonably achieve within one year's time?
4. What objectives will help the student accomplish the goals?
5. How will the goals and objectives be monitored?
6. Is the student placed in the least restrictive environment?

**Individuals Involved**

1. Parent*
2. LEA representative*
3. Special education teacher[†]
4. Student[†]
5. Psychologist
6. Classroom teacher

*mandated

[†]mandated for transition

### III. IEP IMPLEMENTATION AND MONITORING

**Questions to Be Addressed**

1. Are the goals and objectives appropriate? Relevant? Functional?
2. Is the student making progress?
3. Does the IEP need to be amended?

**Individuals Involved**

1. Special education teacher
2. Other service providers as indicated on the IEP
3. IEP team members and appropriate consultants

---

**Box 1.3, Continued**

### IV. ANNUAL REVIEW

| Questions to Be Addressed | Individuals Involved |
| --- | --- |
| 1. Have the goals been achieved? | 1. Special education teacher |
| 2. Does the student still require special education services? | 2. LEA representative |
| 3. What new goals and objectives need to be written? | 3. Parent |
| | 4. Student, when appropriate |

*Source:* Courtesy of North Carolina Department of Public Instruction.

---

## Contents of the IEP

The IEP for each student must contain:

1. Demographic information.
2. The following dates:
   a. The date the IEP document is completed
   b. The entry date to the program (date for initiation of services)
   c. The projected ending date of the IEP (may be no more than one year from the date of the completion of the IEP)
3. A statement of the student's present levels of educational performance, based on formal and/or informal measures.
4. A statement of annual goals.
5. Measurable short-term objectives to be used in implementing each annual goal.
6. Appropriate objective criteria, evaluation procedures, and schedules for determining, on at least an annual basis, whether the short-term instructional objectives are being achieved.
7. A statement of the specific educational and related services to be provided to the student, and the extent (amount of time) to which the student will be able to participate in regular educational programs.
8. The signatures and titles of all participants at the meeting, and the date each one signed.
9. Other information as needed.

   Figure 1.2 is a sample of an IEP.

## Reading sample (middle school)
## INDIVIDUALIZED EDUCATION PROGRAM (IEP)

DEC SHCA
(Part I)

Student  Chris T.

Grade  7  School  Oak Middle

B. Date of Beginning and Duration of Special Education and Related Services

From  September  3,  1991  To  June  7,  1992

    (mo)   (day)   (yr)    (mo)  (day)   (yr)

C. Annual Goal(s)  By using an individualized and linguistic approach, Chris will use phonetic clues to decode unfamiliar words and use strategic routines to summarize main ideas and details.

A  Present Level(s) of Performance
(Summarize evaluation results including strengths and needs or behavioral weaknesses)

- Accurately identifies initial and final consonants and short-long vowels; identifies similarities in word lists; can complete incomplete stories.
- Unable to select main idea in silent reading, use context clues or use phonetic or structural analysis.

D

| Short-Term Instructional Objectives in Measurable Terms | Evaluation Procedures (How) | Evaluation Schedule (When) | Date Attained (Must be completed for each objective) |
|---|---|---|---|
| • Chris will be able to use decoding techniques to "chunk" unknown words with 99% accuracy. | • Informal probes using controlled level materials at the student's instructional level with progress charting. | by December 1 | |
| • Chris will be able to use decoding techniques to attack and identify unknown words with 99% accuracy. | • Informal probes using controlled level materials equal to reading materials used in Chris's mainstreamed classes with progress charting. | by February 28 | |
| • Chris will be able to use comprehension routines to improve recall of main ideas and details with 70% comprehension level. | • Informal comprehension probes using graded controlled reading level materials equal to reading materials used in mainstreamed placement. | by June 7 | |

*Source:* Courtesy of North Carolina Department of Public Instruction.

Figure 1.2

## Confidentiality and Record Keeping

There are provisions under IDEA and other federal laws, such as the Family Educational Rights and Privacy Act (PL 93-380), that guarantee the protection of confidentiality of a student's education records. These provisions address the issues of (1) the use of personally identifiable information, (2) who may have access to the student's records, and (3) parents' right to request that their child's records be amended.

## Other Rights

There are provisions under IDEA for the establishment of a parent surrogate or advocate if the parents are unavailable. Legislation also stipulates that children who are currently receiving no services and are clearly identified as individuals with disabilities have the first priority for obtaining services in competition with already-served children in need of additional services.

Once all of these procedures have been performed and the team agrees with the plan, it is the responsibility of the school in which the child is to be enrolled to implement the plan and protect all those involved.

## LEAST RESTRICTIVE ENVIRONMENT

The final concern is that the services be provided in the least restrictive or isolated setting that the child can successfully tolerate. Students with disabilities are required, to the maximum extent appropriate, to be educated with students who are not disabled. Special classes, separate schooling, or other removal of students with disabilities from the regular educational environment occurs only when the nature and severity of the disability is such that education in regular classes with the use of supplementary aids and services cannot be achieved satisfactorily.

## SPECIAL EDUCATORS: PROFESSIONAL PREPARATION STANDARDS

The final component of this chapter introduces the professionals most responsible for the provision of the services needed by children with exceptionalities: the special education teachers. These professionals may specialize in one or more of the categories of exceptionality listed in Box 1.1. They are certified as competent to provide services by the state in which they work. With the exception of those speech-language pathologists who are certified as clinically competent by the American Speech-Language-Hearing Association in addition to the state in which they provide services, there is no national certification for special educators. Each state determines the criteria a special educator must meet for each of the exceptionalities, and awards the appropriate certification when a candidate meets its criteria. Information about specific guidelines and requirements for any given state can be obtained by contacting the state director of special education at the address listed in Appendix I. Although each state sets its own guidelines for special education teacher certification, this does not mean that each state operates in a vacuum, arbitrarily setting its own independent standards. The Council for Exceptional Children has recently published suggested standards for the initial preparation and certification of teachers of students with exceptionalities (CEC, 1994). Effective teacher training programs must attempt to meet these expectations when training college students who wish to teach students with special needs. The council mandates that university training programs prepare teachers who, upon the completion of their programs of study, will have knowledge and skills in the following eight areas as they relate to the various exceptionalities:

1. Philosophy, history, and legal foundations
2. Characteristics of students with special needs
3. Assessment, diagnosis, and evaluation
4. Instructional content and practices geared toward students with special needs
5. Planning and managing the teaching and learning environment
6. Managing student behavior and social skills
7. Communication and collaborative partnerships
8. Professionalism and ethical practices

Among other skills, special education teachers should be skillful in explaining the current trends in education, interpreting reports and diagnostic information from all professional sources, using and adapting assessment instruments, maintaining reports and records, developing individualized strategies, and choosing and using appropriate technologies to accomplish objectives. Special educators need to be skillful in implementing generalization and maintenance plans and preparing and obtaining specially modified materials. It is their responsibility to lead in the structuring of an optimal learning environment for their students. When it is appropriate, they must be versed in teaching about human sexuality, and recreational, social, and daily living skills. They are often critical in helping with transition services, counseling families, and consulting with appropriate professionals.

The council is hopeful that the areas listed here and the more specific guidelines that accompany them will be adopted by the National Council for Accreditation of Teacher Education (NCATE) and become the national standards for training programs. In addition, the skills and knowledge specified in CEC's *Standards for Professional Practice in Special Education* were designed to serve as a reference for individual states in determining certification requirements for entry level professionals. Each of the chapters on exceptionalities that follow will more specifically detail the contributions that the special education teacher makes as part of the IEP team.

## ❧ CONCLUSION

This introductory chapter has explained the rationale behind the format of this text. We have introduced the exceptional child in a general way and briefly traced the history of special education. A review of the law and special education has provided an understanding of how the current practices in providing service to exceptional children are based on legislative and judicial rulings. We have explained the process by which children are identified and the critical role that families play in educational planning for children with exceptionalities.

The final section of the chapter introduced the special education teacher and described the competencies that are needed to be an effective special educator. Armed with this initial knowledge of special education, special educators, exceptional children, legal standards, and mandated procedures for providing services, we can now turn our attention to several discipline-wide issues that are of importance to all who deal with exceptional children.

## REFERENCES _____

Ballard, J., Ramirez, B. A., & Zantal-Weiner, K. (1987). *Public Law 94-142, Section 504, and Public Law 99-457: Understanding what they are and are not.* Reston, VA: Council for Exceptional Children.

Carl D. Perkins Vocational Education Act, 20 U.S.C. §§ 2331–2342. C.F.R. tit. 34, pts. 1–499 (1991).

IDEA *sails through Congress.* (1997, June). CEC Today, 3, 10.

Council for Exceptional Children. (April 1994) CEC *Standards for Professsional Practice in Special Education.* Reston, VA: CEC.

Council on Children with Behavioral Disorders (CCBD). (1969, April). Position paper presented at the meeting of the Council for Exceptional Children, Denver, CO.

DeStefano, L., & Snauwaert, D. (1989). A *value-critical approach to transition policy analysis.* Champaign, IL: University of Illinois, Secondary Transition Intervention Effectiveness Institute.

Center for the Future of Children. (1996), Los Altos, CA: David and Lucille Packard Foundation.

Heward, W. L. (1996). *Exceptional children: An introduction to special education* (5th ed.). Upper Saddle River, NJ: Prentice Hall/Merrill.

Hobbs, N. (1975). *The future of children.* San Francisco: Jossey-Bass.

Kirk, S. A. (1972). *Educating exceptional children* (2nd ed.). Boston: Houghton Mifflin.

Martin, E. W. (1968). Breakthrough for the handicapped: Legislative history. In J. Jordan (Ed.), A richer future for handicapped children. *Exceptional Children, 34*(7), 493–504.

Meyen, E. L. (1996). *Exceptional children in today's schools* (3rd ed.). Denver, CO: Love.

National Information Center for Children and Youth with Disabilities (NICHCY). (1996, October). Vol.9, pp. 1–6.

North Carolina Department of Public Instruction, Exceptional Children Support Team. (1996). *Individual Education Planning Packet.* Raleigh, NC: Exceptional Children's Division (NCDPI).

Special Education Programs and Academy for Educational Development. Washington, DC, pp. 3–15.

U.S. Department of Education. (1997). *Nineteenth annual report to Congress on the implementation of the Individuals with Disabilities Education Act.* Washington, DC: Author.

Wehman, P. (1997). *Exceptional individuals in school, community, and work.* Austin, TX: PRO-ED.

Wynne, M. D., & Conner, P. D. (1979). *Exceptional children: A developmental view.* Lexington, MA: D.C. Heath.

# 2

# Contemporary Critical Issues in Special Education

The special educators, regular educators, consultants, and families that make up the special education team face profound and often elusive problems that are potential roadblocks in providing the most appropriate educational experience for the child with exceptionalities. In Chapter 1 we summarized the legislative and judicial path that education for exceptional children has taken. In this chapter we wish to share some of the overriding issues facing families and professionals who are committed to the education of the exceptional child. It is clearly beyond the scope of an introductory text to review each issue in the detail it deserves. Nor could we include all the issues that are of concern. We have selected those issues that cross all the areas of exceptionality and that have, in our opinion, the greatest impact on service provision and on the lives of families with children who have special needs. The bibliography at the end of this chapter provides a starting place for those interested in further commentary on each issue we will present. Specific issues that may be of concern for each exceptionality are discussed in the "Issues of Importance" sections of Chapters 3 through 11.

Along with meaningful increases in enabling legislation and judicial activism, the last two decades have witnessed notable challenges to the service-provision structure of education for individuals with exceptionalities. Issues have emerged that have an impact on children in need of special services, their families, and the communities in which they live. In this chapter, we will highlight the following seven issues that affect the process of providing an appropriate educational experience for the exceptional child:

1. Parental roles in special education.
2. Inclusion of children with special needs in the regular classroom.
3. Multicultural concerns in schools.
4. School dropout prevention.
5. School discipline for children with exceptionalities.
6. The impact of technological advances.
7. Transition from school to community integration.

These issues are challenging the training of personnel and the administration of service provision throughout the regular and special education initiative. They directly confront the question of how we can best serve children with special needs in public schools, in the least restrictive manner, while still respecting all the differences children present to educators. These issues will require pragmatic solutions; they have forced and will continue to force innovative responses from schools that are mandated to provide treatment for exceptional children and their families.


## PARENTAL ROLES IN SPECIAL EDUCATION

Historically, parents have probably been the most neglected source of support and expertise in the education of their exceptional children. In the past, schools took it upon themselves to test, place, and educate children, rarely consulting parents to ascertain their needs and desires. Parents were seldom informed of decisions until after the special education program was initiated. However, families would not be denied their rights, and as a result parents of children with disabilities have advocated successfully to obtain an appropriate education for their children. Parents have organized support systems and political groups, and continually engage in lobbying efforts to combat any lingering resistances to their full participation in school activities and decisions that affect their children. Currently and conclusively, educators accept the importance of parental investment in procedural activities of the school relative to special education services. The skills and knowledge that parents possess to assist educators is fully recognized. Most professionals now feel that all parents should be totally involved and committed to the educational programs their children experience (Hardman, Drew, & Egan, 1996). However, in certain unique situations, schools may place students with special needs without parental consent. While this is not the preferred way to operate, it is certainly not illegal and is in fact part of the scope of responsibilities written into laws governing school responsibilities.

## Parent-Teacher Relationships

Despite the great strides detailed in the preceding section, all is not perfect for parents of exceptional children. Many parents express negative feelings when encountering indifference from schools in their search for help for their children. While parents of children with exceptionalities are a diverse group, they share experiences less common to parents of children who are not disabled. They may share initial feelings of denial about their children's differences, and even guilt about responsibility for their children's exceptionalities. Feeling ignored or discriminated against by the educational system, parents may become militant in their quest for satisfaction. This single-mindedness for fairness and perhaps, in some cases, unreasonable expectations of the school system, have caused some parents to be characterized as hostile, uncooperative, disinterested, troublesome, and/or meddlesome by school personnel. There are often understandable reasons driving what appear to be unreasonable behaviors.

When a child is diagnosed with special needs, a series of changes can occur in a family. The parents are required to focus extra energy on the exceptional child to ensure getting help, such as evaluations, medical or clinical follow-ups, and special education services (Buscaglia, 1983). Other children in the family must make allowances for the child with special needs (Atkins, 1987). Professionals "invade" the private workings of the family (Daniels-Mohring & Lambie, 1993). The family feels stigmatized and may be referred to as that family with "little Billy" who is "retarded." These families may become more isolated and withdrawn, feeling "trapped," while believing that they have lost control of their lives to the professionals with whom they have to interact as supplicants (Sloman & Konstantareas, 1990; Kew, 1975). It should not be surprising that interactions with even the most benign and well-meaning professionals can sometimes be volatile.

These negative forces can also lead to a breakdown in optimal parent-child interactions. As a result, schools often must begin to work with children of limited affective response who may have difficulties initiating social interactions. The children may begin schooling with poor pre-verbal signaling skills or communication gestures, limited verbal competencies, feeding difficulties, and delays in motor development exacerbated by home conditions (Fogel, 1984).

Clinical experience strongly suggests that when parents master or are taught specific behaviors that facilitate their children's cognitive and socioemotional behaviors, the resulting gain in confidence increases parental motivation to more actively intervene, which can further increase the gains just described. Training and help from the schools can help parents develop ever-increasing skills that have an observable impact on their children's behaviors. Special education teachers can play a pivotal role in this area. A major goal of the special educator is to improve the quality of parents' interactions with their children, resolve family issues, and secure necessary resources for parents and their children via public school collaboration. A strong parent-teacher partnership is beneficial for all concerned parties, especially the child. A successful partnership can create support and understanding for children and for their parents. This, in turn, can lead to more positive associations with the schools and foster the efforts of child advocacy (Heward, 1996).

## Parent-Teacher Collaboration Responsibilities

Viable and productive parent-teacher collaboration can be described in five steps (Epstein, 1993). First, parents are responsible for providing safe homes and nurturing environments for their children, which helps prepare them for school and supports learning. Second, the school is responsible for communicating to parents any issues surrounding the child's programming, and progress made by the child. Third, parents are encouraged to volunteer at the school and show outward support by attending school functions and sporting events. Fourth, with assistance from teachers, the parent provides learning activities in the home environment. Fifth, parents and teachers collaborate in school policy and education decision making. This recipe of collaboration seems easy enough, but it takes the willingness of both teachers and parents to make it work. Clark (1983) showed that parental involvement in a child's formal education—involvement that was well structured and lasted over several years—helped to improve student achievement.

## Advantages

Parental involvement in a child's education has many advantages for the parent, the teacher, and the child. Involvement with understanding teachers helps the parent increase feelings of self-worth and satisfaction (Epstein, 1993; Murphy, 1981), as well as learn effective educational and behavioral techniques that can be used at home (Moersch, 1978). The teacher, on the other hand, benefits from gaining a more in-depth view into the child's cultural and familial background, as well as receiving information about the child's history, any problems the parents may have with the child, and the ecological makeup of the home environment (Marion, 1981). For the child, parent-teacher collaboration means more consistent expectations and inevitably a much more positive effect upon learning and behavior (Blackard, 1976; Henderson, 1988).

## Communication

Communication is the key element in developing and maintaining parent-teacher collaboration. Communication dispels mistrust. The two overriding issues appear to be that teachers and parents who are consciously aware of the reasons for their commitment to children with special needs are better able to gain self-confidence in what they are doing and be more accepting of each other, and that teachers who are more in tune with their expectations for children from varying cultures become more aware of the different methods of communication needed in sending, receiving, or processing information with the parents of these children (Shea & Bauer, 1991).

Finally, advocacy is probably one of the most difficult elements of collaboration and communication between parents and teachers. Whereas teachers can use their knowledge, energy, and commitment to be an effective advocate for the parent and child, they often must choose between siding with the parent or the school system when they are told that a particular service cannot be offered due to problems with funding or staffing (Cutler, 1993; Shea & Bauer, 1991). However, teachers who are knowledgeable about their legal roles will hopefully be able to give sound advice to parents concerning advocacy issues. Parents can obviously serve as a perfect advocate for their child due to the intimate knowledge of the child they possess. When armed with knowledge of their legal rights, parents can truly be powerful advocates for children with special needs.

## Legislative Influences on Parental Roles

Federal legislation supports the inclusion of most exceptional children in the activities of their communities. Currently, most families take care of their children with disabilities at home. The passage of federal legislation continues to support families that are able to care for children with disabilities at home and keep them in contact with their local communities. Furthermore, education laws provide for active participation by the schools with the families of exceptional children beginning prenatally, continuing through infancy and the child's school years, and providing transitional services including special education services up to age 21.

The Individuals with Disabilities Education Act (IDEA), PL 101-476, and its amendments are also designed to also empower parents and families. Winston and Bailey (1997) indicated that these legislative efforts set the family in the center of the child's experiences in and out of school, and that educational planning should be reflective of the cultural and ethnic origin of the family and the child. Sensitivity to maintaining a family's independence and priorities are essential. Special services should work toward promoting normalization for the child and the family in their community. Parents and professionals should collaborate in the planning, implementation, and evaluation of services for the child, thus minimizing any friction that may arise due to miscommunication of goals.

## Summary

We have tried to explain how critical parent involvement is for the child with exceptionalities. We have also described roadblocks that might prevent parents and teachers from cooperating fully. The overwhelming belief is that parents and teachers together can accomplish more for the exceptional child than either group can by itself.

# INCLUSION

As the rights of students with disabilities to obtain a free, publicly supported education in appropriate educational environments evolved, special education began to take on the form of separate education, with pull-out resource programs and increasingly isolated one-to-one instruction. Madeleine Will, former Assistant Secretary for Special Education in the U.S. Department of Education in the mid-1980s, and other educators saw the possibility of negative consequences occurring when special education students were separated from their normal (nondisabled) peers (Mercer, 1994). Will (1986) stated that special education programs must "establish a partnership with regular education to cooperatively assess the educational needs of students with learning problems and to cooperatively develop effective educational strategies for meeting those needs" (p. 415).

Will's solution is a system of service delivery to special education students that has become known as the Regular Education Initiative (REI). Advocates of the REI suggest that instruction for students with special needs should be delivered within the regular classroom. The concept of educating exceptional students in the least restrictive environment (LRE) has become a focus of emerging legislative initiatives. Educating students with disabilities in general classes is "one of the promising alternatives that has been proposed to implement school reform" (Audette & Algozzine, 1992, p. 11). *Mainstreaming*, the practice of integrating students with disabilities socially and educationally into regular education, emerges from the interpretation of what constitutes the least restrictive environment and was the conceptual support for Will's REI plans.

Regular education and special education teachers are enjoined to work cooperatively within the regular classroom to provide instruction for all students, disabled and nondisabled. The special education teacher and other support specialists provide instruction to students with special needs in the general education classroom rather than in their own separated classrooms (Jenkins, Pious, & Jewell, 1990). Some believe that in the 1990s, the new panacea for educating students with disabilities has become inclusion (Carr, 1993).

However, it is not as simple as it seems. "Least restrictive environment" must be understood in the context of legal requirements established by legislative mandate.

Schools still need to provide the availability of a full continuum of alternative placements, such as resource rooms or self-contained special education classrooms. Then the school must consider whether there is a possibility of harmful effects of such a placement on either the exceptional child, others in his or her environment, or the quality of services. These considerations must be re-evaluated at least annually when determining the Individual Education Plan and the placement decisions for a child (Roberts & Mather, 1995). Interestingly, although the Department of Education's Office of Special Education Programs has not legally defined inclusion, it adamantly requires adherence to the concept of the LRE.

The term *inclusion*, regardless of its legal status, emerged from earlier concepts associated with mainstreaming or the Regular Education Initiative. Part B of the Individuals with Disabilities Education Act (IDEA, PL 101-476) states a strong preference for educating students with disabilities in regular classes with appropriate aids and supports. Although the IDEA does not use the term *inclusion*, the legislation does require an individualized inquiry into the unique educational needs of each disabled student in determining the possible range of aids and supports needed to facilitate the student's placement in the regular educational environment before a more restrictive placement is considered (U.S. OSERS, 1994). This means that when implementing the IDEA's LRE provisions, the regular classroom in the school the student would attend if the student were not disabled is the first placement option that must be considered for a student with a disability before a more restrictive placement is considered. However, if the student's Individual Educational Plan cannot be implemented satisfactorily in that regular classroom, it is not to be considered the LRE placement for that student (U.S. OSERS, 1994).

It is important to understand that even though regular classroom placement is preferred, the IDEA does not require that every student with a disability be placed in the regular classroom regardless of individual abilities and needs. This recognition that regular class placement may not be appropriate for every student with a disability is reflected in the previously mentioned requirement that school districts make available a range of placement options, known as a continuum of alternative placements. This requirement for the continuum of services illustrates the need for individualized programs that meet the needs of individual students with disabilities. These placement options must be available to the extent necessary to implement the IEP of each disabled student.

Opponents of "full inclusion" are concerned that unequivocal full inclusion would eliminate all special education placement options with the continuum of alternative services. They suggest that some services can be most effectively and efficiently delivered in special settings. Only by providing a range of placement options can we hope to provide optimal instructional settings and systems that best meet the individual student's learning needs, styles and interests (NCCPC, 1994). According to York, Doyle, and Kronberg (1992), "Inclusion does not mean that students must spend every minute of the school day in the general education classes (no student should), that students never receive small-group and individualized instruction, or that students are in general education classes to learn the core curriculum only."

Opponents argue that even though the current structure of special education may be flawed, it has worked for some students (Pearman, Huang, Barnhart, & Mellblom, 1992). In a study surveying the beliefs and attitudes regarding the inclusion of all students in special programs in a midsized Colorado school district, results indicated that 49 percent of the educators who responded disagreed or strongly disagreed that inclusion is the best way to meet the needs of all students and that inclusion requires far more and increased cooperation among regular and special educators (Pearman et. al., 1992).

Regular classroom teachers, who by necessity must become more involved with exceptional students as a result of inclusion, do not see themselves as having the skills for adapting instruction and content that meets the needs of regular students but would be inadequate for the instructional needs of students with even mild disabilities. There is concern that regular class teachers may not have the skills to provide the one-to-one instruction and small-group instruction for students with special needs (Semmel, Abernathy, Butera, & Lesar, 1991).

Realistically, full integration of students with severe disabilities has not been realized in most public schools. It appears that general education programs in many public schools are not organized or prepared to serve students with special needs. Classroom teachers haven't been adequately trained to provide instruction to students with a variety of disabilities, and teacher preparation programs have few, if any, requirements regarding integrated inclusive classrooms. Perhaps, most important, educators seem to agree that there are considerable difficulties in (1) establishing good working relationships or collaboration with regular teachers on the aims, goals, and sequences of teaching, and (2) sharing an understanding of the role of the special education teacher and the level of support the special education teacher should provide in the regular classroom (Long, 1994; Kauffman, 1997; Osborne & Dimattia, 1994; Sawyer, McLaughlin, & Winglee, 1994; Kearney & Durand, 1992; Ireson, 1992).

Even the advocates of the full-inclusion position that exceptional children can learn positive social skills from nondisabled classmates and thereby increase their own self-concepts have been challenged. Researchers such as Kauffman, Gerber, and Semmel (1988) have reviewed studies and surveys suggesting that students with mild disabilities placed in regular classrooms will not necessarily experience improved self-concepts.

## Summary

Even though the concept of full inclusion for exceptional children is currently popular with many educators, many questions need to be answered about its efficacy before this new trend in special education becomes a widely implemented and acceptable approach. Local education agencies and school districts need to carefully review and study inclusion practices. Training in the components and implementation of inclusion must be provided for both regular and special educators, students, and parents. The criteria for determining just which students with exceptionalities would most benefit from being served in inclusive programs must be carefully studied.

Researchers, schools, teachers, and parents must remember the overriding goal of special education: that each student with disabilities must be served and educated in the most appropriate individualized placement.

## MULTICULTURAL SOCIETY AND SPECIAL EDUCATION

We live in a multicultural and ethnically diverse society in which individuals develop and often act in accordance with culturally related values. *Culture*, according to Goodenough (1987), is a shared way of perceiving, believing, evaluating, and behaving. When we look at culture this way, it becomes apparent that culture is not limited to race and ethnicity, but is also related to different sources of shared values. Gollnick and Chinn's approach (1994) to understanding culture can serve as an important foundation to understanding diversity. They maintain that within the United States, there exists a macroculture and many microcultures. The macroculture consists of the values on which most political and social structures are based. The ten values that they believe are inherent in the macroculture of the United States are:

1. Status based on occupation, education, and financial worth.
2. Achievement valued above inheritance.
3. Work ethic.
4. Comforts and rights to such amenities.
5. Cleanliness as an absolute value.
6. Achievement and success measured by the quantity of material goods purchased.
7. Egalitarianism as shown in the demand for political, economic, and social equality.
8. Inalienable and God-given rights for every individual that include an equal right to self-governance or choice of representatives.
9. Humanitarianism that is usually highly organized and often impersonal.
10. New and modern perceived as better than old and traditional (p. 13).

Although macrocultural values bind the population together as a whole, they are not sufficient for understanding individual value systems. Each individual not only is a member of a *macroculture*, but also shares values with members of subcultures. These cultures are known as *microcultures*, and each is differentiated from others by specific values, speech and linguistic patterns, learning styles, and behavioral patterns. Gollnick and Chinn (1994) list eight types of microcultures that individuals can identify with:

1. Ethnic or national origin
2. Religion
3. Gender/sex
4. Age

5.  Exceptionality
6.  Urban-suburban-rural
7.  Geographic region
8.  Class (p. 16)

Cultural identification for most Americans involves a blending of various microcultures. This broad interpretation of diversity can be used to encourage people to establish unifying contexts within diversity and strengthen the community that nurtures them (Beckham, 1997, p. 58).

The microculture of exceptionality includes students with special needs from rural and urban areas. It includes wealthy and middle-class children. Some exceptional children live in extreme poverty, are drug dependent, or are homeless. They may belong to one of the 510 federally recognized Native American tribes living on one of 278 reservations where 187 languages are spoken. They may be Asian Americans coming from more than 24 countries and speaking more than 1,000 languages and dialects (Heward, 1996). As different as they may appear from each other, their macro- and microcultural memberships bind them to each other at the same time that they give them separate identities.

The general purpose of multicultural education is to promote understanding of our overall national values and our microcultures. It provides support for the development of positive feelings and attitudes based on knowledge about cultural diversity. The need to appreciate diversity is not an academic one. There are more minorities living in the United States today than any other time in our history. Approximately 60 to 80 percent of these minorities are from low socioeconomic backgrounds (Chinn & Hughes, 1987). The pervasive problem facing families from culturally and ethnically diverse backgrounds is the continued over- and underrepresentation of their children in special education programs. Misrepresentation of minorities in special education is most likely a combination of discrimination in placement decisions and growing up in poverty with malnourishment and inadequate health care (Grossman, 1995).

Overrepresentation is especially prevalent among African Americans, who represent only 12 percent of the elementary and secondary school population, yet represent 28 percent of the total enrollment in special education. European Americans are overrepresented in gifted and talented classes and underrepresented in mental retardation classes. Hispanic and Native American children are overrepresented in classes for the learning disabled and underrepresented in gifted and talented classes. Hispanic children are underrepresented in classes for mild mental retardation, severe emotional disturbance, and speech impairments (Hunt & Marshall, 1994). Non-European Americans with limited English proficiency are also more likely to be overrepresented in special education programs. Asian and Pacific American children are overrepresented in gifted and talented classes and underrepresented in all other classifications of special education (Hunt & Marshall, 1994).

Minorities' high referral rates may be attributed to teachers' lack of understanding of and sensitivity to diverse cultural backgrounds. For example, at school African Americans are typically more active, emotionally responsive, and assertive than European Americans (Grossman, 1995). Different behavioral styles may be misinterpreted as exceptional and in need of being "fixed," when in fact these behaviors are completely acceptable at home and within the student's own culture.

Research indicates that prejudice and racism can also be pervasive problems in our educational system. Bennett and Harris (1982) surveyed teachers at two large urban schools in the Midwest. Both schools had been previously ranked among the country's 100 most problematic schools concerning minority frictions and school discipline. The results of the survey indicated that many of the teachers would not live in a desegregated neighborhood, did not favor mandatory desegregation, thought that the civil rights movement had done more harm than good, and considered the problems of prejudice to be exaggerated. In addition, the majority of teachers considered their European American students to be superior intellectually, socially, and in other school-related characteristics. With findings such as these, it is difficult to deny that racism is a continuing problem within our educational system. Lower expectations for minority students can become a self-fulfilling prophecy and an extreme disadvantage to minority youths. We can only hope that attitudes have changed in the almost two decades since the survey.

Another frequently cited contributing factor to the disproportionate numbers of minorities identified as needing special education services is test bias. Many of the standardized tests used to identify students that need special education were developed by people of European descent based upon norming children of European descent (Bedell, 1991). Since minorities are not represented in the norms, the use of these instruments with minorities is not valid or reliable. Norm-referenced assessment compares a child's performance to a norm sample and assumes that the child

has had an equal opportunity to acquire the skills, concepts, and experiences of the children in the norm sample (Peterson & Ishii-Jordan, 1994). Unfortunately, many minority children and children from low socioeconomic backgrounds have grown up in disadvantaged circumstances and lack many of the opportunities to acquire the skills and prior knowledge that most middle class children of European descent have.

Along with achievement testing, social and psychological measures are used when determining a child's eligibility for special education. These criteria include measured intelligence, achievement, social behavior, social adjustment, and communication skills. For ethnically and culturally diverse groups, the standards by which these attributes are judged lack reliability and validity. One team of educators explained that eligibility requirements are analogous to a rubber yardstick (Gartner & Lipsky, 1986). In some instances, if the test scores do not yield the expected outcome, a sophisticated tester can use other tests to determine that the child is eligible for services. This can obviously be a problem if the teacher or psychologist is consciously or unconsciously biased.

Children who display limited English proficiency (LEP) are at a distinct disadvantage. There is a nationwide shortage of teachers, administrators, and psychologists who are bilingual and aware of multicultural issues, including different learning styles (Grossman, 1995). Since many schools are unable to provide bilingual assessment and educational services, these school districts are often reluctant to refer LEP students for evaluations; as a result, many disabilities go undetected. Bilingual education teachers may also choose not to refer their students to special education programs because they feel that special education programs staffed by teachers who are not bilingual will fail to meet their students' linguistic needs. On the other hand, some teachers refer LEP students to special education even though they are aware that the students are not eligible for such programs. They do so because they hope their LEP students will get the extra remedial and individual attention that they need to master English (Grossman, 1995).

Environmental factors can sometimes explain minority overrepresentation in special education. With a large percentage of minority children growing up in poverty, minorities are more likely to grow up malnourished and without adequate health care (Bedell, 1991). Inadequate prenatal and postnatal health care can also lead to complications during pregnancy and delivery. Prematurity, low birth weight, and learning, emotional and behavioral problems are linked to the poor health care experienced disproportionately by minority children. After birth, poor nutrition can cause general health and specific neurological problems, which in turn can be detrimental to students' school performance and lead to referral to special education (Grossman, 1995). Other evidence suggests that African American and Native American children growing up in poverty are more likely to have parents with substance abuse problems. These children, therefore, have a greater likelihood of being born with birth defects associated with substance abuse and therefore have a need for special education services. Children in less affluent communities also frequently attend failing schools (Bedell, 1991). These schools may have the least resources, deteriorating physical plants, and dispirited teachers who are ill-trained and overwhelmed with large numbers of students.

The political climate of the country and the acceptability of the diagnosis of a learning disability over one of mental retardation have also had an impact on children from ethnically and culturally diverse backgrounds. For example, between 1977 and 1985, the number of students classified as learning disabled (LD) rose 119 percent (Gartner & Lipsky, 1986). This is viewed by many as "classification plea-bargaining," since this rise in children labeled as LD was accompanied by a decrease in the number of children being labeled mentally retarded. Several factors can explain this rise and decline in placements. They may be a result of the increased awareness of the stigmatizing effects of the "mentally retarded" label and the less traumatizing effect of an LD diagnosis. Researchers also suggest that this reluctance to classify minority children as mentally retarded may be a consequence of the recent lawsuits in which school systems have been sued for racial bias. In 1981, 46 percent of African Americans in special education were labeled mentally retarded, while 22 percent of European Americans in special education were labeled mentally retarded (Grossman, 1995). However, only 26 percent of African Americans in special education were labeled LD, while 40 percent of European Americans were labeled LD. This situation is changing as a result of heightened awareness of biases and fear of lawsuits. A decline in the underrepresentation of non-European Americans in gifted and talented classes has also occurred.

Due to numerous court cases regarding the misplacement of minorities in special education, and the fear these cases engender, in many school districts children of non-European descent are now becoming underrepresented in special education. In order to avoid litigation, many teachers and school psychologists are reluctant to refer minorities to special education even when they may be in need of services. Also, some well-meaning teachers wish to protect their students from the abuses that some non-European students have suffered in special education. Thus, we have the concurrent possibilities of overrepresentation and underrepresentation affecting minority children.

## Summary

In this section, we introduced the concept of multiple criteria for determining diversity. We also stressed how the misrepresentation of minority children is a controversial issue in special education today. Despite environmental factors such as poverty that contribute to a disproportionate need for special education services for minority children, there may also be some unfairness in the educational system. Americans of non-European descent are expected to compose one-third of the U.S. population by the year 2000. It is, therefore, especially important that the issue addressed in this segment of the chapter become a priority for schools and educators. Culturally relevant assessment instruments are needed (Peterson & Ishii-Jordan, 1994). Bilingual and multicultural personnel are also necessary if we wish to change the current system, which is failing minority students. A multicultural curriculum needs to be mandated in teacher education programs as well as in elementary and secondary schools. We live in a multicultural society today, and it is essential that our schools reflect this fact.

## SPECIAL EDUCATION SCHOOL DROPOUT

Special education school dropout is a national concern. Students who drop out of school condemn themselves to a life of low wages, unemployment, poverty, criminal activities, and overall diminished social well-being. The problems associated with school non-completion are so grave that reducing the dropout rate has become a national priority (Kortering, Hess, & Braziel, 1997; Wehlage, Rutter, Smith, Lesko, & Fernandez, 1989).

### Definition

The term *school dropout* refers to students who leave high school before completion without re-enrolling in another school or enrolling in a related educational program. Mandatory attendance laws limit the dropout label to students age 16 and older. However, significant numbers of students leave school before age 16 or before reaching the tenth-grade level. These students are referred to as *truants* rather than dropouts. Some students leave school without any forwarding address or information and in essence are "lost" without ever being labeled as dropouts (Kortering et. al., 1997).

Research and professional commentary agree that there is a high rate of school dropout among special education students. The evidence suggests that students with learning disabilities (LD), mental retardation (MR), and behavioral disorders (BD), otherwise noted as the seriously emotionally disturbed (SED), drop out of school at significantly higher rates than their general education peers. Unlike their regular education peers who drop out, these students are rejecting programs that have been specially designed to meet their individual needs (Bartnick & Parkay, 1991; Blackorby, Edgar, & Kortering, 1991). However, the reasons given for dropping out are similar. Jay and Padilla (1987) reported that special education students dropped out of school because they were not doing well in school, they preferred to get out of school to get a job, they were not getting along with their teachers or other students, and their friends or peers dropped out of school. General education students drop out because they don't like school, get poor grades, get a job, can't get along with teachers, become pregnant, marry, and are suspended or expelled (Eckstrom, Goertz, Pollack, & Rock, 1986; Rumberger, 1983, 1987). In summary, both groups were leaving school, generally speaking and in spite of carefully designed programs, because of the rupture of relationships among students and teachers, because of poor academics, and to get a job or get married. However, some surveys and evidence (Kortering, 1993; and Lichenstein, 1983) suggest that students with disabilities are also dropping out of school because of enduring patterns of frustration, school failure, and social alienation from peers and teachers.

The need for positive rapport with the teacher is the single most recurring issue in the education of LD and BD students (Devereaux, 1956; Morse, 1985; Edgar, 1995). The prominence of this issue suggests that for special education students, learning at school seldom takes place without a positive relationship with an adult at the school. For instance, Rogers (1969) presented a compelling commentary about the role of the positive relationship in education:

The initiation of such learning rests not upon the teaching skills of the leader, not upon his scholarly knowledge of the field, not upon his use of audiovisual aids, not upon the programmed learning he uses, not upon his lectures and presentations, not upon an abundance of books. . . . No, the facilitation of significant learning rests upon certain attitudinal qualities which exist in the personal relationship between the facilitator and the learner. (p. 3)

Quality contacts between the student and teacher enhance personal development. Davis (1966) and Mastropieri and Scruggs (1987) reported that student evaluations suggested that effective teachers not only display teaching skills that contribute to scholastic success, but also maintain desirable personal relationships with students. In other words, quality contacts not only are pleasurable, but also help students to learn and improve their lives. These contacts serve to convince students that an education is of value and that one can succeed in school. Such contacts convey the message that the teacher values the student. Students, in turn, seek help and support from educators whom they deem caring and nurturing. These contacts often make the difference between one's decision to stay in or drop out of school. The importance of these contacts is also related to the nature of a student's disability and whether or not he or she has consistent difficulty with success in school and establishing and maintaining interpersonal relationships. Special education students may be particularly needy when they live in environments that fail to provide the levels of emotional support they need. These difficulties make the personalization of schoolwork, anchored by people-to-people service, essential (Kauffman, 1997; Berkowitz & Rothman, 1960).

## Self-Determination

The process of self-determination allows students to be active participants on their IEP team. They have the opportunity to select educational goals for their IEP and transition plan; thus, self-determination represents a source of empowerment for students (Field, 1996). The hope of self-determination is that students will select goals that are appropriate and hold value to them, thus enhancing a program's appropriateness and the student's motivation. Students who have participated in an IEP or even heard of self-determination seem to support this concept. They routinely provide responses in the form of personal changes that represent ideal educational goals, including the need to change their attitude, improve their work habits, and behave better. Each of these areas is also consistent with traditional school goals and the desires of educators. These goals also suggest students' willingness to participate in therapeutic relationships and pursue goals that align with those of the institution. The willingness to participate in a relationship becomes crucial to the student's willingness to persevere despite limitations and to adopt the values of the institution, attitudes that are essential to one's motivation to stay in school.

Smith and Kortering (in press) suggest that appropriate special education would provide programs that address students' perceived limitations. In their study, the limitations focused on were inadequate study habits, limited motivation toward school, and a poor attitude. Students were able to identify their limitations, which suggests an initial understanding of their difficulties. In the school district studied by Smith and Kortering, student participation was not encouraged in IEPs or transition plans. The educators tended to view the IEP and ITP process as bureaucratic requirements, not a means to pursue active student participation. Such a view may not be uncommon among special educators, but it does limit the ability of teachers to see the potential for having students actively involved in the development of IEPs and transition plans. Self-determination can be successful only if it is geared to an appropriate level for each student and if teachers are supporting and nurturing.

## Supportive Services

Kortering and Tompkins (1997) found that students receiving special education services wanted supportive services that offered additional encouragement and assistance. They apparently understood their limitations and viewed encouragement and support as key to successful school experiences and personal development. Given the nature of handicapping conditions, requests for additional support services seem reasonable. The students in this study endured years of failure and bad school experiences. For instance, over three-fourths of the interviewees had not only been identified for special education, but also had been retained at least once (usually within their first three years). Perhaps the key to success lies with helping students overcome their past failures and current limitations, while bridging the gap between perceived needs and actual services. Such an outcome might hinge upon the ability of special educators to ensure that each and every special education student has access to a supportive therapeutic relationship. Box 2.1 illustrates recommended strategies for deploying therapeutic relationships that might prevent school dropouts.

The effects of therapeutic relationships are can be powerful. Initially in the establishment of relationships, the child may exhibit frustration and struggle against forming the relationship, but gradually the supportive therapeutic relationship facilitates the child's becoming a unique individual—a genuine and integrated being, someone who can relate and grow in his or her life with others (Moustakas, 1966). Therapeutic relationships can "assist the child to achieve inner freedom in order to learn and to resume normal development" (Paul & Epanchin, 1982). The child can begin to grow emotionally, which fosters more appropriate behavioral responses. In the interpersonal relationship with the teacher, children develop respect and the desire to take on the admirable qualities of that adult. They develop the idea that they can be acceptable and likable people. Self-esteem is heightened and, therefore, they become more receptive to academic development.

No research exists that tells us whether the interpersonal relationship created in the classroom has lasting value. However, we know from adult reports that many individuals have singled out an experience with a teacher as a turning point toward increased self-esteem, creative accomplishment, originality, and effective living. We also know that the impact of relationships in early life is lasting (Moustakas, 1966).

**Box 2.1**
*WHAT EVERY TEACHER NEEDS TO KNOW*

**Strategies for Deploying Therapeutic Relationships**

| Factor and Definition | Specific Interventions |
| --- | --- |
| *Positive Teacher Contacts*<br>Teachers pursue positive encounters with students. | Attending extracurricular school events in which at-risk students participate |
| | Establishing before- and after-school encounters |
| | Positive encounters in school |
| | Adult or community mentors for students |
| | Orientation interviews with incoming ninth-grade and transfer students |
| *Self-Determination*<br>Students take on an active role in their educational program. | Student-generated IEP/ITP goals and objectives |
| | Self-determination curricula |
| | Active student participation in the IEP process |
| | Linking academic content to postschool plans |
| | Formal vocational assessments that link schoolwork to future occupations |
| | School-sponsored career exploration activities |
| *Supportive Services*<br>Services that help students to experience success in school. | Before- and after-school tutoring services |
| | Peer mentor programs |
| | Test-taking and learning strategy instruction |
| | Peer or community tutors |
| | Computer-based remediation programs |

*Source:* From *Therapeutic Relationships: A Promising Response to School Dropout?* by L. J. Kortering and J. R. Tompkins, 1997, unpublished report, Boone, NC: Appalachian State University.

## Summary

Special education school dropout is an ongoing and critical problem. We have defined the issue, presented some explanations for its occurrence, and suggested some of the newer, more experimental attempts to deal with dropout. We strongly suggest that increasing student interest in the educational process and providing supportive relationships may be critical to maintaining interest in programs that are individually designed for exceptional children.

## SCHOOL DISCIPLINE AND PUNISHMENT

### Corporal Punishment

Corporal punishment is commonly used by school personnel in the public schools to discipline a student for breaking rules or other misbehavior (Polsgrove, 1991; Weilkiewicz, 1986; Wood, 1978). Corporal punishment is more often used with students without disabilities than students with disabilities; however, despite the fact that 27 states have abolished corporal punishment (Evans & Richardson, 1995), students with disabilities are the recipients of corporal punishment as well as nondisabled students (Rose, 1984). Teachers and the general public overwhelmingly support corporal punishment (Hyman, McDowell, & Raines, 1997; McDaniel, 1980; Musemeche & Sauls, 1976).

Whatever the legal or professional opinions are about corporal punishment, little empirical support is available to support applying corporal punishment to children either with or without disabilities. The legal, ethical, and professional issues abound, especially in using corporal punishment with students with emotional and behavioral disorders (Bettelheim, 1985). It is usually seen as unjustifiable.

The Council for Children with Behavioral Disorders, a subgroup of the Council for Exceptional Children (CEC), advocates the continued development of more positive behavior management alternatives to corporal punishment (Wehman, 1997):

> The Council on Exceptional Children supports prohibiting the use of corporal punishment in special education, defining such punishment as a situation in which an authority accuses a child of violating a rule and seeks from him or her an explanation, at which point a judgment of guilt is made, followed by physical contact and pain inflicted on the child. (p. 387)

Despite this position by the Council for Exceptional Children, many educators in the United States appear to be extremely regressive in their attitudes toward corporal punishment and other highly punitive approaches to child discipline (Evans & Richardson, 1995; Hyman, McDowell, & Raines, 1997). A danger is that harsh punishment provokes counteraggression. Some use harsh punishment because the immediate effect frequently results in the cessation of the punished individual's inappropriate behavior. In addition, physical punishment is frequently thought to be more effective than milder forms. These are dangerous misconceptions. Effective punishment does not require inflicting physical pain, psychological trauma, or social embarrassment. Other forms of punishment, such as loss of privileges, can be equally effective. Clumsy, vindictive, or malicious punishment is the teacher's or parent's downfall (Kauffman, 1997).

### School Expulsion and Suspension

Students with emotional and behavioral disorders are being expelled from school at an alarming rate. Expulsion is on the rise, despite the fact that all students with dis-

abilities are entitled to a free, appropriate education. However, at times some exceptional students' behavior is so negative that schools will move to expel them (Wehman, 1997; Katsiyannis & Prillaman, 1989). Before expelling a student, the school must ensure that the student's court-ordered rights have been respected (Yell, 1995).

Suspension consists of temporarily excluding the student from school and classroom work. It may range from in-school suspension from various specific activities to total out-of-school suspension. In high schools, suspension is one of the most widely used school responses to disciplinary problems. The premise for implementing school suspension is that it will be an effective deterrent or punishment for unacceptable behavior. It is used only after the student's behavior has become unmanageable in school (Diem, 1988; Chobot & Garibaldi, 1982).

Unfortunately, suspension as punishment does not significantly reduce serious or recurrent behavior problems for many students and may reinforce some behavior problems (Garibaldi, 1995; Uchitelle, Bartz, & Hillman, 1989). The negative results of suspension include a higher risk for academic failure, reduced opportunity to learn, increased juvenile crime, and loss of opportunity for students to learn self-management (Sulzer-Azaroff & Mayer, 1986).

Students at risk for suspension are those with recurrent behavior problems such as social skill deficits, academic deficits, and adjustment problems associated with anxiety and depression. They are the students most absent from school, those seen as seriously maladjusted, and those most repeatedly disciplined. These students appear to be students with emotional and behavioral disorders (Coie & Koeppl, 1990;

Patterson, 1993; Safer, 1986; Christopher, Mangle, & Hansen, 1993; Frame, Robinson, & Cuddy, 1992). Morgan-D'Atrio, Northup, La Fleur, and Spera (1996) assert that little research attention has been directed toward discovering more effective alternatives than suspension. While the courts have placed restrictions on the schools, they have not prevented them from using disciplinary procedures with students with disabilities. These students are subject to normal disciplinary procedures, such as removal of privileges and short-term suspensions. Procedures such as time out and in-school suspension, when used reasonably and not to excess, are also permissible. Schools can move students to more restrictive environments, but may not use punishments unilaterally or use indefinite suspensions or expulsions. Students cannot be decertified as disabled for purposes of expulsion or use of several suspensions (Yell, 1991, p. 368).

## Other Disciplinary Issues

Discipline of students with disabilities has become one of the most contentious issues in the reauthorized Individuals with Disabilities Education Act (IDEA). The administration has authorized that a child with a disability who brings a dangerous weapon to school or who knowingly possesses, uses, or attempts to sell illegal drugs at school can be removed from the regular school setting and placed in an *interim alternative educational setting* (IAES) for up to 45 days. In addition, a hearing officer can place a student in an IAES for up to 45 days if the student is likely to engage in injury to self or others. However, if it is determined that the child's unacceptable behavior was independent of the child's exceptionality, that child may be disciplined in the same manner as any other child in the school.

In those cases where an interim alternative education setting is selected, the child's IEP team must determine the placement and ensure that the placement enables the child to continue to participate in the school curriculum and still receive the services and modifications that were stated in the IEP (CEC *Today*, 1997).

## SPECIAL EDUCATION AND TECHNOLOGY

Technological changes are a double-edged sword for students with disabilities. At its best, technology allows people with disabilities to enjoy greater participation in all levels of society from school to work to leisure. At its worst, technology makes life more complex. It would not be unreasonable to assume that within the foreseeable future, independent living and the ability to use technology will become intertwined. The ability to use digital telephones, fax machines, microwave ovens, personal computers, and a host of other devices will partially define social competency in our society. Assistive-and adaptive-device mastery, ranging from independent use of hearing aids and corrective lenses to language generating personal computers and reading machines, will define the level of participation open to a person with exceptionalities. Simply stated, if a technology allows people with disabilities to do something they could not do without it, then the technology is in their best interest (Hallahan & Kauffman, 1994).

The Office of Special Education Programs (OSEP) has slowly committed its resources to using technology, educational media, and materials to help people with disabilities discover new learning opportunities, increase their communication effectiveness, enjoy greater physical mobility, and control more of their environment. Computers and other technologies promise to reduce mundane activities and free teachers and other school personnel to spend more time designing instructional and other enriching programs for their students. Computers and other telecommunications technologies make it possible for exceptional students to progress at their own pace, level of interest, and level of motivation. However, some indicators suggest that there is a growing gap between what students are learning in school and what they need to know to succeed in a technological, information-based society (Hauser & Malouf, 1996; *Liaison Bulletin*, 1997).

Using the latest technology available for people with exceptionalities did not begin with the personal computer revolution. There has always been a component of special education that has been committed to using technology in all forms to increase the quality of life for people with exceptionalities. In the 1960s, general research by the Bureau of Education for the Handicapped (now OSEPRS) provided the foundation for implementing the predictably changing face of technology for the disabled. In the 1970s, the Kurzweil reading machine aided the visually impaired. The 1980s brought about increased use of closed-captioned television for the hearing impaired. Assistive devices, from low tech improved feeding utensils to high tech material for sturdy, lightweight wheelchairs, have always been and continue to be part of the treatment plan. As federal and congressional interest grew, more changes developed in legislative efforts. One significant legislative effort was the enactment of Part G of the Education for All Handicapped Children Act of 1986 (PL 99-457), which authorized the Technology, Educational Media, and Materials Program for Individuals with Disabilities and provided $4.7 million for fiscal year 1987. Since then, this program has invested more than $35 million in research and development of technology tools for students with disabilities (Hauser & Malouf, 1996).

OSEPRS initiated its first futures study in 1984 to discover how to better benefit students with disabilities. As an outcome of these investigations, OSEPRS funded projects to use simulation (software and videotape) to teach work-related social competence skills, and to explore robotics and artificial intelligence technologies for people with disabilities. The next round of futures studies will explore technologies ranging from hand-held computers to virtual reality and such technologies as individualized learning systems, word retrievers, telecommunications networks, and databases. There is little doubt that children with disabilities will soon routinely use integrated multimedia technology to study historical figures, times, and cultures; write stories; and take more control of their education (Hauser & Malouf, 1996; Woodward & Gersten, 1992). Technology will help people with disabilities in their role as workers to apply fundamental mathematical concepts, write brief communications, and be able to work effectively as part of a team (U.S. Department of Labor, 1991).

OSEPRS developed a national agenda that will drive future planning and priorities regarding the use of technology, media, and materials to improve outcomes for individuals with disabilities. The use of technology will be advanced by the following commitments for all categories of disabilities:

1. To enable the learner across environments by fostering the creation of state-of-the-art instructional environments.
2. To promote effective policy at all levels in government, schools, and business.
3. To foster use of technology through professional development of training and supporting teachers, administrators, parents, and related service personnel,
4. To create innovative tools by encouraging the development of varied and integrated technologies, media, and materials.

This projected agenda of OSEPRS will be progressive, reflect the state of the art in technology, and meet the needs of children and youth with disabilities (Hauser & Malouf, 1996).

Figure 2.1 provides and illustrates the profile of technology for instruction and the rich possibilities for educational remediation and enrichment.

---

**Applications with Research Verification**

*Calculators*

In addition to arithmetic, algebraic, and trigonometric functions, modern calculators feature plotting and graphing capabilities. These functions enable the student to view computation results in graphic form.

*Computer-Assisted Instruction (CAI)/Integrated Learning Systems (ILS)*

Select drill and practice programs have yielded small but positive effects on learning. In some schools, CAI that features ILS (including individualized academic tutorials) has produced impressive gains with urban students who are underachieving.

*Distance Education*

With distance education, learners in remote locations gather at a site that has cable or satellite receivers, phone lines, and video cameras. This equipment allows one- or two-way audio and video contact with a course provider. Hughes Corporation's Galaxy is a distance education program that beams daily lessons to schools through satellite.

*Laser Videodiscs*

Laser videodisc programs enable the learner to interact with print and still or moving images. These programs do not require a computer. Disc players with remote controls and bar-code readers that select and present images are available at low cost.

*Microcomputer-Based Labs (MBLs)*

These labs use microcomputers and probes to sense temperature, pH levels, and light intensity. Computer labs represent a means for providing hands-on science experiences.

*Presentation Software*

Overhead projectors and other audiovisual technologies effectively support lectures and demonstrations. A computer combined with a large-screen monitor or LCD display panel is a powerful medium for presenting visual material. Adding multimedia capability permits enhancements such as sound, graphics, and video images.

*Telecommunications*

The dissemination of large quantities of information to many people simultaneously is available through telecommunications networks. Students can use telecommunications services for accessing publications, training materials, and collected data.

**Applications with Emerging Support**
*Computerized Adaptive Testing (CAT)*
   With CAT, the test questions vary according to the test taker's responses. An incorrect answer is followed by an easier question, whereas a correct response generates a more difficult question. Initial studies report that CAT provides more accurate results regarding a person's knowledge level, in less time than traditional test formats.
*Interactive Multimedia*
   This computer technology links information from multiple sources and enables the user to interact with program content. Most interactive multimedia programs contain text, line drawings, maps, graphs, animated graphics, voice narration, music, and video clips featuring full motion and color.
*Multi-User Dimensions (MUDs)*
   Using MUDs, individuals with a computer and modem communicate through telecommunications services to play out roles in an imaginary contest. MUDs are able to transport the user to any place in any time. MUDs provide opportunities for individuals to pursue collaborative and creative activities that extend beyond typical writing or drama exercises.
*Text-to-Speech*
   Computers can translate text to speech. This function is a popular enhancement for early grades, students who are visually impaired, and non-English-speaking populations.
*Voice Mail*
   Digital voice-mail systems are commonplace and offer an excellent medium for delivering information to students. Each student can be assigned a private mailbox with a personal information number (PIN), and parents, teachers, and other students can access the individual's mailbox from any touch-tone phone.
*Word Processing*
   Word processing programs are used widely in schools to help students develop written expression skills. These programs have been especially effective with students who are low achievers.
**Future Applications**
*Broadband Networks*
   Through these networks, two-way, delay-free transmissions are delivered to the home through cable or satellite.
*Groupware*
   Groupware allows users in a network to jointly write, share, and disseminate electronic documents, or to join in group decision-making ventures.
*Knowbots*
   Knowbots, which stands for "knowledge robots," are automated systems for collecting, screening, and organizing data.
*Pen-Based Computing*
   Instead of using a keyboard, students enter data through pen-based applications that use touch-screen icons and handwriting recognition.
*Speech-to-Text*
   These voice-aware applications enable users to vocally control computer functions.
*Virtual Reality*
   Users wear special goggles connected to a data input device that engulfs the user in a three-dimensional environment emulating the real world.
*Wireless Connectivity*
   Wireless technology, like the cellular phone, enables teachers and students to share information regardless of their location.

---

Source: From *Students with Learning Disabilities* (5th ed.), (pp. 250–251), by C. D. Mercer, 1997. Reprinted by permission of Prentice-Hall, Inc., Upper Saddle River, NJ.

Figure 2.1
Profile of Technology for Instruction

## Summary

The double-edged sword of technology offers great hope and significant challenges to exceptional populations. Assistive devices bring the hope of compensatory functioning that will be good enough to enable those with exceptionalities to join their peers in the rewarding everyday interactions of living. The challenges of managing the expense of the equipment, taking responsibility for purchasing and caring for it, and attaining the sophistication needed to use it are also part of the equation. The only certainty is that technology will advance our society and that exceptional students will have to master the skills needed to become a productive segment of future society.

## TRANSITION FROM SCHOOL TO WORK

Transition from school to work, community life, and adulthood is as critical a period for students with disabilities as it is for nondisabled students. It is essential to develop and implement effective program plans to help exceptional students develop as independent, productive adults. The purpose of transition planning is to maximize the success of students with disabilities to the greatest extent possible, with cooperative linkages with a variety of postschool opportunities in education, vocational training, employment, recreation, and residential living. The support services during the transition period focus on the need to bridge school and adult life.

The Individuals with Disabilities Education Act (IDEA, PL 101–476) mandates that every student with disabilities over age 16 receiving special education services must have an Individualized Transition Plan (ITP) in addition to an Individualized Education Program (IEP). Transition services are defined by IDEA as a coordinated set of activities for a student, designed within an outcome-oriented process that promotes movement from school to postschool activities, including postsecondary education, vocational training, integrated employment (including supported employment), continuing and adult education, adult services, independent living, and community participation (IDEA 300.18[a]). The legislative effort also encourages transition plan development as early as age 14 if the school personnel and parents feel such planning is appropriate. The transition component is designed to provide instruction and community experiences that lead to successful postschool outcomes in a variety of postschool life experiences (Furney, Hasazi, & DeStefano, 1997).

Prior to beginning transition planning, students, parents, and other interested personnel need information on opportunities and resources available for postschool education, employment, and community life requirements. This suggests that families need help in developing skills in self-advocacy, goal setting, and decision making (Szymanski, 1994; Ward, 1992; Gallivan-Fenon, 1994). Emphasis must be placed on creating a successful interface between the schools and local human-service agencies.

The ITP team is usually composed of the student, parents, special and regular educators and community adult service providers. The plan itself must include long-and short-term goals and objectives and statements of needed transition services. It must be written no later than age 16 (or when appropriate for the individual student, beginning at age 14 or younger) and reviewed annually. The planning statements involve employment possibilities, potential community involvement, and living arrangements. It details the support role of each agency in the student's program. IDEA regulations also state that the IEP team is responsible for providing alternate plans if any agency outside the school does not provide agreed upon services (Browning, Dunn, & Brown, 1993).

Even though the ITP is part of the IEP, some school systems may develop a separate form for writing the ITP, but that form must be attached to the IEP and becomes a part of it. The ITP should include:

1. A statement of goals/outcomes in at least four areas:
   a. Employment
   b. Education/training
   c. Leisure/recreation
   d. Residential (student's living arrangements)

2. Lists of activities and/or sequences of steps to achieve outcomes
3. Timelines for achieving each activity
4. Person or agency responsible for achieving each activity and the interagency co-operation or collaboration plans (Browning et al., 1993).

Transition services for secondary level students may include vocational educa-tion, experience-based career education, community-based employment, supported employment, and college preparation.

The cornerstone of effective transition services is the transition planning process as written in the transition component of the IEP (Halpern, Yovanoff, Doren, & Benz, 1995), and the "best practices" in transition are associated with good planning. Rusch and DeStefano (1989) identified the following characteristic strategies that model programs implement to secure success for students:

1. Early planning
2. Interagency collaboration
3. Individualized transition planning
4. Focus on integration
5. Community-relevant curriculum
6. Community-based training
7. Business linkages
8. Job placement
9. Ongoing staff development
10. Program evaluation (pp. 1–2)

Figure 2.2 is an example of an individualized transition plan.

## Summary

In summary, transition from school for students with disabilities entails the full in-volvement of understanding parents, student input, and active participation by school personnel and community agencies. Despite the diversity of interests and needs in the planning and implementation of the transition process, the essential and foremost issues are the shared vision and the collaborative efforts to plan and provide services. Fully involving parents and students in the process is one critical ap-proach to ensure a smooth transition from school to adult life (Hanley-Maxwell, Whitney-Thomas, & Pogoloff, 1995).

# WATAUGA COUNTY SCHOOLS
# INDIVIDUAL TRANSITION PLAN

**Student's Name:** _____ **Age:** _____ **Date of Birth:** _____

**Projected Graduation/Exit Date:** _____

## *GOALS*

**A. Employment/Training:** _____

_____

_____

_____

**B. Education:** _____

_____

_____

_____

**C. Recreation/Leisure:** _____

_____

_____

_____

**D. Residential:** _____

_____

_____

_____

| Initial Meeting | | | Review Meeting | | |
|---|---|---|---|---|---|
| Signature | Position | Date | Signature | Position | Date |
| | | | | | |
| | | | | | |
| | | | | | |
| Review Meeting | | | Review Meeting | | |
| Signature | Position | Date | Signature | Position | Date |
| | | | | | |
| | | | | | |
| | | | | | |
| | | | | | |

Figure 2.2

| Name _____ | ITP EMPLOYMENT/TRAINING | | |
|---|---|---|---|
| **Objectives** | **Action/Steps** | **Person/Agency Responsible** | **Timelines** |
| _____ Identify local employment opportunities | _____ Contact specific employers<br>_____ Visit job sites<br>_____ Arrange interview<br>_____ Place into:<br>    _____ competitive employment<br>    _____ supported employment<br>    _____ sheltered workshop<br>    _____ community living skills<br>_____ Assist with jobsite training<br>_____ Assist in locating transportation<br>_____ Other: _____ | | |
| _____ Identify student's skills and interests | _____ Administer individual:<br>    _____ interest inventory<br>    _____ vocational assessment<br>_____ Evaluate individual work skills<br>_____ Refer to:  _____ MR/DD<br>    _____ vocational rehabilitation<br>_____ Other: _____ | | |
| _____ Provide student with employability skills training | _____ Follow school vocational-education curriculum:<br>    _____ Regular  _____ Tech prep<br>    _____ ICT  _____ Other<br>_____ Follow functional curriculum<br>_____ Participate in an in-school training program<br>_____ Other: _____ | | |
| _____ Provide student with community-based employability training | _____ Arrange community work experiences: _____ Co-op<br>    _____ Other: _____<br>_____ Assist with jobsite training<br>_____ Assist in locating part-time job:<br>    _____ Summer _____ After school<br>_____ Assist in locating volunteer opportunities<br>_____ Other: _____ | | |

Figure 2.2,
*Continued*

| Name _____ | | ITP EDUCATION | |
|---|---|---|---|
| **Objectives** | **Action/Steps** | **Person/Agency Responsible** | **Timelines** |
| _____ Graduate with:<br>_____ diploma<br>_____ certificate of attendance | _____ Complete functional curriculum<br>_____ Participate in the regular curriculum with support from appropriate exceptional children's classes<br>_____ Complete appropriate vocational courses<br>_____ Complete tech prep courses<br>_____ Complete college preparatory classes<br>_____ Other: _____ | | |
| _____ Identify postsecondary education/training options | _____ Discuss options with counselor<br>_____ Explore entrance requirements for<br>_____ universities<br>_____ community colleges<br>_____ technical schools<br>_____ extended day or night classes<br>_____ Take _____ PSAT _____ SAT<br>_____ Other: _____<br>_____ Complete<br>_____ applications<br>_____ interviews<br>_____ visits<br>_____ Refer to vocational rehabilitation<br>_____ Other: _____ | | |
| _____ Identify military options | _____ Provide information about military service<br>_____ Meet recruiter<br>_____ Take ASFAB<br>_____ Other: _____ | | |

Figure 2.2,
*Continued*

| | ITP | | |
|---|---|---|---|
| **Name** _____ | **RECREATION/LEISURE** | | |
| **Objectives** | **Action/Steps** | **Person/Agency Responsible** | **Timelines** |
| _____ Identify local options | _____ Provide community recreational information:<br>   _____ organizations<br>   _____ clubs<br>   _____ sports teams<br>   _____ other<br><br>_____ Other: _____ | | |
| _____ Identify student's recreation/leisure time interests | _____ Participate in school:<br>   _____ clubs<br>   _____ activities<br>   _____ sports<br>   _____ other _____<br>_____ Participate in community<br>   _____ organizations<br>   _____ clubs<br>   _____ sports teams<br>   _____ other _____<br>_____ Other:_____ | | |
| _____ Match student's interests to community recreation/ leisure time activities | _____ Select a community recreation/leisure time<br>   _____ activity<br>   _____ club<br>   _____ sports team<br>   _____ other<br>_____ Refer to agency (specify) _____<br>   _____ for skills training<br>_____ Assist in locating transportation:<br>   _____ car pool<br>   _____ county transportation system<br>   _____ other _____<br>_____ Assist in obtaining Driver's Education instruction/course<br><br>_____ Other: _____ | | |

Figure 2.2,
*Continued*

| Name _____ | ITP RESIDENTIAL | | |
|---|---|---|---|
| **Objectives** | **Action/Steps** | **Person/Agency Responsible** | **Timelines** |
| _____ Identify local residential options | _____ Discuss types of living arrangements: <br> _____ independent living <br> _____ group home <br> _____ other: _____ <br> _____ Provide local residential information <br> _____ Review entrance requirements/ criteria for residential placement <br> _____ Refer to agency (specify) _____ <br> _____ Investigate housing options for postsecondary-bound students <br> _____ Other: _____ | | |
| _____ Provide student with independent-living skills training | _____ Follow specific independent living skills IEP objectives for <br> _____ self-care       _____ money <br> _____ clothing       _____ housing <br> _____ domestic care <br> _____ other _____ <br> _____ Other: _____ | | |
| _____ Identify available financial assistance | _____ Provide appropriate information <br> _____ Refer to agency (specify) _____ <br> _____ Other: _____ | | |
| _____ Identify need for guardianship | _____ Provide appropriate information <br> _____ Refer to agency (specify) _____ <br> _____ Other: _____ | | |

*Reprinted by permission of Watauga County, NC, Board of Education.*

Figure 2.2,
*Continued*

**Box 2.2**
*WHAT EVERY TEACHER NEEDS TO KNOW*

*Phases of Translation of Knowledge to
Action through Organizational Support*

| Developmental Phase | Purpose | Supporting Organizations |
|---|---|---|
| Research | The discovery of new knowledge about children with disabilities or about those intellectual and personality processes that can be applied to these children | Usually research centers and institutions, often found in universities, which can provide organizational support for long-range attacks on difficult research problems. |
| Development | Knowledge, to be educationally useful, must be organized or packaged into sequences of activities or curricula that fit the needs of particular groups of children. | Sometimes through research and development centers that concentrate on sequencing of existing knowledge; the basic setting is still the university. |
| Demonstration | There must be an effective conjunction of organized knowledge and child. This conjunction must be demonstrated in a school setting to be believable. | A combination of university or government and school operation is required. Usually the elementary or secondary school is the physical setting; additional resources are supplied by the other agencies. |
| Implementation | Local school systems with local needs usually wish to try out, on a pilot basis, the effective demonstrations they have observed elsewhere to establish viability in a local setting. | Additional funds for retraining staff and for establishing a new program locally are needed. Some type of university, state, or federal support is often needed as a catalyst to bring about this additional stage. |
| Adoption | To establish the new program as part of the educational operation. Without acceptance of the new program at the policy level, demonstration and implementation operations can atrophy. | Organized attempts need to be made to involve policy decision-makers (that is, school board members, superintendents, and so on) in the developmental stages so far. Items such as cost-effectiveness need to be developed to help make decisions. |

*Source:* From "A Richer Future for Handicapped Children," by J. J. Gallagher, 1968, *Exceptional Children, 34*(7), p. 486. Copyright 1968 by The Council for Exceptional Children. Reprinted with permission.

## 🐚 CONCLUSION

We have highlighted some of the most important issues facing exceptional children, their families, and their teachers. For meaningful progress to be made, it is critical to attack each issue with a well-formed plan. Dr. James Gallagher, the first Associate Commissioner of the Bureau of Education for the Handicapped (now the U.S. Office of Special Education), made the observations shown in Box 2.2 in the form of a five step plan that suggests an effective way to deal with important issues in special education. He recommended considering these phases in the translation of our knowledge about current issues or problems in special education to action through organizational support.

Following a logical plan whereby research and demonstration generate the facts that indicate the need and beneficial outcomes of services for children, and coupling it with forceful advocacy, will lead federal, state, and local education agencies to be more likely to support solutions to pragmatic issues and dilemmas.

## REFERENCES

Atkins, D. V. (1987). Siblings of the hearing impaired: Perspectives for parents. *Volta Review*, 89(5), 32–45.

Audette, B., & Algozzine, B. (1992). Free and appropriate education for all students: Total quality and the transformation of American public education. *Remedial and Special Education*, 13(6), 8–18.

Bartnick, W., & Parkay, F. (1991). A comparative analysis of the holding power of general and exceptional education programs. *Remedial and Special Education*, 12, 17–22.

Beckham, E. F. (1997, January 5). Diversity opens doors to all: a multi-cultural focus helps stimulate more critical thinking. *New York Times*, Education Life Section 4A.

Bedell, F. (1991). *Educational needs of minorities with disabilities and reactions*. In Tennyson, Wright, Leung, Paul, (Ed); The Unique Needs of Minorities with Disabilities: Setting an Agenda for the Future, Conference Proceedings. Jackson, MS: (ERIC Document Reproduction Service No. ED 358 593)

Bennett, C., & Harris, J. (1982). Suspensions and expulsions of male and black students: A study of the causes of disproportionality. *Urban Education*, 16, 399–423.

Berkowitz, P. H, & Rothman, E. P. (1960). *The disturbed child: Recognition and psychoeducational therapy in the classroom*. New York: New York University Press.

Bettelheim, B. (1985, November). Punishment versus discipline. *Atlantic Monthly*, 17, 51–59.

Blackard, K. (1976). *Introduction to the family training program: Working paper*. Seattle, WA: Experimental Education Unit, University of Washington.

Blackorby, J., Edgar, E., & Kortering, L. J. (1991). A third of our youth? A look at the problem of high school dropout among students with mild handicaps. *The Journal of Special Education*, 25, 102–113.

Browning, P., Dunn, C., & Brown, C. (1993). *School to community transition for youth with disabilities*. Boston: Andover Medical.

Buscaglia, L. (1983). *The disabled and their parents: A counseling challenge* (Rev. ed.). Thorofare, NJ: Slack.

Carr, M. N. (1993). A mother's thought on inclusion. *Journal of Learning Disabilities*, 26, 590–592.

CEC Today. (1997, June), IDEA Sails through Congress. Reston, VA: Council for Exceptional Children, *Copy Editor*, 3(10) 1–9.

Chinn, P., & Hughes, S. (1987). Representation of minority students in special education classes. *Remedial and Special Education*, 8, 41–46.

Chobot, R. B., & Garibaldi, A. (1982). In-school alternatives to suspension: A description of ten school district programs. *Urban Review*, 14(4), 317–336.

Christopher, J. S., Mangle, D. W., & Hansen, D. J. (1993). Social-skills interventions with adolescents. *Behavior Modifications*, 17(3), 314–338.

Clark, R. (1983). *Family life and school achievement: Why poor black children succeed or fail*. Chicago; University of Chicago Press.

Coie, J. D., & Koeppl, G. K. (1990). Adapting intervention to the problem of aggressive and disruptive rejected children. In S. R. Asher & J. D. Coie (Eds.), *Peer rejection in childhood*. New York: Cambridge University Press.

Cutler, B. C. (1993). *You, your child, and "special" education: A guide to making the system work*. Baltimore: Brookes.

Daniels-Mohring, D., & Lambie, R. (1993). Dysfunctional families of the student with special needs. *Focus on Exceptional Children*, 25(5), 1–11.

Davis, R. A. (1966). *Learning in the Schools*. Belmont, CA: Wadsworth.

Devereaux, G. A. (1956). *Therapeutic Education*. New York: Harper & Row.

Diem, R. A. (1988, October–November). On campus suspensions: A case study. *High School Journal*, 36–39.

Eckstrom, R. B., Goertz, M. E., Pollack, J. M., & Rock, D. A. (1986). Who drops out of high school and why? Findings from a national study. *Teachers College Record*, 87(3), 356–373.

Edgar, E. B. (1995, June). *Social bonding and alienation among school dropouts*. Presentation at Keeping Youth in School Conference, Appalachian State University, Boone, NC.

Epstein, J. (1993). How do we improve programs for parent involvement? *Educational Horizons*, 66, 58–60.

Evans, E. D., & Richardson, R. C. (1995). Corporal punishment: What teachers should know. *Teaching Exceptional Children*, 27(2), 33–36.

Field, S. (1996). Self-determination instructional strategies for youth with learning disabilities. In J. Patton & G. Blalock (Eds.), *Transition and students with learning disabilities: Facilitating the movement from school to work*. Austin, TX: PRO-ED.

Fogel, A. (1984). *Infant, family and society*. St. Paul, MN: West.

Frame, C. L., Robinson, S. L., & Cuddy, E. (1992). Behavioral treatment of childhood depression. In S. M. Turner, K. S. Calhoun, & H. E. Adams (Eds.), *Handbook of clinical therapy* (2nd ed.). New York: Wiley.

Furney, K. S., Hasazi, S. B., & DeStefano, L. (1997). Transition policies, practices, and promises: Lessons from three states. *Exceptional Children*, 63(3), 343–355.

Gallagher, J. J. (1968). A richer future for handicapped children. *Exceptional Children*, 34(7), 486.

Gallivan-Fenon, A. (1994). "Their senior year": Family and service provider perspectives on the transition from school to adult life for young adults with disabilities. *Journal for the Association for Persons with Severe Handicaps*, 19(1), 11–23.

Garibaldi, A. M. (1995). Street academics and in-school alternatives to suspensions. In M. C. Wang & M. C. Reynolds (Eds.), *Making a difference for students at risk: Trends and alternatives*. Thousand Oaks, CA: Carven.

Gartner, A., & Lipsky, D. (1986). Beyond special education: Toward a quality system for all students. *Harvard Educational Review*, 57, 367–395.

Gollnick, D. M., & Chinn, P. C. (1994). *Multicultural education in a pluralistic society* (4th ed). Upper Saddle River, NJ: Prentice Hall/Mernill.

Goodenough, W. (1987). Multi-culturalism as the normal human experience. In E. M. Eddy & W. L. Partridge (Eds.), *Applied Anthropology in America* (2nd ed.). New York: Columbia University Press.

Grossman, H. (1995). *Special education in a diverse society*. Princeton, NJ: Houghton Mifflin.

Hallahan, D. P., & Kauffman, J. M. (1994). *Exceptional children: Introduction to special education* (6th ed.). Boston: Allyn and Bacon.

Hanley-Maxwell, C., Whitney-Thomas, J., and Pogoloff, S. (1995). The second shock: A qualitative study of parents' perspective and needs during their child's transition from school to adult life. *Journal of the Association for Persons with Severe Handicaps*, 20(1), 3–15.

Hardman, M. L., Drew, C. J., & Egan, M. W. (1996). *Human exceptionality: Society, school, and family* (5th ed.). Needham, MA: Allyn & Bacon.

Hauser, J., & Malouf, D. (1996). A federal perspective on special education technology. *Journal of Learning Disabilities*, 29(5), 504–505.

Henderson, A. (1988). Good news: An ecologically balanced approach to academic improvement. *Educational Horizons*, 66(2), 60–63.

Heward, W. L. (1996). *Exceptional children: An introduction to special education* (5th ed.). Upper Saddle River, NJ: Prentice Hall.

Hunt, N., & Marshall, K. (1994). Exceptional children and youth: An introduction to special education. Boston: Houghton Mifflin.

Hyman, I., McDowell, E., & Raines, B. (1997). Corporal punishment, an alternative in the schools. An overview of theoretical and practical issues. In J. H. Wise (Ed.), Proceedings: Conference on corporal punishment in the schools. Washington, DC: National Institute of Education.

Ireson, J. (1992). Collaboration in support systems. *British Journal of Special Education*, 19(2), 56–58.

Jay, D., & Padilla, C. (1987). *Special education dropouts: The incidence of and reasons for dropping out of special education in California*. Menlo Park, CA: SRI International.

Jenkins, J. R., Pious, C. G., & Jewell, M. (1990). Special education and the Regular Education Initiative: Basic assumptions. *Exceptional Children*, 56, 479–491.

Katsiyannis, A., & Prillaman, D. (1989). Suspension and expulsion of handicapped students: National trends and the case of Virginia. *Behavioral Disorders*, 15(1), 35–40.

Kauffman, J. M. (1997). *Characteristics of emotional and behavioral disorders of children and youth* (6th ed.). Upper Saddle River, NJ: Prentice Hall.

Kauffman, J. M., Gerber, M. M., & Semmel, M. I. (1988). Arguable assumptions underlying the Regular Education Initiative. *Journal of Learning Disabilities*, 21, 6–11.

Kearney, C. A., & Durand, V. M. (1992). How prepared are our teachers for mainstreamed classroom settings? A survey of post-secondary schools of education in New York State. *Exceptional Children*, 59, 6–11.

Kew, S. (1975). *Handicap and family crisis: A study of the siblings of handicapped children*. London: Pitman.

Kortering, L. J. (1993). *School dropout among youth with learning disabilities or behavior disorders: A look at potential factors and outcomes*. Boone, NC: Appalachian State University.

Kortering, L. J., Hess, R. S., & Braziel, P. M. (1997). School dropout. In G. Bear & K. Minke, (Eds.), *Best practices in school psychology*. Reston, VA: National Association of School Psychologists.

Kortering, L. J. and Tompkins, J. R. (1997). Therapeutic relationships: A promising response to school dropout? Unpublished report. Boone, NC: Appalachian State University.

*Liaison Bulletin*. (1997) Publication of NASDSA, Inc. Alexandria, VA: NASDSA, 26, (6), 1. National Association of State Directors of Special Education, Inc.

Lichenstein, S. (1993). Transition from school to adulthood: Case studies of adults with learning disabilities who dropped out of school. *Exceptional Children*, 59, 336–347.

Long, N. (1994). Inclusion: Formula for failure? Journal of Emotional and Behavioral Problems, 3(3), 19–23.

Marion, R. L. (1981). *Educators, parents, and exceptional children*. Rockville, MD: Aspen.

Mastropieri, M. A., & Scurggs, T. E. (1987). *Effective instruction for special education*. Boston, MA: Little, Brown & Co.

McDaniel, T. R. (1980). Exploring alternatives to punishment: The keys to effective discipline. *Phi Delta Kappan*, 61, 455–458.

Mercer, C. D. (1997). *Students with learning disabilities* (5th ed., pp. 250–251). Upper Saddle River, NJ: Prentice-Hall/Merrill.

Mercer, C. D. (1994). Learning disabilities. In N. G. Haring, L. McCormick, & T. G. Haring (Eds.), *Exceptional children and youth: An introduction to special education* (6th ed.), New York: Macmillan.

Moersch, M. S. (1978). History and rationale for parent involvement. In S. L. Brown & M. S. Moersch (Eds.), *Parents on the team*. Ann Arbor, MI: University of Michigan Press.

Morgan-D'Atrio, C., Northup, J., LaFleur, L., & Spera, S. (1996). Toward prescriptive alternatives to suspension: A preliminary evaluation. *Behavioral Disorders*, 21(2), 190–200.

Morse, W. (1985). The education and treatment of socio-emotionally impaired children and youth. Syracuse, NY: Syracuse University Press.

Moustakas, C. (1966). *The authentic teacher: Sensitivity and awareness in the classroom*. Cambridge, MA: Howard A. Doyle.

Murphy, A. T. (1981). *Special children, special parents: Personal issues with handicapped children*. Upper Saddle River, NJ: Prentice Hall.

Musemeche, R. A., & Sauls, C. (1976). Policies and attitudes on corporal punishment. *Phi Delta Kappan*, 58, 283.

North Carolina Cooperative Planning Consortium (NC-CPC). (1994). *Inclusion: CPC draft statement*. Raleigh, NC: Author.

Osborne, A. G., & Dimattia, P. (1994). The IDEA's least restrictive environment mandate: Legal implications. *Exceptional Children*, 61, 6–14.

Pearman, E. L., Huang, A. M., Barnhart, M. W., & Mellblom, C. (1992). Educating all students in school: Attitudes and beliefs about inclusion. *Education and Training in Mental Retardation*, 27, 176–182.

Peterson, R., & Ishii-Jordan, S. (1994). *Multi-cultural issues in the education of students with behavioral disorders*. Cambridge, MA: Brookline.

Polsgrove, L. (1991). *Reducing undesirable behaviors*. Reston, VA: Council for Exceptional Children.

Roberts, R., & Mather, N. (1995). The return of students with learning disabilities to regular classrooms: A sellout? *Learning Disabilities Practice*, 10, 46–58.

Rogers, C. R. (1969). *Freedom to learn*. Upper Saddle River, NJ: Prentice Hall/Merrill.

Rose, J. (1984). Current use of corporal punishment in American public schools. *Journal of Educational Psychology*, 76, 427–441.

Rumberger, R. W. (1983). Dropping out of high school: The influence of race, sex, and family background. *American Educational Research Journal*, 20, 199–220.

Rumberger, R. W. (1987). High school dropouts: A review of issues and evidence. *American Education Research Journal*, 57, 101–121.

Rusch, F. R., & DeStefano, L. (1989). Transition from school to work: Strategies for young adults with disabilities. *Interchange*, 9(3), 1–2.

Safer, D. J. (1986). The stress of secondary school for vulnerable students. *Journal of Youth and Adolescence*, 15(5), 405–417.

Sawyer, R. J., McLaughlin, M. J., & Winglee, M. (1994). Is integration of students with disabilities happening? An analysis of national data trends over time. *Remedial and Special Education*, 15(4), 204–215.

Semmel, M. I., Abernathy, T. V., Butera, G., & Lesar, S. (1991). Teacher perceptions of the Regular Education Initiative. *Exceptional Children*, 58, 9–21.

Shea, T. M., & Bauer, A. M. (1991). *Parents and teachers of children with exceptionalities* (2nd ed.). Needham, MA: Allyn & Bacon.

Sloman, L., & Konstantareas, M. (1990). Why families of children with biological deficits require a systems approach. *Family Process*, 29, 417–432.

Smith, S., & Kortering, L. (In press). Computer-assisted individual educational programs: Promising practice or bureaucratic expedient? *Journal of Special Education Technology*.

Sulzer-Azaroff, B., & Mayer, G. R. (1986). *Achieving educational excellence with behavioral strategies*. New York: Holt, Rinehart, & Winston.

Szymanski, E. M. (1994). Transition: Life-span and life-space considerations for empowerment. *Exceptional Children*, 60, 401–410.

Uchitelle, S., Bartz, D., & Hillman, L. (1989). Strategies for reducing suspensions. *Urban Education*, 24(2), 163–176.

U.S. Department of Labor (1991). *What work requires of schools*. Washington, DC: U.S. Government Printing Office.

U.S. Office of Special Education and Rehabilitation Services (OSERS). (1994). *Questions and answers on the least restrictive environment requirements of the Individuals with Disabilities Education Act*. Washington, DC: Author.

Ward, M. J. (1992). OSERS initiative on self-determination *Interchange*, 12(1), 1.

Wehlage, G. G., Rutter, R. A., Smith, G. A., Lesko, N., & Fernandez, R. R. (1989). *Reducing the risk: School dropouts as communities of support*. New York: Falmer.

Wehman, P. (1997). *Exceptional individuals in school, community, and work*. (pp. 387). Austin, TX: PRO-ED.

Weilkiewicz, R. (1986). *Behavior management in the schools*. New York: Pergamon.

Will, M. D. (1986). Educating children with learning problems: A shared responsibility. *Exceptional Children*, 52, 411–415.

Winston, P., & Bailey, D. (1997). Family-centered practices in early intervention for children with hearing loss: Strategies for self-examination. In J. Roush & N. Matkin (Eds.), *Infants and toddlers with hearing loss: Identification and family-centered intervention*. Parkton, MD: York.

Wood, F. (1978). The influence of public opinion and social custom on the use of corporal punishment in schools. In F. Wood & K. Lakin (Eds.), *Punishment and aversion stimulation in special education: Legal, theoretical and practical issues in their use with emotionally disturbed children and youth*. Minneapolis, MN: University of Minnesota, Department of Psychoeducational Studies.

Woodward, J., & Gersten, R. (1992). Innovative technology for secondary students with learning disabilities. *Exceptional Children*, 58(5), 407–421.

Yell, M. L. (1991). Reclarify Honig v. Doe. *Exceptional Children*, 57(4), 367–368.

Yell, M. L. (1995). Least restrictive environment, inclusion, and students with disabilities: A legal analysis. *Journal of Special Education*, 28(4), 389–404.

York, J., Doyle, M. D., & Kronberg, R. (1992). A curriculum development process for inclusive classrooms. *Focus on Exceptional Children*, 25(4), 1–16.

# 3

# Children with
# Mental Retardation

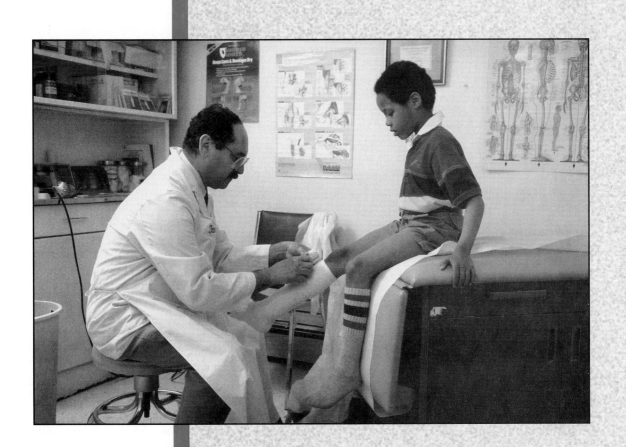

U nderstanding mental retardation (MR), which affects nearly 7 million people in the United States, can be confusing because mental retardation is conceptualized, defined, and diagnosed in a variety of ways by a number of professionals. Professionals other than educators, such as medical personnel, vocational-rehabilitation professionals, and psychologists, are actively involved in the understanding and treatment of individuals with retardation. Individuals with mental retardation come from all levels of society, racial groups, ethnic groups, and especially from families that are at the poverty level or are socioeconomically disadvantaged.

Depending upon the degree of severity, children with retardation are unable to make adequate adjustments to many life circumstances because of their limited intellectual and adaptive capacities (Wehman, 1997). They are characterized by the level of instruction they need in order to learn. This instruction is provided in regular classrooms, sheltered workshops, and other specialized settings. To some extent, the level of functioning of a person with mental retardation is determined by the availability of training or instructional technology and the amount of resources society is willing to provide. Many individuals with mental retardation have areas of normal capability that may be developed or can remain underdeveloped.

Mental retardation does not exist in a vacuum. It is a product of the interaction between heredity and environment, with prolonged exposure to impoverished environments exacerbating the problem (Macmillan, Siperstein, & Gresham, 1996). Poverty is a factor. Grossman and Tarjan (1987) point out that socioeconomically disadvantaged individuals are overrepresented among the mildly retarded. Those with mild levels of retardation constitute approximately 75 percent of the retarded population. Thus, mental retardation is also conceptualized as a sociological phenomenon within society that can be observed through the limited performance of some of the individuals in that society (Gold, 1980).

In this chapter we will introduce you to the major areas related to mental retardation, as well as its causes, classifications, characteristics, definition, diagnosis, and placement options.

## DEFINITIONS

Individuals with mental retardation are by definition those who are inadequate in their intellectual development with concurrent deficits in adaptive behavior. A diagnosis of mental retardation indicates nothing about causality , an individual's past, or his or her future potential. It only tells us that individuals with mental retardation are inadequate in their intellectual and adaptive development and ability at the present time. Often the conceptualization of mental retardation depends upon the specialist defining it. For example, physicians may consider mental retardation as a symptom indicating a chemical imbalance or the inability of the body to assimilate and digest certain foods. Some mental health specialists consider mental retardation a symptom of severe mental illness. Sociologists and developmental psychologists may feel that mental retardation is a reflection of a lack of psychological, environmental, and/or family stimulation. Thus they consider it a symptom of inadequate social concern and an inadequacy of social structure. Some educators feel that mental retardation can be a symptom of poor or inadequate instruction. It might also be a symptom of lack of interest and inattention on the part of the youngster, which results in the child not benefiting from available instruction.

In reality, mental retardation is often associated with one or more of these conceptualizations. Children identified as mentally retarded are incapable of learning the same things as normal children of the same age. However, they can often learn the same material at a later time. The concept of being slow to learn or being a slow learner emerged from this phenomenon (Johnson, 1971). Furthermore, we know that children with mental retardation learn in the same way as normal children. Their motor development follows the same sequence and pattern as it does for normal children. They have the same desires, anxieties, aspirations, and frustrations as anyone else.

The American Association on Mental Deficiency (1992) provided the following new definition for mental retardation:

> Mental Retardation refers to substantial limitation in present functioning. It is characterized by significantly sub-average intellectual functioning, existing concurrently with related limitations in two or more of the following applicable adaptable skills areas: communication, self care, home living, social skills, community use, self direction, health and safety, functional academics, leisure, and work. Mental retardation manifests before age 18. (p. 5)

The following assumptions are essential for the application of this definition: (1) that a valid assessment that considered the wide range of cultural, language, communication, and behavioral diversities has been completed; (2) that impairment of adaptive skills was observed in the person's natural community settings and compared with the behaviors of peers; and (3) that the adaptive profiles indicate strengths as well as weaknesses (Turnbull, Turnbull, Shank, & Leal, 1995; Heward, 1996; Hunt & Marshall, 1994).

The three critical components of the definition deal with intelligence, adaptive behavior, and age of onset.

## Intelligence

The concept of *intelligence* is hypothetical. We define intelligence by tests of observed performance that are based on the assumption that it takes more intelligence to perform some tasks than it does to perform other tasks. Intelligence is the outcome of what we measure regarding an individual's performance (Heward, 1996; Gold, 1980). Technically, intelligence refers to outcome scores of performance on intelligence tests. No one really knows what intelligence is; there are only opinions about which abilities reflect the nature of intelligence. Significantly subaverage general intellectual functioning is determined by one or more standardized intelligence tests and a person scoring at two or more standard deviations from the average or mean IQ score, usually 100, on these tests. The mean score (100) represents the average score of same-age students who have taken the intelligence test. Therefore, the score at the second standard deviation from the mean (100) would fall around or beyond the score of 70. IQ scores then become a rough estimate or indicator of current performance in daily life skills. The lower scores are indications of serious limitations in conceptual, practical, and social intelligence. Thus, a person with an IQ score somewhat higher than 60, with notable deficits or limitations in adaptive behavior, would qualify as mentally retarded (Meyen & Skrtic, 1988; Haring, McCormick, & Haring, 1994).

## Adaptive Behavior

*Adaptive behavior* usually refers to the extent to which a person adapts successfully to various environments, takes care of personal needs, and reflects age-appropriate communication, social, and situational competencies. Some experts suggest that deficits or limitations in adaptive skills are more important issues for a diagnosis of mental retardation than are IQ scores. The deficits or areas of limitation for a fair diagnosis of mental retardation must exist in at least two adaptive skill areas, even though the individual may exhibit strengths in some other skill areas. The ten areas of adaptive skills noted in the AAMD definition are considered essential to socially successful individuals who are reasonably happy and function independently without

substantial support in effectively adapting to environmental demands (Hardman, Drew, & Egan, 1996; Kirk, Gallagher, & Anastasiow, 1993).

Preschool children are expected to grow and mature appropriately within their family. Schoolchildren are expected to learn the three R's and interact socially with peers, forming stable meaningful relationships. Adults are expected to be gainfully employed, pay taxes, get along in the community, and form long-lasting emotional bonds. Adaptive behavior is the individual's response to the demands of the total social environment and the different types of expected adaptive behavioral responses at different ages.

Adaptive behavior deficits vary among individuals relative to their age, cultural group, and socioeconomic status. Adaptive behavior is often difficult to directly assess. Adaptive behavior measures sometimes compare the performance of one individual with that of age or grade peers or the relative position of an individual within the general population, when it can be determined (Cegelka & Prehm, 1982).

## Age of Onset

The American Association on Mental Deficiency defines the *age of onset* for MR as prior to age 18, since it is at this age that people in our society are legally expected to carry out the responsibilities of adult behavior. The condition or disability of mental retardation is manifested during the developmental period but usually (especially with mild mental retardation) initially becomes identified with an IQ test score of 70 or below and with deficits in adaptive behavior (Hallahan & Kauffman, 1991; Berdine, 1993).

Many experts believe that mild mental retardation is not a lifelong condition and that given appropriate assistance, individuals with mild mental retardation will improve (Macmillan et al., 1996). Smith and Luckasson (1995) write that mild mental retardation is a description of present functioning rather than a permanent state of being. Since any individual's functioning will vary depending on circumstance, age, or task, a person with intellectual limitations may (at least in theory) move in and out of the categorization of mental retardation. When at-risk children receive enriching early education programs, they can often escape a diagnosis of mild mental retardation. In this regard, mild mental retardation can be viewed as an individual's present or current adaptive functioning deficit and difficulty in capacity to learn. Individuals with mental retardation live in socially and otherwise demanding environments; their limitations are often an outcome of environmental mismatches, in which the demands of the environment exceed the capacities of the individual. Thus, the competency of individuals may be determined by their experiences in certain environments and their abilities to meet environmental demands (Haring et al., 1994; Hardman et al., 1996).

The terms provided in Box 3.1 are a limited list of the specialized vocabulary used in the area of mental retardation and should help the reader understand some basic concepts to be discussed later.

**Box 3.1**
*WHAT EVERY TEACHER NEEDS TO KNOW*

*Terms*

**adaptive behavior**   How an individual meets standards of self-sufficiency and social responsibility and copes within the environment.

**amniocentesis**   A procedure used to identify certain genetic disorders in the unborn fetus.

**anoxia**   A lack of oxygen that may result in brain damage.

**assessment**   A process for determining a child's strengths and weaknesses. It involves screening, diagnosis, classification, placement, and monitoring.

**at risk**   A term that refers to individuals who are considered to have a higher than usual chance of developing an impairment, disability, problem, and/or deficiency.

**brain injury**   A physical injury or damage to the brain that impedes normal development.

**central nervous system (CNS)**   The brain and spinal cord.

**chromosomal aberrations**   Abnormalities of cell division due to nondisjunctions, translocations, or fragmentation of chromosomes that may result in death or defective offspring.

**cognition**   The understanding of information.

**cultural-familial retardation**   Lowered intelligence of unknown origin associated with a history of MR in one or more family members.

**culture**   The accepted and established knowledge, ideas, and values shared by a society.

**differential diagnosis**   Pinpointing atypical behavior, explaining it, and distinguishing it from problems with similar symptoms.

**heredity**   Genetically inherited characteristics of an individual.

**intelligence**   A hypothetical construct that refers to an individual's ability to perceive, understand, and adapt to his or her environment.

**metacognition**   Self-knowledge about how one learns and the regulation of one's cognition.

**reliability**   Obtaining a relatively similar score when given a test repeatedly.

**standard deviation**   A measurement of the variability of a set of scores of attributes. Small standard deviations mean that the scores are distributed close to the mean; large standard deviations mean that the scores are spread over a wider range.

**trauma**   Physical or psychological damage.

**validity**   Whether a test measures what it is supposed to measure.

## PREVALENCE

The lack of professional agreement about the definition of mental retardation, data collection and reporting problems, and sociocultural and socioeconomic issues all cause problems in estimating the number of school age children who are mentally retarded. Historically, it has been estimated that 3 percent of the general population (approximately 7 million people) were considered mentally retarded. The 50 states report varying estimated figures closer to 4 percent of the population. In addition, mental retardation is a coexisting factor in approximately 13 percent of all students with disabilities. Approximately 90 percent of the mentally retarded population are classified as mildly retarded. Currently, the trend points to decreasing numbers of children with mild mental retardation, due to societal pressures to have these children identified as learning disabled, a more socially acceptable diagnosis. Conversely, children who come from poor families, especially African American families, reveal a rising trend for becoming identified as mentally retarded. The *Nineteenth Annual Report to Congress on the Implementation of* IDEA (U.S. Department of Education, 1997) identifies 584,406 school age children as being classified with mental retardation.

There are other problems influencing prevalence figures, such as bias in testing, prejudice in placement, and litigation (Polloway & Smith, 1983; Smith & Luckasson, 1995). Since most of the children fall in the mild range of mental retardation, there is a higher incidence of identified mental retardation during the school age years and a lower identified incidence during the preschool years and adulthood. There are more males than females identified as mentally retarded, and more mental retardation is identified among ethnic, racial minority, and low socioeconomic groups (Elliott, 1979).

## CHARACTERISTICS

### General Cognition

Aside from being classified as retarded, individuals with mental retardation have little more in common with each other than do people without retardation. The mentally retarded vary physically and emotionally, as well as by personality, disposition, and beliefs. However, despite the diversity of the groups who compose the mentally retarded population, there are some common characteristics of people with mental retardation. Their apparent slowness in learning is related to the delayed rate of intellectual development (Johnson, 1971; Wehman, 1997). For instance, adults with mental retardation may not learn certain skills or concepts efficiently, and as a result tend to perform more poorly than comparative normal groups. Yet when they attend to appropriate aspects of presented learning stimuli versus inappropriate aspects, their rate of learning can be controlled (Wehman, 1997).

Learning is dependent upon intellectual development. Intellectual development, in turn, determines the complexity and level of learning that can take place at any specific time. In comparing the learning ability of two groups of children at the same intellectual developmental level, and assuming the same degree of readiness to learn in terms of background experiences, attitudes, desires, quality of instruction, and similar factors, one would expect that they would learn a skill or concept in the same period of time. However, individuals with MR do not usually learn as rapidly as children who are not intellectually retarded. Yet, if specific educational supports are implemented, students with mild mental retardation can reach the same levels of learnings as their peers (Wehman, 1997). Although the normal and retarded groups differ significantly in such factors as age, physical and motor development, and social development, as long as they are equated for intellectual developmental levels, experiences, and previous learning to ensure equal readiness, they should have similar patterns of learning (Johnson, 1959). Teaching a student with mental retardation requires (1) that successive learning tasks be spaced further apart, extending the sequence of learning over a longer period of time; (2) more practice time in learning; and (3) more total instructional time to learn the entire sequence (skill or concept). The additional time devoted to skill instruction for a student with mental retardation should be in terms of additional practice and rehearsal to overcome the factor of forgetting (Johnson, 1959; Wehman, 1997).

Students with mental retardation score significantly below average on intelligence tests (70 IQ or below). These students have impaired capacities to learn, do not know how to learn, or are not efficient or effective in the learning processes, including attention, memory, linguistic, and generalization skills. They have an impaired ability to acquire, label, classify, remember, and use information appropriately. They are less able to understand abstractions, representations (symbols), and generalizations. They appear to require extensive practice and repeated experiences to learn successfully. They appear impaired at introspection and imagination or imagery relative to their learning experiences (Hallahan & Kauffman, 1991; Hardman et al., 1996).

## Attention

In learning, children must be able to attend to the learning task for the required length of time and be able to control distractions. Children with mental retardation have difficulty doing this. They routinely have difficulty distinguishing and attending to relevant questions in both learning and social situations (Zeaman & Hause, 1979). The problem is not that the child won't pay attention, but rather that he or she can't pay attention or does not know how to attend (Hunt & Marshall, 1994; Meyen & Skrtic, 1988). A related problem is that some children with mental retardation *perseverate*, or can't shift their attention to new material (Berdine, 1993). They can be helped by learning task analysis, in which the learning task is broken down into components and those components are mastered sequentially (Smith & Luckasson, 1995).

## Memory

Children with mental retardation have problems with both long- and short-term memory and the rehearsal processes necessary for placing information in memory. The more severe the retardation, the greater the memory deficit. They do not spontaneously use appropriate learning or memory retention strategies. These children have difficulty in realizing the conditions or actions that aid learning and memory (Smith & Luckasson, 1995; Hunt & Marshall, 1994; Meyen & Skrtic, 1988). Often these children need to learn how to rehearse or practice techniques that will aid in retention of information. They will have trouble recognizing recurring patterns or repetitions and are slower to transfer information to short-term memory and from short-term memory to long-term memory (Berdine, 1993).

## Language

Individuals with mental retardation (depending on the degree of retardation) usually have language comprehension and formulation difficulties. They experience delayed language development and often exhibit less fluent and less articulate speech than their peers. Individuals with mild mental retardation may exhibit few and minor difficulties, while some individuals with severe mental retardation may have severely limited language skills. Depending on the degree of mental retardation, there may be expressive and receptive language problems, problems in conversational skills, giving or receiving directions, determining central or essential issues and telling stories (Meyen & Skrtic, 1988; Turnbull et al., 1995). Individuals with mental retardation show delayed functioning on pragmatic aspects of language, such as turn taking, selecting acceptable topics for conversation, knowing when to speak, knowing when to be silent, and similar contextual skills (Hymes, 1972; Haring et al., 1994). They use mixed up sentences, can't determine main ideas from orally presented materials, and omit common prefixes and suffixes (Wallace, Cohen, & Polloway, 1987). They have limited vocabulary and tend to use a limited number of sentence constructions (Hunt & Marshall, 1994; Berdine, 1993).

## Academic Achievement

The cognitive inefficiencies of children with mild to moderate mental retardation lead to persistent problems in academic achievement (Macmillan et al., 1996: Turnbull et al., 1995). Students with mild and moderate mental retardation typically lag behind their nonretarded peers academically, especially in reading, reading comprehension, computation, and general mathematics.

## Metacognition

Depending on the degree of retardation, some individuals with mental retardation have difficulties in metacognitive skills such as planning how to solve a problem, monitoring their own solution strategy, proceeding with the strategy implementation, and evaluating the outcome. The lack or underdevelopment of these skills notably affects memory, rehearsal skills, organizational ability, and being in control of the process of learning (Sternburg & Spear, 1985; Glidden, 1985; Hunt & Marshall, 1994).

## Motivation

Individuals with mental retardation may approach the learning situation with significant anxiety. Past experiences of failure and the anxiety generated by those failures may make students appear to be less goal/task-directed and lacking in motivation. It is as if they have learned to avoid failure. This avoidance teamed with limited metacognitive skills results in a helplessness in the engagement for learning. They limit their goals and aspirations and become dependent (Zigler & Burack, 1989). The history of failure is likely to lead to a dependence on external sources of reinforcement or reward rather than internal sources of reward. They are less likely to be self-starters motivated by self-approval (Harter, 1978; Smith & Luckasson, 1995).

## Physical Characteristics

The more severe the mental retardation, the more likely the child will exhibit coexisting problems, such as physical, motor, orthopedic, visual, and auditory impairments and health problems (Patton, Beirne-Smith, & Payne, 1990; Drew, Hardman, & Longan, 1996; Hunt & Marshall, 1994). Individuals with mild mental retardation may be below their nonretarded age peers in measures of height, weight, and skeletal maturity. Some children with mental retardation may also have cerebral palsy, convulsive disorders, and sensory impairments. They may be more susceptible than their peers to disease, illness, and dental problems. However, children with mild mental retardation can participate in sports and physical education activities and keep up with other students, and some may even excel in certain sports (Hunt & Marshall, 1994; Haring et al., 1994; Smith & Luckasson, 1995).

## Labels

The terms *mild retardation*, *moderate retardation*, *severe retardation*, and *profound retardation* are most commonly used to characterize the extent of a person's intellectual capabilities and adaptive skills. *Mild mental retardation* refers to the highest level of performance or functioning, while *profound mental retardation* refers to the lowest level of performance. The corresponding numerical IQ scores generally associated with each category are as follows (Hardman et al., 1996; Smith & Luckasson, 1995; Berdine, 1993).

1. Mild retardation = IQ scores of 55–70
2. Moderate retardation = IQ scores of 40–55
3. Severe retardation = IQ scores of 25–40
4. Profound retardation = IQ scores of 25 or lower

The corresponding educational labels used historically were *educable* (mild retardation) and *trainable* (moderate retardation). Despite the current view that all people with mental retardation are educable and trainable, theses terms are persistently used in current professional literature.

## ETIOLOGY

The American Association on Mental Deficiency has identified nine groups of factors that can cause or contribute to mental retardation:

1. Infection and intoxication
2. Trauma and physical agents
3. Metabolism and inadequate nutrition
4. Gross brain disease
5. Unknown prenatal causes or influences
6. Chromosomal abnormalities
7. Gestational disorders
8. Psychiatric disorders
9. Environmental influences (Grossman, 1983)

There may be more than 1,000 known causes of mental retardation. It is not always clear which causes apply to a particular individual. In addition, mental retardation is rarely the result of a single cause, but is more often the result of complex interactions among multiple causes (McLaren & Bryson, 1987; Turnbull et al., 1995).

### Infection and Intoxication

Infections contracted during pregnancy can cause mental retardation. Infections such as rubella, syphilis, meningitis, AIDS (HIV), and toxoplasmosis (blood poisoning) can all have negative affects upon fetal development. Drug usage during pregnancy—including legal prescriptive and nonprescriptive drugs such as alcohol and tobacco, illegal substances such as LSD, heroin, morphine, cocaine, and the ingestion of metals such as lead—can cause mental retardation. Chronic maternal illnesses such as diabetes, kidney disease, thyroid deficiency, and hypertension may affect the nutritional environment of the fetus or cause premature delivery and accompanying mental retardation (Hardman et al., 1996; Hunt & Marshall, 1994; Meyen & Skrtic, 1988). Blood type Rh incompatibility between fetus and mother in pregnancies after the first birth may also cause maternal antibodies to damage the fetus.

Fetal alcohol syndrome can also be a concern. It refers to damage to the fetus resulting from maternal alcohol consumption. The newborn may show facial anomalies, heart problems, low birth weight, and eventually mental retardation (Hardman et al.,1996).

## Trauma and Physical Agents

Injuries that occur to the child before, during, or after birth—for example, anoxia, hypoxia (deprivation of oxygen), physical injuries due to child abuse, and irradiation during delivery and after the baby is born—can cause mental retardation (Haring et al., 1994).

## Metabolism and Inadequate Nutrition

Phenylketonuric disorder (PKU), Tay-Sachs disease, and galactosemia are disorders in which the child's inability to tolerate certain elements in foods may result in brain injury and mental retardation. These problems will be discussed in more detail under chromosomal disorders.

## Gross Brain Disease

Gross brain disease conditions include disorders such as neurofibromatosis (tumors in the skin, peripheral to nerve tissue and the brain). Tuberous sclerosis is growth of tumors in the central nervous system and the degeneration of cerebral white matter (Hardman et al., 1996). These conditions are examples of gross brain disease that can cause mental retardation.

## Unknown Prenatal Influences

Unknown prenatal influences may cause mental retardation. For example, the causes of hydrocephalus and microcephaly are not fully understood. Yet if untreated, both will result in multiple disorders, including mental retardation. Hydrocephalus is the presence of slow-draining cerebrospinal fluid in the skull, which increases the size of the skull while causing pressure on the brain. Microcephaly is a condition in which the skull is significantly smaller than normal, which will also destroy brain tissue (Hunt & Marshall, 1994).

## Chromosomal Abnormalities

Down syndrome, a genetic disorder, occurs when there are 47 chromosomes instead of the normal 46. It routinely leads to mental retardation and a variety of other health problems. The presence of Down syndrome is related to maternal age, with the incidence increasing significantly in children born to mothers age 35 and older. It can also be caused by a chromosomal abnormality called *translocation*. The child may have 46 chromosomes, but one pair breaks, and the broken part fuses to another chromosome. Children with Down syndrome have facial features marked by distinctive epicanthus folds, prominent cheekbones, and a small, somewhat flattened nose (Kirk et al., 1993).

Phenylketonuric disorder (PKU) is another example of a genetic defect that can produce severe retardation. In PKU, the absence of a specific enzyme in the liver leads to a buildup of the amino acid phenylalanine. The effect of PKU, when detected, can be controlled by modifying the child's early infant nutritional intake, especially milk (Hardman et al., 1996).

A final example of the many chromosomal anomalies that can directly lead to mental retardation is fragile X syndrome. Affecting only males, it is the result of a constriction near the end of the long arm of the X chromosome. This anomaly causes mental retardation as well as other physical abnormalities.

## Gestational Disorders

Gestational disorders such as prematurity and low birth weight are risk factors for mental retardation. The more extreme these conditions, the higher the level of risk (Hunt & Marshall, 1994).

## Psychiatric Disorders

The *Diagnostic and Statistical Manual of Mental Disorders* (American Psychiatric Association, 1994) characterizes mental disorders as behavioral or psychological syndromes that currently affect a person's functioning at many levels. In terms of apparent mental retardation, at any given time mental illness can depress intellectual functioning. Psychiatrically involved children will then test as mentally retarded.

## Environmental or Psychosocial Disadvantage

Children with mild mental retardation make up 90 percent of all identified cases. Within this group, etiology is mostly unknown. There is a strong belief that psychosocial disadvantage, the combination of a poor social and cultural environment early in the child's life, may contribute significantly to this population. Pains must be taken to distinguish between social and cultural deprivation and social and cultural difference. There does not appear to be any intrinsic value that makes one rich cultural experience more valid than another. Rather, it is the absence of experiences rather than the type of experiences that appear to be critical. Findings from studies consistently reveal that a large percentage of mild mental retardation is based on environmental causes, most notably deprivation in the early years of life. Poverty and social disorganization in the home environment increase health risks and contribute to early and progressive language deficits and a variety of cognitive problems. Families at the poverty level may also have lower expectations for academic or school achievement. They often are unable to prepare their children for school, receive poor health care, and experience poor nutrition. Some reject dominant cultural values supporting school achievement (McDermott, 1994; Greenwood, Hart, Walker, & Risley, 1994; Ramey & Finklestein, 1981).

## IDENTIFICATION PROCESS

The American Association on Mental Deficiency requires two types of assessment for children to be identified as retarded. Intelligence must be tested and adaptive behaviors must be analyzed. The assessment procedures should include teacher observations of behavior and the results of standardized achievement tests. Other assessment approaches are encouraged, such as curriculum-based assessments, interviewing, and sociometric ratings (Meyen & Skrtic, 1988; Turnbull et al., 1995; Hunt & Marshall, 1994; Kirk et al., 1993).

### Intelligence Testing

Intellectual functioning is measured by standardized intelligence tests, which usually consist of a series of questions and problem solving tasks assumed to require certain amounts of intelligence to answer or solve correctly. The tests sample limited skills and abilities and the outcome score is only a representation of overall intelligence. The intelligence quotient (IQ) is based on the relationship between the individual's chronological age (CA) and mental age (MA). These tests are standardized, which means that they use the same questions and tasks, always presented in the same way, and are scored using the same procedures each time the test is given. A concern is that many IQ tests are culturally biased, favoring white middle-class children by examining prior learning that only a white middle-class child is likely to experience.

Most of the time, IQ scores do not change significantly. However, with children who are mildly retarded, IQ scores can be influenced by experience and can change significantly. Scores in the 70–85 range can change as much as 20 points after a period of significant instruction. Intelligence testing and outcomes can be influenced by motivation, time, the location of the test site, and poor testing procedure (Heward, 1996; Turnbull et al., 1995; Meyen & Skrtic, 1988; Hallahan & Kauffman, 1991).

Intelligence tests are imperfect instruments, imperfectly understood, used for classification purposes, assignment of labels, and placement of children or adults in special programs. They are sometimes of questionable validity, since generally no more than 50 percent of academic achievement is associated with intelligence. The remainder of individual differences are presumably determined by the child's motivation, work habits, experience in taking tests, and acceptability within the school setting. Some educators argue that current school achievement predicts future school

achievement as well as and sometimes better than do intelligence tests (Haywood, 1974; Hobbs, 1975). In addition, intelligence tests may be heavily weighted toward language skills, and the performance portions of the tests require a ready understanding of verbal instructions. Children who speak nonstandard English or are not facile in standard English will most surely do poorly on these tests.

Despite these limitations, intelligence tests, when used appropriately, can be highly useful when making special education eligibility decisions. They can be of real value in the design of appropriate instructional programs (Hobbs, 1975).They are also useful when attempting predictive assessments of future academic success.

Some of the more widely used intelligence tests are:

**The Stanford-Binet Intelligence Scale (SB-IV).**   This test consists of items that progress in difficulty from manipulative skills to verbal and abstract skills, testing memory, perception, information, and logical reasoning (Thorndike, Hagen, & Sattler, 1986).

**The Revised Wechsler Intelligence Scale for Children (WISC-III).**   This test consists of two major areas, verbal and performance. Verbal tasks measure vocabulary, comprehension, and arithmetic skills. Performance tasks measure skills in picture completion, block design, using codes, and solving mazes (Wechsler, 1974).

**The Kaufman Assessment Battery for Children (K-ABC).**   This alternative test of intelligence measures intelligence as manifested by information processing abilities (Kaufman & Kaufman, 1983).

## Adaptive Functioning Assessment

Adaptive functioning measurement is required in the identification of mental retardation. To be classified as mentally retarded, an individual must be clearly below normal in measurements of adaptive behavior. Operationally, this means that there are clear deficits in the effectiveness or degree to which the individual meets the societal standards of personal independence and social responsibility that are expected of his or her age and social group (Grossman, 1983). Adaptive *behavior* refers to how a person meets or fails to meet the challenges and requirements of daily living and the extent to which a child can function and interact with others in his or her environment. "It is not how deprived his home is, how poor he is, the advantages he has or has not been exposed to. It is not asking if he can reason in a certain way or if he can perform certain school tasks. It is asking if he can feed himself, dress himself, get on a bus, or go to the store and buy a loaf of bread" (Windmiller, 1977, p. 44).

Adaptive behavior measures are essential in identifying mild mental retardation and avoiding the misdiagnosis and misplacement of children with problems other than retardation. Adaptive behavior is also a measure of how well children adapt to school as well as to the environment outside of school. Macmillan et al. (1996) make the point that mild mental retardation can be understood only in terms of the child's cognitive inefficiencies and the environmental demands for problem solving. Mild mental retardation is highly contextual and relative to the environment. They suggest that in some contexts, people with retardation may not appear retarded in one setting as opposed to another.

Frequently used instruments that measure the adaptive behavior of school-age children are:

**The Vineland Adaptive Behavior Scale.**    This test uses questions related to age-appropriate self-help, locomotion, communication, occupation, socialization, and self-direction skills. It also attempts to measure social competence (Sparrow, Balla, & Cucchetti, 1984).

**The Adaptive Behavior Scale-Public School Version (ABS-PS).**    This highly regarded and widely used scale is an outgrowth of a project begun in 1965 by Parsons State Hospital and the American Association on Mental Deficiency to develop a measure of adaptive behavior that could be used to help plan programs for patients with disabilities (Debell, 1980). Lambert revised this instrument in 1974 in order to use it with public school children (Lambert, Mihira, & Leland, 1993).

This comprehensive version, using the classroom teacher as the informant, consists of 56 items on Part I and 39 items on Part II.

Part I measures:

1. Independent functioning
2. Physical development
3. Economic activity
4. Language development

5. Numbers and time

6. Vocational activity

7. Self-direction

8. Responsibility

9. Socialization

    Part II measures:

1. Violent and destructive behavior

2. Antisocial behavior

3. Rebellious behavior

4 Untrustworthy behavior

5. Withdrawal

6. Stereotyped behavior

7. Odd mannerisms

8. Inappropriate interpersonal manners

9. Unacceptable vocal habits

10. Unacceptable tendencies

11. Hyperactive tendencies

12. Psychological disturbances

13. Medication use (Coulter & Morrow, 1977)

One of the main strengths of this scale is that it provides an individualized pro-file, which can be then used to develop an educational program for the child (Lambert & Nicoll, 1976; Coulter & Morrow, 1977).

**The Adaptive Behavior Inventory for Children (ABIC).**    This test is part of the *System of Multicultural Pluralistic Assessment* (SOMPA) (Mercer, 1979). The following issues led to the development of SOMPA:

1. Public schools were primary labelers of people with mental retardation, and they relied chiefly on IQ test scores, not medical evaluations, for the diagnosis.

2. Forty-six percent of the classified children with mental retardation had IQs over 70.

3. African American and Spanish-speaking children were more likely to be placed and labeled than Anglo children.

4. Only 19 percent of children with mental retardation returned to the mainstream of regular classes. The remaining 81 percent stayed in self-contained classes.

5. More males than females were labeled.

6. Children from low economic levels were more likely to be identified as "situationally retarded"—70 percent of the children identified were not perceived as mentally retarded by people in their neighborhoods or other agencies (Mercer, 1979).

The study concluded that:

1. A two-dimensional definition of mental retardation should be required (intelligence plus adaptive behavior).

2. People scoring in the lowest 3 percent on a measure of adaptive behavior would be defined as mentally retarded only if their intellectual functioning was also low.

3. Pluralistic norms are needed, so that a child's performance could be compared with others who come from similar sociocultural backgrounds and have had similar opportunities to acquire the knowledge and skills needed to answer test questions (Mercer, 1979).

SOMPA was developed to deal with these concerns and to ensure that children from culturally diverse and economically disadvantaged groups were not unfairly assessed and compared with the dominant Anglo culture, which might in turn cause them to be inappropriately and disproportionately placed in classes for students who are educable or mildly retarded. The ABIC was designed to be given only as part of the total SOMPA assessment, but is often used separately. The ABIC contains 242 questions dealing with home, neighborhood, school, and community functioning. Only those questions appropriate to the child's ability level and age level are asked during the interview.

The adaptive behavior scales are important instruments used in the identification and placement of children with mental retardation. These measures indicate how the child functions outside the school environment. The examiner can determine whether low intelligence and achievement scores are indeed an indication of mild mental retardation or are just reflective of academic problems of origins other than intelligence.

## PROGRAMS

### Educational Services

The special education movement has emphasized the need for children with special needs to be fully or partially included in regular education classrooms and programs to the extent possible and reasonable. These full inclusion or inclusion efforts encompass most children with mental retardation, especially the higher functioning students. Special educators collaborate and cooperate with regular teachers to integrate students with mental retardation into the regular classrooms and provide activities for both educational and social opportunities with normal peers while continuing individualized programs. They participate in all classroom and extracurricular activities with all nondisabled peers (Smith & Luckasson, 1995).

Traditionally, services for students with mental retardation have been offered in regular classrooms, special education resource rooms, self-contained classes, special schools, and hospital or institutional settings. There have been great efforts in the past three decades to provide community-based services for all students with mental retardation and reduce the institutionalized population. Deinstitutionalization programs have resulted in an increase in community-based programs and smaller locally based programs. Emphasis is placed on teaching the mentally retarded, to the extent to which they can learn the functional and academic skills needed and used in everyday life. Emphasis is on transition to community living skills programs for adulthood and especially for employment and socialization (Berdine, 1993; Heward, 1996).

Services for children with mental retardation begin with *early intervention programs* that focus on providing guidance for families and a direct focus on the infant's acquisition of sensory-motor skills. Early intervention programs also provide parents with stimulation techniques that might facilitate intellectual development. *Preschool programs*, such as Head Start programs for children with mental retardation and economic disadvantage, focus on school readiness and socialization activities. *Regular classroom programs* for children with mild and moderate retardation provide individualized programs and interaction with nondisabled peers. *Resource room programs* are provided for some students while they attend a special services program part of the day for remedial help. In *self-contained classroom programs*, students with moderate and severe retardation are in a segregated classroom for most of the day.

In resource rooms and self-contained special education classrooms, placements for lower-functioning students who are mildly or moderately retarded, the curriculum can be designed to most appropriately meet their needs. The curriculum can be organized within the framework of persisting life problems, such as behaving in and managing the home and family, using leisure time, managing money, understanding health and safety issues, and traveling. These life situations are crucial at all age levels and directly involve the individual with his or her environment. The curriculum can be organized around the behaviors and information needed for adequate functioning within the context of life problems. The curriculum can also accommodate traditional subject matter areas, such as reading, arithmetic, science, health, and other school subjects, to facilitate coping in society. In this setting the teacher must be responsive to the following concerns:

1.  The teacher must have a good grasp of each student's status in each ability area so that lessons will have some relationship to the student's fund of knowledge and make it possible for the student to make relevant associations.

2.  The teacher must structure the learning situation and reduce distractions.

3.  The teacher must present material clearly, sequentially, and with positive reinforcement for correct responses.

4.  When the student has an incorrect response, the teacher should encourage the student and re-evaluate whether he or she has overestimated the student's ability, parts of the lesson were confusing, or the student is not ready to engage in that particular learning situation and needs more preparation. In all this, the planning of individualized curriculum and instruction for students with mental retardation considers readiness, motivation, and performance evaluation (Goldstein, 1966; Hunt & Marshall, 1994).

## Full Inclusion Programs

*Full inclusion* is the practice of educating as many students with disabilities as possible in regular classrooms together with their nondisabled peers. This educational approach is critical of the separateness or isolation of regular and special education from each other. Advocates of full inclusion state that the fragmentation of services for students with special needs and segregated classrooms often causes children with disabilities to experience loss of self-esteem, feelings of stigmatization, and negative attitudes about school. The current educational thrust is to ask regular educators to take more responsibility for instruction of students with retardation and other disabilities, while providing appropriate support systems for regular education classroom teachers (Carnine & Kameenui, 1990). Special classes, separate schools, and other restrictive environments for educating students with special needs should be used only when the nature or severity of the disability is such that education in the regular class cannot be achieved satisfactorily.

The increased effort for including some children with mild and moderate retardation is the result of the realization that partial inclusion and resource or self-contained classroom programs are not meeting the needs of some exceptional children, especially children with retardation. Special education and regular education teachers were charged to collaborate on multidisciplinary teams to plan programs for the educational and socialization needs of these students. In fact, these teams met infrequently to review test results, placement options, and other administrative concerns, and not programming issues. This created a breakdown in communication and reduced chances for effective programming for students (Nowacek, 1992). The current belief is that students with mild mental retardation may best be served in inclusion programs that use a functional curriculum and academics, where they can develop the skills necessary to make a successful transition from school to adult responsibilities, including personal/social, daily living, and occupational adjustment skills (Clark, 1994). If students with mental retardation are to be successfully integrated into regular educational settings, they will have to acquire the classroom related survival skills and behaviors required, develop appropriate social skills, and participate in cooperative ventures with nondisabled peers so that they can be perceived as performing reasonably well (Patton et al., 1990). For example, while the class is working on addition of two-digit numbers, the student with mental retardation can use manipulatives to add single digits; or while the class is taking a written spelling test, the student with mental retardation can match written words to pictures. Similarly, while the class is working on Fahrenheit and Centigrade temperatures, the student with mental retardation can work on the concepts of hot and cold. Meyen (1978) reported that more drastic curriculum change will be necessary for students with moderate retardation. A child who needs continued help in self-care skills, such as dressing and traveling independently, will need time to develop and practice such basic behaviors under guidance.

Davis (1994) reported that the Association for Retarded Citizens encourages efforts for the inclusion of youngsters with mental retardation. The Association for Retarded Citizens position is that:

1.  All students have value and should be included in all aspects of school life.

2.  Students can best develop life skills in educational settings designed to meet their individual needs with peers of various abilities and backgrounds.

3.  Students should be educated with nondisabled peers in an age-appropriate setting.

4.  Children have the right to an individualized education that addresses their strengths and needs and provides options and appropriate resources for support (pp. 14–15).

There is also a need to identify programs that successfully include students with retardation and to examine the components of these programs. Early studies have indicated that students with retardation were not socially accepted by nondisabled peers, whether the students with retardation were in the regular classroom or the special education classroom (Kirk & Gallagher, 1986).

## Individualized Educational Programs (IEP)

All children who receive special education services, including children identified as mentally retarded, must have an Individualized Educational Program (IEP) that is designed to detail the services they will receive. This IEP is the result of the collaborative efforts of a team composed of parents, regular and special education teachers, the child, and any other specialists that will be involved in service provision for the child. The IEP details the child's needs and specifically describes how they will be met by the school system. The IEP team meets regularly and modifies the plan as the needs of the child change. One member of the team, usually the special education teacher, is responsible for monitoring the implementation of the IEP and periodically ascertaining from all involved whether or not the plan is effective for the child with mental retardation.

## Behavioral Therapy Programs

In public and other schools, behavior modification is used to decrease disruptive and inappropriate behavior, help the student attend to learning tasks, maintain attention, and shape new learning behaviors by rewarding appropriate behavior. Training procedures incorporating the use of behavioral reinforcement techniques facilitate the cognitive process. This is especially effective when adults model the performance of a task for a child who repeats the task and is reinforced at each stage of performance (Meyen & Skrtic, 1988). These programs provide readiness skills that are prerequisite for learning to attend, follow directions, develop language, develop self-help skills, and acquire socialization skills (Hallahan & Kauffman, 1991; Turnbull, 1995).

The chapter in this text on serious emotional disturbances (Chapter 5) provides a variety of behavioral modification techniques used to assist children in their learning and socialization. It emphasizes positive, rewarding, and pleasant reinforcement procedures. It may be appropriate to read or review that section of the chapter. In this chapter we wish to sensitize the reader to concerns about the appropriate use of punishment as a behavior modifying technique. Punishment is a tool upon which people have relied extensively to suppress inappropriate behavior displayed by students with mental retardation. Punishment may be considered the presentation of an adverse stimulus contingent upon a specific behavior. Punishment serves to reduce the possibility of future inappropriate response and reduces the rate of emission of the behavior (Grossman, 1990; Schloss & Smith, 1994).

Verbal statements in the form of reprimands, warnings, or disapprovals can be punishing. The effectiveness of these statements depends a great deal on the manner in which they are delivered. Reprimands delivered quietly and privately to the student have been shown to suppress disruptive behavior better than loud reprimands delivered either alone or followed by disapproving looks. Loud reprimands shouted across a classroom often draw attention to a child and may reinforce the disruptive behavior (Kazdin, 1980, O'Leary & O'Leary, 1977).

Time-out is a punishment procedure that uses the removal of all positive reinforcers for a certain period of time. Kazdin (1980) states that the crucial ingredient of time-out is delineating a time period in which reinforcement is unavailable as all sources of reinforcement are withdrawn. A variety of different time-out procedures have been used effectively. Schloss and Smith (1994) and Lakey, McNees, and McNees (1973) recommend using a time-out room to suppress obscene verbalizations or noncompliance with classroom rules. Each time the unwanted behaviors occur, the student can be placed in a small room adjacent to the classroom for a specified time period. In another variation of time-out, the child is not removed from the situation. When a disruptive behavior occurs, the child is told that the behavior is inappropriate and removed from the activity. The child is allowed to observe the activities and the other children. After a brief period, the child is allowed to return. This partial removal from an activity can markedly decrease disruptive behavior. Time-out should be limited to approximately two minutes after the child has regained composure. Four or five minutes in time-out should be the maximum exposure (Walker & Shea, 1987; Costenbader & Reading, 1995).

*Response cost* refers to loss of a positive reinforcer or to a penalty involving some work or effort (Schloss & Smith, 1994; Kazdin, 1992). There is no necessary time period in which positive events are unavailable, as in the case of time-out. In using response cost, a penalty of some sort, usually in the form of fines, is required. The following is an example of an effective response cost procedure that was implemented by parents to control a child's behavior during shopping trips. The child was told that he could spend 50 cents at the end of the parents' shopping in the store. However, for each instance of inappropriate behavior, such as inappropriately touching merchandise, roughhousing, or being beyond a certain distance from the parents, a penalty of 5 cents would be subtracted from the original 50 cents. The results indicated that by placing a fine on inappropriate behavior, that behavior rapidly decreased. To be effective, response cost should not be used too frequently. If used too much, the child will become discouraged. In addition, the magnitude of the fines should be within reasonable limits. Discouragement and frustration behaviors are likely to result if the fine is excessive. Gardner (1974) states that the child should also be provided an opportunity to regain reinforcing events following appropriate behavior. This strategy combines a positive reinforcement procedure with the response cost. The combined approach results in the strengthening of appropriate behaviors that will compete with the undesired ones. Understanding the rules of behavior that will govern the removal of the reinforcing events is also vital. In addition, the child should have alternative appropriate behaviors in his or her repertoire and be aware of the rules for using these behaviors to avoid a response cost.

In summary, each of the procedures described has been shown to suppress unwanted behaviors. Kazdin (1980) states that the procedure selected should be determined by the severity of the behavior, the danger of the behavior to the student or to others, the ease of implementing the technique, the training required of the person(s) who will administer the program, and the acceptance of the specific treatment in the setting where it will be applied. Schloss and Smith (1994), Grossman (1990), and Gardner (1974) present the guidelines in Box 3.2 for the use of punishment procedures that will produce the most desirable behavioral effects and the smallest number of negative side-effects.

## An Alternative Program

The French government has developed an extensive program for children with disabilities of all types. An agency called the *Union Nationale des Associations Régionales pour la Sauvegarde de l'Enfance et de l'Adolescence* serves to integrate national special education programs.

"Because of its influence one finds well conceived facilities for children throughout France. These centers are staffed by *Educateurs*, a professional group having no counter-

**Box 3.2**
*WHAT EVERY TEACHER NEEDS TO KNOW*

*Guidelines for Using*
*Punishment Procedures*

1. Punishment must be used infrequently.
2. The inappropriate behavior, the conditions under which it occurs, and its strength must be precisely defined.
3. The punishment procedure to be used should be well articulated.
4. The circumstances in which punishment will be used must be explicit.
5. Alternative behaviors that will replace the punished one, and the reinforcement procedures to be used to strengthen them, should be readily identifiable.
6. Time-out or response cost should be used whenever possible, rather than a procedure involving the presentation of aversive events.
7. The child should be informed in a clear and precise manner about behaviors that will produce positive consequences and those that will result in negative consequences.

8. Rules regarding punishment should be implemented consistently and immediately.
9. The teacher should always provide alternative behavioral possibilities.
10. Maximum intensity of the aversive event must be present from the beginning.
11. When using a punishment procedure, the teacher must be careful to ensure that the consequences are in fact unpleasant to the child.
12. The unpleasantness of the aversive consequences must be stronger than the positive consequences associated with the undesired behavior.
13. After the punishment rule has been presented to the child, routine use of a threat or a warning that the behavior will produce unpleasant consequences if he or she does not stop (or following the next time the inappropriate behavior occurs) is to be discouraged.

part in the United States. The *Educateurs* are carefully selected and trained workers with all types of children with disabilities. Having some of the skills of the teacher, the social worker, the psychologist, and the recreational worker, the *Educateurs* take heavy responsibility for the operation of observation and treatment centers" (Linton, 1969).

This treatment and education model provides services in public schools, children's homes, and institutions for a variety of disabilities and in most public and private agencies. The European approach provides a re-educational model that is directly able to creatively and effectively respond to children's developmental problems. Intervention approaches include behavior modification and social skill training and practice, along with consideration of social and cultural influences on the child.

Prior to placement of children with disabilities or sentencing of delinquent children, the court or the child welfare agency requests an *Educateur* to observe the child's behavior in the child's natural environments or in an observation center. This usually involves home and family life, mealtimes, leisure activities, work settings, friends, and school life. Professionals concerned about the child often collaborate with the *Educateur* (Linton, 1969).

The *Educateur*'s influence is deliberately designed to be positive and re-educative. The *Educateur*'s role is not one of simple judgment of the child. It is a role which involves friendships, counseling, and supportive assistance in any area of the child's life in which the *Educateur* may be needed. This model places a great deal of emphasis on the human relationship as a major modality of development. "The *Educateur* is considered a dominant influence in the growth producing exchange. Therefore, great emphasis is given to the way in which the adult presents him/herself to the child as a representative of the human world" (Rhodes, 1966).

The *Educateur* model directly involves the concepts and practices of social impact, modeling theory, learning theory, and applied behavioral modification. It also involves the influential role of human expectation by this significant person in the child's life as shown by the *Educateur's* behavior, insights, values, and ideas. The objective of this model is the social reintegration of the student. It attempts to alter the environmental forces in the student's life, to the extent that these factors become supportive rather than destructive. The goal is to involve the child's family, friends, and teachers toward changing their expectations so that the child may find greater acceptance in his or her own social system (Rhodes, 1966).

Education, socialization, and vocational training are emphasized. Extensive use is made of physical education training and dance, body rhythm, calisthenics, and indoor and outdoor sports activities. Social, recreational, leisure, theater, music, and work experiences are provided. The *Educateur* can provide special educational or remedial services for the child. The role is to reach the child through re-education and activities. The child and the *Educateur* can arrive at shared interests and human understanding, while applying behavioral modification techniques for coping with the demands of school and attempts at learning age-appropriate behavior.

The North Carolina Department of Human Resources has attempted to replicate this approach by providing paraprofessional educators and mental health specialists to accompany students with special needs who have behavioral disorders, learning disorders, and/or mild retardation in the schools. The program is deliberately integrated and implemented to develop the student's potential for learning and socialization in public schools. In North Carolina, the programs are administered locally by the Human Service Agency of the North Carolina Department of Human Resources, Area Mental Health Programs (N.C. Department of Human Resources, 1996).

## ISSUES OF IMPORTANCE

There are a wide variety of issues and problems in the education of children with mental retardation. These issues and problems range from what constitutes intelligence and mental retardation to what are appropriate placements. We have discussed some of these issues throughout this chapter. However, four major concerns bear emphasis:

1. What is intelligence and how is it measured?
2. The negative stereotyping of individuals with retardation.
3. The absence of standardized educational placement criteria.
4. The paucity of preventive and preschool services.

## Intelligence and Measurement

As you have read in this chapter, there is considerable disagreement as to what intelligence is and how to measure it. Since the theoretical concept of intelligence is not directly observable, we can only infer it from observing acts that are thought to require it. These acts are usually measured by intelligence tests that are often culturally biased and heavily weighted in favor of those with developed language skills. In addition, the scores derived from these tests are not stable, and with young children they are not particularly valid or reliable. The tests also measure performance at only one point in time and do not usually help in determining educational objectives or remedial procedures. Yet despite these problems, deficits in intellectual functioning as measured by intelligence tests are often more heavily weighted than are deficits in the more revealing adaptive behavior of children suspected of being mentally retarded.

## Negative Stereotyping

Individuals with mental retardation differ from each other in more ways than they are similar. The degree of retardation, the environment in which the person functions, and his or her innate characteristics make each child identified as mentally retarded significantly different from every other child, mentally retarded or not. Yet stigmatizing and prejudicial labels such as "stupid" and "moron" are routinely applied by society in general. Dehumanizing myths, such as the inaccurate perceptions that individuals with mental retardation don't get bored while performing repetitive tasks or that mentally retarded people have little pride and don't suffer humiliation when abused, continue to thrive. Perhaps the isolation imposed upon those diagnosed as retarded by separate schools and special classrooms has reinforced these negative stereotypes. The inclusion movement and its mandated requirements for interaction between children who are identified as mentally retarded and their normally intellectually functioning peers will lead to greater understanding and sensitivity. The key seems to be in how the educational system highlights students who are different and how teachers structure the interactions between students who are mentally retarded and their peers.

## Placement Criteria

In spite of AAMD guidelines for identification and placement of students with mental retardation, intelligence levels and adaptive behavior criteria vary widely across states. Quite often, financial pressures placed upon a school system or parental pressures for a more socially acceptable label influence identification and placement. For many, identification of a learning disability is more acceptable than the diagnosis of mental retardation. As a result, the misdiagnosis of many children with mental retardation is occurring. Not only does this tend to mask the occurrence of the real problem for many children, it also leads to the potential provision of ineffective or misdirected services and educational experiences.

## Preventive and Preschool Services

Since the identification of children as mentally retarded, especially mildly mentally retarded, often waits until initial testing at school, preventive programs cannot be introduced until relatively late in the cognitive developmental process for any child. Early identification and early treatment could drastically lower the numbers of children who are identified as mentally retarded by school age. Research indicates that more than 50 percent of all cases of mental retardation could have been prevented (Haring et al., 1994; Smith & Luckasson, 1995; Heward, 1996; Meyen & Skrtic, 1988; Hallahan & Kauffman, 1991, Hardman et al., 1996). A weakness in early identification is the underutilization of educational and treatment services for infants and preschool children with mental retardation. Once again, it is clear that early services for any developmental disability are usually more effective than services after the child has matured. Perhaps as the data about early identification and intervention are accepted by society, parents and professionals will be more willing to make earlier referral for infants and young children who are exhibiting developmental delays.

## MINORITY CONCERNS

Approximately 12 million children live in poverty, live in single-parent families, or are linguistically diverse, speaking a language or dialect other than standard English. The two measures most frequently used to identify children with mental retardation—intelligence testing and adaptive behavior skills—may be influenced greatly by economic disadvantage and cultural and linguistic diversity. Poverty-related issues on a medical level are that high mortality rates of infants, poor nutrition, and poor health care, which lead to a higher incidence of mental retardation in all children, occur at a higher level in poverty group children. Social issues such as overcrowded homes, substandard living environments, lack of stimulation, and instability correlate with low intelligence test scores, regardless of a child's ethnicity. Families preoccupied with survival may appear to be unresponsive to their children's intellectual development and, from their own experiences, have low academic expectations for their children. These restrictions on a child's opportunities to learn are reflected by the disproportionate number of minority children identified as mentally retarded. However, it must be categorically stated that not all of the children of poverty-level families are mentally retarded.

Mercer (1973) dramatized the problems that minority children face with standardized testing. She reported that disproportionate numbers of minority children were placed in self-contained classes for mild retardation as a result of their low IQ scores. She demonstrated that the intelligence tests used to identify the children could be biased against them because:

1. The content of the tests was not valid for the minority children, who might not share the same experiences as their majority group peers, and as a result they failed items not because of lower intelligence but rather because of inexperience.

2.    The predicative validity of the tests was not equally accurate for all culturally diverse groups.

3.    The norms upon which the tests were based did not include representation of minority groups (Mercer, 1973; Meyen & Skrtic, 1988).

Some intelligence tests rely heavily upon linguistic facility and information tied to cultural experiences. Children from culturally and linguistically diverse backgrounds may do poorly on these tests as a result of their different experiences and be misdiagnosed as mentally retarded.

A similar bias may occur with adaptive behavior measures. What is considered socially appropriate, adjusted, or competent behavior for one group may not be for another group (Hallahan & Kauffman, 1991; Heward, 1996). Often minority children identified as mentally retarded in part on the basis of their inappropriate adaptive behaviors are not considered retarded at home or in their neighborhoods.

Obvious solutions to these concerns are the use of intelligence tests that are not culturally biased, such as the previously discussed System of Multicultural Pluralistic Assessment (SOMPA) (Mercer, 1979), and measurement of adaptive behaviors by raters who are familiar with the child's cultural experiences. Minority children are not immune to the debilitating effects of growing up in a hostile environment, any more than any other group of children would be in a similar environment. However, deficits and differences must not be confused. A child who is different is not automatically disordered. Recognition and acceptance of cultural and linguistic differences in schoolchildren is the first step. The second step is to accurately measure the skills and potentials of children using culturally and linguistically appropriate materials. The third step is to provide remediation that distinguishes between differences and deficits and presents information to the child in an appropriate manner.

## PROFESSIONALS

There are many career opportunities for those interested in helping individuals with mental retardation. Intervention programs are geared to infant stimulation, early education, elementary- and secondary-level education, and postsecondary education. There are administrative roles, such as director of special education programs, and teaching positions that provide direct service. There are roles for social service caseworkers, vocational rehabilitation workers, and physical education and physical therapy workers, as well as regular and special education teachers.

As you have read in this chapter, it is becoming more and more common for regular classroom teachers to accommodate students with mental retardation in their regular classrooms. They must be able to modify their lessons to include individualized attention and instruction, alternative learning materials, and appropriate practice sessions to maintain their special students on task (Meyen & Skrtic, 1988).

Resource room and itinerant resource room teachers must have special training and credentials to provide special education services for learners with mental retardation. They emphasize tutorial, one-to-one, remedial instruction combined with some programmed experiences to assist the student with mental retardation in socialization.

Segregated self-contained classroom teachers provide services exclusively to students with mental retardation during the school day. These special education teachers are specially trained and have classes that do not usually exceed fifteen students. The self-contained classroom may be a full day placement, and its curriculum includes life skills programs as well as academic ones.

Teachers in special schools or institutions are specially trained to serve children with moderate to severe retardation. Their concentration of studies differs from that of the resource room special educator or self-contained classroom teacher. The primary concerns in these settings are instruction in practical daily living skills, social skills, and vocational skills (Meyen & Skrtic, 1988).

Vocational rehabilitation agencies provide vocational assessment, counseling, and placement assistance. The professionals in these settings include medical personnel, psychologists, occupational therapists, social workers, rehabilitation counselors, and prospective employers.

Sheltered workshops provide on-the-job training and employment for individuals with mental retardation. The professionals in this primarily adult setting are usually counselors, social workers, volunteers, and employers.

The Council for Exceptional Children's standards for training special education teachers were detailed in Chapter 1. In addition, each professional role has specialized training and certification (licensing) requirements. Appendix I lists the addresses of each state special education director in the United States. Since each state has its own licensing or certification standards, interested readers are encouraged to contact the appropriate state director of special education for information about certification and training requirements to assist students with mental retardation.

## PROFESSIONAL ASSOCIATIONS AND PARENT OR SELF-HELP GROUPS

American Association on Mental Retardation
1719 Kalorama Rd. NW
Washington, DC 20009

Association for Retarded Citizens
P.O. Box 6109
Arlington, TX 76005

Council for Exceptional Children
Mental Retardation Division
1920 Association Drive
Reston, VA 22091-1589

## REFERENCES FOR FURTHER INFORMATION

*American Journal on Mental Retardation*, Education and Training in Mental Retardation and Developmental Disabilities
1719 Kalorama Rd. NW
Washington, DC 20009

Council for Exceptional Children
Division on Mental Retardation
1920 Association Drive
Reston, VA 22091-1589

# REFERENCES   🦈

American Association on Mental Deficiency (AAMR), Ad Hoc Committee on Terminology and Classification (1992). *Classification in mental retardation* (9th ed.). Washington, DC: American Associates on Mental Deficiency.

Berdine, W. H. (1993). Students with mental retardation. In A. E. Blackhurst & W. H. Berdine (Eds.), *An introduction to special education* (3rd ed., pp. 405–453). New York: HarperCollins.

Carnine, D. W., & Kameenui, E. J. (1990). The general education initiative and children with special needs: A false dilemma in the face of true problems. *Journal of Learning Disabilities, 23*(3), 141–144.

Cegelka, P. T., & Prehm, J. J. (1982). *Mental retardation: From categories to people.* Upper Saddle River, NJ: Prentice Hall/Merrill.

Clark, G. M. (1994). Is a functional curriculum approach compatible with an inclusive education model? *Teaching Exceptional Children, 26*(2), 36–39.

Costenbader, V., & Readney-Brown, M. (1995). Isolation timeout used with students with emotional disturbance. *Exceptional Children, 61*(4), 353–363.

Coulter, W., & Morrow, H. (Eds.). (1977). *The concept and measurement of adaptive behavior within the scope of psychological assessment.* Austin, TX: Regional Resource Center, University of Texas.

Davis, S. (1994). *The 1994 update on inclusion in education of children with mental retardation.* Arlington, TX: The Arc.

Debell, S. (1980). Adaptive behavior and its measurement. NASP *Communique, 8,* 4–5.

Drew, C. J., Hardman, M. L., & Longan, D. R. (1996). *Mental retardation: Life cycle approach* (6th ed.). Upper Saddle River, NJ: Prentice Hall/Merrill.

Elliott, R., (1979). Mental retardation. In W. C. Morse (Ed.), *Humanistic teaching for exceptional children: An introduction to special education.* Syracuse, NY: Syracuse University Press.

Gardner, W. (1974). *Children with learning and behavior problems.* Needham, MA: Allyn & Bacon.

Glidden, I. M. (1985). Semester processing, semantic memory, and recall. In N. R. Ellis (Ed.), *International re-view of research in mental retardation* (Vol. 13, pp. 247–278). New York: Academic.

Gold, M. W. (1980). An alternative definition of mental retardation. In M. W. Gold (Ed.), *"Did I say that?" Articles and commentary on the Try Another Way System.* Champaign, IL: Research.

Goldstein, H. (1966). Fostering independent, creative thinking in educable mentally retarded children. In E. M. Kelly (Ed.), *The new and more open outlook for mentally retarded* (pp. 17–29). Washington, DC: Catholic University of America Press.

Greenwood, C. R., Hart, B., Walker, D., & Risley, T. (1994). The opportunity to respond and academic performance revisited: A behavioral theory of developmental retardation theory of developmental retardation and its prevention. In R. Gardner III, D. M. Sainato, J. O. Cooper, T. E. Heron, W. L. Heward, J. Eshleman, & T. A. Grossi (Eds.), *Behavior analysis in education: Focus on measurable superior instruction* (pp. 213–223). Pacific Grove, CA: Brooks/Cole.

Grossman, H. (1983). *A manual on terminology and classification in mental retardation* (Rev. ed.). Washington, DC: American Association on Mental Deficiency.

Grossman, H. (1990). *Trouble-free teaching: Solutions to behavior problems in the classroom* (pp. 133–156). Mountain View, CA: Mayfield.

Grossman, H., & Tarjan, G. (Eds.). (1987). AMA *handbook on mental retardation.* Chicago: American Medical Association.

Hallahan, D. P., & Kauffman, J. M. (1991). *Exceptional children: Introduction to special education* (5th ed.). Upper Saddle River, NJ: Prentice Hall.

Hardman, M. L., Drew, C. J., & Egan, M. W. (1996). *Human exceptionality: Society, school, and family* (5th ed.). Needham, MA: Allyn & Bacon.

Haring, N. G., McCormick, L., & Haring, T. G. (1994). *Exceptional children and youth: An introduction to special education* (6th ed.). New York: Macmillan.

Harter, H. (1978). Effectance motivation reconsidered: Toward a developmental model. *Human Development, 21,* 34–64.

Haywood, H. C. (1974). Distribution of Intelligence. Encyclopedia Britannica (15th ed.), 9, 672–677. Chicago.

Heward, W. L. (1996). *Exceptional children: An introduction to special education* (5th ed.). Upper Saddle River, NJ: Prentice Hall/Merrill.

Hobbs, N. (1975). *The futures of children*. San Francisco: Jossey-Bass.

Hunt, N., & Marshall, K. (1994). *Exceptional children and youth: An introduction to special education*. Boston: Houghton Mifflin.

Hymes, D. (1972). On communicative competence. In J. B. Pride & J. Holmes (Eds.), *Sociolinguistics*. Baltimore: Penguin.

Johnson, G. O. (1959). The relationship of learning rate and developmental rate. *Exceptional Children, 26,* 68–69.

Johnson, G. O. (1971). Psychological characteristics of the mentally retarded. In W. M. Cruickshank (Ed.), *Psychology of exceptional children and youth*. Upper Saddle River, NJ: Prentice Hall.

Kaufman, A., & Kaufman, N. (1983). *Kaufman Assessment Battery for Children, interpreting manual*. Circle Pines, MN: American Guidance Service.

Kazdin, A. E. (1980). *Behavior modification in applied settings*. Homewood, IL: Dorsey.

Kazdin, A. E. (1992). Overt and covert antisocial behavior: Child and family characteristics among psychiatric inpatient children. *Journal of Child and Family Studies, 1,* 3–20.

Kirk, S. A., & Gallagher, J. J. (1986). *Educating exceptional children* (5th ed.). Boston: Houghton Mifflin.

Kirk, S. A., Gallagher, J. J., & Anastasiow, N. J. (1993). *Educating exceptional children* (7th ed.). Boston: Houghton Mifflin.

Lakey, B. B., McNees, P. M., & McNees, M. C. (1973). Control of an obscene verbal tic through time out in a elementary school classroom. *Journal of Applied Behavioral Analysis, 6,* 104–106.

Lambert, N. K., Mihira, K., & Leland, H. (1993). *Adaptive Behavior Scale–School* (2nd ed.). Austin, TX: PRO-ED.

Lambert, N., & Nicoll, R. (1976). Dimensions of adaptive behavior of retarded and nonretarded public school children. *American Journal of Mental Deficiency, 81,* 135–146.

Linton, T. (1969). The European educateur program for disturbed children. *American Journal of Orthopsychiatry, 39* (1).

Macmillan, D. L., Siperstein, G. N., & Gresham, F. M. (1996). A challenge to the viability of mild mental retardation as a diagnostic category. *Exceptional Children, 62*(4), 356–371.

McDermott, S. (1994). Explanatory model to describe school district prevalence rates for mental retardation and learning disabilities. *American Journal on Mental Retardation, 99,* 175–185.

McLaren, J., & Bryson, S. E. (1987). Review of recent epidemiological studies of mental retardation: Prevalence, associated disorders, and etiology. *American Journal of Mental Retardation, 92,* 243–254.

Mercer, J. R. (1973). *Labeling the mentally retarded: Clinical and social system perspectives on mental retardation*. Berkeley, CA: University of California Press.

Mercer, J. R., & Lewis, J. P. (1977). *System of Multicultural Pluralistic Assessment: Parent interview manual*. New York: Psychological Corporation.

Meyen, E. L., & Skrtic, T. M. (1988). *Exceptional children and youth: An introduction* (3rd ed.). Denver, CO: Love.

Nowacek, J. (1992). Professionals talk about teaching together: Interviews with five collaborating teachers. *Interviews in School and Clinic, 25*(5), 262–276.

North Carolina Department of Human Resources, Division of Mental Health, Developmental Disabilities and Substance Abuse, Area Mental Health. (1996). *Individualized habilitation planning system*. Raleigh, NC.

O'Leary, K., & O'Leary, S. (1977). *Classroom management: The successful use of behavior modification* (2nd ed.). New York: Pergamon.

Patton, J. R., Beirne-Smith, J., & Payne, J. S. (1990). *Mental retardation* (3rd ed.). Upper Saddle River, NJ: Prentice Hall/Merrill.

Polloway, E. A., & Smith, J. D. (1983). Changes in mild mental retardation: Population, programs, and perspective. In K. L. Freiberg (Ed.), *Educating exceptional children* (5th ed.). Guilford, CT: Dushkin.

Ramey, C. T., & Finkelstein, N. W. (1981). Psychosocial mental retardation: A biological and social coalescence. In

M. J. Begab, H. C. Haywood, & H. L. Garber (Eds.), *Psychosocial influences in retarded performance: Issues and theories in development*. Baltimore: University Park Press.

Rhodes, W. C. (1966). Preface. In J. Hillmuth (Ed.), *Educational Therapy*. Seattle, WA: Straub & Hillmuth.

Schloss, P. L., & Smith, M. A. (1994). *Applied behavior analysis in the classroom* (pp. 178–196). Needham, MA: Allyn & Bacon.

Smith, D. D., & Luckasson, R. (1995). *Introduction to special education: Teaching in an age of challenge* (2nd ed.). Needham, MA: Allyn & Bacon.

Sparrow, S. S., Balla, D. A., & Cucchetti, D. V. (1984). *Vineland adaptive behavior scales: Interview edition, survey form manual*. Circle Pines, MN: American Guidance Service.

Sternburg, R. J., & Spear, I. C. (1985). A triarchic theory of mental retardation. In N. R. Ellis (Ed.), *International review of research in mental retardation* (Vol. 13, pp. 301–326). New York: Academic.

Thorndike, R. L., Hagen, E. P., & Sattler, J. M. (1986). *Technical manual: The Stanford-Binet Intelligence Scale* (4th ed.). Chicago: Riverside.

Turnbull, A. P., Turnbull, H. R., Shank, M., & Leal, D. (1995). *Exceptional lives: Special education in today's schools*. Upper Saddle River, NJ: Prentice Hall/Merrill.

U.S. Department of Education. (1997). *Nineteenth annual report to Congress on the implementation of the Individuals with Disabilities Act*. Washington, DC: Author.

Walker, J. E., & Shea, T. M. (1987). *Behavioral management: A practical approach for education* (5th ed.). New York: Macmillan.

Wallace, G., Cohen, S. B., & Polloway, E. A. (1987). *Language arts: Teaching exceptional students*. Austin, TX: PRO-ED.

Wechsler, D. (1974). *Manual for the Wechsler Intelligence Scale for Children–Revisited*. New York: Psychological Corporation.

Wehman, P. (1997). *Exceptional individuals in school, community, and work*. Austin, TX: PRO-ED.

Windmiller, M. (1977). An effective use of the public school version of the AAMD Adaptive Behavior Scale. *Mental Retardation*, 15, 42–45.

Zeaman, D., & Hause, B. J. (1979). A review of attention theory. In N. R. Ellis (Ed.), *Handbook of mental deficiency: Psychological theory and research* (2nd ed.). Hillsdale, NJ: Erlbaum.

Zigler, E., & Burack, J. A. (1989). Personality development and the dually diagnosed person. *Research in Developmental Disabilities*, 10, 225–240.

# 4

# Children with Learning Disabilities

A variety of professional and parent groups contribute to a diverse understanding of what it means to be learning disabled (LD). They all appear to agree (1) that LD is a chronic condition of probable neurological origin; (2) that it varies in its manifestations and severity; and (3) that it influences how individuals value themselves (Mercer, 1997; Hammill, 1993). Learning disabilities affect educational, vocational, social, and daily living activities adversely. All interested parties also agree that LD frequently occurs with other handicapping or disabling conditions and that LD can be found in all socioeconomic, racial, and cultural categories. Some feel LD may also be the result of a child experiencing insufficient or inappropriate instruction in addition to being the result of genetic determinants (NJCLD, 1994). Historically, the concept of a child having learning disabilities resulting from neurological impairment was derived from the pioneering work of William Cruickshank at Syracuse University in the late 1950s and early 1960s. In 1968, the Bureau for the Education of the Handicapped, under the leadership of Samuel Kirk, officially sanctioned the term *learning disability*.

Learning disabilities in children are often complicated by problems with adjustment, poor peer interactions, volatile family relationships, and sometimes juvenile delinquency. As these children are identified and interventions are planned for them, many disciplines may be involved, including special education, psychology, psychiatry, social work, and medicine. Children with learning disabilities often experience emotional adjustment and social skill deficits as secondary problems that are manifested by disruptive behavior in the classroom. Their academic deficits have been shown to contribute to poor school adjustment (Gallico, Burns, & Grob, 1988).

There is considerable dissatisfaction with current LD definitions, labels, exclusionary factors, diagnosis, and interventions. Questions surrounding cause or etiology are contentious, and the problems of nature-nurture are also controversial in this special education area. In this chapter, we will discuss these concerns and provide clarifications on conceptual and program approaches. We will also emphasize the issues of definition, identification procedures, and program intervention. We have cross-listed attention deficit/hyperactivity disorder (AD/HD) in this chapter as well as in Chapter 7 (Children with Physical and Health Impairments). Although AD/HD is "officially" listed as a health impairment, the manifestation of the condition is as a learning problem.

## DEFINITIONS

The most influential definitions about learning disorders derived from federal legislation and professional associations, while not exactly the same, share more similarities than differences. These similarities include a recognition of the need for testing, a similar listing of exclusions from service, and a recognition of the possible neurological complications in defining learning disabilities (Hammill, 1990, 1993).

## Legal Definition

The most widely accepted definition of learning disabilities is the one endorsed by the U.S. Office of Special Education and Rehabilitation Services in the Department of Education:

> Specific learning disability means a disorder in one or more of the basic psychological processes involved in understanding or in using language, spoken or written, which may manifest itself in an imperfect ability to listen, think, speak, read, write, spell, or to do mathematical calculations. The term includes such conditions as perceptual handicaps, brain injury, minimal brain dysfunction, dyslexia, and developmental aphasia. The term does not include children who have learning problems which are primarily the result of visual, hearing, or motor handicaps, of mental retardation, of emotional disturbance, or of environmental, cultural, or economic disadvantage. (42 Fed. Reg. 65083 [1977])

There are problems with translating this definition into educationally useful interventions. For example, experts in the area of LD debate the use of the terms *minimal brain dysfunction* and *dyslexia* because these medical terms do not reflect current educational procedures and interventions (42 Fed. Reg. 65082 [1977]; Turnbull, Turnbull, Shank, & Leal, 1995). However, Mercer (1997) suggests that educators continue to need some operational guidelines concerning the possibility of central nervous system dysfunction in the definition and identification process.

We can define *learning disability* as one or more significant defects in essential learning processes, requiring special educational remedial interventions. Children with learning disabilities demonstrate a discrepancy between expected and actual achievement in one or more areas, such as spoken or written language, reading, mathematics, and spatial orientation. The learning disability is not primarily the result of sensory, motor, intellectual, or emotional handicap, or the lack of opportunity to learn.

## National Joint Committee on Learning Disabilities Definition

Educators and other interested professionals and parents often refer to the 1988 definition of specific learning disabilities by the National Joint Committee on Learning Disabilities (NJCLD), which states that:

> Learning disabilities is a generic term that refers to a heterogeneous group of disorders manifested by significant difficulties in the acquisition and use of listening, speaking, reading, writing, reasoning, or mathematical abilities. These disorders are intrinsic to the individual and presumed to be due to central nervous system dysfunction, and may appear across the life span. Problems in self-regulatory behaviors, social perception, and social interaction may exist with learning disabilities but do not themselves constitute a learning disability. Although learning disabilities may occur concomitantly with other handicapping conditions (for example, sensory impairment, mental retardation, serious emotional disturbance) or with extrinsic influences (such as cultural differences, insufficient or inappropriate instruction) they are not the result of those conditions or influences (NJCLD, 1994).

Both this definition and the one previously presented are medically oriented, suggesting that the underlying cause of LD is a neurological condition. Although many experts in the area of LD maintain that there are external or environmental causes for LD, no parallel definitions are available that account for extrinsic influences or experiences being linked to learning disability.

## Definition: Some Qualifications

Most state and local education agencies identify several factors as essential in defining learning disabilities. They include the following factors:

**IQ-Achievement Discrepancy or Aptitude-Achievement Discrepancy.**    IQ-*achievement discrepancy* generally refers to a severe or notable gap in a child's achievements compared to the child's potential as measured by a standardized individual intelligence test. These children exhibit a severe discrepancy between achievement in their school performance in one or more subjects, especially reading and math calculations, and their intellectual potential as measured by standardized tests. Teachers report an unexpected or unpredictable difference or gap between ability and achievement. School failure is not seen as an outcome of intellectual disability or lack of opportunities to learn. Most states propose formulas for determining the discrepancy via mathematical computations using IQ scores, chronological age, and expected grade level equivalency or achievement. For example, the formula used by the North Carolina Division of Exceptional Children's Services, Department of Public Instruction (1993), states that when there "are verbal/performance IQ discrepancies of at least 20 points on the Wechsler Scale, the higher scale IQ may be used to determine the achievement/ability discrepancy providing there is evidence that the higher score accurately reflects the students' intellectual functioning" (p. 32). Thus, when a discrepancy exists between intellectual ability and academic achievement and it can be measured, and the size of the discrepancy exceeds certain levels, a child will be identified as having a learning disability. Neither the formulas nor the levels are uniform from state to state. An obvious conclusion is that as a result of varied formulas, some children would or would not be considered learning disabled if they moved from one state to another (Wehman, 1997). The Council of Exceptional Children opposes the use of these formulas because there is no national, consistent, agreed-upon formula to reliably measure these discrepancies. In addition, the testing instruments used to measure aptitudes and achievements may be unreliable for these children (Haring, McCormick, & Haring, 1994; Mercer, 1997).

**Central Nervous System Dysfunction.**    Some scholars suggest that by definition, children with learning disabilities have some neurological or brain dysfunction, whether it can be documented or not. The neurological disorders associated with children with learning disabilities suggests that the brain, perceptual systems (expressive or receptive), or both are either not functioning or are functioning differently from other nondisabled children. As a result, these children experience difficulty in ac-

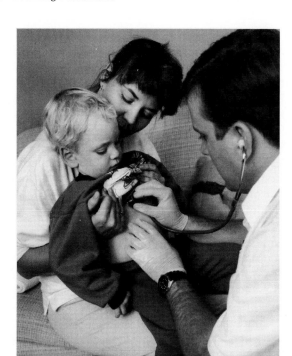

quiring, retaining, and processing information. Some children may show evidence of central nervous system dysfunction, while others exhibit no evidence (Meyen & Skrtic, 1988). However, this view is not held by all experts in special education (Mercer, 1997).

**Psychological Processing Disorders.**    Most educators in the field of learning disabilities assume that children with learning disabilities have deficits in their ability to perceive and interpret stimuli, but do not have learning problems because of visual, hearing, or motor handicaps. Learning disabilities may be the result of a perceptual impairment, in which perceptual skills such as thinking and reasoning are unreliable or unstable. These children demonstrate language problems, especially with listening and speaking. Additional examples of problems in psychological processes are deficits in attention and memory (Hunt & Marshall, 1994; Hallahan, Kauffman, & Lloyd, 1995).

**Exclusions.**    Most definitions of learning disabilities exclude children who are not learning due to economic disadvantage, mental retardation, or emotional disturbance. Outside influences or extrinsic environmental determinants such as poor teaching, poor health, poor home environment, family instability, low motivation, or disadvantaging social, cultural, or ethnic influences are also excluded.

Therefore, a learning disability cannot be the outcome of these debilitating circumstances. However, children with learning disabilities can have additional co-existent handicapping conditions or disabilities that are not the cause of the learning disability.

If you find the preceding paragraph confusing, you are not alone. Highly trained professionals in the area of learning disabilities also have a difficult time sorting out exactly what causes learning disabilities and ruling out irrelevant conditions. Grossman (1978) reports that Kuhn, a noted science historian, suggested that acceptable definitions should be specific enough to rule out the absurd, yet flexible enough to accommodate the creative thoughts that generate new knowledge. Perhaps time and new knowledge will clarify exclusion policies for people with learning disabilities.

**General Issues.**    Learning disabilities are a mixed group of disorders, with subgroups across the major channels used for learning. Problems caused by being learning disabled transcend the school setting and can persist into adulthood. Children with learning disabilities clearly demonstrate a need for special remedial and treatment intervention.

Since these children are generally normal or average in intellectual functioning—that is, there is no incapacity in intelligence—the learning disability lies in their ways of learning, in their perceptual systems, and in how they interpret and integrate information to make sense of their environment. Children with learning disabilities are not lazy, undisciplined, or unmotivated. While they might experience impairments in attending to and remembering information, behavioral problems are not an initial component of their behavior. Only after starting school and becoming frustrated and unserved by specialized remedial interventions will they demonstrate behavioral problems.

Scholars have suggested that the difficulty in defining LD is due to the variety or heterogeneity of this population. In practice, many children labeled as LD have not demonstrated the presence of the hard signs of neurological deficit listed in the legal definitions. Although many special educators advocate for a more restrictive or tighter LD definition to define a distinct population, there is no agreement on what will constitute the definition's conceptual elements (Lilly, 1979). Moreover, while the current definition indicates that the processes associated with learning are deficient, we have no precise indication of how these processes are either impaired, delayed, or qualitatively different. In addition, the previously discussed exclusionary factors, while not seen as primary causes of learning disability, certainly do co-exist in children who are learning disabled (Lorsbach & Frymier, 1992).

Finally, the difficulty of using a significant discrepancy between intelligence and achievement as a reason for inclusion in this population most likely has resulted in our current overidentification of children as learning disabled (Meyen, 1996).

The terms listed in Box 4.1 will be used throughout the rest of this chapter. The brief definitions presented will aid the reader in understanding them when they appear in later discussions.

**Box 4.1**
**WHAT EVERY TEACHER NEEDS TO KNOW**

**Terms**

**aphasia**   Impairment of the ability to use or understand oral language. It is usually associated with neurological impairment.

**brain-injured child**   A child who before, during, or after birth has received an injury to or suffered an infection of the brain that prevents or impedes the normal learning process.

**dyslexia**   A disorder of children who, despite conventional classroom experience, fail to attain the skills in reading. It is believed to have neurological dysfunction as its basis.

**hyperkinesis**   Constant and excessive movement and motor activity. The term *hyperactivity* is also used.

**impulsivity**   Acting upon impulse without consideration of the consequences of an action.

**minimal brain dysfunction**   A mild neurological abnormality that causes learning difficulties in generally average intellectually functioning children.

**modality**   The pathways through which an individual receives information and thereby learns; for example, a child may receive data better through the visual modality than the auditory or hearing modality.

**perception**   The process of organizing or interpreting raw data obtained through the senses.

**perceptual disorder**   A disturbance in the awareness of objects, relations, or qualities, involving the interpretation of sensory stimulation.

**perceptual-motor**   A term describing the interaction of the various channels of perception with motor activity. The channels of perception include visual, auditory, tactile, and kinesthetic.

## PREVALENCE

Estimates of learning disabilities in the U.S. school-age population vary from the modest estimate of 2 percent to extreme ranges of 20 to 40 percent. Moderate estimates and apparently more realistic estimates range from 5 to 10 percent of the school-age population. The forces that drive the confusion about estimates are the result of different definitions, conceptual models, assessment approaches, state education agency guidelines, and professional and parent advocacy group definitions (Turnbull et al., 1995; Hardman, Drew, & Egan, 1996).

Approximately 5 million children with disabilities are served in U.S. public schools; over 2.5 million of these disabled children are classified as learning disabled. This means that approximately 50 percent of children with disabilities who are being served are identified as being learning disabled. Perhaps the lack of serious social stigma associated with learning disability, as compared with the stigma associated with mental retardation and emotional disturbance, is a factor that encourages this classification to be used so frequently (Hallahan & Kauffman, 1991).

Some states report a range of 27 to 64 percent of people with disabilities as learning disabled. Often liberal eligibility criteria include underachievers, children with behavior disorders or reevaluated minority students originally classified as retarded. In general, there are more referrals of children as being learning disabled or at risk than in any other area of special education (Heward, 1996).

# CHARACTERISTICS

Generally, the professional community concerned with the education and treatment of children with learning disabilities has had the most difficulty in validly identifying the characteristics of mild specific learning disabilities and identifying subgroups or subtypes. However, experts appear credible and reliable when identifying subgroups and severity levels among children with moderate to severe learning disabilities. However, these children do not share all the common characteristics usually attributed to people who are learning disabled. There are a wide variety of descriptive characteristics. Each characteristic observed in a given child is chronic and can range from mild to severe. Often children appear unmotivated, passive, or inactive about involving themselves in the learning situation of the classroom, yet they appear to have a higher level of physical activity than do the other children in their classes. There are more males than females (a 3-to-1 ratio) identified as learning disabled. Children with learning disabilities are more often retained in a grade than are their peers. The difficulty is in distinguishing children with learning disabilities from low-achieving children. As we previously mentioned, children with learning disabilities are not emotionally disturbed—that is, behavior problems or emotional problems are not the primary cause of their learning disability. These children may exhibit a learning problem in one area or modality and not in another (Mercer, 1997).

The ten most cited characteristics are:

1. Hyperactivity
2. Perceptual-motor impairment
3. Emotional liability
4. General coordination deficits
5. Disorders of attention
6. Impulsivity
7. Disorders of memory and thinking
8. Specific academic problems (especially in linguistic and calculation skills)
9. Disorders of speech and learning
10. Some central nervous system signs or irregularities (Heward, 1996).

## Intelligence

Generally, children with learning disabilities are thought to be of average or near average intelligence. Some children have above average intelligence and may even be gifted, while some studies indicated IQ scores as low as 94–95 (Hardman et al., 1996). College students are the fastest growing group of adults with learning disabilities who are receiving services (Mercer, 1997).

## Attention Deficit/Hyperactivity Disorder (AD/HD)

Children with AD/HD differ from their peers due to their inability to concentrate or control their impulses. It is officially included with health and physical disabilities, since AD/HD is seen as more of the result of a genetic, biological imbalance than a pure behavioral problem (Comings, 1992). The disorder can be diagnosed by the time the child is approaching age 7. The attention deficit aspect of the disorder is displayed by a child who is typically inattentive and seemingly careless in school-work. Assignments are not completed or appropriately followed through. This behavior is also seen with home as well as school chores. The child avoids sustained mental tasks, loses assignments, appears forgetful, and is easily distracted. The hyperactivity part of AD/HD leads to restlessness, excessive movement (inability to stay seated or running and climbing inappropriately), and excessive talking. Children with AD/HD are impulsive, blurting out answers in class, unable to take turns, and frequently interrupting classroom activities (American Psychiatric Association, 1994).

While not all children with learning disabilities experience AD/HD, many do. Similarly, not all children with AD/HD are automatically learning disabled, but many are. There are three profiles that can describe these children. The first profile is predominantly *inattentive*, with the child displaying the characteristics described in the previous paragraph as attention deficit. The second is predominantly *hyperactive-impulsive*, showing the profile described in the hyperactivity characteristics described earlier. The third type is a *combined* type, with the child showing both types of behavior. Approximately 3 to 5 percent of school-age children, approximately 1.35 to 2.25 million children, are suspected of struggling with AD/HD (Turnbull et al., 1995).

## Perception and Motor Skills

Perception is the ability to organize and integrate sensory stimuli. Children with learning disabilities often experience poor auditory/visual discrimination, which means that they are unable to distinguish one stimulus from another. They may not be perceptually aware of their environment and experience confusion in directional orientation. They tend to be awkward, clumsy, and uncoordinated. They often have poor handwriting and may experience problems in figure-background difficulties, or distinguishing an object or sound from its background. Children with learning disabilities often have problems in attention (the ability to focus on information), memory (acquiring and recalling information), and metacognition (the ability to monitor and evaluate their own performance). Organizing, categorizing, arranging, and planning may not be strong skills. Some children tend to perseverate, repeating or continuing the same response repeatedly. Poor motor skills are also associated with learning disabilities (Smith & Luckasson, 1995).

## Metacognition Skills

Metacognition consists of an awareness of the skills, strategies, and resources needed to perform a task effectively. It requires the ability to use self-regulatory mechanisms such as planning movements, evaluating the effectiveness of ongoing strategies, checking the outcomes of efforts, and remediating difficulties. Metacognitive skills ensure the successful completion of tasks (Mercer, 1997; Baker, 1982). Students with learning disabilities exhibit metacognitive deficits in all areas of self-monitoring (Mercer, 1997).

## Behavior and Affective Characteristics

Children who are learning disabled may be hyperactive (with excessive body activity) or hypoactive (lethargic). They can be easily distracted, have short attention spans, show memory deficits, act impulsively, and overreact with intense and sometimes surprising emotion. They can at times appear to be experiencing serious emotional disturbance or mental retardation. These children can also have serious difficulties in social adjustment because they tend to violate recognized social norms or values by fighting with peers or stealing classmates' property. They are unable to predict the consequences of their behaviors and lack social comprehension skills, which results in their misjudging the feelings of others. They provoke negative reactions from others and become socially undesirable. This inability to interact effectively with others frequently results in low self-esteem. Most researchers have concluded that children with learning disabilities are at a greater risk than their peers to experience low social acceptance. Yet some children who are learning disabled are not rejected and are in fact popular in the class/school milieu. The relationship between the child's misbehavior and academic difficulty is not known. Perhaps much of their misbehavior is a result of frustration, depression, or withdrawal reactions caused by their learning disability (Hallahan & Kauffman, 1991).

## Problems in Academic Learning

Children with learning disabilities are often several years behind their peers in reading achievement, comprehension, fluency, and spelling. They tend to experience number, letter, word, and sound reversals. In general, these children have serious reading problems (dyslexia), in which they have problems identifying words and understanding what they read. These difficulties are often compounded by serious oral and written language impairments. They also exhibit poor handwriting, spelling, sentence structure, and composition skills. Poor math performance is evident in recalling math facts, writing numbers legibly, learning arithmetic terms and concepts, and abstract math reasoning. Some high school level children reach a learning plateau and make little progress in academic skills, have deficiencies in study skills, and reflect ineffective problem solving skills (Hunt & Marshall, 1994).

## Communication Disorders

Children with learning disabilities may have a more difficult time learning to articulate the sounds of language. They may repeat sounds, stumble over words, and in general have halting speech delivery. They may have difficulty in grasping the pragmatic or social aspects of language, such as turn taking and sharing information needed for meaningful communication, which might result in rambling and continuous conversation. These children have problems in language comprehension, processing, and formulation (expression). They often have word-finding difficulties (Haring et al., 1994).

## Memory and Thinking Disorders

Many children with learning disabilities have difficulty memorizing words and remembering the sounds that constitute words. They evidence both short-term and long-term memory deficits for tasks that require semantic processing. However, it is unclear whether learning disabilities result from problems in storing and retrieving information from the long-term memory, or whether they result from a deficit in the memory system itself (Turnbull et al., 1995).

## Specific Academic or Achievement Related Characteristics

The following characterizations are school or achievement related and are oriented to specific areas. For example, students with reading problems can exhibit (1) insecurity with reading tasks, (2) tension manifested physically during the reading activity, (3) inability to keep place during reading, (4) omission of words, (5) insertion of words, (6) substitution of words, (7) reversal of words, and (8) comprehension errors and fluency problems. A student with learning disabilities in reading may exhibit any combination of these characteristics (Reschl, 1987).

According to Mercer (1997), math related learning disabilities are generally characterized by some of the following: (1) motor problems reflected in illegible or slowly written numbers; (2) memory problems including mastery of facts, following steps in an algorithm, and multiple-step problem solving; (3) language problems, which includes processing words with multiple meanings, vocabulary processing, and oral mathematical problem solving; (4) abstract reasoning problems, which includes word problems, comparisons, and symbol meaning; and (5) metacognition problems, which includes the inability to select appropriate preliminary problem solving strategies and a lack of ability for generalization of strategies across mathematical problems.

Written expression problems usually are characterized by the inability to produce written documents that reflect complete sentences, adequate spelling, proper grammar, and thematic writing. These problems are compounded by the inability of children with learning disabilities to remember the sentences they intended to construct. They may also display problems in spacing and paragraphing (Mercer, 1997).

In summary, not all children with learning disabilities share all the noted symptoms or characterizations detailed here. Many of the behaviors identified may also be discovered in children who do not experience learning problems (Frauenheim & Heckerl, 1979). Children with learning disabilities appear to have an immature view of life and a lack of awareness of their potential for personal development and change for the better. They tend to have lower self-evaluations. They do not appear to perceive social situations correctly and consequently act inappropriately and exhibit a general lack of inhibition, causing them to sometimes appear silly or obnoxious to their peers, which results in rejection (Freedman, 1969).

## Labels

Numerous terms and labels are used in reference to children with specific learning disabilities. The more acceptable labels appear to be *specific learning disability* or *learning disabled*. From the historical and medical perspective, the following labels were used and still appear in some professional literature:

- *Brain damage*
- *Minimal brain dysfunction*
- *Brain injury*

- *Psychoneurological learning disorder*
- *Strauss syndrome*
- *Perceptually handicapped* (*disabled*) (Smith & Luckasson, 1995; Mercer, 1997)

Contemporary labels used to identify specific learning disabilities are:

- *Educationally handicapped*
- *Language disordered*
- *Dyslexic* (Slaton & Morsink, 1993).

Confusion about appropriate labels can be circumvented when educators provide descriptions of test results and children's learning profiles when referring to individually suspected children. This approach facilitates comprehension and overall communication about the child and the child's learning problems.

The value of the label *learning disabilities* for these children would seem to be that it makes a renewed plea for good teaching based on an understanding of the child's individual educational needs and of the implied continued advocacy to promote his or her educational and overall welfare.

# ETIOLOGY

Speculations about the causes of learning disabilities are numerous, and the cause of learning disabilities for an individual child may be unknown. The more accepted causes for LD fall into the following categories: environmental/ecological, brain damage, organic and/or biological, and genetic. Research in medicine, psychology, linguistics, and education is ongoing to discover the causes of learning disabilities. Currently, explanations about causes are speculative. Experts suggest that there are various levels of severity, multiple problems, influences, and at-risk vulnerabilities that vary from child to child. The cause of learning disabilities may be embedded in the child as well as in the environment and may be complicated by organic, genetic, or biological anomalies (Haring et al., 1994).

## Environmental/Ecological Model

Poor learning environments, unstable abusive families, disadvantaged environments, and inappropriate school instruction contribute to the learning and socialization problems of children with learning disabilities. Emotional disturbance, lack of motivation, ingestion of lead, drug abuse, school suspension, and/or death in the family appear to contribute to some LD and adjustment problems. On the other hand, direct systematic instruction and removal of painful, unhealthy, or negative influences seem to correct some LD and socialization problems in children. Studies indicated that team teaching, direct instructional procedures, and the use of a teacher aide make significant influences in correcting, preventing, and ameliorating the learning difficulties of children with learning disabilities (Slaton & Morsink, 1993).

Research also indicates that some children with learning disabilities are negatively influenced by poor quality teaching. These learning difficulties are not intrinsic to the child, but are caused by inadequate teaching procedures and lack of appropriate reinforcement for learning. Advocates of this model suggest that perhaps 90 percent of all students labeled learning disabled are a product of poor early instruction. They view learning and socialization as a result of the relationship between the child, the learning environment, and the teacher. There may be a mismatch between the child's predisposition to learn and how the classroom program requires performance to demonstrate the learning. This mismatch can result in poor school performance outcomes. The more vulnerable or disabled the child, the more dramatic the school failure. The greater the teacher's instructional ability and positive relationship to the child, the greater the positive match and subsequent child school success (Turnbull et al., 1995; Smith & Luckasson, 1995). In the final analysis, some experts conclude that these external influences may be the dominant issues surrounding the emergence of some learning disabilities.

Finally, there is evidence that lack of uniform and consistent nurturing, lack of opportunity to learn, absence of personal challenges, and family-related difficulties are more likely to occur with children with learning disabilities than with other children. As these children fail in school, they are seen as "dumb" and "lazy" and often are scapegoated, frustrated, and suspended from school and become dropouts. Within the group of at-risk children, children from minority groups are further discriminated against, academically and socially (Freiberg, 1990; Frauenheim & Heckerl, 1979).

## Brain Damage Model

Some experts believe that 20 percent of children with learning disabilities have sustained brain damage or neurological impairment of the central nervous system. The term *minimal brain dysfunction* is often used, in spite of the lack of evidence for brain or neurological impairment or knowledge of what caused the suspected damage. It is supposed that as a result of complications surrounding the pregnancy and birth, the child experienced injury to the central nervous system (acquired trauma). Other influences could be maternal alcohol, drug, tobacco, or other substance consumption that adversely influenced the fetus. Stresses such as maternal illness, prolonged and difficult labor and delivery, premature birth, hypoxia/anoxia, or instruments used in delivery could explain some resulting learning disabilities (Hallahan & Kauffman, 1991; Heward 1996). Research with children with reading disabilities indicates that some have structural irregularities of the brain's left hemisphere (Hardman et al., 1996; Meyen & Skrtic, 1988; Van Syke & Fox, 1990).

## Organic and Biological Model

There is suspicion that chemical agents found in food colorings or specific food flavorings could cause learning disabilities. Similar speculation exists about the result of vitamin deficiencies, especially the B complex. These possibilities have no scientific support. Theories that there may be imbalances in the neurotransmitters (biochemical), which in turn interfere with neural impulse transmission, thus causing LD, are also inconclusive. Research does not confirm the links between LD and malnutrition; allergies to milk, sugar, and chocolate; salicylates (biochemicals found in certain fruits and vegetables); toothpaste; perfumes; or aspirin. There is an additional position that a developmental or maturational lag (that is, a neurological developmental lag) may underlie some learning disabilities. In this context, the child is cognitively unprepared for certain academic tasks at certain times. Studies do suggest that readiness to learn (neurological development) is related to some emergent learning disabilities (Hunt & Marshall, 1994; Kirk, Gallagher, & Anastasiow, 1993).

## Genetic Model

There is evidence that some families have a history of learning disabilities. Studies of identical (monozygotic) twins indicate in some instances that if one twin is dyslexic, the other twin will likely experience a reading disability. Other evidence suggests that there is an inherited genetic influence on reading and language problems among children and their families. More research is still required to discover relationships between genetic determinants and specific learning disability outcomes (Kirk et al., 1993).

In summary, the causes of learning disabilities are varied; despite technological advances, it is still difficult to ascertain causes for most learning disabilities. Although we have presented the models as separate entities, there is no reason to believe that the causes offered by one model are independent from the causes offered by another model. This interaction may lead to learning disabilities being understood as the result of multiple causes that transcend the limits of any given model (Mercer, 1997).

## IDENTIFICATION PROCESS

Early detection of learning disabilities is imperative. The longer the LD goes unnoticed, the more difficult it will be to remedy the problem and the more at risk the child will be to serious adjustment problems and possible juvenile delinquency. Early detection or screening is dependent on early observation of behavioral and learning characteristics. No person is more qualified in early detection or screening procedures than the classroom teacher. The teacher is with the child throughout the school day and in a key position to screen children with learning disabilities. The symptoms or characteristics of specific learning problems that have been identified and knowledge of them should sensitize the teacher to the possible existence of a learning disability.

Federal and state legislation and other guidelines recommend detailed procedures for identifying and assessing children with suspected learning disabilities. The public school must use a multidisciplinary evaluation team including the child's regular classroom teacher, the school psychologist, and other clinical personnel. The team must determine the degree of discrepancy between intellectual ability and age- or grade-level academic achievement and/or actual performances. By means of appropriate and competent testing, if a severe discrepancy between achievement and intellectual ability is discovered and documented in following areas of oral expression, listening, comprehension, linguistic processing, written expression, basic reading skill, reading comprehension, and mathematics calculation or mathematics reasoning, the child may be considered learning disabled. This child may not be identified LD if the discrepancy is due to other handicaps or impairments and/or environmental, cultural, or economic disadvantage (Turnbull et al., 1995).

Critical to identification procedures are continuous and direct teacher measurements of achievement, especially the use of inventories to assess reading and calculation skills. Some of the tests and materials used in the identification and assessment of LD are the *Wechsler Intelligence Scale for Children–III* (WISC-III), which measures a child's cognitive abilities or intelligence (Wechsler, 1993); the *Woodcock-Johnson Psycho-Educational Battery–Revised* (WJ-R), which measures achievement in reading, writing, and mathematics by age and grade level (Woodcock & Mather, 1989); the *Wide Range Achievement Test* (WRAT), which measures general academic achievement (Jastak & Jastak, 1965); and the *Brigance Diagnostic Inventory of Basic Skills*, which measures a variety of skill sequences in readiness, reading, language arts, and math (Brigance, 1983).

A ideal identification sequence is as follows. A child suspected of being learning disabled may become a concern to teachers when he or she does not meet educational or social-behavioral expectations in school. These concerns may initiate an assessment/diagnostic procedure, with parental approval. A multidisciplinary team evaluates all areas related to the possible learning disability, using appropriate testing instruments administered by highly trained personnel who attempt to control for racial or cultural bias. Both regular and special education teachers must be on the team. They must document the student's present level of functioning, strengths and weaknesses, and unique learning needs (Meyen, 1996). The gap or discrepancy between academic achievement and intellectual ability in one or more areas related to communication skills and math/arithmetic abilities must be clearly demonstrated. Members of the team must observe the child in the regular classroom and confirm that the gap or discrepancy is not a result of sensory or motor impairment, mental retardation, serious emotional disturbance, or other exclusionary factors (Meyen, 1996).

Academic achievement levels can be determined by teacher-made tests and standardized tests (providing grade- or age-level scores). Intellectual ability can be determined by the administration of individual standardized intelligence tests. Criterion-referenced testing is used to examine a student's performance on a specific task—that is, comparing one performance of an individual against a set standard and judging, by the performance, how well the task was mastered. Educational goals and objectives set the standards for instruction and guide the teacher and the team in measuring the student's performance. Once the results of tests and observations are compiled, the team meets and evolves a remediation plan for the child that specifies the type and level of services needed by the child.

The Council for Exceptional Children recommends the following six-step procedure for attempting to identify a child with AD/HD:

*Step* 1. Document behavior observed by both parents and teachers that is indicative of AD/HD.

*Step* 2. Re-evaluate tests such as group intelligence tests, group achievement tests, and vision and hearing tests to determine whether they are accurate measures of potential or whether poor performance may be the result of attention problems. A physician may be consulted to see whether an identifiable physical condition is causing inattention or hyperactivity.

*Step* 3. Attempt classroom management to correct or control behaviors leading to poor academic performance. If these attempts are unsuccessful, request referral for AD/HD placement.

*Step* 4. Conduct psychological evaluations to see whether the student meets criteria for AD/HD placement. Administer individual tests and behavioral rating scales. Review medication recommendations.

*Step* 5. Have the team, including the child's parents, plan for the special educational needs of the child.

*Step* 6 Implement the Individual Education Plan. (Council for Exceptional Children's Task Force on Children with AD/HD, 1992).

## Misidentification

Although the procedures described here may, at first glance, appear relatively straightforward, there is the potential for children to be misidentified as learning disabled due to:

- Confusion about the LD definition.
- Lack of uniformity among the criteria for determining the discrepancy between ability and achievement.
- Misplacement of non-LD children in LD programs to avoid the social stigma associated with the diagnosis of retardation or severe emotional disturbance.
- Confusion between slow learners and children with LD.
- Incompetent testing.
- Confusion in admission or exclusion procedures and guidelines.

However, most states do share common criteria for identification of children with learning disabilities. They recognize and emphasize academic difficulties, are aware of the exclusion factors in the definition, use a discrepancy formula with emphasis on math and language processing deficits, and search for underlying neurological impairments (Turnbull et al., 1995; Hallahan & Kauffman, 1991; Haring et al., 1994).

Teachers often develop their own checklists to prepare for documentation of difficulties that the child demonstrates in class. While waiting for the diagnostic workup, classroom teachers find the following techniques helpful in managing the at-risk child:

1. Discipline the child with kindness in a quiet and firm manner. Spell out, enforce, and reinforce consequences for definite limits on behavior.

2. Allow the child to select a quiet corner in the classroom where he or she will be free from auditory or visual distractions. Try to keep the child's environment relatively free of distractions and interruptions.

3. Make instructions short and to the point.

4. Keep the child's routine highly structural; the child should always know what is expected in behavior and school assignments.

5. Keep the interpersonal relationship gratifying, warm, and fulfilling. The child should receive praise and encouragement for appropriate behaviors, and the manner of relating should be consistent (Freedman, 1969).

## PROGRAMS

Teaching a child with a learning disability requires individualizing learning experiences to his or her unique needs. Using all the information obtained in the assessment procedures, a specific teaching program is designed. As the teacher works with the child, the teacher modifies teaching procedures and plans as new needs become apparent. The following commentary will illustrate some of the more widely used interventions.

### Direct Instruction

Direct instructional approaches consist of data-based instruction, in which specific target learning tasks are identified, behavior analysis is conducted, and progress to achieving targets is charted. These approaches provide a highly structured and organized teaching strategy for children with specific learning disabilities and provides structured phases for lesson delivery. These phases are the provision of the lesson's focus and/or a review of the prior lesson; a clear, succinct statement of the lesson's objective; and the provision of structured, guided, and independent demonstration and practice of skill application with feedback, positive reinforcement, correction, examples, illustrations, and questions/answers directed to the student. Finally, the lesson is reviewed and closure is provided when the student has achieved measurable mastery of the lesson (Hallahan & Kauffman, 1991).

Direct instructional approaches appear to be successful for children in the subject areas of language, reading, handwriting, and mathematics skills. The teacher generates a high rate of student responses and proceeds at a brisk pace, using social praise and other reinforcements as well as modeling the skill or response. Feedback is essential and is provided intermittently as well as through testings and lesson-achievement evaluations (Heward, 1996).

### Cognitive Instruction

In this approach, the teacher uses a highly structured lesson focusing on an identified learning problem. The learning or instructional activities emphasize attending, responding, rehearsal, recall, and transfer of information. The lesson reflects highly structured strategies for monitoring and controlling the thought process. The child with learning disabilities uses a limited number of learning strategies, monitors his or her responses, and progresses with self-correction. The teacher helps with motivation, reinforcement, and progress charting. Direct instructional procedures are used, emphasizing factual content. The teacher provides the child with detailed data profiling strengths and weaknesses and emphasizing successes and achievements. Teachers and children set goals and emphasize self-control, self-recording of progress, and self-reinforcement procedures. Teacher reinforcement for independent learning, coupled with expression of high expectations for the child, is essential. Teachers use lesson content enhancements, which provide the child with visual or graphic means to better identify, organize, understand, and retain information. Content enhancement procedures employed by teachers include graphs, organizers, charts, and diagrams. The cognitive instructional approach demands the reduction of skills into discrete component elements, use of sequential steps in task analysis, use of mnemonic devices to rhyme, and use of acronyms to facilitate recall and self-direction (Lerner, 1976; Turnbull et al., 1995; Kirk et al., 1993).

## Multisensory Approach

Multisensory instructional strategies for children with learning disabilities, often used on an individual basis, highlight learning by seeing, hearing, touching, and movement. This approach may emphasize a high number of repetitions of tasks, reading aloud, tracing letters, and use of fingerpaints and sand trays. This approach employs as many

learning modalities or senses as possible. Some educators recommend the use of combined direct instruction with multisensory training approaches enriched by reasonably sufficient repetitions (Johnson, 1975; Bulgren & Carta, 1994; Hunt & Marshall, 1994).

## Study Skills Training

Study skills training or metacognitive skills training assists the child in learning how to take notes and tests; prepare compositions, projects, and reports; and remember to bring necessary materials (paper, pen, pencil, and so on) to class for assignments. It also helps the child learn to use charts, organizers, outlines, recorders, and computers. This approach helps the child learn to assess and plan how to approach learning tasks (Decker, Spector, & Shaw, 1994; Shields & Heron, 1990). Even more specifically, skills in following oral and written instructions may be necessary. For example, learning how to skim to locate information in a text and remembering when assignments are due might be critical skills. Other skills considered essential are budgeting time, requesting help when it is needed, using library references effectively, and working independently (Knowlton, 1993). In fact, classroom teachers rank the ability to work independently, efficiently, and effectively as a critical study skill (Mercer, 1997). They expect students to be able to organize information and resources such as notes, textbooks, and worksheet information in productive ways that lead to the completion of assignments (Schumaker & Deshler, 1984).

## Social Skills Training

Social skills training, using positive reinforcement and stressing understanding of feelings, helps the child in specific skill areas such as getting along with peers and adults in various settings and circumstances. The affective levels include helping the child achieve self-esteem, self-appreciation, and worthwhileness; control and mastery over his or her feelings and events; and a sense of adequateness and competency. Social skills training focuses the child on skills needed to resolve conflict, manage frustration and aggression, employ conversational skills, express feelings, and learn how to make and keep friends (Hardman et al., 1996; Smith & Luckasson, 1995).

All of the approaches just described use cooperative learning and peer tutoring practices, in which students teach students. Teachers monitor and structure these teaching episodes, which help the children with learning disabilities learn academic content and be better socialized.

## Multifaceted Approach for AD/HD

A multifaceted treatment approach is usually most effective for students with AD/HD. Parker (1988) suggests four phases :

1.  Medical management
2.  Psychological counseling

3. Educational planning
4. Behavior modification

Medical management usually means the prescription of a stimulant such as Ritalin or Cylert, which have been 60 to 80 percent effective in reducing the hyperactivity/impulsivity components (Reeve, 1990). The medication will often increase the child's ability to attend and help control interfering behaviors. This makes the child more available to instruction. However, medications alone do not improve learning and achievement. Too often parents' and teachers' expectations for improvement in learning purely as a result of the effects of medication are unreasonable. Parents and teachers should be alert for possible side effects, including sleeping and eating problems, the appearance of tics, and emotional changes in the child (Swanson et al., 1993). Psychological counseling helps the child understand and cope with AD/HD and the negative evaluations that often result before it is recognized. Educational programming is useful in modifying the learning environment so that it facilitates rather than frustrates the child. Individual modifications can range from establishing quiet zones for study to simplifying and repeating instructions to planning with the student the best ways that he or she can learn (Nussbaum & Bigler, 1990). Behavior management instruction helps the child recognize the behaviors that cause interference with normal functioning. Once the behaviors are recognized, strategies can be developed to monitor for their occurrence and control or eliminate their negative effects upon behavior and learning.

## Program Modifications for Children with LD in Regular Classrooms

Children with learning disabilities are increasingly receiving education experiences outside of special education classes. Numerous intervention programs have demonstrated that children with learning disabilities can be effectively served in the regular class by regular and special education collaboration. However, the resource room is the most frequently used service delivery model in special education and the most widely used option for students with learning disabilities. The resource room is defined as an instructional arrangement that provides part-time academic support to students whose primary placement is in the regular class. The amount of time students spend in the resource room varies as a result of matching available resources to students' needs. The administration of special education programs in the schools mandates a collaborative partnership between regular and special education teachers. Called *full inclusion*, it would reduce or eliminate programs that pull many students with disabilities out of the regular classroom by providing services within the regular classroom (Will, 1986; Vaugh & Bos, 1987; Anderson-Inman, 1987).

## Inclusion Strategies

The Adaptive Learning Environments Model (ALEM) is a popular service delivery model for inclusion. The ALEM consists of the following program components: (1) instruction in regular education settings on a full-time basis; (2) support and services from specialists that are delivered within the regular education setting; (3) highly structured prescriptive learning with built-in diagnostic procedures; (4) social and personal development experiences; (5) individually developed educational plans; and (6) flexibility in arranging parts of the learning environment, such as instructional groups and curricular and staff resources (Wang & Birch, 1984; and Hallahan, Keller, McKinney, Lloyd, & Bryan, 1988). The goal of the ALEM is to provide an effective educational alternative for meeting the needs of individual LD students in regular class settings. It is designed to increase each student's opportunities to master basic academic and social skills. Another model in support of full inclusion is the Integrated Classroom Model (ICM). It is designed to educate students who are mildly disabled, including students with learning disabilities, in the same regular classroom for the entire day. Regular school curriculum and materials are used, and teachers are trained in both special and regular education. A half-time aide is assigned to each integrated classroom; the class consists of approximately one-third students who are mildly disabled and two-thirds average to above average regular education students. Students who are mildly handicapped or disabled include those who are learning disabled or mentally retarded or have behavioral disorders. All students are assigned to the integrated classroom at the appropriate grade level (Affleck, Madge, Adams, & Lowenbraun, 1988). These integrated classrooms are very structured, with clear behavioral and academic expectations. Direct instructional approaches are emphasized, and individualized seatwork, cooperative learning, and independent study techniques are employed. The ICM provides services in a less restrictive environment. It alleviates possible stigmas caused by pull-out resource programs, and it puts an end to scheduling frustrations and coordination of different curricula used in resource rooms and regular classrooms. It sets up the circumstances to improve special and regular education collaboration (Affleck, et al., 1988).

Regardless of the model employed, regular classroom teachers are increasingly expected to teach children with learning disabilities in the regular classroom. Commentators indicate that one guideline for modifying instruction and materials is to make use of whatever it takes to successfully teach children with learning disabilities. This may mean experimentation and creative presentations of curriculum to determine the appropriate instructional approach. Teachers can increase student success by ensuring that the approach and materials are presented at the students' instructional level and that the children are able to and do complete the assignments. Worksheets and exercises should be attractive and interesting and present information in a logical sequence (Winter, 1994; Chalmers, 1991). Teachers may need to repeat instructions more frequently for children with learning disabilities, allow more time for task completion, and divide assignments into smaller-than-usual segments ranging in order from simple to complex. Peer teaching, special seating arrangements, specific and uncomplicated directions, and clarifications at the onset of a learning experience or lesson will increase successful performances (Barrow, Ploghoft, & Shepard, 1989).

Other general instructional modifications may include having a daily assignment sheet posted in view, using charts or graphic organizers, and color-coded materials that highlight directions or changes in assignments. In addition, talking or rehearsing students through tasks, giving samples or illustrations of assignments, and supplying students with a calendar that lists important dates and assignment deadlines may prove to be helpful to students with learning disabilities (Boyle, 1994).

Regular education teachers can prepare students with learning disabilities to read in content areas by using audiotapes, reading aloud to the student, pairing students to work with nondisabled peers in small cooperative groups, and when possible using films and computer programs in place of textbooks (Shumm & Strickler, 1991).

Teachers can help students with learning disabilities in math with numerous simple techniques. For example, they might assign the student with a learning disability fewer problems; grade assignments on different scales; allow the student more time; give the student graph paper to help keep the numbers in line; provide clear, neat examples of the work assignment; keep problems of the same type grouped together; highlight the sign that the student needs to notice $(+, -, \times)$ and provide rewards for completing work (Lambie & Hutchens, 1986; Barrow et al., 1989).

Teachers can modify their programs to help students improve writing by having students read aloud (privately or with the teacher) samples of their own writing, providing samples of finished writing assignments, providing two grades for writing (one for idea and one for technical skills), providing practice with story starters and open-ended questions, setting realistic and mutually agreed-upon expectations for neatness, and providing students with a copy of the teacher's notes (Gajria & Salend, 1995; Bender, 1995; Graham & Harris, 1994).

A wide variety of teaching behaviors can positively influence educational and achievement outcomes for students with learning disabilities and can be integrated in the regular class. These interventions, listed in Box 4.2, appear to successfully meet the instructional needs of these students.

---

**Box 4.2**
***WHAT EVERY TEACHER NEEDS TO KNOW***

***Positive Teaching
Behaviors***

1. Frequent positive feedback to students.
2. Provision of sustaining feedback to students responding incorrectly to questions.
3. Supportive, encouraging response to students in general.
4. Supportive response to low-ability students in particular.
5. Supportive response to problem behaviors indicative of a learning problem (as distinguished from a conduct problem).
6. The asking of questions that students can answer correctly.

7. Provision of learning tasks that students can accomplish with a high rate of success.
8. Efficient use of classroom time.
9. Low incidence of teacher intervention.
10. Infrequent need to discipline students.
11. Limited use of punitive interventions.
12. Minimal punitive response to students.
13. Rare criticism of student responses.
14. Reduced student transition of noninstructional time.
15. Low rate of student off-task time.

*Source:* From "Effective Teaching for Mainstreamed Students is Effective Teaching for All Students," by B. Larivee, 1986, *Teacher Education and Special Education, 94* (4), p. 175.

Finally, the regular educator, by collaborating with the special educator, can make modifications of instruction and overall programming more appropriate to the level of functioning of students with learning disabilities, which will allow students to be more successful and will in turn create a positive learning environment that keeps students on task.

## Providing Structure for the Child with a Learning Disability

The provision of a structured environment appears to be the single most essential condition for the general welfare of children with learning disabilities in special education programs:

> The teacher's primary task is to structure or order the environment for the child in such a way that work is accomplished, play is learned, love is felt, and fun is engaged in by the child and the teacher. Structure and order cannot be provided by allowing the child complete freedom to choose for herself/himself what she/he will do. It must be recognized that children are in difficulty because they have made and continue to make, if unguided, very bad choices about how to conduct themselves. . . . There are two fundamental guiding principles for arranging the environment to teach effectively: choosing tasks that are appropriate for the child (i.e., that are at her level and at which she can succeed) and arranging appropriate consequences for performance. Work, play, love and fun are not learned by failure but by success and mastery. Pride, dignity, and self-worth are not learned by having wishes immediately gratified, but by struggling to overcome difficulties, meeting requirements, and finding that one's own efforts will achieve desired goals. (Kauffman, 1997, pp. 261–263)

Research about effective schools has pinpointed school milieu and climate as an essential variable in effectively sustaining orderliness, discipline, and commitment to academic achievement (Goodman, 1985). Structure and its relationship between the teacher and child permeate the entire teaching concept. For children whose whole lives to date may have been characterized by a lack of structure and of failure, the externally imposed structure of the school, with its programs of curriculum and materials use, sustains them with a real and living fabric in which to invest their lives. The structured school and classroom serve as an "ego bank" for the bankrupt child, from which he or she now can begin to withdraw lessons on how to structure his or her total life (Cruickshank, 1967).

In real life, the necessity of structure is essential for normal development. For example, the realities of coming to class on time and conforming to classroom behavior standards are important prerequisites for learning. "The child who comes to class late and knows he is late must have many negative reactions when the teacher does not bring this to his attention. Am I sick? Am I so different that my teacher does not apply this rule to me?" (Cohen, 1967, p. 72). The child with a learning disability is perhaps more dependent upon the structure and rules of the classroom than is his or her nondisabled peer.

Structure can permeate relationships, including child-to-child, child-to-teacher, child-to-environment, or teacher-to-environment. By providing children with a framework for self-control, the teacher can allow more classroom freedom and offer children greater opportunities to learn.

## Structure as It Relates to Setting Limits

All programs for children with learning disabilities use structure through the setting of limits. Virtually no one argues against the importance of setting consistent and firm limits for these children (Haring & Phillips, 1962; Hewett, 1968; Long, Morse, & Newman, 1971; Parrish & Foster, 1966; Kauffman, 1997). However, there is disagreement on the number and kinds of limits to set. All programs for children with learning disabilities seem to select aggression aimed at others as the first item of prohibition. This is especially true of so-called permissive programs, which usually designate only one limit or rule (Morse, Cutler, & Fink, 1964). Freedom in the classroom does not mean license to do as one pleases, but rather the freedom to grow in a natural way without impeding others. Individuals are allowed to fulfill their needs as long as they do not deprive others of the same fulfillment (Reinert, 1980). Redl and Wineman (1957) believe that "one has to reduce rules to an absolute minimum so as not to set up too much delusional misinterpretation of adult motivation." They feel that the child should be allowed to reflect behavior that is symptomatic of disturbance, behavior that reflects his or her present developmental stage, and regressive behavior. However, the adult "must keep the children from confusing toleration of their symptoms with an actual indifference to or even permissive enjoyment of their problem by the adults, and care must be taken to operate this principle on a sliding scale" (p. 302).

Many teachers set limits relative to academic work. For example, students are required to work before they play, to finish each day's assignments, to exhibit good work habits, and to leave alone others who are working. In addition to "being a student," students must start their work and follow through on their assignments (Hewett, Artuso, & Taylor, 1967). "Scapegoating, severe regressive and primitive behavior, gross misuse of the food situation, and gang campaigns of adult defiance are examples of behavior beyond the limits" (Morse, 1957, p. 22).

It is important to structure the environment so that limits that are set are not broken. The children are told that the limits are for their protection and that they are liked even though their inappropriate behavior is not acceptable. Children need to know what they can do and the sanctions for unnecessary testing of limits. Other ways of structuring the environment so that limits are not broken include providing routines that are reasonable (Long et al., 1971; Morse et al., 1964), having the students share the responsibility of making the rules as a group-based democratic leadership (Morse et al., 1964; Reinert, 1976), and providing meaningful extrinsic and intrinsic rewards (Haring & Phillips, 1972; Hewett et al., 1967; Morse et al., 1964; Parrish & Foster, 1966). One program that makes systematic use of extrinsic rewards is the engineered classroom. In this program, checkmarks, which have an exchange value for such tangible items as toys, candy, and trinkets, are rewarded after each work period (Hewett et al., 1967). Some teachers feel comfortable with a peer group management system that provides structure while offering full participation by the children and a more complete educational experience, because the children have the structure they require and get a much-needed sense of accomplishment from implementing it themselves.

If limits are broken, it is imperative that the problem incident be handled in the most therapeutic way possible (Morse, 1957; Redl & Wineman, 1957) and that the choice of intervention be helpful to the child (Long et al., 1971). This rules out verbal and physical punishment, which have been found to be of little value in dealing with children who have learning or socialization disabilities (Hewett, 1968; Morse, 1957; Morse et al., 1964; Morse & Wineman,1957; Redl & Wineman, 1957). Fenichel (1974) states that

> discipline for the child is more than a system of rewards and punishments, of rules and regulations. It is neither punitive or hostile. Nor is it an instrument of power used by the teacher to dominate a child and make him docile, submissive, or subservient. Controls and limits are not used to block but rather to free a child for more effective learning and functioning. Discipline means constructive goals. It means reducing the child's confusion by setting up clear and reasonable limits to help the child understand exactly what is expected of him. (p. 179)

"We all need structure. Some children need much more than other children before they can feel comfortable and secure. Without these guideposts for behavior, some children become anxious and hyperactive" (Long et al., 1971). Minimally, without a structured environment in which to learn, children with learning disabilities are at an even greater disadvantage.

## Peer Mediated Instruction

Peer mediated instruction is a time-tested technique that uses an alternative teaching arrangement in which students serve as instructional agents for their classmates or other children. Successful programs are logically structured and consistent with principles of effective instructional practice. To be successful, peer teachers, just like their adult mentors, must present information systematically, draw out peer responses, monitor the accuracy of these responses, and provide immediate feedback (Maheady, Harper, & Sacca, 1988).

Although they are not usually used for delivering new instructional content, peer mediated approaches can be used as alternative practice activities after information has been introduced, discussed, and reviewed by the classroom teacher. Two peer programs that have been promoted are Classwide Peer Tutoring (CWPT) and Classwide Student Tutoring Teams (CSTT). Classwide Peer Tutoring, developed at the Juniper Gardens Children's Project in Kansas City, Kansas, was designed to improve the basic skills performance of low-achieving students from minority groups and disadvantaged families and those with mild disabilities. CWPT consists of four major parts: (1) weekly competing teams, (2) highly structured teaching procedures, (3) daily point earning and public display of student performance, and (4) direct practice of functional academic skills (Maheady et al., 1988). Each week the class is randomly divided into two teams. The teacher assigns students within each team to tutoring pairs. While in pairs, students must follow prescribed instructional procedures. When the tutee gives correct answers, the tutor awards points. If the tutee gives incorrect answers, the tutor provides the correct response, requires the tutee to write the answer three times, or gives one point if the tutee corrects the mistake. If the mistake is not corrected, no points are given. Students are encouraged to complete as many items as possible so that they earn more points for themselves and their team. At the end of the week, all points are totaled and the winning team of the week is announced (Maheady et al., 1988).

Use of peer mediated instructional approaches is justified for a number of reasons. These procedures are effective and implementation is feasible. Social relationships and academic performance have the potential to be improved. The existing teacher force is expanded. Finally, peer mediated approaches are advocated because students seem to like them (Maheady et al., 1988).

## Computer Assisted Instruction (CAI)

Computer assisted instruction (CAI) is the use of computer software that is organized to provide a broad range of instruction including drill and practice, tutorial sessions, educational games, simulations, problem-solving experiences, and using word processing programs (Haring et al., 1994). The use of CAI for students with learning disabilities has become a popular, extensively and effectively used teaching tool and a highly rewarding learning activity for students. Montague & Fonseca (1993) indicate that CAI is an attractive and motivating learning approach that appears to engage students with learning disabilities in successful learning experiences. CAI allows teachers to easily analyze student work and detect and correct errors. It also helps reduce emphasis on student handwriting requirements. Computerized speech synthesizers can be useful for students with reading problems. When the students want the text to be read aloud, they can access a speech device and read along with the computerized narrator. The CAI approach facilitates group discussion and cooperative learning and provides a powerful reinforcement for nonjudgmental learning. Vockell and Mihail (1993) demonstrated that CAI programming could be as effective in the implementation of specific instructional strategies with students with learning disabilities as was using direct instructional practices.

Stevens, Blackhurst, and Slaton (1991) and Van Daal and Van der Leij (1992) demonstrated that CAI spelling practice for students with learning disabilities had positive effects on their spelling achievement. It appeared that programs were seen as fun and were able to give immediate feedback. In cooperative group learning situations and in individualized CAI, students with learning disabilities performed better and achieved more significant gains in math skills when CAI was coordinated with formal classroom instruction than they did with traditional instructional practices alone (Mevarech, Silber, & Fine, 1991; Gaurgey, 1987; Messerly, 1986; Braden, Shaw, & Grecko, 1991). Gardner, Simmons, and Simpson (1992) and Majsterek and Wilson (1989) reported that the use of traditional instructional approaches combined with CAI in spelling, reading, and math produced equivalent or significant increased learning with less teacher time than did the use of traditional instruction alone.

It appears that student achievement usually is greater when CAI supplements teacher direct instructional practices. It is a promising attractive instructional intervention for students with learning disabilities, whether presented in group settings or individually. Success seems to be consistent across various academic subjects.

Several procedures are recommended to help teachers establish effective CAI learning environments. Teachers should start their CAI programs at the beginning of the year to establish ground rules and routines. Computer instruction should be made available for students at the same time each day and in the same room. The software that is selected should be attractive and age- and ability-level appropriate. Equipment should be functional and well maintained (Montague & Fonseca, 1993).

## Other Classroom Accommodations

Fagan, Graves, and Tessier-Switlick (1984) provided some suggestions for classroom accommodations for students with learning disabilities that have been recommended by teachers to support full integration in regular classrooms:

### Written Materials: Tests, Worksheets, Textbooks, and Blackboard

Provide copies that are clear and uncluttered.

Seat students close to the blackboard.

Provide a verbal description of printed materials, especially directions and other key points.

Directly teach students how to use the textbook format.

Provide tape recorded textbooks.

### Lectures (Any Subject)

Begin lectures with a review of previous content.

Pause periodically for questions and allow time for notes to be completed.

Close with a review of key points; involve students.

Assist students in detecting key points with tone of voice and gestures.

Allow a peer to use carbon paper to create an extra set of notes for a student who has difficulty taking complete notes.

Use meaningful, informative visual aids.

Use modified tests and worksheets.

### Reading

Systematically introduce new vocabulary.

State a purpose for any independent reading.

Use colored highlighting pens to emphasize key information.

Allow students to work in pairs or cooperative groups.

### Spelling and Written Expression

Maintain a posted list of correct spellings for commonly misspelled words.

Teach students to maintain a personal notebook with correct spellings of words that are troublesome.

Use word processors with spelling checkers.

### Mathematics

Give verbal descriptions of each part of a multistep process or algorithm.

Encourage students to verbalize steps as they work problems.

Highlight operation signs in practice activities involving a mix of operations.

Provide a model problem and solution at the top of practice worksheets (Fagan, Graves, & Tessier-Switlick, 1984).

## ISSUES OF IMPORTANCE

The two issues we will highlight in this section are the implications of children being routinely misdiagnosed as learning disabled and the controversy about the appropriate educational setting for the child with learning disabilities.

### Misdiagnosing Children as Learning Disabled

We have reported in this chapter that the criteria for identification of children as learning disabled are muddled, confused, and inconsistent throughout the United States. There is extensive confusion regarding definitions, prevalence estimates, characterizations, labels used, determination of degrees or levels of severity, diagnostic procedures, etiology, and appropriate program intervention. There appear to be no absolute criteria for diagnosis, and some criteria vary across experts and from state to state. Assessment and testing procedures, especially the use of IQ tests and determination of the discrepancy formula, are questioned regarding validity, relevance, and measurement of error. Some experts even suspect that some children with learning disabilities score in the mild retardation levels because of testing-instrument weaknesses. Yet excessively large numbers of students are identified as being learning disabled, and the numbers are growing each year.

The circumstances suggest that learning disabilities are complex conditions with a wide variety of possible influencing causes, ranging from neurological impairments of various types that cannot be readily diagnosed to negative environmental influences. We know that these children are students who perform below expected academic achievement levels and that they may exhibit social or adjustment difficulties as a result. We know that they are often rejected by peers and can be socially alienated and at risk for juvenile delinquency and/or emotional disturbance. Given the number of uncontrolled variables surrounding the diagnosis of learning disabilities, it is not unreasonable to suspect that large numbers of children having problems in learning and behavior at school are being misidentified and misdiagnosed as learning disabled. It is possible that some children who are mentally retarded, emotionally disturbed, and otherwise sensory impaired are also being grouped as learning disabled. Developmental delays and motivational differences with some non-impaired children also place them at risk for misidentification as learning disabled. Because of the low stigmatizing influences that accompany the diagnosis of learning disability, there has been an extraordinary increase in the number of students identified as learning disabled. Parents who might not accept a diagnosis of serious emotional disturbance, mental retardation, or organic language processing difficulties will often readily accept the less accurate label of *learning disabled*.

This issue is worthy of discussion because misdiagnosed children, with their divergent needs, tend to further confuse the perception of learning disability. In addition, programs and treatments designed for the child with a learning disability may not be successful when applied to children with different needs dictated by their true disabilities. Perhaps most important, misdiagnosis may prevent children from receiving the appropriate special education services they need.

## Appropriate Educational Settings

Despite the current focus on inclusion, there is continued debate about where students with learning disabilities should be educated. A wide variety of curricular and organizational options and instructional strategies are effective for these students. Although full inclusion in the regular classroom is more popular than resource room or special education self-contained classrooms, the demands on regular classroom teachers result in children with learning disabilities receiving poorly conceived, inappropriate instructional programs.

A parallel issue is that program intervention and support for preschool children who will be diagnosed as learning disabled when they reach school age are, on a national scale, modest or non-existent. At-risk preschool children can be helped remarkably through early preschool programs. Yet while early intervention programs continue to grow and show their value in other special education areas, they cannot have the same emphasis in the specific area of learning disability because learning disabilities cannot be diagnosed in early childhood. By their very nature, they relate to academic learning (reading, writing, mathematical calculations) to which the young child has not yet been exposed. One cannot diagnose an academic problem before academic learning has begun.

## MINORITY CONCERNS

The label or term *learning disabilities* is a loose, appealing, cosmetic, and popular label because it carries diminished social stigma and personal parental or child responsibility for its cause. It appears to reduce blame or victimization of families and children when compared with mental retardation or serious emotional disturbance. There is no implication of neglect or abuse. There is no implication of lack of motivation on the part of the child. It is an acceptable middle-class term. Children at a low socioeconomic level in trouble with learning and behavior at school are more likely than their middle-class peers to be regarded as mentally retarded and seriously emotionally disturbed. Thus, it is surprising that Sattler (1988) and Meyen (1996) have indicated that a growing number of children from ethnic minorities are being classified as

LD. There is even a growing concern that children from ethnic minorities are overrepresented in LD programs. The limited commentary about this issue suggests that careful or competent consideration and evaluation of test results, adaptive behavior inventories, classroom performance, and cultural influences on learning and behavior are shoddy, and that children from ethnic minorities are being misidentified and mislabeled as learning disabled. The implication really seems to be that these children simply demonstrate differences in learning and socialization patterns and may indeed demonstrate no real evidence of handicapping conditions.

## AD/HD and Culture

Some cultural issues of importance may need to be considered when determining whether a child from a nondominant culture should be considered for AD/HD classification. Some students exhibit activity levels that may be culturally appropriate but different from the majority culture of their peers. Therefore, the Council for Exceptional Children's Task Force on Children with AD/HD (1992) recommended that at least one member of the evaluation team be either a member of the same minority group as the child (ethnic, cultural, or linguistic) or be familiar with the evaluation of children from that minority group. Evaluation instruments like the Child Behavior Checklist–Direct Observation Form (Achenbach, 1991) allow an evaluator to compare any given child to control peers from the same minority group in the same setting.

## PROFESSIONALS

The professionals most likely to work with students with learning disabilities and their families are regular classroom teachers, special educators, physicians, and psychological counselors. Since most students with learning disabilities are included, as much as possible, with their nondisabled peers, many remedial services are presented in the regular classroom. The regular education teacher provides most of this instruction. A special education teacher, often acting as a consultant, provides the regular teacher with support in remediation activities. In this collaborative role with the regular teacher, the special educator assists in assessment, selecting curriculum materials, and using them in direct instructional activities.

In addition, some special education teachers provide full- or part-time service to students with learning disabilities in self-contained classrooms or resource rooms. Students with the most severe disabilities will obtain special educational services in residential settings that house special educators as well as appropriate medical and counseling personnel.

Medical and paramedical professionals, including family physicians and psychotherapists, depending on their familiarity with the behavioral and other accompanying symptoms often coexisting with learning disability, may provide medication, behavioral therapy, counseling, and other related services. They often assist the regular and special educator in monitoring the effects of medications.

The Council for Exceptional Children provides standards for the preparation and certification of teachers for students with learning disabilities. The program of studies they require of college and university training programs typically includes courses in education philosophy and history; characteristics of students with learning disabilities; assessment, diagnosis, and evaluation knowledge and experience; instructional intervention knowledge; classroom and child behavioral-management knowledge and practice; and knowledge of advocacy and training in collaboration with allied professionals and parents. Coursework in ethical and professional practice is also mandated. These guidelines have been presented in detail in Chapter 1 of this text. While the Council for Exceptional Children sets the guidelines for training programs, each individual state has its own criteria for certification of teachers specializing in working with students with learning disabilities. Appendix I is a listing of the directors of special education for each state. Interested readers may contact their offices to obtain the specific requirements for any specific state.

## PROFESSIONAL ASSOCIATIONS AND PARENT OR SELF-HELP GROUPS

Association for Children with Learning
  Disabilities
Learning Disabilities Association of America
4165 Library Road
Pittsburgh, PA 15234

Attention Deficit Disorder Association (ADDA)
8901 South Ireland Way
Aurora, CO 80016

Children with Attention Deficit Disorder
  (CHADD)
1859 North Pine Island Road, Suite 185
Plantation, FL 33322

Council for Exceptional Children
Division for Learning Disabilities
1920 Association Drive
Reston, VA 20191-1589

Council for Learning Disabilities
P.O. Box 40303
Overland Park, KS 66204

ERIC Clearing House on Disabilities and Gifted
  Education
Council for Exceptional Children
1920 Association Drive
Reston, VA 20191-1589

National Center for Learning Disabilities
99 Park Avenue
New York, NY 10016
(212) 687-7211

National Center to Improve Practice in Special
  Education through Technology, Media, and
  Materials (NCIP)
Education Development Center, Inc.
55 Chapel Street
Newton, MA 02160

Orton Dyslexia Society
Chester Building, Suite 382
8600 LaSalle Road
Baltimore, MD 21286

U.S. Department of Education
National Library of Education
555 New Jersey Avenue NW
Washington, DC 20208-5121
Library Administration

## REFERENCES FOR FURTHER INFORMATION

ADD Warehouse
300 Northwest 70th Avenue, Suite 102
Plantation, FL 33317

*Journal of Learning Disabilities*
PRO-ED
8700 Shoal Creek Boulevard
Austin, TX 78757

LD *Forum*
Council for Learning Disabilities
P.O. Box 40303
Overland Park, KS 66204

*Learning Disability Quarterly*
Council for Learning Disabilities
P.O. Box 40303
Overland Park, KS 66204

*Learning Disabilities Research and Practice*
Lawrence Erlbaum Associates
365 Broadway
Hillsdale, NJ 07642-1487

## REFERENCES ❀

Achenbach, T. M. (1991). *Manual for the child behavior checklist/4-18 and 1991 profile.* Burlington, VT: University of Vermont, Department of Psychiatry.

Affleck, J., Madge, S., Adams, A., & Lowenbaun, S. (1988). Integrated classroom versus resource model: Academic viability and effectiveness. *Exceptional Children, 54*(4), 339–348.

Anderson-Inman, L. (1987). Consistency of performance across classrooms: Institutional materials versus setting as influencing variables. *Journal of Special Education, 21*(4), 9–29.

Baker, L. (1982). An evaluation of the role of metacognition deficits in learning disabilities. *Topics in Learning and Learning Disabilities, 2,* 27–35.

Barrow, E., Ploghoft, J., & Shepard, J. (1989). *Serving students with learning disabilities differences in the regular classroom: A training program.* Chapel Hill, NC: University of North Carolina Press.

Bender, W. N. (1995). Promoting strategic learning by post-secondary students with learning disabilities. *Journal of Learning Disabilities, 28,* 170–190.

Boyle, M. (1994). Two dozen plus ideas that will help special students. *Teaching K–8, 3,* 74–75.

Braden, J., Shaw, S., & Grecko, L. (1991). An evaluation of a computer assisted instructional program for elementary hearing impaired students. *Volta Review, 93* (6), 247–252.

Brigance, A. (1983). *Brigance diagnostic inventory of basic skills.* North Billerica, MA: Curriculum Associates.

Bulgren, J. A. & Carta, J. J. (1994). Examining the instructional contexts of students with learning disabilities. In K. L. Freiberg (Ed.), *Educating exceptional children.* (7th ed.). Guilford, CT: Dushkin.

Chalmers, L. (1991). Classroom modifications for the mainstreamed student with mild handicaps. *Intervention in School and Clinic, 27,* 40–42.

Cohen, S. (1967). Comments on "Hyperactive children: Their needs and curriculum." In P. Knoblock & J. L. Johnson (Eds.), *The teaching-learning process in educating emotionally disturbed children.* Syracuse, NY: Syracuse University Press.

Comings, D. E. (1992). Role of mutant dopamine receptor gene in ADHD: Implications for treatment and relationship to Tourette syndrome. CH.A.D.D.ER, 6(1), 12–15.

Council for Exceptional Children's Task Force on Children with AD/HD. (1992). *Children with AD/HD: A shared responsibility.* Reston, VA: Author.

Cruickshank, W. M. (1967). Hyperactive children: Their needs and curriculum. In P. Knoblock & J. L. Johnson

(Eds.), *The teaching-learning process in educating emotionally disturbed children*. Syracuse, NY: Syracuse University Press.

Decker, K., Spector, S., & Shaw, S. (1994). Teaching study skills to students with mild handicaps: The role of the classroom teacher. In K. L. Freiberg (Ed.), *Educating exceptional children* (7th ed.). Guilford, CT: Dushkin.

Fagan, S. A., Graves, D. L., & Tessier-Switlick, D. (1984). *Promoting successful mainstreaming: Reasonable classroom accommodations for learning disabled students*. Rockville, MD: Montgomery County Public Schools.

Fenichel, C. (1974). Special education as the basic therapeutic tool in the treatment of severely disturbed children. *Journal of Autism and Childhood Schizophrenia*, 4 (2), 179.

Frauenheim, J. G. & Heckerl, J. R. (1979). Learning disabilities. In W. C. Morse (Ed.), *Humanistic teaching for exceptional children*. Syracuse, NY: Syracuse University Press.

Freedman, S. (1969). *Detection of learning disabilities: A guide for the classroom teacher* (pp. 1–5). Knoxville, TN: Birth Defects Clinic, University Hospital Knoxville.

Freiberg, K. L. (1990). *Educating exceptional children*. (5th ed.). Guilford, CT: Dushkin.

Gajria, M., & Salend, S. (1995). Homework practices of students with and without learning disabilities: A comparison. *Journal of Learning Disabilities*, 28, 291–296.

Gallico, R. R., Burns, T. J., & Grob, C. S. (1988). *Emotional and behavioral problems in children with learning disabilities*. Boston: College-Hill.

Gardner, C., Simmons, P., & Simpson, R. (1992). The effects of CAI and hands-on activity on elementary students' attitudes and weather knowledge. *School Science and Mathematics*, 92(6), 334–336.

Gaurgey, A. (1987). Coordination of instruction and reinforcement as enhancers of the effectiveness of computer assisted instruction. *Journal of Educational Computing Research*, 3(2), 219–230.

Goodman, L. (1985). The effective school movement and special education. *Exceptional Children*, 17(2), 104.

Graham, S., & Harris, K. (1994). Implications of constructivism for teaching writing to students with special needs. *Journal of Special Education*, 28, 275–289.

Grossman, R. (1978). LD and the problem of scientific definitions. *Journal of Learning Disabilities*, 11, 120–123.

Hallahan, D. P., & Kauffman, J. M. (1991). *Exceptional children: Introduction to special education* (5th ed.). Upper Saddle River, NJ: Prentice-Hall.

Hallahan, D. P., Kauffman, J. M., & Lloyd, J. W. (1995). *Introduction to learning disabilities*. Needham, MA: Allyn & Bacon.

Hallahan, D., Keller, C., McKinney, J., Lloyd, J., & Bryan, T. (1988). Examining the research base of the regular education initiative and the adaptive learning environments model. *Journal of Learning Disabilities*, 21(1), 29–35.

Hammill, D. D. (1990). On defining learning disabilities: An emerging consensus. *Journal of Learning Disabilities*, 23, 74–84.

Hammill, D. D. (1993). A timely definition of learning disabilities. *Family and Community Health*, 16(3), 1–8.

Hardman, M. L., Drew, C. J., & Egan, M. W. (1996). *Human exceptionality: Society, school, and family* (5th ed.). Needham, MA: Allyn & Bacon.

Haring, N. G., McCormick, L., & Haring, T. G. (1994). *Exceptional children and youth* (6th ed.). New York: Macmillan.

Haring, N. G., & Phillips, E. L. (1962). *Educating emotionally disturbed children*. New York: McGraw-Hill.

Haring, N. G., & Phillips, E. L. (1972). *Analysis and modification of classroom behavior*. Upper Saddle River, NJ: Prentice Hall.

Heward, W. L. (1996). *Exceptional children: An introduction to special education* (5th ed.). Upper Saddle River, NJ: Prentice Hall/Merrill.

Hewett, F. M. (1968). *The emotionally disturbed child in the classroom: A developmental strategy for educating children with maladaptive behavior*. Needham, MA: Allyn & Bacon.

Hewett, F. M., Artuso, A. A., & Taylor, F. D. (1967). *Santa Monica Project: Demonstration and evaluation of an engineered classroom design for emotionally disturbed children in the public schools. Phase 1, Elementary Level*. Project No. 62893: Grant No. OEG 4-7-062893-0377). Los Angeles: University of California. (ERIC Document Reproduction Service)

Hunt, N., & Marshall, K. (1994). *Exceptional children and youth: An introduction to special education*. Boston: Houghton Mifflin.

Jastak, J. F., & Jastak, S. R. (1965). *The Wide Range Achievement Test* (Rev. ed.). Wilmington, DE: Guidance Associates.

Johnson, D. J. (1975). Clinical teaching of children with learning disabilities. In S. A. Kirk & J. McRae-McCarthy, (Eds.), *Learning disabilities: Selected papers.* Boston: Houghton Mifflin.

Kauffman, J. M. (1997). *Characteristics of emotional and behavioral disorders of children and youth* (6th ed.). Upper Saddle River, NJ: Prentice Hall.

Kirk, S. A., Gallagher, J. J., & Anastasiow, N. J. (1993). *Educating exceptional children* (7th ed.). Boston: Houghton Mifflin.

Knowlton, E. K. (1993). *Secondary regular classroom teachers' expectations of learning disabled students.* Research Report No. 75. Lawrence, KS: University of Kansas Center for Research and Learning.

Lambie, R. A., & Hutchens, P. W. (1986). Adopting elementary school mathematics instruction. *Teaching Exceptional Children*, 18(2), 185–189.

Larivee, B. (1986). Effective teaching for mainstreamed students is effective teaching for all students. *Teacher Education and Special Education*, 94(4), 175.

Lerner, J. W. (1976). *Children with learning disabilities* (2nd ed., pp. 291–315). Boston: Houghton Mifflin.

Lilly, M. S. (1979). *Children with exceptional needs.* New York: Holt, Rinehart, & Winston.

Long, N. J., Morse, W. C., & Newmon, R. (1971). *Conflict in the classroom* (2nd ed.). Belmont, CA: Wadsworth.

Lorsbach, T. C., & Frymier, J. (1992). A comparison of learning disabled and nondisabled students on five at-risk factors. *Learning Disabilities Research and Practice*, 7, 137–141.

Maheady, L., Harper, G., & Sacca, M. (1988). Peer mediated instruction: A promising approach to meeting the diverse needs of LD adolescents. *Learning Disability Quarterly*, 11(2), 108–114.

Majsterek, D., & Wilson, R. (1989). Computer assisted instruction for students with learning disabilities: Considerations for practitioners. *Learning Disabilities Focus*, 5(1), 18–27.

Mercer, C. D. (1997). *Students with learning disabilities* (5th ed.). Upper Saddle River, NJ: Prentice Hall/Merrill.

Messerly, C. (1986). The use of computer assisted instruction in facilitating the acquisition of math skills with hearing impaired high school students. *Volta Review*, 88(2), 67–77.

Mevarech, R., Silber, T., & Fine, A. (1991). Learning with computers in small groups: Cognitive and affective outcomes. *Journal of Educational Computing Research*, 7(2), 233–43.

Meyen, E. L. (1996). *Exceptional children in today's schools* (3rd ed.). Denver, CO: Love.

Meyen, E. L., & Skrtic, T. M. (1988). *Exceptional children and youth: An introduction* (3rd ed.).Denver, CO: Love.

Montague, M., & Fonseca, F. (1993). Using computers to improve story writing. *Teaching Exceptional Children*, 25 (4), 46–49.

Morse, W. C. (1957). An interdisciplinary therapeutic camp. *Journal of Social Issues*, 13(1), 15–22.

Morse, W. C., Cutler, R. L., & Fink, A. H. (1964). *Public school classes for emotionally handicapped: A research analysis.* Washington, DC: Council for Exceptional Children.

Morse, W. C., & Wineman, D. (1957). Group interviewing in a camp for disturbed boys. *Journal of Social Issues*, 13(1), 23–31.

National Joint Committee on Learning Disabilities (NJCLD). (1994). *Learning disabilities: Issues on definition.* Position paper of the National Joint Committee on Learning Disabilities. In *Collective perspective on issues affecting learning disabilities: Position papers and statements.* Austin, TX: PRO-ED.

North Carolina Division of Exceptional Children's Services, Department of Public Instruction. (1993). *Procedures governing programs and services for children with special needs.* Raleigh, NC: Department of Public Instruction.

Nussbaum, N., & Bigler, E. (1990). *Identification and treatment of attention deficit disorder.* Austin, TX: PRO-ED.

Parker, H. C. (1988). *The ADHD hyperactivity workbook for parents, teachers and kids.* Plantation, FL: Impact.

Parrish, A. K., & Foster, G. (1966). An approach to emotionally disturbed children: Re-education at Wright School. *North Carolina Journal of Mental Health*, 2(2), 5–20.

Redl, F., & Wineman, D. (1957). *The aggressive child.* Glencoe, IL: Free Press.

Reeve, R. E. (1990). ADHD: Facts and fallacies. *Intervention in School and Clinic*, 26(2), 70–78.

Reinert, H. R. (1976). *Children in conflict. Educational strategies for the emotionally disturbed and behaviorally disordered.* St. Louis, MO: Mosby.

Reinert, H. R. (1980). *Children in conflict.* St. Louis, MO: Mosby.

Reschly, D. (1987). Learning characteristics of mildly handicapped students: Implications for classification, placement, and programming. In M. Wang, M. Reynolds, & H. Walberg (Eds.), *Handbook of special education: Learner characteristics and adaptive behavior.* New York: Pergamon.

Sattler, J. (1988). *Assessment of children* (3rd ed.). San Diego, CA: Author.

Schumaker, J. B., & Deshler, D. D. (1984). Setting demand variables: A major factor in program planning for the LD adolescent. *Topics in Language Disorders*, 4(2), 22–40.

Shields, J. M., & Heron, T. E. (1990). Teaching organizational skills to students with learning disabilities. In K. L. Freiberg (Ed.), *Educating exceptional children* (5th ed.). Guilford, CT: Dushkin.

Shumm, J. S., & Strickler, K. (1991). Guidelines for adapting content area textbooks: Keeping teachers and students content. *Intervention in School and Clinic*, 27, 79–83.

Slaton, D. B., & Morsink, C. V. (1993). Students with learning disabilities. In A. E. Blackhurst and W. H. Berdine (Eds.), *An introduction to special education* (3rd ed.). New York: HarperCollins.

Smith, D. D., & Luckasson, R. (1995). *Introduction to special education: Teaching in an age of challenge* (2nd ed.). Needham, MA: Allyn & Bacon.

Stevens, K., Blackhurst, A., & Slaton, D. (1991). Teaching memorized spelling with a microcomputer: Time delay and computer assisted instruction. *Journal of Applied Behavior Analysis*, 24(1), 153–160.

Swanson, J. M., McBurnett, K., Wigal, T., Pfiffer, L. J., Lerner, M. A., Williams, L., Christian, D. L., Tamm, L., Willcutt, E., Crowley, K., Clevenger, W., Khouzam, N., Woo, C., Crinnella, F. M., & Fischer, T. D. (1993). Effect of stimulant medication on children with attention deficit disorder: A "review of reviews." *Exceptional Children*, 60(2), 154–162.

Turnbull, A. P., Turnbull, H. R., Shank, M., & Leal, D. (1995). *Exceptional lives: Special education in today's schools.* Upper Saddle River, NJ: Prentice Hall/Merrill.

U.S. Office of Education. (1977). Assistance to states for education of handicapped children: Procedures for evaluating specific learning disabilities. *Federal Register*, 42, 65082–65085.

Van Daal, V., & Van der Leij, A. (1992). Computer-based reading and spelling practice for children with learning disabilities. *Journal of Learning Disabilities*, 25(3), 186–195.

Van Syke, D. C., & Fox, A. A. (1990). Fetal drug exposure and its possible implications for learning in the preschool and school-aged population. *Journal of Learning Disabilities*, 23, 160–163.

Vaugh, S., & Bos, C. (1987). Knowledge and perception of the resource room: The students' perspectives. *Journal of Learning Disabilities*, 20(4), 218–223.

Vockell, E., & Mihail, T. (1993). Principles behind computerized instruction for students with exceptionalities. *Teaching Exceptional Children*, 25(3), 38–43.

Wang, M. C., & Birch, J. W. (1984). Effective special education in regular classes. *Exceptional Children*, 50(4), 391–398.

Wechsler, D. (1993). *The Wechsler Intelligence Scale for Children–III.* San Antonio, TX: Psychological Corporation.

Wehman, P. (1997). *Exceptional individuals in school, community, and work.* Austin, TX: PRO-ED.

Will, M. (1986). Educating children with learning problems: A shared responsibility. *Exceptional Children*, 52, 411–415.

Winter, L. (1994). *Successfully including special needs students in the regular classroom: Inclusion strategies that work.* Medina, WA: Institute for Educational Development.

Woodcock, R. W., & Mather, N. (1989). *The Woodcock-Johnson psycho-educational battery–revised.* Allen, TX: DLM Teaching Resources.

# 5

# Children with Emotional and Behavioral Disorders

As generations of children experience abuse, neglect, divorce, broken families, poverty, homelessness, drug and alcohol abuse, and decreased supportive social programs, teachers are confronted with students whose behavior is out of control, and children who are so depressed and withdrawn that they cannot learn or interact with others. School may become irrelevant to students who experience the absence of a parent, a pregnancy, a friend's runaway or suicide, drug addiction, or any of the other multiple problems current in our society.

All teachers confront behaviors that reflect children's home influences, situational and social stresses, and fears and anxieties about new learning tasks. Children with emotional and behavioral disorders, with their additional adjustment problems, may find it difficult to function in schools.

The special education area of emotional-behavioral disorders (EBD) is not easily described or defined. Definitions, prevalence estimates, characteristics, and etiology are often divergent and sometimes the result of a consensus of expert opinion. There is also debate and little agreement about whether a specific philosophy, curriculum, or approach is preferred in the education of children with EBD (Grosenick, George, & George, 1990). Furthermore, children with EBD may have additional impairments that complicate their already difficult circumstances. Children with emotional-behavioral disorders come from all socioeconomic levels, age levels, and ethnic and racial groups. Even the title *emotional and behavioral disorders* is in flux. *Emotional and behavioral disorders* is the preferred term, but much literature and federal legislation refers to *seriously emotional disturbance* (SED). We will refer to the children as having behavioral and emotional disorders. However, some of the literature we quote and governmental mandates will use the term *seriously emotional disturbance* or SED.

## DEFINITIONS

The definitions used in the area of emotional and behavioral disorders vary. Some are subjective and others are educationally irrelevant. The fundamental issue that complicates defining children with EBD is the uncertainty about what constitutes human deviance. The more widely accepted definitions propose that the presenting problem behaviors have the following characteristics:

1. They exist to a marked extent, and are notably serious.
2. They are chronic or exist over a long period of time (three to six months).
3. There is a high rate or frequency of exhibited behavior.
4. There is an intense, dramatic, or overwhelming behavioral response.
5. Unacceptable behavioral episodes last far beyond expected duration.
6. Personal difficulties adversely affect school performances.
7. The behavior is age inappropriate and regarded as deviant from cultural or sociological standards of the child's background (American Psychiatric Association, 1994; Heward, 1996; Hardman, Drew, & Egan, 1996; Hallahan & Kauffman, 1991; Kauffman, 1997).

Children with EBD are notably anxious and depressed children; some act out while others are withdrawn. *Anxiety* refers to feelings of apprehension, fearfulness, or dread, while *depression* refers to feelings of sadness, self-depreciation, or worthlessness. Children who act out are hostile, angry, and sometimes aggressive or assaultive.

Some children should not be considered as EBD. Excluded are children who are experiencing a temporary situational crisis or developmental lags or problems and those whose behavior is a reflection of economic disadvantage or specific social, cultural or ethnic-determined behavioral reactions (Nelson, 1993; Turnbull, Turnbull, Shank, & Leal, 1995).

## Legal Definition

The Individuals with Disabilities Education Act (IDEA) details the following definition:

    (i) "seriously emotionally disturbed" is defined as . . . :

        (1) a condition exhibiting one or more of the following characteristics over a long period of time and to a marked degree, which adversely affects educational performance:

        (A) An inability to learn which cannot be explained by intellectual, sensory or health factors;

        (B) An inability to build or maintain satisfactory relationships with peers and teachers;

        (C) Inappropriate types of behavior or feelings under normal circumstances;

        (D) A general pervasive mood of unhappiness of depression; or

        (E) A tendency to develop physical symptoms or fears associated with personal or school problems.

    (ii) The term includes children who are schizophrenic or autistic. [Autistic is a separate category under IDEA]. The term does not include children who are socially maladjusted, unless it is determined that they are seriously disturbed. (42 Fed. Reg. 478 [1977]).

This legal definition has the potential to be misleading in several ways because children can have emotional-behavioral disturbance and yet still not meet the criteria stated in the definition. For example:

1. Some troubled children can learn as a result of specialized remedial programs. Gifted children who are disturbed may be functioning below their potential but still be at grade level. Intelligence scores that indicate children with EBD to be slow learners or even educable mentally retarded may only be predictive of school failure if special services are not available. While there is a greater likelihood of adjustment problems or EBD for children who are mentally retarded, learning disabled, and sensory or health impaired, these disabilities are not synonymous nor interchangeable with EBD.

2. While troubled children are resistant and suspicious about entering into relationships, with adult persistence, care, and loving affection, these children can be captured in poignant interpersonal relationships.

3.  Judgments of inappropriate behavior are often determined by the subjective personal judgments and opinions of adult observers.

4.  The term *seriously* modifying *emotional disturbance* is unfortunate, since it may discriminate and exclude mildly and moderately troubled children from services. This term may have placed a great burden on interested professionals and parents about what is a fair and inclusive approach in providing services to troubled children.

## The Proposed Definition

An alternate definition developed by the National Mental Health and Special Education Coalition and endorsed by the Council for Children with Behavioral Disorders (CCBD) within the Council for Exceptional Children (CEC) has been proposed. It states that:

> Emotional or Behavior Disorders (EBD) refer(s) to a condition in which:
> (i) behavioral or emotional responses of an individual in school are so different from his/her generally accepted age-appropriate, ethnic, or cultural norms that they adversely affect educational performance in such areas as self-care, social relationships, personal adjustment, academic progress, classroom behavior, or work adjustment. Such a disability is:
> (a) more than a temporary, expected response to stressful events in the environment;
> (b) consistently exhibited in two different settings, at least one of which is school-related; and
> (c) unresponsive to direct intervention in general education or the child's condition is such that general education interventions would be insufficient.
> (ii) Emotional and behavioral disorders can co-exist with other disabilities.
> (iii) This category may include children or youth with schizophrenic disorders, or other sustained disturbances of conduct or adjustment when they adversely affect educational performance in accordance with section (i).
> (CCBD, 1987; Forness & Knitzer, 1992, p. 13)

This proposal has been rejected by Congress. Perhaps the lack of congressional support is because the proposed definition has been developed mainly by non-educators, it has little educational utility, and it does not clearly lead to program interventions (Tompkins, 1996). Furthermore, educational scholars in this special education area recommended that the EBD definition be educationally oriented and school based. They want it to be clearly understood, as positive as possible, appropriate to present school conditions, related to teacher-child relationships, and relevant to important skills such as impulse control and attention, and to important skills in the teacher's role with EBD children (Bower & Kaczynski, 1968). However, Kauffman (1997) believes that the proposed definition does reflect the current professional preference, is inclusive of both emotional and behavioral disorders, is school centered, reflects cultural and ethnic diversity concerns, excludes minor problems in children's lives, and includes the full range of concerns shared by mental health and education professionals.

Any attempt to interpret the definition of EBD to regular educators, special educators, and the lay public must highlight that these children are consistently and seriously troubled and in trouble at home, in school, and in the community.

Children with emotional and behavioral disturbances:

1. Have serious learning problems, are often failing all their subjects, and are often two or more years behind their peers academically.

2. Have serious problems with making or sustaining happy, gratifying relationships with other children and adults.

3. Are often socially alienated and ostracized; some are withdrawn.

4. Exhibit behavior that is often obnoxious and surprisingly inappropriate, and the behavior puzzles, frightens, and disgusts observers.

5. Are often anxious and sad.

6. Complain about psychosomatic illnesses, especially stomach pains, nausea, and headaches.

Descriptions of the unacceptable behavior patterns often illustrate the difficulties these children experience with greater clarity than do clinical diagnostic categories or classification terms. For example, an obsessive-compulsive neurotic child could be characterized as employing a wide range of ritualistic behaviors, such as repeated hand-washing, or the child might be one who reports the inability to suppress thoughts about injuring another person. These typical complaints are more easily understood using the behavioral descriptions than the classification term.

Finally, the EBD concept may be applied to any deviant behavior in the classroom for which there is no other available concept, or children may be so labeled because they violate classroom rules (Trippe, 1966).

## Children with Conduct Disorders

The *Diagnostic and Statistical Manual of Mental Disorders* (American Psychiatric Association, 1994) characterizes conduct disorders or social maladjustment as occurring when there is a repetitive and persistent pattern of behavior that violates the rights of others or violates societal rules or norms that are age-appropriate. Conduct disorders take the form of:

1. Aggression toward people or animals

2. Destruction of property

3. Deceitfulness or theft

4. Serious rule violation

Children with conduct disorders are further classified as "undersocialized" or "socialized" (Quay, 1986a, 1986b). The undersocialized are characterized by impulsivity, irritability, and argumentativeness. They are social isolates, are disobedient, and can be threatening or assaultive. The socialized conduct disorder is displayed by more covert

antisocial behavior typified by lying, stealing, arson, destructiveness, gang membership, truancy, and running away (Kauffman, 1997). Children who are labeled conduct disordered (socially maladjusted) are excluded from special education services (Nelson, Rutherford, Center, & Walker, 1994). These children often get into trouble with the law, go before a juvenile court judge, and become labeled delinquent by the courts. The terms *delinquency*, *social maladjustment*, and *conduct disorder* are used interchangeably. The term EBD is not the same as these terms and it is not interchangeable with them. Kauffman (1997) and Forness and Knitzer (1992) lament the exclusion of children with conduct disorders from the enabling legislation. They represent the viewpoint that socially maladjusted children should be eligible for special education.

The terms defined in Box 5.1 will assist the reader in understanding the concepts used in this chapter.

## PREVALENCE

The most conservative estimates suggest that from 3 to 5 percent of children and adolescents have emotional and behavioral disorders (Turnbull et al., 1995). However, there are notable problems with estimating the number of children with EBD, as a result, estimated figures vary considerably (Wehman, 1997).

**Box 5.1**
*WHAT EVERY TEACHER NEEDS TO KNOW*

*Terms*

**abnormal behavior**   A general term referring to behavior that is unusual and exceeds what society views as normal.

**academic achievement**   The level of success or proficiency attained in school subjects.

**aggression**   Behavior designed to hurt other people or destroy some aspect of the environment. Aggressive behavior may be verbal as well as nonverbal.

**anxiety**   A sense of apprehension or uneasiness, with physiological correlates.

**autism**   A condition that emerges during the second to fourth year of life, reflecting serious developmental problems, social withdrawal, and self-stimulation. There are severe impairments of intellectual, social, and emotional functioning. Such features as speech, language, cognitive, sensory, and relationship impairments are key symptoms.

**behavioral disorder (BD)**   A condition in which actions are so inappropriate, disruptive, and destructive that they interfere with education and social interaction for the individual and those around him or her. This term is often used interchangeably with *serious emotional disturbance (SED)*.

**behavior modification**   The systematic application of consequences to behavior, with the intent of strengthening desired behaviors and extinguishing undesired behaviors.

**compulsion**   An irresistible impulse to perform an act.

**disorder**   Reduced functioning, particularly in academic achievement (for example, learning disorders) or social adjustment (for example, behavior disorders).

**emotional disturbance (disorder)**   Refers to the condition of individuals who are not able to control their emotions and behavior in a socially acceptable manner.

**intelligence quotient (IQ)**   A score obtained from an intelligence test that provides a measure of mental ability in relationship to age. The statistical average for an intelligence test is set at 100 and refers to one regarded at the normal or average IQ.

**neurosis**   An emotional disorder usually characterized by anxiety, guilt, and moderately severe incapacitation.

**psychoeducational approach**   The application of psychological and educational remediation approaches in the school by teachers.

**schizophrenia**   A psychotic reaction with manifestations of loss of contact with reality and severe symptoms of bizarre, nonsensical thought processes and expression and inappropriate behavior.

**withdrawn behavior**   Behaviors that result in both physical and emotional detachments from other people and interfere with the successful development of interpersonal social relationships.

The National Institute of Mental Health in the U.S. Department of Health and Human Services has consistently estimated 10 percent of the school-age population as experiencing mental disorders (Haring, McCormick, & Haring, 1994). Some surveys even extend the estimates of children and youth with EBD to more than 20 percent (Meyen, 1996).

The U.S. Department of Education, Office of Special Education and Rehabilitation Services (OSERS), has estimated that between 1.2 and 2 percent of the school-age population are children with EBD. State program surveys (26 programs in 13 states) in the 1987–1989 school years estimated that about 10 percent of the child population was experiencing emotional disturbances serious enough to warrant the provision of special intervention. Of all the estimate ranges, which potentially identify between 1 and

10 million children disabled by EBD, only approximately 438,000 children with EBD receive special education public school services (U.S. Department of Education, 1997).

Some of the problems in estimating the number of children with severe emotional disturbance are:

1. Lack of agreement on definitional criteria.
2. Governmental confusion and inept data collection.
3. Subjectivity of judgments regarding screening, identification, diagnosis, and placement.
4. Governmental reluctance to include conduct disorders in the operational definition, in spite of gross evidence that children with severe emotional disturbance exhibit these patterns of behavior.
5. Public school personnel rejection of and reluctance to respond to these children, and the resulting tendency to force them out of school (Tompkins, 1996).

Clearly, the legislative requirement to provide educational and related services to all disabled children does apply to children with emotional and behavioral disorders. Even at the 2 percent estimate level, approximately 1,300,000 children would be identified as EBD. With only approximately 400,000 receiving services, there appear to be about 700,000 children with emotional and behavioral disorders going unserved in the public schools (Meyen, 1996). The reasons why these children go unserved are not clear.

## CHARACTERISTICS

### Intelligence and Achievement

Despite the limited research on intelligence of children with EBD compared with normal children, the philosophical problems associated with what is intelligence and the procedural flaws in intelligence testing, the majority of troubled children test only slightly below average in IQ, placing them in the dull normal or mildly retarded range. More compelling studies have indicated that children with disturbances tend to have average to marginally lower-than-average IQs compared with normal children (Bortner & Birch, 1969; Bower, 1981; Duncan, Forness, & Hartsough, 1995; Graubard, 1964; Lyons & Powers, 1963; Motto & Wilkins, 1968; Rubin & Balow, 1978; Kauffman, 1997). The more severe the EBD, the lower the IQ scores appear to be. Reliability studies have not determined whether the IQ scores for these children are stable or are associated with the severity of their mental disorders. The traditional position has been that these children tend to be regarded at the normal or above average intellectual functioning level. Generally, the IQ scores were believed to be depressed as a result of the EBD (Heward, 1996; Hardman et al., 1996).

Academic and school failure is a dominant characteristic of children with emotional and behavioral disorders. Many of these children are two or more academic years behind their peers, fail more courses, evidence higher absenteeism rates, and have a higher dropout rate than other students with disabilities. Troubled children experience social isolation and have difficulty in developing meaningful interpersonal relationships. They appear at the fringe of school extracurricular and social activities. They frequently exhibit antisocial behavior (externalizing their behavioral disorders). About two-thirds of children with serious disturbances who are placed in special education programs exhibit behaviors such as failure to remain seated, fighting, stealing, using profanity, interference with others and the educational program, destroying property, noncompliance, being argumentative, lying, exhibiting temper tantrums, being verbally abusive, and physically and aggressively attacking others. Yet other children with EBD exhibit withdrawal, apprehensiveness, reduced or little social interactions, sad or depressive feelings, daydreaming, and guilt feelings (internalizing behavior disorders). They can be shy, disinterested, and/or immature. Some youngsters frequently exhibit hyperactivity, overactivity, impulsivity, and overall attending problems, depending on the severity of the disability. Most troubled children are characterized as anxious and subject to depressions (Whelan, 1988; Hallahan and Kauffman, 1991; Kirk, Gallagher, & Anastasiow, 1993).

As a result, these children frequently join gangs, become substance abusers, are truant, and/or become delinquent (that is, are adjudicated).

Some common school related behaviors that these children reflect are:

- High rate of absenteeism and tardiness.
- Failing most subjects.
- Being two or more years behind academically.
- Not completing assignments.
- Returning assignments late, soiled, messy, sometimes with written profanity directed toward the teacher.
- Difficulty in following directions and maintaining attention.

Trippe (1966) suggested that children with EBD have the potential to succeed in school but lack the secondary skills such as attending, following directions, and using tools appropriately, which lead to school failure.

## Labels

Many labels or terms are used in reference to children in trouble. The most frequently used labels are *seriously emotionally disturbed, behaviorally disordered, emotional-behavioral disordered,* and *mentally disordered* or *mentally ill.* Other interchangeable labels used in the professional educational literature are *behavioral disabilities, emotionally handicapped, behaviorally handicapped, behaviorally-emotionally handicapped,* and *socioemotionally impaired.* Some professionals prefer to use nonclinical terms, such as *children in conflict* or *troubled children,* to reduce social stigma and confusion in making reference to these children (Meyen & Skrtic, 1988; Hallahan & Kauffman, 1991).

For many educators, it is reasonable to use behavioral descriptors rather than a label in reference to a child. When one describes a child's behavior, the audience will not be misled by a negatively stereotyping label and can draw their own conclusion about the child.

## ETIOLOGY

The following presentation about what causes these children to behave as they do provides a conceptual or theoretical approach to aid our understanding of children with emotional and behavioral disorders. The independent description of influences or causes presented here does not deny the proposition that influences across the models presented may be at play and that their interaction can contribute to a given child's adjustment problems.

Predisposing factors are described in the genetic or organic model, while precipitating factors are described in the psychodynamic model. The predisposing (genetic or organic) influences suggest that there are inherent influences increasing the probability of developing EBD, whereas precipitating influences are those that trigger and support EBD. Although we can identify several conceptual models explaining etiology, the specific causes of individual EBD in any given child are usually difficult to ascertain.

### Organic (Genetic) Factors

Numerous studies worldwide support the proposition that there is an organic or genetic correlation of determinants to mental disorders. While there is no question of a probable genetic cause for schizophrenia and depression, available data does not suggest conclusive proof (Eiduson, Eiduson, & Galler, 1962; Hallahan & Kauffman, 1991). Similarly, depression most likely has a genetic determinant, and it certainly has a biochemical cause (Smith & Luckasson, 1995). However, most experts suggest that the biological, genetic, or organic influences often interact with environmental experiences to produce behaviors (Plomin, 1995; Rutter, 1995). EBD cannot be tied to a single gene or chromosomal anomaly. Even with schizophrenia—where the closer the relationship between a child and a schizophrenic relative, the higher the risk for the child developing the disorder—the exact genetic mechanisms responsible for its predisposition are unknown (Plomin, 1995; Gottesman, 1987; Kauffman, 1997; Brown, 1995).

Studies in the genetics of schizophrenia, infantile autism, depression, anxiety, and related mental problems have often been made through the study of twins. By comparing the similarity between the behavior of monozygotic (identical) and dizygotic (fraternal) twins, medical researchers have established a relationship between serious mental illness (EBD) in children and factors of heredity. The assumption is that if all factors or influences are controlled except the twin relationship, the results will show the contribution or influence of genetics (heredity) to mental illness. While the evidence shows high correlations, it is not 100 percent conclusive. For example, if one identical twin is schizophrenic, the other twin is also likely to be schizophrenic;

studies suggest this relationship occurs in as many as 85 percent of the patients studied (Reinert, 1980; Karlson, 1966).

On an organic level, the ingestion of various toxic substances such as illegal drugs, tobacco, and alcohol by a child or pregnant mother may produce influences on the child's behavior. Gottesman (1987) warns that anyone with a genetic predisposition for mental illness should avoid cocaine, marijuana, LSD, and other hallucinogenic drugs. Additionally, severe nutritional deprivation can cause retardation as well as mental disorders (Haring et al., 1994). Central nervous system dysfunction and brain disorders also can play a role in the development of behavior disorders (Hunt & Marshall, 1994).

An operational definition as well as a statement on etiology for this model is that mental disorders are an inherited predisposition that may be constitutionally (genetically) based or triggered by environmental stress. Within the context of this model, EBD emerges as an outcome of a genetic aberration or a physiological and/or biochemical determinant (Heward, 1996).

## Psychodynamic Model

Psychodynamicists suggest that mental disorders (neuroses) result when the individual has been traumatized very early in life. These traumas generate unresolvable conflicts, from which anxiety emerges. The anxiety in turn causes feelings of apprehension to develop; this apprehension is the basis of subsequent defensive and ultimately neurotic reactions. The unconscious processes and other unobservable intrapsychic events relative to the psychosexual stages of development and personality structures such as the id, ego, and superego play an enormous role in the development of psychopathological responses. The psychodynamic model suggests that the interactional experiences of the mental process are out of balance. Thus the child's "inner life" is replete with conflicts, anxieties, distortions, and defensive gambits that distort reality and diminish cognition. In this model, EBD is regarded as a disease, with symptoms seen as behavioral manifestations that are the result of past unsatisfactorily resolved childhood conflicts, especially those influenced by parents (Meyen & Skrtic, 1988; Hunt & Marshall, 1994).

In psychodynamic terms, the individual unconsciously fears that primitive id instincts (sex and aggression) will overpower the ego (sense of self). Personality organization is thus upset and becomes disorganized, which results in further and excessive anxiety and guilt from the superego (sense of standards for right and wrong behavior). As a result, the child does not successfully resolve intrapsychic and external conflicts during the process of maturation. Theoretically, the child whose transition from the oral stage of development (feeling, learning to make appropriate sounds) to the anal stage (toilet training) has been too severe may experience adjustment problems at subsequent stages of development. Similarly, a child whose progression through the oedipal stage (sexual identification) has been unsatisfactory may have difficulty establishing appropriate relationships with members of the opposite sex later on in life (Reinert, 1980; Rezmierski & Kotre, 1972).

When proponents of the psychodynamic model see disturbance in a child, they search for causes that implicate parents and their child-rearing practices.

## Learning Model

The learning model is based on the idea that behavior is everything a child does. Behaviors are observable, measurable, and elicited by specific activities, and cause consequences in the environment that can be measured. Environmental reactions to behavior can either increase the likelihood of their reoccurrence or decrease this likelihood. Thus, in a negative example, when a child who is asked to sit down in class may instead stand, receiving the attention of classmates and increasing the likelihood of defiant behavior in the future.

Learning model adherents believe that emotional and behavioral disorders are learned maladaptive behaviors. Maladaptive behaviors are responses that are ineffective in coping with a problem or have undesirable side effects, causing failure, withdrawal, confusion, fear, and/or anxiety. Unlike the psychodynamically oriented professional, who looks for past experiences that might influence current behaviors, the learning model teacher is concerned about behavior as it occurs in the here and now, and only about what immediately causes behavior. Behaviors are repeated because of the pay-off, reward, or reinforcement they receive. Behavior is modifiable by changing the reactions it generates. Diagnosis of a behavior problem is based on observation and measurement. The emphasis is on the contingent relationship between the behavior and what supports the behavior—that is, the consequences a child receives depends on the behavior performed (Nelson, 1993).

Since, according to these theorists, maladaptive behaviors are learned, the child's environment must be closely examined. Factors in the environment not only initiate maladaptive behaviors, but also maintain these responses by reinforcing them. Children often learn undesirable behaviors because important people in their lives, including friends, reinforce such behaviors. Children may fail to develop necessary age-appropriate behaviors because such behaviors have not been elicited or reinforced, and they may become confused and erratic in their behavior because they are treated inconsistently (Kauffman, 1997).

Neuroses are seen as learned adjustments to conflicts and result from prolonged tension and conflict. Conflict both maintains itself and causes tension. Therefore, at the heart of neurosis is the self-maintenance of the conflict and tension.

Adherents to the learning model (behaviorists) do not deny the existence of private events, but question the utility of introducing such constructs as explanations for behavior. They emphasize stimuli (events that bring about or elicit behavior), responses (reactions to stimuli), and the use of reactions (consequences) to change behaviors. They admit that there may be underlying conflicts relative to the emergent unacceptable behavior, but they do not try to diagnose the child's underlying unconscious problem. Instead, they attempt to assess the present factors generating the observable maladaptive behavior (Kirk et al., 1993).

In summary, the basic tenets of behavioral theory are that emotional and behavioral disorders are learned through the consequences they generate (reinforcement)

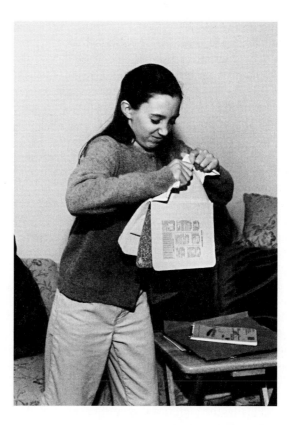

and thus can be shaped and changed through the same process. Behaviors associated with pleasant activities or consequences are most likely to be repeated and sustained. A behavior that is followed by a desirable consequence (positive reinforcement) or by the removal of an ongoing undesired consequence or unpleasant stimulus (negative reinforcement) will increase or become more likely to occur. Conversely, behaviors are less likely to recur when followed by an undesirable or unpleasant consequence (punishment) or the withholding or removal of a desired consequence, or better yet, ignored (extinction) (Zabel, 1991).

## Ecological Model

The ecological model advocates that deviance (disturbance) is the result of a misfit between the behavior of individuals and the dominant values or standards for behavior of the group or overall society that the child lives in. Emotional disturbance is created by discrete social or cultural forces outside the child. It is an interaction between the child and the child's surroundings. In this model, no behavior in itself is inherently "disturbed." Behavior is regarded in the context of the environment and/or living circumstances—that is, children live and act in systems and relationships. Therefore, disturbance is a result of a mismatch between individuals and their context. These environments (settings) contain *inductive forces*, which may be support-ive for desired behavior, or *seductive forces* for unwanted behavior. Change the individ-ual, change the context, or change both and the "disturbance" may be reduced or eliminated. The settings the child lives in, such as his or her home, school, classroom, neighbors, and community are identified as the ecosystem where the child fills a "niche" and plays out a role. This ecosystem seeks, demands, and covets tranquillity and equilibrium within itself by group leaders (parents, teachers, and so on) and members of the group (Smith & Luckasson, 1995; Turnbull et al., 1996).

If the child behaves in a way that is seen as troublesome for the group leader or the group members themselves, a dissonance or discomfort emerges between the child and the group leader or group. The troublesome behavior could be innocent, or it could be significantly difficult, intrusive behavior. At this point, an observer may in-dicate there is a poor fit (lack of "goodness of fit") between the child, the environment, and the "players" in that environment (Haring et al., 1994). For example, a child may be too combative or aggressive and intimidate other children in the group who are more passive, withdrawn, or noncombative.

Ecology theory implies one of two things: (1) all children have a reactive aspect to their behavior even when they have already habitualized considerable impaired be-havior; or (2) if we adequately reduce the external stress or restore balance, children will often recover on their own. The child needs a positive nurturing milieu, which will minimize undesired behavior and also foster normal growth. There is emphasis on the self-fulfilling prophecy that results when stigmatizing labeling communicates nega-tive feelings and expectations for a child, which, inevitably, the child will live out in unacceptable behavioral responses (Hunt & Marshall, 1994).

Finally, the significant contribution of ecological theory and interventions is to balance efforts directed toward the child with intervention directed toward the social settings. The child alone should not be blamed or scapegoated as the single cause of the problem.

In summary, proponents of the ecological theory see the problems of children with EBD as products of all the forces or influences, supportive or restrictive, existing in their environment. Looking at discrete sociocultural forces outside the child and the interactions between the child and the environment, EBD is defined within ecosystems (the child's life spaces at home or in the class, for example) and as a result of mis-matches or a lack of "goodness of fit" of interactions within these ecosystems (Fagen & Long, 1979; Morse & Smith, 1983). Thus, EBD must be reconceptualized in terms of the environment and the social context in which it occurs. Disturbance or "badness" is relative to the "goodness" or "badness" of an environment for a particular child, or the "goodness" of "badness" of the child for a particular environment (Rhodes, 1970). In this model, a variety of high-risk influences and causes for EBD exist, such as:

1. Physical and sexual abuse and neglect.

2. Inconsistent punitive discipline.

3. Rejection and poor adult role models.

4. Inept, hostile, acting-out teachers and other school personnel.

5. Divorce, violent neighborhoods, TV violence, and so forth.

6. Substance abuse.

7. Psychotic parents, death of loved ones, poverty, and/or a severe disabling or handicapping condition.

8. Homelessness. (Smith & Luckasson, 1995; Haring et al., 1994).

## IDENTIFICATION PROCESS

### Screening

Children suspected of having emotional-behavioral disorders are referred for screening only after teachers become concerned about these children's notable misbehaviors. The unacceptable behavior is usually observed for some time and is well documented, with preceding conferences with parents and other school personnel. After the referral, the school assessment team or school based committee composed of teachers and other school staff will observe the child and assessment procedures will be implemented (Barrios, 1993). Typically, behavior rating or inventory scales are used to provide a profile for behavior analysis. This screening procedure should eliminate children who are not truly disturbed and children with adjustment problems. Several widely used screening tests are the *Process for In-School Screening of Children with Emotional Handicaps* (Bower & Lambert, 1962), the *Aschenbach Behavior Checklist* (Aschenbach, 1991), the *Revised Behavior Problem Checklist* (Quay & Peterson, 1987), *Systematic Screening for Behavioral Disorders* (SSBD) (Walker & Severson, 1990), and the *Behavior Rating Profile* (BRP) (Brown & Hammill, 1983).

These inventories or rating scales are organized primarily for teacher use, with some allowing for peers to rate the child. Specific behaviors of notable maladjustment that appear serious and chronic, are in high frequency, and are intense are recorded. Some scales simply note the behavior, while others ask the rater to indicate the behavior as "True" to "Not True." One scale provides a classification system over six clinical dimensions including 89 items. Another scale rank orders children on profiles of two dimensions: externalizing problems (antisocial behavior, acting out, aggression) and internalizing problems (withdrawal, anxiety, social isolation). The most difficult students from the list are tracked by a Critical Events Index, which highlights and characterizes the behaviors. Some scales profile a sociogram that illustrates the child's role and functions in the group. The rating scales vary in the number of items used and in the range of scores for each item. An example is "using sexual profanity." This is rated on a scale of *frequently, sometimes*, or *infrequently*. Teachers' ratings may be very accurate, but they are not sufficient for a complete assessment (Nelson, 1993; Heward, 1996; Meyen & Skrtic, 1988). Rating scales are easy to administer inventories that have varying validity and reliability. They should not be used for diagnostic purposes; they are useful devices to distinguish children who are potentially EBD from other children, but they must be used with other instruments or practices for accurate identification (Kauffman, 1997).

In addition to checklists, the following identification procedures are routinely used:

*Interviews*: A representative of the school or the evaluation team may interview the child and other important people in the child's life to isolate the overriding problem.

*Ecological Assessments*: Observations are conducted at the home, and classroom isolating dynamics that appear to either ameliorate or exacerbate the children's reaction to life circumstances are studied. Very often, social workers perform these evaluations (Brown & Hammill, 1990).

*Self-reports/self-concept measures*: These instruments may inform educators about children's level of anxiety, impulsivity or aggression, or how worthwhile they see themselves (Kauffman, 1997).

The most effective approach in conducting identification and diagnostic procedures is a systematic, comprehensive, and multidisciplinary approach. The child should be evaluated by regular and special education teachers and appropriate clinicians across the cognitive, affective, social, academic, medical, and functional domains. Additional information regarding adaptive behavior, motor skills, neurological functioning, and perceptual abilities may be needed.

When children with EBD are compared with normal peers, they usually tend to score lower on measures of intelligence, language age, and academic achievement, especially in language arts (reading, writing, spelling, and so on). They also display inadequate social skills.

## Diagnosis

**Projective Tests.**    Projective tests are often used in the diagnosis of children with emotional and behavioral disorders. These tests present vague ambiguous stimuli such as inkblots, cartoonlike characters, and sentence or word completion tests. The responses are open-ended, "whatever comes to your mind" responses, and there are no "right" or "wrong" answers. Projective tests are developed to help individuals reveal inner wishes, conflicts, feelings, and/or fantasies. Some projective tests are:

- The *Rorschach Psychodiagnostic Plates* (Rorschach, 1942), which consists of a set of ten cards, each illustrated with an inkblot. The child is asked to construct a story about the inkblot or parts of the inkblot.
- The *Children's Apperception Test* (Wicks-Nelson & Israel, 1991), which requests that the child view a series of pictures and provide a story or narrative about what the figures are doing, saying, feeling, and so on.
- *Draw a Person: Screening Procedure for Emotional Disturbance* (Nagheri, McMeish, & Bardos, 1991), where the child is asked to draw pictures of a man, a woman, and the child.

All of these tests are analyzed by psychologically trained professionals who attempt to determine whether themes indicative of emotional disturbance appear during the responses. Some children may also undergo psychiatric diagnostic interviews conducted by medical or clinical personnel such as psychiatrists, psychiatric social workers, nurses, and clinical psychologists.

**Achievement and IQ Tests.** Children with behavioral-emotional disorders should be tested on an individual basis regarding intelligence and achievement. Achievement tests measure the level of mastery that the child must have to progress to a new skill. Curriculum-based achievement tests use actual items from the classroom curriculum for testing purposes to determine achievement progress. Teacher-made achievement tests or performance assessments determine what the students have learned over a period of time without necessarily using a paper/pencil test (Hardman et al., 1996).

The entire assessment and diagnostic evaluation procedure should cover all of the previously mentioned domains and areas, including screening test results and information from educators, clinicians, and other appropriate personnel. The administrative placement or IEP committee will then convene to review all information to certify the child for a particular placement and for needed services relative to the judged degree of emotional disturbance (Bateman & Chard, 1995).

## Misdiagnosis Possibilities

Children are vulnerable to misdiagnosis and misplacement as a result of:

- *Self-fulfilling prophecy*, in which attitudes, feelings, and expectations of significant people in children's lives can markedly influence outcome behavior.
- *Social/cultural/racial issues*, in which significant adults in children's lives are consciously or unconsciously prejudiced against them relative to race or culture and thereby have a negative influence on behavior.
- *Counteraggressive school personnel*, or adults who act out physically, sexually, verbally, or emotionally and abuse children to retaliate or relieve their own angry, hostile feelings toward the "offending" child.

## PROGRAMS

The previously discussed etiological models used to understand emotional and behavioral disorders often dictate the treatments that children will receive. Programming can be based upon a psychoeducational model, a learning theory or behavioral model, or an ecological model.

## Psychoeducational Programming

Psychoeducational intervention often has its basis in some fundamental psychodynamic conceptual issues. It offers a balance between the clinical or treatment approach and the educational or remedial approach. In terms of clinical/treatment issues, psychoeducational intervention supports:

1. Conflict resolution on both the intrapersonal level (reduction of anxiety) and the interpersonal or group level (reduction of aggression and other antisocial behavior).

2. Emphasis on the affective domain by helping children recognize the authenticity of their feelings and how these feelings influence or determine behavior outcomes.

3. Highlighting the value of relationships and their development as a central component of socialization.

4. Facilitating the development of control of feelings, impulses, and behaviors.

5. Emphasis on self-concept and self-esteem.

6. Program entitlement for the child with no strings—that is, programs are not withheld as a punishment and are quickly restored to the child after a serious behavioral episode (Haring et al., 1994; Kauffman, 1997; Long, 1996).

Programmatically, these influences are planned and implemented via the careful *therapeutic milieu (setting) arrangement*. Management of surface behaviors includes emphasis on structure and tolerating certain "unacceptable" behaviors. Inherent in these practices are the use of the Lifespace Interview, reality therapy, transactional analysis, social skills training, and self-control curriculum. Again, in these approaches, the objectives in helping the child are to resolve conflict and reduce anxiety by allowing the child to express the feelings at the base of his or her behavior. Although there appears to be some emphasis on the treatment issues, these approaches provide equal focus on educational and remedial services (Heward, 1996; Long, 1986).

An important skill needed by teachers who are implementing these programs is the ability to design an effective environment for the school program and to interact effectively with children in a noncritical, accepting, and open-ended manner (Fagen, 1981; Heuchert, 1983; Morse, 1961; Redl, 1969). Such interactions facilitate learning, encourage overall development, and create an environment in which immediate behavior problems can be managed well, thus enhancing student/teacher enjoyment of the classroom environment.

"Children with emotional, behavioral and/or learning problems need much more than specific intervention strategies provided on a piecemeal basis. They need a total intervention aimed at every facet of their lives, their environments, and yes, their ecosystems" (Hewett, 1981). In a therapeutic milieu in the public schools, every aspect of children's lives in the school situation is involved. The milieu is the matrix in which recognition of the value and dignity of children is evident. *Milieu therapy* is the organization of the school environment for the purpose of having a healthy impact on the child. The totality of the child's experience is considered in creating a safe environment that is structured to foster relationships and activities (Hewett, 1981).

Historically, milieu therapy was intended to expose a child or group of children to total environmental design for treatment. The milieu was designed and manipulated with the aim of producing personality changes (Cumming & Cumming, 1966) to meet the special socialization and learning needs of children with serious emotional and behavioral disorders. The environment was designed to nurture, to gratify needs and desires, to encourage and sustain interpersonal relationships, and to help children learn self-regulation and impulse control. Children had the opportunity to master life situations, undistracted by concerns about their basic needs, which were to be recognized and met in the milieu. As they learned to trust in the consistent gratification of their needs, they were also confronted with the strength and comprehensive structure of an environment that could neither be destroyed nor controlled by their misbehavior (Bettelheim & Sylvester, 1949). Thus, they learned that they could safely and effectively have an impact on their world, and that their feelings and wishes did not lead to disaster.

Milieu therapy works through amelioration of a child's previous experiential deficiencies and builds on strengths the child has acquired. No action or practice is too trivial to be considered in proper maintenance of this "good place." Milieu therapy at school identifies the major elements of the classroom and other school settings and analyzes how they act on one another and how each must be adjusted in order for the best of all possible worlds to be attained in fostering the child's socialization and learning.

While therapeutic milieu techniques were developed for troubled children, they can be of immense benefit to all children and to teachers who wish to create a climate that is most conducive to growth and learning. A therapeutic milieu will naturally transform children, acting to prevent potential problems as well as helping to ameliorate problems that are already present.

**The Life Space Interview.**    The Life Space Interview (LSI) is a structured, planned, deliberate way of talking effectively with children about their problems and feelings. The use of this specialized verbal exchange is an important element in a therapeutic environment. It is used for problem solving (Brendtro & Ness, 1983), for control and disciplinary purposes, or for understanding more completely how the child feels, which facilitates mutual insight into his or her behavior. It assists children in understanding and coping with a specific current event that they could not handle on their own (Heuchert & Long, 1981). It is "here and now" intervention, focusing on a clear issue or behavioral incident in the direct life experience of the child at the moment of its occurrence or as close to the time of the problem as possible. Because problem situations in the child's day-to-day life have strategic therapeutic importance when they can be dealt with immediately (Vernick, 1963), the interviewer engages a child at the very time and in the very place, on the spot and in the child's life space, at which the troubling event occurs.

The school milieu is an ideal setting in which to use the Life Space Interview. Teachers' utilization of the Life Space Interview in schools seems a natural supplement in programming for children in trouble. It is a generic technique that can be used with any child in a school setting. The key to improved school mental health, Morse (1961) believed, is the classroom teacher's increased ability to deal effectively and hygienically with day-to-day life events. The Life Space Interview provides the needed focus. While the teacher is not expected to become involved in deep therapeutic interviews, there is much to be said for verbal discourse, on the spot, at times of crisis in day-to-day interaction with children. The Life Space Interview can be used in schools to ease, work through, and learn from critical events transpiring in the classroom or elsewhere in school. It capitalizes on occurrences in the immediate life space of the child and facilitates intervention into problems in a child's life by a person who has direct life experience meaning for the child (Wineman, 1959). Morse (1961) found that the "Life Space Interview embodies a theory and method uniquely suited to the teacher's responsibilities in group management, social adjustment, and social learning. Hence, it is seen as the prototype of adult-child interaction both for generating control and for working through social and personal situations which develop in almost any classroom." (p. 331)

The Life Space Interview technique does not replace the total range of techniques for managing and changing behavior; rather, it supplements them. Life-space theory does not argue that traditional methods are not effective, but rather that the Life Space Interview can be used as a powerful adjunct to these methods or can be used by itself to assist children with troubled and troublesome behavior (Wineman, 1959).

The Life Space Interview is based on noncritical, accepting, and therapeutic principles and is ongoing and open-ended in children's everyday environment. The tools composing the full range of the Life Space Interview are designed to help children get over the rough spots (emotional first aid) or gain insight and motivation to develop more satisfactory means of responding to problems (clinical exploitation of life events). If understood and adapted to individual needs and specific school settings, the methods and techniques of the Life Space Interview can help school personnel deal constructively with a variety of problems. The LSI can provide not only increased understanding of children and youth in schools, but also insight into the professional problems, and their possible solutions, of teachers and administrators (Long, 1990).

In the Life Space Interview, the teacher enters the immediate life experience (or life space) of the child and deals with a crisis whenever it occurs (Wood & Long, 1991). Many children do not remember the details of events long enough and may, indeed, develop distorted recollections too quickly for next Wednesday to be soon enough to talk to them about last Friday's behavior and feelings. Some children do not understand cause and effect and time relationships. If *past* and *future* do not mean much, then *now* is the essential consideration.

The Life Space Interview was developed as a systematic array of responses to children with disturbances. The combination of individual psychotherapy and therapeutic milieu practices was often insufficient in the comprehensive care of children in treatment. The LSI supplemented treatment efforts occurring outside the classroom. While the school counselor, an outside therapist, or others may engage children in therapy or other means of assistance, they may never see either the crises or the opportunities for intervention in the child's everyday life space (Long, Morse, & Newman, 1991).

Although the Life Space Interview originated in work with children with emotional disturbances, it is readily adaptable to many settings. Using the LSI in the school setting capitalizes on its more generic qualities to help children through the usual crises of living and growing up. Cutler and McNeil (1962) found the use of the "emotional first aid" strategies of the LSI during moments of high stress an effective tool in preventive and remedial mental health efforts. The natural first-aid station is in the classroom and school, where the teacher is most available. Significant alterations in the child's basic approach to the world can be brought about by direct life space management techniques. In school, manifestations of a child's problems are likely to be at an action-behavioral level, and the child is developmentally open to acquiring new social tools. Through use of the LSI, the child is offered new opportunities for alternative problem-solving methods.

**Transactional Analysis.**    Transactional analysis is an intervention to help children realize and experience that they are good, worthwhile, or "OK." It is also used to help children relate better and get along with parents, teachers, and other adults. Children are helped to deal with a wide range of their emotions. Older children can be helped with topics such as drugs, sex, rebellion, and striving for independence. Transactional analysis provides a curricular approach to developing interpersonal communication skills in small groups. For example, the children sit in a circle (the Magic Circle Curriculum) and freely discuss human relations topics about themselves and others to arrive at some insight into their feelings, relationships, and other personal concerns (Berne, 1965; Freed, 1977; Bessell & Palomares, 1970).

**Social Skills Self-Control Curriculum.**    Specific social skills need to be taught explicitly and systematically to many students with EBD. Desired conduct needs to be frequently and effectively rewarded (Mayer, 1995; Walker, 1995; Kauffman, 1997). Social skills, especially verbal and conversational skills, are necessary to successfully interact with others. These skills may relate to peers, teachers, or tasks performed at school. The teacher using this curriculum organizes learning tasks such as following directions, asking and answering questions, joining other students in conversation, or resisting peer pressure. These are the skills needed to get along with others in the class group and to control inappropriate behavior by means of self-management. The child is taught how to develop internal controls by means of structure and appropriate modeling of self-control from adults, including self-assessment, self-instruction, self-monitoring, and self-reinforcement (Howell, 1985; Kauffman, 1997).

**Reality Therapy.**    In reality therapy, children's rationalization for unacceptable behavior is rejected by the teacher. Excuses are not valid justifications for "wrong" behavior. Teachers are allowed to make value judgments about wrong or unjustifiable behavior. Glasser (1965) emphasizes that children are responsible for their behavior. Acceptance of society's rules and regulations are required, as is the acknowledgment that there is a "right and wrong" about behavior. Therefore, individuals in this program must learn to view all their behavior as good or bad, adaptive or maladaptive; and must learn, with the teacher's application of consequences for bad behavior, the more acceptable responses. The various procedures of this program recognize the interactional nature between affective and cognitive processes, and bring the teacher and the child together to jointly work out incidents of troubling events at the time and place the trouble occurs.

In summary, the psychoeducational model considers basic needs as motivations in personality development. These include the need for a well developed, positive self-image; the need to feel loved and to feel that one belongs; and satisfaction of physiological needs, safety needs, and the need for self-fulfillment (Zabel, 1991). The psychoeducator uses the tools of education and remediation but does not focus exclusively on increasing cognitive ability and academic skills. An equal emphasis is on affective development and on learning to understand, cope with, and control one's feelings and to promote appropriate expressions of feelings and personality development. Interpersonal and physical/educational environments are manipulated to sustain maximum emotional support for the child. The psychoeducational approach considers both intrapsychic and educational matters in making educational decisions. Group processes and crisis situations are used to develop insight and conflict resolution (Brown, 1981; Cullinan, Epstein & Lloyd, 1991).

## Behavioral Intervention

Behavior modification interventions employ basic reinforcement techniques to assist children's socialization and learning. This intervention is focused on the belief that behavior is a function of its consequences. Typically, reinforcement procedures such as positive reinforcement, when a pleasant or rewarding stimulus is applied immediately following an appropriate behavior, are employed. Of the many positive or rewarding strategies possible, the goal is to provide some type of external reward when the child performs the targeted behavior. Reductions of inappropriate target behavior can be achieved by presenting an unpleasant or aversive experience (punishment) such as time-out or loss of play time after an unwanted behavior. Other procedures such as modeling, performance feedback, or prompting can be used to assist children. This approach encourages the development of a highly structured learning environment where the student's behaviors are carefully observed and measured (counted) and intervention is designed to increase desirable behavior or eliminate undesirable behavior (Hardman et al., 1996).

The initial task of the behaviorist involves assessing the particular behavioral needs of the child. Baseline data (measures taken before any intervention is attempted) must be collected to determine the frequency of those behaviors one wishes to change (targeted behaviors), as well as the context in which those behaviors occur. While standardized assessment instruments can provide information regarding the particular skills that a child has compared to other children, baseline data provide information about a specific child's growth. These data also provide a basis from which to measure the effectiveness of intervention strategies, since frequency of the occurrence of the target behavior can be measured and compared to baseline data as the intervention program proceeds.

Once baselines have been established, it is necessary to identify the undesirable behaviors and those desirable alternative behaviors that one wishes to foster. A teacher needs to be cautious when selecting behaviors for modification. The type, frequency, duration, and intensity of the target behavior must be analyzed. The behaviors most often selected are those that interfere most with classroom processes or the student's overall functioning. The behaviors must be discrete, observable, and measurable (Walker & Shea, 1987). Box 5.2 illustrates potential target behaviors.

***Box 5.2***
***WHAT EVERY TEACHER NEEDS TO KNOW***

# PRE-REFERRAL BEHAVIOR CHECKLIST

Stephen B. McCarney, Ed.D.

Name of Student: _____ _____ _____    Age: _____ _____  Sex: _____
                        (last)            (first)          (middle)              (years)  (months)

School: _____  City: _____  State: _____

Grade Level: _____  Date(s) of Rating: _____ _____ _____
                                                          (month)        (day)         (year)

Has Student Ever Received Special Education Services: _____

_____

Grades Repeated: _____  Reason (if known): _____

Rated by: _____  Position: _____

Student Known to Rater: _____ _____  Length of Time Each Day With Student: _____ _____
                          (from)     (to)                                            (hours)  (minutes)

How Well the Student is Known by the Rater (Indicate type of interactions): _____

_____

_____

## COMMENTS

Copyright © 1988
Hawthorne Educational Services, Inc.

Page 1

## Box 5.2 continued

| TO TEACHER: Check each behavior you have observed the student demonstrate during the last month. |
|---|

### LEARNING

☐ 1. Does not work on assignments during class time

☐ 2. Does not turn in homework

☐ 3. Is disorganized

☐ 4. Performs assignments carelessly

☐ 5. Does not work independently

☐ 6. Fails tests or quizzes

☐ 7. Is not motivated by rewards

☐ 8. Is not prepared

☐ 9. Does not remain on task

☐ 10. Performs below ability level

☐ 11. Does not follow written directions

☐ 12. Does not follow verbal directions

☐ 13. Is reluctant to attempt new assignments or tasks

☐ 14. Limited memory skills

☐ 15. Has difficulty understanding abstract concepts

☐ 16. Does not comprehend what he/she reads

☐ 17. Requires repeated drill and practice

### INTERPERSONAL RELATIONS

☐ 18. Fights with other students

☐ 19. Becomes physically aggressive with teachers

☐ 20. Makes inappropriate comments to teachers

☐ 21. Responds adversely to praise or recognition

☐ 22. Is easily angered, annoyed, or upset

☐ 23. Agitates/provokes peers to a level of verbal or physical assault

☐ 24. Has little or no interaction with teachers

☐ 25. Has little or no interaction with peers

☐ 26. Makes inappropriate comments to peers

☐ 27. Responds adversely to being bumped, touched, brushed against

☐ 28. Responds inappropriately to friendly teasing

☐ 29. Is not accepted by other students

☐ 30. Bothers other students

☐ 31. Responds inappropriately to others' attempts to be friendly, complimentary, sympathetic, etc.

☐ 32. Does not share possessions or materials

☐ 33. Does not allow others to take their turn or participate

### INAPPROPRIATE BEHAVIOR UNDER NORMAL CIRCUMSTANCES

☐ 34. Makes unnecessary comments/noises

☐ 35. Has unexcused absences

☐ 36. Has unexcused tardiness

☐ 37. Makes unnecessary physical contact with others

☐ 38. Blames other persons or materials

☐ 39. Steals or forcibly takes things from others

☐ 40. Behaves inappropriately when others do well or receive praise or attention

41. Inappropriate seat behavior

42. Behaves inappropriately for the situation

43. Avoids situations, assignments, responsibilities

44. Behaves impulsively, without self-control

45. Exhibits extreme mood changes

46. Is unpredictable

47. Does not follow directives from teachers or other school personnel

48. Ignores consequences of his/her behavior

49. Inappropriate sexually-related behavior

50. Is easily overexcited

51. Lies, denies, exaggerates, distorts the truth

52. Brings inappropriate or illegal materials to school

53. Destroys school or other students' property

54. Cheats

55. Has difficulty moving with a group

56. Responds adversely to redirection

57. Has difficulty accepting change

58. Does not follow school rules

59. Does not care about academic performance

60. Needs immediate rewards/reinforcement

61. Does not care for personal appearance

62. Engages in inappropriate behaviors related to bodily functions

63. Does not change behavior from one situation to another

## UNHAPPINESS/DEPRESSION

64. Does not participate

65. Blames self for situations beyond his/her control

66. Is easily upset by a suggestion or constructive criticism

67. Threatens to hurt self or commit suicide

68. Feels no one likes or cares about him/her

69. Does not smile, laugh, or appear happy

70. Is apathetic

71. Is overly critical of self

72. Frowns, scowls, looks unhappy

73. Is pessimistic

## PHYSICAL SYMPTOMS/FEARS

74. Is preoccupied with problems unrelated to school

75. Demonstrates self-destructive behavior

76. Moves about unnecessarily

77. Speaks in an unnatural voice

78. Speaks incoherently

79. Engages in nervous habits

80. Throws temper tantrums

81. Reacts physically when excited (e.g., flaps hands, stutters, trembles, etc.)

82. Becomes pale, may throw up, or passes out when anxious or frightened

83. Demonstrates phobic-type reactions (e.g., fear of school, speaking in front of a group, etc.)

*Box 5.2 continued*

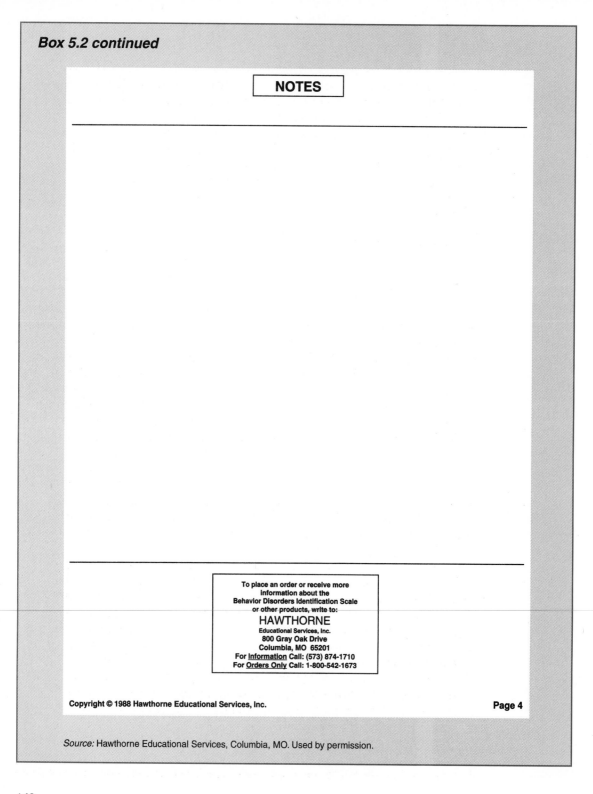

**NOTES**

To place an order or receive more
information about the
Behavior Disorders Identification Scale
or other products, write to:

**HAWTHORNE**
Educational Services, Inc.
800 Gray Oak Drive
Columbia, MO 65201
For <u>Information</u> Call: (573) 874-1710
For <u>Orders Only</u> Call: 1-800-542-1673

*Source:* Hawthorne Educational Services, Columbia, MO. Used by permission.

The effects of various factors in the environment on the child's behavior must be determined by answering questions such as "What immediately precedes the target behavior?" and "What happens just after the behavior occurs?" One must also determine what each child perceives as desirable or undesirable consequences. What may be rewarding to one child may be a neutral or even negative experience for another.

The behavioral approach requires a highly structured program to which the child is expected to attend, comply, and respond. One very important element of this approach is instructional control. Instructions must be clear, consistent, and brief, and the environment must be free from extraneous stimuli (Hewett, 1968). Training sessions are short at first but are gradually extended.

When a new skill is taught, immediate reinforcement of each desired behavior occurs, contingent on the completion of that behavior. Later in the teaching process, the reinforcement can gradually be delayed and presented on a variable schedule. If it is determined that attention is reinforcing some maladaptive behavior, systematically withholding attention (planned ignoring) at each occurrence of the behavior becomes the treatment of choice to facilitate the extinction of the unwanted behavior. The behaviorist makes an effort to attend to the child and reinforce behaviors that are incompatible with the unwanted behavior. For example, if the unwanted behavior is leaving his or her seat, the teacher will ignore the child during this behavior but praise or reward the child when he or she is seated. The child often actively resists this process, and a teacher may see a definite, but temporary, increase in the targeted behavior or the intensity of the behavior in the initial stages of implementing such a plan. Barring unacceptable levels of self-injurious behavior, aggression, or destruction of property, it is best to continue the ignoring program, even in the face of this increased negative behavior. An abandonment of the procedure would be seen as desirable by the child, and the undesirable behaviors would be reinforced.

Social reinforcers such as affection, praise, and attention can be powerful for instilling appropriate behaviors. It may be necessary to use concrete reinforcers such as food or tokens at first; however, they should gradually be replaced by social reinforcers so that ordinary social interactions and reactions will eventually be the cues to which the child is responsive.

*Shaping* is an important technique that springs from behavioral theory. Starting with a response already existing in the child's repertoire, the teacher identifies a number of behavioral steps toward a desired skill. Only after the child acquires stable performance at a given step is the next one introduced. If the child fails to master any step along the way, he or she must return to the preceding step to regain stable performance before advancing toward the goal. This technique can also be referred to as "errorless learning" and gives the learner reinforcement through continued success. When stable performance is obtained on the target skill, the shaping procedure is considered complete. Shaping can be useful in teaching many skills, including language, self-help, motor, academic, pre-academic, and prevocational skills. When a particular behavior has been learned through shaping procedures, it can be linked with other behaviors to form a *behavior chain* under the control of a single instruction. A prompt can be used to guide the child toward the desired response to a directive, thus maximizing the child's opportunities for reinforcement. Prompts may consist of giving the child the correct response, physically assisting (that is, placing the child's body, hand, mouth, and so on in the correct position to perform the activity), modeling the desired response (that is, the instructor performing the expected task), or giving cues that indicate the behavior to be performed. When prompts are no longer needed, they are *faded* (that is, they become less obvious and intrusive until they are no longer used) so that only the training directive remains.

Through a combination of shaping, prompting, and chaining procedures, an effective training program can be developed that is consistent across the various environments a child encounters. Consistency is essential for target behaviors, goals, and procedures to be carried out. A team approach, with communication and continued training opportunities among people in all aspects of the child's environment, is vital. While negative reinforcement may sometimes be used, the use of punishment with human beings is not generally advocated by ethical behaviorists.

## Ecological Intervention

Advocates of this model suggest that classroom, school, home, and community environmental influences should also be targeted for change, along with providing treatments and educational interventions to change the child. Key people close and influential in the child's ecosystem in these settings are encouraged to collaborate and be jointly involved regarding the child's needs.

Project Re-Education is the most notable intervention flowing from the ecological model. Teacher-counselors working in short-term residential treatment with children with emotional and behavioral disorders provide intensive educational remedial academic work for the students. The team of teacher-counselors collaborates and provides activities at the child's home and with the teacher and class to which the child will be returned. All of these influences at home and school will be organized to help the child when he or she is slowly and systematically returned to his or her home, the school, and the community. The goal is to create a better fit between the child and his or her class, school, family, and neighborhood. The central feature to this program is the extensive liaison work with all the major people in the child's life, so that the child can function at his or her return (Turnbull et al., 1995).

Ecological interventions have a common goal of adapting the fit between the setting and the person in order to establish harmony and balance between the child and the surrounding subsystems of the environment. Such interventions operate on the belief that taking the child out of the environment makes it impossible to view or address the problem, because the problem exists within the environment of which the child is an integral part. In this approach, there are no "bad kids" and no behaviors that are essentially disturbed. Badness is relative to the goodness or badness of an environment for a particular child, or the goodness or badness of the child for a particular environment. Interventions do not focus on one set of variables to the exclusion of others; rather, problem behavior is viewed as a global interaction between the individual

and his or her environment. Ideal intervention measures enter the actively disturbed situation, identify the point of convulsive encounter between the child and the surrounding human community, and then trace the problem to its cultural source in the surrounding context, both in terms of people and the cultural practices and influences of the microcommunity and ecological unit (Rhodes, 1970). Because the ecological perspective encourages the development of interventions that reduce interactive disharmony by focusing on the child and the environment simultaneously, it allows integration of practices from sociological, behavioral, organic, and psychodynamic intervention theories.

Rhodes (1967) summarized the goals and impact of the ecological perspective by saying that the emotionally disturbed child affects and is affected by his or her community and that this reciprocal relationship should be taken into consideration in any attempt to describe or treat the disturbance. Changes in environmental components such as physical objects, people, events, or locations may change the child's relationship to the environment, producing either positive or negative changes in behavior. Therefore, focusing attention on the child to the exclusion of family, school, and community can make identification and remediation of difficulties almost impossible. This is consistent with IDEA requirements that school personnel and parents collaborate to develop diagnostic, placement, and IEP procedures.

## Other Interventions

*Cognitive strategy approaches* are procedures and methods referred to as self-monitoring, self-instruction, and/or self-control strategies. When employing these approaches, the child is assisted to deliberate about his or her behavior and how to consciously manage the behavior via self-monitoring, self-evaluation, self-reinforcement, and self-instruction. These approaches are organized to help students develop their self-awareness and self-direction while they are being reinforced to be more socialized and better learners.

*Drug treatment* provides appropriate medications to ameliorate children's depressions, hyperactivity, and other co-existing severe symptoms.

*Instructional methods* and *curriculum content* are often manipulated when attempting to respond to each student's interests and ability level. Curricular emphasis ranges from teaching life, academic, and social skills to helping these children cope with their current problems and prepare for future independent functioning. Direct instructional procedures in concert with direct teaching methods are regarded as effective approaches. Social skills training utilizes behavioral modification, while affective strategies are typically employed using volunteers, parents, and student peers in the academic and socialization programming (Clarke et al., 1995).

Some experts have suggested that the content of the curriculum may not need to be different from that used with children who are not disabled, except that the curriculum may be several grade levels earlier.

Some common therapeutic elements to all of the major remedial interventions are that:

1. Programs are well structured; the arrangement of the learning environment is carefully designed with established routines, rules, and limits. Curricular and other activities are carefully planned and implemented. The experiences of children are characterized by clear directions, expectations that the child will do as directed, and consistent follow-through in applying consequences for behavior.

2. Programs are established so that the adults using them expend vast energy to communicate love, affection, and gratifying experiences with no strings or conditions.

3. Programs of effective remedial education are initiated to enable the child to become a successful student.

4. Programs are developed to increase appropriate socialization and social skills.

5. Parents in collaboration with teachers are included to support the child's programs at home and at school (Tompkins & Tompkins-McGill, 1993).

All of the interventions described support the monumental requirements of the development and maintenance of a positive, meaningful relationship between the child and the teacher, group activities to help children cope with and enjoy relationships with peers in the group, structuring guidelines, scheduling, learning rules, and learning the consequences of behaviors (Meyen & Skrtic, 1988; Kirk et al., 1993; Nelson, 1993).

## ISSUES OF IMPORTANCE

We have already highlighted several critical issues that affect the education of children with emotional and behavioral disorders. Issues for the reader to be aware of are:

- IQ scores of children with EBD are typically depressed, even though the children may in reality be of average intelligence or in some cases intellectually superior to their peers.
- Definitions, characterizations, labels, diagnoses, and etiological beliefs are generally developed from subjective opinions.
- The new and proposed definition of *emotional and behavioral disorder* was constructed or developed by a majority of clinicians, not educators, and could be regarded as educationally irrelevant.
- IQ tests measure past learning, prior opportunity to learn, or enrichment and are good predictors only of future school or academic success.
- Screening, identification, assessment, and diagnosis should be multidisciplinary.
- Prevalence estimates are unrealistic.

The remaining four issues will be highlighted and further developed in this section of the chapter.

### Can Emotional and Behavioral Disorders Be Cured?

When treatment programs are successful, children will be responsive to the therapeutic and educational interventions provided by special educators, counselors, and psychotherapists. As a result of these treatment programs, the children give up symptomatic behaviors, change maladaptive behaviors, and become more socialized. These changes can be considered a cure.

### Why Are Conduct Disorders Excluded from Operational Definitions?

There is no educational or behavioral justification for the exclusion of conduct disorders from the operational definition of serious emotional disturbance. It appears that conduct disorders were omitted from the original definitions and Public Law 94-142 by oversight. Currently there is sentiment to include conduct disorders in the classification system.

### What Are the Implications of Children Being Regarded as EBD on the Basis of Having Violated Classroom Rules?

When children are viewed as disturbed simply on the basis of rule breaking, serious misdiagnosis can occur. Viewing rule-breaking children in the same light as children with behavioral and emotional disorders will often lead to inappropriate placement and exposing the child to inappropriate teaching and behavior modification strategies.

## What Are the Needs of Institutionalized Children?

When children are appropriately institutionalized, they are affected by the most profound mental disturbances. They may be psychotic, perpetrate aggravated aggression, or experience heightened anxiety reactions. The primary need of these children is often the stabilization that can be brought about by medical and pharmacological interventions. In these cases, educational programming is appropriate when it can be tolerated by the child.

## MINORITY CONCERNS

Children from diverse racial and ethnic minorities are especially vulnerable to the effects of negative stereotyped expectations. They are frequently stigmatized and discriminated on the basis of their race, ethnic, or economic status. These children are often misdiagnosed and misplaced in the most restrictive and inappropriate settings on the proposition of perceived divergent social, behavioral, or academic standards. They are often seen in a depreciating point of view and are expected to misbehave and fail in schoolwork. They are often mislabeled and misclassified (Hobbs, 1975; CCBD, 1996).

Social class and socioeconomic status often influence educators and clinicians in schools toward misdiagnosis and misclassification. Antisocial or neighborhood determined behavior from children in a ghetto or lower-class neighborhood may lead them into the correctional system, while white middle-class children enter psychotherapy (Hobbs, 1975).

Culturally and racially diverse students continue to be overrepresented in special education classes for troubled students. They tend to be in more restrictive settings and have a higher dropout rate and earlier arrest rates after leaving school than white middle-class children (Heward, 1996).

## PROFESSIONALS

A wide variety of clinical and educational professionals are involved in the treatment and education of children with behavioral and emotional disorders. Professionals include regular and special education teachers, school psychologists, case or psychiatric social workers, psychiatric nurses, clinical psychologists, and psychiatrists. These professionals work in a variety of settings, such as public schools, residential programs and schools, group homes, and hospital and/or daycare centers; they provide service to all age levels of children and youth. Some collaborate extensively with others, while some work with limited contact outside their professional interests. However, all of these service providers collaborate with the children's families.

## Medical Professionals

Psychiatrists are medical doctors trained in the understanding and treatment of mental illness and disorders via medication, psychotherapy, and other medical practices. Psychiatric nurses and social workers are trained in the clinical aspects of mental illness associated with the particular needs of nursing, casework, and/or therapy in treatment settings and in their own private practices. These medical professionals are trained to determine causes of mental illness and classifications, prescribe and/or administer medications, and/or provide counseling or psychotherapy.

## Educators

The Council for Exceptional Children publishes standards for the preparation and certification of special teachers for the SED (EBD) special education category. The program of studies typically recommended includes academic work in (1) a foundation course in educational philosophy and history; (2) characteristics of SED children; (3) assessment, diagnosis and evaluation; (4) instructional intervention; (5) classroom and child behavioral management; (6) advocacy and consultation-collaboration with professional partnerships; and (7) professional and ethical practices. We have described these competencies in detail in Chapter 1.

## PROFESSIONAL ASSOCIATIONS AND PARENT OR SELF-HELP GROUPS

American Association for the Advancement of
Behavior Therapy
15 W. 36th Street
New York, NY 10018

Council for Children with Behavioral Disorders in the Council for Exceptional Children
1920 Association Drive
Reston, VA 20191-1589

Federation of Families for Children's
Mental Health
1021 Prince Street
Alexandria, VA 22314-2071

Institute of Mental Health
5600 Fishers Lane
Rockville, MD 20852

National Mental Health Association
1021 Prince Street
Alexandria, VA 22314

National Society for Children and Adults
with Autism
621 Central Avenue
Albany, NY 12206

National Society for Children and Adults
with Autism
1234 Massachusetts Avenue NW, Suite 1017
Washington, DC 20005-4599

U.S. Office of Special Education and
Rehabilitation Services Programs (OSERS)
OSERS is divided into:
Office of Special Education Programs and
Rehabilitation Services Administration
National Institute on Disabilities and
Rehabilitation Research
400 Maryland Avenue SW
Washington, DC 20202

## REFERENCES FOR FURTHER INFORMATION

*Behavioral Disorders*  Published quarterly by the Council for Children with Behavioral Disorders.

*Beyond Behavior: A Magazine for Exploring Behavior in Our Schools* Published by the Council for Children with Behavioral Disorders.

*Journal of Emotional and Behavioral Problems* Published by the National Educational Service, 1610 West Third Street, P.O. Box 8, Bloomington, IN 47402.

## REFERENCES _____

Aschenback, T. M. (1991). *The child behavior checklist: Manual for the teacher's report form.* Burlington, VT: University of Vermont, Department of Psychiatry.

American Psychiatric Association. (1994). *Diagnostic and statistical manual of mental disorders* (4th ed.). Washington, DC: Author.

Barrios, B. B. (1993). Direct observation. In T. H. Ollendick & M. Henson (Eds.),  *Handbook of child and adolescent assessment.* New York: Pergamon.

Bateman, B. D., & Chard, D. J. (1995). Legal demands and constraints on placement decisions. In J. M. Kauffman, J. W. Lloyd, D. P. Hallahan, & T. A. Astuto (Eds.), *Issues in educational placement: Students with emotional and behavioral disorders.* Hillsdale, NJ: Erlbaum.

Berne, E. (1965). *Games people play.* New York: Grove.

Bessell, H., & Palomares, V. (1970) *Magic Circle/Human Development Program.* San Diego, CA: Human Development Training Institute.

Bettelheim, B., & Sylvester, E. (1949). Milieu therapy—indications and illustrations. *Psychoanalytic Review, 36,* 54–67.

Bortner, M., & Birch, H. G. (1969). Patterns of intellectual ability in emotionally disturbed and brain-damaged children. *Journal of Special Education, 3,* 351–369.

Bower, E. M. (1981). *Early identification of emotionally handicapped children in school* (3rd ed.). Springfield, IL: Thomas.

Bower, E. M., & Kaczynski, G. (1968, April). *Report on conference on the definition and incidence of emotional disturbance.* Paper presented at the conference sponsored by the Bureau of Education for the Handicapped/USOE, Washington, DC.

Bower, E. M., & Lambert, N. M. (1962). A *process for in-school screening of children with emotional handicaps.* Princeton, NJ: Education Testing Service.

Brendtro, L. K., & Ness, A. E. (1983). *Re-educating troubled youth: Environments for teaching and treatment.* New York: Aldine.

Brown, D. (1995, December 8). Researchers, journalists "oversold" gene therapy: NIH advisers cite nearly uniform failure. *Washington Post,* pp. A1, A22.

Brown, G. B. (1981). Strong educational programs: Laying the foundations. In G. B. Brown, R. L. McDowell, & J. Smith (Eds.), *Educating adolescents with behavior disorders.* Upper Saddle River, NJ: Prentice Hall/Merrill.

Brown, L. L., & Hammill, D. D. (1983). *The behavior rating profile.* Austin, TX: PRO-ED.

Brown, L. L., & Hammill, D. D. (1990). *Behavior rating profile: An ecological approach to behavior assessment* (2nd ed.). Austin, TX: PRO-ED.

Clarke, S., Dunlap, G., Foster-Johnson, L., Childs, K. E., Wilson, D., White, R., & Vera, A. (1995). Improving the conduct of students with behavioral disorders by incorporating student interests into curricular activities. *Behavioral Disorders, 20,* 221–237.

Council for Children with Behavior Disorders (CCBD). (1987). Position paper on definition and identification of students with behavior disorders. *Behavioral Disorders, 13*(1), 9–19.

Council for Children with Behavioral Disorders (CCBD). (1996). Guidelines for providing appropriate services to culturally diverse youngsters with emotional and/or behavioral disorders: Report of the Task Force of the CCBD Ad Hoc Committee on Ethnic and Multicultural Concerns. *Behavioral Disorders*, 21(2), 137–144.

Cullinan, D., Epstein, M., & Lloyd, W. (1991). Evaluation of conceptual models of behavior disorders. *Behavior Disorders*, 16(2), 148–151.

Cumming, J. & Cumming, E. (1966). *Ego and milieu: Theory and practice of environmental therapy*. New York: Atherton.

Cutler, R., & McNeil, E. (1962) *Mental health consultation in schools: A research analysis*. USPHS, Grant #MH6706. Ann Arbor: University of Michigan, Department of Psychology.

Duncan, B. B., Forness, S. R., & Hartsough, C. (1995). Students identified as seriously emotionally disturbed in day treatment: Cognitive, psychiatric and special education characteristics. *Behavioral Disorders*, 20, 238–252.

Eiduson, B. T., Eiduson, S., & Galler, E. (1962). Biochemistry, genetics and the nature-nurture problem. *American Psychologist*, 119, 342–350.

Fagen, S. A. (1981). Conducting an LSI: A process model. *Pointer*, 25(2), 9–11.

Fagen, S. A., & Long, N. J. (1979). A psychoeducational curriculum approach to teaching self-control. *Behavioral Disorders*, 4, 68–82.

Forness, S. R., & Knitzer, J. (1992). A new proposed definition and terminology to replace "serious emotional disturbance" in the Individuals with Disabilities Education Act. *School Psychology Review*, 21, 12–20.

Freed, A. (1977). T.A. *for kids*. Sacramento, CA: Jolmer.

Glasser, W. (1965). *Reality therapy: A new approach to psychiatry*. New York: Harper & Row.

Gottesman, I. I. (1987). Schizophrenia: Irving Gottesman reveals the genetic factors. *University of Virginia Alumni News*, 75(5), 12–14.

Graubard, P. S. (1964). The extent of academic retardation in a residential treatment center. *Journal of Educational Research*, 58, 78–80.

Grosenick, J. K., George, M. P., & George, N. L. (1990). A conceptual scheme for describing and evaluating programs in behavioral disorders. *Behavioral Disorders*, 16(1), 70–73.

Hardman, M. L., Drew, C. J., & Egan, M. W. (1996). *Human exceptionality: Society, school, and family* (5th ed.). Needham, MA: Allyn & Bacon.

Hallahan, D. P., & Kauffman, J. M. (1991). *Exceptional children: Introduction to special education* (5th ed.). Upper Saddle River, NJ: Prentice Hall.

Haring, N. G., McCormick, L., & Haring, T. G. (1994). *Exceptional children and youth: An introduction to special education*. (6th ed.). New York: Macmillan.

Heuchert, C. M. (1983). Can teachers change behaviors? Try interviews! *Academic Therapy*, 18(3), 321–328.

Heuchert, C. M., & Long, N. (1981). A brief history of Life Space Interviewing. *Pointer*, 25(2), 5–8.

Heward, W. L. (1996). *Exceptional children: An introduction to special education* (5th ed.). Upper Saddle River, NJ: Prentice Hall/Merrill.

Hewett, F. M. (1968). *The emotionally disturbed child in the classroom: A developmental strategy for educating children with maladaptive behavior*. Needham, MA: Allyn & Bacon.

Hewett, F. M. (1981). Behavior ecology: A unifying strategy for the 80's. In R. B. Rutherford, Jr., A. G. Prieto, & J. E. McGlothin (Eds.), *Monograph in behavior disorders of children and youth* (p. 3). Tempe: Arizona State University and Council for Children with Behavioral Disorders.

Hobbs, N. (1975). *The future of children*. San Francisco: Jossey-Bass.

Howell, K. W. (1985). A task-analytical approach to social behavior. *Remedial and Special Education*, 6(2), 24–30.

Hunt, N., & Marshall, K. (1994). *Exceptional children and youth: An introduction to special education*. Boston: Houghton Mifflin.

Karlson, J. (1966). *The biological basis of schizophrenia*. New York: Thomas.

Kauffman, J. M. (1997). *Characteristics of emotional and behavioral disorders of children and youth* (6th ed.). Upper Saddle River, NJ: Prentice Hall.

Kirk, S. A., Gallagher, J. J., & Anastasiow, N. J. (1993). *Educating exceptional children* (7th ed.). Boston: Houghton Mifflin.

Long, N. J. (1986). The nine psychoeducational stages of helping emotionally disturbed students through the reeducation process. *Pointer, 30*(3), 4–20.

Long, N. J. (1990). Life space interviewing. *Beyond Behavior, 2*(1), 10–15.

Long, N. J. (1996). The conflict cycle paradigm on how troubled students get teachers out of control. In N. J. Long, W. C. Morse, & R. G. Newman, *Conflict in the classroom: The education of at-risk and troubled students* (5th ed.). Austin, TX: PRO-ED.

Long, N. J., Morse, W. C., & Newman, R. G. (1991). *Conflict in the classroom: The education of at-risk and troubled students* (5th ed.). Austin, TX: PRO-ED.

Lyons, D. F., & Powers, V. (1963). Follow-up study of elementary school children exempted from Los Angeles City Schools during 1960–1961. *Exceptional Children, 30*, 155–162.

Mayer, G. R. (1995). Preventing antisocial behavior in the schools. *Journal of Applied Behavioral Analysis, 28*, 467–478.

Meyen, E. L., & Skrtic, T. M. (1988). *Exceptional children and youth: An introduction* (3rd ed.). Denver, CO: Love.

Morse, W. C. (1961). The mental hygiene dilemma in public education. *American Journal of Orthopsychiatry, 3*(1), 331.

Morse, W. C., & Smith, J. C. (1983). *Understanding child variance* (3rd printing). Reston, VA: Council for Exceptional Children.

Motto, J. J., & Wilkins, G. S. (1968). Educational achievement of institutionalized emotionally disturbed children. *Journal of Educational Research, 61*, 218–221.

Nagheri, J. A., McMeish, T. J., & Bardos, A. N. (1991). *Draw a person: Screening procedure for emotional disturbance.* Austin, TX: PRO-ED.

Nelson, C. M. (1993). Students with behavioral disabilities. In A. E. Blackhurst & W. H. Berdine (Eds.), *An introduction to special education* (3rd ed.). New York: HarperCollins.

Nelson, C. M., Rutherford, R. B., Center, D. B., & Walker, H. M. (1994). Do public schools have an obligation to serve troubled children and youth? In K. L. Freiberg (Ed.), *Educating exceptional children* (7th ed.). Guilford, CT: Dushkin.

Plomin, R. (1995). Genetics and children's experiences in the family. *Journal of Child Psychology and Psychiatry, 36*, 33–68.

Quay, H. C. (1986a). Classification. In H. C. Quay & J. S. Wenry (Eds.), *Psychopathological disorders of childhood* (3rd ed.). New York: Wiley.

Quay, H. C. (1986b). Conduct disorders. In H. C. Quay & J. S. Wenry (Eds.), *Psycholpathological disorders of childhood* (3rd ed.). New York: Wiley.

Quay, H. C., & Peterson, D. T. (1987). *Manual for the revised behavior problem checklist.* Available from H. C. Quay, P.O. Box 248187, University of Miami, Coral Gables, FL 33124-2070.

Redl, F. (1969). Aggression in the classroom. *Today's Education, 5*, 29–32.

Reinert, H. R. (1980). *Children in conflict* (2nd ed.). St. Louis, MO: Mosby.

Rezmierski, B., & Kotre, J. (1972). A limited literature review of theory of the psychodynamic model. In W. C. Rhodes, *A study of child variance.* Ann Arbor, MI: University of Michigan Press.

Rhodes, W. C. (1967). The disturbing child: A problem of ecological management. *Exceptional Children, 33*, 449–455.

Rhodes, W. C. (1970). A community participation analysis of emotionally disturbed children. *Exceptional Children, 37*, 309–314.

Rorschach, H. (1942). *Rorschach psychodiagnostic plates.* New York: Psychological Corporation.

Rubin, R. A., & Balow, B. (1978). Prevalence of teacher identified behavior problems: A longitudinal study. *Exceptional Children, 45*, 102–111.

Rutter, M. (1995). Clinical implications of attachment concepts: Retrospect and prospect. *Journal of Child Psychology and Psychiatry, 36*, 549–571.

Smith, D. D., & Luckasson, R. (1995). *Introduction to special education: Teaching in an age of challenge* (2nd ed.). Needham, MA: Allyn & Bacon.

Tompkins, J. R. (1996). Special education movements in the education of students who are seriously emotionally disturbed: Motto—Move as slowly as you can. In B. L. Brooks & D. A. Sabatino (Eds.), *Personal perspective on emotional disturbance/behavioral disorders.* Austin, TX: PRO-ED.

Tompkins, J. R., & Tompkins-McGill, P. L. (1993). *Surviving in schools in the 1990's: Strategic management of school environments*. Lonhan, MD: University Press of America.

Trippe, M. F. (1966). Educational therapy. In J. Hellmuth (Ed.), *Educational Therapy*. Seattle, WA: Special Child Publications.

Turnbull, A. P., Turnbull, H. R., Shank, M., & Leal, D. (1995). *Exceptional lives: Special education in today's schools*. Upper Saddle River, NJ: Prentice Hall/Merrill.

U.S. Department of Education (1997). *Nineteenth annual report to Congress on the implementation of the Individuals with Disabilities Act*. Washington, DC: Author.

Vernick, J. (1963). The use of the Life Space Interview on a medical ward. *Social Casework*, 44(8), 465–469.

Walker, H. M. (1995). *The acting-out child: Coping with classroom disruption* (2nd ed.). Longmont, CO: Sopria West.

Walker, H. M., & Severson, H. H. (1990). *Systematic screening for behavior disorders*. Longmont, CO: Sopria West.

Walker, J. E., & Shea, T. M. (1987). *Behavior management: A practical approach for educators*. New York: Macmillan.

Wehman, P. (1997). *Exceptional individuals in school, community, and work*. Austin, TX: PRO-ED.

Whelan, R. J. (1988). Emotionally disturbed. In E. L. Meyen & T. M. Skrtic (Eds.), *Exceptional children and youth: An introduction* (3rd ed.). Denver, CO: Love.

Wicks-Nelson, R. & Israel, A. C. (1991). *Behavior disorders of children* (2nd ed., pp. 99–100). Upper Saddle River, NJ: Prentice Hall.

Wineman, D. (1959). The Life Space Interview. *Social Work*, 4(1), 3–17.

Wood, M. M., & Long, N. J. (1991). Life space intervention: *Talking with children and youth in crisis*. Austin, TX: PRO-ED.

Zabel, M. K. (1991). *Teaching young children with behavior disorders*. Reston, VA: Council for Exceptional Children.

# 6

# Children with Communication Disorders

C ommunication is more than just talking. It is understanding others' speech and gestures. It is reading and writing. A child learns to understand his or her world by translating many experiences into language. As the child matures, feelings, thoughts, and discoveries are shared with others by words joined together in ever-increasing complexity. Language and speech make learning an efficient process. Our knowledge, history, culture, beliefs, myths, and fears are passed from generation to generation through some form of language, be it oral or written. It is this exchange of ideas, opinions, and facts between people interacting with each other that defines communication (Bernstein, 1993). Communicative competence is the ability a child develops to use speech and language to uncover how the world works. It is how we obtain, store, analyze, and share information with others. Breakdowns or dysfunctions of this critical communication system make learning an enormously difficult task. Children with untreated communication problems suffer both social and educational isolation from their peers. Yet since much of speech and language are learned, early, structured intervention can help all children with communication disorders compensate for their disability and enable some to completely overcome their handicap.

## DEFINITIONS

Communication disorders include both speech disorders and language disorders. However, before any logical discussion of disorders of communication can be attempted, it is important to discuss what is meant by speech and what is meant by language. Similarly, before we can explain what can go wrong with these processes, it is crucial to understand how the normal acquisition of these skills occurs. The terms listed in Box 6.1 will help the reader understand the concepts discussed initially and throughout the chapter.

## NORMAL DEVELOPMENT OF SPEECH AND LANGUAGE

As they are developing normal speech and language, children pass through a number of well-defined and fairly easily recognized stages. Meaningful speech and language develop over time. The whole process begins with the interactions between the child's normal neurological system and the child's environment.

### Speech

Speech is the systematic use of sounds and sound combinations to produce meaningful words, phrases, and sentences. Specific parts of the body coordinate to produce the sounds. The parts of the body that interact to produce and modify speech sounds are the lungs, larynx, soft palate (*velum*), nasal cavities, tongue, teeth, lower jaw (*mandible*), and lips. Air that is stored in the lungs passes over the vocal cords, which are located in the larynx. This passage of air causes the vocal cords to vibrate

*Box 6.1*
*WHAT EVERY TEACHER NEEDS TO KNOW*

*Terms*

**apraxia**   Difficulty producing speech and other voluntary movements.

**communication**   The interchange of ideas , feelings, facts, or opinions between people sending messages and people receiving messages.

**dysarthria**   Difficulty producing speech and other movements due to neuromuscular damage, weakness, paralysis, or lack of coordination.

**intelligibility**   A listener's rating of the ability to understand the speech and language of a speaker.

**morphology**   Transformation of words with tenses and endings.

**phoneme**   The smallest unit of meaningful sound.

**phonetics**   The sounds of language.

**phonology**   Rules regarding how sounds can be combined.

**pragmatics**   Knowledgeable use of language in socially appropriate contexts.

**primary disability**   A speech or language disability that in and of itself meets the criteria for services under federal and state guidelines.

**secondary disability**   A speech or language disability that arises from other conditions being serviced under federal or state guidelines.

**semantics**   Meaning.

**speech mechanism**   The parts of the body used to produce speech (tongue, lips, teeth, mandible, vocal cords, breathing mechanism).

**syntax**   Rules for sentence structure. The accepted way that words are combined into phrases and sentences.

and produce a noise. This noise (*voicing*) travels up the throat (*pharynx*) and is changed by the movements of the soft palate, lips, lower jaw, and tongue. It is also changed when it travels through the nasal cavities. Figure 6.1 illustrates the speech mechanism and the relationship to each other of the components just described.

The production or generation of sound is called *phonation*. The modification of the sound by the cavities of the body, including the mouth and nasal cavities, is called *resonation*. The final movements of the mouth, lips, tongue, jaw, and soft palate is called *articulation*. It is this whole process that shapes sounds into phonemes, which are the meaningful units of sound that we use in constructing speech. Each language has its own set of phonemes that are used to build words. While many sounds are shared by several languages, not all languages are made up of the exact same sound systems. Learning the phonemes of a language requires motor behavior (physical movements) as well as intellectual understanding. Problems can arise when a child cannot control the physical components of his or her body to produce sounds, cannot hear the differences between sounds, or does not possess the cognitive ability to learn the differences between phonemes.

The sounds of a language are not always accurately represented by the written or orthographic alphabet. For example, the initial sound in the word *photo* is /f/, and the initial sound in *psychology* is /s/, not /p/. As a result, transcription systems called *phonetic alphabets* were derived to accurately transcribe the sounds of language. Tables 6.1 and 6.2 list the sounds of English represented by the phonetic

**Figure 6.1**
The speech mechanism and
respiratory tract

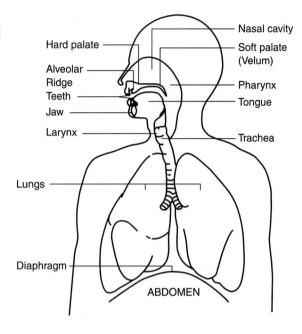

symbols of the International Phonetic Alphabet (IPA). There are three types of phonemes: vowels, diphthongs, and consonants. Each symbol represents only one sound of language. Table 6.1 contains key words illustrating the consonant sounds and provides a timeline for the ages at which the consonant sounds are usually mastered by normally developing children. Table 6.2 contains key words illustrating the vowels and diphthongs of English. Vowels are produced by vocal-cord vibration and changing the shape of the mouth (vocal cavity). Diphthongs are vowel-like productions that combine two vowel sounds in one syllable to create a unique sound. If you carefully listen to the vowel sound in the word *my*, you will hear a movement of sounds that make up the diphthong /ai/, as compared to the single vowel or pure vowel /i/ produced in the word *me*. Consonant sounds are determined by precise movements of the speech articulators, air stream direction, and whether the air stream is vibrated. For example, when the tongue touches the gum ridge behind the front teeth and releases the air stream, the sound /t/ is made. If the back of the tongue touches the soft palate, the sound /g/ is produced. The differences between /s/ and /f/ are dependent upon air stream modification; /p/ and /b/ are made exactly the same, except that there is no vocal cord vibration when making /p/, as there is when making /b/. Fortunately, most speakers learn these subtle distinctions simply by hearing the sounds of their language, and learn how to produce them with little conscious effort. The study of sounds and their production (*phonetics*) is a critical part of the training of professionals who work with children with speech problems.

As Table 6.1 shows, the consonant sounds of language come in over a considerable time period. While all vowel sounds are usually mastered by age 3, some conso-

Table 6.1
Consonant Sounds

| Phonetic Symbol | Orthographic Symbol | Illustrative Word | Age at Which Sound is Produced Correctly by 90% of Children |
|---|---|---|---|
| /p/ | p | *p*ig | 3 |
| /m/ | m | *m*an | 3 |
| /n/ | n | *n*ose | 3 |
| /w/ | w | *w*ater | 3 |
| /h/ | h | *h*at | 3 |
| /b/ | b | *b*ounce | 4 |
| /d/ | d | *d*og | 4 |
| /k/ | k, c | *c*at | 4 |
| /g/ | g | *g*o | 4 |
| /f/ | f, ph | *f*un | 4 |
| /j/ | y | *y*ear | 4 |
| /t/ | t | *t*oes | 6 |
| /ŋ/ | ng | lo*ng* | 6 |
| /r/ | r | *r*ip | 6 |
| /l/ | l | *l*ong | 6 |
| /θ/ | th | *th*ink | 7 |
| /ʃ/ | sh | *sh*oe | 7 |
| /tʃ/ | ch | *ch*ew | 7 |
| /dʒ/ | j | *j*oke | 7 |
| /z/ | z | *z*ipper | 7 |
| /v/ | v | *v*oice | 8 |
| /ð/ | th | *th*is | 8 |
| /s/ | s | *s*oup | 8 |
| /ʒ/ | s, zh | trea*s*ure | 8 |
| /hw/ | wh | *wh*ere | 8 |

nant sounds may not develop in normal children until age 8 (Stoel-Gammon & Dunn, 1985; Olmstead, 1971). Many children are well into the second grade before all consonant sounds are fully developed. However, sound development is not an exact science. The range for individual development is large, with some children completing the process by age 6. We have selected the upper limits by which at least 90 percent of children have developed sounds and have included these figures in Table 6.1 (Stoel-Gammon & Dunn, 1985).

## Language

Language is much more complex than speech. Language puts meaning into speech and is used to express and receive meaning. Although most languages have speech as a component, not all do. Sign language is an example of a language system that fulfills all the requirements of language, yet does not use

**Table 6.2**
Vowels and Diphthongs

| Vowels | | Diphthongs | |
|---|---|---|---|
| **Phonetic Symbol** | **Illustrative Word** | **Phonetic Symbol** | **Illustrative Word** |
| /i/ | sp*ee*d | /ou/ | tone |
| /ɪ/ | h*i*d | /ei/ | take |
| /e/ | h*a*te | /ai/ | m*i*ght |
| /ɛ/ | Fr*e*d | /au/ | sh*ou*t |
| | | /ɔi/ | to*i*l |
| /æ/ | h*a*ve | | |
| /ɔ/ | d*o*g | | |
| /ɑ/ | f*a*ther | | |
| /o/ | h*o*me | | |
| /U/ | b*oo*k | | |
| /u/ | p*oo*l | | |
| /ʌ/ | *u*p | | |
| /ə/ | sof*a* | | |
| /ɚ/ | moth*er* | | |
| /ɝ/ | b*ir*d | | |

speech as the medium to transmit and receive messages. Languages enable communication to work by allowing the composing and sending of messages (*encoding*) from one person to another, who receives them and understands them (*decoding*). Encoding and decoding skills develop over time and are dependent upon intact neurological systems and experiences. Language is innate to all human beings. It is common to all cultures and develops similarly in all people in every society. However, the process doesn't occur in a vacuum. It is social in nature and is dependent upon interactions with the environment. An easy way to understand how humans develop language is to imagine that we each come equipped with a language acquisition device (LAD) in our brain that enables us to shift through all the speech, gestures, and vocal intonations that surround us as we grow. This device helps us attend to what is important and ignore unnecessary distractions. Over time, it helps us learn the systems that surround us, with increasing sophistication, so that we may join in and use them to communicate our own needs and experiences (Chomsky, 1957, 1981).

The major components of language are:

1. Phonology
2. Morphology
3. Syntax
4. Semantics
5. Pragmatics

Each of these components develops as a child matures. Their interaction allows humans of all cultures to express the most complicated concepts in a form that can be readily understood by other speakers and listeners of the same language. *Phonology* is the sound system of a language. The phonological rules of each language determine just what combinations of sounds are permissible in that language to form meaningful words. *Morphology* deals with the rules for transforming words and changing their basic meanings. For example, adding /s/ changes one *horse* to many *horses*, and adding /ed/ changes today's *work* to yesterday's *worked*. *Syntax* is the rule system that governs the order and combination of words to form phrases and sentences. *Semantics* is the meaning of language. "I am hungry" is a sentence that is semantically appropriate to speakers of English. It has meaning. However, "Why is a mouse when it is spinning faster?" is a puzzling statement. It is phonologically appropriate, because it contains sounds of English. It is morphologically sound, since the transformations of the words *spin* and *fast* are allowable. It breaks down on a semantic level because it has no meaning. The final component is *pragmatics*, which is a knowledge of the social aspects of language. It takes into account a knowledge and understanding of the rules of turn taking, starting and ending conversations, choosing and maintaining appropriate topics, being sensitive to miscommunications, and being aware of what experiences are shared by listeners and which need supplemental information for understanding messages. Pragmatics give language life (American Speech-Language-Hearing Association, 1982). Languages have:

1. Form (phonology, morphology, syntax)
2. Content (semantics)
3. Function (pragmatics) (American Speech-Language-Hearing Association, 1993)

A normally developing child's first meaningful words are usually spoken between the ages of 12 and 18 months. Table 6.3 is a schematic outline of the approximate ages and patterns of language development shown by a normally developing child.

By age 6 most normally developing children have mastered the complexity of their native language well enough to use language to learn about concepts that have not been or cannot be directly experienced. Owens (1992) summarizes language development into five age-related phases from birth to age 12. He suggests that the young child (ages 1 to 6 months) is an *examiner* who observes his or her environment with relatively little interaction. The child becomes an *experimenter* (ages 7 to 12 months) and begins to interact with others while beginning to cognitively understand the basics of language. Next comes the *explorer* stage (ages 12 to 24 months), wherein the child begins purposeful interaction with the environment and is learning language at a fast pace. By ages 3 to 5 years, the child has become the *exhibitor*, talking about his or her experiences and feelings in a logical way that can be understood by strangers. From ages 6 to 12, the child is now an *expert*, with a huge vocabulary and the ability to manipulate language to express many complicate and abstract ideas. Table 6.4 is a summary of Owens's conceptualizations of language development (1992).

**Table 6.3**
Language of a Normally Developing Child

| Age | Attainment | Example |
|---|---|---|
| 13 months | First words | here, mama, bye bye, kitty |
| 17 months | 50-word vocabulary | |
| 18 months | First two-word combinations | more juice here ball more T.V. here kitty |
| 22 months | Later two-word combinations | Andy shoe Mommy ring cup floor keys chair |
| 24 months | Mean sentence length of 2.00 words | |
| | First appearance of -ing | Andy sleeping |
| 30 months | Mean sentence length 3.10 words | |
| | First appearance of is | My car's gone! |
| 37 months | Mean sentence length 4.10 words | |
| | First appearance of indirect requests | Can I have some cookies? |
| 40 months | Mean sentence length of 4.50 words | |

*Source:* From "Language Disorders in Preschool Children," by L. Leonard, 1994, in G. Shames, E. Wiig, and W. Secord (eds.), *Human Communication Disorders* (4th ed., p. 179), Needham, MA: Allyn & Bacon. Reprinted by permission.

## DISORDERS OF SPEECH AND LANGUAGE

Speech and language are vulnerable to many disruptions that can lead to disorders. Since the entire communication system depends on neurological systems for cognitive processing of environmental experiences, disruptions in the neurological system, underdevelopment of cognitive skills, or a lack of appropriate language experiences can all lead to speech disorders, language disorders, or both in chil-

Table 6.4
Overview of Language Development: Birth to Age 12

| Age (Months) | Characteristics |
| --- | --- |
| The examiner (1–6 mos.) | Responds to human voice; makes pleasure sounds (1 mo.)<br>Produces strings of consonant-vowel or vowel-only syllables; vocally responds to speech of others (3 mo.)<br>Smiles at person speaking to him/her (4 mo.)<br>Responds to name; smiles and vocalizes to image in mirror (5 mo.)<br>Prefers people games, e.g., peek-a-boo, I'm going to get you; explores face of person holding him/her (6 mo.) |
| The experimenter (7–12 mos.) | Recognizes some words; repeats emphasized syllables (8 mo.)<br>"Performs" for family; imitates coughs, hisses, raspberries, etc. (9 mo.)<br>Obeys some directives (10 mo.)<br>Anticipates caregiver's goal and attempts to change it via persuasion/protest (11 mo.)<br>Recognizes own name; engages in familiar routines having visual cues (e.g., bye-bye); uses one or more words (12 mo.) |
| The explorer (12–24 mos.) | Points to toys, persons, animals named; pushes toys; plays alone; begins some make-believe; has 4- to 6-word vocabulary (15 mo.)<br>Begins to use 2-word utterances (combines); refers to self by name; has about 20-word vocabulary; pretends to feed doll, etc. (18 mo.)<br>Enjoys rhyming games; tries to "tell" experiences; understands some personal pronouns; engages in parallel play (21 mo.)<br>Has 200- to 300-word vocabulary; names most common everyday objects; uses some prepositions (*in, on*) and pronouns (*I, me*) but not always accurately (*in, on*); engages in object-specific pretend play and parallel play; can role-play in limited way; orders others around; communicates feelings, desires, interests (24 mo.) |
| The exhibitor (3–5 yrs.) | Has 900- to 1,000-word vocabulary; creates 3- to 4-word utterances; talks about the "here and now"; talks while playing and takes turns in play; "swears" (3 yrs.)<br>Has 1,500- to 1,600-word vocabulary; asks many questions; uses increasingly complex sentence constructions; still relies on word order for interpretation; plays cooperatively with others; role-plays; recounts stories about recent experiences (narrative recounts); has some difficulty answering *how* and *why* (4 yrs.)<br>Has vocabulary of 2,100–2,200 words; discusses feelings; understands *before* and *after* regardless of word order; play is purposeful and constructive; shows interest in group activities (5 yrs.) |
| The expert (6–12 yrs.) | Has expressive vocabulary of 2,600 words, understands 20,000–24,000 word meanings; defines by function; has many well-formed, complex sentences; enjoys active games and is competitive; identifies with same sex peers in groups (6 yrs.)<br>Verbalizes ideas and problems readily; enjoys an audience; knows that others have different perspectives; has allegiance to group, but also needs adult support (8 yrs.)<br>Talks a lot; has good comprehension; discovers may be the object of someone else's perspective; plans future actions; enjoys games, sports, hobbies (10 yrs.)<br>Understands about 50,000 word meanings; constructs adultlike definitions; engages in higher-order thinking and communicating (12 yrs.) |

*Source:* From *Language Development: An Introduction* (4th ed., pp. 76–111), by R. E. Owens, 1996. Copyright © 1996 by Allyn & Bacon, Needham Heights, MA. Adapted by permission.

dren. Communication disorders include both language disorders (understanding and formulating language) and speech disorders (producing language).

In order to more easily understand communication disorders, we have divided them into speech disorders and language disorders and then further divided speech and language disorders into the discrete types of dysfunction that compose each category. The implication is that this division is mirrored in the children who are seen for services. This is not always the case. Although many children may have a discrete communication disorder, it is also possible to have multiple speech and language problems. Speech and language are co-existing systems. It is quite common for a disruption in one system to have negative effects upon the other.

## Disorders of Speech

A speech disorder is characterized by any impairment of vocal production (voice), speech sound production (articulation), fluency (stuttering and related disorders) or any combination of these impairments (American Speech-Language-Hearing Association, 1993a). Speech disorders are present when a child's speech is so different from what is expected that it calls attention to itself, is so difficult to understand that it interferes with communication, or causes distress to the speaker or listener (Van Riper & Erickson, 1996).

## Disorders of Language

A language disorder is an impairment or abnormal development in understanding and/or using spoken, written, or other symbolic systems. The disorder may involve the form of language (phonology, morphology, or syntax), the content of language (semantics), the function of language (pragmatics) or any combination of form, content, and function (American Speech-Language-Hearing Association, 1993a).

## DEFINITIONS

Federal regulations place communication disorders under both individuals with disabilities and related services. This means that services provided under the Individuals with Disabilities Education Act (IDEA) may be delivered both to children for whom a communication disorder is deemed to be a primary disability served by special education, and also to those children whose speech and language problems are secondary to another condition that is receiving special education. The definition for speech or language impairment is that it is a communication disorder such as stuttering, impaired articulation, a language impairment, or a voice impairment that adversely affects a child's educational performance.

The definitions for communication disorders vary from state to state. However, most require that the child show some deficit in the components of language or in the areas of speech. This must usually be documented on a standardized test or by a sample of communication that was analyzed in the child's normal communication environment.

## DIFFERENCES IN SPEECH AND LANGUAGE

The way children speak is a reflection of their culture (Heward, 1996). Speech and language are learned by interacting with the people in our environment when we are children. We learn to talk the same way that they do. The United States is a linguistically and ethnically diverse country. This diversity is reflected in the language and speech our children learn. Many factors contribute to linguistic diversity. The primary ones can be race, ethnicity, social and economic status, education, occupation, and geographic region. These factors can lead to the development of accents and dialects. *Accents* are sound differences of spoken language and are usually attributed to geographic regions and the influences of foreign languages (Taylor & Payne, 1994). The pronunciation of the word *Cuba* as "Cuber" in certain areas of the Northeastern United States is an example of an accent. *Dialects* are more complex and can be variations of the form, content, and use of a language. They are rule governed differences that are consistently applied by individuals who are members of that geographical, regional, social, cultural, or ethnic group. Dialects are linguistically valid and legitimate ways of communicating. However, they are somewhat different from the Standard English used by most speakers in the United States. The major dialects spoken in the United

States are Black English, Southern English, Southern White Nonstandard English, and Appalachian English. Most dialectal speakers can *code-switch*, which is the ability to move from one language or dialect to another as the situation demands (Gleason, 1973; McCormak & Wurm, 1976). We will give examples of dialectal differences in the "Characteristics and Etiology" section of this chapter.

The critical point is that dialectal speakers are different rather than disordered. The differences in their communication are evidence of a different learned rule system and not evidence of a deviant form of communication. These variations of Standard English are not considered disorders of speech or language (American Speech-Language-Hearing Association, 1993a). However, culturally and linguistically diverse children are more likely to be dialectal speakers, and are often taught by teachers who are unfamiliar with their dialects and consider the speech and language differences they hear to be errors. Sometimes, the opposite occurs and children who are not excused from having communication disorders are not treated because their teachers feel that the disordered speech and language the children are producing is due to dialectal differences and not disordered communication. It is obviously critical that teachers who work in areas where dialects are spoken become knowledgeable about those dialects and gear their instruction appropriately.

## PREVALENCE

Approximately 1 million of the 5 million children between ages 6 and 21 who were served during the 1994–1995 school year under IDEA were diagnosed as having speech or language impairments as their primary impairment (U.S. Department of Education, 1997). However, this 20 percent figure is deceptive because it fails to include the secondary disability status of many children who have communication problems that co-exist with their primary diagnosis. Children with cerebral palsy, mental retardation, severe and multiple disabilities, hearing impairments, and autism almost always have a disordered-communication component to their disability that requires treatment. A study by the American Speech-Language-Hearing Association (Dublinski, 1981) revealed that 42 percent of all children with disabilities who are served by speech-language pathologists have other primary handicaps.

Other surveys suggest that speech disorders affect approximately 10 to 15 percent of all preschool children and 6 percent of all primary school children. Language disorders may be present in 3 percent of the preschoolers and 1 percent of all school-age children (National Institute of Neurological and Communicative Disorders and Stroke, 1988).

When the total population, including adults, is considered, communication problems affect approximately 10 percent of the population of the United States (National Center for Health Statistics, 1988; American Speech-Language-Hearing Association, 1991). The prevalence figures for the entire population include adults, many of whom acquire communication disorders later in life as the result of strokes, hearing loss, accidents, and degenerative diseases that negatively affect communication skills.

# CHARACTERISTICS AND ETIOLOGY

The characteristics of many speech and language problems are directly related to the etiology of the problems. Physical, emotional, or faulty learning causes will affect the speech and language systems in unique ways and often produce different characteristics. This section of the chapter will divide communication problems into speech disorders and language disorders and explain how the different causes of speech and language impairment often manifest themselves with differing symptoms. These characteristics not only help in the identification of the problems but also often point the way to the most effective programming.

## Etiology and Characteristics of Speech Disorders

The most common speech disorders disrupt speech sound production (articulation), vocal sound production (voice), and the smooth flow of speech (fluency). Disorders of articulation, voice, and fluency are each divided into several major subtypes. Beginning with disorders of articulation, we will explore these subtypes, their etiology, and the characteristics common to each of them. The severity of each characteristic can range from being barely noticeable to the listener to being extremely conspicuous.

## Articulation Disorders

Articulation disorders are the most common problem among schoolchildren (Kirk, Gallagher, & Anastasiow, 1993). Children with articulation disorders have difficulty in producing the speech sounds of their language. Speakers with articulation disorders tend to make four types of errors in producing sounds. When speaking, they (1) substitute one sound for another (*wabbit* for *rabbit* or *toup* for *soup*); (2) omit sounds from words (*nake* for *snake* or *oup* for *soup*); (3) distort the normal production of sounds (the "Daffy Duck" kind of /s/ sound); or (4) add sounds that do not belong in words (*balack* for *black*).

Articulation disorders that result from known anatomical or physiological problems are called *organic problems*. Those that result from unknown causes or faulty learning are called *functional problems* (Newman, Creaghead, & Secord, 1985). The most common causes of organic articulation disorders are clefts of the palate, cerebral palsy, traumatic brain injury, and hearing impairment. None of these conditions is in and of itself a speech disorder, yet each is the direct cause of speech disorders. The severity of each condition will determine whether an articulation disorder will result and how severe it will be.

**Clefts of the palate.** A *cleft* is an opening that results from the failure of the facial structures to fuse appropriately during prenatal development. Clefts of the lip and palate result when these structures do not join between the sixth and twelfth weeks of the first trimester of pregnancy. The palate is composed of two structures. The anterior (closest to the face) portion is called the *hard palate*. It is an inflexible structure that forms the roof of the mouth and the floor of the nasal cavity. The posterior (closest to the pharynx) portion is called the *soft palate* and is made up of flexible tissues that bend to seal off the nasal cavities from the pharynx. The *alveolar ridge*, or gum ridge, is directly behind the lips and is the tissue that houses the teeth. Clefts may affect the lips, alveolar ridge, and hard and soft palates. No one single factor has been isolated as the cause of clefts. A multifactor theory that combines genetic predispositions and prenatal environmental factors seems to be currently accepted (Hegde, 1995). The most commonly quoted incidence figure for the occurrence of clefts is 1 in every 750 births (McWilliams, Morris & Shelton, 1990). However, the incidence appears to differ with different racial and ethnic groups. The highest rate in the United States was reported to be 1 in 220 births for Native American children in South Dakota, and the lowest incidence was 1 in 8,600 births for African American children (Hegde, 1995).

Clefts can affect the lip alone, the lip and gum ridge only, the hard palate, or the hard and soft palate, or there may be a total opening that extends from the lip all the way through to the soft palate. Clefts are first and foremost health problems. Depending on the severity of the cleft, the child affected may have significant feeding problems and be susceptible to ear infections because he or she may not be able to suck on a bottle efficiently or close off passages to the nose and ears while eating. Children with clefts may have a difficult time in producing sounds that require firm contact between the soft palate and the pharynx. This results in their inability to close off the nasal passages and means that their speech sounds are partially diverted from the normal pathway through the mouth and are overly influenced by passing through the nasal passages. This excess or hypernasality makes it very difficult to understand the speech of some children with clefts.

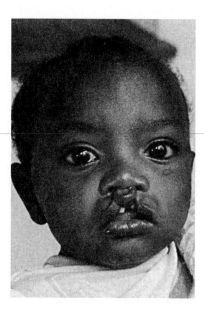
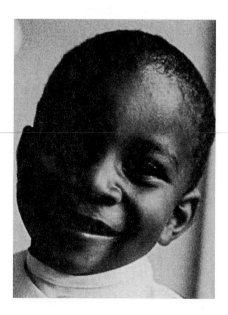

**Cerebral Palsy.**   *Cerebral palsy* is brain damage resulting from infection, poisoning, oxygen deprivation, and/or trauma that occur prior to, during, or immediately after birth. Children with cerebral palsy may have difficulty with coordination and controlling muscular activity. Cerebral palsy does not always cause articulation disorders. It is only when the areas of the brain that control the speech mechanism are affected that articulation disorders are present. If these areas of the brain are damaged, the child may not be able to coordinate the rapid and precise movements necessary for intelligible speech production. He or she may be unable to efficiently use the breath stream in ways necessary to articulate sounds and produce running speech. As a result, individual sounds will be distorted, produced slowly, and slurred together in a manner that will make it difficult for the listener to understand the message. The term *dysarthria* is often used to describe the lack of coordination that is characteristic of the speech patterns of children with cerebral palsy. The brain damage that causes articulation disorders may also cause the child to experience language problems.

**Traumatic Brain Injury (TBI).**   *Traumatic brain injury*, which is caused by any accident or injury to the brain (car accidents, gunshot wounds, child abuse), can also lead to many conditions, including articulation disorders. The observable characteristics may be very similar to those of cerebral palsy. A major difference is that TBI often occurs after sounds have developed normally, whereas in children with cerebral palsy, normal speech and sound development may never have occurred. Children with TBI may evidence the dysarthric speech described previously and in addition may show signs of apraxia. A*praxia* of speech is a weakness and lack of coordination that manifests itself when voluntary movements are attempted. Speech is an activity that, unlike breathing or the circulation of the bloodstream, requires conscious volitional control. Children with apraxia might show little involvement in automatic uses of the speech mechanism in swallowing and chewing food, but may have a difficult time making the sounds of speech and coordinating the speech mechanism. As with cerebral palsy, the brain injury resulting from TBI can also lead to language disorders.

**Hearing Loss.**   The sound system of language is learned by hearing the sounds of language in our environment and learning to mimic them over time. A child with a hearing loss may not hear some sounds or may hear them in a distorted way due to his or her hearing impairment. Children who are deaf may not hear speech or spoken language at any meaningful level. As a result, depending on the severity of the hearing impairment, children will omit sounds, distort sounds, or make inappropriate sounds that are a reflection of what they are hearing. If a child's hearing loss is severe enough, he or she will not spontaneously produce speech sounds at all. The implications of hearing loss and deafness on speech and language development will be discussed at length in Chapter 8, "Children with Hearing Impairments."

Children with functional articulation problems have difficulty making speech sounds without any identifiable structural, neurological, or physiological cause. As many as 80 percent of children identified as having articulation disorders may have functional disorders (Van Riper & Erickson, 1996). One explanation for the etiology of functional articulation disorders suggests that they are in fact phonological disorders that are based on the child's inability to understand the rules used to combine sounds, rather than difficulties in producing sounds. A child with an articulation problem may not be able to physically move his or her tongue to produce the /s/ sound. In contrast, a child with a phonological disorder may not understand that /s/ sounds appear at the end of some words or the child may not have learned the rules for making sounds. The idea that sound problems may be the result of phonological disorders links articulation and language together and suggests that sound-production disorders for children without organic problems may be closely related to language development. Research continues in this area and some treatment approaches are based on helping children with possible phonological disorders learn rules for speaking instead of mastering individually defective sounds (McReynolds, 1990).

Another view is that functional articulation problems are the result of a child learning to say sounds incorrectly, for some unknown reason. The implication is that as a result of poor learning, the child has not mastered the ability to use the speech mechanism to produce sounds of language correctly, even though there is nothing deviant about his or her speech structures or neurological system.

Many conditions and syndromes have articulation problems as one of their components. However, regardless of the cause of the articulation disorder, the penalties for the child can be the same. These children can become frustrated because their listeners cannot understand what they are attempting to say. They may become isolated from their peers because they sound different and are teased when they attempt to communicate. If they have multiple articulation problems (many sounds produced inappropriately), their teachers may not be able to accurately gauge their comprehension of curricular materials or even adequately meet their needs, share their discoveries, or answer their inquiries. In addition, they will have difficulty learning to read when reading is taught using phonically based instruction. Spelling and the comprehension of spoken instruction may also suffer. These negative characteristics will impair the learning process and adversely affect the entire educational process.

## Voice Disorders

Voice disorders are characterized by abnormalities of pitch, loudness, and quality of vocal production. These vocal abnormalities may be transient in nature, lasting only a few days or weeks, or chronic, lasting until help is provided to correct them or the circumstances causing them. The transient nature of some disorders makes it difficult to estimate the incidence of voice problems in school-age children. In addition, many voice problems take time to develop and do not manifest themselves until late adolescence or early adulthood. The largest survey reported places the incidence of voice disorders in children at 6 percent of the population (Senturia & Wilson, 1968). Voice problems are the result of organic factors (structural anomalies and diseases) and functional factors (poor use of structures, serious emotional conflicts, and unknown causes). Voices often mirror inner conflicts and can be a warning sign of emotional distress. Simply listening to a child's voice can often reliably determine whether a problem exists. However, it cannot with any degree of accuracy identify whether the cause of the voice problem is organic or functional. Later in this chapter, we will discuss the identification procedures necessary to pinpoint the possible causes of the abnormal voice characteristics listed here.

**Pitch.**    The pitch of the voice is produced when the vocal folds open and close as air expelled from the lungs rushes over them, causing vocal fold vibration. The more frequently the cords vibrate, the higher the perceived pitch of the voice. Stretching a rubber band and plucking it will mimic vocal fold vibration and pitch production. Each person has an *optimal pitch level*, which is the pitch that results when the most vocal fold vibrations are most efficiently used to make sound. *Habitual pitch level* is the pitch we use most often when making the laryngeal sounds used to form speech sounds. For most people, optimal pitch and habitual pitch are fairly similar most of the time. Most people laugh or clear their throats at their optimal pitch level. The optimal pitch level for a child changes as the child grows. By age 12 or 13, the adolescent vocal structures have matured to the point where adult optimal vocal pitch should be established. Many children, especially males, experience rather dramatic normal shifts (pitch breaks) in the pitch of their voices during puberty. For most, this is a transitory phase requiring no special attention. Disorders of pitch occur when the optimal pitch of the voice and the habitual pitch level do not match each other fairly closely. For the listener, a person with a voice disorder characterized by a pitch problem will have a voice that sounds too high or too low to be appropriate for the speaker's age or sex, or will lack control as evidenced by recurring pitch breaks that draw attention away from the message the speaker is attempting to communicate.

Organic reasons for pitch problems can be failure of the vocal folds to grow properly, paralysis of the vocal cords, growths or diseases affecting the vocal cords, hormonal therapy, or the use of steroids or other muscle-enhancing substances. Functional pitch problems can result from using a pitch level too high or low for the person's age and sex for no known reason or for emotional reasons such as fear of maturity.

**Loudness.**    The loudness of the voice is produced by the amount of energy that is used to produce vocal sounds. Loudness is related to the volume of air that passes over the vocal cords and the tension of the vocal cords. Disorders of voice characterized by loudness manifest themselves in speakers with voices that are too loud or too soft for the situation in which communication occurs.

Organic reasons for loudness problems include hearing losses that make it difficult for the speaker to monitor loudness appropriately. Sometimes children with cerebral palsy or similar coordination disorders cannot control their vocal mechanism well enough to regulate the breath stream in a manner that will result in appropriate loudness levels. Functional loudness problems can result when a child uses an inappropriately loud voice as a result of being reared in an environment where he or she must habitually shout for attention. Other children may use inappropriately soft voices in an attempt to avoid drawing attention to themselves, for any number of reasons from potential child abuse to simple shyness. Our voices call attention to us. If for some reason attention has negative consequences for a child, that child may do all he or she can to avoid the spotlight, including speaking in a very soft voice. As with all other functional voice disorders, a child may use an inappropriately loud or soft voice for no discernible reason.

**Quality.**    The quality of the voice is its most complex feature. Pitch and loudness are a part of quality, but the quality feature of a person's voice is what gives it the unique characteristics that make it different from every other person's voice. The interaction of the vocal sound produced by the larynx with the cavities of the throat (pharynx), nasal cavities, and mouth provide characteristics that are unique to each voice. The range for acceptable voice quality is large. However, at least four parameters can be identified that will isolate deviant voice quality. The acceptable quality of the voice can be disrupted by:

1. Excessive or insufficient nasal resonance
2. Breathiness
3. Harshness
4. Hoarseness

*Nasal resonance* problems are caused when too much or too little air passes through the nose during speech production. Too much air flow (*hypernasality*) can distort speech sounds, as described in the section on articulation disorders. It can also negatively affect voice quality. The opposite of hypernasality is too little air flow into the nasal passages (*hyponasality*). Most speakers have experienced transitory hyponasality when they have colds or allergy reactions. Nasal swelling and blockages hamper normal nasal resonance and give the voice a flat and muffled quality. Chronic hypernasal resonance problems may be caused by clefts of the hard and soft palate or paralysis of the soft palate, which makes it unable to close the nasal passages. Hyponasality can be caused by chronic allergic reactions or by growths in the nasal cavities. Permanent structural damage to the nose can also lead to hyponasality. Either hypernasality or hyponasality can result after surgery to correct soft palate deformities.

*Breathiness* occurs when the vocal folds do not sufficiently hold back enough of the breath stream for vocal fold vibration to occur. As a result, breathy voices have a whisperlike quality. Breathy voicing can occur when the vocal folds are paralyzed and cannot come together to vibrate, when a growth or node appears on the cords and keeps them from vibrating, when a speaker uses the vocal system to affect a breathy voice, or sometimes for no known reason. It is also possible to have a breathy voice for a number of emotional reasons that are unique to each individual.

*Harshness* (stridency) is usually the result of excessive strain or tension. Some children who chronically abuse their voices with excessive loudness and tension over time will develop "screamer's nodes" on their vocal cords. These calluslike growths disrupt vocal fold vibration and will cause the voice to sound harsh or raspy. Some speakers have harsh sounding voices because they do not use their voices efficiently to produce normal voicing.

*Hoarseness* is usually a transitory symptom that most speakers have experienced as the result of shouting too much or cheering too loudly. Another common cause of hoarseness is the swelling of the vocal apparatus that occurs with laryngeal infections (laryngitis). Cheerleaders or poorly trained singers who consistently abuse their voices for long periods of time can develop vocal fold growths that will result in harsh sounding voices. Fortunately, most speakers will automatically desist those activities that lead to vocal damage and allow the tissues to heal before permanent damage can occur.

Pitch, loudness, and quality disorders of the voice do not necessarily occur in isolation from each other. Voice disorders can be characterized by any combination of these components. Each person has unique vocal system strengths and weaknesses. Some children can cheer or yell for hours on end with little or no consequences, while for others even the mildest allergic reaction or common cold will affect their voices. Any vocal difference that persists for an unusual amount of time should be suspect and lead to referral for possible services.

## Fluency Disorders*

*Fluency* is the smooth flow of speech that most speakers experience when talking. Disfluencies take many forms and can result from different causes. Not all disfluencies are abnormal, and they cannot all be treated in the same manner. Stuttering is the most well known type of disfluency. However, it is not the only kind of disfluency. Eight different types of disfluency have been identified. Two types of disfluency are normal, and the remaining six types are abnormal. Figure 6.2 is a listing of the categories and subcategories of disfluency that will be discussed in this section.

**Normal Disfluencies of Speech.**   Normally fluent speech is not perfect speech. All speakers pause, hesitate, repeat, and mis-speak in a variety of ways that are well within the limits of normal communication. When in stressful situations that call for unfamiliar vocabulary use, most speakers may exhibit some disfluent speech. These disfluencies are not stuttering, nor are they abnormal. Speech is a complex activity that requires constant thought and rapid precise movements of many structures. It is not surprising that a process this complex is never fully mastered. Even the most polished and proficient speaker will sometimes pause and hesitate when spontaneously composing and delivering a complicated or emotionally charged message.

**Normal Developmental Disfluencies.**   As children pass through the developmental stages of language learning, they will be more disfluent at certain times than others. These periods of developmental disfluency are normal occurrences. Normally communicating children are most disfluent between the ages of 2.5 and 4 years. These normal disfluencies are characterized by repetitions of whole words and phrases, with occasional interjections of *"ers"* and *"uhs"* and *"ahs"* (Perkins, 1971; Yairi & Lewis, 1984). This is a transitional stage that most children outgrow as they master speech and language.

---

*The concepts discussed in this section were originally discussed in the following works listed in the bibliography: Culatta & Leeper, 1987; Culatta & Leeper, 1989; and Culatta & Goldberg, 1995.

Normal
   Normal disfluencies of speech
   Developmental disfluencies
Abnormal
   Stuttering
   Neurogenic dysfunction
      Motor speech disfluencies
      Neurolinguistic disfluencies
      Chemical reaction disfluencies
   Psychogenic dysfunction
      Emotionally based disfluency
      Manipulative disfluency
      Malingering
   Language delay
   Cluttering
   Mixed types of disfluencies

*Source:* From *Stuttering Therapy: An Integrated Approach to Theory and Practice* (p. 25), by R. Culatta and S. Goldberg, 1995, Needham Heights, MA: Allyn & Bacon.

**Figure 6.2**
Types of disfluency

**Stuttering.**    Stuttering is a disorder that begins in childhood. It becomes more complicated over time, and it follows a fairly predictable developmental path. At first, the behavior is episodic, with weeks passing during which the child's speech is normally fluent. Gradually these fluent intervals shrink until the child is consistently stuttering most of the time. Stuttering begins with simple whole-word and sound repetitions and, if the disorder is untreated, develops into more complicated patterns characterized by blocks, forcings, substitutions of nonfeared words for feared words, avoidances of speaking situations, eye closing, jaw tremors, and other facial and bodily contortions. The internal feelings of a person who stutters also progress through an evolutionary process. The child who is beginning to stutter shows very little reaction or concern about stuttering. This changes to self-identification as a stutterer and eventually strong emotional reactions, including fear of speaking, embarrassment when stuttering, and feelings of victimization (Bloodstein, 1960).

A diagnostic characteristic of stuttering is that the vowels used during repetition are different from those used when normal speakers are disfluent. When a person who stutters repeats a word, he or she tends to insert the schwa vowel /ə/ ("uh") in place of the vowel that would ordinarily occur. Thus "bae-bae-baseball" becomes "buh-buh-baseball." Stuttering can also be manipulated in a number of ways that distinguish it from other types of disfluency. For example, reduction in stuttering often occurs with repeated readings of the same passage. This phenomenon is called *adaptation.* Stuttering can also be reduced when distracting noises are introduced while the person who stutters is speaking. Speaking in time to a metronome, singing, or group recitation can all alter or eliminate stuttering for brief periods of time. In fact, any temporary distraction may produce short-term fluent speech. In addition, people who stutter do not do so on every word they utter. Much of their speech is fluent, and during these fluent periods there is little or no sign of the characteristic behaviors that constitute stuttering.

Stuttering tends to run in families (Kidd, 1980). However, the presence of a "stuttering gene" has not been isolated. The cause of stuttering is unknown. The most widely held belief about the cause of stuttering is that stuttering is the result of environmental experiences that interact with a genetic predisposition to bring about the disorder.

In summary, the following characteristics need to be present to differentiate stuttering from other types of disfluency:

1. The behavior must have a developmental history beginning in childhood.
2. There are no identifiable etiological or maintaining factors.
3. The repetition patterns differ from those of normal speakers.
4. The characteristics of stuttering can be modified in many ways.
5. The characteristics of stuttering are not present during fluent periods.
6. The person who stutters has internalized a belief system about the difficulty of communication in general and specific situations in particular.

**Neurogenic Disfluency.**   Neurogenic disfluency is the direct result of an identifiable neuropathology in a child with no previous history of fluency problems (Culatta & Leeper, 1987). Disfluent behaviors may appear soon after the onset of some neurological trauma or progressive disease. Specific medications have also been reported to affect fluency (Helm-Estabrooks, 1987). Neurogenic disfluencies are often different in form from those presented by stutterers. For example, Rosenbeck (1984), describing the repetitions of apraxic speakers, notes that these repetitions stop once sounds or words are produced correctly. By comparison, children who stutter continue to repeat sounds that are made correctly. Speakers with brain damage who cannot select or code the words they wish to say will be disfluent as they struggle to search for the correct word. These disfluencies cease once the correct word is located. In contrast, children who stutter are well aware of the words they are attempting to say while they are being disfluent.

*Motor speech disorders* caused by cerebral palsy or other conditions that make it difficult for children to plan speech or use their speech mechanisms effectively may also lead to a higher-than-expected frequency of disfluent speech. *Neurolinguistic disfluencies* can appear after children suffer seizures or as the result of direct brain damage that affects language formulation. Reactions to drugs may also cause *chemical reaction disfluencies.* Helm-Estabrooks (1987), Quader (1977), McCarthy (1981), and Nurnberg and Greenwall (1981) all report instances in which the onset of disfluent behavior was correlated to the administration of medication. Most label warnings that accompany medications do not include information about the effects that they have on fluency. Also, children may react differently to different medications and combinations of medications. Parents and teachers should be alert to the sudden onset of disfluency that accompanies the use of a new medication or a shift in the use of ongoing medications.

All three types of disfluencies just described can usually be distinguished by the alert parent, teacher, or clinician. The onset of these disfluencies is usually abrupt, and the child affected will not have a history of fluency problems. Initially, the child experiencing neurogenic disfluencies will feel little concern about speaking as compared to the child who stutters, who is developing self-image and coping strategies that set him or her apart from other children. Many of the speech manipulations that bring about fluent speech with children who stutter will have little or no effect on neurologically based disfluencies.

**Psychogenic Disfluency.**   Speech disfluency can also appear in children for whom no evidence on neurological dysfunction is found and no history of developmental stuttering is reported. The most striking characteristics of this type of disfluency are its sudden onset and its relationship to some identifiable emotional crisis. Psychogenic disfluencies can be grouped into three subcategories: emotionally based, manipulative, and malingering. Emotionally based disfluencies far outnumber manipulative disfluencies and malingering as documented phenomena.

*Emotionally based disfluencies* are allied to a significant event that puts the child under psychological pressures. Their onset is sudden and the behaviors themselves are characterized by a high frequency or repetition of initial sounds or words in sentences and phrases. During these episodes there is little fluent speech and the disfluent behavior is rarely accompanied by the physical contortions and forcings displayed by those who stutter. These children also show little interest in the process of speaking and are not overly concerned about their disfluent speech (Deal, 1982).

*Manipulative disfluency* is speech used to control others. Van Riper (1982) reports that one can sense the controlling, punishing, wheedling, exploitive urges behind the behavior. . . . These [disfluent speakers] . . . suffer less than their listeners. Manipulative disfluency is almost exclusively a childhood occurrence. Characteristics may include unusual and insistent demands for attention while disfluent, lengthy repetition of fluent words and a variety of physical movements and facial grimaces that do not change over time. These children are rarely emotional about their disfluency patterns and do not develop fears of speaking (p. 115).

*Malingering disfluency*, which is disfluency used purposefully to avoid responsibilities or assignments, is rare. Teachers, parents, and speech-language pathologists who suspect malingering should be aware of the situations in which disfluencies occur, whether the behaviors are manipulable under conditions that bring about fluency in those who stutter, and whether any noticeable gains can be achieved by being disfluent.

**Language Delay.**   Childhood language disorders can have an impact on the ability to speak fluently. Hall (1977) and Hall, Wray, and Conti (1986) describe situations where the initiation of therapy to help children with severe language disorders resulted in an increase in disfluency. It appears that the initial rise in disfluency in some children with language disorders when treatment begins is not due to the beginning of stuttering, but rather is due to the children's efforts to learn new language forms. Learning complex language tasks increases the disfluencies of all children (normal developmental disfluency), and language therapy appears to sometimes have the side effect of increasing the disfluencies of children with language delays. The preliminary information available about this type of disfluency indicates that maintaining language-based treatment will result in increasing a child's communication skills and will eventually alleviate the disfluencies that were temporarily created.

**Cluttering.**   This form of disfluency is characterized by speech that is so disorganized that it is difficult to understand. Words are spoken at an extremely fast rate, phrases are left uncompleted, and there are frequent repetitions and omissions of whole words and parts of phrases. Speech is slurred, articulation is disordered, the flow of words is jumbled, and speech is produced in spurts (Van Riper & Erickson, 1996). Children who clutter have little awareness of its effect on their speech or the listener. They do not develop speaking fears, nor do they avoid speaking situations. This lack of concern often results in resistance to help or lack of any real interest in modifying their speech patterns. Unlike children who stutter, children who clutter often have allied reading, language, and writing difficulties and a variety of motor coordination problems.

**Mixed Disfluencies.**   Children who are disfluent for any one of the reasons highlighted previously are not excused from difficulties in any of the other areas. A child who already stutters may suffer neurological damage or emotional trauma, with resulting disfluent behaviors that are independent of the original stuttering. With the exception of the recognized co-existence of cluttering and stuttering, there is little research to document the existence of mixed disfluencies. In practical terms this means that the teacher, parent, or speech-language pathologist who suspects multiple causality for disfluent behavior must share this information with all those concerned about the child and develop logical treatment protocols that account for all the relevant factors contributing to the disfluency pattern.

## Etiology and Characteristics of Language Disorders

Approximately 2 to 3 percent of all preschool children and 1 percent of all school-age children have language disorders (National Institute of Neurological and Communicative Disorders and Stroke, 1988). Language disability is not a disease, but rather a failure to learn (Van Riper & Erickson, 1996). There are many reasons for this failure, some known and others unknown. Language disability may be the result of not having prerequisite conceptual knowledge or adequately developed cognitive processes. It may be developmental or acquired, expressive and/or receptive, and an isolated problem or a component of other disorders.

Conceptual knowledge of the environment is needed when attempting to communicate. It is impossible for a child to linguistically convey what he or she does not know. Children who have limited conceptual knowledge have difficulty symbolizing events (Owens, 1991). Children develop many concepts through play activities. The more sophisticated a child's play, the greater the child's knowledge of the world (Westby, 1988). Children deprived of experiences do not gain the concepts that those experiences teach. A youngster who has never visited a supermarket cannot understand how food gets to stores and from stores to homes. A 10-year-old whose knowledge of the world is at a 3-year-old's level cannot be expected to exhibit language beyond the 3-year-old level.

Several specific cognitive processes are prerequisites for language learning. Deficits in attention skills, memory, and auditory and visual perception will make language acquisition difficult. *Attention* is the ability to focus on one event while excluding all other competing distractions. Children who have difficulty attending will have problems attaching language symbols to their experiences and abstracting meaning from those experiences.

*Long-term memory* and *short-term memory* are the two types of memory needed to learn language. Long-term memory is needed to store the rules, meanings, and structures of language so that they can be accessed when needed. Short-term (working) memory is the brief holding of concepts while processing them. Short-term memory is needed to follow directions or store concepts while searching for meanings that are stored in long-term memory (Wagner and Torgesen, 1987). Children with deficits in long- and short-term processing of information will be unable to store and access the information they need to learn language.

*Perception* is the ability to recognize the commonalities in events. When learning language, children perceive the similarities in their visual and auditory experiences and associate them with the language they are hearing. This is how specific words, word forms, and syntax are learned. If a child does not perceive the similarities in his or her experiences, he or she will not be able to convert these similarities into language symbols (Kemler, 1983).

Developmental language disorders are evidenced by children who have difficulty acquiring any or all of the components of language. Developmental language disability is considered congenital, and many believe that it stems from neurological damage that occurs before or during birth. However, it is not always possible to determine the specific nature of the suspected brain injury, which may be subtle and is often undetectable (Culatta & Culatta, 1993). In addition, children's environments that do not foster language development can play a major role in developmental language disorders.

Acquired or traumatic language disorders are the result of definable injury that affects the language formulation or comprehension areas of the brain. These injuries often occur after normal language has been acquired or during childhood, interrupting or disturbing language as it is being learned.

While speech deals with the production or modification of sounds, language is more complex in that it has both receptive (decoding) and expressive (encoding) components. Receptive language skills are evidenced by a child's ability to receive and translate messages into meaningful information. Receptive language abilities are critical for all language learning. Receptive language skills make it possible for the child to understand the rules of language, the meanings of words, the intent of instructions, and the relationship between experiences and their application to learning. A child's receptive skills must always precede and be more sophisticated than his or her expressive skills for language learning to advance. Expressive language skills are evidenced by the child's ability to formulate what he or she is thinking or feeling into meaningful words, phrases, and sentences. Language relies on speech, in most cases, and gestures and signs in some cases, to transmit the messages that have been formulated. Disorders of a receptive nature can occur when a child is deaf or hearing impaired and does not receive messages or receives them in a distorted fashion.

Receptive language disorders also occur when a child, for a variety of reasons, is unable to store and decode the messages received from others. Expressive language disorders are the result of a child being unable to encode and express thoughts, feelings, and experiences in logical, meaningful, and acceptable ways.

Language disabilities may occur in isolation without other co-existing conditions, or they may be causally linked to any of a number of other conditions. The conditions that are commonly linked with language disabilities are traumatic brain injury, cerebral palsy, hearing impairment, mental retardation, multiple handicaps, autism, severe illness, and environmental deprivations.

Brain damage that has destroyed tissues needed to comprehend and formulate language is a shared cause of traumatic brain injury and cerebral palsy. For both conditions, language disabilities are present only when the language formulation and comprehension areas of the brain are damaged. The damage that causes traumatic brain injury occurs after language has developed or while it is developing. The damage that causes cerebral palsy occurs prior to the child's development of language. Children affected by either condition may have difficulties in attending to messages, decoding them meaningfully, or using language effectively to respond to questions or follow instructions.

Children who are severely hearing impaired or deaf do not hear the language used in their environment. They may be taught language through signing and may learn to master the morphology, syntax, and semantics of language, but will have difficulty with the phonology and pragmatic aspects of spoken language. Since these children have to rely on visual and tactile language learning experiences, they tend to have difficulty with abstractions and tend to be concrete in their linguistic performance (Van Riper & Erickson, 1996).

Children with mental retardation and multiple handicaps, depending upon the severity of the conditions, may have all aspects of language impaired. For children who are mentally retarded, the degree of language involvement will depend on the severity of the retardation. As previously discussed, cognitive skills are necessary to learn the rules of language and the relationship of words to each other. Children with retardation may be slow in developing these needed skills and, as a result, may be slow in developing receptive and expressive language. Children with multiple handicaps may also have cognitive problems and, in addition, may be limited in their conceptual knowledge of the environment. Other prerequisite skills such as attention, memory, and perception may also be inadequate for normal language development.

Children with autism consistently display profound language dysfunctions. Many times a child with autism is suspected of being deaf because he or she fails to attend to voice or speech signals. These children do not learn language at expected rates and have little pragmatic function in their communication. The child's lack of emotionality is mirrored in speech and language that can be devoid of expressions of feeling or totally lacking in attempts to reach out to others. Words that are learned are used in restricted contexts, and the child does not seem to generalize one experience to another. It is suspected that the perceptual problems of children with autism interfere with language learning (Bernstein & Tiegerman, 1989). When they speak at all, children with autism tend to use short, simple sentences, omitting grammatical features such as conjunctions and prepositions. Since the child tends to learn whole phrases as single units, morphological changes are rarely applied (Hegde, 1995).

Children who experience severe illnesses or environmental deprivation may fail to develop language for the same underlying reason. Although for markedly different reasons, both groups may share cognitive deficiencies due to the lack of experiences needed to develop language. The severely ill child who is out of contact or marginally aware of his or her surroundings is not capable of abstracting the experiences needed to learn language. This child must often sacrifice even the most common enriching experiences while battling to survive. Object manipulation, crawling, visiting a shopping center, doing a puzzle, or even playing with blocks may be activities unavailable to the severely chronically ill child. As a result, even if this child lives in the most stimulating environment, he or she might not be able to take advantage of the language learning opportunities that the environment offers. The environmentally impoverished child might be capable of processing, abstracting, perceiving, and conceptualizing, but may not be exposed to activities that lead to developing these prerequisite skills. Children raised in barren environments devoid of toys, educational materials, and language-enriching experiences cannot develop language in a vacuum. Richness of experience does not equate with the expense of toys, but rather with the diversity of experiences to which a child is exposed. Frequent and meaningful conversations with parents or caretakers, travel outside of one's home or neighborhood, looking at pictures, and manipulating toys all add to the conceptual framework that the language developing child is constructing. The fewer experiences the child has, the less information he or she will have for linguistic development and the more restricted that developing framework will become.

## Disorders of Form, Content, and Use of Language

Independent of their cause, the major aspects of language disability can be classified by discussing the components needed to learn language. Disorders of the morphologic, syntactic, semantic, and pragmatic components of language reveal characteristics of language disability that cross the boundaries of any given condition. The form of language may be defective when a child has difficulty acquiring the morphologic and syntactic aspects of language. This is evident in children who are mature enough to have developed a sense of the morphology of their language, yet use words and phrases without the appropriate endings. Children with morphologic problems may not express plurality or appropriate tenses or use articles, pronouns, and prepositions. Syntactic problems arise in faulty sentence construction. Sentences are often reduced in length and the word order used is inappropriate. On a receptive level, the child may be confused by any sentences that are complex or unusual in form.

The content of language is represented by semantic acquisition. Children with language disorders are often slow in learning the meanings of words. Their vocabularies are smaller than those of their peers and they have difficulty remembering the meaning of newly acquired words. Receptively, the child my not understand the meanings of abstract words or the concepts that they represent.

Pragmatics represents the meaningful use of language. Children with pragmatic problems may not know how to initiate or maintain conversations. They may be clumsy in turn taking, knowing how to interrupt, or giving a listener information needed to understand what they are trying to communicate. These children will have problems telling stories, asking questions, and relating the language they hear to personal experiences.

## Characteristics of Speech and Language Differences

This section of the chapter will highlight characteristic speech and language differences that are part of recognized dialects of Standard English. Remember that most dialectal speakers can easily code switch between their dialectal speech and Standard English. However, many children who have little contact with Standard English speakers may come to school as dialectal speakers who are competent in only their particular dialect. It is the task of teachers in these areas of the country to understand what the regional dialect is and be able to determine whether a given child is using language that is different from Standard English yet still valid and not disordered and in need of treatment. Table 6.5 highlights some of the differences between Standard English and the most prevalent dialects. This listing is illustrative of the differences but is by no means complete. Williams and Wolfram (1977) have identified 29 linguistic rules of Black English that differ from Standard English. It is critical to emphasize the fact that dialects are rule governed valid differences

**Table 6.5**

Selected Phonological and Grammatical Characteristics of Black English (B), Southern English (S), Southern White Nonstandard English (SWNS), and Appalachian English (A). Presence of each feature in the dialect is denoted by (X).

| Features | Descriptions | Examples | B | S | SWNS | A |
|---|---|---|---|---|---|---|
| Consonant cluster reduction (general) | Deletion of second of two consonants in word final position belonging to same base word | tes (test) | X | | X | |
| | Deletion of past tense (-ed) morpheme from a base word, resulting in a consonant cluster that is subsequently reduced | rub (rubbed) | X | | X | |
| | Plural formations of reduced consonant cluster assume phonetic representations of sibilants and affricatives | desses (desks) | X | | X | |
| /θ/ phoneme | /f/ for /θ/ between vowels and in word final position | nofin (nothing) Ruf (Ruth) | X | | | |
| /ð/ phoneme | /d/ for /ð/ in word initial position | dis (this) | X | | | |
| | /v/ for /ð/ between vowels and in word final positions | bavin (bathing) bave (bathe) | X | | | |
| Vowel nasalization | No contrast between vowels /ɪ/ and /ɛ/ before nasals | pin (pin, pen) | | X | | X |
| The /r/ and /l/ phonemes | Deletion preceding a consonant | ba: game (ball game) | X | X | | |
| Future tense forms | Use of *gonna* | She gonna go. (She is going to go.) | X | | X | |
| | *Gonna* reduced to *'ngna, 'mana, 'mon* and *'ma* | I'ngma go. I'mana go. I'mon go. I'ma go. (I am going to go.) | X | | | |
| Double modals | Co-occurrence of selected modals such as *might, could, should* | I might coulda done it. (It is possible that I could have done it.) | X | | X | X |
| Intensifying adverbs | Use of intensifiers, i.e., *right, plumb,* to refer to completeness | right large (very large) | X | | X | X |
| Negation | *Ain't* for *have/has, am/are, didn't* | He ain't go home. (He didn't go home.) | X | | | |
| Relative clauses | Deletion of relative pronouns | That's the dog bit me. (That's the dog that bit me.) | X | | X | X |
| Questions | Same interrogative form for direct and indirect questions | I wonder was she walking? (I wonder if she was walking.) | X | | X | X |

*Source:* From *Social Dialects: Differences vs. Disorders* (pp.148–149), by R. Williams and W. Wolfram, 1977, Washington, DC: American Speech and Hearing Association. Adapted by permission of the American Speech-Language-Hearing Association.

in language use and not errors or less correct language. Children who speak a dialect of a language are no less linguistically competent than their Standard English–speaking peers.

## IDENTIFICATION PROCESS

Children with communication disorders are initially identified by referrals to the school speech-language pathologist and by screening examinations conducted by the speech-language pathologist to identify those children who might have communication disorders. Children who are referred and fail screening examinations will then undergo more formal diagnostic procedures to identify the specific aspects of their communication disorder.

### Referral Sources

The major referral source for school-age children is the classroom teacher. The teacher observes the child attempting to communicate in day-to-day situations. He or she observes the child when the child is expressing new information, telling well-known stories, explaining thoughts and feelings, and interacting with other children. In addition, most classroom teachers can compare the communication performance of any given child to that child's peers. Most school-based speech-language pathologists conduct periodic in-service sessions for teachers, during which they highlight the characteristics of children with communication disorders and explain treatment options that are available in the school setting. Teachers are encouraged to contact the speech-language pathologist if they suspect there might be a child with a communication disorder in their class. Checklists and charts outlining normal development are routinely distributed to teachers to help them decide on referrals. Figure 6.3 is a typical checklist that can be used to help teachers identify children who might need special programming.

The next most productive source for referral is parents. Parents have the opportunity to observe their children in a variety of communication settings. Checklists of characteristics of speech disorders that are sent home and invitations to contact the school speech-language pathologist help to identify many children.

Professionals in areas that provide service to children also can refer children for identification. School nurses, pediatricians, dentists, preschool teachers, and coordinators and teachers affiliated with various early intervention programs can be sources for early identification. In some instances, children themselves can initiate a referral by sharing their concerns about how they talk with their parents, teachers, or allied health professionals with whom they come into contact.

### Screening Procedures

Speech, language, and hearing screenings are procedures that briefly sample a child's communication skills and hearing acuity to determine whether a more formal

The following behaviors may indicate that a child in your classroom has a language impairement that is in need of clincial intervention. Please check the appropriate items.

\_\_\_\_\_  Child mispronounces sounds and words.
\_\_\_\_\_  Child omits word endings, such as plural -s and past tense -ed.
\_\_\_\_\_  Child omits small unemphasized words, such as auxilliary verbs or prepositions.
\_\_\_\_\_  Child uses an immature vocabulary, overuses empty words such as *one* and *thing,* or seems to have difficulty recalling or finding the right word.
\_\_\_\_\_  Child has difficulty comprehending new words and concepts.
\_\_\_\_\_  Child's sentence structure seems immature or overreliant on forms, such as subject-verb-object. It's unoriginal, dull.
\_\_\_\_\_  Child's question and/or negative sentence style is immature.
\_\_\_\_\_  Child has difficulty with one of the following:

| | | |
|---|---|---|
| \_\_\_\_\_ Verb tensing | \_\_\_\_\_ Articles | \_\_\_\_\_ Auxiliary verbs |
| \_\_\_\_\_ Pronouns | \_\_\_\_\_ Irreg. verbs | \_\_\_\_\_ Prepositions |
| \_\_\_\_\_ Word order | \_\_\_\_\_ Irreg. plurals | \_\_\_\_\_ Conjunctions |

\_\_\_\_\_  Child has difficulty relating sequential events.
\_\_\_\_\_  Child has difficulty following directions.
\_\_\_\_\_  Child's questions often inaccurate or vague.
\_\_\_\_\_  Child's questions often poorly formed.
\_\_\_\_\_  Child has difficulty answering questions.
\_\_\_\_\_  Child's comments often off topic or inappropriate for the conversation.
\_\_\_\_\_  There are long pauses between a remark and the child's reply or between successive remarks by the child. It's as if the child is searching for a response or is confused.
\_\_\_\_\_  Child appears to be attending to communication but remembers little of what is said.
\_\_\_\_\_  Child has difficulty using language socially for the following purposes:

| | | |
|---|---|---|
| \_\_\_\_\_ Request needs | \_\_\_\_\_ Pretend/imagine | \_\_\_\_\_ Protest |
| \_\_\_\_\_ Greet | \_\_\_\_\_ Request information | \_\_\_\_\_ Gain attention |
| \_\_\_\_\_ Respond/reply | \_\_\_\_\_ Share ideas, feelings | \_\_\_\_\_ Clarify |
| \_\_\_\_\_ Relate events | \_\_\_\_\_ Entertain | \_\_\_\_\_ Reason |

\_\_\_\_\_  Child has difficulty interpreting the following:

| | | |
|---|---|---|
| \_\_\_\_\_ Figurative language | \_\_\_\_\_ Humor | \_\_\_\_\_ Gestures |
| | \_\_\_\_\_ Emotions | \_\_\_\_\_ Body language |

\_\_\_\_\_  Child does not alter production for different audiences and locations.
\_\_\_\_\_  Child does not seem to consider the effect of language on the listener.
\_\_\_\_\_  Child often has verbal misunderstandings with others.
\_\_\_\_\_  Child has difficulty with reading and writing.
\_\_\_\_\_  Child's language skills seem to be much lower than other areas, such as mechanical, artistic, or social skills.

*Source: Language Disorders: A Functional Approach to Assessment and Intervention* (2nd ed., p. 392), by R. E. Owens, 1995. Needham Heights, MA: Allyn & Bacon. Reprinted by permission.

Figure 6.3
Behaviors resulting in teacher referral of children with possible language impairments

diagnostic evaluation should be conducted. Public school speech-language pathologists usually screen children entering kindergarten and those in the primary grades. Receptive and expressive language skills, articulation, voice, and fluency are specifically isolated. Most school systems have guidelines that mandate when initial screening and follow-up screenings must be performed. Children who fail hearing screenings are referred to audiologists for in-depth diagnostic assessment (see Chapter 8).

Children who fail screenings for the other parameters of communication are scheduled for more formal diagnostic testing.

## Diagnostic Procedures

The diagnosis of a communication disorder follows a fairly standard pattern that is modified to meet the needs of any given child. Figure 6.4 is an outline of a typical diagnostic protocol.

## Parental Permission

Parents of children who fail screening tests are usually notified by letter that their child has not passed the speech, language, or hearing portion of the screening examination. The implications of failing the screening tests are usually outlined and permission is requested to conduct a diagnostic evaluation. Parents have the options of granting permission for further testing, not granting permission, or having the diagnostic evaluation performed by a speech-language pathologist of their own choosing outside of the school setting, usually at their own expense. When it is possible, parents are asked to attend the diagnostic evaluation or at least provide pertinent historical data about their child on pre-diagnostic case history forms.

## Case History

The speech-language pathologist, having obtained parental permission, proceeds to construct a case history for the child that focuses on communication. School and medical records may be requested to scan for possible organic, emotional, or environmental experiences the child may have had that could have an impact on present communication. Examples of significant medical events might be a history of

---

Obtain parental permission
Construct case history
   Records
   Interviews
Observations of communication behavior
Evaluations
   Informal (nonstandardized)
   Formal (standardized)
Diagnostic findings
Prognosis
Intervention recommendation

---

Figure 6.4
Diagnostic procedures

seizures, periods of severe illness, specific illnesses such as rubella that have communication consequences, current medications being administered, and a history of diagnosed conditions that are often allied with communication disorders. Emotional episodes and diagnosed emotional conditions can also have an impact upon communication. Environmental experiences of importance might include child abuse, family breakups, or frequent changes in living situations. The speech-language pathologist will also review the pre-diagnostic case history form filled out by the parents to see if any other possible etiological explanations might exist for a child's suspected communication disorder. Most pre-diagnostic forms also request parents to describe the child's communication patterns and to report whether the way the child communicates is of any concern to them. The case history is completed when the speech-language pathologist conducts interviews with parents during the diagnostic session prior to evaluating the child. Questions about school and medical records are discussed at this time, and parents are encouraged to share their view of the child's communication skills and describe in detail any concerns they may have about communication. The child may also be interviewed at this time if the speech-language pathologist feels that the child can help in completing the case history.

## Observations

It is becoming increasingly important to observe the child's communication prior to commencing evaluations. The concern is that relying only on the communication samples obtained and measured during the formal diagnostic setting might not be the most representative sample of the child's "real" communication. Observation can be accomplished in several ways. As a rule, the more natural the setting in which the child is observed communicating, the more valid will be the implications drawn from the sample. Naturalistic contexts for observation include observing the child in group activities, in free-play situations, during task-oriented situations, and in social interactions with parents, peers, adults, and other children. These observations can reveal how the child gains attention, initiates communication, takes turns speaking, and uses speech and language in general (McCormick, 1990). It is not always possible for the speech-language pathologist to observe a child in these naturalistic settings. A compromise might be to ask the parents to send prior to the diagnostic session, or bring to the diagnostic session, an audio- or videotape of the child communicating in natural settings. An advantage of the recordings is that the parents or the speech-language pathologist can point out instances of communication behavior about which there is concern.

Many of the suites used to conduct speech and language evaluations are constructed with one-way observation mirrors. Another common way of observing the child is to ask a parent, sibling, or peer to spend a few minutes in some activity with the child while the speech-language pathologist observes through the observation window. This technique is commonly used to enable observation on the scene during the diagnostic session.

## Evaluation

After completing observations, the usual procedure is to begin informal and formal evaluations of the child. Informal evaluations include attempting to engage the child in conversation, listening to stories or descriptions of pictures, and playing games that elicit speech and language. The speech-language pathologist uses these samples to compare the child's performance to expectations of age-appropriate behavior in communication. The speech-language pathologist will informally assess the child's use of the components of language. He or she will also listen for the correct articulation of sounds and appropriate use of voice and will assess the fluency the child displays. The speech-language pathologist will also observe the ease with which the child is able to perform the movements of the articulators needed for speech.

Formal testing is usually accomplished by using standardized tests that enable the speech-language pathologist to compare any given child's performance on the parameters being tested to similar performance by peers. Many standardized tests are available to test specific aspects of communication. For example, Figure 6.5 is a reproduction of the Screening Test Checklist Form of the Dworkin-Culatta Oral Mechanism Examination and Treatment System (Dworkin & Culatta, 1996), a test routinely used to determine whether a child can manipulate his or her articulators to successfully perform the movements needed for speaking. The inability to perform any of the screening test activities is a signal for the examiner to administer more exhaustive activities in the weak areas.

Speech sound articulation is usually tested by asking the child to identify pictures that contain key sounds. For example, the child might be asked to identify a picture of a *cat* or *kitten* to determine whether the child can produce the /k/ sound correctly. These tests are called *articulation tests*. They provide the examiner with a standardized set of pictures that require the speech sounds of language to be articulated when the pictures are identified. A widely used test is the Goldman-Fristoe Test of Articulation (Goldman & Fristoe, 1986).

Language testing is more complex; many different standardized tests can be used to determine the child's skills in each of the components of language. For example, the Peabody Picture Vocabulary Test (Dunn & Dunn, 1981) will give a standardized measure of a child's receptive vocabulary. The Test of Language Development (TOLD) (Newcomber & Hammill, 1988) will help determine what level a child is at in the development of language skills. The Clinical Evaluation of Language Fundamentals (CELF) (Semel, Wiig, & Secord, 1987) measures language comprehension and expression for fifth- to twelfth-graders. The speech-language pathologist determines from the analysis of the samples collected during observations and from recordings just which language tests are appropriate for a given child.

Evaluations of possible voice problems, unlike those in other areas, begin with a medical evaluation. Since the symptoms (what a listener hears) of voice problems can be the same whether the problem is organic or functional in nature, it is imperative that diagnosis and treatment be a team effort between the otorhinolaryngologist and the speech-language pathologist. Otorhinolaryngologists, or ear, nose, and throat (ENT) specialists, are physicians who specialize in diagnosing and treating

## SCREENING TEST CHECKLIST FORM

Name:_____ ; Sex: _____

Age:_____ ; DOB:_____ ; File #: _____

Address:_____

_____ ; Phone # (___) _____

Referral Source:_____ ; Date of Exam: _____

Examiner:_____ ; Test Location:_____

### SCREENING KEY

**ABNORMAL = YES; NORMAL = NO; QUESTIONABLE = YES**
**[For "YES" response, place ✔ in Deep Test Box.]**

|  | RESPONSE | DEEP TEST |
|---|---|---|
| **I. FACIAL STATUS**<br>1. Does the face look asymmetrical, or possess any abnormal signs at rest? | _____ → | ☐ |
| **II. LIP FUNCTIONING**<br>1. Are the movements of the lips asymmetrical, or are the repetitions too slow, dysrhythmic, or imprecise? | → | ☐ |
| **III. JAW FUNCTIONING**<br>1. Are movements asymmetrical, limited in range, or accompanied by <u>TMJ</u> noises? | → | ☐ |
| **IV. HARD PALATE**<br>1. Is the arch shape or tissue appearance unusual? | → | ☐ |
| **V. TONGUE FUNCTIONING**<br>1. Do movements lack sufficient range and precision, or are the repetitions too slow, dysrhythmic or imprecise? | → | ☐ |
| **VI. VELOPHARYNGEAL FUNCTIONING**<br>1. Are there signs of hypernasal or hyponasal resonance? | → | ☐ |
| **VII. STATUS OF DENTITION**<br>1. Are there gross abnormalities in the alignment and condition of upper/lower teeth or signs of gross gum disease? | → | ☐ |
| **VIII. MOTOR SPEECH PROGRAMMING ABILITIES**<br>1. Are there signs of articulatory groping, or whole or part word transpositions of the sequence? | → | ☐ |
| **LIST EXAMINATIONS TO BE DEEP TESTED** | _____ → | _____ |

COMMENTS:

*Source: The Dworkin-Culatta Oral Mechanism Examination and Treatment System*, by J. Dworkin and R. Culatta, 1996, Farmington, MI

Figure 6.5
Dworkin-Culatta oral mechanism examination and treatment system

disorders of the ear, nose, and throat. Many conditions that reveal themselves through voice problems (laryngeal cancers, vocal nodules, juvenile papilloma) can have serious and even life-threatening consequences. It is therefore imperative that a medical clearance be obtained for the safety of the patient prior to administering speech pathology services.

Fluency evaluations proceed in several stages, depending upon the type of disfluency the child is displaying. Much of the information discussed in the section on the characteristics of disfluency is diagnostic in nature. Instruments such as the Protocol for Differentiating the Incipient Stutterer (Pindzola & White, 1986) help the speech-language pathologist determine whether the disfluencies observed are normal developmental disfluencies or the beginning of stuttering. The Differential Screening Test for Stuttering Checklist (Culatta & Goldberg, 1995) reproduced in Table 6.6 helps the speech-language pathologist decide whether the disfluencies in a child's speech are stuttering or one of the other types of disfluency previously described.

If stuttering is identified as the presenting fluency disorder, many measurements are taken that range from descriptions of the stuttering behavior using instruments such as the Checklist of Stuttering Behavior (Williams, Darley, & Spriestersbach, 1978) to determining how the person who stutters perceives the effects his or her stuttering has on communication, as measured by the Perceptions of Stuttering Inventory (PSI) (Woolf, 1967).

Table 6.6
Differential Screening Test for Stuttering Checklist

| Number | Indicator | Associated with Stuttering | Associated with Other Forms of Disfluency |
|--------|-----------|----------------------------|-------------------------------------------|
| 1 | Onset | Before 7 years of age | After 7 years of age |
| 2 | Stages of development | Progressive | Abrupt |
| 3 | Family history | History of stuttering in family | No history of stuttering in family |
| 4 | Etiology | Unknown | Appears immediately following a specific event |
| 5 | Adaptation | Number of disfluencies reduces through fifth reading | Little or no reduction of disfluencies through fifth reading |
| 6 | Automatic speech—1 (days of the week) | Relatively fluent | Little or no change |
| 7 | Automatic speech—2 (months of the year) | Relatively fluent | Little or no change |
| 8 | Automatic speech—3 (count to 20) | Relatively fluent | Little or no change |
| 9 | Choral reading (reads for 1 minute, 30 seconds; disregard first 30 seconds) | Fluency level improves | No effect on fluency |
| 10 | Singing | Fluency level improves | No effect on fluency |
|    | Total checks | | |

*Instructions:* Check the appropriate responses for each indicator. Although there is no specific number of indicators that unequivocally differentiates a stutterer from a person with another form of disfluency, a preponderance of checked items in one column can provide substantial evidence.

*Source:* From *Stuttering Therapy: An Integrated Approach to Theory and Practice* (p. 97), by R. Culatta and S. Goldberg, 1995, Needham, MA, Allyn & Bacon.

## Diagnosis, Prognosis and Recommendations

Once the case history information, observation information, and results of informal and formal testing are combined and analyzed, the speech-language pathologist is able to state a diagnosis of the communication disorder. For example, a child might be diagnosed as exhibiting a mild to moderate disorder of articulation, severe stuttering, or an expressive language disorder.

As a part of the diagnosis, the speech-language pathologist will usually make a prognostic statement and suggest recommendations for programming. A sample prognostic statement might be that a given child exhibits a moderate functional articulation disorder that will probably improve with treatment, or that a child is severely dysarthric, resulting in the inability to use oral speech, and will need training in alternative forms of communication.

The diagnostic report, including case history information, results of observations, and evaluations, diagnosis, prognosis, and recommendations, is shared with the child's parents and also presented to the IEP team. It is as a result of the collaboration of the parents and the IEP team, of which the speech-language pathologist is a member, that programming decisions are finalized.

# PROGRAMS

## Service Provision Settings

Speech therapy services are presented in all the traditional special educational settings. Speech-language pathologists provide service as consultants to the regular classroom teacher, in resource rooms, separate classes, residential facilities, and home and hospital settings. In addition, speech-language pathology services are provided by private practitioners who work on a fee-for-service basis or with contracts. Training requirements mandate that speech-language pathologists in training be directly supervised by the programs that train them. As a result, speech clinics that provide services while training student speech-language pathologists can be found at many colleges and universities. Students receiving speech therapy are the most highly integrated group of all those receiving special education services. Approximately 88 percent of the children seen for speech or language therapy in the schools attend regular classrooms (U.S. Department of Education, 1997). However, that figure is deceptive, since many of the children seen for speech therapy services—those who are less integrated and whose primary disability is not a communication disorder—are not counted in this tally.

## Type of Service Delivery

Speech therapy services are delivered in several formats. Children with similar communication problems are often grouped together and receive direct service in small groups. Children with unique or more severe problems can be seen individually several times a week during the school year in resource room settings outside of the classroom. This format has been labeled the *pull-out model*; it is the most traditional service delivery model. It can be an appropriate service provision model for developing skills that take a long period to master. For some children, intensive services are provided daily for short periods of time. This is the *block scheduling* model; it can be effective in providing the intensive care some children need to master specific skills that can then be transferred into the classroom.

*Consultation* with regular and special education teachers is becoming an increasingly popular model of service provision. Prior to the implementation of the Individuals with Disabilities Education Act (IDEA), children with severe disabilities were more likely to receive all services, including speech therapy, in segregated facilities. Most of these children are now seen in the schools. Allied with this change in location is the currently popular belief that communication skills can be best mastered in naturalistic settings rather than in the traditional resource room. As a result, more speech therapy services are being delivered using the consultation model than ever before. Speech-language pathologists are increasingly viewing themselves as full participants in the education of the child.

Other trends that affect the type of service delivered to children with communication disorders are the increasing focus on families, literacy, and diversity. There is a growing recognition that children do not "have" communication disorders in a vacuum. The way a child communicates has an impact on his or her family. Successful treatment suggests that the family as well as the child be involved in many aspects of the therapy process, from the initial mastery of new skills to the eventual transferring of those skills to the naturalistic environment. Classroom teachers are often considered "family" in the sense that they are a significant part of the child's communication environment.

Literacy is being seen as a more global concept that supercedes spoken language as the domain of the speech-language pathologist. Literacy is reading and writing as well as speaking and understanding. All of these processes are essentially social procedures that are part of the child's culture. Thus, language and literacy become shared goals for teachers and speech-language pathologists to enhance in a cooperative manner (McCormick, 1990).

A growing sensitivity to the linguistic and cultural diversity of children in the schools is also shaping service provision (Westby & Erickson, 1992). Speech-language pathologists are not only trained to teach children to speak in Standard English, but they are also learning about the dialectal differences discussed earlier in this chapter. Children who might have been treated as disordered a decade ago are now being serviced as competent speakers learning new forms of language.

## Early Intervention Programs

Since much of speech and language development is completed by the time school begins, early intervention for most communication disorders is highly recommended. This is especially true for children who have severe language disabilities or who stutter.

Preschool programs for children with language problems are usually half-day programs that foster cooperative play, encourage spontaneous speech, and facilitate interaction between children. These activities contribute to the conceptual knowledge and cognitive processes needed to develop language. Most of these programs attempt to structure naturalistic settings where children are free to interact and explore. They are usually stocked with a variety of interesting materials and objects that encourage communication (Paul, 1985; Wilcox, 1984). The activities and techniques used are shared with parents so that they might use them at home to encourage communication and language learning.

Children who stutter and do not receive treatment develop more complicated patterns of stuttering and more negative views about the communication process as they mature. The earlier treatments are initiated, the more successful will be their outcome.

If treatment is delayed until adolescence or early adulthood, the disorder is more resistant to treatment and the likelihood of relapse is far greater (Culatta and Goldberg, 1995; Shames & Rubin, 1986). With many speech disorders, the longer the person practices speech errors, the more resistant those errors will be to modification.

## Sample Therapy Techniques

This section of the chapter will sketch a cross-section of the therapy techniques used to treat various speech and language disorders. Most therapy approaches, regardless of the disorder, attempt to make the child aware of acceptable communication behavior, explain how and why the child is not producing the target behavior, model methods for producing the desired speech or language, and structure opportunities to use the newly acquired correct behavior in situations outside of therapy.

## Articulation Therapy

The treatment of articulation disorders caused by clefts of the palate, cerebral palsy, traumatic brain injury, or hearing loss require that the child somehow compensate for a speech mechanism that is not functioning properly. Articulation disorders that are functional in nature require no such compensation.

Prior to initiating articulation therapy for children with clefts, the cleft must somehow be repaired or at least temporarily sealed. For most children with clefts of the palate, this means surgery to seal the cleft. However, surgical repair of a cleft does not guarantee normal functioning of the mechanism or normal speech articulation. Even after surgery, exercises and drill may be necessary to train the newly repaired system to function adequately. Children must be made aware of the sounds that they are misproducing, be taught how to make them correctly, and practice saying them until they become automatic. For some children with clefts of the palate, surgery is postponed for medical reasons. These children will be fitted with prosthetic devices, essentially "false palates" that will achieve the closure necessary to articulate sounds. These devices are usually temporary in nature and require modification as the child grows.

Children who have cerebral palsy and articulation problems must be taught to use their defective articulatory system in as efficient a way as possible. This may mean slowing speech so that they can articulate more clearly, or it may mean that they will have to learn to gain more control over their speech mechanisms through drill and exercise. For many of these children, speech production will improve the intelligibility of their speech, but they will never articulate speech sounds normally. Some children who have severe disabilities may never be able to use oral speech for communication. The section of this chapter on alternative and augmentative communication will describe the options for communication available with technology.

Children who have suffered traumatic brain damage may regain the articulation skills they once had through a well-planned program of speech exercises and drill that will rehabilitate damaged systems. They may have to relearn on a conscious level how to make sounds they originally learned automatically. The degree of improvement will depend upon the severity of the dysarthria that follows the traumatic brain damage and the degree of recovery made within the first six months after the trauma. These children are similar to children with cerebral palsy in that decisions have to be made about how successful any rehabilitation aimed at producing oral speech can be.

Children who are hearing impaired or deaf must learn to produce sounds that they either do not hear or that they hear only in a distorted form. Programs to teach sound production to these children rely upon the use of tactile and visual stimuli to produce sounds, and memorization of where those sounds belong so they can be used in oral communication. A child who cannot hear /s/ can learn to produce it by feeling the air stream on his or her hand or by blowing on a pinwheel. After learning to produce this sound, the child must then learn which words have the /s/ sound and remember to produce it. The more residual hearing a child possesses, the more possible this task is.

Children with functional articulation disorders can be taught to produce correct speech sounds in numerous ways. The success rate for these children is much higher than for those who have the organically based articulation disorders we have just discussed. Many times these children only need to be made aware of the sounds that they are omitting or distorting, and they will use this information to correctly produce those sounds. This process is called *auditory stimulation* and is used to make children sensitive to speech sounds. Other children with functional articulation problems may not only have to be taught to recognize correct sound production but must also be taught how to physically produce the problem sound correctly. This method, called *phonetic placement*, requires a child to consciously learn how sounds are made and use this knowledge when producing speech. Drill and practice are needed to learn to automatically replace the incorrect sound and produce the newly corrected sound.

## Voice Therapy

Treating children with voice problems is always a team effort. If the voice problem is organic in nature, initial treatment is usually medical. If the voice problem is the result of emotional distress, initial treatment will usually be counseling. Even when these preliminary treatments are successful, speech therapy may still be needed. After surgery, the child may need to learn how to use the vocal system as efficiently as possible. Many times, the structures used for voicing are damaged as a consequence of surgical procedures. The child will need instruction on how to prevent further damage to a weakened system. For some children, all that is required after surgery is vocal rest so that tissues may heal.

Children with functional voice problems often have the potential to learn to produce normal-sounding vocal tones. Learning to use an appropriate voice may be a step-by-step process, wherein the speech-language pathologist models appropriate voicing and the child imitates the model, initially in sound production and finally in speech production. Computers and specially designed voice monitors can often be used to graphically represent appropriate voice use for the child as he or she is speaking. Using the appropriate voice must become automatic. Parents, teachers, peers, and siblings are often recruited to aid in this process.

## Fluency Therapy

Different types of disfluency require different treatments. Parents and children who are overly concerned about the normal disfluencies of speech or developmental disfluencies may only need information about the routine nature of normal disfluencies and the transitory nature of developmental disfluency to alleviate their concerns.

More abnormal types of disfluency may need more rigorous treatments. Disfluent speech that results from neurogenic damage will in all probability be treated as a part of the motor planning exercises and language retrieval strategies that focus on the speech and language problems caused by the neurological damage. As these neurogenically involved speakers gain or regain control of their speech and language systems, the disfluencies that they are experiencing will decline. Psychogenic disfluency treatment is in the realm of the psychologist, psychiatrist, social worker, or guidance or family counselor. Since this disfluency is in reaction to emotional stress, it is only tangentially a communication problem and is best treated by professionals other than speech-language pathologists. The disfluencies that arise from language impairment are best treated by techniques that improve language skills. The limited research available seems to indicate that treatment that increases language skills, in spite of emerging disfluencies, will eventually alleviate what appears to be temporarily created fluency failure (Hall et al., 1986; Culatta & Goldberg, 1995).

The treatment of cluttering involves teaching the child who clutters to be aware of his or her problem so that the child will be willing to learn to slow the rapid, jerky, jumbled speech that characterizes cluttering. Over time and with repeated practice, the child will need to build a tolerance for the normal speech being practiced and use it in daily communication.

Children who stutter can be treated by any one of more than 50 separate protocols that are available to speech-language pathologists (Culatta & Goldberg, 1995). However, many of the therapy techniques are similar; when these treatment protocols were analyzed by Culatta and Goldberg, it became apparent that stuttering is treated in a limited number of ways. Speech-language pathologists teach children who stutter to make adjustments of the speech mechanism that will bring about more fluent speech. They teach children to slow their rate of speech to gain control. Speech-language pathologists also use *operant conditioning* techniques to reinforce fluency and fluency generating behaviors and to punish stuttering. By manipulating the length and complexity of a child's utterance, starting from one-word utterances and carefully increasing their length, speech-language pathologists can bring about fluency for some children. In other cases, the negative attitudes that children have developed about communication must be changed before progress can be made. A commonality in all therapy protocols is that they require children to monitor their speech and be aware of whether they are being fluent or are stuttering. Providing treatment for children who stutter and the goals of that treatment have been issues of controversy. Speech-language pathologists have evolved from not being willing to directly treat children who stutter to advocating early intervention. The goals of therapy have vacillated between teaching children to control their stuttering as best they can, to expecting them to be normally fluent as the result of treatment.

## Language Therapy

Developmental disorders of language that affect language acquisition and traumatically acquired disorders of language that result in the loss of linguistic competence are treated differently. When dealing with developmental disorders, the task is one of *habilitation*, or teaching a child to gain skills he or she has never mastered. Traumatically acquired language disorders call for *rehabilitation*, or helping the child regain the skills or potential to develop skills he or she had prior to the accident.

**Therapy for Developmental Disorders of Language.**    The overall goal of language therapy for children who have been identified as having developmental disorders of language is to engage in procedures that will facilitate the acquisition of language. Therapy activities will not be successful if they are administered without the full participation or parents, teachers, and family members. Early intervention objectives focus on preparing parents and caregivers to provide language stimulation in play and routine caregiving activities. Exploring, manipulating objects, and experiencing new situations will provide for later concept development. Preschool language therapy focuses on participating in verbal and nonverbal games and guiding parents in initiating communication activities. Speech-language pathologists, parents, and teachers model how to request objects, respond to the communication of others, and follow directions (McCormick, 1990).

Parents and caregivers are encouraged to engage in *parallel-talk activities*, which provide a running narration of what the child is doing. They are also coached in *self-talk activities*, which provide a running narration of their own activities, and are taught to expand the child's communication attempts. Parallel talk would occur if a parent observes a child playing with blocks and says "Bobby has the red block in his hand. It is a big block." Self-talk would be exemplified by a caregiver making chocolate milk with the following commentary. "I'm putting milk in Bobby's blue cup. Now the powder goes in. Where is the spoon? Here it is. Stir, stir, stir." Expansions occur after a child says, "My book," and the parent replies, "Yes, it is your book, and I would like to read it to you."

Language therapy for school-age children focuses on strengthening the specific components of language that are disordered in the context of the classroom curriculum or ongoing social activities (McCormick, 1990). Box 6.2 illustrates some suggested procedures for facilitating language development.

**Therapy for Acquired Disorders of Language.**    The overall goal of language therapy for children who have been identified as having acquired disorders of language is

*Box 6.2*
## *WHAT EVERY TEACHER NEEDS TO KNOW*

### *Suggestions for Facilitating Language*

1. *Be responsive to the child's spontaneous communicative attempts.* A child learns language by engaging in communicative interactions. If the communication partner is responsive to the child's communicative acts, the language learning process will continue. Being responsive to communicative attempts includes repeating the content, carrying out the child's requests, listening intently, and commenting on the message.

2. *Modify input.* The language trainer should slow speech, pause, repeat, and use gestures as well as intonation to convey meaning. Modified input makes the language signal of more interest to the child. It also permits the child to make associations between words and the aspects of the environment for which they stand.

3. *Provide opportunities for the child to communicate.* A child who communicates a great deal is actively practicing communication skills. There are several mechanisms for increasing the frequency with which the child communicates:
   - *Do not anticipate needs.*
   - *Arrange for unusual or novel events to occur.*
   - *Arrange for the child to convey information to others.*
   - Provide the child with choices.

4. *Model or expand the child's language.* Once the child's communicative attempts are accepted, the trainer or parent can expose the child to a slightly better or more complete way of saying the same thing. If the child says, "I want the big, big ball," the trainer can say, "Yes, you want the *very* big ball."

5. *Talk about things of interest to the child.* Provide language input that corresponds with the child's own intentions. Say the same thing that the child is saying, but in slightly different ways. A spilled drink at lunchtime can become a beneficial language learning experience.

6. *Provide many clear examples of language rules.* If children are learning the word *break,* they should be exposed to many repetitions of the word associated with many examples of things that break. For example, they might break cookies and crackers, encounter objects that keep falling apart, break spaghetti in order to glue the pieces on a picture, and break carrot sticks for lunch.

7. *Use words the child already knows to teach new words.* For a child who doesn't know the meaning of the word *blend,* the trainer can say, "When we blend, we make things go together smoothly." The trainer can then give examples such as, "When we blend *b* and *e* together, we get *beeee,* not *buh-eee.*" By hearing the meanings of new words explained in simple ways, children easily expand their vocabulary.

8. *Reduce complexity.* Language that is too complex is of little or no benefit to the child. To be optimally effective, the language signal must be only slightly more complex than the child's current level of functioning. Thus, if the child is at the single-word level of language development, communication partners should be speaking in simple two-word combinations.

9. *Tell and retell stories and experiences.* Practice in telling and retelling stories and experiences provides the child with the opportunity to relate events in an organized manner. At first, a child's retelling can be prompted with questions and pictures. Children may need several exposures to a simplified version of a story or event before trying to relate it entirely on their own.

10. *In cases where the child has a profound hearing loss or a motor disability, communicate in the child's mode or form of communication.* Children with hearing losses often need to be exposed to several modes of communication, for example, words paired with gestures or signs. Likewise, a child who is using a picture board to communicate will need to have others acknowledge or incorporate that communication board in interactions that occur in all sorts of natural contexts.

to engage in procedures that will facilitate the reacquisition of the specific language skills that are impaired as a result of the brain damage. Analyzing diagnostic test results and samples of the child's spontaneous language will often provide the speech-language pathologist with an outline of a child's strengths and weaknesses in receptive and expressive language skills. Therapy activities can then be targeted to use the child's strengths to compensate for weaknesses. For example, if a child is having difficulties processing complicated instructions, the speech-language pathologist may teach the child how to appropriately ask that instructions be repeated. Rather than say "I don't know what to do," the child might ask, "What do I do on page 25?" Teachers and parents can also be instructed in efficient ways to help the child process information, such as simplifying instructions, writing them on the board, or presenting them slowly. If a child is having trouble retrieving words as the result of brain injury, the speech-language pathologist may help him or her develop strategies, such as thinking of what the word does or who uses the object. These attempts at association often result in successful word retrieval. Language exercises that systematically target the components of form, content, and use previously discussed in this chapter can help strengthen language weaknesses or enable children to learn or relearn lost skills.

## GENERALIZATION AND MAINTENANCE

None of the gains achieved in speech or language therapy will be of any consequence in a child's life unless they are applied outside of the therapy setting (generalized) or become a permanent part of the child's communication (maintained). The current emphasis on naturalistic settings for speech therapy provision is, in part, an effort to foster more efficient generalization and maintenance of therapy gains. Classroom teachers, special educators, and parents must all be active participants in the therapy process so that they are aware of what the child is accomplishing and how the communication gains may be used in daily communication.

## TECHNOLOGY

Technological advances have had an impact on service provision for children with communication disorders in two major areas. The first is in using technology to assist individuals who will not be able to use oral communication effectively. This use of technology is called *alternative and augmentative communication* (AAC). The second is providing equipment that facilitates learning appropriate speech and language.

### Alternative and Augmentative Communication

Alternative and augmentative communication devices can be as low-tech as communication boards with photographs pinned to them, or as high-tech as computers that can be programmed to synthesize speech. Once it is determined that a child requires an alternative to spoken language, it is the responsibility of the speech-language pathologist and IEP team to decide what might best meet the child's needs. Factors that enter into the decision are the cognitive ability of the child, the physical dexterity required to operate the selected device, and the sophistication of the language to be transmitted. It is not unusual for a child to progress from simple to complex devices as he or she becomes more linguistically competent. For example, a communication board with pictures of simple activities and written instructions beneath them might be appropriate in initially helping the child learn vocabulary and how to request basic needs. As the child progresses, a device with selected preprogrammed requests that are produced by the machine might better suit the child's needs. Eventually, the child might learn to use a computer that will generate appropriately complex language that the child composes on the device. Speaking devices can be activated by keyboards, touchpads, and a variety of switches that can be adapted to the manual dexterity the child possesses. Alternative and augmentative communication systems can open new worlds to the child who is unable to use oral communication, but they cannot take the place of learning language. A child cannot use a device beyond his or her level of competence. A sophisticated speech synthesizer will not enable a child functioning linguistically at a 2-year level to compose intricate and complex sentences. However, it can help a child who is linguistically sophisticated but motor impaired express his or her needs in an increasingly acceptable manner. Augmentative and alternative devices and systems are rarely the first choice for teaching a child to communicate. Oral speech or sign language are usually the primary goals in teaching speech or language. (Chapter 8, "Children with Hearing Impairments," discusses the technology available to children who are hearing impaired or deaf). However, the limitations of any given child's ability to use normal communication must be recognized and accepted by the child and the child's parents, teachers, and speech-language pathologists in order to efficiently maximize the child's learning experience.

## Facilitating Devices

Technology in the form of aids to help children master normal communication skills has changed speech therapy provisions. Tape recorders and video recorders are routinely used to demonstrate correct and incorrect production of target behaviors. They help the child understand and practice concepts developed during therapy and provide a way to bring outside experiences with communication to the therapy session. Most speech-language pathologists would not consider conducting therapy sessions without tape-recording or videorecording them for later analysis. Personal computer programs are available to help children learn vocabulary items, develop conceptual knowledge, and practice specific speech and language skills. The materials available range from programs designed to meet special communication needs to programs available to the general public that can be used with little modification. As computers become increasingly sophisticated in speech and sound discrimination ability, they will be increasingly a part of therapy.

Several devices have been designed to specifically help children master the skills needed for normal communication. The Computer-Aided Fluency Establishment Trainer (CAFET), designed by Martha Goebel, director of the Annandale Fluency Clinic in Virginia, uses hardware and software that enables the child to learn speech behaviors needed for fluent speech. Physical movements of the articulatory system are electronically monitored, while age-appropriate programs have been designed for children to practice the required skills. The Visipitch is a complex device that will analyze many components of voice production and provide graphic feedback on a video screen when correct vocal production is produced. This direct and immediate feedback provides initial practice in correct vocal productions and facilitates generalization and maintenance. Many other devices and programs have been specifically designed to help speech-language pathologists obtain the behavior initially needed to correct speech and language disorders. The Society for Augmentative and Alternative Communication and the American Speech-Language-Hearing Association, listed at the end of this chapter, can provide information about alternative and augmentative devices and commercially available devices and programs used in speech therapy.

## ISSUES OF IMPORTANCE

Issues that have an impact on providing effective service to children with communication disorders will be discussed in this section. The issues selected are not the only issues of concern to speech-language pathologists. However, the issues selected provide some insight into controversies affecting the field of speech-language pathology and schoolchildren.

### Appropriate Settings for Service Provision

Most speech therapy is provided in separate therapy rooms using the pull-out model previously discussed. Criticism of the pull-out model is that it isolates students from the natural environment of the classroom, stigmatizes them by focusing attention on their disabilities, and isolates the speech-language pathologist from the educational mission of the schools (Nelson, 1993). The pull-out model is also faulted for weakening generalization and maintenance. Even though the resource room may be highly structured and establish skills, there tends to be little generalization because the skills being learned have little relevance to the children's lives. The pragmatic aspects of communication suffer from lack of peer interaction (McCormick, 1990). Advocates of providing speech therapy in more naturalistic settings suggest that in the future, more speech therapy services will be provided on a consultation and collaboration basis, and in-service training will emphasize how regular classroom teachers can be increasingly responsible for speech and language services. In addition, paraprofessionals, aides, and other support staff will be available to monitor communication in the classroom. A more moderate view acknowledges that while much of what is happening in isolated resource rooms can be transferred to the classroom, there will always be a need for one-on-one therapy conducted in the privacy of the clinical suite or resource room.

## Treatment of Functional Articulation Disorders

A significant proportion of the children seen for speech therapy in the schools are diagnosed as having functional articulation problems that might self-correct as the children mature. The concern is whether treatment should be applied conservatively or withheld until there is no doubt that there is a problem. Initially, this treatment philosophy would free the speech-language pathologist's time for other disorders and help alleviate the chronic shortages of speech-language pathologists in the schools. The downside to this approach is that many of the children who would be denied early service will not self-correct, and thus will present more entrenched problems that are resistant to therapy when it is finally presented. Treating these older children would be more costly and time-consuming in the long run. Clinical judgment, prioritizing provision of services, and using aides and classroom teachers can all have an impact on this concern. Clinical experiences with children who stutter and children with exceptionalities of all types tend to indicate that early intervention is both more effective and less costly in most situations.

## Technology and Augmentative and Alternative Communication

There can be no doubt that the technology applied to designing alternative and augmentative communication devices and systems has had a liberating effect on children who cannot master oral communication. However, providing a child with an augmentative or alternative system is significantly more complex than simply ordering the most appropriate tool and handing it to the family involved. Major problems must be addressed in terms of the costs of the equipment, who pays for the equipment, who updates or replaces it, and how it gets serviced. The complexity of programming many of the devices can be beyond the skill level of the child, his or her parents, and in some cases the speech-language pathologist who recommended it. The portability and reliability of some devices is highly suspect. Some are only usable in restricted situations because of inherent auditory or visual transmission features. Even the most reliable and sturdy machines may be laborious to operate, due to either the speed of the equipment itself or the skills of the user operating it (Beukelman, 1991; Nelson, 1992). Slowness results in frustration for the communicator and the listener. Children who use communication devices often have to rely on the programming and language selections of others who are attempting to guess what the children will wish to say in situations that have not yet been encountered. The cumbersome programming needed to make some devices functional can threaten to turn speech-pathologists into computer technicians and remove them from service provision duties more in line with their training and interests. As anyone who has ever experienced even the most minor glitch in a personal computer can attest, technical service is not only difficult to obtain but also frustratingly complex to apply.

Psychologically, parents, children, teachers, and speech-language pathologists often expect more from devices than they are capable of delivering. It is tempting to hope that a "magic machine" will solve a child's communication problems, and devastating when the reality of the limits of the device become apparent.

The more positive side of the concern is that many of even the most basic devices are still in their infancy. In all fairness, they must still be considered experimental models rushed into service because they are so desperately needed. It is not unrealistic to expect that within the next decade, devices will become less expensive, more portable, less fragile, and easier to operate for both the programmer and the listener. Even in their crudest form, many of these devices do free children from the isolation imposed by not being able to communicate with their peers and enable the children to be included, more than has ever been possible, in the normal activities of the classroom.

## MINORITY CONCERNS

Three of the most pressing minority concerns are the acceptance of the validity of linguistic diversity, the appropriate provision of services to children with linguistic diversity, and the lack of minority professionals available to provide service.

### Validity of Linguistic Diversity

Despite evidence to the contrary and in spite of data that show that the dialects of Standard English are legitimate rule governed forms of English, there is political, social, and educational bias against these forms of English (Taylor, 1986). Dialectal speakers run the risk of being considered disordered rather than different and can be judged cognitively inferior to their Standard English speaking peers. They are discriminated against in the workplace and penalized in the classroom. The fact that many of these children are seen by speech-language pathologists rather than by teachers of English as a second language is in and of itself significant, since the American Speech-Language-Hearing Association has specifically stated that no dialect of English is a disorder or a pathological form of speech or language (American Speech-Language-Hearing Association, 1982). Attempts to recognize that Black English is the primary language of some students and to teach these students to code-switch have been derided as a "cruel joke" by NAACP president Kweisi Mfume and a "ridiculous theory" by the press secretary of California governor Pete Wilson (Leland & Joseph, 1997). Inflammatory rhetoric and uninformed public statements do little to help parents and teachers understand that dialects exist in many languages besides English, and confusion can occur when students and teachers speaking different forms of the same language interact during the educational process. It would appear that it should be necessary for those who teach in Standard English, in areas where dialects of English are commonly spoken, to be aware of the differences in language and the confusions that could occur.

## Service Provision to Dialectal Speakers

Being a dialectal speaker doesn't excuse a child from having communication problems. Disorders exist in minority populations that must not be overlooked. One unintended consequence of sensitivity to dialectal speech is that some minority dialectal speakers with communication disorders are being denied service due to the mistaken belief that their speech disorders are merely speech differences and therefore should not be treated. An interesting and potentially harmful paradox exists where both the inclusion and exclusion of dialectal speakers in special service programs can be viewed as discriminatory (Nelson, 1993). The obvious answer is that the legal requirement that children be evaluated by professionals fluent in the child's native language be applied to dialectal speakers as well as to speakers of foreign languages.

The format of service provision of dialectal speakers is also a concern. Since dialectal speakers don't automatically have speech and language disorders, it would appear that when the only differences in language or speech are dialectal, these children should be as capable as their Standard English–speaking peers in learning the parallel forms of expression that constitute Standard English. Treating or grouping these children with children who have speech and language disorders does not appear to be necessary. Understanding the dialectal form and helping the child translate it into Standard English appears to be the most effective teaching strategy.

## Minority Professionals

Although it is not necessary to be a minority group member to work with minority children, there is no denying that minority professionals can bring a sensitivity and interest to the problems of minority individuals that mainstream speech-language pathologists might not. In addition, minority professionals can serve as role models to minority and majority students alike. Despite active recruiting programs by colleges and university training programs and federally funded minority group grants, minority speech-language pathologists make up fewer than 7 percent of all the members of the American Speech-Language-Hearing Association. Fewer than 2 percent are Hispanic. Fewer than 3 percent are African Americans and fewer than 0.5 percent are Native Americans. Unfortunately, these figures have remained stable even as the number of speech-language pathologists in the United States grows (American Speech-Language-Hearing Association, 1993b).

# PROFESSIONALS

## Speech-Language Pathologists

Speech-language pathologists are the specialists on the educational team who are primarily responsible for the identification, diagnosis, design, and application of programs for children identified as having speech and language disabilities. They provide service directly to children and serve as consultants and collaborators with regular and special education teachers, parents, and allied health and medical practitioners. *Speech-language pathologist* is a professional title conferred by the American Speech-Language-Hearing Association (ASHA). This national professional association is the research and credentialing organization for approximately 90,000 speech-language pathologists and audiologists. *Audiologists* are professionals who deal with children who are hearing impaired and deaf. Their role is explained in Chapter 8 of this text. Approximately 45 percent of all speech-language pathologists work in school settings.

Speech-language pathologists are awarded a nationally recognized certification called the Certificate of Clinical Competence (CCC) once they have completed a course of study that leads to a master's or doctoral degree from an academic institution that has been accredited by the American Speech-Language-Hearing Association. In addition to academic courses, at least 375 hours of supervised clinical practice must be completed with a variety of clients with different speech and language disorders. Upon completing master's training, the speech-language pathologist must complete a Clinical Fellowship Year (CFY) of employment under the supervision of a certified speech-language pathologist and a national examination before the CCC is awarded.

In addition, approximately 45 states require licensing of speech-language pathologists. These licensing requirements are different from the teacher certification requirements that are also mandated in most states to practice in the schools. The American Speech-Language-Hearing Association considers it unethical to provide services in any setting prior to completing or being in the process of completing the requirements for the Certificate of Clinical Competence. However, a diminishing number of states require only a bachelor's degree in communication disorders to obtain teacher certification. Most of these states also require that to maintain a position in the public schools, the bachelor's level service provider must be in the process of obtaining a master's degree in communication disorders. The American Speech-Language-Hearing Association is committed along with most state professional organizations to have the master's degree as the entry level credential for school speech-language pathologists (American Speech-Language-Hearing Association, 1993b).

## Communication Aides or Assistants

Communication aides or communication assistants are support personnel who work under the direct guidance of a speech-language pathologist, who is directly responsible for their actions. The requirements to become a licensed communication assistant vary from state. Approximately 30 states have regulations and laws governing the use of communication aides (American Speech-Language-Hearing Association, 1988). For example, in North Carolina, the communication assistant must have completed an associate's degree in speech-language pathology assisting from a community college or equivalent program, or a BA degree with specific courses outlined in the licensing requirements. The scope of services that the communication assistant may provide are limited to managing the behavior of clients and positioning and escorting patients. They may also complete observation checklists, administer binary screening protocols, record behaviors, and provide prompts. Communication assistants are also empowered to set up appointments, obtain records, organize records, send reports, compile data, arrange the clinical setting, manage and maintain equipment, and program assistive devices (North Carolina Board of Examiners, 1997).

## Educational Professionals

As we have repeatedly mentioned throughout this chapter, classroom teachers and special education teachers are a vital part of the services provided to children with communication disorders. They are vital as collaborators for the generalization and maintenance of gains made in therapy and are becoming increasingly important as members of the team providing direct remediation. Educational professionals have always played a critical role in the identification of students who might need help with communication problems and in helping speech-language pathologists counsel the families of children with communication disorders.

## Medical and Allied Health Professionals

Depending on the type of communication disorder, ear, nose, and throat specialists (otorhinolaryngologists), family counselors, psychologists, psychiatrists, and social workers could all be part of the team that determines what might be the best treatment protocol for the child with a communication disorder.

# PROFESSIONAL ASSOCIATIONS AND PARENT OR SELF-HELP GROUPS

American Academy of Otolaryngology
1101 Vermont Avenue NW, Suite 302
Washington, DC 20005

American Cleft Palate–Craniofacial Association
1218 Grandview Avenue
Pittsburgh, PA 15211

American Speech-Language-Hearing Association
10801 Rockville Pike
Rockville, MD 20852

Division of Children's
   Communication Development
Council for Exceptional Children
1920 Association Drive
Reston, VA 20191–1589

International Fluency Association
457 Old Farm Road
Wyncote, PA 19095

National Center for Neurogenic
   Communication Disorders
University of Arizona
Tucson, AZ 85721

National Center for Voice and Speech
Wendell Johnson Speech and Hearing Center
University of Iowa
Iowa City, IA 52242

National Council on Stuttering
558 Russell Road
DeKalb, IL 60115

National Institute of Communication Disorders,
   Hearing and Deafness
National Institutes of Health
Bethesda, MD 20892

National Stuttering Project
2151 Irving Street, Suite 208
San Francisco, CA 94122

Stuttering Foundation of America
5139 Klingle Street NW
Washington, DC 20016

U.S. Society for Augmentative and
Alternative Communication
202 Barkley Memorial Center
University of Nebraska
Lincoln, NE 68583

## REFERENCES FOR FURTHER INFORMATION

*American Journal of Speech-Language Pathology*
10801 Rockville Pike
Rockville, MD 20852

*Augmentative and Alternative Communication*
P.O. Box 1762
Station R
Toronto, Ontario M4G 4A3
Canada

*Augmentative Communication News*
Sunset Enterprises
One Surf Way, Suite 213
Monterey, CA 93940

*Journal of Childhood Communication Disorders*
1920 Association Drive
Reston, VA 20191–1589

*Journal of Communication Disorders*
Elsevier Science Publishing Co.
655 Avenue of the Americas
New York, NY 10010

*Journal of Fluency Disorders*
Elsevier Science Publishing Co.
655 Avenue of the Americas
New York, NY 10010

*Journal of Speech and Hearing Research*
10801 Rockville Pike
Rockville, MD 20852

*Language, Speech and Hearing Services
in the Schools*
10801 Rockville Pike
Rockville, MD 20852

*Our Voice*
365 W. 25th Street, Suite 13E
New York, NY 10001

## REFERENCES ❧

American Speech-Language-Hearing Association (1982). Definitions: communicative disorders and variations. ASHA, 24, 949–950.

American Speech-Language-Hearing Association (1988). Utilization and employment of speech-language pathology support personnel with underserved populations. ASHA, 30, 55–56.

American Speech-Language-Hearing Association (1991). Fact sheet on communication disorders. Rockville, MD: Author.

American Speech-Language-Hearing Association (1993a). Definitions of communication disorders and variations. ASHA, 35, 40–41.

American Speech-Language-Hearing Association (1993b). Implementation procedures for the standards for the certificates of clinical competence. ASHA, 35, 76–83.

Bernstein, D. K. (1993). The nature of language and its disorders. In D. K. Bernstein & E. Tiegerman (Eds.), *Language and communication disorders in children* (3rd ed). Upper Saddle River, NJ: Prentice Hall/Merrill.

Bernstein, D. K., & Tiegerman, E. (Eds.). (1989). *Language and communication disorders in children.* Upper Saddle River, NJ: Prentice Hall/Merrill.

Beukelman, D. R. (1991). Magic and cost of communicative competence. *Augmentative and Alternative Communication, 7,* 2–10.

Bloodstein, O. (1960). The development of stuttering: Part II developmental phases. *Journal of Speech and Hearing Disorders, 25,* 366–376.

Chomsky, N. (1957). *Syntactic structures.* The Hague, Netherlands: Mouton.

Chomsky, N. (1981). *Lectures on government and binding.* Dordrecht, Netherlands: Doris.

Culatta, B., & Culatta, R. (1993). Students with communication problems. In A. E. Blackhurst & W. H. Berdine (Eds.), *An introduction to special education* (3rd ed.). New York: HarperCollins.

Culatta, R., & Goldberg, S. (1995). *Stuttering therapy: An integrated approach to theory and practice.* Needham, MA: Allyn & Bacon.

Culatta, R., & Leeper, L. (1987). Disfluency in childhood: It's not always stuttering. *Journal of Childhood Communication Disorders, 10,* 96–106.

Culatta, R., & Leeper, L. (1989). The differential diagnosis of disfluency. *National Student Speech-Language-Hearing Association Journal, 17,* 50–59.

Deal, J. L. (1982). Sudden onset of stuttering: A case report. *Journal of Speech and Hearing Research, 47,* 301–304.

Dublinski, S. (1981). Action: School services. *Language, Speech and Hearing Services in Schools, 12,* 192–200.

Dunn, L. M., & Dunn, L. (1981). *Peabody Picture Vocabulary Test–Revised.* Circle Pines, MN: American Guidance.

Dworkin, J., & Culatta, R. (1996). *The Dworkin-Culatta Oral Mechanism Examination and Treatment System.* Farmington, MI: Edgewood.

Gleason, J. B. (1973). Code switching in children. In T. E. Moore (Ed.), *Cognitive development and the acquisition of language.* New York: Academic.

Goldman, R., & Fristoe, M. (1986). *Goldman-Fristoe Test of Articulation.* Austin, TX: PRO-ED.

Hall, D. E., Wray, D. F., & Conti, D. M. (1986, Fall). The language-disfluency relationship: A case study. *Hearsay,* 110–113.

Hall, P. K. (1977). The occurrence of disfluencies in language-disordered school-age children. *Journal of Speech and Hearing Disorders, 42,* 364–369.

Hegde, M. N. (1995). *Introduction to communicative disorders* (2nd ed.). Austin, TX: PRO-ED.

Helm-Estabrooks, N. (1987). Diagnosis and management of neurogenic stuttering in adults. In K. O. St. Louis (Ed.), *A typical stutterer: Principles and practices of rehabilitation.* San Diego, CA: Academic.

Heward, W. L. (1996). *Exceptional children* (5th ed.). Upper Saddle River, NJ: Prentice Hall/Merrill.

Kemler, D. (1983). Wholistic and analytic modes of perceptual and cognitive development. In T. J. Tighe & B. E. Shepp (Eds.), *Interactions: Perception, cognition and development.* Hillsdale, NJ: Erlbaum.

Kidd, R. D. (1980). Genetic model of stuttering. *Journal of Fluency Disorders, 5,* 187–201.

Kirk, S. A., Gallagher, J. J., & Anastasiow, N. J. (1993). *Educating exceptional children* (7th ed.). Boston: Houghton Mifflin.

Leland, J., & Joseph, N. (1997, January 13). Hooked on ebonics. *Newsweek,* 78–79.

Leonard, L. (1994). Language disorders in preschool children. In G. Shames, E. Wiig, & W. Secord (Eds.), *Human communication disorders.* Needham, MA: Allyn & Bacon.

McCarthy, M. M. (1981). Speech effects of theophylline. *Pediatrics, 6,* 5.

McCormak, W. C., & Wurm, S. A. (1976). *Language and man: Anthropological issues.* The Hague, Netherlands: Mouton.

McCormick, L. (1990). Communication disorders. In N. G. Haring, L. McCormick, and T. G. Haring (Eds.), *Exceptional children and youth* (6th ed.). Upper Saddle River, NJ: Prentice Hall/Merrill.

McReynolds, L. (1990). Articulation and phonological disorders. In G. Shames & E. Wiig (Eds.), *Human communication disorders* (3rd ed.). Upper Saddle River, NJ: Prentice Hall/Merrill.

McWilliams, B. J., Morris, H. L., & Shelton, R. L. (1990). *Cleft palate speech* (2nd ed). Philadelphia: Decker.

National Center For Health Statistics (1988). Current estimates from the National Health Interview Survey, United States, 1988. *Vital Health Statistics,* Series 10, No. 173. DHHS Publication No. (PHS) 89-1501.

National Institute of Neurological and Communicative Disorders and Stroke (1988). *Developmental speech and language disorders: Hope through research*. Bethesda, MD: National Institutes of Health.

Nelson, N. W. (1992). Performance is the prize: Language competence and performance among AAC users. *Augmentative and Alternative Communication, 8,* 3–18.

Nelson, N. W. (1993). *Childhood language disorders in context: Infancy through adolescence*. Upper Saddle River, NJ: Prentice Hall/Merrill.

Newcomber, P. L., & Hammill, D. (1988). *Tests of language development* (2nd. ed.). Austin, TX: PRO-ED.

Newman, P., Creaghead, N., & Secord, W. (Eds.). (1985). *Assessment and remediation of articulatory and phonological disorders*. Upper Saddle River, NJ: Prentice Hall/Merrill.

North Carolina Board of Examiners. (1997, February). *Newsletter*. Greensboro, NC: Author.

Nurnberg, H. G., & Greenwald, B. (1981). Stuttering: The unusual side effect of phenothiazines. *American Journal of Psychiatry, 138,* 386–387.

Olmstead, D. (1971). *Out of the mouths of babes*. The Hague, Netherlands: Mouton.

Owens, R. (1991). *Language disorders: A functional approach to assessment and intervention* (2nd Ed.). Needham, MA: Allyn & Bacon.

Owens, R. E. (1996). *Language development: An introduction* (4th Ed.). Needham, MA: Allyn & Bacon.

Paul, L. (1985). Programming peers' support for functional language. In S. F. Warren & A. K. Rogers-Warren (Eds.), *Teaching functional language*. Baltimore: University Park Press.

Perkins, W. (1971). *Speech pathology: An applied behavioral science*. St. Louis, MO: Mosby.

Pindzola, R., & White, D. T. (1986). A protocol for differentiating the incipient stutterer. *Speech and Hearing Services in the Schools, 17,* 2–15.

Quader, S. E. (1977). Dysarthria: An unusual side effect of tricyclic antidepressants. *British Medical Journal, 9,* 97.

Rosenbeck, J. (1984). Stuttering secondary to nervous system damage. In R. Curlee & W. Perkins (Eds.), *Nature and treatment of stuttering: New directions*. San Diego, CA: College-Hill.

Semel, E., Wiig, E., & Secord, W. (1987). *Clinical evaluation of language fundamentals*. San Antonio, TX: Psychological Corporation.

Senturia, B. H., & Wilson, F. B. (1968). Otorhinolaryngic findings in children with voice deviations. *Annals of Otology, Rhinology and Laryngology, 77,* 1027–1042.

Shames, G., & Rubin, H. (1986). *Stuttering then and now*. Upper Saddle River, NJ: Prentice Hall/Merrill.

Stoel-Gammon, C., & Dunn, C. (1985). *Normal and disordered phonology in children*. Baltimore: University Park Press.

Taylor, O. (1986). *Nature of communication disorders in culturally and linguistically diverse populations*. San Diego, CA: College-Hill.

Taylor, O. L., & Payne, K. (1994). Culturally valid testing: A proactive approach. *Topics in Language Disorders, 3(7),* 8–20.

U.S. Department of Education (1997). *Nineteenth annual report to Congress on the implementation of the Individuals with Disabilities Education Act*. Washington, DC: Author.

Van Riper, C. (1982). *The nature of stuttering*. Upper Saddle River, NJ: Prentice Hall.

Van Riper, C., & Erickson, R. (1996). *Speech correction: An introduction to speech pathology and audiology* (9th ed.). Needham, MA: Allyn & Bacon.

Wagner, R., & Torgesen, J. (1987). The nature of phonological processing and its causal role in the acquisition of reading skills. *Psychological Bulletin, 101,* 192–212.

Westby, C. (1988). Children's play: Reflections of social competence. *Seminars in Speech and Language, 9,* 1–14.

Westby, C., & Erickson, J. (1992). Prologue. *Topics in Language Disorders, 12,(3),* v–viii.

Wilcox, M. J. (1984). Developmental language disorders: Preschoolers. In A. Holland (Ed.), *Language disorders in children: Recent advances*. Austin, TX: PRO-ED.

Williams, D. E., Darley, F. L., & Spriestersbach, D. C. (1978). In F. L. Darley & D. C. Spriestersbach (Eds.), *Diagnostic methods in speech pathology*. New York: Harper & Row.

Williams, R., & Wolfram, W. (1977). *Social dialects: Differences vs. disorders*. Washington, DC: American Speech and Hearing Association.

Woolf, G. (1967). The assessment of stuttering as struggle, avoidance and expectancy. *British Journal of Disorders of Communication, 2,* 158–177.

Yairi, E., & Lewis, E. (1984). Disfluencies at the onset of stuttering. *Journal of Speech and Hearing Research, 27,* 155–159.

# 7

# Children with Physical and Health Impairments

The concept of physical and health impairment is a multidimensional one. It consists of two related areas: physical conditions that affect a child's education, and health conditions that affect a child's education. Each of these two large categories (physical impairment and health impairment) is further divided by the many possible diseases and disorders that may be classified as either a physical impairment or a health impairment. The specific disorders may be as unrelated to each other as muscular dystrophy and traumatic brain injury or as different as asthma and hemophilia. Yet children with these uniquely different conditions rely upon the same legislation to guarantee them the right to the best educational experience they are capable of obtaining. The purpose of this chapter is to identify and explain some of the health and physical impairments affecting children and adolescents. How often these conditions occur, what causes them, what their major characteristics are, and what are the most appropriate educational programs for children who are affected will also be discussed. The professionals who help guide the children, their parents, and their families; minority concerns; and issues of importance to this population will be highlighted. The lengthy list of professional and parent or self-help organizations and the wide variety of references for further information presented at the end of the chapter underscore the diversity of the physical and health impairment classification.

There are hundreds of physical and health impairments that can affect children's educational performance (Heward, 1996). The thirty-plus conditions we will highlight are those that are, in general, the most commonly occurring or most illustrative of types of physical or health impairment. Quite often the identification and service obtainment process that children with physical or health impairments experience is similar, even though their conditions may be markedly different.

## DEFINITIONS

This section will explain the legal and educational definitions of health and physical impairments. It will identify how the most common disabilities are classified and provide a basic glossary of terms that will prove helpful when reading the remainder of this chapter. Explanations of the defining characteristics, the causes, and how frequently the impairments occur will be discussed in the next section, which deals with the characteristics, etiology and prevalence of health and physical impairment.

### Differentiating Physical and Health Impairments

A physical disability affects skeletal, muscular, and/or neurological systems. The term *orthopedic disability* is often used interchangeably with the term *physical disability*. In general, federal legislation uses the term *orthopedic impairments*, while special educators and local service agencies use the term *physical disabilities* (Hardman, Drew, & Egan, 1996). Examples of physical/orthopedic impairments are cerebral palsy, epilepsy, and juvenile rheumatoid arthritis. Physical disabilities imply that children have problems with the structure or functions of their bodies. Health impairments put limitations on the body's physical well-being and require medical attention (Smith & Luckasson, 1995).

Health impairments are diseases, infections, or conditions that affect the life-maintaining systems of the body. They can impair the child's ability to perform well at school by their life-threatening or sometimes physically debilitating nature. Examples of health impairments are asthma, cancer, and sickle cell anemia.

## Federal Definitions of Physical and Health Impairments

The Individuals with Disabilities Education Act (IDEA) defines both the categories of physical and health impairment. An orthopedic (physical) impairment is defined as one that "adversely affects a child's educational performance. The term includes impairments caused by congenital anomaly (e.g. clubfoot, absence of some member, etc.), impairments caused by disease (poliomyelitis, bone tuberculosis, etc.), and impairments from other causes (e.g. cerebral palsy, amputations, and fractures or burns that cause contractures)" (23 Fed. Reg. 42478 [1977]).

IDEA defines children with health impairments as "having limited strength, vitality or alertness due to chronic or acute health problems such as a heart condition, tuberculosis, rheumatic fever, nephritis, asthma, sickle cell anemia, hemophilia, epilepsy, lead poisoning, leukemia or diabetes, that adversely affects a child's educational performance" (23 Fed. Reg. 42478 [1977]).

As a result of their impairments, these children may require special school services, including special instruction schedules, counseling, various therapies, special equipment, medication, and technological aids. They are likely to be absent from school with a higher frequency than their peers and may in some cases have to accept and confront their own limited life span or impending death (Smith & Luckasson, 1995).

The terms defined in Box 7.1 are not a complete listing of the specialized vocabulary needed to fully understand all physical and health problems. However, they should pro-

---

### Box 7.1
### *WHAT EVERY TEACHER NEEDS TO KNOW*

#### *Terms*

**Acute**   A condition that develops quickly, usually with intense symptoms.

**Ataxia**   A movement disorder characterized by faulty balance and depth perception.

**Athetosis**   Uncontrolled flailing movements.

**Aura**   A signal that a person with seizure disorders may receive prior to a seizure beginning.

**Chronic**   A long-lasting condition that develops over time.

**Congenital**   Present at birth but not inherited.

**Contractures**   Joints that stiffen so much that motion is limited or lost.

**Meninges**   The balloonlike membranes that cover the brain and spinal cord.

**Seizure**   A spontaneous abnormal discharge of electrical impulses in the brain.

**Shunt**   A drainage tube surgically implanted in the brain that drains excess spinal fluid into the body, where it is absorbed.

**Spasticity**   Uncontrolled tightening of muscles.

**Spinal cord**   The chain of nerves that extends from the base of the brain to the end of the spinal column.

Table 7.1
Classification of Orthopedic (Physical) and Health Impairments

| Orthopedic Impairments | Health Impairments |
|---|---|
| Amputations | Attention deficit/hyperactivity disorder |
| Cerebral palsy | Acquired immunodeficiency syndrome |
| Epilepsy (seizure disorder) | Asthma |
| Juvenile rheumatoid arthritis | Burns |
| Marfan syndrome | Cancer |
| Multiple sclerosis | Child abuse |
| Muscular dystrophy | Congenital heart disease |
| Osteogenesis imperfecta | Cytomegalovirus |
| Polio myelitis | Cystic fibrosis |
| Spina bifida | Fetal alcohol syndrome |
| Spinal cord injuries | Medically fragile/Technology dependent |
| Traumatic brain injury | Hemophilia |
| | Human immunodeficiency virus |
| | Hypoglycemia |
| | Juvenile diabetes |
| | Leukemia |
| | Nephritis |
| | Prenatal substance abuse |
| | Sickle cell anemia |
| | Tuberculosis |

vide enough guidance to help the reader understand the descriptions of the conditions that follow.

Table 7.1 is a listing of how conditions affecting children might be classified.

## PREVALENCE, CHARACTERISTICS, ETIOLOGY, AND TREATMENT OF SELECTED PHYSICAL AND HEALTH IMPAIRMENTS

This discussion of the frequency of occurrence, signs and symptoms, and causes of physical and health impairments differs from the discussions presented in most of the other chapters in this text because the umbrella term *physical and health impairment* comprises so many discrete disorders. As a result, it is more efficient to deal with each of the disorders and highlight its important features in one place in the text rather than in three separate sections. The brief explanations of treatments that follow the descriptions are usually descriptions of medical interventions available. Educational intervention will be discussed more fully in the section devoted to educational programming. The following paragraphs are not meant to be an exhaustive listing of all the possible physical and health impairment possibilities, nor are they meant to be all-encompassing descriptions of the selected conditions described. Instead, their function is to serve as introductory outlines the beginning reader can use on his or her journey to a deeper understanding of how each impairment can affect the social, emotional, and educational life of a child.

## Orthopedic Impairments

**Cerebral Palsy.**    Cerebral palsy is a disorder that affects movement and posture. It is a result of brain damage. The brain damage, usually caused by oxygen deprivation, can occur prior to birth, typically as the result of placental separation; during the birth process, due to birth cord strangulation or by the direct brain damage caused by forceps delivery; or soon after birth as the result of contracting brain damaging viral diseases. Accidental poisoning and direct trauma to the brain early in life while the brain tissues are still developing can also cause cerebral palsy. As a result, children with cerebral palsy, depending on the severity of the condition, may not be able to adequately control their movements. Cerebral palsy is not a disease. It does not become progressively worse, nor is it infectious in any form. The three major types of cerebral palsy are *spastic* (characterized by stiff, tense, poorly coordinated movements), *athetoid* (characterized by purposeless uncontrolled involuntary movements and contorted purposeful movements) and *ataxic* (characterized by balance problems, poor depth perception, and poor fine and gross motor skills). Depending on which areas of the brain are affected, a person with cerebral palsy may exhibit any of the types just described, or it is possible to have a mixture of types.

Estimates of occurrence range from 1.5 to 5 children being affected for each 1,000 live births (Bigge, 1991; Hardman et al., 1996). Approximately 500,000 to 700,000 adults and children currently living in the United States have some degree of cerebral palsy (Smith & Luckasson, 1995).

The problems associated with poor movement and balance skills may complicate educational activities. However, it is common to have associated conditions that further complicate the child's educational experience. Each child with cerebral palsy does not automatically exhibit the following associated conditions, but many do have associated communication, sensory, intellectual, and seizure disorders. The majority of people with cerebral palsy have problems with poor motor coordination, which makes it difficult for them to make the fine movements needed for intelligible speech. Language comprehension and formulation difficulties as a result of the brain damage are also not unusual. Hearing and vision problems of all types are also quite common. Jones (1983) estimates that as many as 30 percent of all people with cerebral palsy have hearing losses. Although it is difficult to accurately measure and not all people with cerebral palsy are automatically intellectually impaired, estimates identify 50 to 60 percent of this population as having cognitive deficits (Capute, 1985). Seizure disorders and their upsetting effect upon the educational experience will be discussed later in this chapter. Children with cerebral palsy exhibit concurrent seizure disorders as an associated condition somewhere between 35 and 60 percent of the time (Healy, 1984; Capute, 1985).

Cerebral palsy cannot be reversed, but proper management of the child can curtail physical damage due to poor posture, increase strength, and compensate for functional skill deficiencies. Braces, canes, crutches, and wheelchairs can facilitate movement and independence. Specially designed tools and augmentative devices can help in self-care and communication. An augmentative device can be any aid or device that replaces natural speech and helps the child communicate. Devices range from simple picture boards that contain pictures of the child's basic requests to sophisticated computers programmed with head pointers that a child can program to produce complicated language.

Each child with cerebral palsy presents a unique pattern of symptoms and resulting needs. For some, the disorder may be a minor inconvenience requiring minimal adjustment to regular classroom education. For others, cerebral palsy may make regular classroom experiences nearly impossible. Between these two extremes, the remaining children will require sensitive team constructed plans that will allow the child to function as well as possible within the restrictions of the disorder.

**Seizure Disorders (Epilepsy).**　Seizures are the result of spontaneous abnormal discharges of electrical impulses in the brain. Epilepsy is a disorder characterized by recurring seizures. Epilepsy is considered to be the most common neurological impairment in school-age children (Smith & Luckasson, 1995). Approximately 2 million people, or 1 percent of the population, are affected with epilepsy (Epilepsy Foundation of America, 1987). Seizures may be of unknown origin or may appear after accidents or high fevers injuring brain tissue (Cross, 1993). Each of the three types of seizure results in different behaviors by the person with the seizure disorder.

*Generalized absence* or *petit mal* seizures often last only a few seconds. The child may not even be aware of them as they occur. The child may appear to be daydreaming or staring into space. A slight eyelid tremor may be the only noticeable physical sign. Children may appear to not be following directions or seem inattentive.

It is possible that generalized absence seizures can develop into more severe forms of seizure behavior, such as *generalized tonic-clonic (grand mal)* seizures. Grand mal seizures are considered the most serious type of convulsion and are characterized by prolonged loss of consciousness and a stiff or *tonic* phase, during which muscles become extremely rigid. The tonic phase is followed by a *clonic* phase characterized by the limbs thrashing about in a purposeless way. During the seizure, teeth grinding and loss of bladder control are common occurrences. Physical injury as a result of the uncontrollable movements is a real possibility. After the seizure is finished, the child may be disoriented and sleepy. The emotional and educational effects of grand mal seizures are both obvious and potentially devastating to the student experiencing them.

*Complex partial* or *psychomotor* seizures result from focal or localized brain electrical discharge. Behaviors may vary, but often the child can appear to be in a stupor or might experience a period of inappropriate and purposeless movement or behavior before returning back to pre-seizure behavior. The following sequence is typical: The child will cease the activity that he or she was doing and replace it with automatic purposeless movements accompanied by incoherent and irrelevant speech (sometimes called *automatisms*). These behaviors are possibly followed by rage attacks of which the child is unaware after the seizure is terminated and normal behavior is resumed

(Cross, 1993). It is not difficult to understand why those exhibiting psychomotor seizures often perform poorly academically and are routinely mislabeled as mentally ill or emotionally disturbed.

Seizures may occur as isolated one-time events or may take place many times each day. Seizures can be initiated by bright lights, certain sound combinations, or even odors. An *aura*, or warning, can sometimes signal that a seizure will be occurring. Auras can take the form of an increase in sensory perception in taste, smell, visual perception, or hearing sensitivity. Occasionally an aura can be used as a signal to engage specific behaviors that prevent seizures from occurring (Clayman, 1989).

Treatment often focuses on control of seizures through medication. There is a possibility of curative surgery to remove the brain tissue thought to be responsible for the seizure activity. Surgery is most successful with infants and young children, who are still neurologically plastic and able to more readily compensate for the tissue loss than are older children and adolescents (Blakeslee, 1992). The primary medical assistive role of the classroom teacher is to monitor the effects of the medication administered to the child. Side effects such as drowsiness, dullness, lethargy, and behavioral change need to be brought to the attention of parents and health care specialists. Often the classroom teacher explains what seizures are to the other children in class or even to the affected child. Seizure disorders alone are not enough of a disability to require special class placement. However, they often occur in conjunction with other disorders such as cerebral palsy.

**Multiple Sclerosis.** Multiple sclerosis is a degenerative neuromuscular disease. This means that as the disease progresses, more and more damage will be done to the nerves that are affected, causing them to fail to transmit messages from the brain or to transmit them inaccurately. Multiple sclerosis destroys the myelin sheathing that surrounds and protects the nervous system. Neither the cause of multiple sclerosis nor a cure for it is known. A currently common theory is that somehow multiple sclerosis is the result of a virus that causes the body to attack and destroy healthy myelin tissue as if it were an invading disease. Multiple sclerosis is not infectious and cannot be transmitted from one person to another by close contact. The disease does not always progress in a systematic way. Some people experience mild attacks and then recover completely. Others have a series of attacks interspersed with periods of remission, during which the myelin damaging process is suspended. However, with each attack more damage is done to the nervous system. Initial symptoms include muscle weakness, poor coordination, and fatigue. If the degenerative process continues, tremors, spasticity, blindness, or severe visual impairment and speech slurring are possibilities. The person may eventually lose bowel or bladder control and become partially or totally paralyzed. Since a person with multiple sclerosis has a good chance of living a normal life span, school years are preparation years that allow the person to knowledgeably anticipate future needs. Between 250,000 and 500,000 people in the United States are affected with multiple sclerosis (Smith & Luckasson, 1995).

There is no known cure for multiple sclerosis. Physical therapy helps keep those affected as strong and healthy as possible.

**Muscular Dystrophy.**    Muscular dystrophy is also a neuromuscular disease. It tends to run in families and is usually transmitted to male children from their mothers (Cross, 1993). The cause of muscular dystrophy is not known. *Muscular dystrophy* is a label used to cover any one of nine hereditary muscle destroying disorders. The Duchenne type, which usually occurs between the ages of 3 and 6, is most common. During the course of the disease, muscles become progressively weaker as muscle tissue is replaced by fat and fibrous cells (Turnbull, Turnbull, Shank, & Leal, 1995).

Muscular dystrophy progresses slowly. Initial signs may include difficulty in walking and climbing stairs and an awkward swaying walking pattern (Bender, Schumaker, & Allen, 1976). Rising from a sitting position can be a problem. Children may grasp at table legs or desktops to pull themselves upright. Muscle weaknesses often force the children to walk on their toes. As the disease progresses, children find it difficult to rise after falling and show back deformities and protruding abdomens. Often by age 10, the child loses the ability to walk and will need a wheelchair to move about (Heward, 1996). During the final stage, children become bedridden and totally dependent on others. They are particularly fragile; even the gentle tension that occurs during lifting can cause dislocations. There is no known cure and death is usually attributed to heart failure or lung failure as a result of muscle weakness.

Muscular dystrophy affects between 1.4 and 2 people per 10,000 births (Batshaw & Perret, 1986). There are approximately 200,000 people with muscular dystrophy in the United States (Hardman et al., 1996).

Muscular dystrophy is not curable. Genetic counseling is the only form of prevention. Active treatment includes exercises that will help maintain range of motion and promote efficient breathing.

**Spina Bifida.**    Spina bifida is a prenatal developmental defect caused by the failure of the spinal column to properly seal around the spinal cord. *Myelodysplasia* is the medical term for the condition. The spinal cord does not close properly during early fetal development, perhaps as early as the first month of prenatal development. The reason this genetically linked disorder occurs is unknown. However, the result is that the spinal cord and the meninges that cover it are unprotected. The resulting damage prevents the nerves of the spinal cord from transmitting messages from the brain to other parts of the body. Depending on just where on the cord the damage occurs (the closer to the neck the more severe the symptoms) and the number of nerve fibers affected, this condition could cause infections, brain damage, and paralysis (Smith & Luckasson, 1995). There are three types of spina bifida. In *spina bifida occulta*, the spinal cord is covered only by skin; the bony aspects of the spinal column never develop. *Meningocele* occurs when a saclike protrusion containing part of the meninges and filled with spinal fluid develops. The spinal cord is not exposed. *Myelomeningocele* results from the partial protrusion of the spinal cord through the unsealed spinal column. This is the most damaging type, usually leading to neurological impairments. These impairments can cause partial paralysis, bowel and bladder control problems, and several associated conditions. The most problematic associated condition is hydrocephalus, a buildup of cerebrospinal fluid on the brain that fails to drain and, if untreated, can cause destruction of brain tissue and subsequent mental retardation.

Estimates are that 80 to 90 percent of children with spina bifida will develop hydro-cephalus (Mitchell, 1983). The use of a shunt surgically implanted in the brain relieves the pressure by transferring the built-up fluid into the bloodstream before it can cause damage. Other associated conditions might include kidney infections or failure, spinal curvature (scoliosis), humpback (kyphosis), or swayback (lordosis). Spina bifida occurs in approximately 1 of every 1,000 live births (Hardman et al., 1996). This affects a total of approximately 2,000 babies per year in the United States (March of Dimes, 1992). Slightly more females than males are born with spina bifida. It rarely occurs in African Americans or Asian Americans (Turnbull et al., 1995). The odds of a second child having the disorder increase if the first child is affected. The incidence of spina bifida is declining due to prenatal detection and parental decisions to terminate pregnancies (Lorber, 1990; Stone, 1987).

Infants with spina bifida usually are candidates for surgical closure of the spinal cord exposure. Surgery helps avoid infection and facilitates normal development by preserving motor, sensory, and intellectual functions. Cosmetically, the back and spine are improved with surgery and are easier to care for postsurgically. Without surgical repair the prognosis is much more guarded, with the possibility of recurring infections that might bring about severe deficits in intellectual functioning. Successful treatment leads to expectations of higher intellectual functioning. Intellectual development is normal in 73 percent of children, and most do not need wheelchairs. Forty-eight percent of those who require shunts to drain brain fluids do not require repeated surgery. On the downside, some combination of crutches and wheelchairs is required for mobility, and 87 percent of children have urinary incontinence (McLone, 1983). Most children require medical monitoring and need clean intermittent catheterization (CIC) to allow their bladders to empty. The CIC procedure is typically performed every three to four hours. The procedure became controversial when children with spina bifida in the public schools met with resistance from teachers who refused to perform the procedure. The Supreme Court ruled that the schools are required to perform CIC either with a school nurse or some other person trained in the procedure (Taylor, 1990; Turnbull, 1990).

**Traumatic Brain Injury (TBI).**    TBI is caused by severe trauma to the head that results in lasting physical and cognitive impairments. Accidents that cause head injuries are linked to alcohol and drug abuse, which in turn cause automobile accidents (the most common cause) and falls. It is also linked to gunshot wounds and other blows to the head that might cause brain damage. It is the most common cause of death for those under the age of 34 (Smith & Luckasson, 1995). Congress added traumatic brain injury as an additional category of disability in the Individuals with Disabilities Education Act (IDEA). According to IDEA, *traumatic brain injury* means:

> an acquired injury to the brain caused by external physical force, resulting in total or partial functional disability or psychosocial impairment, or both, that adversely affects a child's educational performance. The term applies to open or closed head injuries resulting impairments in one or more areas, such as, cognition; language; memory; attention; reasoning; abstract thinking; judgement; problem solving; sensory; perceptual and motor abilities; psychosocial behavior; physical functions; information processing

and speech. The term does not apply to brain injuries that are congenital or degenerative, or brain injuries produced by birth trauma. (34 C.F.R. § 300.7 [b] [12] [1977]).

Traumatic brain injuries are classified as *closed head injuries* when the damage is the result of the brain bouncing against the skull due to rapid acceleration and deceleration in accidents and *open head injuries* where there is direct external trauma to the brain. The specific problems caused by the impairments listed in IDEA might include chronic fatigue, pain, epilepsy, memory impairments, poor judgment, and poor organization skills. Motor problems such as paralysis, poor balance, and poor coordination are common (Smith & Luckasson, 1995). The person affected may be more impulsive, aggressive, or destructive; have temper tantrums; be irritable; be unable to self-monitor; and display high levels of anxiety. After the accident the child may have vision, hearing, and speech problems that were not evident prior to the trauma. The ability to understanding language and producing language may be severely impaired, depending upon which areas of the brain were injured. Some or all of the problems that result from the accident may be transitory or last for the remainder of the person's life. With closed head injuries, there can be a period of spontaneous recovery that lasts up to six months. During this period many functions, skills, and abilities can return. After this time passes, it is less likely that recovery without intensive therapy will occur.

The statistics on TBI are readily available since in most cases the accidents causing the brain damage are severe enough to require the assistance of law enforcement

and medical personnel, either at the scene of the accident or shortly after it occurs. Smith & Luckasson (1995) report that according to the National Head Injury Foundation, 100,000 of the 500,000 cases of TBI that occur each year are fatal. Another 100,000 people become debilitated for life. TBI occurs at the rate of 23 instances per 10,000 people a year (Bigge, 1991). One in 500 school children is expected to be hospitalized with TBI each year (Kraus, Fife, & Conroy, 1987). As many as 3 percent of the adolescent population of the United States have sustained head injuries serious enough to affect school performance (Forness & Kavale, 1993). Child abuse causes more than 60 percent of head injuries among infants. Shaken infant syndrome, in which the caregiver shakes a young child violently enough to cause brain and spinal cord injury, results in 10 to 25 percent fatality and TBI in many of those who survive (Mitiguy, 1991; Schroeder, 1993).

Hardman et al. (1996) list the treatment sequence for TBI as including the following stages:

1. Application of whatever medical procedures are needed to maintain life.
2. Minimizing complications that occur with the traumatic event.
3. Restoring consciousness.
4. Reorienting the patient after coma.
5. Initiating therapies that will help restore lost skills.
6. Preparation for the return home.
7. Providing counseling for family and child.

Depending upon the severity of the damage, children and adolescents with TBI will often need a variety of special education services in addition to medical and rehabilitation therapies. Although restoration of skills to a pre-accident level is always a goal, in many cases the best result possible is to help the child compensate for the traumatically induced weakness. Some children and adolescents will never again return to their level of functioning prior to the accident. Thinking, language, and attending skills, as well as emotional control and judgment and reasoning skills, may all require long-term retraining efforts from a variety of professionals, including speech-language pathologists, psychologists, and special education teachers.

The following briefly outlined orthopedic disabilities occur less frequently than those just described. The reader is encouraged to refer to the sources quoted for information that will provide a deeper understanding of the conditions.

**Marfan Syndrome.**    Marfan syndrome is a genetic disorder that affects approximately 20,000 people each year (Kirk, Gallagher, & Anastasiow, 1993). Children tend to have long, thin arms and legs, prominent shoulder blades, long fingers, and spinal curvature. Most critical is the typical accompanying heart weakness that can lead to heart failure and death. Limited physical exercise is usually prescribed.

**Juvenile Rheumatoid Arthritis.**    Juvenile rheumatoid arthritis is relatively rare, with an estimated occurrence of 3 new cases per 100,000 in the population. It affects female children twice as often as male children. There is complete remission in 75 to 80 percent of all cases (Hallahan & Kauffman, 1994). The disease itself affects muscles and joints, causing inflammation and swelling. As a result, movement becomes painful or impossible due to the resulting stiffness.

**Osteogenesis Imperfecta.**    Osteogenesis imperfecta is also known as *brittle bone disease*. The bones of the children affected are easily fractured. As a result of the repeated fractures, limbs tend to be underdeveloped and bowed. These children are extremely fragile and require frequent hospitalizations. These children may have hearing problems because the bones in the middle ear responsible for transmitting sounds to the brain can be defective (Cross, 1993). As the children mature, their bones become less brittle and the children less fragile. Osteogenesis imperfecta affects approximately 1 in 20,000 children (Heward, 1996).

Treatment of osteogenesis imperfecta relies on bracing the child and surgery when needed. Children may use wheelchairs for ambulation. Their physical activity must be severely restricted. Bones may break even when they are shifting positions in a wheelchair. The children show a normal range of intelligence and, aside from specialized physical accommodations, do not usually require special education classroom placements.

**Polio Myelitis.**    Polio, a viral infection that attacks the nerve cells of the spinal cord that control muscle function, can cause paralysis. It was once a major disease affecting school-age children, but preventive medical treatment in the form of vaccines has made it a rare disease.

**Spinal Cord Injuries.**    Spinal cord injuries usually are caused by auto accidents or falls. Injury to the spinal cord often results in loss of sensation or paralysis. The higher on the cord the injury, the greater the loss of function. Depending upon the injury, a wheelchair may be needed for ambulation. In severe cases, total paralysis may require a respirator to assist in breathing (Heward, 1996). Spinal cord injuries affect approximately 3 of every 100,000 people in the United States (Hardman, et al., 1996). Physical therapy and the use of adaptive devices for mobility and independent living, combined with counseling to adjust to the sudden trauma that caused the injury, constitute the core of the rehabilitative treatment procedures.

Table 7.2 is a summary of the incidence and prevalence of orthopedic impairments that affect children and young adults.

## Health Impairments

**Attention Deficit/Hyperactivity Disorder (AD/HD).**    Children with AD/HD differ from their peers due to their inability to concentrate or control their impulses. It is classified as a health impairment since AD/HD is seen as more of the result of a genetic, biological imbalance than as a pure behavioral problem (Comings, 1992). However, most educators argue to include AD/HD in discussions of children with learning disabilities. In accordance with this preference, we have included our discussion of AD/HD

Table 7.2

Incidence and Prevalence of Orthopedic Impairments

| Orthopedic Impairment | Statistics | Source |
|---|---|---|
| Cerebral palsy | 1.5–5 per 1,000 births | (Bigge, 1991) |
| | 500,000–700,000 adults and children in the United States | (Hardman, Drew, & Egan, 1996) |
| Seizure disorders | 1% of the population of the United States | (Epilepsy Foundation of America, 1987) |
| Multiple sclerosis | 250,000–500,000 active cases | (Smith & Luckasson, 1995) |
| Muscular dystrophy | 1.4–2 per 10,000 births | (Batshaw & Perret, 1986) |
| | 200,000 active cases | (Hardman et al., 1996) |
| Spina bifida | 1 per 1,000 live births | (Hardman et al., 1996) |
| | 2,000 cases per year | (March of Dimes, 1992) |
| Traumatic brain injury | 23 cases per 10,000 | (Bigge, 1991) |
| | 1 of 500 schoolchildren | (Kraus, Fife, & Conroy, 1987) |
| | 500,000 cases a year | (Smith & Luckasson, 1995) |

and its treatments in Chapter 4, "Children with Learning Disabilities." Please refer to that chapter for the discussions of AD/HD.

**Human Immunodeficiency Virus (HIV) and Acquired Immunodeficiency Syndrome (AIDS).** HIV and AIDS are related conditions. HIV is responsible for AIDS. HIV is contracted from the exchange of bodily fluids during unprotected sex or from using contaminated hypodermic needles. It can also be transmitted to a fetus from an infected mother. HIV gradually infects and eventually destroys the body's immune system, which normally protects the body from diseases. HIV progresses through distinct stages. During the earliest stage, the virus is in the bloodstream but there are no outward signs of illness. During the middle stage, minor symptoms appear as the immune system begins to lose its effectiveness. People who have been infected experience unusual fatigue, fevers, night sweats, chronic diarrhea, vaginal yeast infections, swollen glands, and frequent illnesses of all types. During its final stage, HIV becomes AIDS or AIDS related complex. All of the following symptoms are possible: seizures, memory lapses, impaired vision, blindness, weight loss, cancerous lesions, and respiratory infections. Children may lose cognitive skills. Bouts of severe pain and death usually follow. The Centers for Disease Control reported 1 million cases of AIDS in 1993 (Turnbull et al., 1995). Approximately 2 percent of those infected are children. However, the number of infants and children with HIV is on the rise (Smith & Luckasson, 1995). There is no known cure for AIDS.

Treatment for children with HIV infection includes medical care and educational services to families. Although good hygienic practices are critical, there is no evidence that HIV has ever been transmitted from one child to another in a school, daycare, or foster care setting (HIV/AIDS, 1990). Cohen et al. (1991) report that children who became HIV positive as a result of neonatal blood transfusions show an ability to maintain intellectual functioning for years. However, they do show some slowness in motor tasks and have impaired attention abilities and resultant academic problems.

**Asthma.**    Asthma is a chronic condition of breathing difficulty, wheezing, coughing, and shortness of breath. The cause is unknown. Current speculation is that asthma is an allergic response that occurs in those who are predisposed to develop the disorder. It is the leading cause of school absences among all chronic diseases (Altman, 1993). Although emotions can influence the conditions that bring about asthma attacks, they are not thought to be a primary cause of asthma (Cross, 1993). No amount of stress can bring about asthma unless the child already has defective airways. Relaxation, while it is useful in avoiding more lung constriction after an attack begins, by itself cannot prevent asthma (Turnbull et al., 1995). However, a clear relationship does exist between emotional stress and asthma attacks in that stress increases the likelihood of episodes, and attacks produce stress (Heward, 1996). Approximately 6 percent of all children have asthma (Smith & Luckasson, 1995). Twice as many males as females develop severe asthma. However, boys tend to improve as they age, whereas girls develop more complications as they enter adolescence (Paul & Fafoglia, 1988). Of an estimated total of 18 million cases, 4 million are children under age 18 (Turnbull et al., 1995).

Treatment for asthma revolves around eliminating allergens. This might entail special air filtrating, extra classroom cleaning, and vacuuming and wiping of surfaces. Outdoor play might be restricted during certain seasons, class pets may need to be moved, playing materials might need to be screened for content before use, and field trips may need to be more closely monitored (Smith & Luckasson, 1995). Specific medications might be prescribed to help the child resist allergens in general, or they may be used only during asthma attacks to help open closed lung passages. Periodic breathing exercises and mechanical lung drainage activities might be necessary. Often no special educational programming is needed aside from the allergen removing environmental activities described. By consulting with parents and appropriate health care professionals, classroom teachers can be prepared to deal with asthma attacks if they occur at school.

**Cancer.**    Cancer is a condition that causes uncontrollable growth of cells (tumors) in body organs and tissues. Children who develop brain tumors or undergo radiation therapy often develop learning disabilities. Approximately 1,500 children and adolescents a year die from cancerous conditions. Although it is relatively rare in occurrence, it is the primary cause of death by disease of those between ages 1 and 14 (American Cancer Society, 1993). One-third of the cancer deaths reported in 1993 were due to leukemia, a cancerlike blood condition. There are approximately 8,000 cases of childhood cancer a year (Turnbull et al., 1995).

Improved medical treatment has dramatically improved the survival rates of children with cancers. For example, in the 1960s the survival rates for children with leukemia was 4 percent. It is currently at 72 percent. Similarly, the survival rate for Hodgkin's disease, another form of cancer, is between 68 and 88 percent (Turnbull et al., 1995). However, both the chemotherapy and radiation used to control or eliminate cancerous conditions can have side effects that range from physically unpleasant (hair loss) to educationally debilitating (acquired learning disabilities). The American Cancer Society (1988) recommends that all students treated for cancerous conditions have an Individual Educational Plan (IEP) completed before they reenter school. For some children, the plan provides for the eventuality of home schooling. The current practice is to inform even young children about the disease so that they can actively participate in their treatment programs.

**Child Abuse.** Each state has its own definition of child abuse. Public Law 93-247, passed in 1974, defines child abuse and neglect as "physical or mental injury, sexual abuse, negligent treatment or maltreatment of a child under 18 by a person who is responsible for the child's welfare under circumstances which indicate that the child's health or welfare is harmed or threatened" (Hallahan & Kauffman, 1994). Battered children often display suspicious burns, bruises, abrasions, and broken limbs (Solomons, 1983). Long-lasting damage as a result of abuse can affect the central nervous system and the physical and psychosocial development of the child. Children who come to school with repeated swellings and bruises and show sudden onset of behavioral problems, such as sudden acting out episodes or violent aggressive behaviors toward other children, are often in abusive situations. Attempts to disguise injuries and cover bruises should also alert teachers (Chadwick, 1989). Shaken infant syndrome, previously mentioned as a cause of traumatic brain injury in infants and young children, is a significant cause of death and brain injury for abused children.

Child abuse occurs at all socioeconomic levels and affects children from all cultural subgroups. It is estimated that 60 to 90 percent of all adults who abuse children were abused themselves. Child abuse is most likely to occur when there are high levels of stress in a family, when expectations for a child are too high, and when parents or caregivers are emotionally or socially isolated from support services of any type (Hunt & Marshall, 1994). It is the legal responsibility of all citizens to report suspicion of child abuse to social service and law enforcement agencies. Failure to do so is punishable by laws that vary in each state, with punishments ranging from loss of employment to imprisonment. Approximately 1.5 percent of all children under age 18 have experienced abuse (Hardman et al., 1996).

**Cytomegalovirus (CMV).** CMV, a virus of the herpes group, is usually harmless; it is estimated that 40 percent of the children and adults in the United States have contracted CMV with no apparent long-term disability (Taylor & Taylor, 1989). However, when it affects a fetus it is classified as *cytomegalic inclusion disease* and can result in brain damage, blindness, and hearing loss. Although approximately 1 percent of all unborn children may be exposed to CMV, only about 10 to 15 percent of those exposed develop any disabilities (Smith & Luckasson, 1995). It is suspected that the virus is transmitted through bodily fluids. Pregnant women working in daycare settings appear to be at greater risk than others of infecting their unborn children. Although there is no cure, the disease can be identified with prenatal testing. The occurrence of the disease and its resulting disabilities appears to be reduced with frequent hand washing, sanitary diaper disposal, and keeping shared toys and play areas clean.

**Cystic Fibrosis.** Cystic fibrosis is a chronic genetic disorder that can affect either the pancreas, the lungs, or both. When the lungs are affected, mucus matter does not drain properly causing blockages, difficulty in breathing, and susceptibility to lung infection (Hunt & Marshall, 1994). Digestive problems that result in malnutrition and poor growth due to failure to absorb nutrients from food result when the pancreas is involved. Although the responsible gene has been identified and prenatal screening tests are available to determine whether a potential parent carries the disease, no cure is presently available (Cross, 1993). The life expectancy for people with cystic fibrosis is approximately 20 years (Hunt & Marshall, 1994).

Although the long-range outlook is improving for this disease, which was once fatal for children, no reliable cure exists. Proper treatment can retard the progression of the disease. Treatment combines medications that facilitate digestion and solutions that thin and loosen the mucus buildup in the lungs (Heward, 1996). Medications are combined with percussions designed to dislodge the mucus. The child is placed in a position that will make drainage easier and then the chest is clapped vigorously or vibrated. This procedure might be repeated several times a day (Caldwell, Todaro, & Gates, 1989). As a rule, children with cystic fibrosis are of normal intelligence. Educational compensations are usually necessary only for restricting physical activity and for the class time lost during percussions.

**Juvenile Diabetes and Hypoglycemia.** Juvenile diabetes can be an inherited metabolic disorder, or it can develop after a viral infection. In either event, the pancreas does not produce enough insulin to metabolize or absorb the sugar in the bloodstream. Hypoglycemia occurs when too much insulin is produced (Turnbull et al., 1995). As unabsorbed sugar builds in the bloodstream of children with diabetes, it can produce diabetic comas (unconsciousness), nerve damage, and eventually a weakened circulatory system (Little, 1991). Children show increased thirst, frequent urination, weight loss, headaches, and slow healing of incidental cuts and scrapes. Visual and kidney problems are common co-occurrences. Without proper medical intervention, the child with diabetes lacks energy and vitality. Type I diabetes is most common in 10 to 16-year-olds, while Type II is more common to adults and is related to obesity and genetic factors (Heward, 1996). Diabetes affects approximately 5 percent of the population (Hardman et al., 1996) and 1 in 600 school-age children (Winter, 1983).

Appropriate medical intervention for diabetes includes dietary control and doses of insulin administered on a prescribed schedule. Hypoglycemia is more dependent upon dietary modifications. Both disorders require that the child eat appropriate snacks to regulate insulin levels. Teacher observation is critical to spot behaviors that indicate unbalanced insulin levels. Parents and health care professionals can inform the classroom teacher which behaviors are indicative of potential insulin shock, when too much insulin is present, or diabetic coma, when too little insulin is in the child's system.

**Sickle Cell Anemia.** Sickle cell anemia is an inherited blood disease that occurs most commonly among African Americans and Hispanics of Caribbean ancestry. The disease results in oxygen-carrying red blood cells losing their round shape and becoming crescent or sickle shaped. These distorted cells do not circulate as efficiently and cause oxygen transmission to be inefficient. Children experience severe pain in the abdomen, legs, and arms. They are unusually fatigued and vulnerable to infections. The poor blood circulation may lead to degeneration of joints throughout the body. As a result of pain and fevers brought about by infections, school attendance usually suffers (Sirvis, 1996). Sickle cell anemia affects approximately 1 of every 600 African American infants (Hardman et al., 1996). Medical treatment consists of administering massive doses of penicillin until the immune system is capable of warding off infections (Kirk et al., 1993).

**Prenatal Substance Abuse and Fetal Alcohol Syndrome.** A pregnant woman's use of drugs and alcohol can affect her unborn child. The affected children have a greater risk of developing learning and behavioral problems, in addition to the physical damage they are at greater risk of sustaining. Some prescription drugs, illegal drugs, and nicotine can affect the unborn child depending on the drug, the dosage, and when during the pregnancy the child was exposed. For example, prenatal exposure to cocaine can lead to elevated heart and respiratory rates, hyperirritability, poor eating, diarrhea, gastrointestinal problems, and neurological damage of various types (Hardman et al., 1996). A fetus exposed to cocaine is also more likely to be exposed to AIDS and become HIV positive (Smith, 1988). Approximately 1 in 10 newborn babies has been exposed to one or more illegal drugs during its mother's pregnancy (Chasnoff, 1988).

*Fetal alcohol syndrome* is the most common result of prenatal substance abuse. Alcohol abuse and the resultant fetal alcohol syndrome have been blamed for causing 5 percent of all congenital anomalies and from 10 to 20 percent of all cases of mild mental retardation. Yet it is also estimated that even among chronic abusers, 50 to 70 percent of the children born are symptom free (Conlon, 1992). However, even moderate use of alcohol can lead to fetal alcohol syndrome (Glanze, Anderson, & Anderson, 1985). Overall, 2 of every 1,000 children born show signs of fetal alcohol syndrome (Hardman et al., 1996). The affected children tend to be small at birth and remain small after birth. They show a higher evidence of facial deformities, microcephaly, and congenital heart defects (Turnbull et al., 1995). During infancy, children with fetal alcohol syndrome may be more irritable and difficult to handle, feed, and diaper. They may have a high pitched cry and be unresponsive to parental attempts to comfort them. This puts them at higher risk of being abused by frustrated parents (Vincent, Paulsen, Cole, Woodruff, & Griffith, 1991). The majority of children with fetal alcohol syndrome will experience normal development. However, 20 to 30 percent will have language learning problems and attention deficits (Griffith, 1991). Vincent et al. (1991) divide growing children born with fetal alcohol syndrome into three groups. The first group will experience developmental disabilities of all types, including seizure disorders, cerebral palsy, mental retardation, and various physical abnormalities. The second group will develop normally. The final group will be at high risk for developing learning and behavioral problems. These children tend to test the limits of caregivers because they often are socially insensitive, are easily overstimulated, and develop poor peer relationships.

**Technology-Dependent/Medically Fragile.** Children who are medically fragile or technology-dependent require constant attention for survival. These children may both require ongoing medical care and rely on a technological device to replace some vital nonfunctioning body part (Office of Technology Assessment, 1987). Children who are affected fall into four subgroups—those who are sustained by (1) mechanical ventilators (breathing assistance machines); (2) nutrition or medication delivered intravenously; (3) periodic (daily) ventilator or nutritional help; and (4) long-term use of mechanical devices or processes such as kidney dialysis machines, urinary catheters, or any of a variety of life support monitors. The Task Force on Technology-Dependent Children (1988) uses the term *technology-dependent*, while the Council for Exceptional Children (1988) uses the term *medically fragile* to identify the population of children who require special health care and life support during the school day.

Depending upon the severity of the condition, these children may simply require periodic monitoring at school, or they may be able to function only in the most restricted level of special education service, the hospital or home setting. Children who are hospital or home bound are visited by itinerant teachers and, when possible, can interact with peers over closed-circuit television and speakerphone systems. Improvements in miniaturization, durability, and efficiency of medical devices have enabled an increasing number of technology-dependent children to attend school on a regular basis.

Other health impairments that might affect a child's strength, vitality, or alertness or cause negative attention from the nondisabled population and cause adjustment problems are burns, congenital heart diseases, hemophilia, leukemia, nephritis, and tuberculosis.

Table 7.3 is a listing of the incidence and prevalence of health impairments that affect children and young adults.

Table 7.3
Incidence and Prevalence of Health Impairments

| Health Impairment | Statistic | Source |
|---|---|---|
| HIV/AIDS | 1–3 cases per 1,000 live births | (Hardman, Drew, & Egan, 1996) |
| | 1 million active cases | (Turnbull, Turnbull, Shank, & Leal, 1995) |
| Asthma | 6% of all children | (Smith & Luckasson, 1995) |
| | 4 million under age 18 | (Turnbull et al., 1995) |
| | 18 million total cases | |
| Attention deficit/hyperactivity disorder | 3–5% of the school-age population | (Turnbull et al., 1995) |
| | 1.35–2.25 million cases | |
| Cancer | 8,000 children per year | (Turnbull et al., 1995) |
| Child abuse | 1.5% of children under age 18 | (Hardman et al., 1996) |
| Cytomegalovirus | 1% of all fetuses | (Smith & Luckasson, 1995) |
| Cystic fibrosis | 1 in 2,500 live Caucasian births | (Heward, 1996) |
| | 1 in 17,000 live African American births | (Hardman et al.,1996) |
| Juvenile diabetes | 1 in 600 school-age children | (Winter, 1983) |
| Sickle cell anemia | 1 in 600 African American infants | (Hardman et al., 1996) |
| Prenatal substance abuse | 1 in 10 live births exposed to illegal drugs | (Chasnof, 1988) |
| Fetal alcohol syndrome | 2 per 1,000 live births | (Hardman et al., 1996) |
| | | (Turnbull et al., 1995) |

# IDENTIFICATION PROCESS

The initial evaluation that determines whether a child has a particular health or physical impairment is usually performed by a physician. AD/HD identification is an exception in that often educators help in the diagnosis. After a medical diagnosis and identification are completed, school personnel have to decide whether the child needs and qualifies for any of the special educational services supported by the Individuals with Disabilities Education Act (IDEA).

Determining which special services may be needed can be a complex process that will require evaluations and judgments from several paramedical and educational professionals. Children with health and physical impairments require collaboration between professionals more than do children in most other areas identified by the IDEA. Health impairments that affect cognitive skills or behavior will need a multidisciplinary school based team to administer and interpret the appropriate evaluation instruments required to determine what special educational services or classroom modifications are necessary for the child to benefit most from the educational experiences offered. Decisions about the setting, be it a regular classroom, a special classroom, home schooling, hospital based schooling, or some combination, have to be determined and anticipated. Not all children will require all of the services about to be discussed. However, some will. A comprehensive identification would assess all of the following areas to see whether services were necessary in any or all of them.

**Activities of Daily Living.**   Assessment in this area would evaluate the child's daily living potential. Eating, drinking, dressing, toileting, and personal hygiene self-help skills are analyzed to determine current and possible future independent functioning. Later in life, daily living skills expand to cooking, housekeeping, and self-transportation abilities.

**Mobility Assessment.**   A large component of independence is the ability to move about independently. Assessment might consist of evaluating current mobility skills and anticipating any future mobility needs that could be more easily attained with appropriate therapy or education.

**Physical Abilities Assessment.**   The physical potential of a given child needs to be assessed prior to the construction of the IEP. What physical actions a child can currently perform and what limitations the condition affecting the child might impose in the future must be anticipated. Based on the assessment, appropriate professionals can become part of the habilitation or rehabilitation team.

**Psychosocial Abilities Assessment.**   A child's self-image and the ability to initiate and maintain social relationships are only two of many psychosocial processes that may need to be assessed. How well the child adapts emotionally to a disability may be the most facilitative or impeding component to successful education and living.

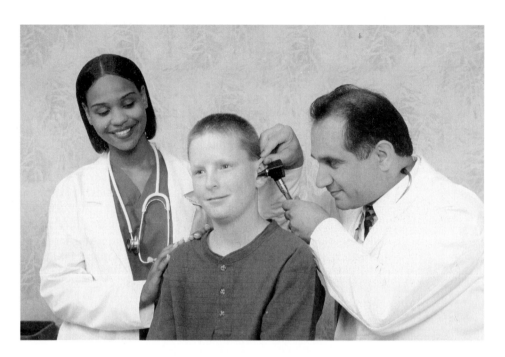

**Communication Assessment.**    The ability to understand language is critical for much of the learning that takes place in the classroom. The skills necessary to formulate thoughts into language and the ability to program the appropriate organs needed to speak are critical for meaningful interaction within the learning environment. A communication assessment can determine a child's language and speech skills and potentials and help educators develop a plan for attainment of deficient skills or suggest compensations for skills that might never be attained.

**Academic Potential Assessment.**    Intelligence testing, reading comprehension skills testing, grade-level achievement tests, and many other measures may be needed to help forecast a child's academic potential prior to the recommendations made in an IEP. Before services can be requested, the IEP team needs an understanding of what academic goals might be appropriate for any child with health or physical impairments.

**Setting Assessment.**    The setting in which learning will take place must also be evaluated to determine whether any modifications will be necessary. Doorway width, lighting, bathroom accessibility, air filtration, extra space for equipment, rest areas, and any other accommodations a child with physical impairments may need will have to be integrated into the setting determined appropriate for that child. Modifications of the learning setting may require the teacher to modify or change teaching techniques or use classroom aids to assist with instruction. A careful review of the curriculum and how it will be presented to the class will pinpoint the modifications necessary to effectively instruct the child with a physical or health impairment.

**Assistive Technology Assessment.** Integrated into the assessments already listed is assistive technology assessment. A determination of the value of available assistive technology and how using it might combine with other areas of assessment must be made. For example, for a child with cerebral palsy that affects the ability to effectively move the speech organs (dysarthria), using an augmentative speech device might be more effective than remediation attempts focused on using natural speech. The potential of the child to function with or without a device, the ability of the child to master the use of a device, the willingness of the family to accept the use of an augmentative system, and the cost and availability of the technology must all be factored into decisions to recommend assistive technology.

The following examples illustrate how the identification and assessment process might be applied to one child with traumatic brain injury and another who may have attention deficit/hyperactivity disorder.

After a student has sustained a head injury that caused either a closed or an open head injury, the medical procedures previously described—ranging from life-maintaining procedures to initial re-orientation—are administered. After a period, when it is felt that spontaneous recovery of previous skills may no longer be a factor, neurologists might perform some brain imaging tests (CAT scans and the like) to uncover the possibility of permanent brain damage. A psychologist or psychometrist might administer tests that measure information processing skills or problems-solving abilities and compare the results to any pre-trauma measures that might exist. Parents will inform the team about how the child is functioning at home. The speech-language pathologist will test for receptive and expressive language abilities as well as evaluating motor speech skills. Physical and occupational therapists might evaluate mobility and the motor skills needed for daily living. The school counselor will contribute information on the child's emotional adjustments. From all of this information and other sources that might be needed for any given child, an appropriate IEP and educational setting recommendation evolve. This plan may deal with short-term needs as well as long-term concerns.

As discussed in Chapter 4 of this text, the Council for Exceptional Children recommends the six-step procedure shown in Box 7.2 for identification of children with possible AD/HD (Council for Exceptional Children, Task Force on Children with AD/HD, 1992).

Some combination or variation of the two examples outlined describes the course that should be taken in the identification and assessment of all children identified as having physical or health impairments that might interfere with academic achievement.

**Box 7.2**
*WHAT EVERY TEACHER NEEDS TO KNOW*
*Identifying Children with*
*AD/HD*

*Step 1.* Document behavior observed by both parents and teachers that is indicative of AD/HD. (See characteristics listed in Chapter 4).

*Step 2.* Re-evaluate tests such as group intelligence tests, group achievement tests, and vision and hearing tests to determine whether they are accurate measures of potential or whether poor performance may be the result of attention problems. A physician may be consulted to see whether an identifiable physical condition is causing inattention or hyperactivity.

*Step 3.* Attempt classroom management to correct or control behaviors leading to poor academic performance. If these attempts are unsuccessful, request referral for AD/HD placements.

*Step 4.* Conduct psychological evaluations to see whether the student meets criteria for AD/HD placement. Administer individual tests and behavioral rating scales. Review medication recommendations.

*Step 5.* Have the team, including the child's parents, plan for the special educational needs of the child.

*Step 6.* Implement the Individual Education Plan.

*Source:* From *Children with AD/HD: A Shared Responsibility* (pp. 1–4), by the Council for Exceptional Children, Task Force on Children with AD/HD, 1992, Reston, VA: Author.

## PROGRAMS

Educational programming and medical treatment for children who have health or physical impairments are related but different processes. Medical treatments stabilize, reverse, and control the conditions causing the children to be identified as physically impaired. Educational programming has as its general goals helping the person gain independence of all types. This includes physical independence and the mastery of daily living skills, self-awareness, and social maturation, including acceptance and coping adjustments, academic growth beyond content mastery and into application of knowledge, and success with life skills such as employment, independent living, community involvement, and leisure activities (Sirvis, 1996). Most children with physical or health related disabilities are included in educational programs on the basis of their learning needs, not their handicaps (Heward, 1996). Even those with the most severe conditions are often best served in the regular classroom. Many are never identified as impaired for special educational purposes. These children don't need curriculum modifications or special related services. Some, however, do require modification of curricula, teaching methods adapted to their needs, and classroom or setting modifications. Of the children identified, approximately 40 percent can be educated in regular classrooms, with resource room help in some cases. Fewer than 30 percent require a separate classroom. Those remaining are best educated in separate schools, hospitals, or residential facilities (U.S. Department of Education, 1997).

## Program Settings

Children with physical or health related disabilities are served within a variety of settings. Most attend school in regular classrooms. Some use resource rooms for part of their education, while others are placed in self-contained classrooms. Home schooling provided by itinerant regular and special education teachers, hospital classrooms, and residential facilities are most appropriate for others. As a society, we have shifted from special classes and schools to more mainstreamed placements. Often, simple adjustments such as additional space for a child's necessary support equipment or a resource teacher to help the child catch up on missed class work can make a regular classroom less restrictive. Depending upon the extent of the modifications needed, regular classroom placement can foster independence, improve social and communication skills development, and even sensitize nondisabled students to the potential of their peers with disabilities (Heward, 1996).

## Program Options

Public Law 99-457 mandates that children under age 3 who need special education are required to have an Individualized Family Service Plan (IFSP) (Hallahan & Kauffman, 1994). Similar to an IEP, this plan must specify how the family will be involved as well as which special educational services will be anticipated. Programs are provided for preschool, primary, and secondary students, as well as those who are transitioning to adulthood.

Early intervention and preschool programs begin as soon as needs are identified. Services often begin at the birth of the child. Initially, support for the family and information about available treatments and service options are provided along with assistance in learning how to care for the child at home. Regardless of the impairment, early programs tend to focus on motor development, self-help in daily living, and social skills (Hanson, 1984). Parents play the most critical role in the early development of their child. Much preschool instruction takes place in the home and is administered by parents. Members of the child's educational team provide support and structure for the interventions applied. Team members may include occupational therapists, speech-language pathologists, physical therapists, and nurses. Constant contact between the habilitation professionals and parents is vital.

The school-age child usually moves beyond the home setting. Schools assume responsibility for educational and physical management, including adapting spaces for wheelchairs, work tables, and other equipment. The school nurse or other informed person may administer medicines. Bathroom stalls, sinks, mirrors, towels, and door handles may need to be adapted to a child's needs. Younger children may require toileting assistance. Academically, children with physical and health impairments often have high absence rates due to the demands of medical treatment and sometimes their own fragile health. Instruction may have to be modified to help these children keep up with their peers. Videotapes of missed experiences, telephone communication, and use of schoolmates as tutors are all critical adaptations that maintain academic and social connections within a classroom. Some children may require untimed exams or need to use specialized equipment to participate in classroom activities. Parents, and most important, the children themselves, are critical members of the IEP team. Quite often, children are best able to describe their difficulties in the classroom and in some cases suggest solutions. Sometime all that is needed are minor environmental manipulations. Wright & Bigge (1991) describe four types of simple environmental manipulations that can be helpful. The first is simply changing the location of materials and equipment so that the handicapped student can reach them without disrupting classroom activities. The second is to modify work surfaces, as needed, so that they become more user friendly. The third is to modify commonly used objects that might be difficult to use in their usual form, and the fourth is to provide aids to help in manipulating objects or sources of frustration. It can be as easy facilitating the use of a water fountain for a student who uses a wheelchair by placing a paper cup dispenser within easy reach.

Many of the adaptations are carried through to middle school and high school instruction. By the middle school and high school years, many of the problems initially encountered in instructional modification and presentation have been solved. Children of middle school and high school age with physical and health related disabilities may be particularly sensitive to being different and be most concerned about their appearance. Both affected children and their peers may need information about a given disability and its effects on physical and intellectual functioning. The affected child must be provided the guidance necessary to realistically accept his or her condition and evolve the best possible coping strategies.

Transition to adulthood continues this process. Employment and independent living are the goals. Legislation has helped make adult living easier by mandating accessibility to public services and making it illegal to discriminate against employment candidates on the basis of a physical handicap. Students with physical disabilities and health impairments have the lowest dropout rates of all special education students (U.S. Department of Education, 1996). Many go on to higher education. Colleges and universities are as responsible as all other agencies for providing appropriate accommodations, both physical and instructional, for these students.

## Technology

Advances in technology have made it possible for children who would not have previously survived to live and attend school. Technology-dependent children may require ventilators that assist in breathing, pacemakers, kidney dialysis, sophisticated insulin delivery systems, urinary catheters, and even organ transplants to survive, remain with their families, attend school on a regular basis, and lead more normal lives. These life-sustaining medical advancements have their educational counterparts. Technology as sophisticated as computers and electronic communication aids and as simple as specially designed spoons can dramatically improve the lives of children with physical impairments and enable them to take advantage of the experiences available in their environment. Computers controlled by any number of inventive switches and head pointers are the newest augmentative communication devices that make writing and programmed spoken communication more possible. Less complex devices, such as communication boards with pictures of frequently used requests, can open up communication channels. Calculators can help in math drill; special switches can turn lights on and off as needed. Newly designed wheelchairs and motorized vehicles of all types provide freedom of movement, increased privacy, and the personal independence needed for many academic and social tasks. Modern braces make it possible to be comfortable enough to read and study. Robotic assistance may be the next wave. Robots may be designed to assist in some tasks currently done by attendants and family members. Some robots exist that can turn pages in books, dial telephones, and hold cups (Kwee, 1986). Cost and maintenance of equipment are the only clouds on the horizon. The technological advances that make living easier for all people will substantially improve the quality of life for people with physical and health related impairments.

## ISSUES OF IMPORTANCE

There are many issues of concern for children and adolescents with physical and health related impairments and their families. Some are not unique to this population and are shared by other disability groups discussed in other chapters of this text. The issues discussed in this section are neither all-inclusive nor sufficiently detailed to be comprehensive presentations. However, they highlight some real and pressing concerns with which families and the professionals who deal with physical and health related impairments struggle daily.

### Prevention

Many physical and health related impairments are easily preventable. The use of seat belts and car seats could drastically lower the incidence of TBI and spinal cord injuries. Education can help us all understand how safety equipment, responsible gun use and weapons training, vaccinations, prenatal care, appropriate supervision of infants and young children, responsible use of medications, and safe sex can all lessen or prevent health and physical impairments. With the exception of stressing safe sex, these actions are not moral issues. They do not require philosophical life modifications or much more than an understanding of the consequences of the failure to routinely employ them. Obviously, sexual issues and the role of genetic counseling in the prevention of health and physically related disorders are more complex. Decisions in these areas are often based on personal beliefs and religious and lifestyle principles. However, even in the most sensitive areas, information and the understanding of consequences can only better prepare families for the outcomes of their decisions.

### Family Management Concerns

We have highlighted the importance of the family in the total management of the child with a physical or health related impairment. However, we have not highlighted the emotional and economic costs that can be placed upon a family attempting to act responsibly. This section will highlight some of the pressing concerns families of children and adolescents with physical and health related impairments must face daily. Martin, Brady, and Kotarba (1992) list the demands that a child's chronic illness can place on a family. Included in the discussion are fatigue, restricted social life, and a preoccupation with the numerous decisions that need to be made about the child. In addition, the economic burdens can be staggering. Employment and career decisions are often made based on the availability of health insurance and maintaining it. Technology is both alluring and expensive. Often the latest technological advances are not paid for by insurance carriers. Motorized wheelchairs, computers, electronic communication aids, and even special spoons can be very costly. The arguments about who should bear the costs of these devices and what might be the limits of a society's responsibility to the handicapped are discussed in Chapter 2. Even when a child is eligible, government regulations are complex, and record keeping for reimbursements can put further strain on a family. Services are not provided equally in all areas of the country or even all areas of a state. Larger urban areas generally can provide more support than can rural areas. Families have had to sever ties with communities and families to move to areas that can provide needed services for a child. Most homes are not designed with the spaces that might be needed for wheelchairs, ramps, or other large equipment needs. Costly remodeling or relocation might become a necessity for a family.

Special planning and complicated arrangements are often necessary for the simplest tasks such as a slumber party, a weekend trip, an adults only dinner, or a family vacation. The frequent absences from school that are a predictable characteristic of many health and physical impairments usually require at least one adult to be with the child, which causes conflicts in two-parent families and often unsatisfactory compromises in one-parent households.

Parent self-help groups and support groups of all types (see the listings provided in this chapter) can help with creative ideas and solutions, joint baby-sitting arrangements, emotional support, and tips for dealing with professionals who may be less than sensitive to a family's conflicts.

## Discrimination

Individuals with physical and health impairments are often noticeably different from those around them in schools, recreational facilities, and the workplace. In addition to their own possible unresolved feelings, they must continually face potentially negative or stereotypical behaviors from people with whom they interact. Fear, rejection, or pity can cause a child to internalize these attitudes and become withdrawn and overdependent.

Equally as troublesome is architectural discrimination in the form of barriers that deny people with physical impairments access to facilities easily available to those without disabilities. The American with Disabilities Act (PL 101-336, 1990) mandates that all new buildings, buildings undergoing renovations, and all public transportation and public facilities must be accessible to people with disabilities. The most

commonly visible result of this legislation are the ramps, street corner pavement breaks, elevators, special parking spaces, special telephones, wheelchair accessible water fountains, and toilet modifications routinely available in many public places and businesses. These modifications have made and continue to make inroads into the often intimidating prospect, for people with disabilities and their families, of traveling from a known environment to an unknown one.

## Death and Grief in the Classroom

Sometimes children do not overcome their disability. Occasionally a disease runs its course prematurely, depriving young children or adolescents of their lives. While death is not a common occurrence in the classroom, it does occur with enough frequency that all participants involved need to be cared for. Obviously the dying child needs support, but so do the child's teachers, parents, and classmates.

Dying children need support during their illness and reassurance that they will not be forgotten. They may need to be absolved of the guilt they feel for the pain and suffering they are causing their friends and families (Turnbull et al., 1995).

Families often feel abandoned while a child is dying and immediately after the death of a child. Surviving siblings need support as much as their parents do. Visits are usually welcomed and are times to show support and refrain from giving advice (Cassini & Rogers, 1990).

Classmates need to be updated on the terminally ill child's condition. Honesty establishes credibility. Code words for death and dying, such as "going away," can confuse young children and can lead to misunderstanding of what is occurring. Reassurance that young children dying is a rare event can be comforting to young children. This is not the time to lecture about safety or give warnings about good health practices. Different age groups will react differently. Preschoolers may not fully comprehend death or dying, but can certainly react to the sadness they are perceiving in the environment. Kindergarten and first grade children may believe that death is reversible or that it may be a consequence of common ailments like head colds or stomachaches. Primary level students need more information than do younger children. They may feel responsible for the death or fear it will bring about other deaths. Middle school children are concerned about how the death affects them personally; they may feel the loss and express it emotionally and openly. High school students can react the same way as adults, experiencing all the feelings of loss and grief without the maturity or experience to handle them (Schaefer, 1988).

Teachers must not be left out of the circle of those affected by a dying child. They also need to grieve and feel anger and frustration. It is not unusual for a teacher who has spent time as a primary figure in a dying child's life to be irritable, depressed or unwilling to confront feelings, or even to withdraw from the dying child. School administrators and fellow teachers should be aware of these characteristic signs and help provide support or, if necessary, recommend counseling.

## MINORITY CONCERNS

### Disabilities and Farm Workers

The children of migrant agricultural workers, many of whom are culturally and linguistically diverse, are at highest risk for disabilities, including physical and health related disabilities (Baca & Harris, 1988). The Education Commission of the States Migrant Education Task Force (1979) reported that the life expectancy of migrant workers is 49 years, as compared to the national average of 79 years, and that infant mortality is 25 percent higher in this group than the national average. The commission noted that among this group, lack of prenatal care and postnatal care resulted in birth injuries and disabilities. In addition, higher instances of poor nutrition and lack of access to health care lead to poor mental and physical development. Many of the health and physical disabilities prevalent in the children of migrant agricultural workers are preventable.

### AIDS and Minorities

HIV infection is currently a growing cause of death in minority infants. The disease and its fatal consequences is growing especially fast among Hispanic and African

American women and children (Indacochea & Scott, 1992). While there is no indication that members of these two minority groups are any more susceptible to HIV or AIDS than any other groups, many members of these minorities are exposed to lifestyle risks that co-exist with the transmission of the viruses. The transmission of HIV and its resultant AIDS could be drastically curtailed by safe sex practices and curtailment of intravenous drug use or even lessening shared hypodermic needle use.

## PROFESSIONALS

Children and adolescents with physical and health impairments and their families come into contact with many medical specialists, educational specialists, teachers, physicians, and therapists. These professionals are part of the interdisciplinary team that shares its expertise to provide the best habilitation and educational plan possible for a child. They are also responsible monitors who make certain that the plans are carried out and modified in the best interests of the child. Individual team members need to communicate with each other as well as with the child's parents to maintain the child's health and, at the same time, develop whatever capabilities the child possesses (Bigge, 1991; Verhaaren & Connor, 1981).

Regular and special education teachers who provide direct instruction to children with physical and health impairments may interact with dozens of specialists and service providers as they help the child achieve his or her maximum potential. Related services and service providers are not always the same for each child. However, related services might include members from the following long list: transportation coordinators, speech-language pathologists, physical therapists, occupational therapists, audiologists, and psychological specialists, recreational therapists, school health service specialists, social workers, early identification and early assessment specialists, music therapists, art therapists, media specialists, vocational education teachers, reading teachers, guidance counselors, assistive technology specialists, mobility specialists, dietitians, and others who may have been inadvertently left off this list. It is not surprising that families often need the assistance of special educators to explain the function of some specialists and to help families become aware of what services are available and necessary for their child. Parents often grant special educators or regular classroom teachers permission to work directly with paramedical and medical specialists. Students whose parents are directly involved with their education are more successful than students whose parents are less involved (Rainforth, York, & Macdonald, 1992). Obviously no one child can be served by all these specialists at once, but it would not be unheard of for a child with serious impairments to have worked with a representative of every field listed here and others not mentioned as well. Any service that directly benefits a child being educated in a school program can be classified as a related service (Turnbull, 1990).

Table 7.4 is a listing of some of the most commonly consulted professionals and the services that they provide.

Table 7.4
Frequently Consulted Professionals

| Professional | Service |
|---|---|
| Speech-language pathologist | Evaluates speech, language, and communication deficits and implements remedial services. Recommends and programs augmentative and adaptive equipment. Provides swallowing therapy. |
| Physical therapist | Directly provides exercises to maintain and enhance range of movement, modify positioning, and perform motor tasks. |
| Occupational therapist | Enhances self-care activities (feeding, dressing, toileting) and fine motor coordination (buttoning, dressing, eating). May also provide counseling related to social and psychological issues. |
| Assistive technology specialist | Assesses needs for assistive and adaptive equipment. Aids in selection and modification of equipment. |
| School nurse | Responsible for health monitoring activities, classroom education, and performing unusual health related procedures. |
| Special educator | Coordinates services and provision of direct instruction. |
| Homebound teacher | Provides direct instruction outside the school setting. |
| Social worker | Assists in family management issues. |
| Resource teachers | Provide direct and indirect services, such as mobility instruction, counseling, and consultation with other professionals. |
| Classroom teacher | Communicates and collaborates with other team members. Evaluates efficacy of programs. Provides direct instruction. |

## PROFESSIONAL ASSOCIATIONS AND PARENT OR SELF-HELP GROUPS

The following list of associations, societies, and programs provides the interested reader with addresses for initial contact with a wide variety of interest groups.

Allergy Foundation of America
801 Second Avenue
New York, NY 10017

American Academy for Cerebral Palsy and
   Developmental Medicine
1910 Byrd Avenue, Suite 10
Richmond, VA 23230

American Allergy Academy
P.O. Box 7273
Menlo Park, CA 94126

American Association for Protecting Children
9725 E. Hampden Avenue
Denver, CO 80231

American Cancer Society
1599 Clifton Road
Atlanta, GA 30329

American Cleft Palate and Craniofacial
   Organization
1218 Grandview Avenue
Pittsburgh, PA 15211

American Diabetes Association
National Service Center
P.O. Box 25757
1660 Duke Street
Alexandria, VA 22313

American Heart Association
7320 Greenville Avenue
Dallas, TX 75231

American Leprosy Foundation
1600 Nebel Street, Suite 210
Rockville, MD 20852

American Lung Association
1740 Broadway
New York, NY 10019

American Occupational Therapy Association
1383 Piccard Drive
Rockville, MD 20805

American Parkinson Disease Association
116 John Street, Suite 417
New York, NY 10038

Amyotrophic Lateral Sclerosis Foundation
21021 Ventura Boulevard, Suite 321
Woodland Hills, CA 91364

Arthritis Foundation
1314 Spring Street NW
Atlanta, GA 30309

Association for the Care of Children's Health
3615 Wisconsin Avenue
Washington, DC 20016

Association of Birth Defect Children
5400 Diplomat Circle, Suite 270
Orlando, FL 32812

Asthma and Allergy Foundation of America
1717 Massachusetts Avenue, Suite 305
Washington, DC 20036

Attention Deficit Disorder Association (ADDA)
8901 S. Ireland Way
Aurora, CO 80016

Center for Children with Chronic Illness and
   Disability
Box 721-UMHC
Harvard Street at East River Road
Minneapolis, MN 55455

CHILD HELP USA, Inc.
6463 Independence Avenue
Woodland Hills, CA 91370

Children's Brain Diseases Foundation
350 Parnassus Avenue, Suite 900
San Francisco, CA 94117

Children's Hospice International
901 N. Washington Street
Alexandria, VA 22341

Children with Attention Deficit Disorder
   (Ch. A. D. D.)
1859 N. Pine Island Road, Suite 185
Plantation, FL 33322

Cystic Fibrosis Foundation
6931 Arlington Road, Suite 200
Bethesda, MD 20814

Division for Physical and Health Disabilities
Council for Exceptional Children
1920 Association Drive
Reston, VA 20191-1589

Epilepsy Foundation of America
4351 Garden City Drive, Suite 406
Landover, MD 20785

Foundation for Children with AIDS
55 Dimock
Roxbury, MA 02119

Huntington's Disease Society of America
140 W. 22nd Street, 6th Floor
New York, NY 10011

International Center for the Disabled
340 E. 24th Street
New York, NY 10010

Juvenile Diabetes Foundation
60 Madison Avenue
New York, NY 10010

Little People of America
7328 Piedmont
Dallas, TX 75227

March of Dimes Birth Defects Foundation
1275 Mamaroneck Avenue
White Plains, NY 10605

Muscular Dystrophy Association
3561 E. Sunrise Drive
Tucson, AZ 85718

Muscular Dystrophy Association of America, Inc.
810 Seventh Avenue
New York, NY 10019

Myasthenia Gravis Foundation
53 W. Jackson Boulevard, Suite 909
Chicago, IL 60064

National AIDS Information Clearinghouse
P.O. Box 6003
Rockville, MD 20850

National Amputation Foundation
12-45 150th Street
Whitestone, NY 11357

National Association for the Craniofacially
    Handicapped
P.O. Box 11082
Chattanooga, TN 37401

National Association for the Physically
    Handicapped
76 Elm Street
London, OH 43140

National Center for the Prevention and
    Treatment of Child Abuse and Neglect
1205 Oneida Street
Denver, CO 80220

National Center for Youth with Disabilities
University of Minnesota
Box 721, UMHC
Minneapolis, MN 55455

National Committee for Prevention of
    Child Abuse
332 S. Michigan Avenue, Suite 950
Chicago, IL 60604

National Council on the Handicapped
800 Independence Avenue SW, Suite 814
Washington, DC 20591

National Cystic Fibrosis Foundation
6931 Arlington Road
Bethesda, MD 20814

National Cystic Fibrosis Research Foundation
3379 Peachtree Road NE
Atlanta, GA 30320

National Easter Seals Society for Crippled
    Children and Adults
2023 Ogden Avenue
Chicago, IL 60612

National Foundation for Asthma
P.O. Box 30069
Tucson, AZ 85751

The National Foundation–March of Dimes
P.O. Box 2000
White Plains, NY 10602

National Head Injury Foundation Inc.
1140 Connecticut Avenue NW, Suite 812
Washington, DC 20036

National Huntington's Disease Association
128-A E. 74th Street
New York, NY 10021

National Kidney Foundation
116 E. 27th Street
New York, NY 10014

National Multiple Sclerosis Society
205 E. 42nd Street, 3rd Floor
New York, NY 10017

National Organization for Rare Disorders
P.O. Box 8923
New Fairfield, CT 06812

National Organization on Disability
910 16th Street NW, Suite 600
Washington, DC 20006

National Organization on Fetal Alcohol
   Syndrome
1815 H Street NW, Suite 710
Washington, DC 20006

National Rehabilitation Association
633 S. Washington Street
Alexandria, VA 22314

National Rehabilitation Information Center
8455 Colesville Road
Silver Spring, MD 20910

National Society for Children and Adults
   with Autism
1234 Massachusetts Avenue NW, Suite 1017
Washington, DC 20005

National Spina Bifida Association of America
1700 Rockville Pike, Suite 540
Rockville, MD 20852

National Spinal Cord Injury Association
600 W. Cummings Park, Suite 2000
Woburn, MA 01801

Osteogenesis Imperfecta Foundation
P.O. Box 24776
Tampa, FL 33623

Spina Bifida Association of America
209 Shiloh Drive
Madison, WI 53705

Tourette Syndrome Association
42-40 Bell Boulevard
Bayside, NY 11361

United Cerebral Palsy Association
1522 K Street NW, Suite 1112
Washington, DC 20005

## REFERENCES FOR FURTHER INFORMATION

The bibliography at the end of this chapter provides a comprehensive listing of the sources compiled in the writing of this chapter. It should serve as a resource for further in-depth study. In addition, the following journals and newsletters may be of interest.

*Accent on Living*
P.O. Box 700
Bloomington, IL 61701

A.D.D. *Warehouse*
300 Northwest 70th Avenue, Suite 102
Plantation, FL 33317

*Assistive Technology*
RESNA
1101 Connecticut Avenue NW, Suite 700
Washington, DC 20036

*Catalogue of Educational Materials*
National Head Injury Foundation
1140 Connecticut Avenue NW, Suite 912
Washington, DC 20036

*Clearinghouse on Disability Information*
Office of Special Education and Rehabilitation
   Services
Room 3132, Switzer Building
330 C Street SW
Washington, DC 20202-2524

*Closing the Gap*
P.O. Box 68
Henderson, MN 56044

*Death and Grief Bibliography*
Good Morning
Juanita Johnson
12 Locust Street
Norwich, NY 13815

*Disability Rag*
P.O. Box 145
Louisville, KY 40201

*Disabilities Studies Quarterly*
Department of Sociology
Brandeis University
Waltham, MA 02254

*Disabled USA*
President's Commission on Employment of the
   Handicapped
1111 20th Street NW, Suite 600
Washington, DC 20036

*Exceptional Parent: Annual Technology and Products-*
   *Services Issues*
Psy-Ed Corporation
209 Harvard Street, Suite 303
Brookline, MA 02146

*International Journal of Rehabilitation Research*
   *Quarterly*
International Society of Rehabilitation of the
   Disabled
Rehabilitation International
432 Park Avenue South
New York, NY 10016

*Journal of Head Trauma Rehabilitation*
Aspen Publishers
200 Orchard Ridge Drive
Gaithersburg, MD 20878

*Mainstream: Magazine of the Able-Disabled*
P.O. Box 2781
Escondido, CA 92025

National Rehabilitation Information Center
8455 Colesville Road, Suite 935
Silver Spring, MD 20910

*NeuroRehabilitation: An Interdisciplinary Journal*
Andover Medical Publishers
125 Main Street
Reading, MA 01867

*New Mobility*
Spinal Network
1911 Eleventh Street, Suite 301
Boulder, CO 80303

*Rehabilitation Literature*
National Easter Seal Society
2030 W. Ogden Avenue
Chicago, Il 60612

*Rehabilitation: Traumatic Brain Injury Update*
University of Washington
Rehabilitation Medicine RJ-30 (Attention TBI
   *Newsletter*)
Seattle, WA 98195

*Spinal Network EXTRA*
P.O. Box 4162
Boulder, CO 80306

*Straight Talk: A Magazine for Teens*
The Learning Partnership
P.O. Box 199
Pleasantville, NY 10507

## REFERENCES _____ 🕸

Altman, L. K. (1993, May 4). Rise in asthma deaths is tied to ignorance of many physicians. *New York Times*, p. B8.

American Cancer Society. (1988). *Back to school: A handbook for teachers of children with cancer.* Atlanta, GA: Author.

American Cancer Society. (1993). *Cancer facts and figures—1993.* Atlanta, GA: Author.

Baca, L., & Harris, K. C. (1988, Summer). Teaching migrant exceptional children. TEACHING *Exceptional Children, 20,* 32–35.

Batshaw, M. L., & Perret, Y. M. (1986). *Children with handicaps: A medical primer* (2nd ed.). Baltimore: Brookes.

Bender, E., Schumaker, B., & Allen, H. H. (1976). *A resource manual for medical aspects of disabilities.* Carbondale,

IL: Rehabilitation Counselor Training Program, Rehabilitation Institute, Southern Illinois University.

Bigge, J. L. (1991). *Teaching individuals with multiple and physical disabilities* (3rd ed.). Upper Saddle River, NJ: Prentice Hall/Merrill.

Blakeslee, S. (1992, September 29). Radical brain surgery, the earlier the better, offers epileptics hope. *New York Times*, p. B6.

Caldwell, T., Todaro, A., & Gates, A. (1989). *Community provider's guide: An information outline for working with children with special health needs.* New Orleans, LA: Children's Hospital.

Capute, A. (1985). Cerebral palsy and associated dysfunctions. In R. H. Haslam & P. J. Valletutti (Eds.), *Medical problems in the classroom* (pp. 243–263). Austin, TX: PRO-ED.

Cassini, K. K., & Rogers, J. L. (1990). *Death in the classroom.* Cincinnati, OH: Griefwork.

Chadwick, D. (1989). Protecting abused kids. NEA *Today*, 8(5), 23.

Chasnof, I. J. (1988, October). A first: National hospital incidence survey. NAPARE U*pdate*, 2.

Clayman, C. B. (Ed.). (1989). *The American Medical Association encyclopedia of medicine.* New York: Random House.

Cohen, C. B., Mundy, T., Karassik, B., Lieb, L., Ludwig, D. D., & Ward, J. (1991). Neuropsychological functioning in human immunodeficiency virus type 1 seropositive children affected through neonatal blood transfusion. *Pediatrics*, 88, 58–68.

Comings, D. E. (1992). Role of mutant dopamine receptor gene in ADHD: Implications for treatment and relationship to Tourette syndrome. CH.A.D.D.ER, 6(1), 12–15.

Conlon, C. J. (1992). New threats to development: Alcohol, cocaine, and AIDS. In M. L. Batshaw & Y. M. Perret, *Children with disabilities: A medical primer* (3rd ed., pp. 111–136). Baltimore: Brookes.

Council for Exceptional Children, Task Force on Medically Fragile Students. (1988). *Policies manual.* Reston, VA: Author.

Cross, D. (1993). Students with physical and health-related disabilities. In A. E. Blackhurst & W. H. Berdine (Eds.), *An introduction to special education* (3rd ed., pp. 351–397). New York: HarperCollins.

Education Commission of the States, Migrant Education Task Force. (1979). *Migrant Health.* Report No. 131. Denver, CO: Author.

Epilepsy Foundation of America. (1987). *Questions and answers about epilepsy.* Landover, MD: Author.

Forness, S. R., & Kavale, K. A. (1993). The Balkanization of special education: Proliferation of categories and sub-categories for "new" disorders. *Oregon Conference Monograph*, 5, ix–xii.

Glanze, W. D., Anderson, K. N., & Anderson, L. E. (Eds.). (1985). *The Mosby medical encyclopedia.* New York: New American Library.

Griffith, D. R. (1991). Intervention needs of children prenatally exposed to drugs. DD *Network News*, 4(1), 4–6.

Hunt, N., & Marshall, K. (1994). *Exceptional children and youth.* Boston: Houghton Mifflin.

Hallahan, D. P., & Kauffman, J. M. (1994). *Exceptional children* (6th ed.). Upper Saddle River, NJ: Prentice Hall.

Hanson, M. J. (1984). *Atypical infant development.* Baltimore: University Park Press.

Hardman, M. L., Drew, C. J., & Egan, M. W. (1996). *Human exceptionality: Society, school, and family.* Needham, MA: Allyn & Bacon.

Healy, A. (1984). Cerebral palsy. In J. A. Blackman (Ed.), *Medical aspects of developmental disabilities in children birth to three* (pp. 31–38). Rockville, MD: Aspen.

Heward, W. L. (1996). *Exceptional children: An introduction to special education* (5th ed.). Upper Saddle River, NJ: Prentice Hall/Merrill.

HIV/AIDS (1990). HIV/AIDS *Education: Resources for Special Educators.* Joint publication of the Council for Exceptional Children and the Association for the Advancement of Health Education. Reston, VA: Council for Exceptional Children.

Indacochea, J. J., & Scott, G. B. (1992). HIV-1 infection and the acquired immunodeficiency syndrome in children. *Current Problems in Pediatrics*, 22, 166–204.

Jones, M. H. (1983). Cerebral palsy. In J. Umbriet (Ed.), *Physical disabilities and health impairment: An introduction* (pp. 41–58). Upper Saddle River, NJ: Prentice Hall/Merrill.

Kirk, S. A., Gallagher, J. J., & Anastasiow, N. J. (1994). *Exceptional children and youth* (3rd ed.). Boston: Houghton Mifflin.

Kraus, J. E., Fife, D., & Conroy, D. (1987). Pediatric brain injuries: The nature, clinical course, and early outcomes in a defined United States population. *Pediatrics, 79*, 501–507.

Kwee, H. H. (1986). Spartacus and Manus: Telethesis developments in France and in the Netherlands. In R. Foulds (Ed.), *Interactive robotic aids—One option for independent living: An international perspective* (pp. 9–17). Monograph 37. New York: World Rehabilitation Fund.

Little, M. (1991).*Diabetes.* New York: Chelsea House.

Lorber, J. (1990). Where have all the spina bifida gone? *Midwife Health Visitor & Community Nurse, 22,* 94–95.

March of Dimes. (1992). *Spina bifida: Public health education information sheet.* White Plains, NY: Author.

Martin, S. S., Brady, M. P., & Kotarba, J. A. (1992). Families with chronically ill young children: The unsinkable family. *Remedial and Special Education, 13,* 6–15.

McLone, D. (1983). Results of treatment of children born with a myelomeningocele. *Clinical Neurosurgery, 30,* 407–412.

Mitchell, D. C. (1983). Spina bifida. In J. Umbriet (Ed.), *Physical disabilities and health impairment: An introduction* (pp. 117–131). Upper Saddle River, NJ: Prentice Hall/Merrill.

Mitiguy, J. (1991). Cycles of abuse: Alcohol and head trauma. *Headlines, 2,* 2–11.

Office of Technology Assessment. (1987) *Technology-dependent children: Hospital vs. home care—A technical memorandum.* OTA-TM-H-38. Washington, DC: Author.

Paul, G. H., & Fafoglia, B. A. (1988). *All about asthma and how to live with it.* New York: Sterling.

Rainforth, B., York, J., & Macdonald, M. A. (1992). *Collaborative teams for students with severe disabilities: Integrating therapy and educational services.* Baltimore: Brookes.

Schaefer, D. (1988). *How do we tell the children? Helping children understand and cope when someone dies.* New York: Newmarket.

Schroeder, H. (1993). Cerebral trauma: Accidental injury or shaken impact syndrome? *Headlines, 4*(5), 18–21.

Sirvis, B. (1996). Physical impairments. In E. L. Meyen, & T. M. Skrtic, (Eds.), *Exceptional children and youth: An introduction.* (3rd ed.). Denver, CO: Love.

Smith, D. D., & Luckasson, R. (1995). *Introduction to special education: Teaching in an age of challenge* (2nd ed.). Needham, MA: Allyn & Bacon.

Smith, J. (1988). The dangers of prenatal cocaine use. *American Journal of Maternal Child Nursing, 13*(3), 174–179.

Solomons, G. (1983). Child abuse and neglect. In J. A. Blackman (Ed.), *Medical aspects of child abuse* (pp. 31–37). Iowa City, IA: University of Iowa.

Stone, D. H. (1987). The declining prevalence of anencephalus and spina bifida: Its nature, causes and implications. *Developmental Medicine and Child Neurology, 29,* 541–549.

Task Force on Technology-Dependent Children (1988). *Fostering home and community-based care for technology-dependent children.* Washington, DC: U.S. Department of Health and Human Services.

Taylor, J. M., & Taylor, W. S. (1989). *Communicable disease and young children in group settings.* Boston: College-Hill.

Taylor, M. (1990). Clean intermittent catheterization. In C. J. Graff, M. M. Ault, D. Guess, M. Taylor, & B. Thompson (Eds.), *Health care for students with disabilities* (pp. 241–252). Baltimore: Brookes.

Turnbull, H. R. (1990). *Free appropriate public education: The law and children with disabilities* (3rd ed.). Denver, CO: Love.

Turnbull, A. P., Turnbull, H. R., Shank, M., & Leal, D. (1995). *Exceptional lives: Special education in today's schools.* Upper Saddle River, NJ: Prentice Hall/Merrill.

U.S. Department of Education. (1997). *Nineteenth annual report to Congress on the implementation of the Individuals with Disabilities Education Act.* Washington, DC: Author.

Verhaaren, P., & Connor, F. (1981). Physical disabilities. In J. M. Kauffman & D. P. Hallahan (Eds.), *Handbook of special education.* Upper Saddle River, NJ: Prentice Hall.

Vincent, L. J., Paulsen, M. K., Cole, C. K., Woodruff, G., & Griffith, D. R. (1991). *Born substance exposed, educationally vulnerable.* Reston, VA: Council for Exceptional Children.

Winter, R. J. (1983). Childhood diabetes mellitus. In J. Umbreit (Ed.), *Physical disabilities and health impairments: An introduction* (pp. 117–131). Upper Saddle River, NJ: Prentice Hall/Merrill.

Wright, C., & Bigge, J. L. (1991). Avenues to physical participation. In J. L. Bigge, *Teaching individuals with multiple and physical disabilities* (3rd ed., pp. 132–174). Upper Saddle River, NJ: Prentice Hall/Merrill.

8

# Children with
# Hearing Impairments

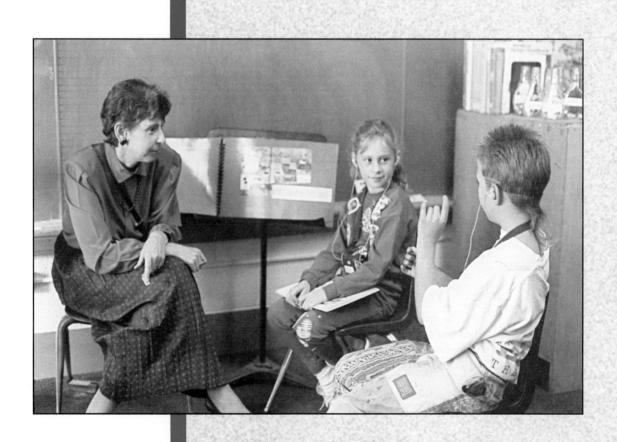

W e hear before we speak. Most children use their hearing as a gateway to learning. One of the earliest links infants develop is between what they hear and what
they see. Our hearing vocabularies, the words we understand, far exceed our
speaking vocabularies. Hearing enables us to know far more than we can say. Language
acquisition and the knowledge of the world that comes with it are naturally occurring
processes for all children. Children who are deaf or hearing impaired will experience their
world in a markedly different way than do their hearing peers. Spoken language may not
be part of that world without early and special help. As a society, we rely upon speech
and language as critical avenues for effective education and socialization. Children with
hearing impairments may be cut off from these processes and become isolated unless
they are identified early and helped to compensate for their hearing loss by learning to
use amplification, undergo corrective medical treatment, learn non-oral ways of receiving and expressing language, or learn to use various types of assistive devices. The purpose of this chapter is to define the parameters of hearing loss and present the options
available for the education of children identified as hearing impaired. We will discuss the
prevalence of hearing impairment, causes of hearing loss, characteristics of people who
are hearing impaired, issues of concern to people who are hearing impaired and their
families, and the professionals who can help those with hearing loss.

## DEFINITIONS

### Normal Hearing

Before we can understand hearing impairment and deafness, we must understand
how normal hearing works. Normal hearing occurs when a listener can change sounds
from his or her environment into signals that are sent to the brain and meaningfully
interpreted. To hear and interpret a sound, we use the ear and its various structures
to receive sound waves; the auditory nerve, which translates sounds into neural signals; and the brain, which decodes these neural signals and translates them into
meaningful information.

Figure 8.1 illustrates the parts of the human ear. The ear is divided into the outer
ear, middle ear, and inner ear. The outer ear consists of the external ear (*auricle*) and
the auditory canal (*external acoustic meatus*). The outer ear collects sound and channels
it through the auditory canal. These sound waves are sent to the middle ear.

The middle ear is composed of the ear drum (*tympanic membrane*) and three small
bones called the hammer (*malleus*), anvil (*incus*), and stirrup (*stapes*). Together these
bones are also called the *ossicles* or *ossicular chain*. The hammer is attached to the
eardrum on one end and the anvil at the other end. The anvil is attached to the stirrup, which in turn is connected to the oval window or entrance to the inner ear. As the

The authors wish to thank Mary Ruth Sizer for her assistance in the preparation of this chapter.

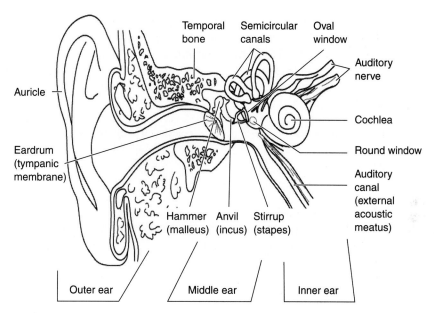

**Figure 8.1**

Parts of the human ear. The external part of the ear and the auditory canal make up the outer ear. The middle ear includes the eardrum, hammer, anvil, and stirrup. The inner ear includes the round window, the oval window, the semicircular canals, and the cochlea. Damage to any part can cause a hearing loss.

*Source:* Heward, *Exceptional Children,* 5th ed., © 1996. Reprinted by permission of Prentice-Hall, Inc., Upper Saddle River, NJ.

sound waves pass through the auditory canal, they strike the eardrum, causing it to vibrate. These mechanical vibrations are passed on to the ossicular chain. The mechanical energy is transferred in turn to the inner ear. The *eustachian tube*, which extends from the back of the throat to the middle ear, opens and closes to equalize the air pressure on both sides of the eardrum.

The inner ear is composed of the *cochlea*, which controls our sense of hearing; semicircular canals, which control our sense of balance; and the beginning of the auditory nerve. The cochlea, which looks like a snail's shell, is a fluid filled cavity lined with small hair cells. As the movements of the ossicular chain enter the inner ear, they disturb the fluid in the cochlea, causing the hair cells to react to the motion of the fluid. The hair cell reactions are sent as signals to the auditory nerve. The impulses from the auditory nerve travel to the brain, where they are processed by the auditory cortex of the brain and become auditory information.

The terms in Box 8.1 are a partial listing of the specialized vocabulary needed to understand hearing impairment and deafness. They will prove helpful in understanding the material presented in the rest of this chapter.

**Box 8.1**
**WHAT EVERY TEACHER NEEDS TO KNOW**

**Terms**

**acquired (adventitious) hearing loss**  A hearing loss acquired later in life.
**amplification**  Use of a hearing aid or other electronic device to make sounds easier to hear.
**audiogram**  A chart that plots the results of hearing testing.
**audiometer**  An electronic device that produces sounds at different levels of frequency and intensity. It is used to test hearing.
**cerumen**  The wax secreted by the ear canal that traps foreign material and keeps the canal lubricated.

**congenital cytomegalovirus**  A herpes virus that infects 1 percent of newborns. It can cause hearing impairment.
**congenital hearing loss**  A hearing loss present at birth.
**otosclerosis**  Growth of spongy bone around the ossicular chain.
**postlingual hearing loss**  Hearing loss acquired after the development of spoken language.
**prelingual hearing loss**  Hearing loss acquired before spoken language could be developed.

## Hearing Loss

Hearing losses can be classified by the degree of hearing loss, the age at which the loss occurs, and the type of hearing impairment the child has acquired. These classifications will be detailed in the sections of this chapter on characteristics, etiology, and identification of hearing impairments. *Normal* hearing occurs in people who are able to hear well enough to understand speech without relying on special aids or techniques (Heward, 1996). Someone who is *hard of hearing* has a significant enough hearing loss that some special adaptation is required to understand speech. Being hard of hearing makes it difficult but not impossible to understand speech with or without amplification (Moores, 1987). People who are hard of hearing still use the auditory channel to learn, even though what they hear may be distorted. Hearing aids can benefit the hard of hearing. A person who is *deaf* cannot use hearing with or without a hearing aid to understand speech, even though that person may be able to hear some sound. *Hearing impairment* is a generic term that is often used to include all hearing loss. Educators may use this term when identifying any child, regardless of severity, who requires special education services. Some educators prefer to use the term *hard of hearing*, since they feel it is less prejudicial a term than is *hearing impaired*.

## Federal Guidelines

The Individuals with Disabilities Education Act defines deafness as a hearing impairment that is so severe that the child is impaired in processing linguistic information through hearing with or without amplification. The hearing impairment adversely affects a child's educational performance. The same act defines hearing impairment as "an impairment in hearing, whether permanent or fluctuating, that adversely affects a child's educational performance, but which is not included under the definition of deafness" (Turnbull, Turnbull, Shank, & Leal, 1995).

# PREVALENCE

Approximately 28 million people in the United States report hearing impairments (Hess, 1991), and 1 percent of the population is severely impaired (Heward, 1996). The vast majority of these people are over age 65. Stein (1988) estimates that over 40 percent of the population over age 75 experiences some hearing impairment. The percentage of school-age children adversely affected by hearing loss is significantly lower. It is difficult to determine exact numbers, because most reports count only children with hearing impairments who receive special educational services. Since many children with hearing loss are unidentified or not severe enough to be included in special education surveys, the estimates are felt to be underinclusive. While students who are deaf are accurately identified and routinely provided service, other students with varying degrees of hearing impairment may only be given special help 20 percent of the time or less (Berg, 1986; Moores, 1987).

The *Nineteenth Annual Report to Congress on the Implementation of the Individuals with Disabilities Education Act* (U.S. Department of Education, 1997) reported that 1.3 percent of all students between ages 6 and 21 who received special education services were served under the hearing impairment disability category. This translates to more than 68,000 of the almost 5 million served. Other estimates, using different, more inclusive criteria, range as high as 5 percent (Bensberg & Sigelman, 1976). Northern and Downs (1991) report that 1 child in 1,000 is born deaf; 2 more children in 1,000 become deaf during their early childhood years; and of the newborns that require intensive care, 1 in 50 become deaf or hard of hearing. They also report that 10 to 15 percent of all children fail the hearing tests that are required by most public schools.

There is a higher incidence of hearing loss among children classified in other special categories than among children not identified as needing special services. This is especially true for children with Down syndrome and children with cerebral palsy. In addition, deafness attributable to hereditary factors and infections such as meningitis appears to be on the rise, as does noise induced hearing loss from repeated exposure to loud noises in the environment and infections such as otitis media (Heward, 1996).

# CHARACTERISTICS

## Degree of Hearing Loss

The degree or severity of a hearing loss will often directly correlate with the characteristic behaviors the child with the hearing impairment will display. Five terms are frequently employed in describing the severity of a hearing loss. The hearing loss may be:

1. Slight
2. Mild
3. Moderate
4. Severe
5. Profound

These descriptive labels are determined by the child's ability to hear sounds at different frequencies and at different intensities. Sound is measured by its *intensity* and *frequency*. Intensity and frequency are physical measures that are most easily understood as loudness and pitch. The loudness of a perceived sound is measured in *decibels*, abbreviated as *d*B. At 0 dB, a person with normal hearing can detect the faintest sound. Whispered speech would be about 10 dB and conversational speech about 50 dB. A sound louder than 125 dB will cause pain and can destroy the hair cells of the cochlea.

The pitch of sound is measured in cycles per second or *hertz*, abbreviated as (Hz). One Hz equals one cycle per second. Although humans can hear frequencies between 20 and 20,000 Hz, many of these sounds fall below or above the frequencies used for speech sounds. Most sounds in our environment fall between 125 and 8,000 Hz. The most important sounds for speech range between 300 and 3,000 Hz. Sounds in this range enable us to hear and understand speech.

The different sounds of our language occur at different pitch levels and intensities. For example, typical sound frequencies and intensities for the sounds /f/, /s/, and /th/ occur at 20 dB at 4,000 to 6,000 Hz. The sounds /g/, /k/, /ch/, and /sh/ are conversationally spoken at 30 dB at 2,000 Hz. The sounds /m/, /b/, /d/, /n/, /ng/, /e/, /l/, and /u/ are measured at 45 dB at 3,000 Hz. Normal running conversation, which is a blend of all sounds, is typically measured at 60 dB. A rigorous dog bark will produce sound at 80 dB at 500 Hz, while the sound of a ringing telephone is typically 85 dB at 2,000 Hz. The loud sound of a lawn mower could be 100 dB at 250 Hz, and a chain saw and jet plane might be measured at 110 dB, 1,000 and 4,000 Hz, respectively.

Translating this information into the five severity categories means the following:

- A *person with normal hearing* will hear sounds between 0 and 20 dB with little difficulty and have no difficulty hearing in any conversational setting.

- A *person with slight hearing loss* will hear sounds at an intensity of 20 to 40 dB or louder and may have difficulty with faint speech. School difficulties are not usually present and can be remediated with careful seating near the teacher.

- A *person with mild hearing loss* will not hear sounds produced at less than 40 to 60 dB and can usually understand face-to-face conversation, but may miss as much as 50 percent of classroom conversations, especially those in noisy environments. The child may have a limited vocabulary and oral speech problems. Special services are usually indicated.

- A *person with moderate hearing loss* cannot hear sounds less intense than 60 to 75 dB, which excludes all but loud conversation. Impaired speech and language are usual and the child will most often require special class placement or a resource teacher.

- A *person with severe hearing loss* cannot hear sounds below 75 to 90 dB as exemplified by loud voices less than one foot from his or her ear. These children may identify environmental noises but cannot hear most consonant sounds. Speech and language is usually impaired or non-existent if the loss occurred prior to one year of age. Special education placement and special classroom placement are most likely.

- A *person with profound hearing loss* cannot hear sounds quieter than 90 dB, which means that he or she cannot hear conversational speech. This child may sense vibrations more than hear sounds and rely upon vision rather than hearing for learning. This child is unlikely to develop oral speech or language and will usually rely on sign language and be placed in a special class or school for the deaf.

The characteristics described here are a general picture that will vary from child to child. Different children will react differently to the same degree of impairment.

## Language Skill Characteristics

By far the most severely affected area of development for a person who is hearing impaired is the comprehension and use of oral language. Both speech and language may be affected. Speech development relies upon the discrimination of the differing sounds in any language and the accurate production of these sounds. Language development is far more complex and requires not only the mastery of the sounds of a language but also its system of rules for combining sounds into words and words into sequences that express thoughts, feelings, intentions, and experiences. Thus, *phonology* (combining sounds meaningfully), *morphology* (putting sounds into words), and *syntax* (combining words into sentences) compose the structure of any language. While semantic development (using language meaningfully) and pragmatic development (using language appropriately) constitute the communicative components of a language, much language learning is the result of experiences combined with hearing the language of others. This automatic combining of hearing and language learning may be absent to differing degrees for each child with a hearing impairment. While all children who are neurologically intact are able to learn some form of language, oral speech and language learning are directly related to the severity of a hearing loss. Wolk and Schildroth (1986) report that 23 percent of people who are hearing impaired are unintelligible, and 22 percent are barely intelligible to ordinary listeners, while 10 percent are unwilling to speak in public. However, 75 percent of those classified as unintelligible are profoundly deaf and only 14 percent of the unintelligible are less than severely impaired. The greatest challenge to those who do not rely upon hearing for information (severely and profoundly hard of hearing) is learning to use the oral language of their society. Most are severely deficient in the languages used by the hearing people with whom they live. We will discuss the compensations made when we discuss the educational approaches used to educate people who are deaf and hard of hearing in the "Programs" section of this chapter. However, depending upon each child's reactions to his or her hearing loss, a general characteristic that children with hearing impairments share is minimally a difficulty in learning the speech system of their native language, and maximally a great deal of difficulty in learning the complexities of oral language in all of its parameters.

## Academic Performance Characteristics

When discussing the academic performance of children with hearing impairment, it is important to remember that most of them possess normal intelligence. They have the same IQ-score distribution as do people who hear (Schlesinger, 1983; Paul & Quigley, 1990). However, they are typically underachievers, lagging far behind their peers in math and reading (Bess, 1988). Studies report that for students in the 16- to 18-year-old age range who are deaf, median reading comprehension is between the second- and fourth-grade level with 60 percent of those tested functioning below the fifth-grade level. Math scores are not as depressed but still fall at the seventh-grade level (Allen, 1986; Gustason, 1990). One obvious problem with performance tests is that they tend to measure language competence along with academic achievement. Since nonverbal IQ tests show that people who are deaf have intelligence scores that approximate those of their hearing peers (Heward, 1996), it becomes obvious that the previously discussed difficulties with language skills are at least partially to blame for the depressed academic performance scores. Five major variables appear to correlate with academic achievement for students with hearing impairment (Box 8.2).

## Social and Psychological Characteristics

Social and personality adjustments of normally hearing children depend heavily upon communication skills and interactions with family members and others in the child's environment. The same rules are true for people who are hearing impaired. Children who are deaf and have parents who are also deaf show higher levels of social maturity, adjustment to deafness, and control of their behavior than do children who are deaf and have normally hearing parents, possibly due to the earlier use of manual communication (Hallahan & Kauffman, 1994; Heward, 1996). The most disruptive children who were deaf were found to also be those with the worst reading-level achievement (Kluwin, 1985), a point that emphasizes that the characteristics being discussed in this section of the chapter are not unrelated to each other. Understandably, children and adults who are deaf have a tendency to associate with each other when possible, to the exclusion of the hearing. Yet, Meadow-Orleans (1985) reports that people with hearing loss frequently express feelings of depression, withdrawal, and isolation. Other characteristics—such as increased reliance on visual cues, which may cause the person who is hard of hearing to appear to stare at the normally hearing person's face, lips, and hands, and the excessive use of gestures and body language—may also be considered rude and further isolate the child with a hearing impairment.

**Box 8.2**
**WHAT EVERY TEACHER NEEDS TO KNOW**

**Five Variables of Academic Achievement**

1. *The severity of the hearing impairment.* The greater the hearing loss, the more likely the child will have difficulty learning language and, in turn, developing academic skills.
2. *The age of onset of the hearing loss.* Hearing lost before language develops (prelingual loss) is much more debilitating than hearing loss after language has developed (postlingual loss).
3. *Intelligence test scores.* The higher a child scores on IQ tests, the better his or her chance at achieving academic success will be.
4. *Socioeconomic status of the family.* Children with hearing impairments and children who

are deaf from higher socioeconomic families are in general more successful academically than their lower socioeconomic counterparts.
5. *Hearing status of parents.* A child who is deaf and has parents who are also deaf is considered likely to have a better chance for academic success than a child who is deaf and has parents with normal hearing. This is especially true if the parents who are deaf are highly educated. This appears to be the result of more appropriate early stimulation for the child and the earlier use of sign language in communication.

*Sources:* From "Educational Programs and Services for Hearing Impaired Children: Issues and Options," by D. F. Moores, 1985, in F. Powell, T. Finitzo-Hieber, S. Friel-Patti, and D. Henderson (Eds.), *Deaf Children in America* (pp. 105–123), San Diego, CA: College-Hill; and *Education and Deafness* (p. 219), by P. V. Paul and S. P. Quigley, 1990, New York: Longman.

## ETIOLOGY

Conditions that cause hearing loss can impair the hearing mechanism to different degrees of severity, can impair the mechanism at different times in a person's life, and can cause different types of hearing loss. Severity has already been discussed. In this section, we will highlight how damage to different parts of the hearing structures will bring about different types of hearing loss to people of differing ages.

It is important to be aware that hearing loss can affect one ear only (unilateral hearing loss) or both ears (bilateral hearing loss), and that each ear may be affected differently. In most instances, the results of bilateral hearing losses are more debilitating than are those of unilateral hearing losses.

### Types of Hearing Loss

As previously discussed, we hear by channeling sounds from the environment into the external ear, convert those sounds into mechanical vibrations in the middle ear, and convert the vibrations into the neural signals that go to the brain. The types of hearing loss parallel these processes. When sounds are prevented from entering the outer or middle ear, the resultant condition is a *conductive hearing loss.* When the inner ear doesn't function appropriately, the result is a *sensorineural hearing loss*. When the brain is unable to interpret the signals sent to it, a *central auditory processing disorder* is the result. It is also possible and likely that there will be a mixture of the types described, leading to a *mixed hearing loss*. Thus the four major types of hearing loss are:

1. Conductive hearing loss
2. Sensorineural hearing loss
3. Central auditory processing dysfunction
4. Mixed hearing loss

Conductive hearing losses can be the result when sound does not get through the outer and middle ear structures efficiently. Any blockage of the ear canal, such as a buildup of excessive ear wax (cerumen) or the failure of the canal to develop at birth, can interfere with sound transmission. Conductive hearing loss is often caused by a buildup of fluids in the middle ear due to infections (otitis media). This buildup of fluid impedes the work of the ossicular chain in transmitting sound to the inner ear. Infections and diseases may also cause the eardrum or the ossicles to work inefficiently. Otosclerosis, a disease characterized by the growth of spongy bone on the ossicles, prevents them from vibrating in a way that will send sound to the cochlea efficiently. Quite often, conductive loss can be overcome by surgery, medical treatment, or amplification of incoming sounds so they can get past the middle ear and stimulate the inner ear structures. Many conductive losses are transitory, lasting no longer than several days. Repeated untreated infections can lead to permanent damage of the hearing mechanism.

Sensorineural hearing losses occur when sound that gets to the inner ear is not transmitted to the brain or is transmitted in a distorted manner. Damage to the cochlea and the auditory nerve will bring about sensorineural hearing loss. The most common causes of this damage are viral diseases, Rh incompatibility, medications that have the side effect of harming the hearing mechanism (ototoxic medicines) while correcting other conditions in the body, normal aging, and repeated exposure to loud noise. Sensorineural hearing loss is usually permanent; it is treated with amplification but is not treatable medically or surgically.

Mixed hearing losses occur when any one person has a combination of both a conductive hearing loss and a sensorineural hearing loss.

Central auditory processing problems do not result from the inability of the mechanism to deliver the auditory signal to the brain, but rather the inability of the brain to process or interpret the signals that are delivered. This symbolic processing disorder may show itself in the inability of a person to perceive sounds, discriminate sounds, or even comprehend language that is received. It can be easily seen how people with auditory processing problems will have difficulty learning or using language. Central auditory processing problems are the result of lesions or growths within the nervous system or direct damage to those parts of the brain and nervous system that are dedicated to the processing of auditory signals.

Table 8.1 is a listing of some of the most common causes and conditions associated with hearing impairments in school-age children.

Emotions may also enter into the causation of hearing disorders. For a small number of people, hearing may be impaired due to causes unrelated to any structural anomaly. For these people, the apparent loss in the ability to hear is a reaction to emotional disturbance. Quite often this conversion of emotional disturbance into the unwillingness to hear can happen without the conscious consent of the person affected. This type of hearing problem is called a *functional hearing loss* in recognition of the fact that the hearing mechanism is apparently functioning appropriately. The most appropriate treatment is usually counseling rather than special educational placement for hearing impairment. When a person consciously pretends not to hear to avoid some task or responsibility, such as being inducted into military service, the condition is labeled as *malingering*.

## Age of Onset

The onset of hearing loss at different times in a child's development can have markedly different implications. Onset is usually identified as being either *prelingual* or *postlingual*.

Prelingual hearing losses occur before a child develops linguistic skills and the reliance on hearing to obtain information from the environment. Prelingual hearing loss makes the acquisition of speech and language a much more difficult process. Some of the most prevalent causes of prelingual hearing loss are:

1.  *Maternal rubella (German measles).* When contracted during pregnancy, especially the first trimester, rubella can cause deafness, visual impairment, and heart deficits.

Table 8.1

Some Causes and Conditions Associated with Hearing Impairments in School-Age Children

### Conductive Hearing Impairment

| | |
|---|---|
| Otitis media (including middle ear fluid) | Impacted cerumen (wax) |
| Otitis externa | Blockage of the external auditory meatus by foreign |
| Discontinuity of the ossicles | object |
| Congenital malformation of the outer ear | Cholesteatoma |
| Congenital malformation of the middle ear | Cleft palate |
| Genetic syndromes (e.g., Down syndrome, Hunter's | Traumatic head injury |
| syndrome) | Eustachian tube dysfunction |
| Perforation of the tympanic membrane | |

### Sensorineural Hearing Impairment

| | |
|---|---|
| Congenital viral infections | Encephalitis |
| Maternal rubella | Scarlet fever |
| Cytomegalovirus | Measles |
| Prematurity and low birth weight | Mumps |
| Perinatal anoxia or hypoxia | Influenza |
| Hyperbilirubinemia | Other viral infections |
| Rh-factor incompatibility | Cerebrovascular disorders |
| Maldevelopment of inner ear | Drug ototoxicity |
| Hereditary familial hearing impairment (congenital or | Congenital syphilis |
| acquired) | Unexplained high fever |
| Noise-induced hearing loss | Auditory nerve tumors (e.g., neurofibromatosis) |
| Genetic syndromes (e.g., Waardenburg's syndrome, | |
| Hunter's syndrome) | |
| Meningitis | |

*Source:* From "Auditory Dysfunction," by B. Friedrith, 1987, in K. Kavale, J. Forness, and M. Bender (Eds.), *Handbook on Learning Disabilities: Vol. 1* (p. 316), Austin, TX: PRO-ED. Copyright © 1987. Used by permission of the publisher, PRO-ED, Inc.

The most recent major epidemic, from 1963 to 1965, accounted for more than 50 percent of the students with hearing impairments receiving special education services during the 1970s and 1980s.

2. *Heredity.* Even though 90 percent of children who are congenitally deaf are born to hearing parents, about 30 percent of school-age children who are deaf have close relatives who are deaf or hearing impaired (McKusick, 1983). Hereditary childhood deafness can be related to more than 150 distinct genetic syndromes. It is estimated that at least 50 percent of those with moderate to profound prelingual sensorineural hearing loss acquire it as the result of genetic factors (Shaver, 1988). In residential schools for the deaf, it is not uncommon to find students who are the second or third generation of their families attending the school. The high incidence of marriage between people with hearing impairments is a contributing factor in the genetic transmission of deafness and hearing impairment (Lowenbraun & Thompson, 1990).

3. *Prematurity and complications that arise during pregnancy.* These are also directly related to prelingual hearing impairments of differing levels of severity.

4. *Viral infections.* Meningitis in particular can destroy the inner-ear hair cells and lead to early and permanent damage.

5. *Congenital cytomegalovirus.* This herpes related virus infects approximately 1 percent of all newborn babies. For almost 3 percent of all children under age 6 who report hearing loss (approximately 10,000), cytomegalovirus is listed as its cause, and 4,000 of those children have hearing losses ranging from mild to profound (Pappas, 1985). Of the students who require special educational services, approximately 90 percent have been affected by prelingual hearing loss (Commission on the Education of the Deaf, 1988).

Postlingual hearing loss occurs after a child or adult has developed linguistic skills and learned to use sound for learning. Educational treatment for postlingual hearing loss usually centers on the maintenance of speech and learning skills that were developed prior to the onset of the hearing problem. Some of the most prevalent causes of postlingual hearing loss are:

1. *Infections of all types.* Meningitis, a leading cause of prelingual hearing impairment, is also a leading cause of postlingual impairment. *Otitis media* is a generic term for infections of the middle ear that cause fluid buildup in that chamber. If these infections are untreated, the fluids can not only disrupt sound transmission but also burst the eardrum, leading to conductive hearing problems.

2. *Side effects of medication.* Some medications may be ototoxic and cause permanent damage to the hearing mechanism. These drugs, if identified, are usually prescribed when the disorder being treated is of such a serious nature that the risk to hearing is an acknowledged factor.

3. *Noise induced hearing loss.* Sustained levels of noise can bring about sensorineural hearing loss. Recognition of this fact has lead many industrial settings (airports, construction sites, and so on) to require that their employees wear protective sound absorbing ear protectors. Young males are at greater risk than young females, due to male oriented activities such as gun firing and automobile engine repair activities (Hess, 1991).

4. *Unknown causes.* Almost 50 percent of all postlingual hearing losses are of undetermined origin (Smith & Luckasson, 1995). It is often difficult to determine the etiology of many hearing losses, since they either take time to develop or are the result of repeated exposure to several circumstances or conditions, each of which could result in hearing loss.

## IDENTIFICATION PROCESS

For some children the identification process begins at birth. Although most states do not require that the hearing of newborns be tested, fourteen states do require that newborns who are considered at risk be tested. Rhode Island requires that all infants undergo hearing testing (Clarkson, Vohr, Blackwell, & White, 1994). However, most children experience their first hearing testing at preschool centers, pediatricians' offices, or routine school screenings. Most public schools and many preschools offer routine hearing testing programs. Often these programs are run in cooperation with university training programs to help university students with an interest in hearing and communication disorders gain practical experience testing children. Most children with severe hearing losses are identified by parents or others in their environment prior to school screenings. However, school and preschool screenings do discover children with mild and moderate losses who have not been previously diagnosed. Children detected by these screening examinations are usually referred for more intensive audiometric and other testing.

## Early Detection

Significant hearing losses are often discovered by parents or caregivers who notice that the child is not attending to environmental sounds or speech. Perhaps the child does not startle when loud noises occur or doesn't respond to people he or she is not looking at. Green and Fischgrund (1993) list many signs that can be clues to parents and others in the child's environment that hearing may be of concern. Chief among these signs are that the child:

1. Does not appear to attend.
2. Has frequent earaches or any discharge from the ears.
3. Makes speech sounds poorly or omits age appropriate sounds completely.
4. Often misinterprets verbal requests.
5. Doesn't respond to direct attempts at communication.
6. Appears to attend better when facing a speaker.
7. Frequently requests repetition.
8. Sets the volume on electronic equipment to levels that are unreasonably loud.

Children suspected by parents of having hearing loss are usually referred for audiometric testing.

## Audiometric Testing

**Pure-Tone Audiometry.**   Initial hearing testing is usually performed by a procedure called *pure-tone audiometry*, using a machine called an *audiometer*. Audiometers are electronic devices capable of generating sounds at different levels of intensity (dB) and at differing frequencies (Hz). When the person being tested hears a tone being produced by the audiometer, usually through earphones, he or she signals the examiner that the sound was heard. Normally hearing children will usually respond to tones presented at most frequencies between 0 and 15 dB (Northern & Downs, 1991). A child with a hearing loss of 45 dB at 1,000 Hz will not respond to the signal from the audiometer until it exceeds 45 dB in loudness.

**Bone Conduction Testing.**   Another component of the testing procedure is called *bone conduction testing*. Bone conduction testing allows the examiner to bypass the outer and middle ear and present signals directly to the inner ear by vibrating the bones of the skull. This procedure helps the examiner to determine the presence of sensorineural components of hearing losses.

The results of pure-tone audiometry hearing tests are mapped out on *audiograms*. Audiograms are graphic representations of a person's hearing ability (acuity) at different frequencies. Figures 8.2, 8.3, and 8.4 are samples of typical audiograms representing the hearing acuity of children with moderate, severe, and profound hearing losses, respectively. The circles (O) and crosses (X) represent the responses of the left and right ears, respectively. As the hearing loss becomes more severe, the symbols appear lower on the audiogram, indicating decreasing hearing acuity.

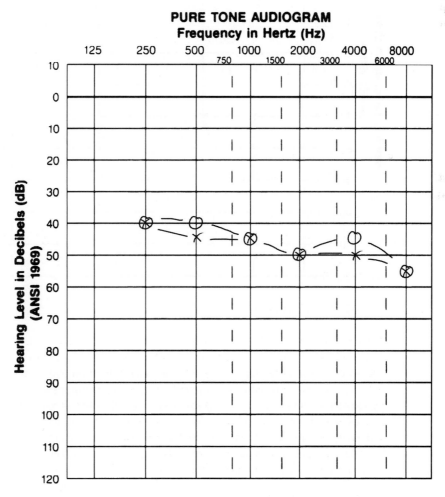

Figure 8.2
Moderate hearing loss

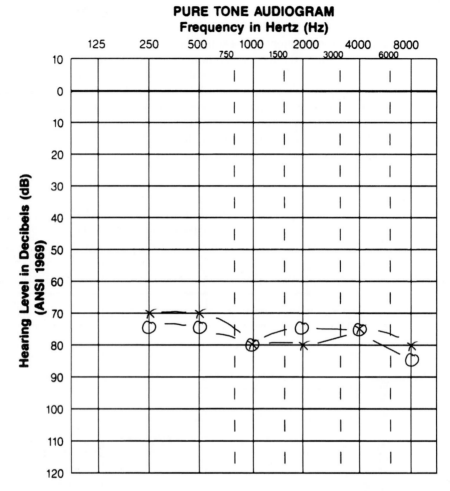

Figure 8.3
Severe hearing loss

**Other Types of Hearing Tests.** *Play audiometry* is often used with children who are too young to use earphones or who will not tolerate earphones. During play audiometry, usually administered in a sound treated booth, the child is taught to respond actively to presented tones. For example, an assistant will place a block in a pail each time a sound is presented and teach the child to perform the same activity. By carefully noting the intensity and frequency of the sounds responded to by the child, the examiner can determine the child's hearing acuity.

*Speech audiometry* provides a measure of a listener's ability to hear and understand speech. By presenting a series of two-syllable words at different intensity levels, the examiner can establish a child's speech recognition threshold (SRT), which is the level at

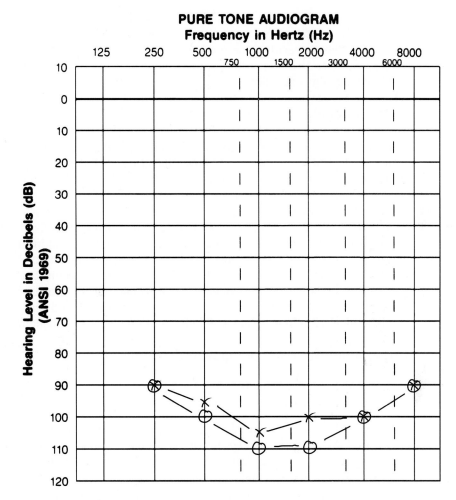

**Figure 8.4**
Profound hearing loss

which he or she can understand 50 percent of the words presented. *Discrimination tests* present similar sounding words and measure how well the listener can tell them apart at varying loudness levels. Speech discrimination abilities can also be tested by presenting information at various loudness levels to determine what the optimal conditions might be to maximize the understanding of speech.

*Immittance audiometry* helps to determine how well the middle ear is functioning by testing how the eardrum (tympanic membrane) is working. This information is particularly helpful in diagnosing middle ear problems such as otitis media.

*Evoked-response* audiometry is a procedure that uses electronic sensors to determine whether the auditory nerve is sending signals to the brain. This procedure is most applicable to very young children and infants or those who cannot respond accurately or consistently.

Once hearing acuity is determined to be below the levels expected for a child, the next step is to determine what, if any, compensations must be made to help the child obtain a quality education.

## Educational Assessment

Each child will react differently to a hearing impairment. Simply measuring a child's hearing level will not always provide all the information necessary to construct an educational program that will meet the child's needs. It is often difficult to compile a valid educational assessment for a child who is severely hearing impaired or deaf, because the child's English language competencies are often significantly delayed. Test questions written in English often test English mastery as well as content (Paul & Quigley, 1990). Attempts to change instructions run the risk of invalidating the tests and, as a result, test scores cannot be used for comparisons with children who are not hearing impaired (Salvia & Ysseldyke, 1991). Intelligence, achievement, and communication and language assessments are vital in helping members of the educational team determine how the child is using his or her hearing and what might be appropriate plans to help meet any unfilled educational needs the child may have.

## Communication and Language Assessments

Assessment of the linguistic abilities of a child with hearing impairment must provide information in at least the following three areas:

1.   *Expressive and receptive vocabulary skills.* How much can the child understand and how well can he or she express his or her needs? A fair assessment will test not only spoken and hearing abilities but also abilities in sign language, finger spelling, speechreading, reading, and writing.

2.   *Syntactical or grammatical skills.* The planning team needs some measure of how well the child can string words together in English or grammatically correct American Sign Language.

3.   *Nonlinguistic language competence.* At what level can educators expect the child to understand and use nonlinguistic communication channels such as gestures, postures, and facial expressions that are situationally and socially appropriate?

If the child uses spoken language, some assessment must be made of articulation skills, or the ability to say the sounds of a language correctly and with phonological competence, which is the ability to use the rules for combining sounds in acceptable ways (Mayer, 1996).

## Intelligence Testing

The Performance Scale of the Wechsler Intelligence Scale for Children–Revised (WISC-R) has been normed on students who are deaf (Ray, 1979) and as a result is the most commonly used standardized test to measure IQ status of children who are deaf (Blennerhassett, 1990).

## Achievement Testing

The test used most frequently to assess achievement of students who are hearing impaired or deaf is the Stanford Achievement Test–Hearing Impaired Version (SAT-HI) (1989). It has been normed and standardized on students who are deaf and covers primary grades and high school students.

Once the results of these and similar tests have been studied by the educational planning team and combined with information solicited from parents, teachers, peers, and consulting professionals, educational programming plans can be designed, proposed and, if accepted by those responsible for the child's welfare, implemented with periodic review to determine whether they are effective.

# PROGRAMS

Answers to the following questions are often necessary before any educational program can be devised and implemented for students who are hard of hearing: When should children with hearing impairment begin formal instruction? Where should they be taught? What should they be taught? How should they be taught? (Turnbull et al., 1995) The belief systems of a society at any given time as well as the information that any given child presents will often interact when decisions are made. The brief historical review that follows will illustrate how the views of a society can determine the programming available, sometimes in direct opposition to the data generated by a child.

## History of Educational Programming for Students with Hearing Impairment

A brief summary of educational practices for children living in the United States who are severely hard of hearing and deaf begins by noting that the American Asylum for the Education of the Deaf and Dumb opened in Hartford, Connecticut, in 1817. The governing philosophy at this time was that people who were deaf were best served in special schools that were isolated from normal (hearing) society. The word *Dumb* in the title reflects the mistaken idea that people who were deaf were incapable of learning oral speech and thus were mute. Most schools were residential and were established in small communities. In the 1850s, attempts at instructing the children to use speech and lipreading became a part of the curriculum. In fact, there was such an overreaction to the use of speech instruction that there was a movement to outlaw sign language (Heward, 1996). In 1864, Abraham Lincoln signed legislation creating the National Deaf Mute College, known today as Gallaudet University (Lowenbraun & Thompson, 1990). Located in Washington, D.C., Gallaudet offers a wide variety of undergraduate and graduate programs for students with hearing impairments. Approximately 100 years later, the National Technical Institute for the Deaf (NTID) was established in

Rochester, New York. NTID provides technical training in business and vocational fields such as computer science, hotel management, and medical technology. Both schools are supported by federal funds and each enrolls approximately 1,500 students.

With the passage of Public Law 94-142 (Individuals with Disabilities Education Act) in 1975, the concept of providing the least restrictive environment in which to educate children with special needs came into focus. For most special education placements, this meant that the least restrictive educational environment was one wherein the special child was afforded as much interaction with nondisabled children as possible. This conceptualization of *least restrictive educational environment* may not always be appropriate for children who are deaf. In recognition of this fact, in 1988 the Commission on the Education of the Deaf recommended to Congress that the regular education classroom not be automatically interpreted as the least restrictive educational environment for children who are deaf. Parents now can choose between residential placement, local public school placement, or day placement in residential schools. Approximately 80 percent of children who are deaf in the United States attend local public schools; about 50 percent of these children are integrated into a regular classroom for at least a part of the school day (U.S. Department of Education, 1997). Of the approximately 12 percent of the students with hearing impairments who attend residential schools, about one-third do so as day students who live at home (Schildroth, 1986).

A recent moment of historical significance for the Deaf community occurred in 1988, when, after much unrest and political activism, Gallaudet University became the first and only university in the world to have a president who is deaf.

## Early Identification and Early Intervention

Early identification and intervention is critical for children who are deaf and severely hearing impaired. Since communication skills develop from early infancy, withhold-

ing service until the school years will put children who are hearing impaired irretrievably behind in the development of speech, oral language, and reading skills. The connection between what a child says and the use of hearing begins long before a child's first words are ever spoken. Even though first words usually are spoken between 12 and 18 months of age, children as young as 3 months begin to use their hearing skills to repeat the nonlinguistic sounds they are producing. This patterned babbling stage of speech development appears to be critical in the development of speech. Children who are severely hard of hearing and deaf and are unable to hear their early babbling sounds will fall silent at this stage of development. If left untreated, they will begin to fall behind their hearing peers in the development of speech and language. Children with adequate hearing have learned the basics of spoken language by age 3 and are stable enough in their linguistic skills by age 6 to use language to learn the academic concepts presented in early schooling. Children need language skills to develop the reading skills that are their main way of obtaining information about the world in which they live.

Preschool early intervention programs are not only for the child. Direct parent and family instruction is a vital reason for their existence. Much needs to be done with parents, especially hearing parents of children who are severely and profoundly hard of hearing and deaf. These parents will probably not know or use sign language or be aware of the reliance that their child will have on the visual rather than auditory aspects of his or her environment. Hearing parents of children who are deaf may have a greater tendency than parents who are deaf with children who are deaf to see their children in a negative light, and as a result treat them as more abnormal than the hearing impairment may warrant (Hallahan & Kauffman, 1994). Bodner-Johnson (1987) suggests that early intervention programs should focus on helping the child with hearing impairment develop within the structure of the family just as the normally hearing child does. To facilitate this development, parents must be aware of normal child development as well as what their child's hearing abilities will allow. They will need help in developing the skills needed to accomplish this assimilation of the child with a hearing impairment. Most critical are skills in developing communication, knowledge of language development, and the transmission of a positive self-concept to the child (Smith & Luckasson, 1995).

Preschool programs are equally vital for the children. For many children with hearing impairments, preschool programs provide the first opportunity for the child to interact with other children, both hearing and hard of hearing. They become the vehicle for the child to learn group functioning skills; the rules of group interaction such as how to play, share, and take turns; and the variety of social skills needed for later success in the classroom (Mayer, 1996). On a pre-academic level, preschool programs provide a place for children and parents to practice signing, learn how to use residual hearing through auditory training and hearing aid operation, and develop readiness skills in English, reading, and arithmetic (Kirk, Gallagher, & Anastasiow, 1993). Without these experiences, the child's transition to any of the educational placement options will be difficult and the chances of success will be diminished.

## Placement Options

Children with unilateral hearing losses (one ear affected) usually learn speech and language, even though they may have problems identifying where some sounds originate or hearing in noisy environments. It is the students with bilateral hearing loss (in both ears) that most often require special services.

Five basic educational placement options are available to children with hearing impairment. Many factors go into helping parents and other members of the educational placement team decide what might constitute the least restrictive educational environment for any given child with a hearing impairment. The five options are:

1. Full-time placement in a regular classroom
2. Part-time placement in a regular classroom and part-time placement in a special education classroom
3. Special class placement in a regular school
4. A separate day school placement
5. Separate residential school placement

## Regular Classroom Placement

Depending on the severity of the hearing loss and a given child's ability to compensate for her or his hearing loss, regular classroom placement must be considered as an option. Children with mild to moderate hearing loss may be able to function in a regular classroom with appropriate support. This support may consist of special seating that will help the child hear the majority of what the teachers present, and hearing aids or other amplification systems such as FM amplification systems that allow teachers wearing transmitting microphones to broadcast what they are saying to children wearing special receivers. The children might require the services of speech-language pathologists to help them use speech and language to their maximal potential. In some instances, educational interpreters or note takers may accompany a child to regular classrooms. The regular education classroom teacher may need to periodically consult with an itinerant teacher of the deaf for information on how to present or modify lessons to help the child. The child may also require tutoring after class to help explain material that might not have been understood. Regular classroom placement does not mean putting children with hearing impairments into a regular classroom and ignoring the hearing loss, thereby placing the burden for compensation solely on the children and their families.

## Part-Time Regular Classroom Placement and Part-Time Special Class Placement

When this type of placement is employed, students who are hard of hearing may spend a part of their school day in special resource rooms where special educators will address each child's special needs, and the rest of the day in a regular classroom that has been modified as listed earlier. This type of placement requires coordination between the regular and special education teachers to make sure that they are working in concert to maximize learning.

## Special Classes in Regular Schools

Children who are hearing impaired in special classes may spend most of their school day in a special education class but may be included in one or more academic classes, perhaps with the help of an interpreter. They may also participate in nonacademic activities such as library study or gym. Social inclusion for lunch, recess, and other school activities may be stressed. Children in special classes may be taught with special educational approaches and be exposed to separate curricula that will be discussed in the following sections of this chapter.

## Separate Day Schools

A child with a severe or profound hearing loss may, depending on his or her needs, attend a separate day school with other children with hearing impairments. Separate day schools are both public and private in nature. In these schools, usually in cities large enough to have groups of children with hearing impairments, inclusion opportunities with peers who are normally hearing may be limited to after school hours or those special occasions when the students with hearing impairments may be transported to adjacent general education facilities. Special approaches to teaching will routinely be used in these settings. Specially trained teachers of the deaf will most likely be employed to present specially modified curricula.

## Separate Residential Schools

There are approximately 60 public residential schools for the deaf in the United States and a group of privately financed residential schools. These schools tend to be large and independent in their functioning. It is possible for some students who live close enough to a given residential school to use it as a day school placement. These schools are often the centerpieces of Deaf communities that surround them. Members of the Deaf community will gravitate toward areas that have special residential schools. They argue that by putting together enough students in a supportive environment, it is more possible to obtain the special services needed for quality education (Higgins, 1992; Kluwin, 1992). Some argue that residential schools are critical in fostering the supportive concept of a Deaf community, which combats the difficulty to succeed in environments and the isolation that inclusion attempts often bring about (Lane, 1992; Padden & Humphries, 1988). We will discuss these views in greater depth in the "Issues of Importance" section in this chapter. Residential schools employ specially trained teachers of the deaf and use any of a number of educational approaches designed exclusively to teach students who are severely hard of hearing and deaf.

There are conflicts over which placements serve children who are hearing impaired best, and there is conflicting evidence to bolster all points of view. Placements in regular public schools have grown with the passage of federal legislation making it possible for children with hearing impairment to attend them, better hearing aid and other technological assistance availability, and increased demands for public-school placement by parents and citizens who are deaf. Although 77 percent of children with hearing impairments are educated in local schools, fewer than 50 percent are integrated into regular classrooms. Most of those integrated have hearing losses less than 90 dB (Schildroth & Holt, 1991). Successful experiences in regular classrooms for children with hearing impairment seems to correlate with their possessing good oral communication skills, strong parent support, average or above average intelligence, self-confidence, and adequate support services (Davis, 1986).

## Academic Curriculum

The academic content presented to children who are hard of hearing parallels the content presented to students who hear normally. However, specially modified programs and materials do exist for subject areas such as math, science, and the arts. Luetke-Stahlman and Luckner (1991) contend that educators have the following five choices in the selection and implementation of a curriculum for students who are hard of hearing. They may:

1. Use a curriculum that has been specifically designed for students who are hearing impaired or deaf.
2. Use the general education curriculum, attempting to meet the same standards as for other students by allowing for special services and special teaching methods.
3. Use the general curriculum, but reduce the level of complexity of material presented.
4. Use a curriculum from a lower grade level.
5. Use curricula that have been developed for students with other exceptionalities.

Of major concern is the language curriculum. Even though students who are hearing impaired learn language the same way other students do, they may have special problems with spoken and written English. They might need to learn about language through curricular activities that stress the structure and grammar of English, since they may not learn the complexities of grammar through hearing (Quigley & Paul, 1990). In addition, the language curriculum may need to be stressed to a greater extent than it would be with normally hearing children. Some educators believe that some of the poor achievement results displayed by children with hearing impairments in academics is due in part to the fact that so much instructional time is spent on communication and language skills that the academic areas are compromised. Table 8.2 is a listing of the effects that different degrees of hearing loss may have on speech and language mastery and the educational needs consistent with different degrees of hearing impairment

**Table 8.2**
Effects of Different Degrees of Hearing Loss on Speech, Language, and Probable Educational Needs

| Faintest Sound Heard | Effects on Understanding Language and Speech | Probable Educational Needs and Programs |
|---|---|---|
| 27 to 40 dB (slight loss) | • May have difficulty hearing faint or distant speech<br>• Will not usually have difficulty in school situations | • May benefit from a hearing aid as loss approaches 40 dB<br>• Attention to vocabulary development<br>• Needs favorable seating and lighting<br>• May need speechreading instruction<br>• May need speech correction |
| 41 to 55 dB (mild loss) | • Understands conversational speech at a distance of 3 to 5 feet (face to face)<br>• May miss as much as 50% of class discussions if voices are faint or not in line of vision<br>• May have limited vocabulary and speech irregularities | • Should be referred for special education evaluation and educational follow-up<br>• May benefit from individual hearing aid and training in its use<br>• Favorable seating and possible special education supports, especially for primary-age children<br>• Attention to vocabulary and reading<br>• May need speechreading instruction<br>• Speech conservation and correction, if indicated |
| 56 to 70 dB (moderate loss) | • Can understand loud conversation only<br>• Will have increasing difficulty with group discussions<br>• Is likely to have impaired speech<br>• Is likely to have difficulty in language use and comprehension<br>• Probably will have limited vocabulary | • Likely to need resource teacher or special class<br>• Should have special help in language skills, vocabulary development, usage, reading, writing, grammar, etc.<br>• Can benefit from individual hearing aid through evaluation and auditory training<br>• Speechreading instruction<br>• Speech conservation and speech correction |
| 71 to 90 dB (severe loss) | • May hear loud voices about 1 foot from the ear<br>• May be able to identify environmental sounds<br>• May be able to discriminate vowels but not all consonants<br>• Speech and language likely to be impaired or to deteriorate<br>• Speech and language unlikely to develop spontaneously if loss is present before 1 year of age | • Likely to need a special education program for children with emphasis on all language skills, concept development, speechreading, and speech<br>• Needs specialized program supervision and comprehensive supporting services<br>• Can benefit from individual hearing evaluation<br>• Auditory training on individual and group aids<br>• Part-time regular-class placement as profitable for student |
| 91 dB or more (profound loss) | • May hear some loud sounds but senses vibrations more than tonal pattern<br>• Relies on vision rather than hearing as primary avenue for communication<br>• Speech and language likely to be impaired or to deteriorate<br>• Speech and language unlikely to develop spontaneously if loss is prelingual | • Will need a special education program for children who are deaf, with emphasis on all language skills, concept development, speechreading, and speech<br>• Needs specialized program supervision and comprehensive support services<br>• Continuous appraisal of needs in regard to oral or manual communication<br>• Auditory training on individual and group aids<br>• Part-time regular-class placement may be feasible |

*Source:* W. L. Heward. (1996). *Exceptional Children.* Reprinted by permission of Prentice-Hall, Inc., Upper Saddle River, NJ.

## Educational Approaches

A variety of approaches are available to transmit information to students who are hard of hearing. In this section of the chapter, we will explain some of the different approaches used with these students. The "Issues of Importance" section will highlight how the selection of which approach is used may be equally dependent on the belief systems of educators and members of the Deaf community and on whether or not an approach is educationally effective.

## Oral/Aural, Manual (Non-Oral), and Simultaneous Communication Approaches

*Oral/aural approaches* emphasize speech and sound as a part of the curriculum. Oral language is used as a vehicle to transmit information. Teachers use their voices and rely on speechreading skills and students' use of their residual hearing. Amplification in the form of hearing aids and other assistive amplification devices are employed in the teaching process. Students are encouraged to use their voices when they speak. Approximately one-third of the programs for students who are hard of hearing use an oral/aural approach (Reagan, 1985).

*Manual approaches* rely more exclusively upon sign language and non-oral means to communicate information to students. The use of signs to transmit information is on the rise in all educational programs (Connor, 1986).

*Simultaneous communication* approaches use both speech and signing at the same time. They often use finger spelling along with sign.

## Auditory Training

Auditory training programs help children make better use of their residual hearing. Many children with hearing impairments have more auditory potential than they actually use. Auditory training, with its emphasis on amplification of sounds, can help them maximize the hearing potential they have, with the goal of developing oral skills. Auditory training can focus on basic sound detection (awareness of sounds), discrimination between sounds, and identifying sounds that are critical in comprehending messages. It focuses on listening as well as hearing (Heward, 1996). A significant amount of time is spent with the parents of younger children, familiarizing them with hearing aid use and maintenance.

Hearing aids are the most widely used technology for the hearing impaired. Essentially, hearing aids are amplification instruments that make sounds louder. Dozens of different types of hearing aids are available. Each attempts to amplify sounds in ways that are most helpful to a given person. Some aids amplify sounds across the entire speech frequency band. Others emphasize the lower, middle, or higher ranges of frequencies, hoping to match their amplification of those sounds to the particular child's hearing loss. Some aids are worn in the ear canal and some behind the outer ear. Hearing aids increase the awareness of sounds as well as simply amplifying them. However, hearing aids do not "cure" hearing problems. They can make sounds louder but not more clear. It is the task of the person who is using one to interpret the sound being amplified by the aid. The earlier a child is fitted with hearing aids, the sooner he or she can begin to use the aids for awareness of environmental sounds and learning. Advocates of amplification feel that for aids to be maximally effective, they should be worn throughout the day so that a child can learn to process all sounds, not just speech (Heward, 1996).

For some children, classroom amplification systems can overcome the problems caused by teachers moving about while they talk and room noise that cancels or masks speech signals. A typical system will use an FM broadcasting system that the child can receive either through an earpiece or a hearing aid equipped to receive FM signals. The teacher wears a lapel microphone and can be totally mobile. These systems do not usually interfere with other classroom activities and have the potential of bringing amplified sounds to the child who is hearing impaired without forcing him or her to sacrifice mobility.

## Speechreading

Speechreading was once called *lipreading*. However, the skill involves more than just looking at someone's lips as he or she is talking. In reality, it is careful observation of the entire face that helps the speechreader decipher a message. Visual cues are more helpful in discriminating some sounds than others. When speechreading is combined with residual hearing, familiarity with the listener, and some familiarity with the context of the message, it can be helpful. Students need to be trained in the tactic of speechreading. Since many sounds and words look similar and different people use facial expressions and gestures in a multitude of ways, speechreading is a difficult skill to acquire and the concentration it requires is often tiring to its user. It is estimated that the best speechreaders can get as much as 25 percent of a message through speechreading (Walker, 1986), whereas the average child who is deaf might only get as much as 5 percent of a message through speechreading (Vernon & Koh, 1970).

## Cued Speech

Cued speech is a system that relies on learning and using a specific set of hand signals to supplement oral speech. These signals, which are different from sign language or finger spelling, are given by hand positions used near the chin while speaking. The signals do not stand alone and must be used with oral speech. Basically, there are eight hand shapes that are used to indicate consonant sounds and four hand positions around the mouth and chin to indicate vowels. The hand shape and its location near the mouth and chin provide cues in understanding the speaker's oral message. Although this system has a degree of popularity throughout the world, it has never been particularly embraced by people who are hard of hearing or educators in the United States.

## Sign Language

Sign languages use gestures to represent words, ideas, and concepts. Some signs are *iconic*, which means that they look like what they represent or that they act out a message. Most signs are not iconic. There are several sign languages. American Sign Language (ASL) is the language of the Deaf culture of the United States and Canada. It is estimated that ASL has a vocabulary of more than 6,000 signs that represent concepts. Advocates consider it the natural language of people who are deaf (Hardman, Drew & Egan, 1996). ASL is a valid linguistic form with its own rules of syntax, semantics, and pragmatics (Turnbull et al., 1995). The shape and movement of the hands in relation to the body, the intensity of the movements made, and the accompanying facial expressions all convey meaning. Space and movement are the linguistic elements. The rules of ASL do not correlate with those of spoken English. Translating ASL is similar to translating a foreign language. Most children who are deaf learn ASL from other children in residential schools and not from their parents, who are usually hearing. Grammatical problems can occur when some systems use Pidgin Sign English, which is the use of ASL signs in oral English grammatical forms. Advocates of ASL feel that this practice has a detrimental effect upon the effective use of ASL.

## Finger Spelling

Finger spelling, or the *manual alphabet*, consists of 26 special hand and finger positions that represent English letters. A person using finger spelling spells out each word letter by letter, using one hand almost like a typewriter. Sign language uses finger spelling for proper names and when it is necessary to clarify specific concepts. Figure 8.5 shows the hand positions required to finger spell each letter of the alphabet.

## Total Communication

Total communication relies upon the simultaneous presentation of signs and speech. It uses residual hearing, amplification systems, and speechreading in combination with manual systems. Total communication provides students with the most options. Since its introduction in the 1960s, it has become the predominant method used in schools for students who are deaf (Luterman, 1986). Currently most educators favor this method, which is the approach of choice at Gallaudet University. Wolk and Schildroth (1986) found that of the students they surveyed, 62 percent used both speech and sign for learning, 21 percent used speech only, and 17 percent relied on sign systems exclusively.

Regardless of the approach or combination of approaches used in presenting information to the child with hearing impairment, several common sense modifications in the classroom setting can help facilitate the transfer of information. Visual aids along with lectures help provide cues, as does the use of overhead projectors rather than blackboards, which often cause teachers to turn away from students. Appropriate lighting as well as seat placement close to the teacher will make speechreading easier. Swivel chairs help students more easily position themselves to follow classroom discussion. The assignment of alert peers to give cues when fire alarms ring or class bells chime can also be helpful (Turnbull et al., 1995).

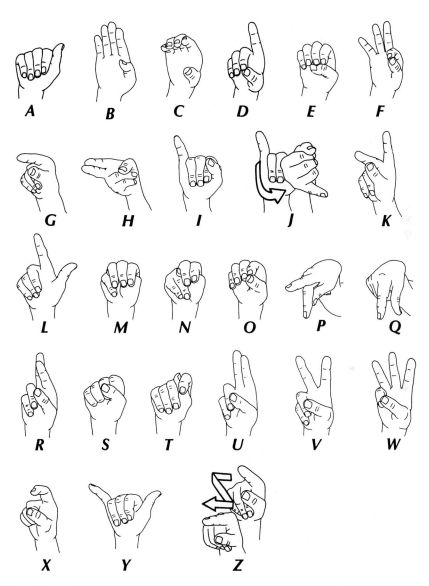

Figure 8.5
The American Manual Alphabet

## Technology

The technologies most closely associated with people who are hearing impaired are hearing aids and amplification systems. We have already discussed hearing aids and amplification systems such as the FM amplification system. In this section of the chapter, descriptions of current medical and assistive technology will be highlighted.

Specifically, cochlear implants, microcomputers, assistive devices, and captioning and alerting devices will be discussed.

**Cochlear Implants.**  Surgical implants are available to those with severe and profound sensorineural hearing loss. When performing this procedure, a surgeon will implant a set of electrodes into the patient's cochlea. These electrodes are connected to a receiver that captures sounds and encodes them into electrical stimulation, which the electrodes then transmit through the neural pathways to the brain for processing. When this process is successful, it allows the recipient to hear environmental sounds such as telephone bells, automobile horns, and traffic noise. Cochlear implants may also make it easier for children who are severely and profoundly hearing impaired to learn speech. This is a relatively new procedure and it has sparked some controversy; it is expensive, and long-term data documenting its effectiveness is not yet available. Some members of the Deaf community are opposed to the procedure for these reasons, and because they believe that it is an attack on the cultural identity of people who are deaf, undermining their self-concepts as healthy, competent members of society.

**Microcomputers.**  Microcomputers and the educational programs written for them help children who are hearing impaired in many of the same ways that they help hearing students. In addition, specific programming targeted for children with hearing impairments is useful in helping them learn reading and writing skills and become more proficient in finger spelling and sign language (Prinz, Pemberton, & Nelson, 1985). Microcomputer programs can also help normally hearing users learn sign language (Slike, Chiavacci, & Hobbis, 1989). An advantage to these programs is that they allow family members and peers to practice without having to have a professional available to monitor their practice sessions.

**Assistive Communication Devices.**  Teletypewriters (TTY) or telecommunication devices for the deaf (TDD) are essentially specially designed telephone systems that allow users to type messages into the telephone system and receive typed replies. These devices are also called text telephones (TT). Special 800 numbers allow people who don't own a TTY or TDD to communicate by telephone with people who are hard of hearing. Special operators act as translators, reading messages to the hearing listener or writing them for the listener who is hearing impaired. An increasing number of businesses have their own systems as part of their telephone service and as a result do not need to use the interpreting operator. The Americans with Disabilities Act (PL 101-336) of 1990 requires that all telephone companies offer this service all day and every day.

**Captioning.**  Captions are written transcriptions of dialogue that is occurring that appear on a screen during television programs, films, and even some operas. Most television entertainment, sports, and news shows are *closed captioned*. This means that viewers with a decoder on their television can receive these transcriptions of dialogue as they watch. Since July 1993, all television sets 13 inches or larger sold or built in the United States have been equipped with a caption chip that allows viewers to choose whether they want to see the captions accompanying all available programs (Bowe, 1991). Captioning has enabled people who are hearing impaired to learn

about current events and social issues without delay. Many normally hearing people use captions when they wish to watch television in circumstances that make listening to the soundtrack difficult.

**Alerting Devices.**   Most alerting devices used by hearing people have been adapted for use by people who are hard of hearing. Doorbells have been adapted so that they flash lights as well as chime. Vibrating pillows respond to the sounds of alarm clocks. Fire detectors can be modified to give visual signals as well as auditory ones. Catalogs offering many types of ingenious and constantly improving alerting devices are available from all professionals who provide services to the hearing impaired.

## ISSUES OF IMPORTANCE

There are many issues of importance that have an impact on the education of people who are hearing impaired. We have already discussed some of them in the body of this chapter. In this section, two particularly critical issues will be highlighted. We will focus on (1) the controversy surrounding the effectiveness of educational practices and (2) the special meaning that *least restrictive environment* may have for students who are hard of hearing.

### Effectiveness of Academic Instruction

The most difficult problem in educating students who are deaf is teaching them spoken language. Many students who leave school are unable to read or write in English proficiently. The average student with hearing impairment who completes a secondary education program reads at a level equal to that of a 9- to 10-year-old hearing student (Paul & Quigley, 1990). Many students who are deaf cannot communicate effectively with their hearing family members or hearing peers. Their rate of unemployment and underemployment is high. Advocates of oral/aural and simultaneous communication approaches believe that their way of teaching helps the student who is severely hearing impaired or deaf integrate better into mainstream society. However, students with severe or worse hearing losses who develop good speech are a select group. They typically score above average on IQ tests, have parents who are highly involved in their education, and have access to the resources and support services that higher socioeconomic status provides (Geers & Moog, 1989).

Advocates of non-oral instruction fundamentally disagree about the extent to which learning spoken English is necessary. They are skeptical about the value of spending so much time teaching children who are severely impaired to express themselves through speech and attempting to perceive the communication of others through speechreading and the use of residual hearing. They argue that greater-than-ever numbers of hearing people are learning sign language and finger spelling. In fact, coursework in sign language and finger spelling is offered in many schools, colleges, and universities as a part of the curriculum for hearing students. Public service professionals such as police, firefighters, and emergency medical technicians are becoming more proficient in sign language and finger spelling, and the mass media are using captioning and interpreters as a matter of course in many presentations. Most significantly, the data quoted earlier seem to indicate that current methods do not seem to be producing literate graduates with hearing impairments from secondary schools. There is no hard evidence that the use of sign language by children who are deaf inhibits their acquisition of speech (Moores, 1987; Rooney, 1982). However, some specialists feel that it is difficult for children to process both oral language and sign language when they are presented together. Ling (1984) suggests that children should learn oral and manual skills at different times rather than concurrently, to avoid possible confusion.

There is no existing proof that either of these two approaches is better than the other. Some students become frustrated with oral/aural programs only. Others may not develop good oral skills because they weren't given the opportunity to use their potential auditory and oral skills. A goal appears to be to develop methods to determine what approach or approaches might provide the best educational opportunity for any given child. Thus far, this goal has not been attainable. The congressional Commission on the Education of the Deaf reported in 1988 that the present state of education for people who are deaf in the United States is unacceptable.

## Least Restrictive Environment

For most exceptional children, the least restrictive educational environment translates into mainstreaming and the opportunity to take part in as many regular classroom and school activities as are feasible. However, this may not be the case for many students who are severely and profoundly hearing impaired. Some feel that inclusion in regular classrooms, due to the low incidence and resulting small number of children, is really exclusion and isolation. If students who are deaf are placed in an environment where they are unable to communicate with their peers and with most of the educational staff, this isolation might lead to loneliness and depression. Perhaps residential schools for the deaf with staff and peers able to communicate with the child are in fact less restrictive (Bowe, 1991). Any setting, including a regular classroom, that prevents the child who is deaf from receiving an appropriate educational experience, including communication, may not be the least restrictive environment for that child. Special services might also be more readily accessible when more students who are deaf are in one central location. Inclusion in a regular classroom does not always guarantee that all support services will be automatically supplied. The following examples illustrate how court rulings about support services can be mixed. The courts ruled in *Board of Education of the Hendrik Hudson Central School District v. Rowley* (1982) that the local school district was not required to provide, at its expense, an interpreter for a child with hearing impairment performing adequately in regular classes without an interpreter. However, in *Barnes v. Converse College* (1977) it was ruled that a private college had to provide, at its own expense, an interpreter for a student who was hearing impaired.

Unlike oversight groups for other exceptionalities, the Commission on the Education of the Deaf (1988) urged that the Department of Education reconsider the focus on least restrictive environment and instead look toward the most appropriate placement for each student who is deaf. This issue is still being debated by parent and professional groups. It is not an easy decision to legislate and most probably can only be decided on a child-by-child basis.

## MINORITY CONCERNS

Two concerns isolated from the general concerns we have been discussing in this chapter are the needs of minorities within the hard of hearing population and the concept of whether or not the Deaf community forms a distinct cultural minority within the United States.

### Needs of Minorities

Approximately 30 percent of all students in programs for people who are deaf and hearing impaired are children representing racial, linguistic, or ethnic minority groups (Cohen, Fischgrund, & Redding, 1990). Nationally, about 15 percent of students with hearing impairments come from non-English speaking families. Estimates for some areas of the country are as high as 40 percent (Smith & Luckasson, 1995). An explanation for these high incidence figures is probably tied to the limited health care and access to timely medical care experienced by a disproportionately large number of families within these groups. Educational programming for many of these children is particularly challenging. Until relatively recently, children from non-English speaking families were included in special programs with English speaking peers with little or no thought to their special linguistic needs (Mayer, 1996). Although many programs seek to meet the needs of children from culturally diverse backgrounds, it is a particularly complex problem to teach English communication skills to a child who is deaf when a language other than English is spoken at home (Heward, 1996). Blackwell and Fischgrund (1984) warn that insensitive placement can bring about conflicts that will interfere with service provision. Non-English speaking families may be struggling on many fronts and unable to fully utilize available services. Some may be struggling with feelings of isolation in their adopted communities. Others may be limited by economic constraints that curtail the amount of time they can devote to participating in the educational process available for their child. Still others may not understand the benefits of early amplification and resist it as unnecessary. Cultural insensitivity and the lack of understanding of how different cultural groups will react to a child in need of special services can further complicate an already formidable task.

## Deaf Culture

Some consider people who are deaf as a distinct minority population and deafness as a defining cultural characteristic. The rationale is that Deaf people, like people of other cultural groups, are united by their common physical characteristics (deafness and hearing loss), a common language (sign language), and common needs (special accommodations in communication) (Commission on the Education of the Deaf, 1988; Dolnick, 1993; Reagan, 1992). Advocates of Deaf culture feel it is appropriate to capitalize the D when referring to themselves as a specific population; they use the word *Deaf* as an adjective. Thus, Deaf people have hearing losses. Others are careful to refer to themselves as *people who are deaf*, emphasizing their cultural bond (Turnbull et al., 1995). The members of this Deaf community see American Sign Language (ASL) as the Deaf child's first language and believe that English is a second language. English is best taught, they contend, as a second language after the child has mastered ASL. Paul and Quigley (1990) present the argument that total communication programs that use codes along with speech provide inappropriate linguistic models for children who are deaf, because these codes may not be grammatically consistent with ASL grammar. They report that these approaches have done little to promote English literacy or academic achievement.

Others have reported that mainstreaming often isolates children who are deaf from the Deaf community and puts them at risk of isolation, loneliness, and depression because they may have few people with whom they can communicate (Charlson, Strong, & Gold, 1992; Loeb & Sarigiani, 1986). Students who are deaf feel more secure if they are in consistent contact with other people who are deaf with whom they can communicate (Stinson & Whitmire, 1992). As a result, many people who are deaf socialize to a great extent with others who are deaf. This contact has lead to the transmission of sign language and the learning of the Deaf culture.

In the past, this self-imposed isolation from the hearing community was seen as a social pathology. Some professionals now see this as a natural condition arising from the common bond of sign language. However, common language is but one bond. Reagan (1992) outlines other factors that may validate the Deaf culture. It may be described as a bilingual group comparable to the Hispanic culture, except that the two languages are American Sign Language and English instead of Spanish and English. There are attitudes and perceptions about deafness not shared by the hearing community, such as the view that hearing impairments are not a sickness or disability that needs to be cured (Smith & Luckasson, 1995). There are specific behavioral norms that differ from mainstream cultures, such as the degree of eye contact and physical touching appropriate when communicating. Members of this culture marry each other at rates as high as 90 percent and pass on a social awareness of the Deaf and events that are of particular significance to them. There are volunteer and social organizations for the community such as the National Association of the Deaf, the National Theatre of the Deaf, and the Deaf Olympics (Hallahan & Kauffman, 1994). Members of the Deaf community advocate for each other and feel that they have gained many of the benefits they now enjoy such as greater access to jobs, legislation for captioning, and the availability of assistive technology in public places (Smith & Luckasson, 1995). Since the transmission of Deaf cultural values most easily occurs in residential schools for people who are deaf, there is even concern that Deaf culture is under attack by policies such as educational inclusion and the interpretation of the least restrictive educational environment for education as being placement in regular classrooms. Some are seeking to have classes in Deaf history and culture for children who are isolated from the community and taught in nonresidential schools (Gaustad & Kluwin, 1992; Janesick & Moores, 1992).

There is no society wide agreement about the argument for a separate cultural assignment. Arguments and counterarguments may continue forever among professionals and deaf people. Dr. I. King Jordan, the president of Gallaudet College and the only president of a university who is deaf, writes about the conflict with the following words: "*Any labels that define one group to its satisfaction, . . . exclude another. While Deaf is a pronouncement to the world of great pride in culture, Deaf can also be used to exclude those who describe themselves as deaf. . . . We will constantly be defining and refining ourselves and seeking new language to reflect that expanded vision*" (Jordan, 1992).

## PROFESSIONALS

The needs of families with children who are hard of hearing will vary, depending upon the degree of hearing loss a child has and his or her accommodation to it. All or most of the professionals described in this section will probably have at least cursory contact with each child who is hearing impaired. Other services provided by other professionals may be needed for co-existing conditions that are either related or unrelated to hearing impairments.

### Educational Team Members

An educational team is responsible for producing an individualized education program (IEP) for each identified child with a hearing impairment severe enough to warrant special educational services. Audiologists, in cooperation with otorhinolaryngologists or otologists, must assess the hearing loss and its physical and functional dimensions. Speech-language pathologists can assist the child in reaching his or her potential in speechreading and speech production. Special teachers for students who are deaf or hard of hearing will develop the IEP and help carry it through with the regular education teacher. Interpreters and teachers of students who are deaf who present curricular subjects may also be part of the team. Parents will need to be in close contact with each of these professionals and may also require counseling by genetic specialists.

## Audiologists

Audiologists are specially trained professionals who are concerned with the evaluation of a child's hearing ability. They can be responsible for planning and implementing treatment that will help the child hear as efficiently as possible. They will identify the degree of hearing loss, determine the child's perceptual abilities, and chart this information on audiograms. Some audiologists are aural rehabilitation specialists, who provide training in the use of residual hearing and the use of hearing aids. Counseling activities include an emphasis on the social and educational impact of hearing loss. National certification is provided by the American Speech-Language-Hearing Association and is obtained after completing coursework at the master's degree level and serving a one-year clinical fellowship year while employed.

## Otorhinolaryngologists

Otorhinolaryngologists, also known as ENT specialists, are physicians who specialize in disorders of the ears, nose, and throat.

## Otologists

Otology is a medical subspecialty of otorhinolaryngology. Otologists specialize in the diagnosis and treatment of disorders and diseases of the ear.

## Speech-Language Pathologists

Speech-language pathologists are professionals trained to work with students to develop skills in articulating the sounds of language, using their voices efficiently, and developing both receptive and expressive language skills. Parental counseling usually focuses on explaining the impact of speech and language problems and providing structured information for helping parents to help their children develop and use speech and language most effectively. National certification for speech-language pathologists is acquired from the American Speech-Language-Hearing Association after successfully completing masters-level training and serving a paid clinical fellowship year.

## Deaf Educators

Deaf educators provide a variety of services. Some are classroom teachers who present curricular content to students who are deaf, similar to regular education math, history, and science teachers. Others may provide service as special education coordinators, ensuring that IEPs are followed and reviewed as needed. They may serve as resource personnel for regular educators or staff resource rooms. The Council for Exceptional Children (1995) has proposed guidelines for the approximately 80 colleges and universities in the United States that offer training programs in the education of people who are deaf and hard of hearing. The council believes that graduates of these training programs should possess knowledge and skills in at least the following eight areas:

1. Philosophical, historical, and legal aspects of education of people who are hard of hearing and deaf. This would include knowledge of incidence, identification techniques, theories of teaching, cultural knowledge, educational placement options, and the rights and responsibilities of parents and educators.

2. Characteristics of children who are deaf and hard of hearing, including the cognitive, emotional, and social impact of deafness and hearing impairment on students and their families.

3. Assessment, diagnosis, and evaluational procedures, including the appropriate terminology used and the legal guidelines concerning referrals and placements.

4. Instructional content and practice, including sources of specialized materials; knowledge of nonverbal communication systems, including American Sign Language, and familiarity with language development and practices to maximize residual hearing.

5. Planning and managing the teaching environment, including knowledge of model programs and cultural factors that might influence classroom management.

6. Management of student behavior and social interaction skills, and the facilitation of interaction between students who are deaf and communities that are deaf.

7. Communication and collaborative partnerships, including how to obtain governmental and nongovernmental resources for parents and knowledge of responsibilities of regular teachers and support personnel.

8. Professional and ethical practices, including proficiency in obtaining information on education, philosophy, and knowledge of relevant consumer and professional organizations for people who are hard of hearing and deaf.

Teachers of students who are hard of hearing and deaf are certified by state departments of education. The credentials needed vary, with some states requiring at least master's-level training in deaf education before granting certification.

## Educational Interpreters

These professionals, who sign the spoken content of what teachers and other speakers say, became a recognized professional group in 1964. Their umbrella organization is called the Registry of Interpreters for the Deaf (RID) (Heward, 1996). The RID sets standards for the competencies needed to become a certified interpreter. Freelance interpreters work primarily with adults in needed medical or legal situations. Educational interpreters, also called educational transliterators, make it possible for students who are deaf to enroll in postsecondary educational programs. Educational interpreters are being used in increasing numbers in elementary and secondary class-rooms, where their duties can vary from strictly translating to tutoring, assisting regular and special education teachers, keeping records, and supervising students with hearing impairments (Salend & Longo, 1994; Zawolkow & DeFiore, 1986).

## Genetics Specialists

A significant percentage of hearing losses are either inherited or occur during prenatal, perinatal, or postnatal development. The geneticist plays an important role in family counseling and prenatal screening to determine which families are at risk and informing them of the current knowledge available about hereditary transmission and its consequences.

## Professional Organizations

The next section of this chapter lists professional organizations, parent and self-help groups that are concerned with the needs and rights of the hard of hearing. Two organizations that provide direct service to the Registry of Interpreters for the Deaf and the individual state vocational rehabilitation departments will be highlighted in this section.

**Registry for Interpreters of the Deaf (RID).**　The RID maintains a national listing of members who are skilled in the use of American Sign Language and other sign systems. It will also provide information about interpreting and the certification of interpreters.

**Vocational Rehabilitation Departments.**　Each state has a vocational rehabilitation office that will provide assistance in vocational evaluations, availabilities, and eligibility requirements for financial assistance, educational training, and job placements. The addresses for the vocational rehabilitation offices in each state are provided in Appendix I.

## PROFESSIONAL ASSOCIATIONS AND PARENT OR SELF-HELP GROUPS

Alexander Graham Bell Association for the Deaf
3417 Volta Place NW
Washington, DC 20007

American Athletic Association of the Deaf
1134 Davenport Drive
Burton, MI 48529

American Deafness and Rehabilitation
　Association
P.O. Box 55369
Little Rock, AR 72225

American Society for Deaf Children
814 Thayer Avenue
Silver Spring, MD 20910

American Speech-Language-Hearing Association
10801 Rockville Pike
Rockville, MD 20852

American Tinnitus Association
1618 S.W. First Avenue, Suite 417
Portland, OR 97201

Beginnings for Parents of Hearing Impaired
    Children
3900 Barrett Drive, Suite 100
Raleigh, NC 27609

Better Hearing Institute
P.O. Box 1840
Washington, DC 20013

Center on Deafness
3444 W. Dundee Road
Northbrook, IL 60062

Cochlear Implant Club
P.O. Box 464
Buffalo, NY 14223

Deaf Artists of America
87 N. Clinton Avenue, Suite 408
Rochester, NY 14604

Deafness Research Foundation
9 East 38th Street
New York, NY 10016

Deafpride Inc.
1350 Potomac Avenue SE
Washington, DC 20003

Dogs for the Deaf
10175 Wheeler Road
Central Point, OR 97502

Gallaudet University
800 Florida Avenue NE
Washington, DC 20002

Hear Now
9745 E. Hampden Avenue, Suite 300
Denver, CO 80231

National Association for Hearing and Speech
    Action
10801 Rockville Pike
Rockville, MD 20852

National Association of the Deaf
814 Thayer Avenue
Silver Spring, MD 20910

National Center for Law and the Deaf
Gallaudet University
800 Florida Avenue NE
Washington, DC 20002

National Cued Speech Association
P.O. Box 31345
Raleigh, NC 27622

National Foundation for Children's Hearing
    Education and Research
928 McLean Avenue
Yonkers, NY 10704

National Information Center on Deafness
Gallaudet University
800 Florida Avenue NE
Washington, DC 20002

National Technical Institute for the Deaf
One Lomb Memorial Drive
Rochester, NY 14623

Paws with a Cause
Home of Ears for the Deaf, Inc.
1235 100th Street SE
Byron Center, MI 49314

Registry of Interpreters for the Deaf
51 Monroe Street, Suite 1107
Rockville, MD 20850

Self-Help for Hard of Hearing People
7800 Wisconsin Avenue
Bethesda, MD 20814

## REFERENCES FOR FURTHER INFORMATION

*American Annals of the Deaf*
814 Thayer Avenue
Silver Spring, MD 20910

*The Endeavor*
American Society for Deaf Children
East 10th and Tahlequah
Sulphur, OK 73086

*Journal of the American Deafness and Rehabilitation Association*
P.O. Box 251554
Little Rock, AR 72225

*Our Kids Magazine*
Alexander Graham Bell Association for the Deaf
3417 Volta Place NW
Washington, DC 20007

*Sign Language Studies*
Linstok Press
9306 Mintwood Street
Silver Spring, MD 20910

*Volta Review*
Alexander Graham Bell Association for the Deaf
3417 Volta Place NW
Washington, DC 20007

## REFERENCES

Allen, T. (1986). Patterns of academic achievement among hearing impaired students: 1974 and 1983. In A. N. Schildroth & M. A. Karchmer (Eds.), *Deaf children in America* (pp. 161–206). San Diego, CA: College-Hill/Little, Brown.

Barnes v. Converse College, 436 F. Supp. 635 (1977).

Bensberg, G. J., & Sigelman, C. K. (1976). Definitions and prevalence. In L. L. Lloyd (Ed.), *Communication assessment and intervention strategies*. Baltimore: University Park Press.

Berg, F. S. (1986). Characteristics of the target population. In F. S. Berg, J. C. Blair, S. H. Vieweg, & A. Wilson-Vlotman (Eds.), *Educational audiology for the hard of hearing child* (pp. 1–24). Orlando, FL: Grune & Stratton.

Bess, F. H. (1988). *Hearing impairment in children*. Parkton, MD: York.

Blackwell, P. M., & Fischgrund, J. E. (1984). Issues in the development of culturally responsive programs for deaf students from non-English-speaking homes. In G. L. Delgado (Ed.), *The Hispanic Deaf: Issues and challenges for bilingual special education* (pp. 154–166). Washington, DC: Gallaudet University Press.

Blennerhassett, L. (1990). Intellectual assessment. In D. F. Moores & K. P. Meadow-Orlans (Eds.), *Educational and developmental aspects of deafness* (pp. 255–280). Washington, DC: Gallaudet University Press.

Board of Education of the Hendrik Hudson Central School District v. Rowley, 102 S. Ct. 3034 (1982).

Bodner-Johnson, B. (1987). Helping the youngest ones. *Gallaudet Today*, 18, 8–11.

Bowe, F. (1991). *Approaching equality: Education of the deaf*. Silver Spring, MD: TJ Publications.

Charlson, E., Strong, M., & Gold, R. (1992). How successful deaf teenagers experience and cope with isolation. *American Annals of the Deaf*, 137(3), 261–270.

Clarkson, R. L., Vohr, B. R., Blackwell, P. M., & White, K. R. (1994). Universal hearing screening and intervention: The Rhode Island program. *Infants and Young Children*, 6(3), 65–74.

Cohen, O., Fischgrund, J., & Redding, R. (1990). Deaf children from ethnic, linguistic and racial minority backgrounds. *American Annals of the Deaf*, 135(92), 67–73.

Commission on the Education of the Deaf. (1988). *Toward equality: Education of the deaf*. Washington, DC: U.S. Government Printing Office.

Council for Exceptional Children (1995). *What every special educator must know: The international standards for the preparation and certification of special education teachers*. Reston, VA: Council for Exceptional Children.

Davis, J. M. (1986). Academic placement in perspective. In D. M. Luterman (Ed.), *Deafness in perspective* (pp. 205–224). San Diego, CA: College-Hill.

Dolnick, E. (1993). Deafness as a culture. *Atlantic Monthly*, 272(3), 37–53.

Friedrith, B. (1987). Auditory dysfunction. In K. Kavale, J. Forness, & M. Bender (Eds.), *Handbook of learning disabilities: Vol. 1*. Austin, TX: Pro-Ed.

Gaustad, M. G., & Kluwin, T. N. (1992). Patterns of communication among deaf and hearing adolescents. In T. N. Kluwin, D. F. Moores, & M. G. Gaustad (Eds.), *Toward effective public school programs for deaf students: Context, process, & outcomes* (pp. 107–128). New York: Teachers College Press.

Geers, A., & Moog, J. (1989). Factors predictive of the development of literacy in profoundly hearing-impaired adolescents. *Volta Review*, 91, 69–86.

Green, W. W., & Fischgrund, J. E. (1993). Students with hearing loss. In A. E. Blackhurst & W. H. Berdine (Eds.), *An introduction to special education* (3rd ed., pp. 271–309). New York: HarperCollins.

Gustason, G. (1990). Signing exact English. In H. Bornstein (Ed.), *Manual communication: Implications for education*. Washington, DC: Gallaudet University Press.

Hallahan, D. P., & Kauffman, J. M. (1994). *Exceptional children* (6th ed.). Upper Saddle River, NJ: Prentice Hall.

Hardman, M. L., Drew, C. J., & Egan, M. W. (1996). *Human exceptionality: Society, school, and family* (5th ed.). Needham, MA: Allyn & Bacon.

Hess, D. (1991, July 23). Say what? *Albuquerque Journal*, pp. A1–A2.

Heward, W. L. (1996). *Exceptional children* (5th ed.). Upper Saddle River, NJ: Prentice Hall/Merrill.

Higgins, P. C. (1992). Working at mainstreaming. In P. M. Ferguson, D. L. Ferguson, & S. J. Taylor (Eds.), *Interpreting disability* (pp. 103–123). New York: Teachers College Press.

Janesick, V. J., & Moores, D. F. (1992). Ethnic and cultural considerations. In R. N. Kluwin, D. F. Moores, & M. G. Gaustad (Eds.), *Toward effective public school programs for deaf students: Context, process, & outcomes* (pp. 49–65). New York: Teachers College Press.

Jordan, I. K. (1992). Language and change. *Viewpoints on deafness: A deaf American monograph*, 42, 69–71.

Kirk, S. A., Gallagher, J. J., & Anastasiow, N. J. (1993). *Educating exceptional children*. (7th ed.). Boston: Houghton Mifflin.

Kluwin, T. N. (1985). Profiling the deaf student who is a problem in the classroom. *Adolescence*, 20, 863–875.

Kluwin, T. N. (1992). What does "local public school" mean? In R. N. Kluwin, D. F. Moores, & M. G. Gaustad (Eds.), *Toward effective public school programs for deaf students: Context, process, & outcomes* (pp. 30–48). New York: Teachers College Press.

Lane, H. (1992). *The mask of benevolence: Disabling the Deaf community*. New York: Knopf.

Ling, D. (Ed.). (1984). *Early intervention for hearing-impaired children: Total communication options*. San Diego, CA: College-Hill.

Loeb, R., & Sarigiani, P. (1986). The impact of hearing impairment on self-perceptions of children. *Volta Review*, 88(2), 89–100.

Lowenbraun, S., & Thompson, M. (1990). Hearing impairments. In N. G. Haring, L. McCormack, & T. G. Haring (Eds.), *Exceptional children and youth*. Upper Saddle River, NJ: Prentice Hall/Merrill.

Luetke-Stahlman, B., & Luckner, J. (1991). *Effectively educating students with hearing impairments*. White Plains, NY: Longman.

Luterman, D. M. (Ed.). (1986). *Deafness in perspective*. San Diego, CA: College-Hill.

Mayer, M. H. (1996). Children who are deaf or hard of hearing. In E. L. Meyen (Ed.), *Exceptional children in today's schools* (pp. 315–350). Denver, CO: Love.

McKusick, V. (1983). *Mendelian inheritance in man* (6th ed.). Baltimore: Johns Hopkins Press.

Meadow-Orleans, K. P. (1985). Social and psychological effects of hearing loss in adulthood: A literature review. In H. Orleans (Ed.), *Adjustment to adult hearing loss* (pp. 35–57). San Diego, CA: College-Hill.

Moores, D. F. (1985). Educational programs and services for hearing impaired children: Issues and options. In F. Powell, T. Finitzo-Hieber, S. Friel-Patti, & D. Henderson (Eds.), *Deaf children in America* (pp. 105–123). San Diego, CA: College-Hill.

Moores, D. F. (1987). *Educating the deaf: Psychology, principles, and practices*. Boston: Houghton Mifflin.

Northern, J. L., & Downs, M. P. (1991). *Hearing in children* (4th ed.). Baltimore: Williams & Wilkins.

Padden, C., & Humphries, T. (1988). *Deaf in America: Voices from a culture*. Cambridge, MA: Harvard University Press.

Pappas, D. (1985). *Diagnosis and treatment of hearing impairment in children.* San Diego, CA: College-Hill.

Paul, P. V., & Quigley, S. P. (1990). *Education and deafness.* New York: Longman.

Prinz, P. M., Pemberton, E., & Nelson, K. (1985). The Alpha Interactive Microcomputer System for teaching reading, writing, and communication skills to hearing-impaired children. *American Annals of the Deaf,* 130(4), 441–461.

Quigley, S. P., & Paul, P. V. (1990). *Language and deafness.* San Diego, CA: College-Hill.

Ray, S. (1979). *An adaptation of the Wechsler Intelligence Scale for Children–Revised for the deaf.* Northridge, CA: Steven Ray.

Reagan, T. (1985). The deaf as a linguistic minority: Educational considerations. *Harvard Educational Review,* 55, 265–277.

Reagan, T. (1992). Cultural considerations in the education of deaf children. In D. F. Moores & K. P. Meadow-Orleans (Eds.), *Educational and developmental aspects of deafness* (pp. 73–84). Washington, DC: Gallaudet University Press.

Rooney, T. E. (1982). Signing vs. speech: What's a parent to do? SEE *What's Happening,* 1(1), 6–8.

Salend, S. J., & Longo, M. (1994). The roles of the education interpreter in mainstreaming. TEACHING *Exceptional Children,* 26(4), 22–28.

Salvia, J., & Ysseldyke, J. E. (1991). *Assessment* (5th ed.). Boston: Houghton Mifflin.

Schildroth, A. N. (1986). Residential schools for deaf students: A decade in review. In A. N. Schildroth & M. A. Karchmer (Eds.), *Deaf children in America* (pp. 83–104). San Diego, CA: College-Hill/Little, Brown.

Schildroth, A. N., & Holt, S. A. (1991). Annual survey of hearing-impaired children and youth: 1989–90 school year. *American Annals of the Deaf,* 136(2), 155–163.

Schlesinger, H. (1993). Early intervention: The prevention of multiple handicaps. In G. Mencher & S. Gerber (Eds.), *The multiply handicapped hearing-impaired child* (pp. 83–116). New York: Grune & Stratton.

Shaver, K. A. (1988). Genetic causes of childhood deafness. In F. H. Bess (Ed.), *Hearing impairment in children* (pp. 15–32). Parkton, MD: York.

Slike, S. B., Chiavacci, J. P., & Hobbis, D. H. (1989). The efficiency and effectiveness of an interactive videodisc system to teach sign language vocabulary. *American Annals of the Deaf,* 134, 288–290.

Smith, D. D., & Luckasson, R. (1995). *Introduction to special education: Teaching in an age of challenge* (2nd ed.). Needham, MA: Allyn & Bacon.

Stanford Achievement Test (8th ed.). (1989). Hyattsville, MD: Psychological Corporation.

Stein, L. (1988). Hearing impairment. In V. B. Van Hasselt, P. S. Strain, & M. Hersen (Eds.), *Handbook of developmental and physical disabilities* (pp. 271–294). New York: Pergamon.

Stinson, M. S., & Whitmire, K. (1992). Students' views of their social relationships. In T. N. Kluwin, D. F. Moores, & M. G. Gaustad (Eds.), *Toward effective public school programs for deaf students: Context, process, & outcomes* (pp. 149–174). New York: Teachers College Press.

Turnbull, A. P., Turnbull, H. R., Shank, M., & Leal, D. (1995). *Exceptional lives: Special education in today's schools* (pp. 550–593). Upper Saddle River, NJ: Prentice Hall/Merrill.

U.S. Department of Education. (1997). *Nineteenth annual report to Congress on the implementation of the Individuals with Disabilities Education Act.* Washington, DC: Author.

Vernon, M., & Koh, S. D. (1970). Effects of manual communication on deaf children's educational achievement, linguistic competence, oral skills, and psychological adjustment. *American Annals of the Deaf,* 115, 527–536.

Wolk, S., & Schildroth, A. N. (1986). Deaf children and speech intelligibility: A national study. In A. N. Schildroth & M. A. Karchmer (Eds.), *Deaf children in America* (pp. 139–159). San Diego, CA: College-Hill/Little, Brown.

Zawolkow, E., & DeFiore, S. (1986). Educational interpreting for elementary- and secondary-level hearing-impaired students. *American Annals of the Deaf,* 131, 26–28.

# 9

# Children with Visual Impairments

"**M**onkey see, monkey do!" Quite an inelegant and possibly offensive way to describe a major part of the incidental learning process that guides the acquisition of social and education competencies valued in our society. Yet in some ways, those four simple words pinpoint what may be the most critical obstacle for the children and adolescents with visual impairments discussed in this chapter. The normally sighted automatically depend on and use vision for many tasks. Educationally, we learn from the printed and visual materials that give us a greater understanding of our world and its many wonders. Environmentally, we move from place to place based on visual signs we recognize. Socially, we read each other's faces and body language to help determine whether our behavior is appropriate, and we change it if it isn't. We select friends, play sports, work, and relax with the help of the visual information we hardly pause to consider. Obviously, this is not so for children and adolescents with visual impairments. Depending on the amount of residual vision each individual possesses, modifications in learning, socialization, recreation, and career choices must be implemented in a logical and meaningful way to help compensate for the information lost by the visual impairment.

## DEFINITIONS

As a part of defining blindness and visual impairment, it is necessary to understand how normal vision works. It is also helpful to master some of the many terms that make up the vocabulary for defining visual impairment. Once the normal vision system is understood and the most appropriate terms are familiar, it will be easier to define misfunctions of the system. As with many other areas covered in this text, different definitions of visual impairment and blindness are employed for different purposes. The differing legal and educational conceptualizations and their implications are fairly straightforward and reasonably understandable once this prerequisite knowledge is mastered.

Unimpaired vision has four components:

1. The object to be viewed.
2. The light that reflects from the object to the eye.
3. A normally functioning eye to receive the reflections.
4. The occipital lobes of the brain to interpret the signals transmitted from the eye (Chalkley, 1982; Kirk, 1981).

As light reflects off an object and strikes the eye, the reflected image is converted into electrical impulses that are received by the brain and translated into what we perceive. Figure 9.1 is a schematic illustration of the parts of the eye and how they work. You may wish to refer to it as you read the next few sentences. The reflected light rays enter the eye through the transparent curved part of the front of the eye, which is called the *cornea*. They pass through the watery *aqueous humor* on the way to the hole in the center of the eye, which is called the *pupil*. The pupil is housed in the center of the *iris*, the colored part of the eye. The pupil changes size by expanding

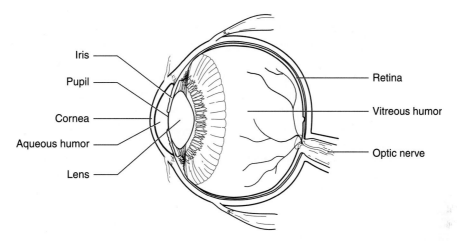

Iris

Pupil

Cornea

Aqueous humor

Lens

Retina

Vitreous humor

Optic nerve

**Figure 9.1**
The Human Eye

and contracting, which allows differing amounts of light into the eye. The *lens*, which is behind the iris changes in thickness and brings the reflected light rays into focus. This process is called *accommodation*. These focused light rays pass through the *vitreous humor*, a transparent gelatinous substance, and onto the *retina* or inside lining of the eye. The job of the cells of the retina is to translate the reflected visual information into electrical impulse messages that are sent via the *optic nerve* to the *occipital lobe* of the brain. The occipital lobe is located in the back of the brain. It is where the messages are interpreted so that the viewer can interpret what is being seen. The movements of the eyes are controlled by six pairs of muscles that enable the eye to move from side to side and up and down. While gazing straight ahead, a normal eye can see objects within a range of about 160 degrees. This is called the *visual field*. When the eyes are functioning normally, a person can maintain *visual attention*, which means that he or she is alert enough to be visually sensitive to the environment, is able to select the visual information the environment offers, is attentive enough to change from one visual stimulus to another, and has the processing ability to decode the information he or she is receiving from the visual channel (Smith & Luckasson, 1995).

The terms listed in Box 9.1 are not a complete listing of the entire specialized vocabulary that has developed to define visual impairment. However, an understanding of these basic concepts should provide enough information to help the reader understand the definitions that follow.

## Legal and Educational Definitions of Visual Impairment

Students with visual impairment may be described in a number of ways for differing purposes. The two major categorizations define children and adolescents with visual

**Box 9.1**
*WHAT EVERY TEACHER NEEDS TO KNOW*

*Terms*

**adventitious blindness**    Refers to children or adults blinded after age 3. People who are adventitiously blind may retain some visual memories that can be helpful in learning.

**age of onset**    When the disability occurs.

**congenital blindness**    Refers to a child who was blind at birth and will retain no visual memories.

**functional blindness**    Refers to people who may be able to perceive only shadows or limited amounts of movement visually. Education must occur through tactile or other senses.

**legal blindness**    Refers to people who have central visual acuity of 20/200 or less in their better eye and/or a visual field that is no greater than 20 degrees. (20/200 means that they can see at 20 feet what a normally sighted person can see at 200 feet. The normal visual field is approximately 160 degrees.)

**low vision capacity**    Refers to partially sighted individuals who may be able to use sight for many activities, including reading.

**peripheral vision**    How wide a field of vision a person can maintain while gazing ahead.

**residual vision**    The amount and degree of vision that is functional despite any visual impairment. Residual vision measurement can be influenced by light conditions, fatigue, distance from objects, and other factors.

**tunnel vision**    Inadequate peripheral vision, causing the visual field to be restricted to a narrower-than-normal arc.

**visual acuity**    How sharp and clear vision is at various distances.

**visual capacity**    What can actually be seen. It is a combination of visual acuity, visual field, and the ability to respond to visual stimulation.

**visual efficiency**    An educational term similar to *visual capacity* that describes how well a person can use the sight he or she has.

impairments for legal purposes and for educational purposes. The legally blind are eligible for a wide variety of services, materials, and benefits from government agencies. For example, they may be provided with tapes, record players, and audio recorded books from the Library of Congress. Their schools can obtain specialized materials and books from the American Printing House for the Blind. They are also eligible for free occupational training, free mail service, and special income-tax exemptions (Heward, 1996). Educational definitions are most concerned with the modifications that will be needed to ensure that a child will receive the most appropriate and effective educational experience. The vision impairments of a person who is legally blind meet or exceed the acuity and field-of-vision restrictions previously described in Box 9.1.

Educational definitions are more varied. According to Public Law 101-467 (IDEA), a *visual handicap* is a "visual impairment that, even with correction, adversely affects a child's educational performance. The term includes both partially seeing and blind children" (42 Fed. Reg. 42474 [1977]). Two widely used defining terms are *low vision* and *blind*. Both groups can use braille, but most students with low vision use some form of print for reading. The American Foundation For the Blind defines those with low vision as possessing visual acuity between 20/200 and 20/70 in their better eye with the best possible correction, or those who in the opinion of an eye specialist need temporary or permanent special education services (American Foundation for the Blind, 1961). Some have proposed slightly differing definitions in an attempt to clarify the needs of children with low vision. For example, Corn (1989) defines low vision as a level of vision that, with standard correction, hinders an individual in the planning and/or execution of a task, but permits enhancement of functional vision through the use of optical or nonoptical devices and environmental modifications or techniques. Individuals with low vision can generally read print, although they may depend on optical aids such as magnifying glasses. Some use both braille and print. In any case, they are able to use vision to learn (Lewis, 1995).

Children who are blind are those whose visual loss indicates that they should be educated chiefly with braille or other tactile or auditory materials (American Printing House for the Blind, 1981). Individuals who are totally blind do not receive meaningful information through the visual sense. They need to use auditory and tactile learning methods. Those who are functionally blind typically use braille for efficient reading and writing. They may use their residual sight for other tasks such as traveling and doing other daily chores. Their limited vision supplements the tactual and auditory learning to which they are exposed (Lewis, 1995).

Additionally, each state has its own definition of visual impairment that specifies which children are eligible for special services that the schools can provide. In general, these definitions are consistent with those discussed in this section.

There is another way of defining and grouping people who are visually impaired that might be helpful for educational planning. Barraga (1986) proposed the concept of moderate, severe, and profound visual impairments. Moderate visual impairments can almost entirely be corrected with the help of visual aids or special lighting in regular classrooms or resource rooms. Severe visual disability is helped only marginally with aids. However, the child can still use vision for learning, with additional time and energy needed to perform visual tasks. Severe visual disability is the rough equivalent of low vision. Profound visual disability occurs when a student cannot use vision as an educational tool. Touch and hearing are the primary channels. Although possible, the performance of most gross visual tasks may be difficult. Detailed tasks cannot be performed visually. This is the equivalent of legal blindness.

Although the definitions and categorizations differ for legal and educational reasons, the single most defining characteristic is a visual restriction of sufficient severity that it interferes with a child's normal progress in a regular education setting without some modification (Scholl, 1986). The student must exhibit one or more of the following characteristics: visual acuity loss, visual field loss, or a changing or degenerating visual condition.

## PREVALENCE

About 1 child in 10 begins school with some degree of visual impairment. However, a large majority of these children can be helped with corrective glasses or direct medical treatment. As a result, their vision problems have little or no effect on social or educational development. Approximately 1 in 1,000 has a visual problem so severe that it cannot be corrected (Kirk, Gallagher, & Anastasiow, 1993). During the 1995–1996 school year, 25,443 students between ages 6 and 21 received special education services as a result of their visual impairments (U.S. Department of Education, 1997). These children have low vision but are not legally blind. The annual registration of people who are legally blind by the American Printing House for the Blind revealed that in 1992, 51,813 people from birth to age 21 qualified for inclusion in this population (Hunt & Marshall, 1994). The figure most often used is 0.1 percent of the school-age population (U.S. Department of Education, 1997), although some report an incidence of as high as 1.5 percent of the school-age population (Nelson & Dimitrova, 1993).

Visual impairments are fairly evenly divided between boys (55 percent) and girls (45 percent). Incidence figures may vary somewhat, due to unidentified children with visual impairment, varied state definitions for inclusion in the visually handicapped population, and counting individuals with multiple disabilities who have visual impairments in other categories of disability (Smith & Luckasson, 1995). Kirchner (1983) believes that many students with mild or perhaps even moderate visual disabilities are not being identified and are therefore not receiving services. The base population around which figures fluctuate remains stable due to the high rate of visual impairment caused by hereditary factors (Kirchner, Peterson, & Suhr, 1988). However, there does appear to be a steady increase in the number of children reported as visually impaired since the late 1970s (Kirchner, 1990). The data collected by the American Printing House for the Blind indicate a 9 percent increase between 1987 and 1991. The data also reveal that enrollment in infant programs increased by 25 percent and the number of preschool children in programs increased by 41 percent (American Printing House for the Blind, 1987, 1992b). This rise can be credited in part to better and earlier identification of children with visual impairments and in particular to the ability of the medical community to save premature infants and sustain the lives of neonates with severe medical problems to a greater extent than ever before. Some of these children have congenital visual impairments or sustain visual impairments as a result of the procedures used to keep them alive. This will be further discussed in the "Etiology" section of this chapter. Finally, it must be noted that visual impairments are highly correlated with increasing age. The vast majority of people who are legally blind and visually handicapped are over age 65 (Genensky, Berry, Bikson, & Bikson, 1979).

## CHARACTERISTICS

Assigning characteristics to children with visual impairments must be done cautiously. Adaptations and reactions to limited sight vary from child to child. Most children with visual impairment are more like children who are normally sighted than they are different from them. They are a diverse and multicultural population. Some are gifted and talented, while others are average in most ways. While this section of the chapter will highlight their uniqueness, the reader should bear in mind the similarities of students with visual impairments to children who are sighted. Still, as a group, youngsters with visual impairment have a higher than average number of concomitant multiple disabilities, and all share a limited capacity for incidental environmental learning (Harrell & Curry, 1987).

## Motor Development

There is no indication that the motor development and innate motor skills of children with visual impairments are different from those of children with normal sight. However, the child with visual impairment, depending on the severity of the impairment, may not be motivated to move and explore. The lack of visually driven imitative behaviors and the restrictions of an environment that is overly protective may retard the development of some motor skills (Caton, 1993).

## Academic Skills

The intelligence of children who are visually impaired does not appear to be significantly different from their sighted peers (Caton, 1993). However, measuring their intellectual abilities can be challenging when using measurement instruments standardized on their seeing peers. Many items on the most popular intelligence tests can be unfair to people who are visually impaired, since they often cannot respond appropriately in providing the information or performing the tasks required. Obviously, tasks used to measure abilities that range from color sorting to describing pictures or other visually presented stimuli might place the child with visual impairment at a disadvantage. However, there does not appear to be a reason to believe that any innate intellectual impairment exists in this population of children (Hallahan & Kauffman, 1994).

Language abilities of children with visual impairments do not seem to differ in regard to acquisition and development of the major components of language. Minor differences tend to revolve around the restricted experiences these children may suffer because of their impairment and the corresponding lack of linguistic experiences that are related to their lack of interaction with their environment. Some differences are logical and predictable. For example, Warren (1984) suggests that the language of those with visual impairment is more self-centered and refers to fewer objects and people than does the language of their sighted peers.

Children with visual impairment may indulge in *verbalism* (Cutsforth, 1951), which is a tendency to use words about which they have no firsthand knowledge. They may describe the rise and fall of the ocean waves or the darkening of the sky before a storm approaching with no real understanding of what they are describing. Language development and cognitive or concept developments are intertwined for most children who are visually impaired. Some concepts may never be fully understood without vision. Height, distance, and the atmosphere of a candlelit room can be examples of visually based concepts. Often, special educational experiences can and must be devised to help compensate for the information lost through the visual channel. However, touch and hearing information tends to be perceived in sequences; for example, you feel a puppy from nose to tail in some order and hear a kitten purr when you stroke it. It requires mental imagery to integrate these experiences into a meaningful whole. Vision

provides the whole and its parts simultaneously and automatically. Relationships do not have to be constructed, because they are visible. Construction of concepts from hearing and touch is not only less efficient, but it is also more prone to error and misunderstanding (Sacks, Rosen, & Gaylord-Ross, 1990).

These learning difficulties are often reflected in academic performance. Unless there are multiple disability factors that cause other learning problems, there is no reason to believe that children with visual impairment, with appropriate modifications in the learning environment, will not perform well academically (Hodges, 1983). However, as a group these children do tend to lag behind their sighted peers but not because of basic intellectual abilities. Ashcroft (1963) points out that children with visual impairments usually enter school later than their age peers, are often educated in inappropriately modified environments, miss school for repeated surgeries and other related medical treatment, and perhaps most critically, use braille and other curriculum modifications that slow or otherwise restrict their ability to gather information quickly and efficiently. These roadblocks to quick and efficient learning take their toll when students with visual impairments attempt to keep pace with their sighted classmates, who can obtain and process material much more quickly using visual skills.

## Social Skills

The development and practice of social skills is the area in which students with visual impairment tend to differ most from their peers. Some believe the lack of social skills directly relates to negative attitudes transmitted by our society to people who are visually impaired. The image of a helpless and dependent blind person, coupled with parental overprotection, can retard social development. So can isolation and lack of contact with sighted people (Caton, 1993). While there do not appear to be innate personality problems automatically associated with visual impairment, older people with visual impairments are often characterized as socially immature, self-conscious, isolated, passive, withdrawn, and dependent (Tuttle, 1981). Many skills acquired automatically by sighted children must be taught to children with visual impairment. Eye contact provides sighted children with information about the appropriateness of behavior that children with visual impairment cannot access. Appropriate smiling and facial expression and postural messages are all a part of socialization that are difficult for people with visual impairments (Hallahan & Kauffman, 1994). Often children with visual impairments are rejected by their classmates because they lack social skills. They may ask too many questions or engage in inappropriate acts of affection (Jones & Chiba, 1985; Kekelis, 1992). They may also be rejected because their knowledge of play experiences is limited. Because they often find it difficult to hold sighted playmates' interests, their conversations become brief and self-centered rather than focused on shared activities (MacCuspie, 1992). Rejection might even begin when parents react negatively to children who don't reinforce them with smiles and appropriate eye contact (Fraiberg, 1977; Warren, 1984). A final and critical impediment to social adjustment may be the stereotypical behaviors that some children with visual impairment display. Body rocking, eye rubbing, and inappropriate hand and finger movements are all distracting and off-putting to peers and interfere with attempts at social interaction. Aside from their social consequences, these behaviors can interfere with learning by using up the time needed for other activities (Bambring & Troster, 1992). Stereotypical behaviors, once learned and ingrained into the child's behavior pattern, are often very difficult to eliminate.

As with all the other disabilities covered by this text, the list of characteristics discussed here will not be found in all children or even in any one child. However, the composite picture presented here should help the reader understand some of the consequences of being visually impaired.

## ETIOLOGY

We have defined the categories of visual impairment, shared the prevalence statistics, and sketched some of the most common characteristics of visually impaired children and adolescents. Unlike some of the other disabilities covered in this text, we can at least accurately describe most of the conditions that lead to visual impairments. Unfortunately, we are not always aware of what causes each condition that in turn results in visual impairment. While this section on the causes of visual impairment covers many of the most commonly occurring conditions, it does not cover all possible causes or every condition that can lead to blindness or visual impairments.

Heredity is by far the largest causal link in visual impairments and is responsible for more than 37 percent of the most serious visual disabilities in young children.

Infectious diseases during pregnancy cause another 15 percent of impairments, and approximately 10 percent more are due to injuries and the oxygen poisoning that results from attempts to sustain premature infants. Another 10 percent of visual impairments are attributable to tumors and other neoplasms affecting the optic nerve (Kirk, Gallagher, & Anastasiow, 1993). The 30 different causes and types of the eye dysfunctions discussed in this section can be grouped into major categories. The causal category deals with injuries, infections, substance abuse problems, and nutrition problems that might affect vision. The major types or conditions are grouped as being primarily refractive disorders, retinal and optic nerve problems, eye muscle disorders, and central vision insufficiencies. These categorizations and a listing of causes and conditions appear in Figures 9.2 and 9.3. Figure 9.2 lists potential causes of visual impairment, such as vitamin A deficiency and substance abuse. Figure 9.3 lists the most frequently seen conditions of impairment, such as myopia and retinitis pigmentosa. This attempt to present a comprehensive listing is intended as a useful checksheet for understanding the causes of visual dysfunction.

| | |
|---|---|
| EYE INJURIES | INFECTIONS |
| NEOPLASMS | Measles |
| Tumors | Trachoma |
| MALNUTRITION | Onchocerciasis |
| Vitamin A deficiency | AIDS |
| SUBSTANCE ABUSE | Chlamydia |
| SYSTEMIC DISEASES | Gonorrhea |
| Diabetes | POISONING |
| | Excess oxygen |

Figure 9.2
Causes of Visual Impairment

| | |
|---|---|
| REFRACTIVE DISORDERS | RETINAL AND OPTIC NERVE PROBLEMS |
| Hyperopia | Retinal degeneration |
| Myopia | Retinal detachment |
| Astigmatism | Macular degeneration |
| Cataracts | Retinitis pigmentosa |
| Aniridia (ocular albinism) | Coloboma |
| EYE MUSCLE PROBLEMS | Glaucoma |
| Strabismus | Optic nerve atrophy |
| Nystagmus | Color vision problems |
| CENTRAL VISION LOSS | Retrolental fibroplasia |
| Visual cortex damage | Retinoblastoma |
| | Diabetic retinopathy |
| | Optic tumors |

Figure 9.3
Conditions of the Eye

## Injury, Infections, Substance Abuse, and Malnutrition

These conditions are not eye impairments themselves, but they can cause vision problems. For example, injuries to the prenatal nervous system and fetal alcohol syndrome are not vision problems, but both can lead to optic nerve hypoplasia, which is a visual problem (Sacks, Rosen, & Gaylord-Ross, 1990). *Eye injuries* of all types can lead to visual impairment or blindness. Most eye injuries are preventable and can be avoided with the proper use of safety goggles and other safety measures. *Neoplasms* (tumors) are a variety of growths that can affect an organ. An example is a retinoblastoma, a malignant tumor of the eye. It usually affects both eyes and occurs before age 3 (Sacks, Rosen, & Gaylord-Ross, 1990). *Malnutrition* in a severe form can lead to blindness. Vitamin A deficiency is particularly critical as a cause of visual impairment. Vitamin supplements, as well as increasing the child's intake of fruits, vegetables, milk, protein, and eggs when possible in a deficient diet, can prevent nutritional blindness, also known as *xerophthalmia*. *Substance abuse* during pregnancy, especially during the first trimester, can cause visual impairments in the neonate and is partially responsible for the current increase in visual impairments (Smith & Luckasson, 1995). *Systemic diseases* such as diabetes, if untreated or treated inconsistently, can lead to visual impairment or blindness. *Diabetic retinopathy* is causally linked to diabetes and results when the blood supply to the retina is compromised due to the diabetic condition. A host of *viral infections* can cause visual problems. Measles (rubella) can affect the vision of children when contracted by pregnant women during the first trimester of pregnancy. A major outbreak of rubella in the early 1960s left many children with varying degrees of visual impairment. Trachoma and river blindness (*onchocerciasis*) are both spread by infection bearing flies and lead to scarring of the cornea and blindness if untreated. More common in underdeveloped countries, they can be controlled, when possible, by keeping a child's eyes clear of flies and, in the case of river blindness, using the medications ivermectin and amocarzine to kill the parasites that damage vision (Smith & Luckasson, 1995). Sexually contracted and transmitted infections such as the AIDS virus, chlamydia, and gonorrhea can be passed from a mother to her neonate. Modification of delivery procedures or, in cases of chlamydia or gonorrhea, application of topical ointments can prevent damage if the infection is diagnosed soon enough. Finally, *poisoning* can occur as a result of excessive amounts of oxygen administered to some premature infants in an attempt to keep them alive. The resulting condition, called retinopathy of prematurity (ROP), causes damage to the retina and can range from mild impairment to blindness.

## Refractive Problems

Beginning with refractive problems, we will highlight the more commonly occurring conditions that affect vision. Refraction is the ability of the eye to focus light rays on the retina. Several visual conditions can be classified as refractive disorders. For the purposes of this section we have classified hyperopia, myopia, astigmatisms, cataracts, and ocular albinism as refractive disorders.

*Hyperopia*, most commonly known as farsightedness, results from the failure of the cornea and the lens of the eye to focus light appropriately and allows the individual to focus on objects at a distance but not when they are close. *Myopia*, or nearsightedness, is similar, except in this condition the individual can focus on objects that are close but not at a distance. *Astigmatisms* result in blurred vision. They are caused by an uneven curve of the cornea or lens of the eye. This produces images on the retina that are not equally in focus. Astigmatisms occur frequently and are almost always correctable with surgery or corrective glasses. They are a serious problem and, if undetected or uncorrected, can lead to visual and educational difficulties. *Cataracts* occur when the lens becomes clouded and vision is masked. The opacity of the lens can cause severe visual loss. Surgical procedures are usually the major course of treatment. *Ocular albinism*, also called *aniridia*, is characterized by a lack of color in the iris of the eye. This leads to extreme sensitivity to light, reduced visual acuity, and sometimes nystagmus (defined in a following section). Color vision may also be impaired. Aside from the modifications needed in the classroom and the use of light reducing lenses, this condition is often not an educational problem of real consequence (Ashley & Cates, 1992).

## Retinal and Optic Nerve Problems

There are numerous conditions of the retina and optic nerve that have serious consequences on vision and, in turn, on education. The following is only a partial listing and definition of the most commonly occurring retinal and optic nerve problems. The most common retinal and optic nerve disorders are *retinal degeneration* and *retinal detachment*. Retinal degeneration can be the result of infection or it may be inherited. Often, the underlying cause of the deterioration is unknown. This is a particularly difficult condition because there is no widely accepted treatment and the rate of degeneration is often uncontrollable. Children with retinal degeneration are usually enrolled in special educational placements as soon as the condition is diagnosed (Caton, 1993). A similar but somewhat less devastating condition is *macular degeneration*, a condition that causes the macula, a small area near the center of the retina, to gradually deteriorate. A result is that peripheral vision is retained while central vision is lost, causing difficulties in writing and reading. Fortunately, macular degeneration is rare in children (Heward, 1996). Retinal detachments occur when the retina becomes separated from the outer layers of the eye tissue. This condition causes interruption in the transmission of visual signals for the brain to interpret. This condition, when correctly diagnosed, can often be repaired surgically. *Retinitis pigmentosa* is a hereditary disorder that causes degeneration of the retina and a resulting narrowing of the field of vision. It is progressive in nature and leads to eventual blindness. One of its earliest symptoms is night blindness or extreme difficulty seeing in dimly lit environments. *Coloboma* is another congenital disorder wherein the retina is malformed, resulting in both visual field and visual acuity problems. *Glaucoma* occurs when the flow of fluids in the eye is restricted. This causes pressure to build and, if untreated, can eventually sever the blood supply to the optic nerve, damaging the retina and causing blindness. The cause of glaucoma is unknown; onset may be gradual or sudden. Glaucoma can be prevented if detected early. During its earliest stages, those affected report that light bulbs and other illumination sources appear to have halos surrounding them (Thomas, 1985). *Optic nerve atrophy* or weakening will cause the optic nerve to function less efficiently and can result in reduced visual efficiency of many types, depending upon its severity. Less severe in terms of their impact on educational and social functioning are *color vision problems*. Problems at the retina can cause a person to have diminished abilities to differentiate colors. Usually these problems have little or no effect on visual acuity at all. They can cause problems at the primary level of education, where many curriculum activities revolve around color-matching tasks and the identification of learning-center materials by color. Color vision problems occur in varying degrees of severity. It is rare that a child will experience total color loss (Sacks, Rosen, & Gaylord-Ross, 1990). We have listed retrolental fibroplasia, retinoblastoma, diabetic retinopathy, and the effects of optic tumors in Figure 9.3. Each of these conditions can cause visual impairment of varying degrees of severity.

## Eye Muscle Problems

The two major eye muscle problems are *strabismus* and *nystagmus*. Strabismus is the result of improper muscle functioning that causes either or both eyes to be directed inward. When this occurs, two separate images may be sent to the visual cortex of the brain. The brain disregards one of the images sent by the affected eyes, which can lead to eventual blindness in one eye. Nystagmus is characterized by rapid, involuntary movements of the eyes, usually laterally. These movements make it difficult to focus upon objects and cause dizziness and nausea. Nystagmus is often a sign of concomitant inner ear or brain dysfunction (Hallahan & Kauffman, 1994).

## Central Vision Loss

Damage to the visual cortex, the area of the brain responsible for decoding the signals sent along the optic nerve, can lead to visual insufficiency at many different levels. It can result in figure/ground discrimination problems, an inability to distinguish items in the foreground from items in the background, which in turn makes it difficult to distinguish objects from one another. In addition, cortical visual problems usually occur with other disorders, such as cerebral palsy or epilepsy. A given child's co-existing attention span difficulties might lead to visual functioning fluctuations, making the measurement of the visual impairment a difficult task.

## IDENTIFICATION PROCESS

The most widely used institutional strategies for identifying children with visual impairments are acuity screenings and functional visual assessments. Often, these screenings and assessments are used together to obtain the information needed prior to suggesting educational placement modifications. In addition, parents, teachers, and family members should be alert for specific signs of potential visual difficulty.

## Visual Acuity Screenings

All states require that all school-age children participate in vision screening programs (Harley & Lawrence, 1984). The screening test used most often uses the Snellen chart, and is routinely administered by the school nurse or a pediatrician. The two most popular versions use the letter E presented in different sizes and placed in different positions, or alphabet letters of different sizes. The chart or sometimes a projection of the chart is placed 20 feet from the person being tested. The eight rows of symbols or letters correspond to normal vision at 15, 20, 30, 40, 50, 70, 100, and 200 feet (Smith & Luckasson, 1995). Normal visual acuity is measured by how accurately a person can see a symbol or letter at 20 feet. Thus, normal vision is 20/20. A score of 20/40 means that the person being tested can see at 20 feet what a person with normal vision can see from a distance of 40 feet away. The distance of 20 feet is used because at this distance, when light rays enter the eyes no accommodation is required of the eye to focus the rays; the eye is at rest. This is thought to give the truest measure of sharpness and clarity of vision (Caton, 1993). People with visual acuity measures between 20/70 and 20/200 in the better eye with correction are considered to have low vision. Acuity below 20/200 classifies a person as legally blind (Rogow, 1988). Referrals are usually made when children screened using the Snellen chart obtain the following results: 3-year-olds, 20/50 or less; 4-year-olds, 20/40 or less; and 5-year-olds, 20/30 or less (National Society for the Prevention of Blindness, 1990).

The Snellen chart procedure, despite its relative ease of administration and widespread use, has some limits in identification of visual impairment. Most obvious is that it measures visual acuity at a distance. Distance vision is not nearly as critical for school activities as is the near vision required for reading and other activities. The procedure also does not provide the schools with any measure or prediction about a child's ability to use sight to learn to read. Visual acuity and visual efficiency are not the same skill (Hallahan & Kauffman, 1994). Another measure of visual acuity is called contrast sensitivity. Size alone as measured by the Snellen chart procedure may not be an adequate measure of acuity. It may also be necessary to determine how well a person can see something in contrast to its background (Sacks, Rosen, & Gaylord-Ross, 1990).

## Functional Vision Assessments

Children who share similar visual impairments may utilize their residual vision in markedly different ways. Although visual acuity is certainly important, it does not in and of itself determine how well or poorly a child is going to compensate and function in his or her environment. Visual capacity, visual attention, and visual efficiency are other factors that are often considered when conducting a functional vision assessment. *Visual capacity* is in some ways an expansion of visual acuity. What can actually be seen includes acuity, the amount of usable visual field, and how the child responds to information presented visually. *Visual attention* comprises four distinct parameters:

1. *Visual alertness*, or how sensitive a child is to environmental visual stimuli.
2. *Visual selection*, which is the ability to select information from different sources.
3. *Degree of attention*, which is measured by the ability to change attention from one visual stimulus to another.
4. *Processing capability*, or the ability to make sense of visual input.

*Visual efficiency* depends on how well the individual can use instructional modifications or alternate methods that depend on auditory or tactile stimuli (Smith & Luckasson, 1995). Efficiency can be enhanced by changing seat placement, adapting materials, using specialized equipment, and modifying classroom teaching techniques.

Assessment of functional vision can be complicated with children who have not fully developed their language skills or who have multiple handicaps that make accurate assessment very challenging (Bishop, 1990). Examples of the types of test items that provide information for the functional vision assessments discussed here might be learning at what distance a child can imitate facial expressions, testing the ability to identify classmates, or even monitoring the ability to use sight to locate a cubby or personal possessions in a closet. Can the child visually track moving objects? Can he

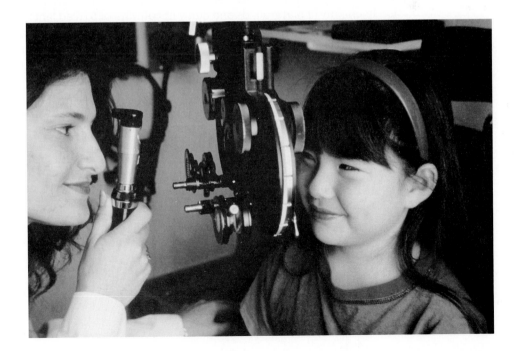

---

### Box 9.2
### *WHAT EVERY TEACHER NEEDS TO KNOW*

### *Nine Warning Signs*

Does the child exhibit:

1. Clumsiness and trouble walking in unfamiliar settings?
2. Holding the head in an awkward position or holding material close to the eyes to see it?
3. Lack of attention to written information on blackboards or other visual presentations?
4. A constant need for explanation of what is happening at events.

5. Extreme sensitivity to glare, or loss of vision in different types of light?
6. Extreme squinting?
7. Excessive eye rubbing?
8. Poking the eyes with fingers or knuckles?
9. Physical anomalies such as swollen eyes or strabismus?

*Source:* From *Handbook for Preschool Vision Screening* (p. 17), by the Kentucky Society for the Prevention of Blindness, 1990, Louisville, KY: Author.

---

or she move efficiently over different surfaces? Is the child able to visually complete puzzles? Functional evaluations also try to test the ability to use visual skills in different settings and for different activities. Different visual skills are needed to function in brightly lit playgrounds and dimly lit hallways or to read labels on cans and direction signs on walls. A well conceived assessment will enable the team working with the child and parents to make decisions about whether to use print or braille, the level of assistive services needed, and the type of educational placement required for the most optimal educational experience.

Even before the vision screenings mandated by law are conducted, parents and others in a child's environment should be alert for specific signs that suggest visual impairment. The Kentucky Society for the Prevention of Blindness (1990) lists nine signs that may be significant (Box 9.2).

The National Society for the Prevention of Blindness (1972) adds recurring styes; reports of dizziness, headaches, or nausea following close eye work; and reports of blurred or double vision to the list of potentially serious signs of visual impairment.

In summary, systematic identification processes should involve comprehensive screenings, referrals for complete evaluations, and follow-up activities to be certain that recommendations are followed (Harley & Lawrence, 1984). The usual steps in the process can be outlined as follows:

1. Parental concern about vision
2. Visual acuity screening test failure
3. Ophthalmologist determination of disorder

4.  Optometrist and low vision expert determination of whether the impairment can be corrected

5.  Functional evaluation of low vision

6.  Evaluation by an orientation and mobility specialist

7.  Intelligence testing by a school psychologist

8.  Comprehensive determination of the potential effects of the visual impairment on academic, communication, social/emotional, sensorimotor, and orientation and mobility functioning by a teacher of the visually impaired, an orientation and mobility specialist, a speech-language pathologist, and a regular education teacher

9.  Estimate of social and daily living skills needs by a teacher of the visually impaired, an orientation and mobility specialist, a daily living professional, and parents.

## PROGRAMS

Understanding educational programming for students with visual impairments requires more than simply looking at curriculum modifications. This section of the chapter will explore some introductory information about the settings and service delivery models in which educational experiences are offered to students with low vision and students who are blind, and the educational assessments beyond identification needed to construct meaningful, individually designed educational programs. Programming initiated through early intervention and preschool services, primary, secondary, and postsecondary curriculum modifications, and finally transition services in the form of adult living instruction will be discussed. The special listening, orientation, and mobility skills that are vital to independent functioning and socialization will be highlighted. No discussion of programming for people who are visually impaired can ignore the role of technology, from the use of canes to the latest computer wizardry.

The primary goal of special education for children with visual impairments is to reduce as much as possible the vision-related handicaps they experience (Caton, 1993). Although this primary goal is simple to state, implementing it for each individual with visual impairment requires a willingness to amass diagnostic information, sensitivity to children and their families, and access to the necessary facilities and equipment needed to insure success. Students who are visually impaired constitute the smallest group of children being served by the Individuals with Disabilities Act (IDEA) (U.S. Department of Education, 1997). The majority of children who are eligible for special education services have some useful vision. Students classified as having low vision account for between 75 and 80 percent of school-age children who are visually impaired (Bryan & Jeffrey, 1982). In addition, within the group more than 80 percent who are classified as blind use print as their primary way of learning. They use their residual vision to read, watch television, and function in society (Kirchner, 1988).

## Educational Settings for the Visually Impaired

There are 52 residential schools for blind students in the United States (Heward, 1996). Most of the students attending them are multiply handicapped or have visual problems that their parents are unable to handle. Some lack the necessary services in their home communities. Some are enrolled because their parents prefer the concentration of special services the residential schools can provide. It wasn't always this way. In 1940, only 10 percent of children with visual impairments were in the public schools. By 1992, 80 percent were enrolled in the public schools and 9 percent were in residential schools (American Printing House for the Blind, 1992a). The increase in children with visual impairments during the 1960s due to a rubella epidemic strained the capacity of the residential schools. At the same time, parents began to lobby for mainstream education for their children. They believed that there were many social and life skill advantages in functioning in regular classrooms, living at home, and being a more integral part of normal family life (Sacks, Rosen, & Gaylord-Ross, 1990). As a result, students with visual impairments are now enrolled in regular classrooms at their neighborhood public schools. They and their teachers receive itinerant or consultative special education services to support their regular classroom placements (Smith & Luckasson, 1995).

This migration of students has changed the role of the residential schools drastically. They now serve as statewide resource centers, providing materials and specialists to consult with regular education teachers. They are able to offer short courses and special intensive summer programs for teachers and students. Often they are responsible for maintaining all types of outreach programs designed to meet family needs. The remaining full-time educational programs for residential students characteristically maintain a "separate but equal" approach to education from kindergarten through grade 12. Their students are usually isolated from sighted children except for any classes in which the residential students may be enrolled at the local public schools (Caton, 1993). The programming at residential schools allows for a concentration of specialized services, such as orientation, mobility, and independent living skills training managed by on-site specialists. A current issue of importance is whether these special services outweigh the benefits of inclusion in regular schools. This issue is more fully discussed in the "Issues of Importance" section of this chapter.

Local schools operate under some combination of the following five plans to provide an educational setting for children with visual impairments. The first plan is the *special class plan*, sometimes called the *self-contained classroom*. In this setting, students are housed in a special classroom and receive most instruction there. There may be some non-academic integration, but it is not usually the practice to provide academic integration with sighted children. This setting is most appropriate for children with multiple disabilities who are not able to benefit from regular education classes. The second plan is known as the *cooperative class plan*. In this rarely used plan, the children are grouped into a visually impaired class and divide their time between the special class and the regular classroom for academic subjects. Most nonacademic experiences are with regular educators. The third plan is the *resource room setting*. Children with visual impairments are placed in regular education settings and leave them to go to a resource room for special help in academic areas in which they are having difficulty. Thus, they spend most of their time in the regular classroom, leaving only when it is necessary. The fourth plan is the *itinerant teacher plan*. Students are housed in a regular classroom, and a specially trained teacher who serves several schools provides special instructions and materials. The fifth plan, the *teacher-consultant plan*, is similar to the itinerant plan except that with the teacher-consultant plan, the itinerant specially trained teacher works with regular teachers and other school personnel rather than directly with the children (Caton, 1993).

In practice, schools employ combinations of the plans described, varying the setting depending on the needs of the child and the resources available to the school district. Placement decisions are always made by IEP committees, who use the data from eye examinations and medical, developmental, social history, and behavioral reports provided by parents, teachers, and other appropriate specialists. These plans and settings change as the child changes and becomes more independent, needing fewer special services.

The settings for preschoolers and toddlers can be center based in self-contained classrooms or in other locations where children with visual impairments can be integrated into play and other activities with sighted peers. Early intervention services are usually home based, with itinerant specialists providing information and programs for parents and children in the home (Hatlen, 1980; Sacks, Rosen, & Gaylord-Ross, 1990).

## Educational Assessments

Once a setting is determined, a plan must be developed to guide professionals and parents. The identification process described previously has determined that the child has visual impairments and possibly has assessed how the child uses his or her residual sight to learn. Now the task is to determine what, if any, special educational experiences the child requires. Educational assessments help determine what special services are needed. They can be based on a given student's specific needs in academic skills, communication skills, social/emotional skills, sensory/motor skills, orientation and mobility skills, daily-living skills, or career and vocational skills. Figure 9.4 is a listing of the needs that children with visual impairment might have in each of the areas just mentioned.

As an IEP team comprising professionals and parents evaluates each of these areas, a plan will evolve to meet the individual needs of each child. Lewis (1995) believes that the school evaluation team should minimally consist of a school psychologist, a speech-language pathologist, an orientation and mobility specialist, and a teacher of students with visual impairments. Specific characteristics displayed by any given child might also call for the inclusion of an occupational therapist, a behavior specialist, an audiologist, a low vision specialist, or a physical therapist, among others on the evaluation and planning team. Parents, caretakers, and other family members form the vital nonprofessional part of the team.

Each professional will use assessment tools specific to his or her specialty area. In general, the assessment tools will be either specially designed for the student who is visually impaired, adapted for the student's needs, or used in their original form with no accommodation for the visual impairment (Caton, 1993). Assessment tools

**Concept Development and Academic Skills**
- Maximum use of vision
- Development of concepts
- Determination of learning mode
- Academic support
- Listening skills
- Organization and study skills
- Reading charts, maps, graphs
- Use of reference materials

**Communication Skills**
- Handwriting
- Development of legal signature
- Use of braille writer
- Use of slate and stylus
- Use of word processors
- Use of adaptive equipment
- Note-taking skills

**Social/Emotional Skills**
- Knowledge of self
- Knowledge of human sexuality
- Knowledge of visual impairment
- Knowledge of others
- Development of interaction skills
- Development of social skills
- Lifelong recreation and leisure skills
- Self-advocacy skills

**Sensory/Motor Skills**
- Development of gross motor skills
- Development of fine motor skills
- Development of strength, stamina, and endurance in legs, arms, hands
- Identification of textures tactually and underfoot
- Identification of kinesthetic sources
- Identification of olfactory sources

**Orientation and Mobility Skills**
- Development of body image
- Development of concrete environmental concepts
- Development of spatial concepts
- Development of directional concepts
- Understanding traffic and traffic control
- Trailing techniques
- Sighted guide techniques
- Use of vision for travel and orientation
- Development of orientation skills
- Use of long cane
- Independent travel in a variety of environments
- Public interaction skills

**Daily Living Skills**
- Personal hygiene
- Eating
- Dressing
- Clothing care
- Food preparation
- Housekeeping
- Basic home repair
- Money identification and management
- Use of telephone and information
- Use of desk tools
- Time and calendar activities
- Shopping skills
- Restaurant skills
- Community skills
- Knowledge and use of community services

**Career and Vocational Skills**
- Knowledge of relationship between work and play
- Understanding of value of work
- Knowledge of characteristics of valued workers
- Awareness of the variety of jobs people hold
- Awareness of jobs people with visual impairments often hold
- Awareness of jobs teenagers hold
- Job acquisition skills (want ads, resumes, applications, interviews)

- Typical job adaptations made by workers with visual impairments
- In-depth knowledge of a variety of jobs of interest
- Work experience
- Laws related to employment
- Management of readers, drivers

Source: From *Exceptional Lives: Special Education in Today's Schools* (p. 614), by A. P. Turnbull, H. R. Turnbull, M. Shank, and D. Leal, 1995, Upper Saddle River, NJ: Prentice-Hall/Merrill. Reprinted by permission of Prentice-Hall, Inc.

Figure 9.4
Potential Unique Needs of Students with Visual Impairments

designed specifically for young children with visual impairments include tests such as the Maxfield-Bucholz Social Maturity Scale for Blind Preschool Children (Maxfield & Bucholz, 1957); the Reynell-Zinkin Scales, which is a parent observation protocol (Reynell, 1983); the Mangold Developmental Program of Tactile Perception and Braille Letter Recognition (Mangold, 1977); and the Revised Peabody Mobility Scale (Harley, Wood, & Merbler, 1981).

Other factors considered during the educational assessment include the etiology of the impairment, since some conditions require a special setting or modifications such as bright lighting or highly contrasted print; whether the condition is degenerative and will eventually lead to blindness and a reliance on braille; and the age of onset of the condition, so that teachers will know how much sight memory the child may have (Caton, 1993).

## Curricular Modifications and Special Programming

Once the educational assessment is completed, teachers and other specialists can begin to help children and their parents by implementing the plan they have cooperated in conceiving. While each child may have different needs, no one child is so different that his or her needs cannot be anticipated and provided for with either curricular modifications or special programming. In addition, the degree of impairment will also dictate the level and intensity of programming. Regardless of their classification, all children with visual impairments share the same goals. They need to learn to read, write, and move about in their environment. The degree of visual impairment doesn't change this need; it only structures how children, their parents, and their teachers go about accomplishing these goals.

The most dramatic change has been in how children with low vision are being educated. Most educators credit Barraga (1964, 1970, 1980, 1983) with changing the basic philosophy and implementation of intervention strategies for children with low vision. Prior to her work, "sight conservation classes" were the norm for children with visual impairment. These classes were designed to help the children preserve their sight, as if it were a limited commodity that could be exhausted if not used sparingly. Barraga demonstrated that children with low vision should be helped to use their vision in a proactive way. For most of the children, this meant getting the maximum use of their residual vision rather than attempting to ration it. The children needed to be taught how to get information directly from visual experiences. They also needed to learn to appreciate visual input and use their vision when planning and carrying out tasks (Corn, 1989).

## Early Intervention

Special services begin with early intervention. There are valid reasons to begin to offer early assistance to families that go beyond kindness. Failure to provide experiences and information early in the life of a child with visual impairment can complicate all the attempts to achieve normal functioning that follow. Primary behaviors such as crawling and early socialization may be delayed, due to a lack of motivation that is innate to sighted children. Infants and toddlers with visual impairment explore close to their bodies and need to be stimulated to reach beyond themselves (Fraiberg, 1977). It is also critical to prevent secondary disabilities from developing. These problems are not automatically part of visual impairment, but can be the result of failure to compensate for visual deficits. Examples might be the failure of infants to bond with parents, delays in ear and hand coordination, or the development of inappropriate self-stimulating behaviors (Ferrell, 1986). Parents are critical in early intervention programs. They often need support in physically managing the child and in understanding the extra effort that will be required to provide needed experiences, from early socialization to providing games that help in all types of exploration. The line between overprotection, which disables a child's development, and poor judgment, which places a child in danger, must be constantly redrawn. The fears that all parents feel for their children are magnified when visual impairment may be seen as preventing the most primary of self-protective behaviors from developing.

## Preschool Programs

Preschool programs in both the home and the center continue the work begun with early intervention. In the best of circumstances, preschool programs are staffed by a teacher of students who are visually impaired, an orientation and mobility specialist, a speech-language pathologist, an occupational therapist, and/or a physical therapist. All these professionals should be available to parents and encourage their involvement in the preschool activities (Sacks, Rosen, & Gaylord-Ross, 1990). A goal of preschool programs is to help children develop the skills needed to transfer successfully from the home to the school setting. Very often, preschool activities are practice for the behavior that will be necessary at school. They can be as specific as drill in language and listening skills, preacademics, initial literacy skills, and fine and gross motor play. They might deal with utilization of residual vision for mobility or for planning and executing tasks. At times, socialization, confidence building, and independence fostering activities are appropriate. Preschool programs might also introduce unfamiliar assistive technology that will later aid in learning. As with early intervention programs, preschool programs focus on continuing to support families in their efforts to rear children in the most positive environment possible. Through these programs and the experiences, support, and counseling they offer, children will develop and gain a strong sense of themselves and their capabilities (Smith & Luckasson, 1995).

## Reading and Writing

Once school formally begins, the program emphasis shifts to the reading, writing, and listening skills necessary to learn. The social emphasis is on the development of peer relationships and friendships. Orientation and mobility skills are now needed as much as ever to help navigate the school setting as well as the after school environment (Lewis, 1995). Reading and writing skills have traditionally been presented with some combination of modified type size and braille.

*Braille* uses a coded system of raised dots to represent letters, words, numbers, special contractions, and codes for different types of reading. This system was developed in 1829 by Louis Braille, who was blind. Braille is a fairly complicated system to learn and takes a good deal of practice to master. Training in braille with a teacher of students who are visually impaired usually begins during kindergarten (Sacks, Rosen, & Gaylord-Ross, 1990). Writing in braille requires the use of a *slate* and *stylus*. The slate is a metal frame that holds paper in the appropriate position while the stylus, a pen-like device, punches the code onto the paper held on the slate. A *brailler* or *braillewriter* can also be used to write in braille. The braillewriter is a six-key machine that embosses braille dots onto paper in the coded form or cells necessary to spell in braille. Writing in braille requires the manual dexterity that is usually developed by the fifth grade (Sacks & Rosen, 1990). Microcomputers have also been developed that can print and translate regular print into braille. Using braille is a comparatively slow process. The average blind high school student can read only 86 to 90 words per minute in braille (Nolan, 1967). It was once the primary system of literacy for the blind (Heward, 1996); however, braille is now less popular than in the past. In 1963, more than 50 percent of students who were severely visually impaired used braille to read and write. In 1978, the figure had dropped to 20 percent; by 1992 only 10 percent of students who were blind relied on braille (American Printing House for the Blind, 1992).

*Modified type size* is the other major alternative for developing literacy skills. Figure 9.5 provides some examples of different sizes of type. The goal with large type is to use the smallest magnification that will be useful and then try to transfer to normal-size type as the child matures (Heward, 1996).

All modification systems have advantages and disadvantages: large type is easy to use, funds are available to get books and materials, and the materials themselves are not particularly delicate and are sometimes easy to carry. The problems include the following: magnification often distorts printed material; when photocopies are used to magnify print, the material is usually limited only to black-and-white reproductions; and despite their portability, large-type books often become unwieldy and difficult to manage. The most serious drawback is the limited availability of large-type works after the school years. People who rely only on large type run the risk of becoming nonfunctional readers (Heward, 1996). Audiocassette versions of material and personal readers are also available but limited options. For some, minor modifications such as book placement or special lighting enable the use of normal print for learning. Regardless of the method, many students have difficulty learning to read. It can be a fatiguing process and they often require more practice, more drill, and more repetition than their sighted peers (Harley, Truan, & Sanford, 1987). It is a challenge for teachers to provide these experiences without overusing any one type of drill. Troubling statistics released by the American Printing House for the Blind (1992) reveal that 22 percent of the population sampled were considered at the prereading level and 31 percent were considered nonreaders. These low literacy figures are used to support the wishes of those who want to reinstill the use of braille. The debate about bringing braille back into the mainstream will be more fully discussed in the "Issues of Importance" section of this chapter.

Students with visual impairments must rely on auditory (listening) skills as well as tactile skills in their attempts to compensate for the information they might miss

This is an example of 12 point type.
AN UPPERCASE SAMPLE.
A lowercase sample.

This is an example of 14 point type.
AN UPPERCASE SAMPLE.
A lowercase sample.

This is an example of 18 point type.
AN UPPERCASE SAMPLE.
A lowercase sample.

This is an example of 24 point type.
AN UPPERCASE SAMPLE.
A lowercase sample.

This is 36 point type.
AN UPPERCASE SAMPLE.
A lowercase sample.

**Figure 9.5**
Examples of Different Sizes of Type Fonts

visually. Listening skills do not develop automatically, and are becoming more and more critical as the availability of recorded material is increasing. Smith (1972) divides listening skills into five categories: attentive, analytic, marginal, appreciative, and selective. *Attentive listening* takes place when the listener focuses on one form or source of communication. Telephone use requires attentive listening, as does following directions. *Analytic listening* requires that the listener not only listen but also prepare to analyze or interpret the information received. Asking a child to explain what the author meant by a "slippery character" in a story means the child must not only attend to the story but also interpret the author's intent. *Appreciative listening* occurs when listening purely for the sake of enjoyment. *Marginal listening* takes place when the auditory signal is part of the background and not a primary part of activity. Background music in a restaurant during a conversation requires marginal listening. *Selective listening*, on the other hand, requires focusing on one signal and disregarding others. Selective listening for a person with visual impairment takes place when he or she ignores the background music on an elevator and listens for the chimes that announce the number of each floor. Listening skills need to be a part of the curriculum for the visually impaired. An understanding of the type of listening required for the various situations the child will encounter can guide the teacher in structuring learning experiences that will hone the needed auditory skills.

Developing peer relationships for many students who are visually impaired does not occur without some parental or teacher help (Sacks, 1992b). Informal interactions are particularly difficult to initiate. These interactions, which usually occur during lunch, physical education, or recess periods are often visually and auditorally confusing for the child who is visually impaired. Quite often, such interactions emphasize the child's weaknesses, such as shooting a basketball or playing tag. Teacher-initiated activities that call for pairing allow for social- as well as task-related conversations. One-to-one interactions are always easier than group interactions. It is important for teachers and parents to attempt to keep the skills needed to complete a task balanced so that the sighted child is not always the leader. Peer interactions with other children who are visually impaired are often helpful because they can provide a forum for sharing experiences (Lewis, 1995).

## Orientation and Mobility Training

Orientation and mobility skills allow students with visual impairments to move about in their environment and interact within it for many types of learning and for socialization, concept development, and independence (Caton, 1993). The special instruction necessary is intensified during the primary school years. In addition to using residual sight to its maximum extent, there are essentially four aids to help in establishing mobility: long canes, guide dogs, human guides, and electronic devices. The long cane or *Hoover cane* was developed by Richard Hoover in 1944. This long white cane is swept in front of you touching the ground lightly, as you walk. Users get cues by echo and tactile feedback about uneven surfaces, holes, stairways, and other barriers. The cane is reliable, with no batteries or moving parts to fail. However, its efficient use does not occur without training. The traditional approach of waiting until school age to train users is being reconsidered. A more current view suggests that its use be implemented as soon as a child begins to walk independently (Skellenger & Hill, 1991). Cane sizes and other modifications need to be employed with some youngsters. *Guide dogs* are not recommended very often for school-age children. The size of the dogs, their relatively fast walking pace, and their need for care are drawbacks for young people. However, they do provide faster reactions to potential danger

than do walking canes. *Human guides* provide the greatest freedom of movement. However, dependence on human guides is not practical in most cases. In addition, some feel that the use of human guides can disrupt or retard the development of orientation and mobility skills (Hallahan & Kauffman, 1994). *Electronic devices* may be the wave of the future for enhancing orientation and mobility. Many that are currently available are both expensive and experimental in nature. Typically they use some form of laser beam or sonic wave to provide feedback. Orientation and mobility training is a well-developed specialty taught by orientation and mobility specialists, described in the "Professionals" section of this chapter.

## Daily Living Skills

Daily living skills such as eating, bathing, dressing, and toileting are not usually taught in the school setting but rather at home. For sighted children, many of these skills are acquired by observation and incidental learning. However, they require special effort during home teaching with as much assistance as parents need for those with visual impairments (Caton, 1993). Acquisition of skills is monitored by teachers and reported to the parents and the educational team if intervention is necessary. When failure to acquire daily living skills occurs, the responsibility falls to the schools and more specifically the teacher of students who are visually impaired to teach them (Hatlen & Curry, 1987). Obviously, daily living skills are needed in the classroom as well as at home. Programs and curriculum guides, such as the Texas School for the

Blind's Living Skills Curriculum (Loumiet & Levack, 1991) help teachers and parents in developing and maintaining appropriate living skills.

## Middle and Secondary Schools

Middle and secondary school experiences follow the guidelines established during the primary years. However, there may need to be greater emphasis on experiences that will reinforce self-confidence and self-esteem. The learning process should parallel that of normal sighted students, using whatever accommodations are needed to master the information presented. Special curricular packages such as MAVIS (Materials Adaptation for Students with Visual Impairments in the Social Studies) and SAVI (Science Activities for the Visually Impaired) are available to assist teachers and can be obtained from agencies, residential school libraries, or itinerant teachers.

Since the majority of students who are visually impaired are placed in regular classroom settings, many suggestions are available to help the regular classroom teacher be as effective as possible in reaching these students with as little disruption in teaching style as possible. For example, all students learn better when given previews of information that will be presented. All are helped by advanced organizers such as highlighting critical vocabulary, giving appropriate background information, and presenting outlines of information to be presented (Deshler, Warner, Schumaker, & Alley, 1983; Lenz, Alley, & Schumaker, 1987). Students with low vision benefit from teacher attempts to use descriptive oral language, rather than speech that refers to visually based material. For example, a teacher who says, "Look at the number next to the letter I have written on the board," would be more effective if she said, "Look at the number 4 next to the letter A that I have written on the board." The habitual reading aloud of information on blackboards and overheads will not disrupt class teaching, but it will help a student with visual impairment. Large type overheads and handouts, when possible, will also help yet not disrupt regular classroom activity. Sometimes special actions such as giving written copies of orally presented material and audiotaping lectures may be necessary (Smith & Luckasson, 1995).

Students who are blind can be accommodated in regular classrooms with minor modifications. Suggestions from experts (Barraga & Morris, 1980; Harley et al., 1987; Sacks & Kekelis, 1992; Sacks & Reardon, 1992) range from making certain that the student is seated close to the teacher's desk, blackboard, and door to explaining the social rules of the classroom to the child as often as it is necessary. Providing adequate lighting and space necessary for special equipment and making the classroom as obstacle free as possible will also enhance the learning environment. Simple rules such as opening and closing all doors fully, placing materials in consistent places, and keeping distracting noises to a minimum will also reduce the amount of time needed to care for the needs of the student who is blind. Routinely checking with students to find out whether their classroom needs are being met will often short-circuit problems before they can develop. Specialists and consultants are almost always available to share the concerns of students and their teachers and assist in solving problems.

## Transition to Independent Living

The transition from the educational system to independent living is also a critical time in the life of a person with visual impairment. Some educators, like Hatlen (1976, 1978) are concerned that there is too much emphasis on providing academic skills and too little on living skills such as cooking, shopping, financial management, decision making, personal hygiene, social behavior, and recreational activities. The process of obtaining needed services itself is complicated. Despite the low incidence of visual handicaps, more than 1,000 agencies provide services and programs in the United States alone (Heward, 1996). Accessing these programs and obtaining eligibility to use their services can be an educational experience in and of itself. Winer (1978) suggests that people who are blind should take courses in how to access the services of the variety of programs available to them. Career counseling is needed to help people with visual handicaps become a productive part of the workforce. Only 30 percent of adults with visual impairments and no other complicating condition are employed in competitive settings. Many others are underemployed, working at jobs below their skill levels (Kirchner & Peterson, 1989). It appears obvious that some guidance is needed to help people with visual impairments make the transition from the sheltered school environment to independent adult living. A relatively new professional called a *transitional living specialist* is becoming available to help with this process. A description of this specialist's role appears in the "Professionals" section later in this chapter.

## Technology

Including technology as a subheading of programming is merely a convenient way to provide the information. Technology does not exist in a vacuum but rather attempts to provide better ways to accomplish the goals previously listed. Identifying aids to mobility, daily living, information accessing, and recreation will be the focus of this section of the chapter.

Probably the most simple and effective aid to mobility is the Hoover cane, previously discussed in this chapter. High-tech offshoots of the basic cane are devices like the Mowat Sensor (Hill, 1986) and the Sonic Guide, produced by Wormald International Sensory Aids (1979). Both of these aids provide electronic feedback to the user about their distance from objects and other spatial information. Daily living can be made easier by devices like the Note Teller ("Talking Wallet," 1992), which will identify the denomination of paper money, or the Personal Companion, which will access and dial phone numbers, keep an appointment schedule, and even turn appliances on and off (Feinsilber, 1989).

Technology has made its most important contributions in the area of information transmission for educational and recreational purposes. Tactile, auditory, and visual enhancing aids, as either independent devices or parts of microcomputers, provide access to the printed information vital to functioning in our society. The Optacon (*opt*ical to *tac*tile *con*verter) consists of a hand held scanner that when passed over printed material will convert the print into tactile letters that can be felt on the fingers of the hand. The Optacon II scans computer screens and provides similar tactile translations. These devices are easily portable. However, they tend to work slowly and are expensive to purchase (Hallahan & Kauffman, 1994). The Kurzweil Reader, first produced in 1975 and updated and improved since then, converts print into synthesized speech. The Xerox/Kurzweil Reader PC, the latest improvement, also produces voice when a scanner moves over a line of type. The rate of speech and the gender of the voice are programmable. An obvious advantage for students using this device is that they can use the same materials as their classmates without waiting for special versions. The downside is that exclusive use of this or similar devices can have a negative impact on reading skills or the desire to improve them. The current price for the PC/Reader is about $4,000. For braille readers, the VersaBraille saves time and space by converting braille onto tape cassettes, then replaying those tapes onto the machine's reading board. The VersaBraille II+ (4 Telesensory Systems Inc.) is a portable laptop on which students can take notes, complete tests, or prepare papers. It can print in braille or conventional type. This enables more rapid communication with teachers not proficient in braille. The VersaBraille II+ can also be connected to talking word processors to obtain printed information (Heward, 1996). Closed circuit television (CCTV) is being used to enlarge print size and broadcast it onto a television screen for almost instant access to printed materials (Holbrook & Healy, 1994).

Less sophisticated but most highly used are *talking books*. Available since 1934, these recordings are readings of a large catalog of books of many types. In their latest form they allow for speech compression, which in turn allows greater amounts of

information to be transmitted in shorter periods of time (Smith & Luckasson, 1995). A service that parallels captioning for people who are deaf called *audiodescription* is now available for making television, plays, and movies more understandable for people who are visually impaired (Cronin & King, 1990). Descriptive Video Services of Boston (Telability Media, 1992), developed by WGBH, the National Public Radio station in Boston, provides a narration about television shows, plays, and movies that fills in the information missing when listening to the soundtracks alone. It provides descriptions of costumes, scenes, actors' body language, and other critical visual information. The narration is provided during silences in the action.

The future of technology is constrained only by the cost of the devices and the ability of those who need them to select the appropriate equipment. Currently, these are formidable drawbacks. Financial resources are limited for many people with visual impairments, and it is not clear whether social service agencies are responsible for providing and upgrading the latest in technology at the expense of the public. Providing services and programs is not a cut-and-dried science. Many controversies exist, and attempts are always being made to improve services. The next section of this chapter will highlight some of these issues.

## ISSUES OF IMPORTANCE

The four issues discussed in this section are not the only issues of importance. However, they represent major concerns of educators, parents, and people who are visually impaired. Doubts have arisen about whether or not full inclusion in the public schools is truly the least restrictive environment. Some feel that a return to the residential school concept might be more effective. The decline in literacy that has accompanied the rejection of braille has led to a backlash and the proposal of the so-called Braille Bills, which call for increased availability of braille for people who are visually impaired. The sexual information deficits and vulnerability that seem to accompany visual impairments are the third issue to be highlighted. Finally, technological advances are both exciting and expensive; the issue is who is responsible for paying for the new technology.

### Inclusion

The movement of students with visual impairments from residential to public schools was discussed in the previous section. It was a time of optimism. Educators hoped that the isolation imposed by the segregation of students who were visually impaired would evaporate as they became a more integrated part of the regular education system and a more functional part of their own families. However, despite the obvious advantages of family and educational integration, many educators are voicing concerns that the graduates of regular school systems do not attain the skills needed for independent living. They are concerned that children who are visually impaired need direct, intensive special instruction in social skills, use of assistive technology, career education, leisure education, braille, and orientation and mobility, which are not a part of the regular curriculum (Curry & Hatlen, 1988; Sacks, Kekelis, & Gaylord-Ross, 1992). Sacks (1992a) reports that even though students with visual impairments have spent their entire academic careers with sighted peers, they are still socially isolated and academically limited. Physical proximity does not automatically ensure that social and living skills will be met. Sacks believes that the current practices might even be more restrictive for students who are visually impaired. Some, like Silverstein (1985), are advocating that centers or residential schools might be the best placement for children with moderate and severe visual problems. Silverstein feels this is especially true for those living in rural areas, who may not have access to the special services they require. Other educators take a more conciliatory view (Turnbull et al., 1995), refusing to select one placement over another and voicing the opinion that a student's needs should dictate placement. Representatives from eight North American associations concerned about this issue formed a Joint Organizational Committee (1993) and issued the position paper reprinted in Figure 9.6.

Although the viewpoints presented in Figure 9.6 are well conceived and motivated, there is little data available to support any of the recommendations about which settings are most successful (Kirk et al., 1993). Harrell & Curry (1987) report that there is no compelling evidence that integrated programs are of more benefit than the segregated residential programs that offer only limited and carefully planned opportunities to interact with nondisabled peers. Until more persuasive, data based arguments can be presented, this issue will remain unresolved.

## Back to Braille

One of the side effects of the work of Barraga (1964) that placed more of an emphasis on the use of residual vision was a decrease in tactile learning. Children whose level of impairment falls between low vision and blindness are in danger of becoming functionally illiterate, unable to read print, and untutored in braille (Caton, 1993). The use of braille is in decline. It is not being taught in the public schools, where other methods to access information (electronic books, closed circuit television, audio aids) are preferred. Along with the decline in the use of braille, a parallel decline in the literacy capabilities of students with visual impairments has occurred (Smith & Luckasson, 1995). Previously quoted statistics from the American Printing House for the Blind indicate that 53 percent of people with visual impairments polled were nonreaders (1992). A reaction to this disturbing trend is an increasing debate over returning to more of a reliance on braille for literacy skills (de Witt, 1991). Advocates feel that braille readers have advantages over those who rely on current technology in that they can skim read, take notes, and financially afford the system. Twenty-two states have either passed or are considering implementing "Braille Bills" (Schroeder, 1993). These legislative initiatives do not mandate the use of braille. Rather, they stress that students not be denied the opportunity to learn braille or to have braille learning made part of their IEPs. The two major components of most bills are that braille is to be available for students if any members of the IEP team, including parents, feel that it is indicated, and that teachers of students with visual impairments be proficient in braille (Hallahan & Kauffman, 1994).

**STATEMENT BY THE JOINT
ORGANIZATIONAL EFFORT**

"Full inclusion," a philosophical concept currently advanced by a number of educators, is not a federal requirement of special education law. Proponents of "full inclusion" nevertheless take the position that all students with disabilities must receive their total instruction in the regular public school classroom regardless of individual needs. Unfortunately, "full inclusion" would eliminate all special placements, including "pull out" services, resource rooms and specialized schools. Such an arrangement would be seriously detrimental to the educational development of many students with disabilities.

We, the national organizations of and for the blind listed below are firmly committed to appropriate educational opportunities designed to provide students with the competencies necessary to ensure full participation in society. It is significant to recognize that our field was the first to develop a broad range of special education options beginning with specialized schools as early as 1829, and extending to public school programs since 1900. These options have provided critically important educational preparation for several generations of highly successful and independent blind people. Based on this long and impressive record of success in making optimal use of both special and public school programs to meet the diverse needs of blind students, we strongly agree upon the following:

- If provided with timely and adequate specialized services by appropriately certified teachers, students who are blind or visually impaired can develop skills that will enable them to achieve success and independence as responsible citizens in a fully integrated society. If these students do not receive appropriate instruction designed to develop competencies that meet the sensory deficits of blindness and low vision, critical learning opportunities will be lost, thus diminishing the potential for future accomplishments. In this context, ample opportunities for instruction in such areas as braille, abacus, orientation and mobility, and use of prescribed optical devices must be made available to students, as needed.
- Educational decisions must be made on a case by case basis consistent with the Individuals with Disabilities Education Act (IDEA) which guarantees a Free Appropriate Public Education in the "Least Restrictive Environment" (LRE) from among a "Full Continuum of Alternative Placements," based on the Individual Education Plan for each student. Educational decisions should not be made simply on the basis of philosophy, limited school budgets, administrative convenience, or concerns about socialization.
- Full inclusion in regular education classrooms for all students with disabilities irrespective of individual needs is in sharp conflict with procedural guarantees of IDEA.
- Least Restrictive Environment and Full Continuum of Alternative Placements are critically important IDEA

**Figure** 9.6
Making a Difference

## Sexuality

Sex education and vulnerability to sexual assault are critical issues for people with visual impairments and those interested in their welfare. Children with visual impairments often mature with serious misconceptions and knowledge gaps about sex in general and reproduction in particular (Heward, 1996). Parents and teachers are uncomfortable giving information, and modesty makes getting information by touch impractical. Heward reports that in some European countries, live human models are used to familiarize students who are blind with anatomy. This is not a common practice in the United States. The visually impaired not only need information about the social and emotional aspects of sexuality, but they also need information about the genetic transmission of visual impairments. Sexual safety is also a concern in what appears to be an increasingly hostile sexual environment, where AIDS and other sexually transmitted diseases are occurring in what some consider to be epidemic proportions. The vulnerability to sexual assault, especially for women who are visually provisions. LRE is not one sole physical location. It is, rather, a principle, which if properly applied, matches the need of the student with an appropriate school setting which provides meaningful challenges, realistic expectations, and maximum opportunities for achievement and development of healthy self-esteem.

- The regular education classroom may be considered the LRE if the student possesses sufficient readiness and survival skills and can be provided adequate supports, specialized services (from personnel trained in education of the visually impaired), and opportunities to develop skills commensurate with his or her potential. Extreme caution must be exercised so that full inclusion does not result in "full submersion," social isolation, "lowered" self-esteem, poor performance, or a setting in which services are unavailable.

- In cases where the needs of the student cannot be met in the regular classrooms, an alternative education must be provided and be recognized as the LRE for that particular student. Such alternative placements should not be negatively viewed as discriminatory or as "segregated" settings when legitimately warranted to develop the needed skills for future integration in school and society.

- Since it has been clearly demonstrated that blind children benefit from interacting with disabled and non-disabled children, both interaction opportunities should be fully encouraged in whatever setting that is considered appropriate. We believe that the mandate in IDEA which states that "to the maximum extent appropriate, children with disabilities [should be] educated with children who are nondisabled," does not intend that blind children avoid interaction with each other.

We strongly urge that decision makers carefully consider and be sensitive to the impact of reform initiatives on the education of students with visual disabilities. Caution must be exercised to insure that educational philosophy and trends such as full inclusion do not seriously endanger appropriate and specialized services for students who are blind or visually impaired. If properly implemented, IDEA can provide legal safeguards to insure that all individual children can realize their full potential for independence and success.

**AMERICAN COUNCIL OF THE BLIND**
**AMERICAN FOUNDATION FOR THE BLIND**
**ASSOCIATION FOR EDUCATION AND REHABILITATION OF THE BLIND AND VISUALLY IMPAIRED**
**BLINDED VETERANS ASSOCIATION**
**CANADIAN COUNCIL OF THE BLIND**
**CANADIAN NATIONAL INSTITUTE FOR THE BLIND**
**NATIONAL FEDERATION OF THE BLIND**
**NATIONAL LIBRARY SERVICE FOR THE BLIND AND PHYSICALLY HANDICAPPED**

Source: Joint Organizational Committee, *Full Inclusion of Students Who Are Blind or Visually Impaired: A Position Statement*, Author, 1993.

impaired, should also be of concern. Pava (1994) reports survey results that indicate that 1 of 3 respondents had been targets of either attempted or actual sexual assault. Pava, Bateman, Appleton, and Glascock (1991) have developed a rape prevention and self-defense curriculum for women with visual impairments.

Privacy, morality, religious beliefs, community standards, and a host of other societal concerns and taboos make it difficult to implement any standardized policies or guidelines for sexuality and people who are visually impaired. The difficulty in coping with the area does not lessen its priority or necessity for attention.

## Responsibility for Providing Needed Technology

The marvels of technology that are becoming available for people with visual impairments come with a curse for many who need them. The costs of these devices and aids are often beyond the means of the families that need them most. Although some agencies and community charitable organizations will help in providing needed equipment, most costs still fall on the individual or his or her family. Some equipment can be loaned only during the school year and must be returned during school breaks or permanently at graduation. Finding out about new equipment and choosing wisely among options is a task that requires technological sophistication that is not readily available to most families. Even equipment that is obtained needs to be repaired or upgraded often, as it rapidly becomes obsolete. The question is a simple one: Who should pay for equipment that will enhance the lives of people who are visually impaired when they cannot afford to buy their own equipment? The answer is a jumble of reasons why specific agencies and institution cannot be responsible. State educational institutions simply don't have the funds. The Individuals with Disabilities Education Act (IDEA) does not automatically provide the money. Some feel it should; others feel it should not. Even when charitable organizations can purchase equipment initially, they cannot afford to maintain it or routinely replace it. The more militant feel that people with visual impairments should not be dependent on the kindness of charity for devices that will ensure that they are productive citizens. The more conservative may believe that there are many ways to make everyone's life, disabled or not, more productive, but that the costs of these life improving sources are not and should not be the burden of taxpayers, beyond providing equal educational opportunities. Arguments and counterarguments can be made from all perspectives. Perhaps all have some degree of merit. However, regardless of philosophy, the problem remains that a good deal of the latest technology is beyond the means of those for whom it was designed.

## MINORITY CONCERNS

A greater percentage of school-age children from culturally and linguistically diverse backgrounds have severe visual impairment than do their peers from the mainstream culture (Kirchner & Peterson, 1988). The reasons for the higher incidence are not clear. However, speculation points toward higher rates of inadequate prenatal care, higher instances of prematurity for minority women, and less adequate health care in general for this population (Kirchner & Peterson, 1981). It appears that linguistically and culturally diverse families would benefit from improved preventive health care procedures more than others.

Educational concerns for minority children with visual impairments are in reality no different than the concerns for sighted minority children. Culturally biased assessments and instructional techniques should be avoided. Sensitivity to familial structures needs to be developed and unique cultural attitudes need to be respected. This is especially true since a large part of the programming during early intervention and the preschool years takes place in the home setting. Respect for individuals and their culture is a teacher characteristic highly correlated to student success (Plata, 1982). Since the numbers of minority professionals who work with children with visual impairments from culturally diverse backgrounds are not proportionately equal to those of their students, these professionals must make attempts to understand how insensitivity to diversity can have a negative impact on service provision. Scorn for the Asian family that turns to a traditional healer before accepting programming or failure to understand the resistance to encourage independence for a Hispanic child can only lead to mistrust and delay in providing the best possible plan for a minority child with visual impairment (Chan, 1986; Correa, 1989).

## PROFESSIONALS

Although many professionals can be a part of the life of a child with visual impairments, the primary ones we will discuss are medical (ophthalmologists, optometrists, opticians), educational (teachers of students who are visually impaired), orientation and mobility specialists, and transitional specialists. Any given child may also need the care of physical therapists, occupational therapists, speech-language pathologists, dietitians, social workers, family counselors, and many other related professional workers who will provide care directly to the child who is visually impaired and his or her family.

### Medical Professionals

The physical care of the vision falls to ophthalmologists, who are medical doctors who specialize in eye disorders. They are trained to perform surgery, conduct physical examinations, and prescribe medications and corrective lenses. Optometrists are able to measure vision and prescribe corrective lenses. Opticians fill prescriptions for glasses and corrective lenses.

### Educators

The Council for Exceptional Children has published suggested standards for the initial preparation and certification of teachers of students with visual impairments (CEC, 1996). The council mandates that university training programs prepare teachers who, upon completion of their program of studies, will have knowledge and skills in the following eight areas as they relate to students who are visually impaired:

1. Philosophy, history, and legal foundations
2. Characteristics of learners who are visually impaired
3. Assessment, diagnosis, and evaluation of students with visual impairment
4. Instructional content and practices geared toward students who are visually impaired
5. Planning and managing the teaching and learning environment
6. Managing student behavior and social skills
7. Communication and collaborative partnerships
8. Professionalism and ethical practices

Among other skills, teachers of students who are visually impaired should be skillful in explaining the current trends in education, interpreting reports and diagnostic information from all professional sources, using and adapting assessment instruments, maintaining reports and records, developing individualized strategies, and choosing and using appropriate technologies to accomplish objectives. They need to be skillful in implementing generalization and maintenance plans and preparing and obtaining specially modified materials. It is their responsibility to lead in structuring an optimal learning environment for their students. They should be proficient in all aspects of braille and handwriting for students with low vision. Teachers of students who are visually impaired must be current in methods used to teach sexuality, recreational skills, social skills, and daily living skills. They are often critical in helping with transition services, counseling families, and consulting with appropriate professionals.

Certification of teachers of students who are visually impaired occurs at the state level. Information about the specific guidelines and requirements for any given state can be obtained by contacting the state director of special education at the address listed in Appendix I.

## Orientation and Mobility Professionals

We have already discussed the tasks of the orientation and mobility specialist in the section of this chapter on programming. The Association for Education and Rehabilitation of the Blind and Visually Impaired (AER) certifies orientation and mobility specialists. It also recognizes the orientation and mobility assistant, who provides selected services to students who are visually impaired under the direction and supervision of the orientation and mobility specialist. Specific requirements for certification can be obtained from the AER, which is listed in the "Professional Associations" section of this chapter. Generally speaking, certification usually requires at least two years of study at either the undergraduate or graduate level.

## Transitional Specialist

Transitional specialists are a relatively new arrival on the care provision team. They are usually housed in school districts or within a state department of rehabilitation (Sacks & Pruett, 1992). Many have specialized training in helping those with visual impairments. The transition specialist monitors the implementation of an Individualized Transition Program (ITP) with respect to the establishment of the student's relationships with adult agencies and employers. They are available for follow-up services and career counseling, referrals for continuing education, and similar necessary services (Sacks & Reardon, 1988; Siegel, Greener, Prieuer, Robert, & Gaylord-Ross, 1989). It is apparent, given the high levels of unemployment and underemployment of people who are visually handicapped and the increasing complexity in selecting technological equipment and even locating agencies to help, that the role of transition specialists is becoming increasingly critical for full service provision.

## PROFESSIONAL ASSOCIATIONS AND PARENT OR SELF-HELP GROUPS

The following list of associations, societies, and programs should provide the reader the means to establish initial contacts with a variety of interest groups.

AFB Information Network
American Foundation for the Blind
1515 M Street NW, Suite 250
Washington, DC 20036

American Council of the Blind
1155 15th Street NW, Suite 720
Washington, DC 20005

American Foundation for the Blind
15 W. 16th Street
New York, NY 10011

American Printing House for the Blind
P.O. Box 6085
1839 Frankfort Avenue
Louisville, KY 40206

Association for Education and Rehabilitation of the Blind and Visually Impaired (AER)
206 N. Washington Street, Suite 320
Alexandria, VA 22314

Descriptive Video Services
114 Western Avenue
Boston, MA 02134

Division for the Visually Handicapped
Council for Exceptional Children
1920 Association Drive
Reston, VA 20191-1589

Division of the Blind and Visually Impaired
Rehabilitation Services Administration
U.S. Department of Education
330 C Street SW
Washington, DC 20202

National Association for Parents of the
Visually Impaired
2180 Linway Drive
Beloit, WI 53511

National Association for Parents of the
Visually Impaired
2011 Hardy Circle
Austin, TX 78756

National Association for Parents of the
Visually Impaired
P.O. Box 317
Watertown, MA 02272-0317

National Association for the
Visually Handicapped
22 W. 21st Street
New York, NY 10017

National Braille Association, Inc.
1290 University Avenue
Rochester, NY 14607

National Federation for the Blind
1800 Johnson Street
Baltimore, MD 21230

National Society to Prevent Blindness
500 E. Remington Road
Schaumburg, IL 60173

U.S. Association for Blind Athletes
33 North Institute Brown Hall, Suite 105
Colorado Springs, CO 80903

## REFERENCES FOR FURTHER INFORMATION

The bibliography at the end of this chapter provides a comprehensive listing of the sources compiled in writing this chapter. It can serve as a resource for more in-depth study. The following journals, newsletters, and sources of general information may also be of interest.

American Printing House for the Blind, Inc.
1839 Frankfort Avenue
Louisville, KY 40206

Blind Children's Center
4120 Marathon Street
P.O. Box 29159
Los Angeles, CA 90020

Braille Book Bank of the National Braille
  Associates
422 Clinton Avenue South
Rochester, NY 14620

Braille Institute of America
741 N. Vermont Avenue
Los Angeles, CA 00029

Carroll Center for the Blind
770 Centre Street
Newton, MA

DVH *Newsletter*
Division for the Visually Handicapped
Council for Exceptional Children
1920 Association Drive
Reston, VA 20191-1589

*Journal of Visual Impairment and Blindness*
15 W. 16th Street
New York, NY 10011

Library of Congress National Library Service for
  the Blind and Physically Handicapped
1291 Taylor Street NW
Washington, DC 20542

National Braille Press
88 St. Stephen Street
Boston, MA 02115

Radio Reading Services
University Avenue
St. Paul, MN 55104

Recordings for the Blind Inc.
20 Roszel Road
Princeton, NJ 08540

Reed Reference Publishing
P.O. Box 31
New Providence, NJ 07974
Complete directory of large-print books and
  serials.

RE:*view* (formerly *Education of the Visually
  Handicapped*)
Association for Education and Rehabilitation of
  the Blind and Visually Handicapped (AER)
206 N. Washington Street
Alexandria, VA 22314

*Sight-Saving Review*
National Society to Prevent Blindness
500 E. Remington Road
Schaumburg, IL 60713

Taping for the Blind
3935 Essex Lane
Houston, TX 77027

# REFERENCES ✵

American Foundation for the Blind. (1961). *A teacher education for those who serve blind children and youth.* New York: Author.

American Printing House for the Blind. (1981). *English braille, American edition, 1959.* Louisville, KY: Author.

American Printing House for the Blind. (1987). *Distribution of federal quota based on the January 1987 registration of eligible students.* Research report. Louisville, KY: Author.

American Printing House for the Blind (1992a). *Annual report.* Louisville, KY: Author.

American Printing House for the Blind. (1992b). *Distribution of federal quota based on the January 1992 registration of eligible students.* Research report. Louisville, KY: Author.

Ashcroft, S. C. (1963). Blind and partially seeing children. In L. M. Dunn (Ed.), *Exceptional children in the schools.* New York: Holt, Rinehart & Winston.

Ashley, J. R., & Cates, D. L. (1992). Albinism: Educational techniques for parents and teachers. *RE:view,* 24, 127–131.

Bambring, M., & Troster, H. (1992). On the stability of stereotyped behaviors in blind infants and preschoolers. *Journal of Visual Impairment and Blindness,* 86(2), 105–110.

Barraga, N. C. (1964). *Increased visual behavior in low vision children.* New York: American Foundation for the Blind.

Barraga, N. C. (1970). *Teacher's guide for development of visual learning abilities and utilization of low vision.* Louisville, KY: American Printing House for the Blind.

Barraga, N. C. (1980). *Source book on low vision.* Louisville, KY: American Printing House for the Blind.

Barraga, N. C. (1983). *Visual handicaps and learning* (Rev. ed.). Austin, TX: Exceptional Resources.

Barraga, N. (1986). Sensory perceptual development. In G. T. Scholl (Ed.), *Foundations of education for blind and visually handicapped children and youth: Theory and practice.* New York: American Foundation for the Blind.

Barraga, N. C., & Morris, J. E. (1980). *Program to develop efficiency in visual function: Sourcebook on low vision.* Louisville, KY: American Printing House for the Blind.

Bishop, V. E. (1990). Evaluating functional vision in infants and young children. In S. A. Aitken, M. Buultjens, & S. J. Spungin (Eds.), *Realities and opportunities: Early intervention with visually handicapped infants and children.* New York: American Foundation for the Blind.

Bryan, W. H., & Jeffrey, D. L. (1982). Education of visually handicapped students in the regular classroom. *Texas Tech Journal of Education,* 9, 125–131.

Caton, H. R. (1993). Students with visual impairments. In A. E. Blackhurst & W. H. Berdine, (Eds.), *An introduction to special education* (3rd ed.). New York: HarperCollins.

Chalkley, T. (1982). *Your eyes: A book for paramedical personnel and the lay reader* (2nd ed.). Springfield, IL: Thomas.

Chan, S. (1986). Parents of exceptional Asian children. In M. Kitano & P. Chinn (Eds.), *Exceptional Asian children and youth.* Reston, VA: Council for Exceptional Children.

Corn, A. L. (1989). Instruction in the use of vision for children and adults with low vision: A proposed program model. *RE:view,* 21, 26–38.

Correa, V. (1989). Involving culturally diverse families in the educational process. In S. H. Fradd & M. J. Weismantel (Eds.), *Meeting the needs of culturally and linguistically different students: Handbook for educators.* Boston: College-Hill/Little, Brown.

Council for Exceptional Children. (1996). *What every special educator must know: The international standards for the preparation and certification of special education* (2nd ed.). Reston, VA: Author.

Cronin, B. J., & King, S. R. (1990). The development of the Descriptive Video Service. *Journal of Visual Impairment and Blindness,* 86(2), 101–104.

Curry, S. A., & Hatlen, P. H. (1988). Meeting the unique educational needs of visually impaired pupils through appropriate placement. *Journal of Visual Impairment and Blindness,* 82, 417–422.

Cutsforth, T. D. (1951). *The blind in school and society*. New York: American Foundation for the Blind.

Deshler, D. D., Warner, M. M., Schumaker, J. B., & Alley, G. R. (1983). Learning strategies intervention model: Key components and current status. In J. D. McKinney & F. Feagans (Eds.), *Current topics in learning disabilities* (Vol. 1, pp. 245–283). Norwood, NJ: Ablex.

de Witt, K. (1991, May 12). How best to teach the blind: A growing battle over braille. *New York Times*, p. A1.

Feinsilber, M. (1989, June 28). New machine can be big help for visually impaired. *Albuquerque Journal*, p. B3.

Ferrell, K. A. (1986). Infancy and early childhood. In G. T. Scholl (Ed.), *Foundations of education for blind and visually handicapped children and youth: Theory and practice*. New York: American Foundation for the Blind.

Fraiberg, S. (1977). *Insights from the blind: Comparative studies of blind and sighted infants*. New York: New American Library.

Hallahan, D. P., & Kauffman, J. M. (1994). *Exceptional children* (6th ed.). Upper Saddle River, NJ: Prentice Hall.

Harley, R. K., & Lawrence, G. A. (1984). *Visual impairment in the schools* (2nd ed.). Springfield, IL: Thomas.

Harley, R. K., Truan, M. B., & Sanford, L. D. (1987). *Communication skills for visually impaired learners*. Springfield, IL: Thomas.

Harley, R., Wood, T., & Merbler, J. (1981). *Peabody Mobility Scale*. Chicago: Stoelting.

Harrell, L., & Curry, S. A. (1987). Services to blind and visually impaired children and adults: Who is responsible? *Journal of Visual Impairment and Blindness, 81*(8), 368–376.

Hatlen, P. H. (1976, Winter). Priorities in education programs for visually handicapped children and youth. *Division for the Visually Handicapped Newsletter*, 8–11.

Hatlen, P. H. (1978, Fall). The role of the teacher of the visually impaired: A self-definition. *Division for the Visually Handicapped Newsletter*, 5.

Hatlen, P. H. (1980). *Important concerns in the education of visually impaired children*: MAVIS sourcebook (p. 5). Boulder, CO: Social Science Education Consortium.

Heward, W. L. (1996). *Exceptional children* (5th ed.). Upper Saddle River, NJ: Prentice Hall/Merrill.

Hill, E. W. (1986). Orientation and mobility. In G. T. Scholl (Ed.), *Foundations of education for blind and visually handicapped children and youth: Theory and practice*. New York: American Foundation for the Blind.

Hodges, H. L. (1983). Evaluating the effectiveness of programs for the visually impaired: One state's approach. *Journal of Visual Impairment and Blindness, 77*(1), 97–99.

Holbrook, C., & Healy, M. S. (1994). Children who are blind or have low vision. In N. Hunt, & K. Marshall, *Exceptional children and youth: An introduction to special education*. Boston: Houghton Mifflin.

Hunt, N., & Marshall, K. (1994). *Exceptional children and youth: An introduction to special education*. Boston: Houghton Mifflin.

Joint Organizational Committee. (1993). *Full inclusion of students who are blind or visually impaired: A position statement*. Author.

Jones, L., & Chiba, C. (1985). *Social skills assessment and intervention*. Final report. Bethesda, MD: National Institute of Child Health and Human Development.

Kekelis, L. S. (1992). Peer interactions in childhood: The impact of visual impairment. In S. Z. Sacks, L. S. Kekelis, & R. J. Gaylord-Ross (Eds.), *The development of social skills by blind and visually impaired students*. New York: American Foundation for the Blind.

Kentucky Society for the Prevention of Blindness. (1990). *Handbook for preschool vision screening*. Louisville, KY: Author.

Kirchner, C. (1983). Special education for visually handicapped children: A critique on numbers served and costs. *Journal of Visual Impairment and Blindness, 77*, 219–223.

Kirchner, C. (Ed.). (1988). *Data on blindness and visual impairment in the U.S.: A resource manual on social demographic characteristics, education, employment and income, and service delivery* (2nd ed.). New York: American Foundation for the Blind.

Kirchner, C. (1990). Trends in the prevalence rates and numbers of blind and visually impaired schoolchildren. *Journal of Visual Impairment and Blindness, 84*, 478–479.

Kirchner, C., & Peterson, R. (1981). Estimates of race-ethnic groups in the United States visually impaired and blind population. *Journal of Visual Impairment and Blindness, 75*, 73–76.

Kirchner, C., & Peterson, R. (1988). Estimates of race: Ethnic groups in the U.S. visually impaired and blind population. In C. Kirchner (Ed.), *Data on blindness and visual impairment in the* U.S.: *A resource manual on social demographic characteristics, education, employment and income, and service delivery* (2nd ed.). New York: American Foundation for the Blind.

Kirchner, C., & Peterson, R. (1989). Employment: Selected characteristics. In C. Kirchner (Ed.), *Blindness and visual impairment in the* U.S. New York: American Foundation for the Blind.

Kirchner, C., Peterson, R., & Suhr, C. (1988). Trends in school enrollment and reading methods among legally blind school children, 1963–1978. In C. Kirchner (Ed.), *Data on blindness and visual impairment in the* U.S.: *A resource manual on social demographic characteristics, education, employment and income, and service delivery* (2nd ed.). New York: American Foundation for the Blind.

Kirk, E. C. (1981). *Vision pathology in education.* Springfield, IL: Thomas.

Kirk, S. A., Gallagher, J. J., & Anastasiow, N. J. (1993). *Educating exceptional children* (7th ed.). Boston: Houghton Mifflin.

Lenz, B. K., Alley, G. R., & Schumaker, J. B. (1987). Activating the inactive learner: Advance organizers in the secondary content classroom. *Learning Disability Quarterly, 10,* 53–62.

Lewis, S. (1995). Blindness and low vision. In A. P. Turnbull, H. R. Turnbull, M. Shank, & D. Leal, *Exceptional lives: Special education in today's schools.* Upper Saddle River, NJ: Prentice Hall/Merrill.

Loumiet, R., & Levack, N. (1991). *Independent living: Self-care and maintenance of personal environment.* Austin, TX: Texas School for the Blind.

MacCuspie, A. P. (1992). The social acceptance and interaction of visually impaired children in integrated setting. In S. Z. Sacks, L. S. Kekelis, & R. J. Gaylord-Ross (Eds.), *The development of social skills by blind and visually impaired students: Exploratory studies and strategies.* New York: American Foundation for the Blind.

Mangold, S. (1977). *Mangold Developmental Program of Tactile Perception and Braille Letter Recognition.* Castro Valley, CA: Exceptional Teaching Aids.

Maxfield, K., & Buchholz, F. (1957). *Social Maturity Scale for Blind Children: A guide to its use.* New York: American Foundation for the Blind.

National Society for the Prevention of Blindness (1972). *Teaching about vision.* Schaumburg, IL.

National Society for the Prevention of Blindness (1990). *Vision screening in schools.* New York: Author.

Nelson, K. A., & Dimitrova, E. (1993). Severe visual impairment in the United States and in each state. *Journal of Visual Impairment and Blindness, 87,* 80–85.

Pava, W. S. (1994). Visually impaired persons' vulnerability to sexual and physical assault. *Journal of Visual Impairment and Blindness, 88,* 103–112.

Pava, W. S., Bateman, P., Appleton, M. K., & Glascock, J. (1991). Self-defense training for visually impaired women. *Journal of Visual Impairment and Blindness, 85,* 397–401.

Plata, M. (1982). *Assessment, placement, and programming of bilingual exceptional pupils: A practical approach.* Reston, VA: ERIC Clearinghouse on Handicapped and Gifted Children, Council for Exceptional Children.

Reynell, J. (1983). *Manual for the Reynell-Zinkin Scales.* New Windsor, Berkshire, United Kingdom: NFER-NELSON.

Rogow, S. M. (1988). *Helping the visually impaired child with developmental problems: Effective practice in home, school, and community.* New York: Teachers College Press.

Sacks, S. (Ed.). (1992a). *The development of social skills by blind and visually impaired students: Exploratory studies and strategies.* New York: American Foundation for the Blind.

Sacks, S. Z. (1992b). The social development of visually impaired children: A theoretical perspective. In S. Z. Sacks, L. S. Kekelis, & R. J. Gaylord-Ross (Eds.), *The development of social skills by blind and visually impaired students: Exploratory studies and strategies.* New York: American Foundation for the Blind.

Sacks, S. Z., & Kekelis, L. S. (1992). Guidelines for mainstreaming blind and visually impaired children. In S. Z. Sacks, L. S. Kekelis, & R. J. Gaylord-Ross (Eds.), *The development of social skills by blind and visually impaired students: Exploratory studies and strategies.* New York: American Foundation for the Blind.

Sacks, S. Z., Kekelis, L. S., & Gaylord-Ross, R. J. (Eds.). (1992). *The development of social skills by blind and visually impaired students: Exploratory studies and strategies.* New York: American Foundation for the Blind.

Sacks, S. Z., & Pruett, K. M. (1992). Summer transition training project for professionals who work with adolescents and young adults. *Journal of Visual Impairment and Blindness, 86,* 211–214.

Sacks, S. Z., & Reardon, M. (1988). Maximizing social integration for visually handicapped students. In R. J. Gaylord-Ross (Ed.), *Integration strategies for students with handicaps*. Baltimore: Brookes.

Sacks, S. Z., & Reardon, M. P. (1992). Maximizing social integration for visually impaired students: Applications and practice. In S. Z. Sacks, L. S. Kekelis, & R. J. Gaylord-Ross (Eds.), *The development of social skills by blind and visually impaired students: Exploratory studies and strategies*. New York: American Foundation for the Blind.

Sacks, S. Z., Rosen, S., & Gaylord-Ross, R. J. (1990). Visual impairment. In N. G. Haring & L. McCormick (Eds.), *Exceptional children and youth* (5th ed.), Upper Saddle River, NJ: Prentice Hall/Merrill.

Scholl, G. T. (1986). Growth and development. In G. T. Scholl (Ed.), *Foundations of education for blind and visually handicapped children and youth: Theory and practice*. New York: American Foundation for the Blind.

Schroeder, F. K. (1993). *Braille usage: Perspectives of legally blind adults and policy implications for school administrators*. Unpublished doctoral dissertation, University of New Mexico, Albuquerque.

Siegel, S., Greener, K., Prieuer, J., Robert, M., & Gaylord-Ross, R. (1989). The community vocational training program. *Career Development for Exceptional Individuals, 12*, 48–64.

Silverstein, R. (1985). The legal necessity for residential schools serving deaf, blind, and multiply impaired children. *Journal of Visual Impairment and Blindness, 79*, 145–149.

Skellenger, A. C., & Hill, E. W. (1991). Current practices and considerations regarding long cane instruction with preschool children. *Journal of Visual Impairment and Blindness, 76*, 133–143.

Smith, D. D., & Luckasson, R. (1995). *Introduction to special education: Teaching in an age of challenge* (2nd ed.). Needham, MA: Allyn & Bacon.

Smith, J. A. (1972). *Adventures in communication*. Needham, MA: Allyn & Bacon.

(1992). Talking wallet. *Journal of Visual Impairment and Blindness, 86*, 411.

Telability Media. (1992, January). *Home videos described for blind people*. 1, p. 1.

Thomas, C. L. (Ed.). (1985). *Taber's cyclopedic medical dictionary* (15th ed.). Philadelphia: Davis.

Turnbull, A. P., Turnbull, H. R., Shank, M., & Leal, D. (1995). *Exceptional lives: Special education in today's schools*. Upper Saddle River, NJ: Prentice Hall/Merrill.

Tuttle, D. W. (1981). Academics are not enough: Techniques of daily living for visually impaired children. In *Handbook for teachers of the visually handicapped*. New York: American Printing House for the Blind.

U.S. Department of Education. (1997) *Nineteenth annual report to Congress on the implementation of the Individuals with Disabilities Education Act*. Washington, DC: Author.

Warren, D. H. (1984). *Blindness and early childhood development* (2nd ed.). New York: American Foundation for the Blind.

Winer, M. (1978). A course on resources for the newly blind. *Journal of Visual Impairment and Blindness, 72*, 311–315.

Wormald International Sensory Aids (1979). *Electronic travel aids*. Bensenville, IL: Author.

# 10

# Children with Severe or Multiple Disabilities

C hildren with severe and multiple disabilities may have an extensive range of physical problems and co-existing intellectual challenges. These children experience more than one disability. Some of these children's disabilities are so severe that they need intensive assistance or support for their entire lives. Many are also profoundly mentally retarded. However, some children with severe and multiple disabilities may be cognitively gifted and talented. Some are ambulatory; others need wheelchairs or other prostheses such as crutches or braces. They may experience mild physical or neurological difficulties, severe impairments of language, other communication disorders, or impairment of body movements (Kirk, Gallagher, & Anastasiow, 1997; Batshaw & Perret, 1992). It is difficult to provide an all-inclusive definition of children with severe and multiple disabilities, since no one definition would include all the prevailing multiple conditions. Sailor and Guess (1983) suggest that this population has the distinction of being everybody who is not someone else.

## DEFINITIONS

IDEA (PL 94-142) has separate definitions of multiple disabilities and of severe disabilities. The section of IDEA that specifies the thirteen different categories of exceptionality defines multiple disabilities (but not severe disabilities) as follows:

> Multiple disabilities means concomitant impairments (such as mental retardation–blindness, mental retardation–orthopedic impairment, etc.), the combination of which causes such severe educational problems that they cannot be accommodated in special education programs solely for one of the impairments. The term does not include deaf-blindness (34 C.F.R., pt. 300, § 300.7).

Another part of IDEA describes programs and services for students with severe disabilities:

> The term "children with severe disabilities" refers to children with disabilities who, because of the intensity of their physical, mental, or emotional problems, need highly specialized education, social, psychological, and medical services in order to maximize their full potential for useful and meaningful participation in society and for self-fulfillment.
>
> The term includes those children with disabilities with severe emotional disturbance (including schizophrenia), autism, severe and profound mental retardation, and those who have two or more serious disabilities such as deaf-blindness, mental retardation and blindness, and cerebral palsy and deafness.
>
> Children with severe disabilities may experience severe speech, language, and/or perceptual-cognitive deprivations, and evidence abnormal behaviors such as failure to respond to pronounced social stimuli, self-mutilation, self-stimulation, manifestation of intense and prolonged temper tantrums, and the absence of rudimentary forms of verbal control; and may also have intensely fragile physiological conditions (34 C.F.R., pt. 300, §315.4[d]).

The two major defining themes are that the extent of disability is beyond mild or moderate levels, and that there typically are two or more disabilities occurring simultaneously.

A most useful definition of severe and multiple disabilities is offered by the Association for Persons with Severe Disabilities, formerly known as of the Association of Persons with Severe Handicaps (TASH). Their definition is as follows:

> Persons with severe handicaps include individuals of all ages who require extensive ongoing support in more than one life activity in order to participate in integrated community settings and to enjoy a quality of life that is available to citizens with fewer or no disabilities. Support may be required for life activities such as mobility, communication, self-care, and learning as necessary for independent living, employment, and self-sufficiency (Kirk et. al., 1997, p. 470; Meyer, Peck, & Brown, 1991, p. 19).

Hardman, Drew, and Egan (1996) characterize individuals with severe and multiple disabilities as those who are experiencing

> physical, sensory, [possible] intellectual, and/or adaptive skill deficits significantly below average; performance deficits evident in all environmental settings and across several areas of performance; identifiable causes in most cases; and substantially altered patterns of required support and treatment. (p. 316)

Guess and Siegel-Causey (1988) point out that there is no generally agreed-upon, educationally oriented definition for students with severe and multiple disabilities and that definitions vary among the 50 states in the United States and among local education districts or agencies.

## Special and Major Categories: Severe and Multiple Disabilities

There are several special and major categories associated with children and adults with severe and multiple disabilities. These problems are unique and challenging, and they often require special services that are notably different and more sophisticated than those routinely provided to people with exceptionalities. What follows is a listing and brief outline of these categories.

## Children with Autism and Pervasive Developmental Disorders (NOS)

Autism and pervasive development disorders, often referred to as *not otherwise specified* or NOS, are neurological disorders of unknown origin that lead to deficits in the child's ability to communicate, understand language, play, develop social skills, and relate to others (NICHCY, 1994). The Individuals with Disabilities Education Act (IDEA) defines autism as

> a developmental disability significantly affecting verbal and non-verbal communication and social interaction usually evident before age 3, that adversely affects a child's

educational performance. Other characteristics often associated with autism are engagement in repetitive activities and stereotyped movement, resistance to environmental change or change in daily routines, and unusual sensory experiences(NICHCY, 1994, p. 1).

Symptoms generally become apparent between the second and fourth year. Experts feel that there is a neurological underpinning and/or biochemical imbalance influencing perception and understanding. A pervasive aspect of autism is the individual's social or interpersonal detachment or unrelatedness to others in his or her environment. These children usually have impaired or delayed speech and language; show sensory disabilities; and can be overresponsive or underresponsive to light, noise, touch, or pain. They exhibit either inappropriate behavior or a flat affect and engage in repetitive self-stimulatory behaviors that can interfere with learning. Often, they fail to develop normal, appropriate play behaviors and will exhibit obsessive ritualistic behaviors that make these individuals extremely resistant to change (Kirk et al., 1997, p. 473).

At present, the treatment of autism is experimental. There are many approaches; some are effective with some individuals and others are not. Approaches as diversified as the use of operant techniques to punish unwanted stereotypical

behaviors while reinforcing selected appropriate behaviors to auditory integration training (AIT), which relies on systematic exposure to a variety of sounds, have been used with varying degrees of success (Rimland & Edelson, 1994). Detailed explanations of attempts to provide behavioral management and the subsequent education of children with autism are beyond the mission of this text. Interested readers may contact the National Society for Children and Adults with Autism (listed at the end of this chapter) to acquire initial sources for study. Minimally, individual programs need to be developed to meet family needs and the needs of children with autism (Kirk et al., 1997).

## Children with Deaf-Blind Impairment

IDEA (PL 101-476) defines children who are deaf-blind as:

> having auditory and visual impairments, the combination of which creates such severe communication and other developmental and learning needs that they cannot be appropriately educated in special education programs solely for children and youth with hearing impairments, visual impairments or severe disabilities, without supplementary assistance to address the educational needs due to these dual concurrent disabilities (PL 101-476, 20 U.S.C. ch. 33, § 1422 [2]).

The Helen Keller National Center defines a person who is deaf-blind more specifically as someone

> (1) with central vision acuity of 20/200 or worse in the better eye with corrective lenses and/or a visual field of 20 degrees or less in the better eye . . . or with a progressive visual loss . . . ; (2) who has either a chronic hearing impairment so severe that most speech cannot be understood . . . ; (3) and for whom the combination of impairments . . . causes extreme difficulty in daily life activities. . . . (Everson, 1995).

Some causes of deaf-blindness are listed in Box 10.2 later in this chapter.

For the person who is deaf-blind, help begins at a most basic level. The child must be helped to maintain sufficient focus to realize that (1) he or she exists; (2) others exist; (3) he or she has needs; (4) these needs can be met; (5) some of the needs will be met by himself or herself; and (6) some, if not most, of these needs will be met by others (Murphy & Byrne, 1983). Many infants who possess deaf-blind impairments can go beyond point 6 and, as they develop, begin to meet many of their own needs. With the infant who is deaf-blind, joint attention begins through touch, which is augmented by any residual hearing or vision through the use of hearing aids and glasses or sonic directional devices, which give the infant vibrational feedback about the location of objects (Bower, 1989). Without intervention, infants who are deaf-blind focus on their own bodies and show little interest in object use. They do little exploration of the environment and resist new stimuli, becoming prone to self-stimulation (Taylor, 1988).

Changes occur with maturity; a child without the ability to see or hear is deprived of the normal sensory stimulation that facilitates normal growth. Without early intervention to offset these deprivations, the developmental changes in the neuroanatomical systems are degenerative and abnormal (Murphy & Byrne, 1983).

## Children with Mental Retardation and Cerebral Palsy

A diagnosis of mental retardation in youngsters with cerebral palsy can be suspect if the intelligence tests used were designed for and tested on children with adequate speech, language, and motor abilities, because many children with cerebral palsy have problems in both speech and psychomotor areas. In general, IQ tests have serious limitations when evaluating children with multiple disabilities.

Often the poor speech and uncontrolled movements of children with cerebral palsy give the lay person the impression that these individuals are mentally retarded. Actually, there is little relationship between the degree of physical impairment and intelligence in children with cerebral palsy. A child who is severely impaired may be intellectually gifted; another with mild physical involvement may be severely retarded (Kirk et al., 1997).

The terms in Box 10.1 will help the reader better understand the concepts discussed in this chapter.

### Box10.1
### WHAT EVERY TEACHER NEEDS TO KNOW

### Terms

**assistive technology**   Tools such as computers, adaptations, and switches supporting and enhancing the functioning, communication, and management of daily-living skills for people with disabilities.

**community-based instruction**   The educational approach that focuses on learning and applying skills in community settings.

**community-based employment**   The placement of students in jobs where they receive training while in school.

**de-institutionalization**   The effort to bring individuals out of institutions and into more normal or mainstreamed (inclusive) settings within their communities.

**dual-sensory impairments**   Refers to people with two impairments, such as the child with both vision and hearing impairments or the child with both deafness and blindness.

**ecological inventory**   A process for developing and individualizing functional curriculum (domestic,

vocational, and recreational) for individuals with severe and multiple disabilities. Sometimes this term is interchangeable with *environmental inventory or analysis.*

**functional skills**   Skills, tasks, and activities required for a person to function appropriately in normal or routine settings.

**generalization**   The application of prior knowledge to new situations.

**multiple-sensory impairments**   A variety of difficulties in sensory modalities such as hearing, vision, touch, taste, or smell.

**normalization**   The care, education, and services for people with disabilities that allows them to function in a manner equal or nearly equal to what is normal in society.

**support networks**   Types of assistance or support for individuals with severe or multiple disabilities that enable inclusion into local schools and communities.

# PREVALENCE

Students with severe and multiple disabilities account for less than 0.5 percent of the total special education population (Kirk et al., 1997; Meyer, Peck, & Brown 1991). Of the approximately 5 million children with disabilities between ages 6 and 21 served during the 1995-1996 school year, a total of 124,199 were identified as experiencing multiple disabilities (94,034), autism (28,813), or deaf-blindness (1,352) (U.S. Department of Education, 1997). Gast and Berkler (1981) indicated that 1 person in 1,000 of the total population can be regarded as severely and multiply disabled.

Baldwin (1993) reported that there are only slightly more than 8,000 people with deaf-blindness throughout the nation and that approximately 2 out of every 1,000 individuals have sensory impairments. Landesman-Dwyer and Butterfield (1983) reported a 7 per 1,000 birth incidence for severe or profound mental retardation. Autism has an incidence of 5 out of every 10,000 births (Knoblock, 1982; and Haring, McCormick, & Haring, 1994).

# CHARACTERISTICS

Individuals with severe and multiple disabilities exhibit wide behavioral differences and characteristics due to sensory and motor impairments, physical and orthopedic anomalies, communication deficits, and cognitive delays, and often exhibit accompanying inappropriate or bizarre behaviors. They may also be severely mentally retarded, with seizure disorders, cerebral palsy, or other motor disabilities. Other individuals included in this category may be deaf-blind. Many students with severe disabilities will likely experience adjustment problems or be self-injurious or self-abusive (Kirk et al., 1997; Hardman et al., 1996; Giangreco, Edelman, Macfarland, & Luiselli, 1997). The difficulty in defining severe and multiple disabilities carries over into attempts to describe all characteristics of all individuals with severe and multiple disabilities. It may be that the variances among individuals with severe and multiple disabilities are greater than the similarities (Guess & Siegel-Causey, 1988). But we can categorize characteristics such as intellectual functioning, adaptive behavior, physical and sensory development, health care needs, and communication needs. Throughout this section the reader must keep in mind that some individuals with severe and multiple disabilities may have normal intelligence, be ambulatory, and become fully integrated into society. The following paragraphs provide a comprehensive but brief review of characteristics of individuals with severe and multiple disabilities by focusing on the skills most critical for normal functioning.

## Intellectual Functioning

Many, but not all, individuals with severe and multiple disabilities have severe impairments in intellectual functioning as determined by intelligence test scores. However, there are individuals with normal or high intelligence who may yet be discriminated against by ineptly trained evaluators using typical intelligence testing instruments who are dealing with this population (Turnbull, Turnbull, Shank, & Leal, 1995).

## Academic Skills

Most individuals with severe and multiple disabilities cannot perform traditional academic tasks, although some of these students can benefit from functional, educational, and academic skill programs (Giangreco et al., 1997). Students with severe or multiple physical disabilities with sufficient cognitive abilities can succeed in general education classes. (Giangreco et al., 1997; Turnbull et al., 1995).

## Self-Care Skills

Many individuals with severe and multiple disabilities, with appropriate support, can learn to care for their own needs such as dressing, personal hygiene, toileting, and feeding, and may successfully master some household chores (Kirk et al., 1997; and Meyer & Eichinger, 1994).

## Social Skills

The majority of individuals with severe and multiple disabilities do not have typical social skills nor the opportunities for the social interactions that might enable them to develop social skills. Also, some are withdrawn, or conversely, too assertive. However, reports do indicate that these individuals can engage in reciprocal interpersonal relationships with teachers and family. The facilitating key appears to be providing enriching opportunities for participation in the community, with appropriate employment and living situations if possible (Hardman et al., 1996; Bradley & Knoll, 1995).

## Delayed Motor Development

Individuals with severe and multiple disabilities usually exhibit a significant delay in motor development, including sensorimotor impairments and abnormal orthopedic muscle tone. However, many of these individuals can learn to walk with assistance (Turnbull et al., 1995; Nisbet, 1992).

## Sensory Impairment

Hearing and vision impairments are common among individuals with severe and multiple disabilities, with the most impaired individuals being deaf-blind. Downing & Eichinger (1990) indicate that there may be diverse combinations of sensory impairments that occur with normal or gifted individuals.

## Health Care Needs

Students with health care needs who experience severe and multiple disabilities may need school and other staff members to assist with intermittent catheterization, gastrostomy tube feeding, respiratory ventilation, and administration of medications for seizures, hyperactivity and muscle relaxation. Clean intermittent catheterization involves inserting a catheter (tube) into the urethra to the bladder to drain off urine. Gastrostomy tube feeding is used with individuals who cannot ingest adequate nutrition normally. Respiratory ventilation involves suctioning mucus from the respiratory tract by machine through a small tube (Turnbull et al., 1995; Kirk et al., 1997). These life sustaining duties may become the responsibility of aides or special education or regular classroom teachers.

## Communication Skills

The majority of individuals with severe and multiple disabilities display serious communication problems or even a failure to acquire speech and language. In spite of their speech and language problems, they can and do communicate with others. Some may point at pictures on communication boards containing critical objects and needs. Some develop sign language. A growing number have access to assistive

technology and computerized communication devices (Turnbull et al., 1995; Nisbet, 1992; Haring & Romer, 1995).

## Summary

In summary, educators need to be aware of the multiple factors that may affect the learning of students with severe or multiple disabilities. Often learning is not only possible but probable, because there are more similarities between these students and their typical peers than differences. The many possible characteristics exhibited by individuals with severe and multiple disabilities that we have just sketched will appear in a variety of combinations for any given child. These life needs must be met with substantial assistance from society if the child is to attain any measure of integration into society (Hardman et al., 1996).

## ETIOLOGY

There are multiple causes for the many conditions that result in severe and multiple disabilities. Prior to conception, there are genetic determinants. Prior to birth, maternal substance abuse, blood incompatibility, or viral diseases may be factors. During the birth process, oxygen deprivation and extremely low birth weights associated with prematurity can contribute to severe and multiple disabilities. After-birth accidents, infections, poisonings, malnutrition, or physical and emotional child abuse can also cause severe and multiple disabilities (Kirk et al., 1997; Evans, 1991; Hardman et al., 1996; Seligman, 1975). However, the majority of known causes of severe and multiple disabilities relate to prenatal biomedical factors such as chromosomal abnormalities, genetic metabolic disorders, disorders of the central nervous system, and prenatal noxious environmental influences. Unfortunately, there is no identifiable cause for these disabilities in an estimated 40 percent of all children born with them (McLaren & Bryson, 1987; Turnbull et al., 1995). Box 10.2 illustrates some of the more identifiable causes of severe and multiple disabilities, indicating the time of injury, affecting agent, agent activity, and the typical results.

Some but not all causes are preventable. Generally, the causes of severe and multiple disabilities are related to randomly occurring genetic or medical conditions and not cultural factors. It is often difficult to determine or document causality; the conditions affect all social, economic, racial, and linguistic groups equally (Haring et al., 1994, pp. 268–270).

## IDENTIFICATION PROCESS

### Medical Evaluation

Infants with severe and multiple disabilities are usually detected at birth during administration of the screening processes required by physicians in checking for

**Box 10.2**
*WHAT EVERY TEACHER NEEDS TO KNOW*
*Causes of Multiple Handicaps*

| Time of Injury | Affecting Agent | Agent Activity | Typical Results |
|---|---|---|---|
| Conception | Genetic disorder; inherited; inborn errors of metabolism | Serious change in embryo and fetus; inability to carry out normal metabolic processes | Down syndrome; Tay Sachs; many other disorders that if untreated will lead to severe mental retardation |
| Prenatal | Mother has German measles or other viral infection; uses toxic substances (crack, heroin); or has RH blood incompatibility | Interferes with development of central nervous system | Visual, hearing, and motor impairments; mental retardation |
| Natal | Anoxia | Destroys brain cells | Cerebral palsy, mental retardation, and other defects |
| | Low birth weight (less than 5.5 lb); prematurity | Immature organism not ready for environmental stimulation | From normal to severe mental retardation and disabilities |
| | Very low birth weight (less than 3 lb) | Damage to brain organization | From normal to severe and profound disabilities |
| Postnatal | Encephalitis, meningitis, physical abuse | Damage to brain cells | Epilepsy, mental retardation, motor disabilities |

*Source:* S. A. Kirk, J. J. Gallagher, N. J. Anastasiow. From *Educating Exceptional Children* (8th ed.), Copyright © 1997 by Houghton Mifflin Company. Used with permission.

observable disabilities, genetic and metabolic disorders, and potential developmental problems (Turnbull et al., 1995; Campbell, 1989). An example of a screening process for newborns is the Apgar test. The physician ranks the child on five physical traits (heart rate, respiratory effort, muscle tone, gag reflex, and skin color) at one minute and at five minutes after birth. Each child receives a rating based on the scores that indicate the risk to being disabled. The neonate may also have disabilities common to a given syndrome or show symptoms that are easily recognizable. Parents may report that the child is having unusual difficulties sleeping, eating, or attaining developmental milestones. These reports will lead to genetic investigations and physical evaluations that might include vision and hearing tests, blood tests, metabolic workups, and a variety of other screening procedures that might reveal the presence of disabling conditions (Turnbull et al., 1995).

## Educational Evaluation

Concurrent with medical identification and assessment procedures, the child is referred to educational and therapeutic specialists who are experts in remediation and treatment (Gaylord-Ross & Holvoet, 1985). For example, as a result of screening procedures, a child at birth may be suspected of having respiratory problems with possible neurological impairments along with low Apgar scores. The child is referred for indepth testing; if the presenting problems indicate cerebral palsy or other physical impairments, these results will lead to vision and hearing tests. The possible combination of problems and their potential severity will prompt a variety of specialists to become part of the service provision team that will evaluate and plan to treat the child. In addition to medical personnel, speech-language pathologists, physical therapists, special educators, family counselors, and other appropriate professionals will begin to prepare for the child's future educational and therapeutic needs. Early intervention programs will be notified and they will add the family to their caseloads and begin to provide supportive services during infancy and the preschool years.

The educational placement procedures that will be set in motion parallel those described in previous chapters of this text. Assessment activities for students with severe and multiple handicaps or disabilities should analyze students' performance under natural, normal situations and settings where they learn, live, work, and recreate. Individualized intelligence tests will be administered, following guidelines to ensure that the most accurate scores can be obtained. Most students with severe and multiple disabilities have IQ scores that indicate severe cognitive impairments (Turnbull et al., 1995). However, examiners must be cautious about applying test scores that were derived from tests designed for children with intact neurological and sensory systems. Commercial assessment devices may need to be adjusted to each child's age and type(s) of disabilities to the teacher's qualifications, the kind of school, and the community and home environment of the child (Kirk et al., 1997; Haring et al., 1994).

Adaptive behavior scales will also be a part of the assessment battery. Adaptive behavior tests focus on behaviors important to an individual's adjustment to cultural, social, and age standards of performance.

Many assessment tools are available for determining developmental problems, educational diagnosis, and programming. Some diagnostic instruments are:

- AAMD *Adaptive Behavior Scale: Public School Version* (Lambert, Windmiller, Cole, & Figuerra, 1975).

- The TARC Assessment Inventory for Severely Handicapped Children (Sailor & Mix, 1976).

- *The Behavior Rating Instrument for Atypical Children* (BRIAC) (Ruttenberg, Kalish, Wenar, & Wolf, 1977).

- A Manual for the Assessment of a Deaf-Blind Multiply Handicapped Child (Collins & Rudolph, 1975).

These instruments are useful in the evaluation of students with severe and multiple disabilities because they rely, to some extent, on the developmental approach and the ecological assessment model, wherein the teacher considers what particular skills the student needs to perform a particular behavior and the settings within which a student is expected to function. Severe and multiple disabilities are often diagnosed when a student scores significantly below average in two or more areas of adaptive behavior. This usually indicates problems in areas such as communication, daily living skills, socialization, and coordination abilities.

The educational team must also consider the intensity of support that the child will require. The major areas to be considered are communication, self-care, social skills, home living, community involvement, health, and safety (Turnbull et al., 1995).

From all of these tests and observations and in consultation with family members and the multidisciplinary team, an Individualized Educational Program (IEP) evolves that will be the guideline for the child's educational experience.

## PROGRAMS

Historically, services for those with severe and multiple disabilities were primarily focused on protection and care. Children with severe and multiple disabilities were often isolated from their community and society in large institutions. Current emphasis in education practices is to include children with disabilities as much as is possible and reasonable in their communities and local schools.

Hardman et al. (1996) have identified several aspects of instructional emphasis illustrating quality school programs for students with severe and multiple disabilities:

> Student preferences and needs are taken into account in developing educational objectives; the school values and supports parental involvement; instruction focuses on frequently used functional skills that are meaningful to everyday life activities; and there are continual opportunities for interaction between students with severe and multiple disabilities and their nondisabled peers. (p. 322)

### Curriculum

Current curriculum emphasis for children with severe and multiple disabilities focuses on the critical environments in which the student is expected to function and identifies the skills and activities he or she needs to participate successfully in these identified environments (Snell, 1992; Orelove & Sobsey, 1991). The emphasis on functional curriculum content is concerned not only with what is taught, but also with how and where teaching occurs. Educators are taking responsibility for teaching domestic skills along the entire range of self-care so that the child will be better able to function within a home environment. School skills now include not only traditional academic areas but also activities related to successful functioning in schools, such as interacting with peers, working in groups, participating, communicating, and complying with schedules and adult requests. Community skills such as mobility within the community (for example, transportation), going shopping, recreation and leisure, spending time in socially acceptable and enjoyable ways, and vocational training focused on getting and keeping a job are also the responsibility of the educational team and the plan that they evolve for the child (Rainforth, York, & Macdonald, 1992; Haring et al., 1994).

## Instructional Priorities

Teachers of children with severe and multiple disabilities agree that instructional time must be spent teaching skills that are used frequently in children's everyday lives at home or in the community. These skills are critical for successful integration and personal survival. Sailor, Goetz, Anderson, Hunt, and Gee (1988) provide guidelines for selecting important skills. The critical components are that:

- The skill to be learned has immediate utility for the student.
- The skill has desirability, as it will produce something for the student that he or she would likely choose.
- The skill is acquired in a social context and is the product of social interactions.
- The skill is acquired in the actual physical contexts that the student will use when requested.
- The skill is practical and will be used when needed and frequently.
- The skill is age-appropriate, supporting independence.
- The skill is adaptable and can be generalized in different situations (pp. 68–69).

## Instructional Methodology

After the identification of relevant skills, Meyen (1996) and Bateman (1971) suggest that a task analysis be performed. A task analysis is the process of isolating, describing, and sequencing all of the subtasks that need to be mastered that will enable a student to acquire a skill. The teacher begins with the simplest step and proceeds sequentially to the more difficult steps until the whole task is accomplished. It consists of breaking down the skill to be learned into simpler, easier, and/or smaller steps. Teaching skills in related clusters promotes the student's understanding of the interdependence of some naturally occurring behaviors (Meyen & Skrtic, 1988).

As a component of this systematic instruction, teachers follow a series of specific procedures and collect performance information to document the effectiveness of their instruction (Orelove & Sobsey, 1991). The teachers help students learn the correct steps in a skill sequence with abundant use of positive reinforcement, prompts, cues, and demonstrations. Immediate rewards are necessary in the beginning of skill mastery sequences. It is hoped that natural cues in the environment will eventually trigger the performance of the behaviors being learned (Turnbull et al., 1995; Giangreco, Dennis, Cloninger, Edelman, & Schattman, 1993).

An additional consideration is that students with severe and multiple disabilities should not be denied access to daily routine activities simply because they cannot function independently. Appropriate modifications that include these children can often enable them to participate and learn with their peers. Parents and teachers are currently taking the position that full participation (as far as is reasonable) in the whole range of school and other experiences is required for an appropriate educational experience. Assistive technology has contributed to increased opportunities for community participation (William, 1991; Bishop, Eshelian, & Falvey, 1989).

## Technology

There is widespread national support to foster the development and use of computer technology for people with disabilities in education, assessment, vocational training, and transition from school to employment. There are numerous programs designed for students with learning, hearing, vision, motor, and cognitive disabilities. Adaptive devices such as head pointers allow some students to type, while some can use their limited dexterity to use software that aids in reading and responding to curriculum materials (Greenwood, 1994; Cary & Sale, 1994; Kirk et al., 1997). Communication boards, typewriters, and other electronic devices can be adapted electronically or mechanically through the use of ingeniously designed switches that enable people with disabilities to enhance their motor skills and compensate for poor coordination.

Video game technology and videotaping can be used with students to teach social skills and communication and to simulate community-based instruction and behavioral management. Teachers can use current technology for administrative tasks and in obtaining data from which they can make instructional and other decisions about their students (Fox & Williams, 1991; Wehman, 1997).

## Placement

Determining the most appropriate, reasonable, and natural settings for the education of students with severe and multiple disabilities has engendered serious debates in special education and educational circles. Children with severe and multiple disabilities are guaranteed educational services by legislation and court decisions in the least restrictive environment, including their home or local schools, community programs, partial or full participation in chronological age-appropriate environments, and activities that are educationally responsive to their special needs. There are no definitive answers as to what constitutes the least restrictive environment for these children. Considerable evidence supports the educational and socialization benefits of integration for students with severe disabilities into the regular classroom. Kirk et al. (1997) have reviewed many studies indicating that integration influences positive changes in attitudes of nondisabled individuals toward their peers with severe and multiple disabilities at various age levels, shows improvement in social and communication skills of children with severe and multiple disabilities, improves positive interactions among all students, and facilitates adjustment to the community settings as adults. Children with severe and multiple disabilities become more responsive to others, increase reciprocal interactions, and increase displays of affection toward others. Brown et al.

(1989) argue for placing students in home schools "to engender a pluralistic society, to use the most meaningful instructional environments, to enhance family access and to develop a wide range of social relationships with nondisabled peers" (pp. 2–3).

In practice, students with severe and multiple disabilities may have full-time placement in regular classes, part-time placements in regular classes and resource rooms, or placements in special self-contained programs. The Individual Education Plan, based on professional judgments that consider the wishes of the family, the age and abilities of the child, the services available, the content of instructional approaches, and the child's need for a more or less structured educational, community, and work environment will determine the placement that is in the child's best interests (Giangreco et al., 1997; Buysse & Bailey, 1993).

The question of where to teach students with severe and multiple disabilities centers on selecting the setting that will maximize skill development and use. Therefore, depending upon the severity, number, and kinds of disabilities, these students could be provided services (education and treatment) in institutions, residential settings, and/or in their community or home schools.

Students with severe and multiple disabilities are increasingly being educated in general education classes. These students' schedules are designed so that they receive supportive services such as speech-language and physical therapy, orientation and mobility services, and other services unique to their disabilities while attending their home schools. The reliance on specialists to assist these children is critical.

However, the traditional use of specialists who work in isolation in separate classes or schools may not work well in the context of the regular classroom. Many special service providers are having to learn to integrate their services within regular classroom instruction (Giangreco et al., 1997).

The low incidence of this population, the limited availability of special teachers and specialists, and budgetary constraints will sometimes dictate placement for children with severe and multiple disabilities. Other factors, such as conflicting educational goals and different agendas between specialists and regular classroom teachers, specialists disrupting the regular classes, and incompatible school schedules and routines can also interfere with full inclusion (Giangreco et al., 1993). However, there is a great deal of support and advocacy for full access to homes, neighborhoods, local schools, regular classrooms, and job sites. These support and advocacy activities maximize the importance of specialized services in inclusive settings (Nisbet, 1992; Giangreco et al., 1997; Meyen, 1996).

## ISSUES OF IMPORTANCE

### Confusing Mental Retardation with Other Disabilities

An individual with a hearing loss may be mentally retarded. However, a careful and appropriate assessment of a child with a hearing loss may reveal that the child's poor academic performance is primarily the result of hearing loss. The child's low score on a standardized IQ test may reflect that he or she is not able to accurately hear spoken language or that test instructions were inappropriately administered orally.

Another possibility is confusing mental retardation and mental illness. One of the major concerns of the Association for Persons with Severe Disabilities is the faulty assumption that people with mental retardation are mentally ill, an assumption often based on these individuals' challenging behaviors. Individuals with mental retardation are prone to magical thinking and confusion of reality because of their cognitive deficits, but this is not mental illness (Menolascino, Levitas, & Greimer, 1986). People with retardation may have some rigid rule-oriented, or ritualistic behaviors, but not be emotionally or behaviorally disordered. Mental retardation does not necessarily include mental illness.

### Collaboration

Students with severe and multiple disabilities and their families need a complicated and extensive array of support and services from educators, physical and occupational therapists, vocational counselors, speech-language pathologists, and medical personnel. The many interested professionals and paraprofessionals need to cooperate in special health-related services that range from the administration of medication to assistance with respiratory ventilation. Turnbull et al. (1995) report that if students with severe and multiple disabilities are to be successful in integrated schools and communities, collaboration between families and professionals and between professionals and each other is essential. Since a greater number of families are keeping their children at home, professionals must provide enabling support either directly to the families or through community schools and agencies. The era of the independent professional treating his or her "part" of the child in isolation from the entire rehabilitation program does not seem to have a place in modern service provision to children with severe and multiple disabilities.

Collaboration may also mean enlisting the support and friendship of the exceptional child's peer group. Adults in the lives of children with severe and multiple disabilities can encourage social interpersonal relationships with other students in the school by fostering peer tutor programs, cooperative small group learning, and buddy systems (Villa & Thousand, 1992; Turnbull et al., 1995). The efforts of cooperation and collaboration on behalf of children with severe and multiple disabilities cannot be dramatized enough, especially the profound benefits of engendering peer relationships for these children.

## Early Intervention and Preschool Caregivers

Children with severe and multiple disabilities are generally identified at birth and require extensive early health and medical care. However, a problem for families is that few preschool programs will accept young children with severe and multiple handicaps. Parents are forced to hire, when possible, individual caregivers. There is a danger that, unlike trained teachers interacting with children with severe and multiple handicaps, caregivers may be inflexible and less permissive with the children in their care. In some cases, caregivers tend to provide unnecessary assistance for the child, be more intrusive, and encourage the child's dependency. Children in their care tend to be more withdrawn, less active, and less willing to engage in play than their peers in preschool programs. Early intervention specialists need to help families and paraprofessional caregivers learn to encourage more independence and overcome their potential lack of involvement in the child's independence (Kirk et al., 1997; Turnbull et al., 1995).

## Generalization, Maintenance, and the Use of Aversive Procedures

A persistent concern in the education and treatment of students with severe and multiple disabilities is that students often fail to generalize the behaviors targeted in their programs and that they seem unable to maintain learned behaviors after reinforcement and other procedures have been discontinued. Generalization and maintenance programs, when applied at all, are often haphazardly constructed and poorly monitored. Attainment of behaviors in the controlled safety of the classroom is a far cry from the active utilization of an acquired behavior in everyday life outside the classroom. For behaviors to generalize and be maintained, they must be meaningful and under the control of the student. Parents, teachers, and peers are an underutilized resource in generalizing and maintaining newly learned skills.

A disquieting and troubling co-existing situation is the use of many aversive or punishing procedures, including electric shock, ammonia spray, pinching, and forced body movements to control unwanted behaviors. The effectiveness of these procedures is questionable and the process is ethically suspect (Meyen & Skrtic, 1988). Teaching and rewarding alternatives that are incompatible with unwanted behaviors, as compared to punishing inappropriate behaviors, is more desirable and effective. Positive intervention is constructive and teaches the student what to do rather than what not to do. Non-aversive procedures, such as rewarding sought-after behavior, facilitate generalization and maintenance of behaviors incompatible with those formerly punished (Snell, 1988; Meyen, 1996; Kirk et al., 1997; Hunt & Marshall, 1994).

## Family Issues

Families with a child with severe and multiple disabilities face many pressures and heartrending issues that most families never need to confront. The realization that a child with severe and multiple disabilities might require extensive lifelong care means that families of children with severe and multiple disabilities require more financial and professional support and services to than do other families, just to help them keep their children at home. They need information about how to deal with their children's needs and how to become more cogent advocates for their children. The families of children with severe and multiple disabilities also may need direct physical assistance in caregiving time, to give them some respite and release time from the constant demands of caregiving for their children (Turnbull et al., 1995).

When making demands of the families of children with severe and multiple disabilities, professionals must become sensitive to the effect that their mandates might have on the already-strained family dynamic that raising a child with severe and multiple disabilities causes.

## PROFESSIONALS

It is conceivable that every professional that we have described in each of the preceding chapters of this text might be on the service provision team for any given child with severe and multiple disabilities. However, no one team will require all of the services available to all exceptional children. Coordination of the array of personnel requires a team that can work supportively. Typically, members of the team will be a regular education teacher, a special education teacher, a speech-language pathologist, and a physical therapist. Other professionals can include physicians, occupational therapists, vision specialists, audiologists, vocational rehabilitation counselors, movement specialists, and medical and nonmedical paraprofessionals of all types. The composition of the team is obviously driven by the combination and severity of the multiple disabilities. How any given team functions is critical to efficient service provision to the family and the child.

There are three popular team approaches:

1. Multidisciplinary
2. Interdisciplinary
3. Transdisciplinary

The *multidisciplinary team* involves separate disciplines providing independent evaluations and treatment recommendations from each individual discipline's perspective. This team is often involved in the screening and identification of children with disabilities. The team can be medically or clinically oriented, and therapy services are usually provided outside the home and school.

The *interdisciplinary team* has a case coordinator and there is collaboration between specialists on the team, who share evaluation outcomes and make recommendations that lead to the development of a single overall educational plan.

The *transdisciplinary team* involves each discipline working cooperatively from the outset of program design and implementation. Team members exchange information, share skills, and train each other to implement specialized programs. Specific team members, especially parents, teachers, and paraprofessionals, have continuous contact with the student and deliver the educational and therapeutic services with support and training from the specialist team members. Programs are implemented in school, home, and community as well as in specialized settings (Meyen & Skrtic, 1988).

## PROFESSIONAL ASSOCIATIONS AND PARENT OR SELF-HELP GROUPS

American Association of the Deaf-Blind
814 Thayer Avenue
Silver Spring, MD 20910

Association for Persons with Severe Handicaps
11201 Greenwood Avenue N
Seattle, WA 98133

Association of Birth Defect Children
3526 Emerywood Lane
Orlando, FL 32812

Helen Keller National Center for Deaf-Blind
Youths and Adults
111 Middle Neck Road
Sands Point, NY 11050

National Society for Children and Adults with Autism
621 Central Avenue
Albany, NY 12206

United Cerebral Palsy Association
66 East 34th Street
New York, NY 10016

## REFERENCES FOR FURTHER INFORMATION

*Autism Screening Instrument for Educational Planning* (1997). By D. Krung, J. Grick, and P. Almond. Austin, TX: PRO-ED.

*Choosing Options and Accommodations for Children* (1994). By M. Giangreco, L. Cloninger, and V. Iverson. Baltimore: Brookes.

*Critical Issues in the Lives of People with Severe Disabilities* (1991). Edited by Luanna H. Meyer, Charles A. Peck, and Lou Brown. Baltimore: Brookes.

*Curriculum Considerations in Inclusive Classrooms: Facilitating Learning for All Students* (1992). Edited by Susan Stainback and William Stainback. Baltimore: Brookes.

*Educating Children with Multiple Disabilities: A Transdisciplinary Approach* (1991). By Fred Orelove and Dick Sobsey. Baltimore: Brookes.

*Instruction of Students with Severe Disabilities*, 4th ed. (1993). By Martha E. Snell. Upper Saddle River, NJ: Prentice Hall/Merrill.

*Mental Retardation and Developmental Disabilities* (1997). Edited by P. McLaughlin and P. Wehman. Austin, TX: PRO-ED.

*The Advance*
Association for Persons in Supported Employment
5001 W. Broad Street, Suite 34
Richmond, VA 23230

*Focus on Autism and Other Developmental Disabilities*
PRO-ED
8700 Shoal Creek Boulevard
Austin, TX 78757

*Supported Employment InfoLines*
Training Resource Network
316 St. George Street
St. Augustine, FL 32084

*Journal of the Association for Persons with Severe Handicaps*
Association for Persons with Severe Handicaps
11201 Greenwood Avenue North
Seattle, WA 98133

# REFERENCES

Baldwin, V. (1993, October). *Population/demographics.* Paper presented at the National Project Directors Meeting on Educational Services for Children and Youth with Deaf-Blindness, Washington, DC.

Bateman, B. D. (1971). *The essentials of teaching.* San Rafael, CA: Dimensions.

Batshaw, M. L., & Perret, Y. M. (Eds.) (1992). *Children with handicaps: A medical primer.* (3rd ed.) Baltimore: Brookes.

Bishop, K. D., Eshelian, L., & Falvey, M. A. (1989). Motor skills. In M. A. Falvey (Ed.), *Community-based curriculum: Instructional strategies for students with severe handicaps.* Baltimore: Brookes.

Bower, T. G. R. (1989). *The rational infant.* New York: Freeman.

Bradley, V., & Knoll, J. (1995). Shifting paradigms in services to people with disabilities. In O. Karan & S. Greenspan (Eds.), *Community rehabilitation for people with disabilities.* Newton, MA: Butterworth-Heinemann.

Brown, L., Long, E., Udvori-Solner, A., Schwarz, P., VanDeventer, P., Ahlgren, C., Johnson, F., Gruenwald, L., & Jorgensen, J. (1989). Should students with severe intellectual disabilities be based in regular or in special education classrooms in home schools? *Journal of the Association for Persons with Severe Handicaps, 14,* 8–12.

Buysse, V., & Bailey, D. B. (1993). Behavioral and developmental outcomes in young children with disabilities in integrated and segregated settings: A review of comparative studies. *Journal of Special Education, 26,* 434–461.

Campbell, P. H. (1989). Dysfunction in posture and movement in individuals with profound disabilities: Issues and practices. In F. Brown and D. H. Lehr (Eds.), *Persons with profound disabilities: Issues and practices.* Baltimore: Brookes.

Cary, D., & Sale, P. (1994). Notebook computers increase communication. TEACHING *Exceptional Children, 27* (1), 62–69.

Collins, M. T., & Rudolph, J. M. (1975). *A manual for the assessment of a deaf-blind multiply handicapped child* (Rev. ed.). Denver, CO: Mountain Plains Regional Center for the Deaf-Blind.

Downing, J., & Eichinger, J. (1990). Instructional strategies for learners with dual sensory impairments in integrated settings. *Journal of the Association for Persons with Severe Handicaps, 15,* 98–105.

Evans, I. M. (1991). Testing and diagnosis: A review and evaluation. In L. H. Meyer, C. A. Peck, & L. Brown (Eds.), *Critical issues in the lives of people with severe disabilities.* Baltimore: Brookes.

Everson, J. (Ed.). (1995). *Supporting young adults who are deaf-blind in their communities.* Baltimore: Brookes.

Fox, T., & Williams, W. (1991). Implementing best practices for all students in their local school. Burlington, VT: University of Vermont, University Affiliated Program of Vermont. (ERIC Document Reproduction Service No. ED 361 977)

Gast, D., & Berkler, M. (1981). Severe and profound handicaps. In A. E. Blackhurst and W. H. Berdine (Eds.), *An introduction to special education.* Boston: Little, Brown.

Gaylor-Ross, R. J., & Holvoet, J. F. (1985). *Strategies for educating students with severe disabilities.* Boston: Little, Brown.

Giangreco, M. F., Dennis, R., Cloninger, C., Edelman, S., & Schattman, R. (1993). "I've counted Jon": Transformational experiences of teachers educating students with disabilities. *Exceptional Children, 59,* 359–372.

Giangreco, M. F., Edelman, S. W., Macfarland, S., & Luiselli, T. E. (1997). Attitudes about educational and related services for students with deaf-blindness and multiple disabilities. *Exceptional Children, 63*(3), pp. 329–342.

Greenwood, C. (1994). Advances in technology-based assessment within special education. *Exceptional Children, 61*(2), 102–104.

Guess, P. D., & Siegel-Causey, E. (1988). Students with severe and multiple disabilities. In E. L. Meyen & T. M. Skrtic (Eds.), *Exceptional children and youth: An introduction* (3rd ed.) Denver, CO: Love.

Guess, P. D., & Mulligan, M. (1988). The severely and profoundly handicapped. In E. L. Meyen and T. M. Skrtic (Eds.), *Exceptional children and youth: An introduction* (3rd ed.). Denver, CO: Love.

Hardman, M. L., Drew, C. J., & Egan, M. W. (1996). *Human exceptionality: Society, school, and family* (5th ed.). Needham, MA: Allyn & Bacon.

Haring, N., & Romer, L. (1995). *Welcoming students who are deaf-blind into typical classrooms: Facilitating school participation, learning, and friendships.* Baltimore: Brookes.

Haring, N. G., McCormick, L., & Haring, T. G. (1994). *Exceptional children and youth: An introduction to special education* (6th ed.). New York: Macmillan.

Hunt, N., & Marshall, K. (1994). *Exceptional children and youth: An introduction to special education.* Boston: Houghton Mifflin.

Kirk, S. A., Gallagher, J. J., & Anastasiow, N. J. (1997). *Educating exceptional children* (8th ed.). Boston: Houghton Mifflin.

Knoblock, P. (1982). Teaching and mainstreaming autistic children. Denver, CO: Love.

Lambert, N., Windmiller, M., Cole, L., & Figuerra, R. (1975). AAMD *adaptive behavior scale: Public school version.* Washington, DC: American Association of Mental Deficiency.

Landesman-Dwyer, S., & Butterfield, E. C. (1983). Mental retardation: Development issues in cognitive and social adaptation. In M. Lewis (Ed.), *Origins of intelligence: Infancy and early childhood* (2nd ed., pp. 479–519). New York: Plenum.

McLaren, J., & Bryson, S. E. (1987). Review of recent epidemiological studies of mental retardation: Prevalence, associated disorders, and etiology. *American Journal of Mental Retardation, 92,* 243–254.

Menolascino, F. J., Levitas, A., & Greimer, C. (1986). The nature and type of mental illness in the mentally retarded. *Psychopharmacology Bulletin, 22,* 1060–1071.

Meyen, E. L. (1996). *Exceptional children in today's schools* (3rd ed.). Denver, CO: Love.

Meyen, E. L., & Skrtic, T. M. (1988). *Exceptional children and youth: An introduction* (3rd ed.). Denver, CO: Love.

Meyer, L., & Eichinger, J. (1994). *Program quality indicators (PQI): A checklist of the most promising practices in educational programs for students with disabilities* (3rd ed.). Syracuse, NY: Syracuse University, School of Education.

Meyer, L. H., Peck, C. A., & Brown, L. (1991). *Critical issues in the lives of people with severe disabilities.* Baltimore: Brookes.

Murphy, K., & Byrne, D. (1983). Selection of optimal modalities as avenues of learning in deaf, blind, multiply disabled children. In G. Mencher & S. Gerber (Eds.), *Multiply handicapped hearing-impaired child.* New York: Grune & Stratton.

National Information Center for Children and Youth with Disabilities. (1994, March). *Learning Disabilities.* Fact Sheet N.7. Washington, DC: Amos.

Nisbet, J. (1992). *Natural supports at home, school and in the community for people with severe disabilities.* Baltimore: Brookes.

Orelove, F. P., & Sobsey, D. (1991). Curriculum and instruction. In F. P. Orelove & D. Sobsey (Eds.), *Educating children with multiple disabilities: A transdescriptionary approach* (2nd ed.). Baltimore: Brookes.

Rainforth, B., York, J., & Macdonald, C. (1992). *Collaborative teams for students with severe disabilities: Integrating therapy and educational services.* Baltimore: Brookes.

Rimland, B., & Edelson, S. (1994). Auditory integration training and autism. *Autism Research Review, 8* (2)., 5–7.

Ruttenberg, B. A., Kalish, B. I., Wenar, C., & Wolf, E. G. (1977). *Behavior rating instrument for atypical children (BRIAC).* Chicago: Stoelting.

Sailor, W., Goetz, L., Anderson, J., Hunt, K., & Gee, K. (1988). Research on community intensive instruction as a model for building functional, generalized skills. In R. H. Horner, G. Dunlap, & R. L. Koegel (Eds.), *Generalization and maintenance: Lifestyle changes in applied settings.* Baltimore: Brookes.

Sailor, W., & Guess, D. (1983). *Severely handicapped students.* Boston: Houghton Mifflin.

Sailor, W., & Mix, B. J. (1976). *TARC assessment system.* Lawrence, KS: H & H Enterprises.

Seligman, M. E. P. (1975). *Helplessness: On depression, development, and death.* San Francisco: Freeman.

Snell, M. A. (1988). Curriculum and methodology for individuals with severe disabilities. *Education and Training in Mental Retardation, 24* (4), 302–314.

Snell, M. A. (1992). *Systematic instruction of persons with severe handicaps* (4th ed.) Upper Saddle River, NJ: Prentice Hall/Merrill.

Taylor, R. (1988). Assessment policies and procedures. In L. Sternberg (Ed.), *Educating students with severe or profound handicaps* (pp. 103–118). Austin, TX: PRO-ED.

Taylor, S. J., & Racino, J. A. (1991). Community living: Lessons for today. In L. H. Meyer, C. A. Peck, & L. Brown (Eds.), *Critical issues in the lives of people with severe disabilities.* Baltimore: Brookes.

Turnbull, A. P., Turnbull, H. R., Shank, M., & Leal, D. (1995). *Exceptional lives: Special education in today's schools.* Upper Saddle River, NJ: Prentice Hall/Merrill.

U.S. Department of Education. (1997). *Nineteenth annual report to Congress on the implementation of the Individuals with Disabilities Education Act.* Washington, DC: Author.

Villa, R. A., & Thousand, J. S. (1992). Student collaboration: An essential for curriculum delivery in the 21st century. In S. Stainback & W. Stainback (Eds.), *Curriculum considerations in inclusive classrooms: Facilitating learning for all students.* Baltimore: Paul H. Brookes.

Wehman, P. (1997). *Exceptional individuals in school, community, and work.* Austin, TX: PRO-ED.

Williams, R. R. (1991). Assistive technology in the eye of the beholder. *Journal of Vocational Rehabilitation, 1*(9), 9–12.

# 11

# Children Who are
# Gifted and Talented

The special gifts and talents that some children possess can, with nurturing and care, blossom into the contributions a society values, or they can be ignored and wither on the vine. Unlike other exceptionalities that affect children, giftedness is a difference that a society should strive to encourage. It is not as easy as it might seem to define giftedness, identify those who are gifted and talented, and then provide meaningful programs that will enhance their development as human beings. There are unresolved conflicts about which children should be identified, what training experiences and skills are necessary, and even whether the school systems should assume any responsibility for providing special educational opportunities for these children. All of these questions are debated, concerns discussed, and ultimately decisions made, while generations of gifted and talented children mature. Some are never identified. Others' chances to excel evaporate in poverty. Many are too culturally distinct for their teachers to appreciate them. A number suffer disabilities that may mask their talents, while others, for a variety of reasons, are unable to achieve their potential. As a result, they do not learn how to lead us in evolving toward a better society.

## DEFINITIONS

The definition of who is gifted and talented is evolving and becoming less restrictive. The earliest definitions were based exclusively on intellectual potential as measured by intelligence tests. More recently proposed definitions are wider in scope and recognize many facets of giftedness and talent. They stress multiple evaluation measures and encourage parent and community input. However, regardless of the definition, they all seem to agree that students who are gifted and talented need services not ordinarily provided by schools.

Definitions are of practical importance. Hardman, Drew, and Egan (1996) suggest that how we define giftedness and talent will ultimately have an impact on:

1. The number of students labeled to receive services.
2. Which tests are used to evaluate potential students.
3. The cutoff scores needed to qualify.
4. Which students are specifically offered help.
5. What type of education is provided.
6. The funding allocated by school systems for programs for the gifted and talented.
7. The experiences needed by teachers who wish to instruct children and youth who are gifted and talented.

Unfortunately, there is little agreement on how to define children who might be gifted and talented (Gallagher, 1985; Maker, 1986). While factors such as intelligence, creativity, and talent are the keys to many definitions (Howell, Heward, & Swassing, 1996), they are not universal to all definitions, nor are all the definitions available limited to using those three terms exclusively. The most efficient way to deal with this potentially confusing issue is to divide the information available. First, we will share some of the many terms that make up the vocabulary defining children who are gifted and talented. Then we will illustrate some of the many federal government and state educational agency definitions. Finally, we will end this section on definitions with a sampling of how some of the most influential scholars define the children with gifts and talents whom they study.

The terms listed in Box 11.1 are not a complete listing of the specialized vocabulary that has developed to define giftedness and talent. However, they should provide enough information to help the reader understand the definitions that follow.

By understanding this partial listing of terms and their definitions, the reader can now more meaningfully interpret the following federal, state, and individual expert definitions of what it means to be gifted and talented.

---

### Box 11.1
### WHAT EVERY TEACHER NEEDS TO KNOW

### Terms

**cognition**   Understanding based on the ability to integrate perceptions, memory, insights, judgments, and similar learning processes.

**convergent thinking**   The ability to blend apparently unrelated information into a unified concept (Smith & Luckasson, 1995).

**creativity**   Ability to sense relationships that are not readily apparent, ask critical questions, and generate novel or unexpected responses to situations. Creativity may be noticed in the child's ability to produce many alternative ideas in problem-solving tasks (Hallahan & Kauffman, 1994; Guilford, 1977).

**divergent thinking**   The ability to start from a given idea or concept and branch into different directions from the starting point (Smith & Luckasson, 1995). This skill is vital in the demonstration of creativity.

**evaluative thinking**   The ability to make logical decisions by comparing and contrasting the components of the information one has available (Smith & Luckasson, 1995).

**genius**   A markedly exceptional aptitude or capacity in any area; usually used in reference to intellectual aptitudes.

**giftedness**   Often considered present in a child who shows cognitive or intellectual superiority, creativity,

and motivation to succeed to a degree sufficient to separate that child from most of his or her age mates (Renzulli, Reis, & Smith, 1981; U.S. Senate Report, 1972).

**high intelligence**   The result of a number of characteristics, such as the ability to think on abstract levels, solve complicated problems, perceive complicated relationships and expand and develop these outstanding abilities (Smith & Luckasson, 1995).

**high performance capability**   A term applied to children who might be extraordinarily gifted or talented, but are not currently showing their potential abilities in their performance (Kirk, Gallagher, & Anastasiow, 1993).

**specific academic ability**   Exceptional ability in one area but not in all areas traditionally measured (Kirk et al., 1993).

**talent**   Superlative skills, aptitudes, or accomplishments, usually in the fine arts or performing arts. These skills may not always correlate with high scores on general intelligence tests (Hallahan & Kauffman, 1994; Council of State Directors of Programs for the Gifted, 1991; Gallagher, 1985; Stanley, 1977; Tannenbaum, 1992).

## Federal and State Definitions of Giftedness

In 1972, Sidney Marland, who was then the U.S. Commissioner of Education, proposed a definition of giftedness and talent that signaled that educators should be aware of more than just superior intellectual ability when determining which children in their school systems were to be considered for special programming. His definition remains the most widely accepted and the basis for most state definitions (Smith & Luckasson, 1995). Marland proposed the following:

> Gifted and talented children are those identified by professionally qualified persons who by virtue of outstanding abilities are capable of high performance. These are children who require differentiated educational programs and services beyond those normally provided by the regular school program in order to realize their contributions to self and society. Children capable of high performance include those with demonstrated achievement and/or potential ability in any of the following areas singly or in combination:
> 1. General intellectual aptitude.
> 2. Specific academic aptitude.
> 3. Creative or productive thinking.
> 4. Leadership ability.
> 5. Visual and performing arts. (Marland, 1972, p. 1)

Marland stressed that students who are gifted and talented require and deserve different educational experiences than their age peers. With the passage of PL 95-561 in 1978 and PL 100-297, the Jacob K. Javits Gifted and Talented Children's Education Act of 1988, Congress incorporated Marland's conceptualizations into law. According to PL 95-561 and its similarly worded mate, PL 100-297:

> Gifted and talented means children, and whenever possible, youth who are identified at the preschool, elementary, or secondary level as possessing demonstrated or potential abilities that give evidence of high performance capability in areas such as intellectual, creative, specific academic or leadership ability, or in the performing or visual arts, and who by reason thereof require services or activities not ordinarily provided by the school. (Congressional Record, 1978)

A recent attempt on the federal level to define this special group was proposed by the U.S. Department of Education in 1993. In *National Excellence: A Case for Developing American Talent* (U.S. Department of Education, 1993), this proposed definition states that:

> Children and youth with outstanding talent perform or show the potential for performing at remarkably high levels of accomplishment when compared with others of their age, experience or environment. These children and youth exhibit high performance capability in intellectual, creative and/or artistic areas, possess an unusual leadership capacity or excel in specific academic fields. They require the services or activities not ordinarily provided in the schools. Outstanding talents are present in children and youth from all cultural groups, across all economic strata and in all areas of human endeavor.

The word *gifted* is most noticeable by its absence from this definition. *Gifted* implies that the child needs to have a mature or developed power rather than a developing ability. In stressing the developing aspect of abilities, the case for services to nurture these abilities is underscored. This definition stresses that teachers need to look into all disciplines of endeavor for students with talents and not just traditional academic areas. This would entail using a variety of measuring instruments and providing accessibility to special programs to those with less obvious potential. This definition explicitly mandates a sensitivity to multicultural and diverse populations, who may not automatically meet the expectations of the prevailing cultural standards and who are currently underrepresented in gifted and talented programs.

Since 1984, 48 states have established their own definitions for children who are gifted and talented. They appear either in statutes or in state department of education regulations, many of which require special education for those identified as gifted and talented (Wolf, 1990). Most of the states have incorporated aspects of the federal definitions into their definitions. However, they are by no means uniform in their selection of criteria for inclusion in their individual programs. The most common elements in the individual state definitions are that the gifted and talented children must show (1) general intellectual ability, (2) specific academic aptitudes, (3) creative thinking skills, (4) advanced abilities in the fine or performing arts, and (5) leadership abilities (Council of State Directors of Programs for the Gifted, 1991). The most efficient way to obtain and study the definition of any given state is to contact the state department of special education and request a copy of the definition and guidelines for inclusion in gifted and talented programs. A listing of the addresses and phone numbers for each state appears in Appendix I.

We have summarized in the following section the conceptualizations of some of the most influential scholars who have devoted their efforts to better understanding children who are gifted and talented. It is from their work, both historical and current, that our understanding of the nature of these children arises.

## Scholarly Definitions

Terman (1925, 1947, 1959) was most influential in the early defining of giftedness in terms of performance on individual IQ test scores. IQ scores in the 98th or 99th percentile came to define giftedness and also served to identify those who were to be eligible for special services. IQ scores of 145 or 150 were and are still used as a numerical way to describe the intellectual capabilities of children who are gifted. Seaberg and Stafford (1991) report that most states still focus on intellectual ability in defining giftedness. However, as scholars became more knowledgeable about the way children who are gifted and talented function, components other than intellectual functioning exclusively were added to the definition of giftedness. In fact, even the conceptualization of intelligence has been expanded. Witty (1951) expanded the definition to include special skills and talents when he described children who are gifted and talented as those who show performance that is remarkable not only in intellectual functioning but also in any area valuable to society. Guilford (1959) added that creativity should be considered; he found it to be the driving force behind the contributions of scientists and inventors who were gifted. The belief among those who study individuals who are gifted and talented has become that intelligence and giftedness are more complex than tests alone can measure. IQ test scores may not accurately reflect thinking ability or insight-fulness (Reis, 1989; Sternberg & Davidson, 1983). Sternberg (1991) reports that giftedness cannot be captured by a single number. In his view, it is a multifaceted combination of different types of abilities. The person who is gifted will show *analytical understanding*, which allows for dividing problems into their critical components; *synthetic insights*, shown by the intuitive ability to cope with novel situations; and *practical application skills*, which make it possible to use the analytic and synthetic skills to solve problems.

Renzulli (1978) expanded the definition to include children who might not achieve high IQ scores but who do evidence above average ability in an area, combined with task commitment and creativity. This combination of talents should make these children eligible for the special programming provided for students who are gifted and talented.

Gardner and Hatch (1989) have expanded the definition of intelligence so that it includes seven different dimensions. This widely accepted acknowledgment of the multiple components of intelligence recognizes *logical-mathematical intelligence*, evidenced by high level inductive and deductive reasoning and computational skills; *linguistic intelligence*, seen in written and oral language performance; *musical intelligence*, the ability to understand and manipulate components of music, either in performance or composition; *spatial intelligence*, the ability to perceive and manipulate visual-spatial configurations; *bodily-kinesthetic intelligence*, evidenced by the ability to control body movements or handle objects with great skill; *interpersonal intelligence*, shown by abilities to understand an act insightfully in response to other people's actions or feelings; and *intrapersonal intelligence*, the ability to use one's own feelings and perceptions as guides to understanding. Table 11.1 is a reproduction of the seven components of intelligence, emphasizing their core components and giving examples of possible vocational outcomes.

Kauffman (1997) has attempted to synthesize some of these emerging definitions. His global definition of what it means to be gifted and talented stresses *high abilities* (including high intelligence as an ability), *high creativity* (as seen in the generation of novel ideas and applying them as solutions to problems), and *high task commitment* (shown in the ability to see projects through to their conclusion). As we proceed with the rest of this chapter, we will see how many of the concepts just presented have an impact on the lives of children who are gifted and talented and the parents and teachers responsible for their well-being.

## PREVALENCE

There appear to be two figures repeated most often in the literature that identify how many of the children currently in school should be eligible for special education as gifted and talented children. The first, more conservative figure is approximately 3 to 5 percent (Marland, 1972; Mitchell & Erickson, 1978; Sisk, 1981, 1987). The second, more inclusive figure, suggests that approximately 15 percent of all children currently

Table 11.1
The Seven Intelligences

| Intelligence | End States | Core Components |
|---|---|---|
| Logical-mathematical | Scientist<br>Mathematician | Sensitivity to, and capacity to discern, logical or numerical patterns; ability to handle long chains of reasoning |
| Linguistic | Poet<br>Journalist | Sensitivity to the sounds, rhythms, and meanings of words; sensitivity to the different functions of language |
| Musical | Composer<br>Violinist | Abilities to produce and appreciate rhythm, pitch, and timbre; appreciation of the forms of musical expressiveness |
| Spatial | Navigator<br>Sculptor | Capacities to perceive the visual-spatial world accurately and to perform transformations on one's initial perceptions |
| Bodily-kinesthetic | Dancer<br>Athlete | Abilities to control one's body movements and to handle objects skillfully |
| Interpersonal | Therapist<br>Salesman | Capacities to discern and respond appropriately to the moods, temperaments, motivations, and desires of other people |
| Intrapersonal | Person with detailed, accurate self-knowledge | Access to one's own feelings and the ability to discriminate among them and draw upon them to guide behavior; knowledge of one's own strengths, weaknesses, desires, and intelligences |

*Source:* "Multiple Intelligences Go to School: Educational Implications of the Theory of Multiple Intelligences," by H. Gardner and T. Hatch, 1989, *Educational Researcher, 18*(8), p. 6. Copyright 1989 by the American Educational Research Association; reproduced with permission from the publisher.

enrolled in the public schools are eligible for consideration (Renzulli & Reis, 1991). Current enrollment figures, as can best be determined, come closer to but do not reach the first figure of 3 to 5 percent. Each state has its own guidelines or formula for the identification of children with giftedness, and this also contributes to the variance in the estimates.

## CHARACTERISTICS

Common stereotypes of children who are gifted and talented as little adults with thick glasses, pocket protectors, and arcane mathematics textbooks in each hand do not mirror reality. Being considered gifted and talented may cover a wide variety of possibilities, abilities, and skills, each occurring individually or in combination with others. As a result, a correspondingly wide variety of characteristics are applicable to children who are gifted and talented. However, characteristics do exist. The traits are generalizations, based for the most part on observations, standardized tests, and the individual researchers' familiarity with children who are gifted and talented. Like all generalizations, they fail to describe each individual child, but rather provide large inclusive categories that help parents, teachers, and other interested community members recognize the behavioral characteristics these special children are likely to exhibit.

Beginning in 1920, Terman (1925, 1947, 1959) studied 1,528 children with average IQ scores of 151. His discoveries over a more than 40-year period helped to contradict the most widely held stereotypes of children who are gifted and talented. He discovered that these children tended to be superior to their age mates in almost every measure he applied. They were not intellectually gifted at the cost of being physically weak, socially timid, or emotionally immature. In fact, as a group, they were taller, heavier, stronger, more energetic, and healthier than their age mates. They were more emotionally stable and even showed, as measured by Terman, superior moral character (Terman, 1926). It must be noted that Terman's children were selected as the result of their performance on group intelligence scores and teacher recommendations. It was largely a white middle class group of children who were high achievers. Culturally diverse and economically disadvantaged children did not make up a significant portion of the sample. It must also be emphasized that these are general characteristics. Children who are gifted show as much individual variation as any other group of children. As we recognize more types of giftedness, the relationships that Terman described may be less observable. However, others, including Gallagher (1985), also reported that the children they observed who were gifted were socially and emotionally equal to or ahead of their age peers' developmental levels and above average in their concerns about moral and ethical issues and behaviors. They tended to be well liked by peers, be social leaders, be self-sufficient, and show a wide variety of interests; although not immune to problems, they were less prone to neurotic or psychotic episodes than their contemporaries (Coleman & Fultz, 1985; Janos & Robinson, 1985; Piechowski, 1991; Gallagher, 1985).

Creativity, in many different forms, appears repeatedly as a characteristic of students who are gifted and talented. The characteristics of creativity are varied. We often see gifted and talented children who produce large numbers of novel, often wild and silly ideas and solutions to problems (Lucito, 1974; Renzulli & Hartman, 1971). These sometimes unusual or unexpected ideas can be produced rapidly in great detail, and can be paired with unlikely alternative solutions to problems (Guilford, 1987). Creativity is difficult to measure. The Torrance Tests of Creative Thinking (Torrance, 1966) attempt to elicit original responses to questions and problems. Rather than looking for "correct" answers, it looks for the production of unusual and creative answers to questions requiring the child to be imaginative and demonstrate understanding of the problems presented.

Children who are gifted and talented can show exceptional academic skills in general, as they are able to grasp concepts, generalize, analyze, and synthesize new ideas or problems with greater facility than their age peers (Bloom, 1956; Clark, 1992), or they may have unusual aptitude only in a given area or areas. They sometimes learn to read easily, before entering school, either teaching themselves or with minimal input from parents. Their reading skills are often far more advanced than their concomitant above average performance in writing or math. (Gallagher, 1985). Reading is often also a preferred leisure activity (Van Tassel-Baska, 1983). These children learn a great deal of information quickly, retain and use what they learn, have an excellent command of language, enjoy acquiring and manipulating

abstract material, and are excited by the learning process in general. Children who are gifted and talented characteristically do more than just absorb knowledge. They have the ability to see the "big picture," as evidenced by their ability to deal with a variety of concepts at any time and organize these concepts into large meaningful patterns. They have an intellectual curiosity that fires a need for mental stimulation and an intuitive sense of appropriateness reflected in good judgment. (Terman & Oden, 1959; Clark, 1992; Gallagher & Gallagher, 1994; Piirto, 1994; Silverman, 1995; Guilford, 1987).

Children who are gifted are often confident children, exhibiting advanced appreciation of humor along with an intellectual playfulness that brings a sense of relaxation to their creative pursuits. They do not fear being different and will uninhibitedly express opinions and, if sufficiently challenged, express their opinions in a spirited and tenacious manner (Lucito, 1974; Renzulli & Hartman, 1971).

We can more easily catalog the characteristics of children who are academically gifted than we can those of who are extremely talented. *Talents* usually refers to outstanding skills or potentials, primarily those of the visual or performing arts. Children who are talented show highly developed nonverbal skills, exceptional physical coordination, and spatial talents. They might also display skills in music, dance, storytelling, drawing, or painting (Turnbull, Turnbull, Shank, & Leal, 1995). The parents of children who are musically talented report that their children displayed a natural feeling or sensitivity and emotional responsiveness to music at a very young age (Bloom,

1982). Children who are visually talented seem to show more control over artistic media of all types than do their age mates. This is often most noticeable in early drawing skills (Clark & Zimmerman, 1984). Key characteristics that might bring dance and dramatic talents into focus early are not yet as clear, as are some of the others we have been cataloging in this section.

Children who are gifted and talented often show the potential for leadership. Although there are many different types of leaders and many skills appropriate to leadership, some characteristics have emerged. Highly developed communication skills seem to head the list, along with co-existing social skills, empathy, superior decision-making skills, the ability to motivate others, and the skills needed to keep groups united and on task; these all appear to be a part of the leadership component of giftedness (Turnbull et al., 1995). Even though these children may show leadership skills, they are often very independent (Lucito, 1974). They can plan and execute projects with little need for or interest in supervision. They not only have the ability to work alone, but they often prefer solitude for both scholarly and artistic tasks (Bloom, 1982; Getzels, 1979). As a result, they often rely upon their own judgment and self-evaluation more than on the evaluations of their peers or teachers (Wolf, 1990). Box 11.2 is a brief compilation of some of the abilities and personality attributes that children who are gifted and talented might exhibit. Notice how the outstanding abilities and personality characteristics are similar for some talent areas but markedly different for others.

It would appear that being gifted and talented excuses children from the negatives of life. This is not the case at all. Children who are gifted are, in many ways, like all other children in many ways. They suffer emotional traumas, have physical problems, and evidence all the types of behavior that their less talented peers bring to childhood. In addition, their talents often bring some special problems. These children are often impatient with the routines of regular classroom life. Although they may do very well in analysis, argument and debate tasks and rote exercises are often met with resistance and noncompliance (Tidwell, 1980). Conforming to routines in general may be difficult for some of these children. Programmed instruction, unless it is challenging enough, will often not capture the attention of children who are gifted (Strom & Torrance, 1973). Their self-evaluations may lead them toward perfectionism and to applying unreasonably high standards not only to their own efforts, but also to the efforts of others in their environment (Whitmore, 1980). *Driven*, *domineering*, and *aloof* are not terms unfamiliar to children who are gifted and talented (Howell et al., 1996). Clark (1992) synthesized the work of many investigators and developed a comprehensive listing of the characteristics of children who are gifted and talented and the problems that might arise as a consequence of outstanding ability. She summarized their characteristics and potential problems into five domains: cognitive (thinking), affective (feeling), physical (sensation), intuitive, and societal. Table 11.2 is a reproduction of these findings. It is critical to remember that this and all other listings form a composite picture of children who are gifted and talented, in general. They are not a snapshot of any one child.

### Box 11.2
*WHAT EVERY TEACHER NEEDS TO KNOW*

### Characteristics of Children with Special Talents

| Talent Area | Abilities | Personality Attributes |
|---|---|---|
| Mathematics | Ability to manipulate symbolic material more effectively and more rapidly than classmates | Highly independent<br>Enjoy theoretical and investigative pursuits<br>Talented girls less conforming than other girls |
| Science | Ability to see relationships among ideas, events, and objects<br>Elegance in explanation; the ability to formulate the simplest hypothesis that can account for the observed facts | Highly independent, "loners"<br>Prefer intellectually rather than socially challenging situations<br>Reject group pressures<br>Methodical, precise, exact<br>Avid readers |
| Language arts | Capability of manipulating abstract concepts, but sometimes inferior to the high general achiever in working with mathematical material<br>Imagination and originality | Highly independent<br>Social and aesthetic values (girls)<br>Theoretical and political values (boys)<br>Avid readers |
| Leadership | Ability to effect change<br>Good decision-making ability<br>Proficiency in some area, such as athletics or academics<br>Ability to communicate | Empathic<br>Sensitive<br>Charisma—can transform the group through their enthusiasm and energy<br>Superior communication skills |
| Psychomotor ability | Gross motor strength, agility, flexibility, coordination, and speed<br>Excellence in athletics, gymnastics, or dance<br>Fine motor control, deftness, precision, flexibility, and speed<br>Excellence in crafts—jewelry making, model building, mechanics, working with electronic equipment, etc.<br>Ability to use complicated equipment with little or no training | Enjoy and seem to need considerable exercise<br>Competitive<br>Interested in mechanics, electronics, or crafts<br>Have hobbies such as model building, origami, pottery<br>Early participation in sports |
| Visual or performing arts | Ability to disregard traditional methods in favor of their own original ones<br>Resourcefulness in use of materials<br>Ability to express their feelings through an art form<br>Attention to detail in their own and others' artwork<br>Responsive to music, sculpture, etc. | Self-confident<br>Competitive<br>Prefer working alone<br>Sensitive to their environment<br>Gain satisfaction through expressing their feelings artistically |

*Source:* From *An Introduction to Special Education* (3rd ed.), by A. E. Blackhurst and W. H. Berdine. Copyright © 1993 by HarperCollins/College Publishers. Reprinted by permission of Addison-Wesley Educational Publishers Inc.

Table 11.2

Representative characteristics of people who are gifted and potential concomitant problems

| Domains | Differentiating Characteristics | Problems |
|---|---|---|
| Cognitive (thinking) | Extraordinary quantity of information, unusual retentiveness.<br>High level of language development.<br>Persistent, goal-directed behavior.<br>Unusual capacity for processing information. | Boredom with regular curriculum; impatience with waiting for group.<br>Perceived as showoff by children of the same age.<br>Perceived as stubborn, willful, uncooperative.<br>Resent being interrupted; perceived as too serious; dislike for routine and drill. |
| Affective (feeling) | Unusual sensitivity to the expectations and feelings of others.<br>Keen sense of humor—may be gentle or hostile.<br>Unusual emotional depth and intensity.<br><br>Advanced levels of moral judgment. | Unusually vulnerable to criticism of others; high level of need for success and recognition.<br>Use of humor for critical attack on others, resulting in damage to interpersonal relationships.<br>Unusual vulnerability; problem focusing on realistic goals for life's work.<br>Intolerance of and lack of understanding from peer group, leading to rejection and possible isolation. |
| Physical (sensation) | Unusual discrepancy between physical and intellectual development.<br><br><br>Low tolerance for lag between standards and athletic skills. | Result in adults who function with a mind/body dichotomy; children are comfortable expressing themselves only in mental activity, resulting in a limited development both physically and mentally.<br>Refusal to take part in any activities where they do not excel, limiting experience with otherwise pleasurable, constructive physical activities. |
| Intuitive | Early involvement and concern for intuitive knowing and metaphysical ideas and phenomena.<br>Creativity apparent in all areas of endeavor. | Ridiculed by peers; not taken seriously by elders; considered weird or strange.<br>Seen as deviant; become bored with mundane tasks; may be viewed as troublemaker. |
| Societal | Strongly motivated by self-actualization needs.<br>Leadership.<br><br><br><br>Solutions to social and environmental problems. | Frustration of not feeling challenged; loss of unrealized talents.<br>Lack of opportunity to use social ability constructively may result in its disappearance form child's repertoire or its being turned into a negative characteristic (e.g., gang leadership).<br>Loss to society if these traits are not allowed to develop with guidance and opportunity for meaningful involvement. |

*Source:* From *Human Exceptionality: Society, School, and Family* (5th ed.), by M. L. Hardman, C. J. Drew, and M. W. Egan, 1996. Needham, MA: Allyn & Bacon.

## ETIOLOGY

At this time, we can only make some informed guesses and point out what seem to be important factors for those already diagnosed as gifted and talented. We are unable to predict or perfectly explain why giftedness occurs. Three factors do seem to be important: (1) heredity, (2) prenatal and perinatal care, and (3) early childhood envi-

ronment. It is the interaction between heredity and environment that seems to be the key to helping giftedness develop (Tannenbaum, 1992).

## Heredity

The statistical probability of a child being gifted increases when the parents of the child have higher than average intelligence and are able to provide a nurturing environment (Kauffman, 1997). Studies of higher incidence of giftedness in both children in twin births and the close relationship between the talents of adopted children and their natural, rather than custodial, parents forces recognition of some inherited properties in giftedness (Plomin, 1989).

## Environment

Talent may be shaped by heredity, but most researchers believe that it is nurtured and developed by the environment (Kirk et al., 1993). The proportions in the mix of heredity and environment that are necessary to produce and develop a child who is gifted remain unknown. The nurturing environment includes not only intellectual and artistic stimulation, but also more basic components such as appropriate nutrition and escaping the often devastating effects of neurological trauma. It is not possible to simplistically state that just because we are aware that malnutrition can bring about mental deficiency in children who might have otherwise been normal or even above average, that we can hypothesize that a superior diet and health care system will bring about children who are gifted who might not ordinarily be gifted. Parents, families, peer group interactions, and even community experiences can have a strong influence on the development of a child's talents. Bloom (1982) and Bloom and Sosniak (1981) traced what they believed to be critical experiences in the developing years of children who were eventually identified as gifted. As adults, these formerly gifted children were able to recall some or many of the following experiences:

1. A specific person in their family who took personal interest in their development and provided support for that development.
2. Parents who were role models in a skill or talent area.
3. Parents who encouraged an exploration of interests and curiosities.
4. Parents who communicated their belief that the child would do well in a given talent area.
5. Expectations of high performance standards with enforced schedules of accomplishment.
6. A variety of learning experiences, often informal.
7. Provision of private tutors and mentors to guide in the attainment of performance standards.
8. Direct parental observation of practice sessions, with rewards for accomplishment.
9. Parental encouragement to participate in public events to showcase talents.

These reports seem to undermine any argument for leaving children who might potentially be gifted and talented to their own devices, with the expectation that they will somehow blossom as highly productive talented adults.

## IDENTIFICATION PROCESS

The most common strategies for isolating children who are gifted and talented usually include some combination of the following tactics, which are used to obtain information that is then evaluated before placement is decided:

1. Standardized tests are administered to identify potential candidates.
2. Nominations are solicited from creditable sources.
3. A product illustrating outstanding potential is studied.

### Testing

Four types of tests are used most frequently. *Achievement tests* are designed to indicate whether a child demonstrates aptitudes in particular subject areas. *Group intelligence tests* and *Individual intelligence tests* often point out potential when achievement has not been outstanding. Many individual intelligence tests measure both verbal and non-verbal potential. *Tests of creativity* often measure divergent thinking processes by seeking creative rather than "correct" responses.

Tests have both benefits and liabilities. The most traditional method of identifying students who are gifted and talented has been to use intelligence tests administered in a group setting and then limit the pool of children eligible to those with IQ scores in the 98th or 99th percentile (Howell et al., 1996; Pendarvis, 1993). Both group aptitude tests and group intelligence tests can be administered without the services of a psychologist, and are thus less costly for initial screening. The interpretation of the results of individual tests can be critical in the evaluation of potential. Group tests are not as reliable as individually administered tests. Most of the tests used have been designed for average students and may not be sufficiently discriminative for children who are gifted. Achievement tests will only isolate those students doing well academically, and neither type of test will routinely measure creative thinking in areas other than academic subjects. Some children, regardless of how gifted they are, simply do not do well on timed tests. Many researchers also believe that culturally diverse children do not perform well on these tests (Kirk et al., 1993). Tests of creativity might deal with some of these concerns. For example, the Torrance Tests of Creative Thinking (TTCT) (Torrance, 1966) test giftedness by measuring fluency (the ability to give many answers to questions), flexibility (different types of answers or the ability to shift from one type of answer to another), originality (responding in unique yet appropriate ways), and elaboration (developing answers in detail). However, there is a lack of data on the reliability and validity between these measures and outstanding creative performance (Silverman, 1986).

More culturally sensitive tests have been designed, such as the Subcultural Indices of Academic Potential (Renzulli, 1973) and the Kranz Talent Identification Instrument (Kranz, 1982). The System of Multicultural Pluralistic Assessment (SOMPA) (Mercer, 1978) compares its results not only to standardized norms but also to the results of children of the same age and similar sociocultural background. All types of tests, when used with some degree of sensitivity, help to provide some information, but cannot be the sole criterion for identification. A more multifaceted approach using tests, nominations, and student generated products is currently in vogue.

## Nominations

Children who might be gifted and talented may be nominated by classroom teachers, parents, other students, or in some instances the children themselves. A checklist or questionnaire is usually provided to help with the nomination. The checklists often rely upon observations of performance that will help document the request for inclusion. Classroom teachers may mention grades, academic awards earned, outstanding test scores, and other achievements. Typically, behaviors and observations are rated on a scale of *seldom* (rated 1), *sometimes* (rated 2), *often* (rated 3), or *always* (rated 4). Items

**In the classroom, does the child**
- Ask a lot of questions?
- Show a lot of interest in progress?
- Have lots of information on many things?
- Want to know why or how something is so?
- Become unusually upset at injustices?
- Seem interested and concerned about social or political problems?
- Often have a better reason than you do for not doing what you want done?
- Refuse to drill on spelling, math facts, flash cards, or handwriting?
- Criticize others for dumb ideas?
- Become impatient if work is not "perfect"?
- Seem to be a loner?
- Seem bored and often have nothing to do?
- Complete only part of an assignment or project and then take off in a new direction?
- Stick to a subject long after the class has gone on to other things?
- Seem restless, out of seat often?
- Daydream?
- Seem to understand easily?
- Like solving puzzles and problems?
- Have his or her own idea about how something should be done? And stay with it?
- Talk a lot?
- Love metaphors and abstract ideas?
- Love debating issues?

This child may be showing giftedness cognitively.

**Does the child**
- Show unusual ability in some area? Maybe reading or math?
- Show fascination with one field of interest? And manage to include this interest in all discussion topics?
- Enjoy meeting or talking with experts in this field?

- Get math answers correct but find it difficult to tell you how?
- Enjoy graphing everything? Seem obsessed with probabilities?
- Invent new obscure systems and codes?

This child may be showing giftedness academically.

**Does the child**
- Try to do things in different, unusual, imaginative ways?
- Have a really zany sense of humor?
- Enjoy new routines or spontaneous activities?
- Love variety and novelty?
- Create problems with no apparent solutions? And enjoy asking you to solve them?
- Love controversial and unusual questions?
- Have a vivid imagination?
- Seem never to proceed sequentially?

This child may be showing giftedness creatively.

**Does the child**
- Organize and lead group activities? Sometimes take over?
- Enjoy taking risks?
- Seem cocky, self-assured?
- Enjoy decision making? Stay with that decision?
- Synthesize ideas and information from a lot of different sources?

This child may be showing giftedness through leadership ability.

**Does the child**
- Seem to pick up skills in the arts—music, dance, drama, painting, etc.—without instruction?
- Invent new techniques? Experiment?
- See minute detail in products or performances?
- Have high sensory sensitivity?

This child may be showing giftedness through visual or performing arts ability.

*Source:* Reprinted with the permission of Prentice-Hall, Inc. from *Growing Up Gifted*, 5th ed by Barbara Clark, pp. 55–59. Copyright© 1997 by Prentice-Hall, Inc., Upper Saddle River, NJ. Adapted by permission.

**Figure 11.1**
Sample questions for identifying children who are gifted and talented

such as the child's ability to learn rapidly, work unsupervised, use vocabulary skills beyond classmates, be imaginative, show curiosity, complete and exceed assignment requirements, and use advanced and original oral and/or written language are often included in the checklists (Delisle, 1994). Figure 11.1 is a reproduction of some sample questions that may appear on teacher checklists.

Teachers may have a difficult task in nominating children when the curriculum doesn't challenge a child enough to obtain an outstanding performance (Stanley, 1977) or if a child does not readily participate in group activities (Roedell, Jackson, & Robinson 1980). Ysseldyke and Algozzine (1982) report that attractive children are referred more by teachers than are children they find unattractive. Parents may be more familiar with their children and as a result be a creditable referral source. This appears to be especially true in the early grades (Jacobs, 1971; Roedell et al., 1980). There is only limited research available on the validity of peer and self-nominations. Behavioral checklists, parent interviews, and direct observations of a child's performance may be less formal than standardized tests, but are especially important for culturally different or disabled children who might be gifted (Wolf, 1990).

## Products

Stories, poems, paintings, and videotapes of outstanding performances often compose a portfolio of products, which is becoming a more common and useful method employed in discovering gifts and talents. This is proving to be most critical in the evaluation of outstanding performances in non-academic areas (Reis & Renzulli, 1991). Specialists outside of the normal decision-making process can be more easily asked for their input on a portfolio than on the other strategies outlined earlier.

Table 11.3 is a summary of the most common methods used to identify children who may be eligible for services. It highlights both the strengths and weaknesses of the methods being used.

States are not required by federal legislation to provide services to children who are gifted and talented. Nor are they are required to report the number of children they identify or serve. As a result, priorities are determined at the individual state level and often at levels lower than state level. Some recognize only academic achievement, while others favor a blend of their own choosing. Breadth or depth models may be used. In *breadth models*, children who are multitalented but not necessarily outstanding in each area are selected. The goal of this model is to help produce well rounded students. The *depth model* may use a single measure of outstanding performance in any one area for inclusion (Dirks & Quarfoth, 1981).

A final concern in the identification process is the relative lateness of most identification systems for all but the children who are most exceptionally gifted and talented. Children with the potential to develop talents are often not identified until the third or fourth grade. Early identification may prove to be important, both to help schools prepare for the eventual enrollment of children who are gifted and talented (Eby & Smutny, 1990) and to help the individual child begin as early as possible to develop his or her potential.

Table 11.3

Summary of Commonly Used Methods of Evaluation

| Method | Strengths | Limitations | Comments |
|---|---|---|---|
| Teacher evaluation via behavior checklists or questionnaires | Familiar with student's work. Familiar with "normal" performance for grade level. | Teacher perceptions may be influenced by irrelevant factors such as appearance, willingness to conform, and attitudes toward classwork. | Teachers may fail to recognize as many as half of gifted students. Teacher nomination may be improved through in-service training on the characteristics of gifted children. |
| Peer evaluation via behavior checklists or questionnaires | Familiar with student's work. May be aware of interest or abilities of which the teacher is unaware. | Students' perceptions may be influenced by whether they like or dislike their classmate and whether or not the teacher appears to like their classmate. | Little research has been done on the effectiveness of peer evaluation. |
| Parent evaluation via behavior checklists or questionnaires | Familiar with child's development, interests, and abilities. | Parents may not know how their child's behavior compares with that of other children of the same age. | In kindergarten and at the primary level, parents may be better than teachers at identifying gifted children. |
| Grades | Information is readily available. | Review of grades fails to identify underachievers and children who are gifted in non-academic areas. | Referral of children with an average of "B" or better results in the inclusion of most gifted children, but many nongifted children are referred as well. |
| Work samples | Can be collected in all talent areas, including the visual or performing arts. | Requires availability of experts such as music teachers and art teachers to judge the work sample. | Work samples reflect both the student's ability and commitment. |
| Interest inventories | Seem to be more "culture-fair" than IQ or achievement tests. | Ability level may not be as high as interest level. | One of the few measures that reflect commitment to an area of art or science. |

## PROGRAMS

### Historical Background

Interest in children who might be gifted and talented began in France in the early 1900s when Binet and Simon, at the request of the French government, developed the first developmental assessment test to identify children with intellectual disabilities. They began to look at children's ability to attend, remember, use judgment, reason, and understand. As a result, they were able to differentiate among children who differed in these

| Method | Strengths | Limitations | Comments |
|---|---|---|---|
| Achievement tests | Indicate academic aptitude in particular subject areas.<br>Test scores are usually on record in children's cumulative folders. They are a readily available source of information. | May fail to identify underachievers, especially children from culturally different environments and gifted children with disabilities. | Success on most achievement tests requires superior verbal comprehension. |
| Group intelligence tests | Can indicate aptitude even when achievement is low.<br>Test scores are often on record in children's cumulative folders. | If high cutoff points (e.g., 130 IQ or above) are used, as many as half of gifted children may be overlooked.<br>Fails to differentiate the highly gifted from the moderately gifted. | For screening purposes, a relatively low cutoff point such as 115 IQ can reduce the number of gifted children missed. |
| Creativity tests | Usually considered more "culture-fair" than IQ or achievement tests. | Administration and interpretation often require special personnel.<br>May be difficult to distinguish "original" but relevant responses from "bizarre" and irrelevant responses. | The relationship between ability to do well on a creativity test and consistent, outstanding creative performance hasn't been established. |
| Individual intelligence tests | Is most reliable single indicator of intellectual giftedness in middle- and upper-class socioeconomic levels.<br>Many individual tests measure both verbal and nonverbal ability. | Require special personnel for administration and interpretation.<br>Can be biased against minority groups and gifted children with disabilities.<br>Fail to assess important abilities such as specific artistic or academic aptitude. | Interpretation of the quality and character of responses by a competent tester can provide considerable insight into a child's ability. |

*Source:* From *An Introduction to Special Education* (3rd ed., pp. 578–579), by A. E. Blackhurst and W. H. Berdine, Copyright© 1993 by HarperCollins College Publishers. Reprinted by permission of Addison-Wesley Educational Publishers Inc.

measures of intelligence (Binet & Simon, 1905a, 1905b). Soon American psychologists were using this test to measure mental abilities (Davis & Rimm, 1985). At Stanford University, Terman modified and Americanized the Binet-Simon test; in 1916 he published the Stanford-Binet Intelligence Scale and developed the term *intelligence quotient* (IQ). Terman identified some 1,500 children with outstanding IQ scores. This group became the first gifted group to be identified and were and still are the most studied group of individuals in the world ever identified as gifted (Davis & Rimm, 1985; Hardman et al., 1996). In the years that followed, others have added to the criteria used to isolate those who might be considered gifted. Memory, divergent thinking, and vocabulary usage were considered, as was the idea that intelligence is the result of multiple factors. Creativity measures were developed and notable skills in visual and performance arts were recognized as components of giftedness (Hardman et. al., 1966).

In 1957, Russia launched the Sputnik satellite. Many scholars and politicians in the United States felt this accomplishment was a technological defeat for the United States' education of its brightest scholars. Commissions, reports, and books indicated that the United States educational system was providing meager intellectual stimulation for children who were gifted. As a result, there was an initial and short-lived "talent mobilization" (Tannenbaum, 1979), with emphasis placed on teaching gifted and talented students in math and science, primarily at the high school and college levels. Interest waned and relatively little funding has survived for gifted education at the present.

Currently, no nationally adopted curriculum or standardized set of instructional procedures exist for the gifted and talented. Programs are often intuitively designed and based on the opinions of leading educators, with little data to support their validity (Gallagher, 1988). However, there does seem to be agreement that early and advanced education does facilitate the development of talents (Bloom, 1982; Feldman, 1979; Pressey, 1955). All but two states have programs for the gifted, but only 30 have mandated these programs as a part of their educational mission (Mitchell, 1982; Schmidt, 1993). More ominously, a *Newsweek* report (Beck & Wingert, 1993) suggests that the number of funded programs may decline as the public schools eliminate programs in response to budgetary crises.

Programs for children who are identified as gifted and talented are usually composed of experiences with curriculum enrichment, special classes, special schools, and special educational experiences.

## Curriculum Enrichment

*Enrichment* may have several meanings and may be used to describe any of a variety of attempts to extend or broaden a child's knowledge (Aylward, 1987; Schiever & Maker, 1991). It most often refers to attempts made within the classroom setting, by the classroom teacher, to add depth, detail, and challenges to the curriculum in place for children at a given grade level. Acting independently or with the aid of specially trained consultant teachers, the classroom teacher might provide the children in the class who are gifted and talented with special activities such as independent study with advanced texts, independent small group projects, or access to computer programs that can replace drills. To be successful, enrichment activities need a purpose and specified outcomes. They should be systematic in extending student learning and stress higher order thinking skills (Schiever & Maker, 1991). In-class enrichment allows the child who is gifted to study in depth and detail and still maintain social contact with his or her age peers. However, enrichment in the classroom and clustering small groups of children for advanced study within a classroom is not in favor because many teachers, administrators, and parents believe that the regular classroom teacher is already too burdened with regular classroom responsibilities to provide the necessary meaningful enrichment activities (Kirk et al., 1993).

*Compacting the curriculum* occurs when a teacher deletes many of the repetitions, drills, and practices unnecessary for children who can grasp concepts quickly. Compacting could allow the child who is gifted the opportunity to spend the time saved in more challenging activities and could perhaps counteract the boredom and underachievement that often plague the child who is gifted (Clark, 1992). Compacting requires an intimate knowledge of the curriculum and a sensitivity to exactly what is critical to concept mastery and what may be unnecessarily redundant. Reis (1995) found that the 436 teachers in his study were able to eliminate 40 to 50 percent of content without any detrimental effects on the 738 students they taught who were gifted and talented. In fact, the children achieved higher scores in math and science concepts after the critical areas were compacted.

## Special Classes within the Regular School Setting

The two most frequently used types of special classes are the resource room and the self-contained classroom. In the self-contained classroom, children who are gifted and talented are grouped together and receive specialized instruction from a specially trained teacher or teachers. There are not very many self-contained classrooms, since they are dependent upon a school system identifying enough children to fill a full-time classroom. In addition, many children who are gifted may not be above average in all subjects and thus may be ineligible for full class participation. Some educators report that being isolated in a self-contained classroom may contribute to an increase in social problems for the children and may even have a negative impact on overall school morale in high schools due to its exclusionary nature (Delisle, 1994).

The resource room is a popular method of providing special instruction, since it provides a special education experience and still allows the individual child to remain with age mates within the regular classroom environment. Children who are gifted and talented leave their home classroom on a regular basis to go to a resource room where they receive instruction from a specially trained teacher. This pull-out method of instruction is usually assigned on a once- or twice-a-week basis, often for only one or two hours at a time. The teacher of the gifted and talented is usually an itinerant teacher assigned to several schools in a district. Although this model may not offer much continuity or in-depth instruction, it is the method most often used at the elementary school level (Cox, Daniel, & Boston, 1985). It requires some cooperation on the part of the classroom teacher. The potential social isolation problems still exist, since the child is pulled out of class to go to the resource room—sometimes, depending on scheduling, missing out on desirable activities or important assignments. An even more critical concern is that classroom teachers may feel that the resource room and special teacher have the sole responsibility to care for the needs of children who are gifted and give up responsibility as a team member in the children's overall program.

## Special Schools

There are two kinds of special schools available to some children who are gifted and talented: *magnet schools* and *state sponsored schools*. Magnet schools offer both regular programming and accelerated classes in specific subjects within the same school. Children enrolled in magnet schools are not expected to be outstanding in all areas and are assigned to a variety of classes during the school day. Magnet schools are often found in large urban areas, since they require a large pool of students and reasonable efficient transportation.

State sponsored or governor's schools are often residential schools with a special emphasis on science or arts. They feature special programming, and specially trained teachers and are usually located close to universities with access to special experiences for their students. Even though these schools offer intense special instruction, they are often not popular with parents, since their residential format separates children from their communities and families. Large urban areas may also have commuter high schools such as the High School of Performing Arts, the Bronx High School of Science, or Brooklyn Technical High School, available to residents of New York City.

## Special Experiences

Students who are gifted and talented are often eligible for special educational experiences that are both curriculum and noncurriculum based. The most controversial special experience for a child who is gifted is *acceleration*, where the child is allowed to move through academic levels or grades at his or her own pace. This entails skipping grades, cross-grade placement, being allowed to attend advanced classes, or early entrance into kindergarten, high school, or college. The concerns about children accelerating beyond the experiences of their age mates are obvious. There is fear of social isolation, negative social and emotional experiences, and a loss of perspective. However, acceleration is the most efficient way to provide content without special classes or schools. Educators researching the effects of acceleration are stressing that when acceleration is implemented wisely, children show increased interest in school and higher levels of academic achievement. They also receive more recognition of their accomplishments and complete higher levels of education in less time (Kulick & Kulick, 1984; Robinson & Noble, 1991; Southern & Jones, 1991). Acceleration with dual enrollment in high school and college seems to be most effective for students who excel in math (Stanley, 1989; Brody & Stanley, 1991). Fears about premature burnout and undue pressure seem to have no basis in fact. There is no evidence that acceleration harms students who are willing to participate in it socially, academically, or emotionally (Swiatek, 1993; Feldhusen, 1992a). For some children, not only academic achievement but also extracurricular activities and social and emotional adjustments are positive experiences (Brody & Benbow, 1987; Stanley, 1985). Some educators suggest that accelerated placement spares these children the negative experiences of always being first to answer or being most correct and may lead to a more reasonable self-concept and toleration for the weaknesses of others (Southern & Jones, 1991). Benefits or problems cannot be generalized. Acceleration requires sensitivity to the individual student's needs. Counseling and support services are critical (Brody & Stanley, 1991; Noble & Drummond, 1992). Children who are gifted and talented are still children, and they require the concern and protection of adults. Gross (1992) feels that acceleration is most effective when combined with enrichment. This allows children both appropriate social experiences as well as academic programs equal to their abilities.

As might be expected, the counseling and interest of those most concerned about any given child often prove critical in structuring that child's experiences. Traditional programs such as advanced placement (AP), in which high schools offer college level instruction on the high school campus, are fairly widespread. Often the student can receive college credit for these courses by "testing out" of the college course of similar content. In some instances, high school students are allowed to enroll in classes taught at local colleges or universities. Larger schools are often able to sponsor special interest clubs either as part of the school day or as extracurricular activities. Periodically, in-depth seminars can be offered on topics not in the regular curriculum. These seminars can be presented along with independent study, in which a teacher assists the student in locating resources and defining topics and goals for independent projects. Tutorials are more formal, individually designed relationships between a selected student and an expert who meet to share interests in a given topic. The experts can be adult volunteers or older students knowledgeable in a content area and willing to share expertise with a younger student. A more hands-on experience can be provided through *mentorships* and *internships*, in which students who are gifted and talented are placed in settings or with willing community experts at the site where the experience is to be offered. Both internships and mentorships provide the opportunity to learn in depth from practitioners, often while the service is being performed or the product created.

For younger students, the extracurricular Odyssey of the Mind program provides a nationally sponsored, competitive program in which children are guided by volunteer coaches to present solutions to complex problems, perform self-generated skits, and construct projects illustrating scientific or artistic concepts. The Junior Great Books Program employs teachers specifically trained to help children produce sophisticated analysis and discussion of classical, philosophical, fictional, and poetic works of literature. Addresses to contact for more information about these programs can be found in the listings of parent and self-help groups at the end of this chapter.

The addition of a personal computer to the world of the child who is gifted and talented has opened up pathways to knowledge that are just beginning to be explored. Appropriately used, computers can help dissolve distances and rural or urban disadvantages to learning and allow communication to take place globally. The evaluation of the possibilities for learning and perils of enhanced computerized educational experiences for children who are gifted and talented are only beginning to be studied. Programs such as the Fifth Dimension (Nicopolou & Cole, 1993; Cole, 1995) are enabling primary level schoolchildren to experience affiliation, play, education, and peer interaction while being introduced to computers and computer networking.

Programs such as the Schoolwide Enrichment Model (Renzulli & Reis, 1986), the Integrated Curriculum Model (Maker, 1993), the Responsive Learning Environment (Clark, 1986), and the Autonomous Learner Model (Betts, 1985) were designed by scholars attempting to establish more fully integrated systems of education for students who are gifted. Interested readers are encouraged to learn about these programs by consulting the readings listed in the bibliography at the end of the chapter.

Several goals of programming seem to be shared by educators. The student who is gifted needs to be helped in mastering the appropriate analytical, expressive, and conceptual prerequisite skills to facilitate the ability to learn. He or she needs to learn to develop strategies and skills that will allow for independence and foster creativity. Students who are gifted and talented should develop a joy for and excitement about learning that will carry them through the drill and routine that are also a part of the learning process (Kirk et al., 1993). The concept of the *differentiated curriculum* is currently gaining favor as a way of accomplishing these goals. The differentiated curriculum uses a variety of curricular targets and a combination of instructional techniques, models, and practices individually designed to meet the needs of the child who is gifted and talented (Clark, 1992; Van Tassel-Baska, 1992; Yong & McIntyre, 1992). The combination seems to be the key. Success seems to be dependent upon cooperation between the regular classroom teacher, the teacher of gifted and talented students, administrators, parents, and community agencies.

## ISSUES OF IMPORTANCE

The issues to be discussed here are not an all-inclusive list of all the conflicts and unresolved problems facing those responsible for educating children who are gifted and talented. They represent only some of the concerns and are only briefly presented.

## Responsibility for Providing Services

Should the public educational system further tax its limited resources by providing special educational services for children who are gifted and talented? Those who believe that special programming is not necessary stress that these children will succeed without it and that the programs are elitist and unfairly exclusionary since many children are not identified (Gear, 1978). An even more troubling concern is that children are often not identified fairly, due to cultural and economic prejudice. Those who are identified are often separated from their age mates and community, risking potential social and emotional problems. Also, there is not much research evidence that special educational programs contribute to the development or maintenance of giftedness (Weiss & Gallagher, 1982).

Proponents argue that some children who are gifted will perform at high levels without special help, but most will not come close to achieving their potential unless they are challenged by programs that will foster the development of their advanced abilities (Kauffman, 1997). Most children who are gifted and talented do not succeed on their own. Some become dropouts (Marland, 1972), delinquents (Seeley & Mahoney, 1981), counseling problems (Sanborn, 1979), and underachievers (Gowan, Demos, & Kokaska, 1979). The idea that students who are gifted and talented will automatically learn is persistent. Ideas and the strategies needed to learn efficiently must be explicitly taught. They are not likely to be spontaneously discovered by an individual who is gifted and talented. Occasionally, a student who is gifted will intuitively perform in an innovative manner, but unless the potential is recognized and honed, the student will not likely develop the strategies needed for consistent performance. Many educators believe that it is the responsibility of the public schools to help these students develop their skills and abilities. The research shows that the concern that the schools will be training an "elite" group of students at taxpayer cost does not appear to be valid. Giftedness is often accompanied by an unusually strong sense of responsibility, obligation, and empathy for others (Dabrowski, 1964). Identifying characteristics of children who are gifted and talented often include a high degree of morality, concern for others, and heightened emotional sensitivity in general (Terman, 1925; Marland, 1972; Silverman, 1983). A more basic argument is that students who are gifted and talented are entitled to a public education that meets their special needs. Denying them denies the right to equal opportunity to fulfill their potential. Society is best served when these children achieve their potential and become productive adults (Hallahan & Kauffman, 1994).

As Silverman (1988) reports, the attitudes toward the gifted and talented are on a perpetual roller coaster. She notes that they are alternately applauded and attacked, mined as a resource and then ignored. This issue remains unresolved. As a society we have not determined whether we have the same moral obligation to the gifted and talented that we do to those with other exceptionalities.

## Terminology

The use of the word *gifted* in identifying or placing children is beginning to be a cause for concern. Some educators are beginning to call for the deletion of the term *gifted*.

The most recently proposed definition (U.S. Department of Education, 1993) does not include the term *gifted*. The Department of Education felt that the term *gifted* implied that the skills or abilities isolated are already developed and might not need special services to fully develop. Others believe that the term implies that the talents these children might have are totally predetermined and will not result or benefit from efforts aimed at further development. This would facilitate ignoring the needs of this special population and could lead to further underachievement (Howell et al., 1996). Feldhusen (1992b) argues that "there is no physiological, genetic or neurological justification for a diagnostic category called 'gifted.' The very term implies hereditary transmission, for how else could a 'gift' be placed in a child?" (p. 3) Perhaps, as Ring and Shaughnessy (1993) suggest, the trend toward deleting the term *gifted* comes in response to the public perception of elitism that is implied with the term *gifted*. Heward (1996) suggests that deleting references to giftedness may be the start of movement away from giftedness as a unidimensional perception of high intellectual functioning and toward a recognition of many types of special talents and aptitudes.

## Underachievement

Since the potential for children who are gifted and talented is so great, their apparent underachievement is particularly troubling. The discussions of underachievement fall into several categories. There is a concern that the children identified as gifted and talented are disproportionately underachievers. More specifically, there is the issue that females are not achieving their potential as often as their male peers. In addition, minority students seem to be at more of a risk to underachieve than their dominant culture counterparts. A more basic concern with minority children is the failure to identify them at all. The next section of this chapter will highlight this concern. This section will focus on the issues of underachievement by students who are gifted and talented as a group and the specific concerns about the lack of success of female children who are gifted.

Children who are gifted and talented become underachievers, regardless of their talents, for the same reasons that cause all children to fail. They are not immune to emotional conflicts; debilitating family situations; hostile home, school, or community environments; and specific physical or social impairments. Some children who are gifted may have specific learning disabilities that contribute to underachievement (Fox, Brody, & Tobin, 1980; Redding, 1990; Whitmore, 1980). Maker (1977) points out that communication disorders in particular can mask giftedness and frustrate potentially gifted children. Like all children, children who are gifted may develop poor study habits and lack the self-confidence needed to achieve their potential. Children who are gifted and talented are more likely to underachieve because the instruction they receive is too easy or slow paced. An unchallenging or monotonous curriculum might foster poor attitudes toward the learning process for children who grasp concepts quickly (Delisle & Berger, 1991; Delisle, 1984). Minority children and children from diverse cultural environments may lack enough exposure to the mainstream culture to thrive in its educational system (Richert, Alvino & McDonnel, 1982; Ruiz, 1989). The special challenges faced by children with exceptional talents need to be recognized and dealt with by parents and professionals with an understanding and sensitivity to the needs for both support and challenge these children require.

Females who are gifted face some unique challenges to achieving their potential. Although there is little evidence of biological differences, boys' and girls' achievements are different. At the primary level of education, girls achieve better grades than boys (Wentzel, 1988). However, by junior and senior high school, boys outperform girls on achievement tests (Hallinan & Sorensen, 1987). More adult males than females are identified as gifted and creative. Perhaps social and cultural experiences shape females differently than males, causing them to increasingly yield to boys and men in achievement and competitiveness. This may explain their occasional failure to pursue advanced studies or careers commensurate with their abilities (Pendarvis, Howley, & Howley, 1990; Conroy, 1989; Eccles, 1985). Sex role stereotyping, as evidenced by lack of equal opportunity or lack of motivation to enter traditionally male fields, may establish barriers to the development of female giftedness. Cultural barriers and expectation also seem to play a role in limiting female achievements (Eccles, 1985). Conflicts between careers and marriage and family responsibilities can also act as barriers (Kerr, 1985). The "fear of success" studied by Butler-Por (1987) illustrates how the negative consequences of outstanding achievement, such as animosity of classmates and pressure from others to succeed, produced girls who were more fearful of success than boys.

Solutions to these problems may be to provide the motivation to achieve for girls who are gifted and talented by making them aware of role models who challenge sex stereotypes and by providing, early in the educational programming, information about careers in nonstereotypical fields and disciplines (Callahan, 1979). Single sex classrooms for math and science classes may cancel the incentives to underachieve for females who are gifted. Parental education may be necessary to alter attitudes toward girls who are gifted and their potential to choose nontraditional fields of endeavor. Teachers may need to be sensitized about potentially damaging sex-based instructional practices (Fox, Brody, & Tobin, 1980). In the operating room, not all brain surgeons are male, nor nurses female. Math professors may be male or female. It appears that progress is being made. Kerr (1991) reports that young women who are gifted are choosing professional careers in almost equal proportions to men. In the same report, the author states that business has replaced education as the most popular career choice of bright young women.

More information on the issue of achievement for gifted and talented women can be found in a special issue of the journal *Gifted Education International* (Vol. 19, No. 3, 1994) which focuses on girls and women who are gifted and talented.

## Early Identification

The evidence available overwhelmingly supports the notion that children who are gifted and talented need special nurturing to achieve their potential. Other areas of exceptionality are discovering that early intervention leads to a more successful result. However, there appears to be no comprehensive plan for early identification of children who are gifted. There is no equivalent of Project Child Find or similar programs for early identification. While programs such as early admissions to kindergarten and primary levels might offer advantages, relatively few preschoolers who are gifted can overcome the age restrictions needed for admission. This is especially true since their social and motor development might be age-appropriate, making placement burdensome to the teachers of these classes. Worse still, it might place preschool children who are gifted and talented in situations where expectations of their social and emotional skills would be equal to expectations for their advanced cognitive and language skills. Little thought has been given to perhaps teaching social skills to precocious children to make them eligible for accelerated placements (Baum, 1986; Roedell, 1985). It appears logical that children who are gifted and talented will not only profit from but may require early intervention (Wolf, 1990). It also appears logical that the arguments that special experiences are necessary to help achieve potential during the school years can be extrapolated to the preschool years. In fact, it may prove that preschool experiences or the lack of preschool experiences may prove to be the most critical issue in the development of gifted children's talents.

## MINORITY CONCERNS

The most overriding issue for minority groups is that they are underrepresented in gifted and talented programs (Perrone & Male, 1981; Howell et al., 1996). "Gifts and talents exist in children of every race, culture, and socioeconomic group. However, gifted program planners have often been criticized for not looking hard enough to find talents in children who may not represent the majority culture or its values" (Delisle, 1994, p. 592). As an example, Baldwin (1985) reports that African American children

are overrepresented in all categories of special education except giftedness. The underidentification seems to be a result of an interaction between tests, teachers, and opportunities.

## Tests

The cultural bias inherent in many of the tests used to identify students who might be gifted and talented often makes it difficult to obtain a fair estimate of minority children's abilities. While totally culture fair tests may not be possible, special procedures might be appropriate in the identification of minority children who are potentially gifted and talented. Suggestions range from using separate norms for large minority groups or those who are economically disadvantaged to including the top scoring 2 to 5 percent of minority students, regardless of their test scores (Pendarvis et al., 1990; Maker, Morris, & James, 1981). Special tests such as the previously discussed Subcultural Indices of Academic Potential (Renzulli, 1973), the Kranz Talent Identification Instrument (Kranz, 1982), the System of Multicultural Pluralistic Assessment (SOMPA) (Mercer, 1978), and the DISCOVER problem solving system (Maker, 1993) have been suggested as alternative instruments to measure the potential of minority children. Most programs use traditional methods and tests to identify potentially gifted and talented children (Scott, Prior, Urbano, Hogan, & Gold, 1992).

## Teachers

Negative teacher attitudes may be a significant factor in the underidentification of culturally diverse children. Due to a lack of cultural sensitivity, minority children may be passed over because they do not always display giftedness in the same manner as their dominant-class cohorts (High & Udall, 1983; Rhodes, 1992; Plummer, 1995; Van Tassel-Baska, Patton, & Prillaman, 1991). Their teachers may not recognize the signs of their giftedness. Haring, McCormick, and Haring (1990) suggest that dominant culture teachers educating minority students may need specific training that will enable them to identify culturally different children who have the potential to be gifted. Culturally different children may be raised in environments that conflict with the conventional ideas of giftedness. For example, in some Hispanic families, highly verbal children may not be (as prized) for their verbal skills as are their dominant culture peers.

## Opportunities

Children reared in poverty, regardless of race, may not have the opportunity to interact with toys or reading materials. They might not have positive traveling experiences. They may be malnourished and receive inadequate medical care. They may be denied many or all of the opportunities and experiences that facilitate the development of talents (Kauffman, 1997). Their basic skills may suffer from this impoverishment and mask their superior abilities. When Standard English is not the child's primary language, this lack of facility might in and of itself be enough to deny the child access to programs for the gifted (Maker, 1977). Despite the increasing use of computers and their ability to bring information into the classroom, children who are gifted in isolated or rural areas may not have access to the resources necessary to develop their potential.

All of these factors contribute to the underidentification of minority children. Underidentification, in turn, prohibits them from participating in critical experiences that might help in the full development of their potential. This lack of inclusion appears to make other minority issues secondary in nature.

## PROFESSIONALS

The certification of teachers of students who are gifted and talented is individually administered by each state. Karnes and Whorton (1991) were able to report specific certification requirements for only 21 states. As of 1991, their inquiries revealed that 25 states had no specific requirements for obtaining a teaching certificate for teaching this population. Information about the specific guidelines and requirements for any given state can be obtained by contacting the state director of special education at the address listed in Appendix I.

Should teachers of students who are gifted be gifted themselves? Most educators feel that a teacher of students who are gifted need not be gifted in the same way the children are, but must have enough intellectual capability to understand the child's thinking processes. A shopping list of proposed characteristics includes intellectual curiosity, a developed literary and cultural interest, a high tolerance for ambiguity, high quality verbal skills, a variety of interests, appreciation for achievement, a high energy level, a good sense of humor, enthusiasm, and a love of learning (Lindsey, 1980; Piirto, 1994; Story, 1985).

It is also felt that effective teachers of students who are gifted and talented must also show some combination of the following skills and practices in their classroom instruction: They must demonstrate a high quality and quantity of verbal interactions with their students, be flexible and open to new ideas and unusual responses, and be process oriented rather than content-driven, yet still maintain appropriately high standards and respect high quality work. However, they also need to be well prepared in content, have mastered teaching techniques, and be flexible in time scheduling. They should want to teach children who are gifted and talented and be comfortable with the idea that for any given topic, students may be more knowledgeable than the teacher. Silverman (1983) suggests that Renzulli's (1978) characteristics for giftedness (above average intelligence, creativity, and task commitment) are appropriate criteria for the selection of the teachers of students who are gifted. She also stresses that the teacher of students who are gifted and talented is often more of a facilitator than a director and needs to be comfortable in that role.

These lists form quite an impressive profile. Effective teacher training programs must attempt to meet these expectations when training college students who wish to teach the gifted. The Council for Exceptional Children has recently published suggested standards for the initial preparation and certification of teachers of students with gifts or talents (CEC, 1996). The council mandates that university training programs prepare teachers who have knowledge and skills in the following eight areas as they relate to students who are gifted and talented:

1. Philosophy, history and legal foundations
2. Characteristics of students who are gifted and talented
3. Assessment, diagnosis, and evaluation of potentially gifted students
4. Instructional content and practices geared toward students who are gifted
5. Planning and managing the teaching and learning environment
6. Managing student behavior and social skills
7. Communication and collaborative partnerships
8. Professionalism and ethical practices

## PROFESSIONAL ASSOCIATIONS AND PARENT OR SELF-HELP GROUPS

The following list of associations, societies, and programs should provide the reader with a series of initial contacts for a variety of interest groups.

American Association for Gifted Children
New York City Partnership
200 Madison Avenue
New York, NY 10016

American Association for Gifted Children
c/o Talent Identification Program
Duke University
1121 W. Main Street, Suite 100
Durham, NC 27701

American Creativity Association
P.O. Box 26068
St. Paul, MN 55126

Future Problem Solving
Future Problem Solving International
315 W. Huron, Suite 140B
Ann Arbor, MI 48103-4203

Gifted Children's Information Office
12657 Fee Fee Road
St. Louis, MO 63146

Gifted Child Society
190 Rock Road, Suite 6
Glen Rock, NJ 07425

Junior Great Books Foundation
40 E. Huron
Chicago, IL 60611

Mensa
Gifted Children Program
2626 E. 14th Street
Brooklyn, NY 11235

National Association for Creative Children and
    Adults
8080 Spring Valley Drive
Cincinnati, OH 45236

National Association for Gifted Children
1155 15th Street NW, #1002
Washington, DC 20005

National Association for Gifted Children
4175 Lovell Road, Suite 140
Circle Pines, MN 55014

National Research Center on the Gifted and
   Talented (NCR/GT)
University of Connecticut
Stoors, CT 06269

National/State Leadership Training Institute on
   the Gifted and Talented
One Wilshire Building, Suite 1007
624 S. Grand Avenue
Los Angeles, CA 90017

Odyssey of the Mind
OM Association
P.O. Box 547
Glassboro, NJ 08028

The Association for the Gifted (TAG)
c/o Council for Exceptional Children
1920 Association Drive
Reston, VA 20191-1589

The Association for the Gifted (TAG)
2216 Main Street
Cedar Falls, IA 50613

World Council for Gifted and Talented Children Inc.
Lamar University
P.O. Box 10034
Beaumont, TX 77710

World Council for Gifted and Talented Children Inc.
HMS, Room 414
University of South Florida
Tampa, FL 33620

## REFERENCES FOR FURTHER INFORMATION

The bibliography at the end of this chapter provides a comprehensive listing of the sources compiled in the writing of this chapter. It should serve as a resource for further in-depth study. In addition, the following journals and newsletters may be of interest.

*Gifted Child Newsletter*
Gifted and Talented Publications Inc.
213 Hollydell Drive
Sewell, NJ 08080

*Gifted Child Quarterly*
National Association for Gifted Children
4175 Lovell Road, Suite 140
Circle Pines, MN 55014

*Gifted Child Today*
P.O. Box 637
Holmes, PA 19043

*Gifted Education International*
A.B. Academic Publishers
P.O. Box 42
Bicester, Oxon OX6 7NW, England

*Gifted International*
Trillium Press, Inc.
Box 209
Monroe, NY 10950

*Journal for the Education of the Gifted*
Association for the Gifted
University of North Carolina Press
Box 2288
Chapel Hill, NC 27515

*Journal of Creative Behavior*
Creative Educational Foundation, Inc.
1050 Union Road
Buffalo, NY 14222

*Prufrock Journal: The Journal of Secondary Gifted
   Education*
1617 N. Valley Mills Drive, Suite 237
Waco, TX 76710

*Roeper Review*
Roeper City and County Schools
2190 N. Woodward
Bloomfield Hills, MI 48013

# REFERENCES ❊

Aylward, M. (1987). Enriched-students' program: Nova Scotia, Canada. *Gifted Child Today, 10*(4), 271–285.

Baldwin, A. Y. (1985). Programs for the gifted and talented: Issues concerning minority populations. In F. D. Horowitz & M. O'Brien (Eds.), *The gifted and the talented: Developmental perspectives*. Washington, DC: American Psychological Association.

Baum, S. (1986). The gifted preschooler: An awesome delight. *Gifted Child Today, 9*(4), 42–45.

Beck, M., & Wingert, P. (1993, June 28). The young and the gifted: Are our schools nurturing talented kids? *Newsweek*, pp. 52–53.

Betts, G. (1985). *The autonomous learner model*. Greeley, CO: Autonomous Learning Publications Specialists.

Binet, A., & Simon, T. (1905a). Méthodes nouvelles pour le diagnostic du niveau intellectuel des anormaux. *L'Année Psychologique, 11*, 191–244.

Binet, A., & Simon, T. (1905b). Sur la nécessité d'établir un diagnostic scientifique des états inférieurs de l'intelligence. *L'Année Psychologique, 11*, 191–244.

Blackhurst, A. E., & Berdine, W. H. (1993). *An introduction to special education* (3rd ed.).New York: HarperCollins.

Bloom, B. S. (Ed.). (1956). *Taxonomy of educational objectives. Handbook 1: Cognitive domain*. New York: McKay.

Bloom, B. S. (1982). The role of gifts and markers in the development of talent. *Exceptional Children, 48*(6), 510–522.

Bloom, B. S., & Sosniak, L. A. (1981). Talent development vs. schooling. *Educational Leadership, 39*, 86–94.

Brody, L. E., & Benbow, C. P. (1987). Accelerative strategies: How effective are they for the gifted? *Gifted Child Quarterly, 31*, 105–110.

Brody, L. E., & Stanley, J. C. (1991). Young college students: Assessing factors that contribute to success. In W. T. Southern & E. D. Jones (Eds.), *Academic acceleration of gifted children*. New York: Teachers College Press.

Butler-Por, N. (1987). *Underachievers in school: Issues and intervention*. New York: Wiley.

Callahan, C. M. (1979). The gifted and talented woman. In A. H. Passow (Ed.), *The gifted and the talented: Their education and development. Seventy-eighth yearbook of the National Society for the Study of Education, Part 1*. Chicago: University of Chicago Press.

Clark, B. (1986). The integrative education model. In J. S. Renzulli (Ed.), *Systems and models for developing programs for the gifted and talented*. Mansfield Center, CT: Creative Learning.

Clark, B. (1992). *Growing up gifted: Developing the potential of children at home and at school* (4th ed.). Upper Saddle River, NJ: Prentice Hall/Merrill.

Clark, G., & Zimmerman, E. (1984). Identifying artistically talented students. *School Arts, 83*(3), 26–31.

Cole, M. (1995). Socio-cultural-historical psychology: Some general remarks and a proposal for a new kind of cultural genetic methodology. In J. Wertsch, P. del Rio, & A. Alveron (Eds.), *Sociocultural studies of mind*. Cambridge, MA: Cambridge University Press.

Coleman, J. M., & Fultz, B. A. (1985). Special class placement, level of intelligence, and the self-concepts of gifted children: A social comparison perspective. *Remedial and Special Education, 6*(1), 7–12.

Conroy, M. (1989). Where have all the smart girls gone? *Psychology Today, 23*(2), 20.

Council for Exceptional Children. (1996). *What every special educator must know: The international standards for the preparation and certification of special education* (2nd ed.). Reston, VA: Author.

Council of State Directors of Programs for the Gifted. (1991). *The 1990 state of the states gifted and talented education report*. Washington, DC: Author.

Cox, J., Daniel, N., & Boston, B. (1985). *Educating able learners: Programs and promising practices*. Austin, TX: University of Texas Press.

Dabrowski, K. (1964). *Positive disintegration*. London: Gryf.

Davis, G. A., & Rimm, S. B. (1985). *Education of the gifted and talented*. Upper Saddle River, NJ: Prentice Hall.

Delisle, J. (1994). Children who are gifted and talented. In Hunt, N., & Marshall, K., *Exceptional children and youth: An introduction to special education*. Boston: Houghton Mifflin.

Delisle, J. R. (1984). *Gifted children speak out*. New York: Walker.

Delisle, J. R., & Berger, S. (1991). Underachieving gifted students. In S. Berger (Ed.), *Flyer files for the gifted and talented*. Reston, VA: Council for Exceptional Children.

Dirks, J., & Quarfoth, J. (1981). Selecting children for gifted classes: Choosing for breadth vs. choosing for depth. *Psychology in the Schools, 18,* 437–449.

Eccles, J. S. (1985). Why doesn't Jane run? Sex differences in educational and occupational patterns. In F. D. Horowitz & M. O'Brien (Eds.), *Gifted and talented: Developmental perspectives*. Washington, DC: American Psychological Association.

Feldhusen, J. F. (1992b). *Talent identification and development in education* (TIDE). Sarasota, FL: Center for Creative Learning.

Feldman, D. (1979). The mysterious case of extreme giftedness. In A. H. Passow (Ed.), *The gifted and the talented: Their education and development. Seventy-eighth yearbook of the National Society for the Study of Education, Part 1.* Chicago: University of Chicago Press.

Fox, L., Brody, L., & Tobin, D. (Eds.). (1980). *Women and the mathematical mystique*. Baltimore: Johns Hopkins University Press.

Gallagher, J. J. (1985). *Teaching the gifted child* (3rd ed.). Needham, MA: Allyn & Bacon.

Gallagher, J. J. (1988). National agenda for educating gifted students: Statement of priorities. *Exceptional Children, 55,* 107–114.

Gallagher, J. J., & Gallagher, S. (1994). *Teaching the gifted child* (4th ed.). Needham, MA: Allyn & Bacon.

Gardner, H., & Hatch, T. (1989). Multiple intelligences go to school: Educational implications of the theory of multiple intelligences. *Educational Researcher, 18*(8), 4–9.

Gear, G. (1978). Effects on training on teacher's accuracy in the identification of gifted children. *Gifted Child Quarterly, 22*(1), 90–97.

Getzels, J. W. (1979). From art student to fine artist: Potential, problem finding, and performance. In A. H. Passow (Ed.), *The gifted and the talented: Their education and development. Seventy-eighth yearbook of the National Society for the Study of Education, Part 1.* Chicago: University of Chicago Press.

Gowan, J. C., Demos, G. D., & Kokaska, C. J. (Eds.). (1979). *Guidance of exceptional children: A book of readings* (2nd ed.). New York: McKay.

Gross, M. U. M. (1992). The use of radical acceleration in cases of extreme intellectual precocity. *Gifted Child Quarterly, 36,* 91–99.

Guilford, J. P. (1959). Traits of creativity. In H. H. Anderson (Ed.), *Creativity and its cultivation*. New York: Harper & Brothers.

Guilford, J. P. (1977). *Way beyond the IQ*. Buffalo, NY: Creative Education Foundation.

Guilford, J. P. (1987). Creativity research: Past, present and future. In S. Isaksen (Ed.), *Frontiers of creativity research*. Buffalo, NY: Bearly.

Hallahan, D. P., & Kauffman, J. M. (1994). *Exceptional children: Introduction to special education*. Needham, MA: Allyn & Bacon.

Hallinan, M. T., & Sorensen, A. B. (1987). Ability grouping and sex difference in mathematics achievement. *Sociology of Education, 60,* 64–72.

Hardman, M. L., Drew, C. J., & Egan, M. W. (1996). *Human exceptionality: Society, school, and family* (5th ed.). Needham, MA: Allyn & Bacon.

Haring, N. G., McCormick, L., & Haring, T. G. (1990). *Exceptional children and youth* (6th ed.). Upper Saddle River, NJ: Prentice Hall/Merrill.

Heward, W. L.(1996). *Exceptional children: An introduction to special education*. (5th ed.). Upper Saddle River, NJ: Prentice Hall.

High, M. H., & Udall, A. J. (1983). Teacher ratings of students in relation to ethnicity of students and school ethnic balance. *Journal for the Education of the Gifted, 6,* 154–166.

Howell, R., Heward, L., & Swassing, R. (1996). Gifted and talented students. In W. L. Heward, *Exceptional children: An introduction to special education*. Upper Saddle River, NJ: Prentice Hall/Merrill.

Jacobs, J. C. (1971). Effectiveness of teacher and parent identification of gifted children as a function of school level. *Psychology in the Schools, 8,* 140–142.

Janos, P. M., & Robinson, N. M. (1985). Psychosocial development in intellectually gifted children. In F. D. Horowitz & M. O'Brien (Eds.), *The gifted and talented: Developmental perspectives*. Washington, DC: American Psychological Association.

Karnes, F. A., & Whorton, J. E. (1991). Teacher certification and endorsement in gifted education: Past, present and future. *Gifted Child Quarterly*, 35, 148–150.

Kauffman, J. (1997). *Exceptional children* (7th ed.). Needham, MA: Allyn & Bacon.

Kerr, B. (1985). Smart girls, gifted women: Special guidance concerns. *Roeper Review*, 8(1), 30–33.

Kerr, B. (1991). Educating gifted girls. In N. Colangelo & G. A. Davis (Eds.), *Handbook of gifted education*. Needham, MA: Allyn & Bacon.

Kirk, S. A., Gallagher, J. J., & Anastasiow, N. J. (1993). *Educating exceptional children* (7th ed.). Boston: Houghton Mifflin.

Kranz, B. (1982). *Kranz Talent Identification Instrument*. Moorehead, MN: University of Minnesota Press.

Kulick, J. A., & Kulick, C. L. (1984). Effects of accelerated instruction on students. *Review of Educational Research*, 54(3), 409–425.

Lindsey, M. (1980). *Training teachers of the gifted and talented*. New York: Teachers College Press.

Lucito, L. (1974). The creative. In R. Martinson (Ed.), *Identification of the gifted and talented*. Ventura, CA: Office of the Ventura County Superintendent of Schools.

Maker, C. J. (1977). *Providing programs for the gifted handicapped*. Reston, VA: Council for Exceptional Children.

Maker, C. J. (1986). Education of the gifted: Significant trends. In R. J. Morris & B. Blatt (Eds.), *Special education: Research and trends*. New York: Pergamon.

Maker, C. J. (1993). Creativity, intelligence, and problem solving: A definition and design for cross-cultural research and measurement related to giftedness. *Gifted Education International* 9(2), 68–77.

Maker, C. J., Morris, E., & James, J. (1981). The Eugene field project: A program for potentially gifted young children. In National/State Leadership Training on the Gifted, *Balancing the scale for the disadvantaged gifted*. Ventura, CA: Office of the Ventura County Superintendent of Schools.

Marland, S. (1972). *Education of the gifted and talented*. Report to Congress by the U.S. Commissioner of Education. Washington, DC: U.S. Government Printing Office.

Mercer, J. (1978). SOMPA: *System of Multicultural Pluralistic Assessment*. New York: Psychological Corporation.

Mitchell, B. (1982). An update on the state of gifted/talented education in the U.S. *Phi Delta Kappan*, 64, 357–358.

Mitchell, P., & Erickson, D. K. (1978). The education of gifted and talented children: A status report. *Exceptional Children*, 45, 12–16.

Nicopolou, A. & Cole, M. (1993). The Fifth Dimension, its playworld, and its institutional contexts: The generation and transmission of shared knowledge in the culture of collaborative learning. In E. A. Foreman, N. Minnick, & C. A. Stone (Eds.), *Contexts for learning: Sociocultural dynamics in children's development*. New York: Oxford University Press.

Noble, K. D., & Drummond, J. E. (1992). But what about the prom? Students' perceptions of early college entrance. *Gifted Child Quarterly*, 36, 106–111.

Pendarvis, E. (1993). Students with unique gifts and talents. In A. Blackhurst & W. Berdine, *An introduction to special education*. (3rd ed.). New York: Harper-Collins.

Pendarvis, E., Howley, A., & Howley, C. (1990). *The abilities of gifted children*. Upper Saddle River, NJ: Prentice Hall.

Perrone, P. A., & Male, R. A. (1981). *The developmental education and guidance of talented learners*. Rockville, MD: Aspen.

Piechowski, M. M. (1991). Emotional development and emotional giftedness. In N. Colangelo & G. A. Davis (Eds.), *Handbook of gifted education*. Needham, MA: Allyn & Bacon.

Piirto, J. (1994). *Talented children and adults: Their development and education*. Upper Saddle River, NJ: Prentice Hall/Merrill.

Plomin, R. (1989). Environment and genes: Determinants of behavior. *American Psychologist*, 44, 105–111.

Plummer, D. (1995). Serving the needs of gifted children from a multicultural perspective. In J. L. Genshaft, M. Bireley, & C. L. Hollinger, (Eds.), *Serving gifted and talented students: A resource for school personnel*. Austin, TX: PRO-ED.

Pressey, S. L. (1955). Concerning the nature and nurture of genius. *Scientific Monthly*, 81, 123–129.

Redding, R. E. (1990). Learning preferences and skill patterns among underachieving gifted adolescents. *Gifted Child Quarterly*, 34(2), 72–75.

Reis, S. (1995). What gifted education can offer the reform movement. In J. L. Genshaft, M. Bireley, & C. L.

Hollinger, (Eds.), *Serving gifted and talented students: A resource for school personnel*. Austin, TX: PRO-ED.

Reis, S. M. (1989). Reflections on policy affecting the education of gifted and talented students: Past and future perspectives. *American Psychologist, 44*, 399–408.

Reis, S. M., & Renzulli, J. S. (1991). The assessment of creative products in programs for gifted and talented students. *Gifted Child Quarterly, 35*, 128–134.

Renzulli, J. S. (1973). Talent potential in minority group students. *Exceptional Children, 39*, 128–134.

Renzulli, J. S. (1978). What makes giftedness? Reexamining a definition. *Phi Delta Kappan, 84*, 180–185.

Renzulli, J. S., & Hartman, R. K. (1971). Scale for rating behavioral characteristics of superior students. *Exceptional Children, 38*, 243–248.

Renzulli, J., & Reis, S. (1986). The enrichment triad/revolving door model: A schoolwide plan for the development of creative productivity. In J. Renzulli (Ed.), *Systems and models for developing programs for the gifted and talented*. Mansfield Center, CT: Creative Learning.

Renzulli, J. S., & Reis, S. M. (1991). The schoolwide enrichment model: A comprehensive plan for the development of creative productivity. In N. Colangelo & G. A. Davis (Eds.), *Handbook of gifted education*. Needham, MA: Allyn & Bacon.

Renzulli, J., Reis, S., & Smith, L. (1981). *The revolving door identification model*. Mansfield Center, CT: Creative Learning.

Rhodes, L. (1992). Focusing attention on the individual in identification of gifted black students. *Roeper Review, 14*, 108–110.

Richert, E. S., Alvino, J. J., & McDonnel, R. C. (1982). *National report on identification: Assessment and recommendations for comprehensive identification of gifted and talented youth*. Sewell, NJ: Educational Improvement Center–South.

Ring, B., & Shaughnessy, M. F. (1993). The gifted label, gifted children, and the aftermath. *Gifted Education International, 9*(1), 33–35.

Robinson, N. M., & Noble, K. D. (1991). Social-emotional development and adjustment of gifted children. In M. C. Wang, M. C. Reynolds, & H. J. Walberg (Eds.), *Handbook of special education: Research and practice. Volume 4: Emerging Programs*. New York: Pergamon.

Roedell, W. C. (1985). Developing social competence in gifted preschool children. *Remedial and Special Education, 6*(4), 6–11.

Roedell, W. C., Jackson, N. E., & Robinson, H. B. (1980). *Gifted young children*. New York: McGraw-Hill.

Ruiz, R. (1989). Considerations in the education of gifted Hispanic students. In C. J. Maker & S. W. Schiever (Eds.), *Critical issues in gifted education: Defensible programs for cultural and ethnic minorities*. Austin, TX: PRO-ED.

Sanborn, M. P. (1979). Differential counseling needs of the gifted and talented. In N. Colangelo & R. T. Zaffrann (Eds.), *New voices in counseling the gifted*. Dubuque, IA: Kendall/Hunt.

Schiever, S. W., & Maker, C. J. (1991). Enrichment and acceleration: An overview and new directions. In N. Colangelo & G. A. Davis (Eds.), *Handbook of gifted education*. Needham, MA: Allyn & Bacon.

Schmidt, R. (1993, May 20). Seeking to identify the gifted among LEP students. *Education Weekly*, pp. 1, 12.

Scott, M. S., Prior, R., Urbano, R., Hogan, A., & Gold, S. (1992). The identification of giftedness: A comparison of white, Hispanic and black families. *Gifted Child Quarterly, 36*, 131–139.

Seaberg, V. T., & Stafford, P. B. (1991, April). *Council of State Directors of Programs for the Gifted—Nationwide trends in gifted education; The state of the states*. Presentation to the Council for Exceptional Children International Convention, Atlanta, GA.

Seeley, K. R., & Mahoney, A. R. (1981). Giftedness and delinquency: A small beginning toward some answers. In R. E. Clasen, *Programming for the gifted, talented, and creative: Models and methods* (2nd ed.). Madison, WI: University of Wisconsin Extension.

Silverman, L. K. (1983). Personality development: The pursuit of excellence. *Journal for the Education of the Gifted, 6*(1), 5–19.

Silverman, L. K. (1986). What happens to the gifted girl? In C. J. Maker (Ed.), *Critical issues in gifted education: Defensible programs for the gifted*. Austin, TX: PRO-ED.

Silverman, L. K. (1988). Gifted and talented. In E. L. Meyen & T. M. Skrtic (Eds.), *Exceptional children and youth: An introduction* (3rd ed.). Denver, CO: Love.

Silverman, L. K. (1995). Highly gifted children. In J. L. Genshaft, M. Bireley, & C. L. Hollinger, (Eds.), *Serving gifted and talented students: A resource for school personnel.* Austin, TX: PRO-ED.

Sisk, D. (1981). Educational planning for the gifted and talented. In J. M. Kauffman & D. P. Hallahan (Eds.), *Handbook of special education.* Upper Saddle River, NJ: Prentice Hall.

Sisk, D. (1987). *Creative teaching of the gifted.* New York: McGraw-Hill.

Smith, D. D., & Luckasson, R. (1995). *Introduction to special education: Teaching in an age of challenge* (2nd ed.). Needham, MA: Allyn & Bacon.

Southern, W. T., & Jones, E. D. (Eds.). (1991). *The academic acceleration of gifted children.* New York: Teachers College Press.

Stanley, J. C. (1977). Rationale of the study of mathematical precocious youth (SMPY) during its first five years of promoting educational acceleration. In J. C. Stanley, W. C. George, & C. H. Solano (Eds.), *The gifted and creative: A fifty-year perspective.* Baltimore: Johns Hopkins University Press.

Stanley, J. C. (1985). How did six highly accelerated gifted students fare in graduate school? *Gifted Child Quarterly, 29,* 180.

Stanley, J. C. (1989). A look back at educational non-acceleration: An international tragedy. *Gifted//Creative/Talented, 12*(4), 60–61.

Sternberg, R. J. (1991). Giftedness according to the triarchic theory of human intelligence. In N. Colangelo & G. A. Davis (Eds.), *Handbook of gifted education.* Needham, MA: Allyn & Bacon.

Sternberg, R. J., & Davidson, J. E. (1983). Insight on the gifted. *Educational Psychologist, 18,* 51–57.

Story, C. (1985). Facilitator of learning: A microethnographic study of the teacher of the gifted. *Gifted Child Quarterly, 29*(4), 155–159.

Strom, R. D., & Torrance, E. P. (1973). *Education for effective achievement.* Chicago: Rand McNally.

Swiatek, M. A. (1993). A decade of longitudinal research on academic acceleration through the study of mathematically precocious youth. *Roeper Review, 15*(3), 120–123.

Tannenbaum, A. J. (1979). Pre-Sputnik to post-Watergate concern about the gifted. In A. H. Passow (Ed.), *The gifted and the talented: Their education and development.*

*Seventy-eighth yearbook of the National Society for the Study of Education,* Part 1. Chicago: University of Chicago Press.

Tannenbaum, A. J.. (1992). Early signs of giftedness: Research and commentary. *Journal for the Education of the Gifted, 15,* 104–133.

Terman L. M. (Ed.). (1925, 1947, 1959). *Genetic studies of genius: Vols. 1, 4, 5.* Stanford, CA: Stanford University Press.

Terman, L. M. (1926). *Genetic studies of genius: Vol. 1. Mental and physical traits of a thousand gifted children* (2nd ed.). Palo Alto, CA: Stanford University Press.

Terman, L. M., & Oden, M. (1959). The gifted group at midlife: Thirty-five years' follow-up of the superior child. In L. M. Terman (Ed.), *Genetic studies of genius: Vol. 5.* Stanford, CA: Stanford University Press.

Tidwell, R. (1980). A psycho-educational profile of 1,593 gifted high school students. *Gifted Child Quarterly, 4*(2), 63–68.

Torrance, E. P. (1966). *Tests of creative thinking.* Princeton, NJ: Personnel.

Turnbull, A. P., Turnbull, H. R., Shank, M., & Leal, D. (1995). *Exceptional lives: Special education in today's schools.* Upper Saddle River, NJ: Prentice Hall/Merrill.

U.S. Congress. (1978). Educational Amendment of 1978. [PL 95-561, IXCA].

U.S. Department of Education. (1993). *National excellence: A case for developing American talent.* Washington, DC: Author.

U.S. *Senate report of the Gifted and Talented Subcommittee on Labor and Public Welfare.* (1972, March). Washington, DC: U.S. Department of Health, Education, and Welfare.

Van Tassel-Baska, J. (1983). Profiles of precocity: The 1982 Midwest talent search finalists. *Gifted Child Quarterly, 27*(3), 139–144.

Van Tassel-Baska, J. (1992). *Planning effective curriculum for gifted learners.* Denver, CO: Love.

Van Tassel-Baska, J., Patton, J. M., & Prillaman, D. (1991). *Gifted youth at risk: A report of a national study.* Reston, VA: Council for Exceptional Children.

Weiss, P., & Gallagher, J. J. (1982). *Report on education of gifted: Vol. 2.* Chapel Hill, NC: University of North Carolina, Frank Porter Graham Child Development Center.

Wentzel, K. R. (1988). Gender differences in math and English achievement: A longitudinal study. *Sex Roles*, 18(11/12), 691–699.

Whitmore, J. (1980). *Giftedness, conflict, and underachievement*. Needham, MA: Allyn & Bacon.

Witty, P. A. (Ed.). (1951). *The gifted child*. Boston: D. C. Heath.

Wolf, J. (1990). The gifted and talented. In N. G. Haring, L. McCormack & T. G. Haring, *Exceptional children and youth*. Upper Saddle River, NJ: Prentice Hall/Merrill.

Yong, F. L., & McIntyre, J. D. (1992). A comparative study of the learning style preferences of students with learning disabilities and students who are gifted. *Journal of Learning Disabilities*, 25, 124–132.

Ysseldyke, J. E., & Algozzine, B. (1982). *Critical issues in special and remedial education*. Boston: Houghton Mifflin.

# Appendix 1

# Addresses of State Offices of Teacher Licensure and Certification

The addresses and phone numbers of the state offices that can supply you with information about the requirements for licensing and certification are listed in this appendix.

## STATE OFFICES OF TEACHER LICENSING AND CERTIFICATION

**Alabama**
Certification—Division of Professional Services
Department of Education
Gordon Persons Building
50 N. Ripley Street
Montgomery, AL 36130-3901
(205)242-9977

**Alaska**
Teacher Education and Certification
Department of Education
Alaska State Office Building
Pouch F
Juneau, AK 99811-1894
(907)465-2831

**Arizona**
Teacher Certification Unit
Department of Education
1535 W. Jefferson Street
P.O. Box 25609
Phoenix, AZ 85007
(602)542-4368

**Arkansas**
Office of Teacher Education and Licensure
Department of Education
#4 Capitol Mall, Room 106B/107B
Little Rock, AR 72201
(501)682-4342

**California**
Commission of Teacher Credentialing
1812 9th Street
Sacramento, CA 95814
(916)445-7254

**Colorado**
Teacher Certification
Department of Education
201 E. Colfax Avenue
Denver, CO 80203-1799
(303)866-6628

**Connecticut**
Bureau of Certification and Accreditation
Department of Education
P. O. Box 2219
Hartford, CT 06145
(203)566-4561

This list is drawn from D. Haselkorn and A. Calkins, *Careers in Teaching Handbook*. Belmont, MA: Recruiting New Teachers, 1993, pp. 65–69.

**Delaware**
Office of Certification
Department of Public Instruction
Townsend Building
P.O. Box 1402
Dover, DE 19903
(302)739-4688

**District of Columbia**
Division of Teacher Services
District of Columbia Public Schools
415 12th Street NW
Room 1013
Washington, DC 20004-1994
(202)724-4250

**Florida**
Division of Human Resource Development
Teacher Certification Offices
Department of Education, FEC, Room 201
325 W. Gaines Street
Tallahassee, FL 32399-0400
(904)488-5724

**Georgia**
Professional Standards Commission
Department of Education
1454 Twin Towers East
Atlanta, GA 30334
(404)656-2604

**Hawaii**
Office of Personnel Services
Department of Education
P.O. Box 2360
Honolulu, HI 96804
(808)586-3420

**Idaho**
Teacher Education and Certification
Department of Education
Len B. Jordan Office Building
650 W. State Street
Boise, ID 83720
(208)334-3475

**Illinois**
Certification and Placement
State Board of Education
100 N. First Street
Springfield, IL 62777-0001
(217)782-2805

**Indiana**
Professional Standards Board
Department of Education
State House, Room 229
Indianapolis, IN 46204-2790
(317)232-9010

**Iowa**
Board of Education Examiners
State of Iowa
Grimes State Office Building
Des Moines, IA 50319-0146
(515)281-3245

**Kansas**
Certification, Teacher Education & Accreditation
Department of Education
120 S.E. Tenth Avenue
Topeka, KS 66612
(913)296-2288

**Kentucky**
Teacher Education and Certification
Department of Education
500 Mero Street, Room 1820
Frankfort, KY 40601
(502)564-4606

**Louisiana**
Teacher Certification
Department of Education
P.O. Box 94064
626 N. 4th Street
Baton Rouge, LA 70804-9064
(504)342-3490

**Maine**
Department of Education
Certification and Placement
State House Station 23
Augusta, ME 04333
(207)289-5800

## Maryland
Division of Certification & Accreditation
Department of Education
200 W. Baltimore Street
Baltimore, MD 21201
(410)333-2142

## Massachusetts
Bureau of Teacher Certification
Department of Education
350 Main Street
Maiden, MA 02148
(617)338-3300

## Michigan
Teacher/Administrator Preparation
and Certification
Department of Education
P.O. Box 30008
608 W. Allegan Street
Lansing, MI 48909
(517)373-3310

## Minnesota
Personnel and Licensing
Department of Education
616 Capitol Square Building
550 Cedar Street
St. Paul, MN 55101
(612)296-2046

## Mississippi
Office of Teacher Certification
Department of Education
P.O. Box 771
Jackson, MS 39205
(601)359-3483

## Missouri
Teacher Education
Missouri Teacher Certification Office
Department of Elementary and Secondary Education
P.O. Box 480
Jefferson City, MO 65102-0480
(314)751-3486

## Montana
Certification Services
Office of Public Instruction
State Capitol
Helena, MT 59620
(406)444-3150

## Nebraska
Teacher Certification/Education
301 Centennial Mall, South
Box 94987
Lincoln, NE 68509
(402)471-2496

## Nevada
Teacher Licensure
Department of Education
1850 E. Sahara, Suite 200
State Mail Room
Las Vegas, NV 89158
(702)486-6457

## New Hampshire
Bureau of Teacher Education and Professional Standards
Department of Education
State Office Park South
101 Pleasant Street
Concord, NH 03301-3860
(603)271-2407

## New Jersey
Teacher Certification and Academic Credentials
Department of Education
3535 Quakerbridge Road, CN 503
Trenton, NJ 08625-0503
(609)292-2070

## New Mexico
Educator Preparation and Licensure
Department of Education
Education Building
Santa Fe, NM 87501-2786
(505)827-6587

## New York
Office of Teacher Certification
Department of Education
Cultural Education Center, Room 5A11
Albany, NY 12230
(518)474-3901

**North Carolina**
Division of Certification
Department of Public Instruction
114 W. Edenton Street
Raleigh, NC 27603-1712
(919)733-4125
(919)733-0377

**North Dakota**
Teacher Certification Division
Department of Public Instruction
600 E. Boulevard Avenue
Bismarck, ND 58505-0440
(701)224-2264

**Ohio**
Teacher Certification
Department of Education
65 S. Front Street, Room 1012
Columbus, OH 43266-0308
(614)466-3593

**Oklahoma**
Department of Education
2500 N. Lincoln Blvd., Room 211
Oliver Hodge Education Building
Oklahoma City, OK 73105-4599
(405)521-3337

**Oregon**
Teacher Standards and Practices Commission
580 State Street, Room 203
Salem, OR 97310
(503)378-3586

**Pennsylvania**
Bureau of Teacher Preparation and Certification
Department of Education
333 Market Street, 3rd Floor
Harrisburg, PA 17126-0333
(717)787-2967

**Puerto Rico**
Teacher Certification Division
Department of Education
Box 190759
Hato Rey, PR 00919
(809)758-4949

**Rhode Island**
School and Teacher Accreditation, Certification
and Placement
22 Hayes Street
Roger Williams Building, 2nd Floor
Providence, RI 02908
(401)277-2675

**South Carolina**
Teacher Education and Certification
Department of Education
1015 Rutledge
1429 Senate Street
Columbia, SC 29201
(803)734-8466

**South Dakota**
Office of Certification
Division of Education and Cultural Affairs
Kneip Office Building
700 Governor's Drive
Pierre, SD 57501
(605)773-3553

**Tennessee**
Office of Teacher Licensing
Department of Education
6th Floor, North Wing
Cordell Hull Building
Nashville, TN 37243-0377
(615)741-1644

**Texas**
Division of Personnel Records
William B. Travis Office Building
1701 N. Congress Avenue
Austin, TX 78701
(512)463-8976

**Utah**
Certification and Personnel Development
State Office of Education
250 East 500 South
Salt Lake City, UT 84111
(801)538-7740

## Vermont
Licensing Division
Department of Education
Montpelier, VT 05620
(802)828-2445

## Virginia
Office of Professional Licensure
Department of Education
P.O. Box 2120
Richmond, VA 23216-2120
(804)225-2022

## Washington
Director of Professional Preparation
Office of the Superintendent of Public Instruction
Old Capitol Building
Box 47200
Olympia, WA 98504-7200
(206)753-6775

## West Virginia
Office of Professional Preparation
Department of Education
Capitol Complex, Room B-337, Building 6
Charleston, WV 25305
(304)558-2703
(800)982-2378

## Wisconsin
Bureau of Teacher Education, Licensing and
Placement
Department of Public Instruction
125 S. Webster Street
P.O. Box 7841
Madison, WI 53707-7841
(608)266-1027

## Wyoming
Certification and Licensing Unit
Department of Education
2300 Capitol Avenue
Hathaway Building
Cheyenne, WY 82002-0050
(307)777-6261

## St. Croix District
Department of Education
Educational Personnel Services
2133 Hospital Street
Christianstead
St. Croix, Virgin Islands 00820
(809)773-5844

## St. Thomas/St. John District
Educational Personnel Services
Department of Education
44-46 Kongens Grade
St. Thomas, Virgin Islands 00802
(809)744-0100

## U.S. Department of Defense Overseas Dependent Section
Teacher Recruitment
2461 Eisenhower Avenue
Alexandria, VA 22331-1100
(703)325-0690

# Appendix II

# National Toll-Free Numbers

Following is a selected list of toll-free numbers for national organizations concerned with disability and children's issues. Inclusion on this list does not imply endorsement by NICHCY or the Office of Special Education Programs. There are also many national disability organizations providing services and information that do not have toll-free numbers. If you would like additional help in locating assistance, contact NICHCY at (800)695-0285 (Voice/TT).

Note: Telephone numbers are designated either voice (V) or text telephone (TT), indicating their accessibility to TT users. Spanish-language resources are also indicated.

## AIDS

CDC National AIDS Clearinghouse
(800)458-5231 (V; English/Spanish)
(800)243-7012 (TT)

CDC National AIDS Hotline
(800)342-2437 (V)
(800)344-7432 (V; Spanish)
(800)243-7889 (TT)

Hemophilia and AIDS/HIV Network for
Dissemination of Information
(800)424-2634 (V)

## ALCOHOL AND OTHER DRUG ABUSE

National Institute on Drug Abuse Helpline
(800)662-4357 (V)

OSAP National Clearinghouse for Alcohol
and Drug Information
(800)729-6686 (V)
(800)487-4889 (TT)

## AMERICANS WITH DISABILITIES ACT (ADA)

Disability Rights Education and Defense Fund
ADA Technical Assistance Information Line
(800)466-4232 (V/TT)

Equal Employment Opportunity Commission
(800)669-3362 (V)
(800)800-3302 (TT)

Job Accommodation Network
(800)526-7234 (V/TT)
(800)232-9675 (V/TT; ADA information)

National Information Center for Children and Youth with Disabilities
P.O. Box 1492, Washington DC 20013-1492
(800)695-0285 (Toll-Free, Voice/TT)
SpecialNet User Name: NICHCY **Internet: nichcy@capcon.net

U.S. Architectural and Transportation Barriers
Compliance Board—Access Board
(800)872-2253 (V)
(202)728-5483 (TT)

U.S. Department of Housing and Urban
Development—HUD User
(800)245-2691 (V)

## ASSISTIVE TECHNOLOGY/DEVICES

AbleNet
(800)322-0956 (V)

Apple Office for Special Education Material
(800)732-3131, ext. 950 (V)

AT&T Accessible Communications Product Center
(800)233-1222 (V)
(800)833-3232 (TT)

IBM Special Needs Information Referral Center
(800)426-4832 (V)
(800)284-4833 (TT)

Techknowledge
(800)726-9119
(404)894-4960 (V; Atlanta metro area)

## BLINDNESS/VISUAL IMPAIRMENTS

American Council of the Blind
(800)424-8666 (V/TT)

American Foundation for the Blind
(800)232-5463 (V)

Blind Children's Center
(800)222-3566 (V)
(800)222-3567 (V; in CA)

Hadley School for the Blind
(800)323-4238 (V)

Job Opportunities for the Blind
(800)638-7518 (V)
(410)659-9314 (V; in MD)

Lighthouse National Center for Vision
and Child Development
(800)334-5497 (V)
(212)808-5544 (TT)

National Association of Parents
of the Visually Impaired
(800)562-6265 (V)

National Society to Prevent Blindness
(800)331-2020 (V)

Recording for the Blind
(800)221-4792 (V)

Retinitis Pigmentosa Foundation
(800)683-5555 (V)
(410)225-9400 (V; in MD)
(410)225-9409 (TT)

## BURNS

Phoenix Society
(800)888-2876 (V)

## CANCER

Cancer Information and Counseling Line
(800)525-3777 (V)

Candlelighters Childhood Cancer Foundation
(800)366-2223 (V)

National Cancer Information Service
(800)422-6237 (V; English/Spanish)

## CHILD ABUSE

Clearinghouse on Child Abuse and
Neglect/Family Violence Information
(800)394-3366 (V)

National Resource Center on Child Sexual Abuse
(800)543-7006 (V)

## COMMUNICATION DISORDERS

National Institute on Deafness and Other
Communication Disorders Clearinghouse
(800)241-1044 (V)
(800)241-1055 (TT)

## CRANIOFACIAL SYNDROMES

Children's Craniofacial Association
(800)535-3643 (V)

FACES—National Association for the
Craniofacially Handicapped
(800)332-2373 (V)

National Foundation for Facial Reconstruction
(800)422-3223

## DEAFNESS/HEARING IMPAIRMENTS

American Society for Deaf Children
(800)942-2732 (V/TT)

Better Hearing Institute
(800)327-9355 (V/TT)

Deafness Research Foundation
(800)535-3323 (V/TT)
(212)684-6559 (V/TT; in NY)

Hear Now
(800)648-4327 (V/TT)

John Tracy Clinic
(800)522-4582 (V/TT)
(213)748-5481 (V; in 213 area)
(213)747-2924 (TT; in 213 area)

National Hearing Aid Society
(800)521-5247 (V)

National Institute on Deafness and Other
Communication Disorders Clearinghouse
(800)241-1044 (V)
(800)241-1055 (TT)

TRIPOD (Information for parents of deaf children)
(800)352-8888 (V/TT)
(800)346-8888 (V/TT; in CA)

## DISABILITY AWARENESS

Kids on the Block
(800)368-5437

## EDUCATION

American Association for Vocational
Instructional Materials
(800)228-4689 (V)

Association for Childhood Education International
(800)423-3563 (V)

HEATH Resource Center
(800)544-3284 (V/TT)
(202)939-9320 (V/TT; in DC)

National Center for Research in Vocational Education
(800)762-4093 (V)

National Center for School Leadership
(800)643-3205 (V)

National Committee for Citizens in Education
Clearinghouse
(800)638-9675 (V)
(800)532-9832 (V; Spanish)

U.S. Office of Educational Research and Improvement
(800)424-1616 (V)

## EMPLOYMENT

Equal Employment Opportunity Commission
(800)669-3362 (V)
(800)800-3302 (TT)

Job Accommodation Network
(800)526-7234 (V/TT)
(800)232-9675 (V/TT; ADA Information)

Job Opportunities for the Blind
(800)638-7518 (V)
(410)659-9314 (V; in MD)

## FINANCIAL COUNSELING

National Foundation for Consumer Credit
(800)388-2227 (V)

## HOSPICE

Children's Hospice International
(800)242-4453 (V/TT)

HOSPICELINK
(800)331-1620
(203)767-1620 (V; in CT)

## INFORMATION SERVICES

ABLEDATA/National Rehabilitation Information
Clearinghouse
(800)346-2742 (V/TT)

ACCESS ERIC
(800)538-3742 (V)

BRS Information Technologies
(800)289-4277 (V)

National Center for Youth with Disabilities
(800)333-6293 (V)
(612)624-3939 (TT)

National Easter Seal Society
(800)221-6827 (V)
(312)726-4258 (TT)

National Information Clearinghouse for Infants with
Disabilities and Life Threatening Conditions
(800)922-9234, ext. 201 (V/TT)
(800)922-1107, ext. 201 (V/TT; in SC)

ODPHP National Health Information Center
(800)336-4797 (V)

Office of Minority Health Resource Center
(800)444-6472 (V)

## LITERACY

National Literacy Hotline
(800)228-8813 (V)
(800)552-9097 (TT)

## MEDICAL/HEALTH DISORDERS

American Association of Kidney Patients
(800)749-2257 (V)

American Brain Tumor Association
(800)886-2282 (V)

American Diabetes Association
(800)582-8323 (V)

American Kidney Fund
(800)638-8299 (V)

American Liver Foundation
(800)223-0179 (V)

American Lupus Society
(800)331-1802 (V)

Asthma and Allergy Foundation of America
(800)727-8462 (V)

Chronic Fatigue and Immune Dysfunction
Syndrome Association
(800)442-3437 (V)

Federal Hill-Burton Free Hospital Care Program
(800)638-0742 (V)
(800)492-0359 (V; in MD)

Leukemia Society of America
(800)955-4572 (V)

Lupus Foundation of America
(800)558-0121 (V)
(800)558-0231 (V; Spanish)

National Association for Sickle Cell Disease
(800)421-8453 (V)

Shriners Hospital for Crippled Children
(800)237-5055 (V)
(800)282-9161 (V; in FL)

United Ostomy Association
(800)826-0826 (V)

## MENTAL HEALTH

National Alliance for the Mentally Ill
(800)950-6264 (V)

National Clearinghouse on Family Support and
Children's Mental Health
(800)628-1696 (V)

National Mental Health Association
(800)969-6642 (V)

## MENTAL RETARDATION

American Association on Mental Retardation
(800)424-3688 (V)

The ARC
(800)433-5255 (V)

## NUTRITION

Beech-Nut Nutrition Hotline
(800)523-6633 (V)

Gerber Consumer Information
(800)443-7237 (V)

## PHYSICAL DISABILITIES

American Paralysis Association
(800)526-3456 (V)

Human Growth Foundation
(800)451-6434 (V)

Physically Challenged Resource Center
(800)255-9877 (V)

## RARE SYNDROMES

Alliance of Genetic Support Groups
(800)336-4363 (V)

National Information Center on Orphan Drugs and
Rare Diseases
(800)456-3505 (V)

National Organization for Rare Disorders
(800)999-6673 (V/TT)

## RECREATION

Adventures in Movement for the Handicapped, Inc.
(800)332-8210 (V)

Magic Foundation
(800)362-4423 (V)

North American Riding for the Handicapped, Inc.
(800)369-7433 (V)

Sunshine Foundation
(800)767-1976 (V)

## REHABILITATION

Clearinghouse for Rehabilitation and
Technology Information
(800)638-8864 (V)
(800)852-2892 (TT)

National Clearinghouse of Rehabilitation
Training Materials
(800)223-5219 (V/TT)

National Rehabilitation Information
Clearinghouse/ABLEDATA
(800)346-2742 (V/TT)

## RESPIRATORY DISORDERS

National Jewish Center for Immunology and
Respiratory Medicine—LUNGLINE
(800)222-5864 (V)

## RESPITE CARE

Access to Respite Care and Help (ARCH)
National Resource Center
(800)473-1727 (V)

## RURAL

ERIC Clearinghouse on Rural Education
and Small Schools
(800)624-9120 (V)
(800)344-6646 (V; in WV)

Rural Institute on Disabilities (Montana University
Affiliated Program)
(800)732-0323 (V/TT)

## SPECIFIC DISABILITIES

Attention Deficit Disorder Association
(800)487-2282 (V)

Cleft Palate Foundation
(800)242-5338 (V)

Cooley's Anemia Foundation
(800)221-3571 (V)
(800)522-7222 (V; in NY)

Cornelia de Lange Syndrome Foundation
(800)223-8355 (V)
(800)753-2357 (V; in CT)

Cystic Fibrosis Foundation
(800)344-4823 (V)

Epilepsy Foundation of America
(800)332-1000 (V)

Little People of America
(800)243-9273 (V)

National Down Syndrome Congress
(800)232-6372 (V)

National Down Syndrome Society
(800)221-4602 (V)

National Fragile X Foundation
(800)688-8765 (V)

National Multiple Sclerosis Society
(800)532-7667 (V)

National Organization for Albinism and
Hypopigmentation
(800)473-2310 (V)

National Reye's Syndrome Foundation
(800)233-7393 (V)

National Tuberous Sclerosis Association
(800)225-6872 (V)

Orton Dyslexia Society
(800)222-3123 (V)

Prader-Willi Syndrome Association
(800)926-4797 (V)

Spina Bifida Association of America
(800)621-3141 (V)

Stuttering Foundation of America
(800)992-9392 (V)

Sudden Infant Death Syndrome Alliance
(800)221-7437 (V)

Tourette Syndrome Association
(800)237-0717 (V)

United Cerebral Palsy Associations
(800)872-5827 (V/TT)

United Leukodystrophy Foundation
(800)728-5483 (V)

United Scleroderma Foundation
(800)722-4673 (V)

## SUPPLEMENTAL SECURITY INCOME (SSI)

Social Security Administration
(800)772-1213 (V)
(800)325-0778 (TT)
(800)392-0812 (TT; in MO)

Zebley Implementation Project
(800)523-0000 (V)
(215)893-5356 (V; Philadelphia metro area)

## TRAUMA

American Trauma Society
(800)556-7890 (V)

National Head Injury Foundation
(800)444-6443 (V)

National Spinal Cord Injury Association
(800)962-9629 (V)

## VIETNAM VETERANS/AGENT ORANGE

Access Group for Children of Vietnam Veterans
(800)821-8580 (V)

National Information System for Vietnam Veterans
and Their Families
(800)922-9234, ext. 401 (V/TT)
(800)922-1107, ext. 401 (V/TT; in SC)

This list is made possible through Cooperative Agreement #H030A30003 between the Academy for Educational Development and the Office of Special Education Programs, U.S. Department of Education. The contents of this publication do not necessarily reflect the views or policies of the Department of Education, nor does mention of trade names, commercial products, or organizations imply endorsement by the U.S. government.

# Name Index

# Subject Index